Eclectic Philosophy of Education

Eclectic
Philosophy of Education
SECOND EDITION

A Book of Readings

Edited by **JOHN S. BRUBACHER**

Professor of Education,
The University of Michigan

PRENTICE-HALL, INC.

Englewood Cliffs, N. J.   1962

PRENTICE-HALL EDUCATION SERIES

John S. Brubacher, *Editor*

22253—C

Preface

In picking up this revision of *Eclectic Philosophy of Education,* the reader should not look for radical changes from the first edition. The principal change is the addition of new materials from the literature of the past decade. Some of these materials present points of view new to the book; others are simply better statements of points of view already included. Outmoded materials have been withdrawn, and some of the selections have been rearranged. Extended use of the book convinced me that some of them belonged in different chapters while others needed rearrangement in the chapter in which they now appear.

The reader will observe that a few chapters have been omitted. The materials of these chapters, however, have generally not been dropped but rather merged in other chapters. For instance the chapters on "Democratic Education" and "Non-Democratic Education" have been merged in a single new one entitled "Political Basis of Education." The student will now have to make discriminations which formerly the chapter organization made for him. A last but minor alteration to which the reader will attend is some reformulation of the study questions at the beginning of each chapter. Here again some questions are new, some have been dropped, and still others have been restated.

In spite of these revisions the major purpose of the volume remains the same, that is, to offer the student a rich variety of the best writings available in educational philosophy. It is principally by comparing and contrasting these different viewpoints that the student learns to think for himself. Little thinking is required so long as the continuity of thought is unbroken. It is only when this continuity is interrupted by contradiction and contrast that it becomes urgent to think. On this account it seems to me that a book like this, an "eclectic" one, should be used, not as a supplementary, but rather as a primary text. The student's initial contact with educational philosophy should be in problematic form. After he has puzzled over these problems, and what various eminent minds have said about them, then is the best time for him to turn to some systematic account of educational philosophy to true up his own budding systematization.

J.S.B.

Contents

1. The Role of Educational Philosophy   1

2. Traits of Reality   22

    I.   The Nature of Being   23
   II.   The Natural and Supernatural   25
  III.   Static and Dynamic   34
  IV.   Temporal and Eternal   41
   V.   Novel and Primordial   43
  VI.   Origin and Destiny   47

3. Human Nature   60

    I.   Mind and Body   61
   II.   Original Nature   66
  III.   The "Whole Child" and Integration   72
  IV.   Freedom and Determinism   76

4. Learning   89

5. The Nature of Knowledge   108

    I.   Truth   108
   II.   Ways of Knowing   123
  III.   The Role of Intelligence   136

6. The Theory of Value   142

7. Educational Aims   165

   I.   Function and Determination of Aims   165
   II. Leading Values as Aims   177

8. Ethical Principles of Education   195

9. Political Basis of Education   207

10. Education and the Production and Ownership of Wealth   233

11. Education and Socio-Economic Class Structure   261

12. Public and Private Education   277

13. Church and State in Education   298

14. Nationalism and Education   308

15. The School and Social Progress   317

16. Teaching Controversial Issues   334

17. Academic Freedom   347

18. Method of Instruction   374

19. Logic and the Order of Instruction   391

20. Interest, Effort, and Discipline 402

21. Freedom as Method 420

22. Measurement and Evaluation 431

23. The Curriculum 443

24. Play and Art in Education 456

25. Student Discipline and Government 473

26. Moral Education 493

27. Religious Education 512

Index of Authors 540

Index 555

Eclectic Philosophy of Education

1

The Role of Educational Philosophy

Problems in the Philosophy of Education Discussed in this Section

1. Does every teacher and administrator have a philosopy of education whether he is aware of it or not?
2. How does a "common-sense" viewpoint on educational problems differ from a "scientific" one? A "philosophic" one? How are all three viewpoints related to the art of education?
3. What function or functions does a philosophy of education perform for teachers and administrators? Is philosophy of education ever the source of new facts?
4. Is the critical examination of assumptions employed in education a function of the scientist as well as of the philosopher?
5. Which is more reliable, scientific or philosophic knowledge?
6. Must the scope of educational philosophy contract as the domain of educational science expands?
7. How accurately can language express educational realities?
8. How can a person be sure his educational philosophy is sound?
9. When educational philosophers disagree, what should the individual teacher do? When the faculty of a school differs on educational philosophy how should school policy be settled? Would it be desirable for all teachers in a given school to have the same philosophy of education?

1. Philosophy is Inescapable

As we look upon life so we teach. What we believe, the loyalties to which we hold, subtly determine the content and the method of our teaching. Each of us has a philosophy whether or not he has thought it through and definitely phrased it. Everything we say and do as well as what we think reflects that philosophy.

1. Harold O. Rugg, *The Great Technology* (New York: John Day Company, 1933), p. 258.

1

2. Practicality of Theory

Theory is in the end, as has been well said, the most practical of all things, because this widening of the range of attention beyond nearby purpose and desire eventually results in the creation of wider and farther-reaching purposes and enables us to use a much wider and deeper range of conditions and means than were expressed in the observation of primitive practical purposes.

3. Philosophy and Common Sense

The difference between a common-sense philosophy and a critical and systematic one is somewhat analogous to the difference between common-sense knowledge and scientific knowledge; that is, the latter is more thorough than the former, is made more carefully, its parts articulate better, it gives us a larger world which has more depth and steadfastness in it.

4. Functions Performed by Philosophy of Education

. . . Looking back over its history, it appears that philosophy has done three sorts of things. It has sought to work out a conception of the universe as a whole in all of its aspects, and of man's place in it. In this endeavor it has been synthetic, making use of the results of the various sciences of the day and adding to them the fruits of the aesthetic, moral, and religious experience of mankind, in order to see life steadily and see it whole. It has also been speculative, venturing more or less questionable hypotheses in order to fill out the picture or to find a meaning where none was obvious.

Besides seeking such "world-hypotheses," as S. C. Pepper has called them, philosophers have sought to afford some wisdom in the conduct of human affairs. That is, they have tried to provide, not only a picture

2. John Dewey, *Sources of a Science of Education* (New York: Liveright Publishing Corporation, 1931), p. 17.
3. Ernest Carroll Moore, *What is Education?* (Boston: Ginn and Company, 1915), p. 13.
4. William K. Frankena, "Toward a Philosophy of the Philosophy of Education," *Harvard Educational Review*, 26:94–97, Spring, 1956.

of the world we live in, but a guide to action, whether individual or social, by discovering and formulating goals, norms, or standards to serve as pillars of cloud by day and pillars of fire by night.

In their twofold pursuit of the real and the ideal, philosophers have often been engaged in a less exciting but still essential kind of enquiry —analysis or criticism. This includes a critical evaluation of the assumptions and methods used by philosophers, as well as by scientists and common sense people, and a careful attempt to define such terms as "real," "true," "good," "right," "cause," "matter," "substance," and "time," which play so important a part in both ordinary and systematic thinking. Here, whatever his ultimate goal may be, the proximate goal of the philosopher is simply conceptual clarity and methodological understanding.

✿　　　✿　　　✿

The connection of philosophy with each of these parts of the discipline of education is now readily apparent. Consider the factual science of education. For the most part, this will be scientific, not philosophical in character, and will belong among the social sciences. But one of the fields from which it may borrow facts or hypotheses is speculative philosophy (including for the moment theology). For example, it may borrow from philosophy the naturalistic-humanistic view of life and the world, as so much of our recent educational philosophy does; or, like traditional theories of education, it may adopt the beliefs in a superior reality, a spectator theory of knowledge, and an immortal destiny, which Dewey has so long decried. To the extent to which it depends on or applies such doctrines, a "science" of education will not be really scientific, it will be philosophical; in fact, it will be an adjunct of speculative philosophy, whether it is aware of this or not (in saying this, I do not mean to bury such educational philosophy, nor even to dispraise it).

There is another possible connection between education and speculative philosophy. One might derive from a study of the process of education some hypothesis about the nature of the world, for example, the idealistic thesis that the history of the universe is the self-education of Mind. Here, however, the goal of enquiry is not insight into education but insight into the nature of the universe, and hence such thinking cannot properly be called philosophy of education, even though thinking of the reverse sort may be.

As for the normative part of education—this seems to me to contain the heart of the philosophy of education. All of it may with some propriety be called philosophy, since it consists of judgments about what should or should not be done in the process of education, together with the reasons for these judgments; indeed, it is really nothing but a

branch of normative philosophy as a whole. However, some hesitate
to include recommendations about the means to be used by the schools
under philosophy, and would prefer to regard the science of education
as consisting of two parts, as political science does, viz., a factual part
and a part which makes recommendations about means. But, in any
case, theories about the ends of the process of education are properly
called normative philosophy.

It should be pointed out that the recommendations made by the
philosopher of education, whether they concern means or ends, will
normally be based partly on normative premises taken from ethics
(and so from philosophy, though, of course a given philosopher of
education may work out his own ethics in his capacity as a philosopher,
and need not borrow from anyone *else*), and partly on factual premises
derived from common sense, science, or philosophy. For example, any
recommendation he may make about the treatment of religion in the
schools will depend in part on his views about the aims of education,
which will rest on his moral and social philosophy in general, and
in part on his views about the validity of religious beliefs and the importance of religious literacy.

The analytical part of education as a discipline belongs entirely to
philosophy—analytical philosophy. In so far as it is concerned to study
the methods of educational science it is just a part of the philosophy of
science in general, and there is no point in speaking of it as philosophy
of education, unless the science of education has features which are
peculiar to it. The analysis of the concepts and methods of the normative part of education, again, is to a considerable extent just a part of
ethical theory; it is not as such philosophy of education, although
philosophers of education should be at home in it. However, there is
left as a proper part of the philosophy of education the analysis of
concepts which are peculiarly central to either the scientific or the
normative parts of education, for example, "growth," "learning," "independence," "intellectual freedom," etc.

5. Comprehensiveness of Philosophy

As we might expect, then, philosophy has generally been defined in
ways which imply a certain totality, generality and ultimateness of
both subject matter and method. With respect to subject matter, philosophy is an attempt to *comprehend*—that is, to gather together the

5. John Dewey, *Democracy and Education* (New York: The Macmillan Company, 1916), pp. 378–384.

varied details of the world and of life into a single inclusive whole, which shall either be a unity, or, as in the dualistic systems, shall reduce the plural details to a small number of ultimate principles. On the side of the attitude of the philosopher and of those who accept his conclusions, there is the endeavor to attain as unified, consistent, and complete an outlook upon experience as is possible. This aspect is expressed in the word "philosophy"—love of wisdom. Whenever philosophy has been taken seriously, it has always been assumed that it signified achieving a wisdom which would influence the conduct of life. Witness the fact that almost all ancient schools of philosophy were also organized ways of living, those who accepted their tenets being committed to certain distinctive modes of conduct; witness the intimate connection of philosophy with the theology of the Roman church in the middle ages, its frequent association with religious interests, and, at national crises its association with political struggles.

This direct and intimate connection of philosophy with an outlook upon life obviously differentiates philosophy from science. Particular facts and laws of science evidently influence conduct. They suggest things to do and not do, and provide means of execution. When science denotes not simply a report of the particular facts discovered about the world but a *general attitude* toward it—as distinct from special things to do—it merges into philosophy. For an underlying disposition represents an attitude not to this and that thing nor even to the aggregate of known things, but to the considerations which govern conduct.

Hence philosophy cannot be defined simply from the side of subject matter. For this reason, the definition of such conceptions as generality, totality, and ultimateness is most readily reached from the side of the disposition toward the world which they connote. In any literal and quantitative sense, these terms do not apply to the subject matter of knowledge, for completeness and finality are out of the question. The very nature of experience as an ongoing, changing process forbids. In a less rigid sense, they apply to *science* rather than to philosophy. For obviously it is to mathematics, physics, chemistry, biology, anthropology, history, etc. that we must go, not to philosophy, to find out the facts of the world. It is for the sciences to say what generalizations are tenable about the world and what they specifically are. But when we ask what *sort* of permanent disposition of action toward the world the scientific disclosures exact of us we are raising a philosophic question.

From this point of view, "totality" does not mean the hopeless task of a quantitative summation. It means rather *consistency* of mode of response in reference to the plurality of events which occur. Consistency does not mean literal identity; for since the same thing does not happen twice, an exact repetition of a reaction involves some mal-adjustment. Totality means continuity—the carrying on of a former habit of action with the readaptation necessary to keep it alive and growing. Instead of signifying a ready-made complete scheme of action, it means keeping the balance in a multitude of diverse actions, so that each borrows and gives significance to every other. Any person who is open-minded and sensitive to new perceptions, and who has concentration and responsibility in connecting them has, in so far, a philosophic disposition. One of the popular senses of philosophy is a calm and endurance in the face of difficulty and loss; it is even supposed to be a power to bear pain without complaint. This meaning is a tribute to the influence of the Stoic philosophy rather than an attribute of philosophy in general.

*   *   *

More specifically, the demand for a "total" attitude arises because there is the need of integration in action of the conflicting various interests in life. Where interests are so superficial that they glide readily into one another, or where they are not sufficiently organized to come into conflict with one another, the need for philosophy is not perceptible. But when the scientific interest conflicts with, say, the religious, or the economic with the scientific or aesthetic, or when the conservative concern for order is at odds with the progressive interest in freedom, or when institutionalism clashes with individuality, there is a stimulus to discover some more comprehensive point of view from which the divergencies may be brought together, and consistency or continuity of experience recovered. Often these clashes may be settled by an individual for himself; the area of the struggle of aims is limited and a person works out his own rough accommodations. Such home-spun philosophies are genuine and often adequate. But they do not result in systems of philosophy. These arise when the discrepant claims of different ideals of conduct affect the community as a whole, and the need for readjustment is general.

*   *   *

If we are willing to conceive education as the process of forming fundamental dispositions, intellectual and emotional, toward nature and fellow men, philosophy may even be defined as *the general theory of education*. Unless a philosophy is to remain symbolic—or verbal—or a sentimental indulgence for a few, or else mere arbitrary dogma, its auditing of past experience and its program of values must take effect in conduct. Public agitation, propaganda, legislative and administrative action are effective in producing the change of disposition which a philosophy indicates as desirable, but only in the degree in which they are educative—that is to say, in the degree in which they modify mental and moral attitudes. And at the best, such methods are compromised by the fact they are used with those whose habits are already largely set, while education of youth has a fairer and freer field of operation. On the other side, the business of schooling tends to become a routine empirical affair unless its aims and methods are animated by such a broad and sympathetic survey of its place in contemporary life as it is the business of philosophy to provide.

6. Clarifying the Role of Educational Philosophy

It has become obvious to philosophers in the past fifty years that a great many of the unprofitable controversies of the past can take on a new and enlightening aspect if we look at them from this point of view. The metaphysicians who debated about God, morality, human destiny and so on were assuming that these problems were similar to scientific questions at least in being clear questions about definite matters of fact to which answers were in principle possible. Yet it is obvious from the history of philosophy that equally honest, intelligent and well-informed men may have all the supposedly relevant facts at their disposal and still disagree profoundly about such matters. This indicates that the facts which they supposed to be relevant were not really relevant at all. If they had been, it is incredible that generally acceptable answers on these matters should not by now have been reached. For it is important to notice that facts are never relevant in philosophy in the way that they are in history or in science. Historians and scientists may, and often do, disagree on the way in which the available facts are to be interpreted. But these disagreements can, in principle, always be resolved by the discovery of *further* relevant facts; and no historical or scientific disagreement could outlive the knowledge of *all* the facts, if these were ever obtainable. Yet this can and does happen in metaphysical disputes. It is indeed one sure way by which we may recognize that the dispute is metaphysical.

There are two ways of proceeding from this point. We can say that questions and statements of this sort to which no generally acceptable evidence seems at all relevant, are simply meaningless or nonsensical, that they are grammatically correct forms of words which carry no meaning whatever of an informative kind. This was the view of the logical positivists, a pre-war school of philosophy which no longer

6. Daniel J. O'Connor, *Introduction to Philosophy of Education* (London: Routledge & Kegan Paul, 1957), pp. 35–36.

survives in its original hard-shelled form. Under this ruling, only two kinds of statement retain any cognitive meaning, statements of empirical fact that can be confirmed by sensory observation and statements of logic and mathematics that can be checked by calculation. Every other kind of statement is ruled out as lacking any kind of cognitive content. This is clearly a very rough way of dealing with the statements of ethics, politics, religion and criticism of literature and the arts as well as the writings of the metaphysicians. And it shows perhaps a rather cavalier and unsympathetic attitude to matters which have excited men of ability and integrity since the beginning of history.

A more tolerant point of view which is now quite widely accepted among philosophers, may be expressed as follows: 'These statements are certainly misleading in looking grammatically like statements of observable fact. But perhaps we are being misled by their linguistic form. After all, language has many uses and fact-stating is only one of them. Let us consider all the other possible uses of language to see if we can re-interpret such apparently empty propositions in such a way that we can see what they are really asserting and so come to some agreed decision about their value.' This is one of the ways in which modern philosophers have come to be very interested in questions of language. And investigations of this kind have proved very fruitful in putting some of the oldest controversies of philosophy in quite a new light. Unfortunately, it is not easy to give in a summary way any adequate idea of the methods and results of the contemporary linguistic approach to philosophy. A general description of this work would be too vague to be informative. It can be appreciated only by seeing it in action.

7. The Accuracy of Language

. . . briefly the position is that many of the classical philosophers assumed that our thinking about the world mirrored what we found there, at least when our thinking was not mistaken and that our language mirrored our thinking. It was believed that thinking, correct or mistaken, was a sort of mapping of the universe and that the map was a good one when our thinking was true and a bad or distorted or even totally misleading one when our beliefs were false. Moreover, language was a sort of externalized model of our internal cogitations, the map, as it were, in its published form. This view was first stated in an em-

7. Daniel J. O'Connor, *Introduction to Philosophy of Education* (London: Routledge & Kegan Paul, 1957), p. 40.

bryonic form by Aristotle and was later canonized into what was called
the Correspondence Theory of Truth. There is just enough in this kind
of metaphor to make it easy for us to press it too far. The real harm of
this three-level view of knowledge, thinking mirroring fact and language mirroring thinking, is not so much in the metaphor of the mirror
or the map, though this is a misleading way of explaining even very
elementary kinds of knowledge. The danger lies rather in the supposed
split between thinking and its expression as if thinking is some sort of
mysterious inner process that can proceed apart from language or from
any other kind of symbolism whatever. Both the sources of this error
and its consequences are too complicated to dwell on here. One of its
most damaging results is to make us suppose that the actual grammatical and syntactical structures of natural languages are a key to the
nature of reality. For language, on this view, is a picture of the world,
or rather, a picture of a picture. And what we find in the structure of
languages may fairly be supposed to correspond to the structure of the
world. Thus to take one example, some metaphysicians seem to have
taken the grammatical distinction between subject and predicate as
evidence for the philosophical theory that the world consisted of a
number of substances characterized by different properties.

8. The Task of Philosophy

Philosophy is frequently presented as the systematic endeavor to
obtain knowledge of what is called Ultimate and Eternal Reality.
Many thinkers have defended this conception of its task and aim on
the ground that human life can derive stable guidance only by means
of ideals and standards that have their source in Ultimate Reality. On
the other hand, scepticism about the worth of philosophy usually
rests upon denial of the possibility of attaining such knowledge. When
the business of philosophy is conceived in this manner, philosophical
oppositions and controversies are believed to spring from conflicting
conceptions of the nature of Ultimate and Perfect Reality. One school
holds that it is spiritual; another that it is material. One school of
thought holds that the particulars of the Universe are held together
only externally by mechanical bonds; another school holds that they
are organically united because of common subordination to a final

8. John Dewey, "The Determination of Ultimate Values or Aims through Antecedent or a Priori Speculation or through Pragmatic or Empirical Inquiry," National
Society for the Study of Education, Thirty-Seventh Year Book, Part II, *The Scientific Movement in Education* (Chicago: University of Chicago Press, 1938), pp.
471–482.

controlling end and purpose that they all serve. Such divisions are inevitable as long as philosophy is defined as knowledge of supreme reality supposed to be beyond and beneath the things of experience.

But there is an alternative conception of philosophy, and the deepest philosophic divisions do not have their origin in a different conception of ultimate reality, but in the conflict between two opposed conceptions of what philosophy is about, its aim and task. According to this alternative view, the work of philosophy is confined to the things of actual experience. Its business is criticism of experience as it exists at a given time and constructive projection of values, which, when acted upon, will render experience more unified, stable, and progressive. Defects and conflicts in experience as it exists demand thoroughgoing criticism of its contents and procedures. This phase of inquiry is not, however, final; criticism does not end with mere intellectual discrimination. It provides the basis for projection of values as yet unrealized, values that are to be translated into ends that move men to action. Philosophy thus conceived does not involve a flight and escape to that which is beyond experience. It is concerned with making the most possible out of experience, personal and social. Everyday homely objects and occupations of everyday life are possessed of potentialities that, under the guidance of deliberate and systematic intelligence, will make life fuller, richer, and more unified.

There are defects and conflicts in abundance in experience as it exists at any time. But they are to be dealt with in terms of experience, not by running away from it. They are a challenge to project, through systematic reflection, a better ordered and more inclusive experience. Systematic endeavor to meet this challenge constitutes the reality of genuine philosophy. The first-mentioned idea of the work of philosophy rests upon distrust of the capacity of experience to generate fundamental values and to direct deliberate effort in behalf of their realization. This distrust involves lack of loyalty to practical intelligence, substituting in its place dependence upon so-called *a priori* intuitions and upon an alleged faculty of pure Reason that grasps absolute non-empirical truth.

Hence, there is a further fundamental difference between the two ideas of the business of philosophy. According to the first-mentioned view, knowledge, provided that it is knowledge of ultimate reality, is the final goal, complete in independence of practical activity. According to the other view, thought and knowledge cannot themselves resolve the discords of existence and life. Even if there were a Reality beyond and behind the things of the experienced world and even if knowledge of it were possible, knowledge would leave the defects and inconsistencies of the world in which we live just what they were before. Only action can change things in the direction of unity and stability. To accomplish this result, action must be directed by leading principles, and such action, as the fruit of reflection upon actual experience, reveals new and as yet unrealized possibilities. The systematic critical work that is philosophy has its constructive phase in projection of values and ends that, by their very constitution, demand application in action and guide the active operations they project.

There is a practical effect of absolute philosophies. But it is that of promoting conflicts and strengthening appeal to external authority as the sole agency for establishing order and unity in experience. Every absolute philosophy must claim to be in exclusive possession of *the* ultimate truth or else go back on its own pretensions. Absolute philosophies cannot tolerate rivals or learn from opposed philosophies. History shows that such philosophies have met with general acknowledgment only when they have had the support of powerful institutions, political and ecclesiastical. Their practical logic calls for external authority to enforce submission and punish heretical deviations. Absolute truth exacts absolute obedience. Recognition of the relation of philosophic ideas to the conditions set by experience furthers, on the contrary, intercommunication, exchange, and interaction. Through these processes differences of belief are modified in the direction of consensus. They are negotiable.

The most important practical difference that follows from the two opposed conceptions of the aim of philosophy (especially with respect to the philosophy of education) concerns the relationship of philosophy and science. Since natural and humane sciences are based upon experience, and since, according to the first view of philosophy, the subject matter of experience is intrinsically inferior to that of Ultimate Reality, philosophy and science are, according to it, necessarily rivals unless science is willing to accept the dictates of metaphysics as a servant obeys his master. Adherents of this philosophy speak with lofty disdain of science as being "merely empirical."

From the standpoint of the other view, there is no competition between science and philosophy. They exist, so to speak, in distinct, although connected, dimensions. As far as knowledge is concerned, the primacy and ultimacy of science is admitted. For what "science'" means is simply the most authentic knowledge of nature, man, and society that is possible at any given time by means of the methods and techniques then and there available. The work of philosophy as critical and constructive does not attempt to furnish additional knowledge beyond the reach of science. Its concern is rather with the values and ends that known facts and principles should subserve. This concern is manifested in ideas whose claim is to have authority over *action* in effecting realization of the ends and values in question, not to be authoritative in presenting any kind of superior "reality" and knowledge.

This is the sense and the only sense in which philosophy can claim to be more comprehensive than science. This greater comprehensiveness exists because every intelligent systematic attempt to determine the values and uses to which ascertained knowledge should be put is philosophical as far as it goes, not because of any prerogatives inherent in a separate domain labelled "philosophy."

           *   *   *

It is not, then, an accidental matter that the present-day adherents of absolutistic, super-empirical philosophies base their criticisms of existing education and their proposals of reform upon appeal to Greek and Medieval tradition. For it was in ancient Greece that a philosophy of super-empirical Reality, and of truths about it that are identical under all conditions of experience, was formulated; and it was in the Middle Ages that, because of the sanction and support of a powerful social institution, philosophy actually flourished in the organized constitution of society. The conflict of the two philosophies of education is, therefore, a conflict between the intellectual and moral attitudes of a prescientific past and those consonant with the potentialities of the living present. Insistence upon the necessity of making a sharp separation between liberal and vocational education, upon the importance of literary classics in contrast with scientific subjects (with the exception of mathematics treated as an exemplar of a system of absolute truths instead of as an ordered system of deductions from freely chosen postulates), and lack of faith in anything approaching first-hand experience in the schools, all flow logically from the philosophy that rests upon return to the past. The function of a philosophy of education based upon experience is, on the contrary, constructive exploration of the possibilities of experience directed by scientific method.

For the only way out of existing educational confusion and conflict is just the critical and constructive exploration of the potentialities of existing experience as that experience is brought under the fuller control of intelligence represented by scientific method. The existing school system presents, like existing life and culture, an incoherent mixture of values and standards derived from the old and the new. The school has neither the benefit of values inherent in a culture that existed centuries ago nor yet of the values inherent in those possibilities of present experience that can be realized by a more thoroughgoing use of scientific method. On the one hand, schools are so peculiarly subject to the power of tradition and of uncriticized custom that they embody the subjects and ends of the past. On the other hand, pressure of demands arising from existing conditions, especially those arising from contemporary industrial and economic institutions, has compelled the introduction of new subjects and new courses of study. The educational response in the latter case has been, however, almost as uncritical as the response that is exhibited in the adoption of values and ends having the sanction of tradition. Science and the applications of science that ushered in first the machine age and now the age of power have forced by their sheer social pressure the introduction into the educational system of scientific subjects and of occupational training. But to a large extent these new subjects overlay the older ones as a recent geological stratum overlays, with "faults" and distortions, older deposits.

❉   ❉   ❉

The issue of the relation of knowledge to experience is strikingly raised by the two opposed philosophies of education. According to one of them, knowledge is a final end in itself and nothing has a right to the name of "knowledge" (in its full sense) unless it is attained by a faculty of reason and rational intuition supposed to be independent of experience. To treat knowledge as an end in itself is equivalent to isolating it from activity. Hence, the conviction of those who hold this philosophy that education is "intellectual" only as knowledge is pursued apart from connection with practical experience. The other philosophy demands with equal insistence that education be made to nurture and develop intelligence. But intelligence is not supposed to be that separate faculty to which classic traditional philosophy gave the name "intellect"; it is trained power of judgment in choosing and forming means and ends in all the situations that life presents. The alternatives to formation of the fundamental attitudes and habits of life experience and of values and ends that give life whatever ordered articulation it possess through the use of science are convention, prejudice, custom, and desire to believe that which it is agreeable to believe, either because of its harmony with personal wishes or its conformity with the expectations and requirements of the particular group of which one is a member.

The philosophy that holds knowledge to be inherently related to experience, when experience is informed by scientific method, requires that the schools provide a place for first-hand experience. It is not enough, as is sometimes assumed by so-called "progressive" schools, that any kind of experience, as long as it is first-hand, will do. Nor is it enough to assume, as schools under the influence of routine tradition are given to assuming, that the function of experience is to produce forms of automatic skill. First-hand experience must be such as to evoke reflective observation and suggest ideas to be tested in appropriate forms of action. There must be continuity, not a stab at one thing one day and a jab at another thing the next day. Experience had outside school walls provides many opportunities for introduction within the school of activities under conditions that will utilize familiar everyday experiences for ends and values not subserved in the experiences had outside, values such as intellectual habits that are in harmony with the demands of scientific method and ability to understand social conditions and relations.

9. Philosophy Follows Rather than Leads

. . . Actually educational theories follow rather than lead—they are the rationalizations of pre-existing conditions. In the light of the attempt of German philosophers to develop a science of education which is autonomous, self-contained, and having its own ends, the point of view here presented must be emphasized. It is no accident or no mere coincidence that the pragmatic philosophy of education is peculiarly American and that American education is founded on the idea of progress, while the French emphasize the progress of ideas and the cult of reason.

10. Value Judgments by Scientists

We have, then, in connection with value judgments, a situation where attitudes are in the course of being altered; and since one of the ways of altering attitudes is *via* an alteration of beliefs, all science, with its careful attention to the truths of beliefs, has a bearing on what value judgments we will make and accept. And that, in essentials, is why it seems to me that scientists, so far from backing away from evaluations, should be particularly insistent on making them.

This is not to say, of course, that a scientist can altogether "prove" his evaluative contentions. He can't. . . . In other words, between the reasons I give and the evaluative judgment I'm trying to back up there's not a logical connection but only a psychological one. And the

9. Isaac L. Kandel, *Comparative Education.* Used by permission of the publishers (Boston: Houghton Mifflin Company, 1933), p. 24.

10. Charles L. Stevenson, "The Scientist's Role and the Aims of Education," *Harvard Educational Review,* 24:237–238, Fall, 1954.

same is true on all evaluative issues. If some one says scientifically that a discipline in Latin transfers to other things, we are always free to say that we don't give a hang about this transfer. But it remains the case that very often we *don't* elect to exercise this freedom—that the psychological, rather than logical, connection is quite enough for us. We aren't so different, psychologically, that an appeal to these not-quite-logical reasons is always unavailing; and that's why evaluations illuminated by science have a point to them.

You might still feel, however, that a scientist needn't actually *make* evaluations—and that you, approaching the study of education in a scientific spirit, can also be absolved from them. "Let us," you may say, "be content to have our scientists as pure scientists. Let us have them write up their results in encyclopedic form, and leave it to others to select from all the encyclopedia the established beliefs which, as inter-mediaries, will guide people in evaluating. The scientists needn't do the selecting at all."

I think that's impractical. . . . There is a full time job in *selecting* the data. And similarly for evaluative judgments, and in particular for deciding what education *ought* to aim at. The scientists best know their way among the factual beliefs; *they* must certainly be *among* those who select them, and adduce them as reasons that, serving as intermediaries, will get our attitudes straightened out under the guidance of beliefs that are well verified.

I think it would be a great pity, then, if those studying education should become so enamoured of pure science that they should suppose that value judgments were only for "others." But at the same time, I think it would be a great pity to fail to distinguish between value judgments and scientific conclusions. When a man goes from a scientific conclusion to a value judgment it seems to me that he should carefully give notice that the value judgment is *more* than a scientific conclusion, and that his repute as a scientist does not entitle him to an evaluation that purports to be the last word of adequacy. For the reasons that back up evaluations are not only less than logically related to the evaluation, but are often rebellious of being limited to any special field of science.

11. Philosophy as a Temporary Stop-Gap

Ordinarily a decision, though made in the light of an executive's entire experience, must be promptly made and can not wait to be

11. Truman L. Kelley, "The Scientific Versus the Philosophic Approach to the Novel Problem," *Science*, 71:298–299, March 21, 1930.

verified by a time-consuming study. Herein we may look for a difference between the philosophic and the scientific mental process.
I will quote the distinction that Dr. Kilpatrick draws in this connection. He states that science ordinarily postulates the question, "If I do
this what will happen," but that philosophy can not wait to see what
will happen. He says, "Philosophy in contrast faces a situation of
necessary action . . . Note that any situation confronting is actual and
must be met, and that any choice or course whatever, including refusal
to act, is *an* answer which carries with it its appropriate harvest of
consequences. Philosophy then asks, 'In the light of all this what shall
I do?'" I believe that Dr. Kilpatrick has here stated *the* essential difference between science and philosophy—other differences follow
therefrom. Philosophy is willing to attack any problem, any time,
anywhere, and give an immediate answer. Science is not. I would
not cite this as to the credit of either the one or the other, but do
cite it with Kilpatrick and Dewey as a difference of great moment.

The philosophic question, "In the light of all this what shall I do?"
may be paraphrased without inaccuracy as, "In the ignorance as to
consequences that enshrouds me, what shall I do?" for, of course, the
"appropriate harvest" is not known at the time the decision and resulting act are made. The philosophic answer to an issue is, "Do something
and the best you can," while the scientific answer is, "If in doubt delay
decision and investigate." Each procedure has its place in this life, this
hurly-burly in infinite time. It is something of a travesty upon the mind
of man that it is philosophy, sometimes thought of as the enduring, that
responds to the hurly-burly, and it is science, changing science, that
seeks to be judged by the standards of the permanent. Let us note some
of the consequences of these outlooks.

The scientist procrastinates decisions, is other worldly, is of little aid
in time of stress. He functions where deliberation and experimentation are possible, and his method is that of experimental analysis,
synthesis and verification. On the other hand, the philosopher provides
an almost immediate solution. He counsels in times of stress and rides
every emergency. His method is that of inadequate analysis, because
logical only . . . Knowing that he has a unique situation to deal with
he makes much of "integrations" and "total situations." His total picture, to which he reacts, may be grossly at variance with the real total
situation present, but of this he knows nothing because no experimental
synthesis of factors has been made.

The statement that "the (philosophical) effort is, as far as may be
possible, to find a course of action which will save all the interests
which will integrate all into one course of action that best saves all"
is also an excellent statement of the purpose of multiple correlation

and of any scientific attempt to explain total outcomes. Though science moves more slowly and with greater assurance here, not being free to synthesize except as experimentation gives warrant, still it moves with the same purpose as does philosophy. In connection with this issue Dr. Kilpatrick implies that science deals only with parts of situations, while philosophy deals with them entire. Now there is no logic that deals with wholes as wholes. If a problem case involving a cross-eyed, untrustworthy, brilliant, crippled, butcher's boy presents itself, what technique can treat this as a whole and without analysis? A logical or experimental analysis must be incorporated in any reasonable attempt to arrive at a solution of the total problem. How will you ever get the case referred to the oculist and how, unless there is analysis, will you ever get the cooperation of the father unless you call upon the butcher, etc.? Philosophy at its best must involve very detailed logical analysis followed by equally careful synthesis . . .

12. Philosophy is not Limited by Scientific Advance

. . . There has arisen the opinion, widely held in certain circles, that the advance of science, having thus at times cleared up doubt and so abolished old philosophic problems, will, given time enough, clear up all such problems and so, as it were, "push philosophy off the map." The contention—or hope—might be more tenable if we lived in a finite world, with nothing new happening in it. In such a world there may, for aught I know, be a finite number of problems with the possibility of solving at least some of them so that they would stay solved. So far as we can yet tell, however, our world is not finite, but has infinite possibilities for new problems. In fact, each significant advance of science, in general, adds more problems for philosophy than it subtracts, and besides makes many an old problem still more tangled. For instance, man in his philosophizing has not yet digested the doctrine of evolution, and now comes the new physics with the promise of enough problems to keep us busy for generations to come. In a smaller way, the testing movement in education has added to the number of problems facing the philosophy of education. Testing has helped to solve some problems in education, but it has added more than it has settled.

As long as the world remains infinite and science will oblige us by continuing to grow, philosophy has no fears of running out of problems.

12. William H. Kilpatrick, "The Relations of Philosophy and Science in the Study of Education," *School and Society*, 30:42–43, July 1929.

13. Philosophy as a Source of Educational Science

Philosophy of education is . . . a source of the science of education
in the degree in which it provides working hypotheses of comprehensive application. Both "working" and "hypotheses" are important. It
is hypotheses, not fixed and final principles or truths, that are provided; they have to be tested and modified as they are used in suggesting and directing the detailed work of observation and understanding.
They are working ideas; special investigations become barren and one-
sided in the degree in which they are conducted without reference to
a wider, more general view. This statement is particularly applicable
in the early stages of formation of a new science. Physics, chemistry,
biology, all have behind them a history that has put them in possession
of relatively tested and solid general principles. Just because educational science has no such achievement of laws to fall back upon, it is
in a tentative and inchoate state which renders it especially in need of
direction by large and fruitful hypotheses. No matter how these are
obtained, they are intrinsically philosophical in nature, good or bad
philosophy as the case may be. To treat them as scientific rather than
as philosophic is to conceal from view their hypothetical character and
to freeze them into rigid dogmas that hamper instead of assisting actual
inquiry.

14. A Traditionalist's View of Philosophy and Science

Where the modernist asserts the exclusive validity of the scientific
method, the traditionalist maintains that there are many valid methods
of inquiry, each appropriate to its own subject matter. All these
methods have certain fundamental features in common—objectivity,
intellectual honesty, care and precision in methodology, and the aggregation and consideration of all available evidence. . . .

In this sense of the term the traditionalist divides valid methods of
inquiry into two large groups, in one of which the method of empirical
science is the archetype. . . .

In contradistinction is the group of methods used by mathematics,

13. John Dewey, *The Sources of a Science of Education* (New York: Liveright
Publishing Corporation, 1931), pp. 54–55.

14. Mortimer J. Adler and Milton Mayer, *The Revolution in Education* (Chicago: University of Chicago Press, 1958), pp. 164–168.

philosophy, and theology. If investigation may be said to be the common characteristic of the first group, reflection (and, perhaps, discussion) may characterize the second, although the traditionalist would also use the terms "speculative thought," "insight," "analysis," and so on. His is popularly called "the armchair method" in contrast to "the laboratory method," and if the armchair is thought to be less powerful or precise than the laboratory, the traditionalist would remind his opponent that the great instruments of precision and power—including nuclear power—are the end products of the mathematician's armchair.

The traditionalist does not mean that experience plays no part in the methods of the mathematician, the philosopher, and the theologian, any more than the modernist means that reflective thinking plays no part in empirical research. But the distinction is still clear between what for brevity may be called "the investigative method" and "the reflective method" if it is remembered that the former uses special, specifically controlled, or specially arranged experiences as its materials, while the latter uses the common experience of mankind.

If philosophical investigation is to be conducted by a method different from that of science, then there is no necessity for a reconstruction of philosophy in an age of science—at least, not in so far as method is concerned. Philosophical inquiry must take account of new scientific knowledge, but the method by which the philosopher does his own characteristic work is unaffected. Neither the tremendous development of empirical science nor the application of its methods to new fields of inquiry alters the relationship of philosophy and science, although the clarification of that relationship may become more difficult and more important.

✱   ✱   ✱

What is uniquely modern about modern science, says the traditionalist, is not science itself but the modernist's attitude toward it. The real difference between a culture that is "modern" or "scientific" in this sense and the "pre-scientific" culture of the past is to be found in the fact that the modernist in philosophy has abandoned the method of philosophy for that of science. In short, the traditionalist would not call ours "the age of science" as if science were itself new, but, rather, the age of scientism or positivism, to the extent that the positive sciences have been taken as the only valid source of knowledge and their method as the only valid method of learning.

The assertion that there are sources of knowledge and methods of learning other than science and the scientific has two consequences that widen the breach between the traditionalist and the modernist.

The first is that the intellectual tradition may contain truths that are still true, judged by the criteria of philosophical inquiry. The second is that practical wisdom or knowledge of moral values cannot be acquired in the same way as scientific knowledge about matters of fact or real existence.

❖ ❖ ❖

The traditionalist makes three claims for philosophy, . . . The first is that philosophy is knowledge, not opinion or conjecture, and that it has the validity of knowledge as much as science. The second is that philosophical knowledge is independent of the empirical sciences in that the latter's methods are incapable of answering philosophical questions or of refuting philosophical conclusions. The third is that philosophical knowledge is superior to empirical science both theoretically and practically—theoretically, in that it is concerned with the ultimate nature of things, whereas science is concerned with their phenomenal aspects; and practically, in that it is concerned with directing human life and society to its ends or goals, while science is concerned with technological applications in the sphere of productivity for man's use en route.

It is in this last area—that of the practical—that values or ideals are found, and to which belongs the whole realm of moral philosophy (i.e., ethics, politics, and the first principles of jurisprudence, education, etc.). Because moral philosophy is practical thinking with regard to the ends of life and society, it has a logic that is different from that of the theoretical branches of philosophy (such as metaphysics or the philosophy of nature) as well as from the logic of science. Practical judgments of what should be done, are inherently different from theoretical judgment or judgments of fact, judgments of what is. Therefore moral problems, although their solution proceeds in part by the "armchair" method of all philosophy, cannot be solved in the same way as those either of the theoretical branches of science or of their technological applications to production.

15. One or Many Educational Philosophies?

The criteria for judging the several contributions to this volume must be the critical standards appropriate to philosophical inquiry, whereby truth is distinguished from falsity. This means, furthermore,

15. Mortimer J. Adler, National Society for the Study of Education, Forty-First Yearbook, *Philosophies of Education* (Chicago: University of Chicago Press, 1942), pp. 199–200.

that there cannot be many equally true, though opposed, philosophies of education. With respect to education, as with respect to every other matter which the philosopher considers, there can be only one set of true principles and conclusions. To say this is to say there is only one true philosophy of education, only one body of philosophical knowledge about education, and not a variety of equally entertainable "systems," each with its own arbitrary "postulates" and "definitions." In this field, as in any other, the philosopher must proceed from principles evident to all, and from real, not nominal, definitions, to conclusions validly drawn. This does not mean that those who endeavor to do philosophical work cannot make errors; otherwise, how would there be so many false philosophies of education? It means only that philosophical truth is demonstrable—much more so than scientific findings are, and even more than the sort of mathematical conclusions which depend upon postulates, as in various modern geometries. It means that every error which is made in the philosophy of education can be shown to be false, and must be rejected when it is so revealed. And, above all, it means that those who accept the obligation of being philosophers must accept nothing which has not been seen or been proved to be true, and reject nothing which has not been conclusively shown to be false.

No part of what is *strictly* the philosophy of education is either a matter of faith or of opinion. Although philosophy differs from science in both object and method, it is like science in this fundamental respect —that every one of its propositions is true only in the light of experienced fact and in terms of the canons of rational procedure. Like science, it differs not only from opinion, but also from dogmatic theology which proceeds in terms of a higher light than reason or experience can provide—the light of *supernatural* faith, the gift of God who has revealed Himself to men. In short, philosophy, like science, is *knowledge* and, as knowledge, is entirely *natural*. The principles of religious education cannot be *established* by the philosopher. They ultimately rest upon religious (supernatural) faith, and are matters properly for the theologian. . . .

Although I must hold that there is only one true philosophy of education, because no other position is compatible with the conception of philosophy as knowledge rather than as opinion, I cannot say, *for the same reason*, that what I am here going to offer as an account of the philosophy of education is *the* true *one*. I would not be offering it, of course, if I did not think it true, but whether it is true or false depends upon whether it does or does not satisfy all the criteria relevant to a critical judgment on philosophical work. Each reader must ultimately decide that for himself.

2

Traits of Reality

Problems in the Philosophy of Education Discussed in this Section

1. Is the world of nature to be taken as the ultimately real? Are there laws of nature according to which educational controversies can be adjudicated? Does the parent or teacher interfere with these laws at his peril?
2. Do educational controversies have to be appealed to the supernatural as a court of last resort?
3. What is it that makes the predictability of educational outcomes more or less uncertain? Is the contingency in the educational environment genuine or is it merely the result of human ignorance?
4. Can there be learning without novelty? What is a "novel" learning situation? Is novelty apparent only to the learner? Are individual differences between pupils to be considered as really unique? Can education be genuinely "creative"?
5. Is change the ultimate character of reality, or merely the finite appearance of an underlying reality that is immutable? Would it be preferable to base a philosophy of education on something that is fixed and immutable?
6. Can the great differences between pupils, learning situations, pressure groups, educational values, and the like be ultimately reconciled in some grand synthesis, or is a certain amount of contradiction (chaos, irrationality) inescapable for the educational philosopher?
7. Is it necessary for the educator to make any commitment as to the initial origin or ultimate destiny of the pupil?
8. How should "progressive education" be conceived? Might progressive education some day become outmoded? Under what circumstances? Will education inevitably progress? Is it evolutionary? Is its progress governed by some fixed external end?
9. Can anything evolve in the course of educational history which was not already involved at some prior point of time? Does the "recapitulation" or the "culture epoch" theory of education follow from such a premise?

I. THE NATURE OF BEING

16. Personalism as an Ultimate Explanation

Personalism has an intimate relationship with education because it teaches that all reality including the school is personal. The school is spiritual in nature, the unity of selves or persons, and is truer to life than any presupposition of impersonalism. The problem of educational personalism is to determine the nature, number and relations of selves which make up the school and ascertain whether the thought of literature and other subjects is personal or impersonal. Since thought from its nature must be personal the world which is but an expression of the thought of God is personal, and the thought of all literature, science and history must also be personal because it is the thought of some thinking mind. The teacher knows he is a person; and as one ethical school says, must respect other beings as persons, therefore, the school which is merely the organization of persons is itself a person "writ large." Teaching is an activity existing between persons and has many personal elements, and personal freedom for its supreme end.

17. Education Explained in Terms of Will

A standard must next be sought by which the value of educational processes and influences may be judged. I find this standard in the conclusion, common, I am confident, to the best philosophy and to the soundest science alike, that the facts of nature must be explained, in the last resort, in terms of energy, and that energy in turn can be conceived only in terms of will, which is the fundamental form of the life of mind or spirit.

18. Experience as Reality

The most fundamental value in the experimentalist philosophy is its method. This method is the method of experience. It is radically

16. Arthur C. Fleshman, *The Metaphysics of Education* (Boston: Mayhew Publishing Company, 1914), pp. 143–144.
17. Nicholas M. Butler, *The Meaning of Education* (New York: Charles Scribner's Sons, 1915), p. 5.
18. John L. Childs, *Education and the Philosophy of Experimentalism* (New York: Appleton-Century-Crofts, Inc., 1931), p. 30.

empirical. It boldly takes the things of ordinary experience as evidential of the nature of reality. The doings and undergoings of men, the
things men suffer and enjoy—everyday human experience—is said to
be just as evidential of the nature of nature as is an electron or a star.
Reality is not considered to be something back of, ulterior to, essentially
different in kind from, this world of man's experience; but is held to
be precisely this world of common experience in all of the myriad
forms that experience takes.

19. Mind as an Ultimate and Eternal Reality

To take the second familiar fact (since philosophy presents us with
no new facts) which may provide us with a thread of meaning, to lead
us through the labyrinth of the phenomenal into the open place of the
noumenal, viz., education shows us a development, the unrealized
powers of mind through exercise becoming actualized. But what in
the nature of things is the possibility of development? . . . Can something develop from nothing? In disobedience of the dicta alike of
medieval scholasticism and modern biology? Can mind come from
something not itself mental? the unlike giving birth to the like. Can
maturity of mind develop out of simple immaturity? time thus making
additions to the sum total of reality as against what might be called
the law of the unity and conservation of the Absolute? Can that
develop in the temporal process which is not eternally realized? as
against the doctrine of the Stagirite that there is no δύναμις without
ἐνέργεια. Education finds itself unable to understand how the development of unrealized mind which it secures can occur without implying
that, underneath its whole process and giving power at every point, is
the one realized mind. Not a first cause in a temporal series of events
does education reflectively and vainly seek, but an adequate cause
of its great central fact of development. This it satisfactorily finds only
in the existence of a mind which needs no development itself, and so
can guarantee the fruitfulness of all educational efforts for development. Thus education upon reflection is forced to hold that the reality
it declares mental it must also declare actual.

19. Herman H. Horne, *The Philosophy of Education* (New York: The Macmillan Company, 1927), pp. 264–265.

II. THE NATURAL AND SUPERNATURAL

20. Education According to Nature

God makes all things good; man meddles with them and they become evil. He forces one soil to yield the products of another, one tree to bear another's fruit. He confuses and confounds time, place, and natural conditions. He mutilates his dog, his horse, and his slave. He destroys and defaces all things; he loves all that is deformed and monstrous; he will have nothing as nature made it, not even man himself, who must learn his paces like a saddle-horse, and be shaped to his master's taste like the trees in his garden.

Yet things would be worse without this education, and mankind cannot be made by halves. Under existing conditions a man left to himself from birth would be more of a monster than the rest. Prejudice, authority, necessity, example, all the social conditions into which we are plunged, would stifle nature in him and put nothing in her place.

       ❁   ❁   ❁

Plants are fashioned by cultivation, man by education. If a man were born tall and strong, his size and strength would be of no good to him till he had learnt to use them; they would even harm him by preventing others from coming to his aid; left to himself he would die of want before he knew his needs. We lament the helplessness of infancy; we fail to perceive that the race would have perished had not man begun by being a child.

We are born weak, we need strength; helpless, we need aid; foolish, we need reason. All that we lack at birth, all that we need when we come to man's estate, is the gift of education.

This education comes to us from nature, from men, or from things. The inner growth of our organs and faculties is the education of nature, the use we learn to make of this growth is the education of men, what we gain by our experience of our surroundings is the education of things.

       ❁   ❁   ❁

Now of these three factors in education nature is wholly beyond our control, things are only partly in our power; the education of men is the only one controlled by us; and even here our power is largely

20. Jean Jacques Rousseau, *Émile*, Barbara Foxley, translator (New York: E. P. Dutton & Co., Inc., Everyman's Library, 1911), pp. 5–9.

illusory, for who can hope to direct every word and deed of all with whom the child has to do.

Viewed as an art, the success of education is almost impossible, since the essential conditions of success are beyond our control. Our efforts may bring us within sight of the goal, but fortune must favour us if we are to reach it.

What is this goal? As we have just shown, it is the goal of nature. Since all three modes of education must work together, the two that we can control must follow the lead of that which is beyond our control.

✻   ✻   ✻

The natural man lives for himself; he is the unit, the whole, dependent only on himself and on his like. The citizen is but the numerator of a fraction, whose value depends on its denominator; his value depends upon the whole, that is, on the community. Good social institutions are those best fitted to make a man unnatural, to exchange his independence for dependence, to merge the unit in the group, so that he no longer regards himself as one, but as a part of the whole, and is only conscious of the common life.

✻   ✻   ✻

He who would preserve the supremacy of natural feelings in social life knows not what he asks. Ever at war with himself, hesitating between his wishes and his duties, he will be neither a man nor a citizen. He will be of no use to himself nor to others. He will be a man of our day, a Frenchman, an Englishman, one of the great middle class.

✻   ✻   ✻

Our inner conflicts are caused by these contradictions. Drawn this way by nature and that way by man, compelled to yield to both forces, we make a compromise and reach neither goal.

✻   ✻   ✻

In the natural order men are all equal and their common calling is that of manhood, so that a well-educated man cannot fail to do well in that calling and those related to it. It matters little to me whether my pupil is intended for the army, the church, or the law. Before his parents chose a calling for him nature called him to be a man. Life is the trade I would teach him. When he leaves me, I grant you, he will be neither a magistrate, a soldier, nor a priest; he will be a man. All that becomes a man he will learn as quickly as another. In vain will fate change his station, he will always be in his right place.

21. Naturalistic Aims are Unsatisfactory

The form of a system of education, e.g., the naturalistic, is determined by its goal. But what is the goal of naturalistic education? Since the naturalistic educators deny existence outside of nature, it follows that the goal must be found within nature. But where, in nature, should we locate our goal? If in man, who is a part of nature, then the naturalistic system breaks down into either individualistic or social education, depending upon whether we make individual man or generic mankind the center of education. If we locate our goal in the non-man part of nature, we fall into the dilemma of drawing an aim for the education of man, who is on the highest stage in the evolutionary process, from the lower evolutionary stages. Lastly, if we locate our goal in nature as a whole, then education would be nothing more than living according to nature; for man, being a part of nature, is evolving according to natural laws. But if we adopt this viewpoint, which is that of the thoroughgoing naturalist, we theoretically can't do anything about man's education; for man, being a part of nature, will live according to natural law, no matter what he does, or in what direction he grows. All will be "natural development." Practically, however, the teacher watches the child's development, and either encourages or discourages traits which the child evinces from time to time. But to do that, the teacher must have a criterion, which he can't draw from nature because the child's traits, good or bad, are "natural" and they manifest themselves and develop according to nature. Accordingly naturalistic pedagogues usually draw their criteria from ethics, with the result that naturalistic education again fails to find a goal for itself within nature.

22. Naturalism as the Uniform and Essential

Naturalism in one form or another is the doctrine that has lately come to prevail in American education. It is the doctrine that holds that the natural world, the world of sensible things and physical

21. Gustav G. Schoenchen, *The Activity School* (New York: Longmans, Green & Company, 1940), p. 77.

22. Robert M. Hutchins, "The Philosophy of Education," in R. N. Montgomery, editor, *The William Rainey Harper Memorial Conference* (Chicago: University of Chicago Press, 1938.)

change, is all there is. The supernatural is superstition. As the boundaries of knowledge are extended, those of superstition must necessarily contract. Since John Dewey the leaders of our profession have insisted that the scope of education be limited to the world of physical and social change. They hold that we have outgrown the superstition that this world is preparation for the next. The end of man is no longer that beatitude which comes through the vision of the Divine Essence. The end of man is restricted to what may be accomplished here on earth. We must devote ourselves to those studies which, we think, will prepare our pupils to live in the here and now.

Naturalism should stand for an educational program based upon and directed toward the nature of things. Oddly enough American educational naturalism does nothing of the sort. It is really a false naturalism which turns us away from nature; it is an empiricism which leads us to concern ourselves not with nature but with experience. Empiricism is content with experience. True naturalism would pass through experience to the nature of things.

✳   ✳   ✳

The ancient sophists held that fire was natural because it burned in Greece and Persia alike, today and long ago. Laws, they said, were conventional because they vary with the time and place. In this saying there is a true insight and a false note. The true insight is that nature is the uniform, the permanent. It is not static, but its changing countenance shows regular features and a certain fixity of expression. The false note is that conventions are not entirely fortuitous and irregular. Convention, like art, must have a natural basis, and in that basis, human nature is the source of uniformity in the variegated practices of men.

This brings us to one more distinction involved in the notion of nature. The nature of anything is that which is essential to its constitution; what makes it a thing of a certain sort. But we know that things are not only of a certain sort; they are also individual and unique things of that sort. We are forced to distinguish the nature of things from all accidents of their individuality. The nature of man does not exhaust the character of John Smith; but we do not know John Smith by knowing only his individual characteristics. We must know him as a man, having a human nature in which all other men participate.

All these distinctions are related to another: the distinction between knowledge and opinion. Knowledge has nature for its object: the essential, the universal, the uniform. Opinion is concerned with conventions and particulars. An educational program is soundly naturalistic if it seeks primarily to inculcate knowledge rather than opinion; if it directs students to the understanding of nature instead of giving them information about conventions; if it deals with the universal and the uniform rather than the particular and the variable. I do not mean that the study of convention is not part of education. I mean only that it must be a subordinate part and that it must be studied not for its own sake but for the sake of the contribution it can make to the comprehension of nature. The false naturalism that now prevails is so occupied with the startling variety of the changing world that it does not penetrate to the nature of things. That is what I mean by saying that contemporary naturalism is not naturalism at all; it is empiricism.

Contemporary naturalism in education often appeals to the natural scientists for support. The appeal is specious. The good scientist always holds the universal and the invariant to be the object of his research. It is the generalizations with which research concludes that constitute the grand scheme of science. Scientists attempt to formulate the principles underlying change, and in doing so they separate the essential from the accidental, the universal from the particular. We must not be misled by what scientists say or by the wildly empirical character of some of their teaching. Science, when it is true science, is not the collection of data; it is the determination of general laws.

Nor can contemporary naturalists in education appeal for help to the theory of evolution. Nothing in *The Origin of Species* or since justifies the view that everything is in flux, or, I may add, that all change is beneficial. It is naive to suppose that evolution denies constants and uniformities. The problem of the origin of species would be meaningless if there were no species. A species is the constant and uniform nature of an indefinite number of animals. A group of animals belong to a species because they have this nature. If you deny that there is nature in this sense, you deny the existence of species and you make nonsense out of the problem and theory of evolution. So long as a species exists, it is a constant, a set of related characteristics essentially the same for all the individuals occurring in that species. Now man is a biological species. All men belong to this species and their specific human nature is a constant in the world of change. This constant must be the object of the science of man and of all the studies of human affairs, for conventions can be grasped only in terms of it. To use the theory of evolution or indeed any of the ideas or methods of natural science as an argument in behalf of naturalism as we now use the term in education is simply unsophisticated.

It is in those disciplines dealing with man and society that the naturalists have produced the greatest emphasis on convention. The process is about as follows. We are going to study nature. Nature is

those things which can be touched, observed, and measured. Since the
only aspects of man that can be investigated this way are physiological,
psychology is a physiological science. In so far, then, as psychology
deals with anything of importance, it is physiology—all about muscles
and the central nervous system. The nature of man as distinguished
from the other animals scarcely appears in it.

The result is that there is no such thing as the intellectual life of
man. The mind is regarded as a biochemical mechanism developed to
solve practical problems. There is no such thing as the truth. All the
ideas that men have had were conventions of their time and place and
may be disregarded, since we live in a different time and usually in a
different place. The thing to do is to get together and pull for the
benefit of the community. But what is the benefit of the community?
Science cannot tell us. It may secure us the control of nature; but it
cannot tell us what to do with it after we have got it. The wisdom of
our forefathers cannot tell us. By definition they lived in a different
time. The naturalists say that philosophy cannot tell us because it is
mere words; it isn't about "scientific facts"; science is always correcting
it and limiting its scope just as it is always restricting religion and
other superstitions. It is, therefore, in those fields in which the aim of
the activity as well as the laws of it is important that the doctrine of
naturalism has caused the most confusion. In courses in law, ethics,
politics, economics, and history, we have descriptions of what is and
has been because we can have nothing else. The critic must have some
standard for criticism. What works is an unworkable standard. What
is in accordance with man's nature, and hence best for man, is inadmis-
sible because our naturalists will have nothing to do with man's nature.
There is nothing left but description which makes no distinction between what is natural and what is conventional. It is impossible to
reconcile insistence on convention with the possibility of principles in
human action. Yet a contemporary economist tells us that "we must
remember that there are certain economic principles which have
validity irrespective of the historical framework in which they operate."
If this is so, it must be because of the consistency of human nature and
of the world in which we live. If there are such principles, it would
appear that there must be principles of equal validity in law, history,
sociology, ethics, and politics, for these disciplines also deal with man.
If human nature is constant in economics, it must be constant in these
other disciplines, too. In these other disciplines, too, our principal
aim should be to communicate these principles.

I hasten to add that I by no means am to be taken as saying that the
sole aim of instruction in these or any other fields is the communication
of general principles. Convention is as important in daily life as nature

is. But unless nature is understood, convention is incomprehensible. It is something to be memorized and that is all. If we had to choose (as we do not) between teaching general principles and teaching conventions illustrating them, we should, however, be forced to choose general principles, because with a grasp of those a student might understand conventions as he met them after graduation. He is not likely to come to an understanding of general principles without the guidance which the educational system was intended to provide.

I hasten to add, also, that I am not here discussing pedagogical method. It is perfectly possible to consider convention first, such as the government of the pupil's city, state, or country, and pass from it to a consideration of the nature of the state. I should not feel moved to protest unless the pupil never got to the nature of the state or unless the teacher left him with the notion that the convention described was nature. The problem here is not how to teach. This question is subordinate to the question what to teach, the question which in our excitement about educational housing, administration, method, and finance we have most neglected.

In education with a capital E, education as a whole, as distinguished from education in any particular branch of knowledge, the doctrine of naturalism has led to most unfortunate results. I shall mention only two. It has produced emphasis on the immediately useful. It has destroyed the curriculum. If there is nothing true except what works; if there is no knowledge except information about the past and present; if there are no principles, then certainly what we should do is to train our pupils to earn a living. They should be familiar with current technological conventions. They should study salesmanship and typewriting . . .

Naturalism has destroyed the curriculum in the same way. There is nothing to be taught except things obviously not worth teaching. Therefore we must have great men and women to do the teaching. Only they can make the insignificant significant. If the student learns no subject matter, his life will at least be illumined by the radiance of these great personalities. Pay no attention to what you should teach. Get Solomon in all his glory to sit behind the desk, and your pupils will get an education.

I think they would. The trouble is that there is only one Solomon, and he has been a long time dead. What chance have ordinary teachers like us to light up the dark recesses of the cosmetic industry or enliven the reports of the Census Bureau? If the curriculum can be about convention, there is no convention it cannot be about. There is no triviality too slight for us. If the major premise is that convention shall be taught, a perfectly good syllogism justifying a curriculum including everything from table manners to surrealism can be readily developed. It is thus that the course of study has sunk in the morass of the insignificant. There is nothing to tell us what is significant and what not.

There is another way in which the destruction of the curriculum is defended which takes its origin from the same source. If nature means convention, then we are not dealing with human nature in the classroom. We are dealing with individuals. Individuals are different. Hence no curriculum is worth developing. Each individual must receive different treatment. The way to determine what treatment to give him is to determine what interests him. Whatever interests him is what he should study. This is a doctrine of what is called Progressive Education.

The trouble is that, though individuals are different, they are also the same. The sameness is their human nature. If, as the Progressive Educators say they wish to do, we want to "socialize" our pupils, we are not likely to accomplish it by emphasizing their conventional as against their natural characteristics. We do not wish, if this is our aim, to indulge individuality. We wish to develop humanity. Such a desire will require us to have a course of study which will emphasize the common qualities of man and the constant qualities of his nature rather than the accidents of an individual.

Progressive Education has made great contributions to the method of education. It has restored interest to its role in learning. It is probably fair to say that without interest nothing can be taught. It does not follow that whatever is interesting must be taught. We must discover what the subjects are that must be taught and teach them in as interesting a way as we can.

At this point I beg to say that I deprecate the appropriation by the Progressive Educators of the word "progressive." By inference everybody who does not agree with them is reactionary.

                            *   *   *

To the naturalist-become-conventionalist there is no truth except relative truth tested by what works. This is supposed to be a "liberal" position. We see at once that in theoretical matters nothing can be said for it. One who holds that two and two make five is not a liberal; he is a fool. In practical matters there is no doubt that more than theory is required. Practical wisdom is, in effect, theory plus experience. But there must be some standard of what constitutes "working." Fascism seems to be working in Italy today. Injustice seems to be prevailing in China. Are these things right or true because they have not yet been stopped? Convention as the test of morals, custom as the test of law, "success" as the test of truth—these are the criteria to which, oddly enough, naturalism has brought us.

We are sometimes given to understand that nobody can be a liberal unless he holds that everybody is entitled to his own opinion. Of course, nobody actually believes this. Nobody would say that a person who had never studied a subject was entitled to an opinion about it. Liberal professors claim freedom only for other professors; they do not think the uninitiated layman is entitled to an opinion of their work. And frequently in faculty meetings I have heard them suggest that professors in other departments were not competent to pass judgment upon them. Of course, we are all liberals in the sense that we do not want to shoot anybody who disagrees with us. We will let him live. But we do not really believe that his opinion is as good as ours. We do not think he may be right. In fact, we know he is wrong.

True liberalism springs from an understanding of man, his rights, his duties, his powers, and his ends. It springs, too, from a comprehension of the difference between knowledge and opinion. On matters of opinion men may differ, though it is to be hoped that they will make some effort to make their opinions intelligent. Nor should we be forced to hold that the opinion of a dunce and a dullard, even on a matter of opinion, was as valuable as the opinion of a wise man. On matters of knowledge men should agree. The object of education is to help them toward agreement. If men were perfectly rational, they might still disagree on matters of opinion. They would no longer disagree on matters of knowledge. The aim of education is to increase the rationality of the race.

23. Naturalism is False Apart from the Supernatural

. . . Every form of pedagogic naturalism which in any way excludes or weakens supernatural Christian formation in the teaching of youth, is false. Every method of education founded, wholly or in part, on the denial or forgetfulness of original sin and of grace, and relying on the sole powers of human nature, is unsound. Such, generally speaking, are those modern systems bearing various names which appeal to a pretended self-government and unrestrained freedom on the part of the child, and which diminish or even suppress the teacher's authority and action, attributing to the child an exclusive primacy of initiative, and an activity independent of any higher law, natural or Divine, in the work of his education.

If any of these terms are used, less properly, to denote the necessity

23. Pius XI, "The Christian Education of Youth," *Catholic Educational Review*, 28:149–150, March 1930.

of a gradually more active cooperation on the part of the pupil in his own education; if the intention is to banish from education despotism and violence, which, by the way, just punishment is not, this would be correct, but in no way new . . .

But alas! it is clear from the obvious meaning of the words and from experience, that what is intended by not a few, is the withdrawal of education from every sort of dependence on the Divine law. So today we see, strange sight indeed, educators and philosophers who spend their lives in searching for a universal moral code of education, as if there existed no Decalogue, no Gospel law, no law even of nature stamped by God on the heart of man, promulgated by right reason, and codified in positive Revelation by God himself in the Ten Commandments. These innovators are wont to refer contemptuously to Christian education as "heteronomous," "passive," "obsolete," because founded upon the authority of God and His holy law.

Such men are miserably deluded in their claim to emancipate, as they say, the child, while in reality they are making him the slave of his own blind pride and of his disorderly affections, which, as a logical consequence of this false system, come to be justified as legitimate demands of a so-called autonomous nature.

III. STATIC AND DYNAMIC

24. A Curriculum Based on Unchanging Reality

. . . Since the properties of number appear to have the power of leading us towards reality, these must be among the studies we are in search of. The soldier must learn them in order to marshal his troops; the philosopher, because he must rise above the world of change and grasp true being, or he will never become proficient in the calculations of reason . . . They are to practice calculation, not like merchants or shopkeepers for purposes of buying and selling, but with a view to war and to help in the conversion of the soul itself from the world of becoming to truth and reality.

❋   ❋   ❋

. . . For such [military] purposes a small amount of geometry and arithmetic will be enough. We have to ask whether a much more advanced study will help towards a comprehension of the essential Form of Goodness. Any study, as we have said, will have that tendency, if

24. Plato, *The Republic*, Cornford translation (Oxford University Press, 1955), p. 236.

it forces the soul to turn towards the region of that beatific reality, which it must by all means behold. So geometry will be suitable or not, according as it makes us contemplate reality or the world of change. . . .

In this respect, then, no one who has even a slight acquaintance with geometry will deny that the nature of this science is in flat contradiction with the absurd language used by mathematicians, for want of better terms. They constantly talk of "operations" like "squaring," "applying," "adding," and so on, as if the object is to do something, whereas the true purpose of the whole subject is knowledge—knowledge, moreover, of what eternally exists, not of anything that comes to be this or that at some time and ceases to be.

25. Permanence Stems from Man, Change from Society

Once this concept of the curriculum as the tool in the hands of the teacher to be used in the realization of educational aims is accepted, the question immediately arises, "Is this a perfect tool, or is it subject to continued improvement?" In other words, is it to be expected that the curriculum will be constantly undergoing changes; or, on the contrary, can we ever expect that some day it will reach perfection, and the only task of the teacher will be to improve his technique in its use? In answering this question there are two principles which give us guidance, one which we may call the principle of *permanence,* the other the principle of *change.* The principle of permanence arises from the nature of man; the principle of change, from the nature of society. No one questions that society is constantly undergoing changes. These changes during the last half century have been so manifold and so important, that we could hardly expect the curriculum of the school to keep up with them, even if it were thought desirable that all social changes should be immediately reflected by changes in the curriculum. Any school that tries to keep up with all social changes, introducing them before they have proved their worth for the betterment of social living, would be so lacking in stability that it would be ruinous for the lives of the individual pupils who form its clientele and for the welfare of the society in which they are soon to be the adult members. We have the other principle, however, to offset the inherent dissipating tendencies of the principle of change, and this is the principle of permanence. As said above, it arises from the nature of man. In spite

25. William F. Cunningham, *The Pivotal Problems of Education* (New York: The Macmillan Company, 1940), pp. 282–285.

of the statement of some psychologists so-called, who tell us that human nature is constantly undergoing changes, and that the business of the new education is to accelerate these changes, we contend that just the contrary is the true statement of the case. Psychologically, the forces resident within man are the same today as they have been from the beginning, and the same as they will be tomorrow. It is the forces outside of man that are constantly undergoing changes. On this principle, there are certain elements within the curriculum, if it is to be an instrument for the perfection of man's nature as it unfolds through childhood and adolescence into adulthood, which will always remain substantially the same. Thus, language study will aways remain the core of the curriculum of general education, though, of course, the particular language that constitutes that core will change from people to people. In China it will be Chinese, but in the United States of America it will be English; and language study, taught either formally in language classes or informally in other classes in which it is the medium of instruction, will always be one of the essential elements of the curriculum in general education.

The reason for this is obvious. In our concept of the nature of man there is a duality. Man is matter and spirit, united in substantial union to form the being we call man. On this basis, man, therefore, is an animal carrying on many activities in common with the members of brute creation, but the matter of chief concern to the school is that he is a *rational* animal. From this rationality arise two powers which mark man off from animals of the lower orders, namely, the power of thought and the power of expression. When we say the power of thought, we mean, of course, the ability to do abstract thinking. Thinking in the concrete may be ascribed to animals of the lower order. After all, a dog knows his master; and knowing, even on this level, is a kind of thinking. But conceptual thought, abstract thinking, is an entirely different affair, and this is peculiarly characteristic of man. In the same way, expression on a very low level is characteristic of the lower animals, but only in a metaphorical sense can they be said to have a language; and nowhere do we find even the slightest trace of anything resembling a written language. Perhaps even more important for human kind is the fact that language is not only a tool for communication; it is a tool for thinking. Words are labels for ideas, and as labels they are of particular importance in the realm of abstract thinking. Without such labels it is hard to see how the mind could hold ideas before it, comparing one with another, discovering relationships between ideas, that is, making inferences, and this is the very nature of abstract thinking. Hence we repeat: on the level of general education, language must always be the core of the curriculum.

26. Education as a Realization of the Eternally Self-Realized

The reasonable, the divine, has absolute power to realize itself. It has run its perfect course from eternity. It is not so powerless that it must wait for some far-off beginning. The world stands as the realization of the divine reason; only upon the surface rules the play of unintelligent caprice. It, therefore, may be considered complete and independent; at least with as much, and, perhaps, with more, correctness than may the individual just growing into manhood. Thus the man acts with reason in giving up his plan of making the world anew, and in striving instead to work out his personal aims, desires and interests only as a member of the world. Even so there is room for honorable, far-reaching, creative activity. For, although the world must be regarded as complete, still it is no dead thing, nor inert. But, like the life-process in general, it ever renews itself while at the same time it is ever advancing. The man's work is a part of his renewal and advancement.

So, while it is true that a man can bring forth only what is already present, it is also true that progress is the result of his activity. But it takes an enormous lever to move the world. A vast number of individuals must labor at it. However, if a man after a half century of work looks back, he will see that there has been progress . . . For this it is necessary, above all things, that the training of the young man be adequate.

27. Genuine Novelty in Change

It becomes now necessary to inquire regarding the nature of the world we live in. The older educational view, which formed also the starting point for the scientific (measuring) movement, expected, as we have seen, to set before the young what they were to study and learn. This view began back in such days as Boas tells us about, when man could go thirty thousand years without perceptibly changing his culture. In such days, and much later, each generation so nearly repeated the preceding that conscious education largely restricted itself to handing

26. George William Frederick Hegel, quoted in F.L. Luqueer, *Hegel as Educator* (New York: The Macmillan Co., 1896), pp. 125–126.
27. William H. Kilpatrick, "The Essentials of the Activity Movement," *Progressive Education,* 11:349–351, October 1934.

on to the rising generation what the elders had previously received from their parents.

Later, when knowledge began to be seriously studied, it was largely thought of as authoritatively fixed either by revelation or by necessary laws of nature and thought. In any case, it was the individual's duty to acquire and accept and act accordingly. Now this outlook implicitly supposed a fixed-in-advance future:

> Yea, the first Morning of Creation wrote
> What the last day of reckoning shall read.

Until very recently these words perhaps held for most of us, some seeing the fixing as fore-knowledge and predestination and others as the working of nature's eternal and inclusive laws. To be sure, novelty was a fact, but somehow it was negligible. To the orthodox theologian, everything was predestined. To the classical philosopher who looked at things *sub specie aeternitatis*, change was unreal. To the physical scientist, all apparent change was but the motion and recombination of eternal elements, all of which we might in time hope to foretell with certainty.

From this point of view, education was specific, consisting of training in distinct skills, habits, facts, etc. Thinking was soft-pedaled; in any event, it was limited to the few. Personality was slighted. Education was to make people efficient according to a prearranged plan. This fixedness in advance might reach also further. The system of social institutions was often conceived as already substantially fixed. Education, as stated by one writer, was to be thought of as a process "of transforming individuals so that they will conform to institutions." Schools were devised to "insure the transformation of every child so far as possible, into a being able and willing to conform to the social pattern of action and thought," this social pattern not being thought of as in process of change.

*   *   *

We do not have to suppose that any proponent of this position accepted all the implications inherent in it. (Fortunately, perhaps, people are not so consistent.) The tendencies are there, however, and school work has suffered accordingly.

But is life so fixed-in-advance that a "complete science of psychology," as one author suggests, is conceivable? Are our existing institutions so fixed and perfect that education exists simply or even primarily to transform individuals into conformity with them? Is life so fixed in advance that its problems and their solutions can be blue printed? Is the human personality to be constructed in the same mechanical fashion as the engineer makes a bridge? A generation ago when the science of physics seemed perfected and all phenomena were expected by scientists to come under the fatalism of its iron laws (Psychology to be reduced to physiology, and physiology in its turn to chemistry and physics) it required hardihood for Peirce and James and Dewey to uphold the doctrine of an unsettled and contingent future. But they took the stand. And now physics itself renouncing practically all its former fundamental assumptions, has joined them. Out of better thinking there has come a practical consensus that actually novel events are still in the making.

We feel safe, then, in asserting that the future with which man deals is not fixed, but is in continual process. The world of affairs, both as a whole and in its significant details, gives us always a process of unique becoming. Life develops novelly, always mingling the familiar and unfamiliar. By means of the old and familiar, we see somewhat into the situation at hand and can, in some measure, control it. But there are limits beyond which we cannot see or control, and these limits are never known beforehand. These several characteristics of the total life process affect crucially the situation which education faces and so affect crucially our conception of education and how it should be managed. For one fundamental thing, widespread creative thinking follows as a necessary corollary. No mere fixed-in-advance responses could take care of our kind of world. Being novelly developing, it requires thinking and not mere habit to deal with it.

The opposed position (more or less set out above.) is that the stream of life and affairs consists entirely of the recombination of eternal elements, seeming novelty being due solely to human ignorance. On this basis, expanding science would gradually encroach upon man's ignorance and master more and more of the combinations so as to foretell ever better what to expect and how to meet it. Education then would call, on the one hand, for experts to identify and foretell the problems and find the answers and, on the other, for teachers to pass on the expert-made answers to the rest of us. The expert few would have need of thinking, the rest of us could rely sufficiently on the answer-habits drilled into us by our teachers.

During the generation just past those who adopted this position sought in varying degrees to impose that kind of education on our schools. But with novelty playing the continual part it does in ordinary life, it becomes impossible to foreknow the answers so that mere habit-drill will suffice. Take so simple a thing as crossing a busy street which has no traffic lights. No mother, however wise, could stay at home and make a nonthinking plan whereby her young child might safely cross this street when he comes to it. The problem cannot be solved in advance, but only on the spot in terms of what is then and there going on. The same is characteristic of life in all its significant aspects. Whether to start walking, where to walk and how fast, when to stop, are all matters of conscious control adjusted to the ends which one is pursuing.

The conclusion from this is an emphasis upon thinking as the rule of life. And education becomes primarily the process of building up good thinking with, of course, the correlative habits of acting obediently to the best thinking one can do. Acting upon thinking may then be taken as the unit element of the educative process. Our aim would accordingly be that the child have such varied opportunities of acting on thinking as would promise best to build up in him good thinking always with correlative appropriate action.

28. Change Implies the Changeless

What we want to know is whether there really is a world of reality, changeless in character, which is grasped by the intellect, which remains despite man's denial and social change, which is implied even by the process of change itself.

Now thought does possess just such a world, and it can be shown to do so. In general, it is the realm of concepts, essences, universals. The very notion of change implies the changeless. Without the permanent there is no impermanent. The only constant may be change, yet there is a constant. If there were only change, we might not be conscious of it, as we are not conscious of the weight of the air which is always present but never sensed. Certain characteristics even of changing phenomena do not change, for example, all phenomena have both form and content, both figure and stuff. Here is a formal changeless truth about our changing world . . . The changeless conceptual order is one thing, the changing perceptual order is a different thing. And the changeless conceptual order permeates the changing perceptual order as changeless space permeates changing matter. These views remain in any actual or conceivable form of human society. Educationally, they mean that there is an intellectual which is concerned, as the pragmatic philosophy says, with the changing practical; and also that there is an intellectual, denied by the pragmatic philosophy, which is concerned with the changeless order of things. Our education should adjust us to the changeless as well as the changing. That is the kind of world we live in.

28. Herman H. Horne, *The Democratic Philosophy of Education* (New York: The Macmillan Company, 1935), pp. 366–367.

IV. TEMPORAL AND ETERNAL

29. Being and Becoming

The category of ultimate reality is being; of temporal reality, and so of education, is becoming. Through education the individual becomes in time what he eternally is. Never-ending life is God's education of man into His own likeness.

30. Education is a Temporal Process

Reality is the heavenly city of philosophy and education is one of its signboards.

What then is the reality as indicated by education? Attempting first to put the facts of education all together so as to view them as one, two things are seen, viz., education is a world-process, and it is a temporal process. Education is a world-process; it is the world at work developing a man into the fulness of his stature . . .

. . . Education belongs decidedly to the temporal process. In that reality where is no time, any educational process is unimaginable . . . Time is the presupposition of education, without which as the logical condition of succession, of change from less to more, no development could take place.

31. The Eternal Dimension of Education

. . . The conception that the process is identical with the product is incomplete. It assumes that the process is all the reality there is, and that all reality is temporal in character. These are large assumptions indeed and run counter to much good philosophical thinking, both of other days and of to-day. Are the principles of the process also in process? Eddington says that Einstein does not deny absolutes; he only affirms they are harder to find than had been thought. All-devouring space, not time, would seem to be one of them. Mathematics has its

---

29. Herman H. Horne, *The Philosophy of Education* (New York: The Macmillan Company, 1927), p. 286.
30. *Ibid.*, pp. 259–261.
31. Herman H. Horne, *The Democratic Philosophy of Education* (New York: The Macmillan Company, 1935), p. 101.

unchanging limits as well as its changing curves. Plato has his unchanging concepts as well as his changing sensations. We ourselves have an unchanging centre of reference in ourselves; in a sense, though changing, we remain the same. Now the recognition of this non-temporal or eternal aspect of experience makes it impossible for us to regard the process, even when including its own product, as the sum of reality. And our education, to be complete, must consequently adjust us to the whole of reality of which we are a part. Our education would then be viewed as progress in the consciousness of our relation to the whole of reality of which the process is indisputably a part. Our definition might run: *Education is the increasing realization of the temporal and eternal values of life.*

32. Artistic Teaching is Indifferent to Time

. . . Sad to tell, education sometimes follows the lead of fashion rather than that of art . . .

The artist teacher seeks, then, to see his work in its eternal aspect . . .

Nothing is more characteristic of true art than a fine indifference to time. The artist works for the far future because he works for that which abides—for that which conquers time. And as he works for all the future, he lays tribute on all the past, rejecting nothing merely because it hath been before. And then, how patiently he labors on, spending his days freely as if they were his without stint. He knows "to bide his time, and can his fame abide." There are teachers who cannot wait; who must have immediate and striking success or their spirit is gone. Their chief educational agency is suggestion in its more hypnotic form; and when that fails, all is lost.

33. The Space-Time Location of Education

Being a form of social action, education always has a geographical and cultural location; it is therefore specific, local, and dynamic, not general, universal, and unchanging; it is a function of a particular

32. Elmer E. Brown, "The Fine Art of Teaching," *Educational Review*, 16:334–335, November 1898.

33. American Historical Association, *Report of the Commission on the Social Studies, Conclusions and Recommendations of the Commission* (New York: Charles Scribner's Sons, 1934), p. 31.

society at a particular time and place in history; it is rooted in some actual culture and expresses the philosophy and recognized needs of that culture.

V. NOVEL AND PRIMORDIAL

34. Certainty and Probability

We cannot usefully discuss the organization of universities, considered as educational institutions, apart from a preliminary survey of the general character of human knowledge, and of some special features of modern life . . .

In the first place, there is the division into certainty and probability. Some items we are certain about, others are matters of opinion. There is an obvious common sense about this doctrine, and its enunciation goes back to Plato. The class of certainties falls into two subdivisions. In one subdivision are certain large general truths,—for example, the multiplication table, axioms as to quantitative "more or less,"—and certain aesthetic and moral pre-suppositions. In the other subdivision are momentary discriminations of one's own state of mind: for example, a state of feeling—happiness at this moment; and for another example, an item of sense perception—that colored shape experienced at this moment. But recollection and interpretation are both deceitful. Thus this latter subdivision just touches certainty and then loses it. There is mere imitation of certainty.

In the class of probabilities there are to be found all our judgments as to the goings on of this world of temporal succession, except so far as these happenings are qualified by the certainties whenever they are relevant.

❋   ❋   ❋

The bearing of these doctrines on the procedures of education cannot be missed. In the first place: Develop intellectual activities by a knowledge of the certain truths, so far as they are largely applicable to human life. In the second place: Train the understanding of each student to assess probable knowledge in respect to those types of occurrences which for any reason will be of major importance in the exercise of his activities. In the third place: Give him adequate knowledge of the possibilities of aesthetic and moral satisfaction which are open to a human being, under conditions relevant to his future life.

34. Alfred N. Whitehead, "Harvard: The Future," *Atlantic Monthly*, 158:261–262, September 1936.

35. Emergent Evolution and Education

The basic presupposition of the creation hypothesis—either special or continuous—is that there must be an adequate explanation for everything by reference to a prior agency. It is taken as self-evident and indisputable that no thing can come out of nothing, and thus that whatever exists must be referable to some prior reality. To imagine otherwise, it is held, would be to abandon hope for rational understanding.

It is the denial of this fundamental premise that marks the view of cosmic development as a process of *emergence*. According to this position, new things progressively emerge either by genuine origination or by novel combinations and arrangements of prior entities. There is no agency which produces the emergent entities. They simply arise of themselves in the course of natural interaction. It does no good to invoke as explanation of changes some mysterious creative power, since nothing is known beyond the observed effects in the natural order. It is more reasonable, then, simply to organize what does occur naturally and to seek no explanation elsewhere.

The emergence hypothesis rests on the conception that the higher forms come from the lower forms—that the more complex orders of being are derived from the simpler ones by a natural process of development. The creation hypothesis, on the other hand, regards it as axiomatic that the river cannot rise higher than its source, and thus that the production of the successive levels of being requires the existence of a higher level of being which includes all the lower ones.

Education and emergence. What, now, of education within the context of cosmic emergence? Under this hypothesis, the emphasis would tend to be on originality and inventiveness. While the learners would usually be expected to tread familiar paths, emergence might lead one to be alert for the appearance of really creative personalities from whose activities important new suggestions could come. The world would be viewed as wide open to fresh possibilities. No one knows in advance what these are, hence the importance of the experimental method. It is only as a variety of approaches is tried that the emergent possibilities become clearly evident. A philosophy of emergence places man at the top of the cosmic scheme and gives him no superhuman powers upon which to depend. Thus upon education rests the heavy obliga-

35. Philip Phenix, *Philosophy of Education* (New York: Henry Holt & Co., 1958), pp. 537–540.

tion of developing persons who are mature, self-governing, and responsible. The most important of all educational objectives is to develop competence in making decisions. Since no creator makes man, man must learn to make himself and to remake his world according to his own will and desire.

The educational outlook associated with the philosophy of emergence depends to some extent on the type of emergence mechanism one accepts. The theory of chance is hardly consonant with education of any kind, for the whole point of directing human development is to avoid purely haphazard influences. The belief in chance would then mean that education has nothing to do with cosmic development. It would also tend to rob human attainment of any special dignity and would fail to provide any basis for preferring one condition of things over another, since every state of being would be only a random combination of world-elements.

36. Creation and Discovery

While the fullest recognition needs to be given, if education is to remain vital, to independent thought, creative activity, experiment, and adventure, it has to be borne in mind at the same time that the adventure is always a search for a reality which, while in one sense it has to be created, in another sense already exists. What the prophetic mind creates is not entirely its own creation, but rather something which it is able to create because it has first been found.

37. Unexpected Results of Experimentation

It is often imagined that educational experiments are unnecessary, and that a judgment as to whether a thing will be good or not can be reached on rational grounds alone. This is a great error, and experience teaches that with our experiments there very often appear effects entirely different from those which were expected. Since it all depends upon experiments, it is clear that no one generation can present a complete educational plan.

36. International Missionary Council, *Jerusalem Meeting*, Vol. II. (New York: The Council, 1928), p. 30.
37. Immanuel Kant, quoted in Edward F. Buchner, *The Educational Theory of Immanuel Kant* (Philadelphia: J. B. Lippincott Company, 1904), p. 126.

38. No Two Children are Alike

One of the most striking results of biological research is the discovery that every sexually produced individual in the world is unique, the first and last of its identical kind. This results from the fact that the inheritance units and their possible permutations are so numerous and the environments are so varied that no two persons in the world are identical, unless they have come from one and the same egg by a process of fission or budding. Psychical personalities and characteristics differ as much as physical ones, and consequently no single kind of environment or education is best for all persons. Wise parents and teachers can help children to discover their aptitudes and limitations, but in the main and especially with older pupils this is and should be a process of self-discovery. The motto of Socrates, "Know thyself," is still the motto of every wise teacher, and probably no other knowledge is so important as the knowledge of one's own peculiar self.

39. Irreducible Uniqueness of Individuality

Experience discloses that nature is a process. "It is a scene of incessant beginnings and endings" in which unique, individualized events emerge. No analysis, no matter how far it is carried, can legitimately eliminate these qualitatively unique occurrences. Individuality is therefore considered to be an "irreducible trait" of all existence. In the process of interaction, which is nature, novel events emerge. These later events are in no sense less real than those which preceded them. Each occurrence is to be taken at full face value for whatever traits it exhibits in its behavior. The nature of a thing is found in what it does, not in some alleged underlying substance from which it is supposed to be made.

40. Imperfection and Uncertainty are Unavoidable

At the outset of life the human being is a chaos of impulses, each useful in itself, but all relatively independent. From the point of view of the highest ideal of growth, these impulses are to be brought from

38. Edwin G. Conklin, "Contributions of Biological Research to Education," *School and Society*, 31:752, June 1930.

39. John L. Childs, "Whither Progressive Education?" *Progressive Education*, 13:584, December 1936.

40. Josiah Royce, "Is There a Science of Education?" *Educational Review*, 1:19–20, January 1891.

chaos to such complete order that not only in the individual, but in his relations to society, there shall be no chaos left, and only complete unity of life. And the educator is to do what he can to further such a growth in the child. Could we now describe in definite and material terms the content of this ideal of the perfect unity of character, could we tell what the man, and what the social order, would be like, in which the ideal were thus absolutely realized, then indeed we should have that "universal" theory of society and of education which the eighteenth century dreamed of. As a fact, however, we cannot describe the perfectly organized character because we have never seen it, and are subject in our judgment of what tends toward it to the vicissitudes and the accidents of our age and our nation. Any concrete account and picture of the ideal state that we may attempt will, therefore, have elements of chaos left in it. Any complete plan of education that we may devise will, furthermore, have defects, and only a transient significance. But there remains a sense in which the undertakings of pedagogy will be capable of scientific and general discussion. To the educator we in effect say: "Work against the chaos of impulses, by using the very impulses themselves as the material for good order. In a word, organize." Meanwhile, although the actual content of any attempted organization of life will be "historically determined," and so imperfect and transient, relatively general accounts can be given of processes that *do* increase the orderliness of the life of the child . . . In short, scientific pedagogy, far from telling the teacher finally and completely just what human nature is, and must be, and just what to do with it, will be limited to pointing out what does, on the whole, tend toward good order and toward the organization of impulses into character. "This is the whole province of pedagogy," as a general science. Its application to the conditions of a particular time, nation, family, and child, will be a matter of art, not of science. And "therefore, no concrete educational questions can be solved in terms of a universally valid science." Such questions will always contain elements of uncertainty, will always require the practical skill of the individual educator, and will always receive answers that will vary with time and occasion.

VI. ORIGIN AND DESTINY

41. Education as a Realization of Divine Spirit

An eternal law pervades and governs all things. The basis of this all-controlling law is an all-pervading, living, self-conscious and therefore

41. Friedrich Froebel, in S.S.F. Fletcher and J. Welton, translators, *Froebel's Chief Writings on Education* (London: Edward Arnold & Co., 1932), pp. 31–32. Used by permission of the publishers.

eternal Unity. This Unity is God. God is the source of all things. Each thing exists only because the divine spirit lives in it and this divine spirit is its essence. The destiny of every thing is to reveal its essence, that is, the divine spirit dwelling in it. It is the special function of man as an intelligent and rational being to realize his essence fully and clearly, to exercise, practise, and reveal the divine spirit in him, freely and consciously in his own life.

The Theory of Education is the body of doctrine derived by thoughtful men from insight into this law, as a guidance in the apprehension and attainment of man's true calling.

The Art of Education is the free application of this knowledge and insight to the development of rational beings and their training towards the fulfilment of their destiny.

The Purpose of Education is the realization of a faithful, pure, inviolate, and therefore holy, life.

Education, then, must develop the divine spirit in man and make him conscious of it, so that his life may become a free expression of that spirit. Education, in other words, should lead man to a clear knowledge of himself, to peace with nature, to unity with God.

42. Dignity of Education Stems from the Origin and Destiny of Man

Philosophers have held a number of different views, among them being that life arose as a chance occurrence; that it arose as an absolute necessity under the reign of impersonal physical law; that it arose by creative fiat, or the act of a Supreme Intelligence (Creationism); or, that it arose as a new expression of an immanent Purpose in the world, as a part of the Spiritual Order of the universe.

*   *   *

Educationally speaking, on the basis of the former alternatives, our pupils are behaving organisms and children of time. On the basis of the latter alternatives, our pupils are,—*in addition*, be it observed— images of their Great Original and children of eternity. Our sense of the dignity of teaching as a profession and life career thus depends considerably on our conception of the origin and nature of life. A thoroughgoing philosophy of education should therefore include the theories of the origin of life.

42. Herman H. Horne, *The Democratic Philosophy of Education* (New York: The Macmillan Company, 1935), pp. 8–9.

43. God as the Origin and Destiny of Man

Supernatural revelation supplies three fundamental truths about man that are requisite for the science of education:

1. **Man's origin and nature.** Man was created by God. Man is a creature composed of body and soul, and made to the image and likeness of God. This truth is in contrast to the evolutionary theory of man, and the materialistic conception of his nature.

2. **Man's natural condition.** As a result of original sin, man is born with an intellect less able to attain truth, a will less able to seek good, and, consequently, a nature subject to bodily corruption and inclined to disorderly affections. In opposition to this truth is the theory, prevalent especially since the time of Rousseau, of man's natural perfection and perfectibility, which has led to the consequent overemphasis in education on self-discovery and self-expression. Such a theory fails to recognize the absolute need for self-repression and discipine in the life experiences of the individual.

3. **Man's final end.** Man was created to praise, reverence, and serve God, and by so doing, attain eternal happiness with Him in heaven. Thus, man has a supernatural destiny, and everything in the world is secondary to it. The materialistic conception of man, which is contradictory to the foregoing truth, restricts man's purpose to his life on earth, and contends that the function of education is concerned only with life here below.

These fundamental truths are essential to the science of education, because they provide facts about man himself that are of primary importance in understanding the true nature and purpose of the human being who is the subject of education. Of course, by means of unaided natural reason one might arrive at some particular glimmer and even attain some light concerning these basic truths; but one could never attain full certainty about them. From reason alone, one could arrive at the conclusion that man's nature was good in the beginning, and that sin, therefore, did not necessarily belong to that nature, but unaided natural reason could never come to the knowledge that man was created in a state of original innocence endowed with supernatural gifts of holiness and perfection; and that these gifts were lost to man by original sin. So, too, natural reason might conclude that man's nature, in its present condition, is not in perfect

43. John D. Redden and Francis A. Ryan, A *Catholic Philosophy of Education* (Milwaukee: The Bruce Publishing Company, 1955), pp. 48–50.

order. However, natural reason alone could not arrive at complete truth about man's original state, of the tragedy and consequences of original sin, and of restoration to the adopted sonship of God through the merits of Jesus Christ through baptism and supernatural grace. This knowledge falls exclusively within the domain of truths supplied by supernatural revelation, and would be unknown to man if it were not divinely revealed.

Finally, in determining man's last end, one might reasonably conclude, from a consideration of man's nature, that he has a final destiny; but a perfect understanding of that destiny would remain a mystery without the full light of divine revelation. The fundamental dogmas of natural theology, namely, the existence of God, the freedom of the will, and the immortality of the soul, might be deduced by natural reason; but man's origin, his present condition as a result of original sin, his final destiny, could be perceived with absolute certainty only through the light of supernatural revelation. Such revelation illumines the whole purpose of this world, and gives knowledge concerning the inner life and workings of the soul.

44. Education as Actualization of Potentiality

As Aristotle, the fulfiller of the Platonic system, showed, the idea toward which the organism grows is already in the organism itself potentially. The ideal of a thing is the perfection of that thing, not the making of it into something else. A thing can become by development only what it is already in germ . . . The young mind has within it already in latent form all the powers it can ever hope to reach by development. The school cannot send real men into society unless the home sends potential men into the school. Education can neither create nor endow, it can only develop . . . Men are not made after the fashion of the factory, but of the garden . . . Education was the ancient Roman's method of bringing *up* his child; it is our method of bringing *out* the child.

45. Education as Unfolding

Now concerning education as unfolding, it is important to recognize an indisputable element of truth in it. A child is a potential man;

44. Herman H. Horne, *The Philosophy of Education* (New York: The Macmillan Company, 1927), pp. 208–209.
45. Herman H. Horne, *The Democratic Philosophy of Education* (New York: The Macmillan Company, 1935), pp. 70–71.

under no conceivable conditions is the human infant capable of becoming a lower animal really, or a plant of course. Why not? Because
of his implanted nature, his potentialities, which predestine him to
belong to *genus homo*, though reared like Romulus and Remus by a
she-wolf. The kind of human creature he becomes depends on his
environment, but he becomes a human creature through his native
heredity. To this he is destined by circumstances and predestined by
the germ-cells which constitute his essence. Here is first an enfolding,
then an unfolding that is inescapable. Many hold the inspiring view
that this native original being is a potential image of the divine, and
that this image should unfold in accordance with the model of perfect
manhood. This view may be rejected; it has not been disproven. There
is much to commend it.

46. Education as Recapitulation

To linger at leisure in each recapitulatory stage, so that each individual
may experience all the life the race has experienced, is the ideal. This
is also the most practical education, for the individual thus completed
is the most mature, the most efficient and therefore the most economical
for any society to produce in the greatest abundance possible . . . In a
word, to repeat what cannot be too strongly impressed, the biological
principle demands that the child be allowed to live in and enjoy to the
full each stage, while we provide for him whatever makes it more full,
joyous, and free, at the same time moulding his energy and directing
it toward the best ends. In this way the child is educating himself in
ways of which he knows nothing. He is practising, in a harmless way,
the great sins of the race, and fortifying himself against their later
influence. He is draining off rudimentary impulses, and unfolding from
the energy, thus set free, powers that he will later use in practical life.

47. An Infinite End Need Not Be Static

The pragmatic criticisms of the idealistic philosophies of Froebel
and Hegel mistakenly treat those philosophies as static; they are really
organic. The whole system of reality is organic. Human society is
becoming so. Progress toward the infinite goal is without limit and no

46. George E. Partridge, *Genetic Philosophy of Education* (New York: Sturgis
and Walton Company, 1912), pp. 116–117.
47. Herman H. Horne, *The Democratic Philosophy of Education* (New York:
The Macmillan Company, 1935), pp. 72–73.

"arrest of growth" is implied. In mathematics an asymptote approaching its limit is not "arrested" in its directed movement because it is said to reach its limit at infinity. If the infinite goal is an absolute self-consciousness, embracing all experience of value, can a finite individual progressing through infinite time toward the fulfillment be said to be "arrested" or limited in his growth? The concept of progress, unfolding, toward the infinite is an organic, not a static category. The finite changes and is dynamic, the changeless infinite containing the changing finite is both static and dynamic, it is organic. As Plato said, "time is the moving image of eternity."

48. Progressive Education is Predicated on Reality of Change

Do we continue to progress by giving up one new and extreme position for another, like Eliza crossing the river on cakes of ice? Is "progressive education" after all just a series of fads which pass before us in bewildering succession of ballyhoo and oblivion?

Using the words not in any copyrighted, in-quotes meaning, but in the plain, every-day sense of alert, adaptive, forward-looking educational thought and practice, in tune with the authoritative culture of this generation, this writer is of the opinion that progressive education to-day is something new and big and sound.

❋   ❋   ❋

It seems probable that the adherence of most persons to what we are calling progressive education rests upon their commitment to the new psychology and its educational meanings. There is, however, a second aspect of that movement which is hardly less influential, even though less conspicuously accepted, than the directions accepted from psychological signposts. There is an intellectual method underlying progressive education which likewise goes back to the influence of Charles Darwin and which represents as complete a break with traditional modes of philosophic thought as that which occurred in the case of psychological theory. Darwin's theory of the evolution of species was the *coup de grâce* to a moribund, but lingering, rationalism. This brought to an end the reign of those ghostly concepts which had been gratuitously set up as a means of explaining the universe. When eternal and unchangeable patterns of existence demonstrably changed

---

48. Edward H. Reisner, "What Is Progressive Education?" *Teachers College Record* (Bureau of Publications, Teachers College, Columbia University), 35:194–199, December 1933.

under the eye of man enlarged to take in a long sweep of time, they went into bankruptcy with their alleged function discredited. The cozy universe with its movements referable to a rational center and plan was gone, and with it were gone those patterns of perfect truth and absolute goodness which were supposed to legislate for mankind and which mankind might hope to discover as the clue to knowledge and as the law of conduct. From Darwin on, metaphysical speculation, whether on the severe and simple lines of Aristotelian rationalism or in the grandiose and hazy systems of absolute idealism, was on the defensive. The full implications of the Darwinian hypotheses for the entire realm of philosophic thought were slow to be realized. They were suggested by Charles Peirce, furthered by William James, and comprehensively developed as the life achievement of John Dewey.

Perhaps the central position of the new order of philosophic thought was its treatment of the concept of change. The old order of thinking had consistently attempted to minimize change and to explain it away in terms of cyclical movement or as process of planned fulfillment. The new order recognized the reality of change, seeing it as the natural and universal fact of experience. Even truth, in any sense in which it could be humanly significant, was seen to derive from experience, and, accordingly, to take on that aspect of changeableness and relativity which is a fundamental characteristic of experience. Truth was seen to be a function of human adjustment. It represented those happy and successful means which human beings could bring to their aid in understanding their environment, in adjusting to it, or in mastering it. But in such relationships the adjustment which is satisfactory at one time ceases to be so as the environment changes, or as the person changes. So truth is relative and subject to change in the light of experimentation and new experience. In the same way good, which had been regarded as "eternal in the heavens," was seen to be a changeable function of human conduct. "Time makes ancient good uncouth," and the mores that spell favorable adjustment for one generation may mean chains and injustice for its successor.

49. Myth of Progress Criticized

It is no play on words to say that *the myth of universal progress, progress in all things, lies at the heart of progressive education.* This myth of progress is a nineteenth-century notion, due partly to posi-

49. Mortimer J. Adler, "The Crisis in Contemporary Education," *The Social Frontier*, 5:141–144, February 1939.

tivism and partly to illicit extensions of the doctrine of evolution. Progress differs from change in that it is change in a definite direction and is measured by standards which evaluate stages in a process as better and worse. The growth of a plant or animal is a progress from infancy to maturity, to the point where the organism reaches its biological perfection. But everywhere in nature growth is followed by decline, maturity by senescence. The one possible exception to the rule that natural progress is not interminable is that which the panorama of evolution appears to present. But even here, taking the facts as they are usually told in the story of evolution, it is only by a questionable extrapolation of the curve that one could conclude that there is interminable progress in the development of forms of life. Yet it was just this uncritically reached conclusion which propagated the notion that the law of progress rules all things, and that as we move into the future we go endlessly from worse to better, from lower to higher.

The other source of this myth of progress was a view of cultural history, dictated by positivism. If one supposes, as the positivists do, that science is the only form of valid, general knowledge about the world, and that the technical application of science to the control of things is the only kind of utility which knowledge has, then there appears to be uninterrupted and interminable progress in human affairs as well as in nature. For does not Auguste Comte tell us that there are three stages in human history—the superstitious or religious; the speculative, conjectural, or philosophical; and the stage of positive knowledge, or the scientific—and is this not progress? In the era of science itself does not every century see the ever increasing scope of scientific knowledge and the ever enlarging domain of technology? As the years roll by, we have more and better knowledge, bigger and better inventions or utilities. The positivists are so enraptured by this picture of progress and by the dreams of the future it generates that they are somehow able to forget that in our moral and political affairs a Hitler and a Mussolini and their followers are not much of an improvement upon a Nero or a Caligula and the gangs they led. But this flaw in the picture must not be forgotten, for it is the clue to one of the two great exceptions to the law of progress in human affairs which make the notion of universal and perpetual progress a deceptive illusion.

The first exception is human nature itself. If we can discriminate between nature and nurture, we can understand the sense in which human nature is constant throughout all the variations of culture and all the transformations of history. Man is a biological species, and if a species means anything it means a constant nature which is transmitted from generation to generation. When that constancy fails, when another specific nature is generated, we have, whether by mutation or otherwise, the origin of a new species. It must follow, then, that so long as what is generated remains specifically man, human nature remains constant from generation to generation. By human nature I mean the native abilities and the organic needs which everywhere constitute the same animal, known as man.

✸   ✸   ✸

If man is a rational animal, constant in nature throughout history, then there must be certain constant features in every sound educational program, regardless of culture or epoch. The basic education of a rational animal is the discipline of his rational powers and the cultivation of his intellect. This discipline is achieved by the liberal arts, the arts of reading and listening, of writing and speaking, and, perforce, of thinking, since man is a social animal as well as a rational one and his intellectual life is lived in a community which can exist only through the communication of men. The three R's, which always signified the formal disciplines, are the essence of liberal or general education. They cannot be inculcated by college courses in logic or mathematics or classical languages. That was the error of classical education, which the progressivist rightly condemned. One learns to write and read only by performing these acts, but since reading and writing are intellectual arts, the habits must be formed under the discipline of rules of art; moreover, intellectual habits cannot be formed intelligently unless the rules themselves are understood. The program of liberal education consists of the liberal arts, acquired as habits through performance under intelligible disciplines. In short, the A.B. degree should be awarded for competence in reading, writing, and reckoning.

But one cannot learn to read and write without subject matter. The reason is trained in its proper operations by these arts, but the intellect is not cultivated by them. That can be accomplished only through furnishing it with knowledge and wisdom, by acquainting it with truth, by giving it a mastery of ideas. At this point, the other basic feature of liberal education appears, namely, the great books, the master productions in all fields, philosophy, science, history, and belles-lettres. They are not only the material which must be used to teach students how to read and write, but they constitute the cultural tradition by which the intellects of each generation must first be cultivated.

Note, here, how the myth of progress is denied. If there is philosophical wisdom as well as scientific knowledge, if the former consists of insights and ideas that change little from time to time, and if even the latter has many abiding concepts and a relatively constant method, if the great works of literature as well as of philosophy touch upon the permanent moral problems of mankind and express the universal convictions of men involved in moral conflict—if these things are so, then the great books of ancient and medieval, as well as modern, times are a repository of knowledge and wisdom, a tradition of culture which must initiate each new generation. The reading of these books is not for antiquarian purposes; the interest is not archaeological or philological. That was the type of interest which dominated the humanistic course in the German *gymnasium,* and was "classical education" at its worst. Rather the books are to be read because they are as contemporary today as when they were written, and that because *the problems they deal with and the ideas they present are not subject to the law of perpetual and interminable progress.* The fact that the ancients and medievals were wrong in many matters of scientific knowledge, the fact that even Newton and Galileo were wrong in their turn, makes no difference to the philosophical accomplishments of these periods, nor even to the insights and procedures of the great masters of science.

50. Classical Metaphysics and Progressive Education

. . . What about those who clearly and consciously subscribe to some set of classical metaphysical views but who appear to subscribe just as clearly and consciously to the principles of Progressive Education? Some in this group are probably not really embracing Progressive Education. They are impressed by the results of certain Progressive principles but turn to their own philosophy in search of equivalent principles. The principles thus discovered (or "rediscovered") often bear similar names to Progressive principles, as illustrated by the recent emphasis of scholastic educators on "activity" and "interest"; but, because of their different philosophical contexts, they are probably not equivalent in either intent or use. But other educators in this group are apparently adopting actual Progressive principles while at the same time insisting that they are not in conflict with a classical metaphysics. One of the more popular arguments for this point of view is worth presenting in outline here.

First of all, these "Classical-Progressives" contend that their educational aims in practice are really not static or fixed. They still hold that the true aims are ultimately fixed in the cosmos, but that there is always considerable human error in perceiving what the true aims

50. Lawrence G. Thomas, "What Metaphysics for Modern Education?" *The Educational Forum,* 6:127–130, January 1942.

should be. Consequently, aims are often changed, revised, reconstructed because a rational examination of human experience reveals that any current set of aims contains many imperfections—imperfections which Reason knows ought not to be there if these aims were the True Aims. Thus, new aims designed to eliminate the observed imperfections are set up. Since even the wisest seers are only human and cannot see the whole of ultimate truth, man must do the best he can with his experiences. Gradually, over the course of history, the ultimate truth will be painstakingly distilled out of man's experience, rationalistically interpreted. Actually, therefore, these people do about as much selecting, changing and reconstructing of aims as thorough-going experimentalists do.

For these people, then, the nature of the aims, the technique of their selection and the basis of their revision are, in much actual practice, indistinguishable from the practical procedures of the experimentalists. When this is the case, it easily follows that the teaching methods used and the bases of selecting and organizing the subject matter of the curriculum are similarly influenced. The rigorous, formal methods . . . assigned to the classicists could be used only if one were certain that the ultimately true aims had been revealed to him. This the persons mentioned above deny, and so they accept with high enthusiasm and serene conscience the methods of teaching and curriculum construction espoused by the experimentalists.

Plausible as this argument may appear, it either proves too much or proves too little. On the one hand, it would mean that one's metaphysics has no necessary, characteristic significance for practice—that it does not give guidance to the practical problems of action and is not subject to verification and reconstruction in the light of the results of that action. Metaphysics then would be at most a leisure-time pursuit, quite separable from other aspects of living. Such a conclusion, even if it were acceptable to this group, would ignore the psychological need that most people experience for achieving a set of metaphysical views as a functional adjustment to their universe. On the other hand, if this group agrees that one's metaphysics actually does have a peculiar and characteristic expression in practice, then a foreign metaphysical system cannot be superimposed on the principles of modern education. If a person claims to accept both Progressive Education and a classical metaphysics, he can only mean that he is really shuttling between two metaphysical frames of reference—one in his teaching and the other perhaps in some especially personal area, such as morals or a religious creed. This latter alternative is very probably the case. Thus, those who *consciously* adhere to a classical metaphysics are in the same position as those who *unconsciously* cling to the classical metaphysics they learned as children. Both, if they are really trying to understand and practice Progressive Education, are unavoidably dividing their allegiance between two metaphysical frames of reference.

These people, who believe they are devoted to the cause of Progressive Education and yet who strongly prefer a classical metaphysics to that of experimentalism, might still raise one final question: Why not maintain this dual loyalty? How important are the objections? Are there any real hazards and dangers in it?

The first major objection concerns the very heart of the relationship between metaphysics and education. The attempt to live in reference to a classical metaphysics while presumably practicing an experimentalistic program of teaching fails to capitalize on the most important function of a philosophy. Reflection and action complement each other in any experience. Philosophy is an extensive elaboration of the reflective phase of experience. Its great function is to interpret, criticize, rationalize and formulate the bases of action. The completed action, in turn, verifies the validity and dependability of the philosophical preview and provides the basis for further criticism and interpretation. Those who hold metaphysical views unrelated to or inappropriate to their professed bases of action in practical situations are foregoing the mutually reconstructive value of free and complete interaction between their philosophies and their courses of action. Besides the bifurcating effect on the person's personality, it contributes to that anomalous situation where he affirms his enthusiasm for some liberal, progressive-minded end but is willing to accept means to achieve it which are inappropriate and even subversive to that end. Most cases of self-deluding lip-service to a goal sought by Progressive Education are examples of this disjunction between philosophy and action.

The second major objection concerns the dependability and predictability of persons attempting to live in two frames of reference. From the mental hygiene standpoint, such persons are likely to back away from the full implications of one view or the other and, when the inevitable situation arises in which their two viewpoints conflict, attempt a hopeless reconciliation between opposing emotional commitments. From the standpoint of educational and social progress, such persons are unreliable allies. On some unexpected occasion they may desert honestly and critically examined experience in favor of unquestionable emotional convictions. Certain things will be considered good or bad, desirable or undesirable, regardless of their long-run consequences. When problems are at the most critical stage, this tendency may become acute, in which case there is a frantic retreat to reliance on uncriticized authority. Such persons on these occasions may care little about the method proposed; all they want is a guarantee of certainty and order, and they will give allegiance usually to the one who is most dogmatic in his assertions. Nothing could be more subversive to the growth—even the existence—of democracy. When democracy most needs them to be experimentalistic, they are most likely to develop a craving for authoritarianism in action as well as in metaphysics.

The third major objection to a classical metaphysics for those who would promote the cause of Progressive Education raises the question of whether a classical metaphysics is really appropriate to the needs and demands of modern living. Both the intent and the method of the classical tradition in metaphysics tend to offer an intellectual and emotional escape from the overwhelming problems of the present instead of giving a hard spur to action. The classical tradition seeks certainty and security for man in the total environment by postulating an ultimate, immutable reality which is favorably disposed toward man, which guarantees the immortality of his most cherished desires and ideals and upon which he can rely with the confidence of a child upon his father. This view, in its way, offers man something big and important to live for, rewards his sacrifices, sustains him in his disappointments and relieves him of the crushing weight of too much responsibility for how things go in this world. In sum, it offers man a theoretically pre-established security—something which experimentalism cannot and will not offer.

There is no denying the emotional appeal of this security-for-the-asking, but does it contribute to better living here and now? To some it does, for this guaranteed certainty provides them with the necessary motivation to live useful, constructive lives. But for others it *permits* a very unfortunate misdirection of effort and attention away from the pressing problems of achieving security and progress in the immediate present to the more remote, speculative problems posed by their classical metaphysics.

3

Human Nature

Problems in the Philosophy of Education Discussed in this Section

1. How do you account for the fact that although the child grows or changes as he learns, nonetheless he seems to maintain his identity?
2. What difference will it make in education whether or not one regards the child as having a "self," personality, individuality, or character? To what extent is each of these an original datum? A social product?
3. Is the pupil one or many selves? Is an integrated self desirable? Is integration a datum or an achievement? Is an integrated environment essential to the growth of an integrated personality, or is a certain degree of conflict morally necessary?
4. What educational differences will it make whether the mind is conceived of as material or immaterial? Whether the psyche of the learner has a supernature or soul? Whether original nature be described in terms of faculties or of instincts and impulses?
5. Is human nature everywhere and at all times the same? How inflexible are the limits imposed on education by heredity? Should eugenics form a part of an educational program?
6. How is the will involved in learning? How is it related to preference and judgment? To effort? Is it free? Can it be trained? If there is freedom of the will, what does it mean to teach the child to act "voluntarily," to be "self-directing," to be morally "autonomous"?
7. To what extent can children be held individually responsible for errors, mistakes, or wrongs committed in the course of their education? For what consequences of his teaching that issue in pupil conduct can the teacher be held responsible?
8. When a child's case history is examined, is it to be assumed that determinism has been operating, that for every deed there is an antecedent cause? If not, is it worthwhile for the teacher to predicate his instruction on psychological laws?
9. Should the educator assume, with Rousseau, that child nature is fundamentally good? Is this a warrant for the child's doing anything he desires? What significance would a theory of original sin have for educational aims and methods?

I. MIND AND BODY

51. Man is Composed of Body and Soul

. . . The Catholic teacher must have a true conception of human nature. Here again we turn to Catholic philosophy. Man is a creature composed of body and soul. The soul is a spiritual entity, owing its existence to a special act of creation. It is incorruptible and immortal by nature; united to the body in such a way as to be its single substantial form. It determines the nature of man, giving him all that differentiates him from other beings. It is the principle of all human activity. Because he has a soul, man has an intellect, which is not the result of organic evolution but which is *intrinsically independent* of any organism. Because man has a body, he has many things in common with lower animals, mechanisms and drives, instincts and reflexes, tropisms and reactions, but his mental life is not completely explainable in terms of these. His psychology differs specifically from that of the brute.

Though not intrinsically dependent on the organism, and capable of existing without the organism, the human intellect, because man is a composite being, is, during this life, *extrinsically dependent* on the nervous system, on the brain, the sense organs, the afferent and efferent nerves, for the materials out of which it fashions its knowledge. Sense perception, memory, imagery—all of these have a neurological explanation. But abstraction, which gives us the real meaning of things, is the active function of the intellect, the *intellectus agens,* and is not a passive reaction.

Intellect is not the only faculty of the soul; it also has a capacity we call the will, the power to choose what we intellectually apprehend as good. That choice is free, though this freedom is often limited because our intellectual apprehension is cloudy, or because of the clamor of the passions, desires and impulses that minister more directly to the body, or because of habits of acting previously acquired. But in spite of these handicaps, the will always has the essential power of self-direction, and barring cases that are distinctly pathological may assert its independence. A weak will may be strengthened by exercise. Self-discipline is the process whereby we bring all our vagrant impulses to heel and direct our lives and actions in accordance with the dictates of reason.

51. George Johnson, "Fundamentals of Catholic Teacher Training," *Catholic Education Review*, 21:453–454, October 1923.

52. Body and Soul are Necessary for Learning

The view which makes the body a mere instrument of the soul was not accepted by St. Thomas and it is not prevalent among Catholic philosophers. Pious exaggerations which refer to the body as the prison-house of the soul should not be regarded as sober philosophy and need not be taken into account in the philosophy that concerns itself with the educative process.

It is true that the immortality of the soul is essential to the Catholic's belief in a hereafter but we have little means of knowing the nature or operations of the soul after its separation from the body. St. Thomas found reason for believing that it is so incomplete as to be unable to acquire new truths or to come in contact with the physical world except by miracle until it shall be again united with the body.

Analogies to St. Thomas' view of the relation of soul to body are not difficult to find. Oxygen and hydrogen unite to form water, but water exhibits none of the characteristic qualities or actions of either hydrogen or oxygen. We are not dealing in the school with the souls of children nor are we dealing with their bodies. The schoolroom is neither a morgue nor a limbo for disembodied spirits. It is a place where we are confronted with living, moving children; with beings possessed of souls and bodies, indeed but possessing these two elements of their nature in a solidarity and a unity which can be severed only by death. Whatever divergency may exist in the views of psychologists and philosophers concerning the nature of spirit and the nature of matter, there is practical unanimity among them in the belief that in the present life of man, soul and body are inseparably united and must be dealt with as a unit presenting divergent aspects.

53. Fallacy of Locating the Mind

The reason for "locating" the mind in the brain is not fundamentally better than the reason for locating it in the heart or the liver, as some of the ancients thought, for the simple reason that it is absurd to try to locate it anywhere. It is much the same as it is with energy in the

52. Thomas E. Shields, *Philosophy of Education* (Washington, D. C.: The Catholic Education Press, 1921), pp. 194–195.

53. Henry C. Morrison, *Basic Principles in Education* (Boston: Houghton Mifflin Company, 1934), pp. 112–113. Used by permission of the publishers.

physical world. He would be an unimaginative physicist indeed who could form no conception of energy apart from a steam engine or electric generator.

Perhaps the first confident step we should take is to exclude the notion of mind as a separable organ after the analogy of the physical organs with which we are familiar. We can be sure of mental processes, and physical processes in general of which mental processes are but one category. We can study in the laboratory the phenomena which they yield and find that the latter hold together in reasonable relationships much as do the phenomena which we study in other laboratories. So far we can cultivate scientific patience and restraint.

For the student of education, one of the first advantages lies in the fact that we shall cease thinking about "educating the mind," not to say the brain. When we have once taken that step, we shall find the pathway to a comprehensible theory of instruction in general and of the curriculum in particular a good deal clearer.

Another advantage, fraught with the eradication of almost incalculable injustice to the individual and with a decidedly more optimistic view of social possibilities, is in abandonment of such notions as the "child mind," "mental age," and "types of mind."

54. The Materialism of Behaviorism

More specifically, the situation invites us to try explaining human behavior in terms of bodily processes alone. Why not ignore what we call "mind" altogether and confine ourselves to a description of how the organism behaves? A procedure of this kind has the advantage of being strictly objective, in the sense that different observers can watch the same fact and can verify what they see. This is not true in the same sense in introspection. If a person watches what is taking place in his own inner consciousness, other observers cannot share in the observation, and cannot check in any direct fashion on the report that the introspecting observer may see fit to make.

The movement in the direction of substituting physical processes for mental processes as terms of description and explanation in psychology has gained considerable headway and is now known as Behaviorism. At the outset this movement was content to make the assertion that mental or psychic facts need not be considered, since all

54. Boyd H. Bode, *Conflicting Psychologies of Learning* (Boston: D. C. Heath and Company, 1929), pp. 128–129. Reprinted by special permission of the publishers.

the relevant facts can be secured by a study of behavior and of physiology. We may admit the existence of "consciousness," but nothing is gained by taking it into account. As time went on, however, the movement gained courage, and presently the claim was advanced, more or less frequently, that "mind" could be ignored, not merely because it was irrelevant to the purposes of the psychologist but because it was really non-existent. The assertion was made that what is called mind is in reality reducible to a bodily process. Physics, for example, reduces the phenomena of light and sound to terms of wave motions; and a similar reduction is possible with mental phenomena. Thus a pain, an emotion, or the perception of a sound or a color is in reality nothing but a physical process going on in the cerebral cortex. Mind and matter are fundamentally the same thing. Everything that we call personal experience is reducible to forms of movement.

A doctrine of this sort is bound to have considerable significance for our interpretation of the educative process. If this doctrine is true, then obviously the emphasis in teaching should fall not on the organizing or relating of "ideas," but on the cultivation of modes of behavior. From the point of view of behaviorism, education consists of a process of substituting new forms of behavior for old ones. The forms of behavior with which we are born are known as reflexes; the forms of behavior which are substituted for them are designated by such names as "acquired reflexes," "conditioned reflexes," or habits. Habit becomes the fundamental category in education.

55. The Materialistic Basic of Learning

. . . "How do men gain knowledge?" . . . (a) the materialist basis of sensation and activity will provide postulates for a theory of learning, and (b) neither the individual inheritance nor the supposedly automatic effect of environment will be acceptable as an understanding of the development of the individual child. Neither nature nor nurture will do, for the latter is not a rigidifying limit on the growth of the child's humanity and the former is itself being changed by the child and his society. The direction of this technical thinking may be indicated by a brief statment of Pavlov, written in 1930: "The chief, strongest, and most permanent impression we get from the study of higher nervous activity by our methods is the extraordinary plasticity

55. Robert S. Cohen, "On the Marxist Philosophy of Education," in 54th Yearbook of the National Society for the Study of Education, Part I, *Modern Philosophies and Education* (Published by the Society, Chicago, 1955), p. 207.

of this activity, and its immense potentialities; nothing is immovable or intractable, and everything may always be achieved, changed for the better, provided only that the proper conditions are created." The result of knowledge that confirms and carries on this impression would obviously be of utmost significance for education.

56. Evils of Mind-Body Dualism

It would be impossible to state adequately the evil results which have flowed from this dualism of mind and body, much less to exaggerate them . . . In part bodily activity becomes an intruder. Having nothing, so it is thought, to do with mental activity, it becomes a distraction, an evil to be contended with. For the pupil has a body, and brings it to school along with his mind. And the body is, of necessity, a wellspring of energy; it has to do something. But its activities, not being utilized in occupation with things which yield significant results, have to be frowned upon. They lead the pupil away from the lesson with which his "mind" ought to be occupied; they are sources of mischief. The chief source of the "problem of discipline" in schools is that the teacher has often to spend the larger part of the time in suppressing the bodily activities which take the mind away from its material. A premium is put on physical quietude; on silence, on rigid uniformity of posture and movement; upon a machine-like simulation of the attitudes of intelligent interest. The teachers' business is to hold the pupils up to these requirements and to punish the inevitable deviations which occur.

❀   ❀   ❀

On the intellectual side, the separation of "mind" from direct occupation with things throws emphasis on *things* at the expense of *relations* or connections. It is altogether too common to separate perceptions and even ideas from judgments. The latter are thought to come after the former in order to compare them. It is alleged that the mind perceives things apart from relations; that it forms ideas of them in isolation from their connections—with what goes before and comes after. Then judgment or thought is called upon to combine the separated items of "knowledge" so that their resemblance or casual connection shall be brought out. As a matter of fact, every perception and every idea is a sense of the bearings, use, and cause, of a thing. We

56. John Dewey, *Democracy and Education* (New York: The Macmillan Company, 1916), pp. 165–168.

do not really know a chair or have an idea of it by inventorying and enumerating its various isolated qualities, but only by bringing these qualities into connection with something else—the purpose which makes it a chair and not a table; or its difference from the kind of chair we are accustomed to, or the "period" which it represents, and so on. A wagon is not perceived when all its parts are summed up; it is the characteristic connection of the parts which makes it a wagon. And these connections are not those of mere physical juxtaposition, they involve connection with the animals that draw it, the things that are carried on it, and so on. Judgment is employed in the perception; otherwise the perception is mere sensory excitation or else a recognition of the result of a prior judgment, as in the case of familiar objects.

II. ORIGINAL NATURE

57. Faculties of the Soul

The faculties are the principles of action, the instruments by means of which the powers of the soul are manifest. One mind, the principle of all conscious states, has a multitude of capabilities. So the faculties may be defined as the capabilities possessed by the mind for engaging in a particular kind of activity.

The Classification of the Faculties:
  A. Cognitive Faculties

    1. Sensuous and Organic
       (a) External Senses:
           Sight, hearing, touch, taste, smell
       (b) Internal Senses:
           Instinct, imagination, memory
    2. Spiritual and Inorganic
       (a) Acts of the Intellect:
           Concept, judgment, reasoning
  B. Appetitive Faculties
    1. Sensuous Passions or Feelings and Emotions
    2. Rational Will

There are two divisions of faculties, the cognitive and the appetitive. The foundation for this classification is the fact that the mind both receives impressions from without and reacts to impressions from

57. William A. Kelly, *Educational Psychology* (Milwaukee: The Bruce Publishing Company, 1933), pp. 15–16.

within. The cognitive faculties react to impressions from without. The appetitive faculties manifest the reaction of the mind to the impressions received. The cognitive faculties are those by which the human beings know, and the appetitive faculties are those by means of which they strive after or seek things.

58. Faculties and Functions

Psychologically the American theory bases itself on a denial of the old "faculty psychology." You cannot train the Memory or the Will or any other supposed faculty because these are merely hypostatised abstractions . . . We should naturally expect the next step in the argument to be that, since this is so, we must assume some principle of unity in us which coordinates the different senses and "faculties," and that the aim of education should be to train this so that it can do its work of judgment and comparison efficiently . . . It would seem, in fact, that the denial of the "faculty psychology" should lead naturally to a keen sense of the importance of general education, but, on the contrary, we find that the comparatively limited number of faculties recognized by the old-fashioned psychology is replaced by a whole host of specific "functions" or sub-faculties, if we may call them so. There are many memories and so on which are quite independent of one another . . . Nothing is really gained by speaking of functions instead of faculties. No one who knew what he was talking about ever meant more by faculty (δύναμις) than the possibility of a function (ἐνέργεια), and a function has no independent existence any more than a faculty. It must be a function of something, and that something is best called the soul. It seems to me, then, that the psychology on which the new doctrine is based is open to the very same objections as the old faculty psychology, and in an even higher degree.

59. Mind, the Unity of Its Manifestations

The mind reveals its nature in its processes and its products. The difficulty in defining mind is mainly due to considering it abstractly, apart from its manifestations. The attempt at such a definition can end

58. John Burnet, *Higher Education and the War* (London: Macmillan and Co. Ltd., 1917), pp. 41–43.
59. Herman H. Horne, *The Philosophy of Education* (New York: The Macmillan Company, 1927), p. 106.

only in synonyms, like consciousness, the state of being aware, intelligence, etc. Mind is the unity of its appearances. It is no thing-in-itself, lying back of the phenomena of consciousness, unknown and unknowable. It is the synthesis of those concrete experiences known to all as sensation, perception, memory, thought, feeling, will, and the rest. Mind is not one of its own aspects; it is the real unity of all conscious experience . . .

60. Mind as an Immaterial Substance

Apparently the reason for this solicitous insistence that the existence of the self is not really open to doubt lies in the fact that the traditional conception of the self or "mind" includes some elements which are not known in . . . immediate and indubitable fashion. In other words, the traditional conception is a mixture of intuition and inference. This conception holds, not merely that a self is present in every moment of experience, but that this self is simple and immaterial, that it is permanent throughout experience and cannot be destroyed except by an act of God, that it exists in relative independence of matter, and that it is a source of energy or power. This is about what is meant by the doctrine that the mind is an immaterial substance or entity.

❉   ❉   ❉

If we undertake to interpret the learning process in terms of a substantive mind, the suggestion lies at hand that all learning must represent some activity on the part of the mind. But this is only a point of departure. When we inquire into the nature of this activity, we find that it varies according to circumstances. The activity of the mind expresses itself through the use of the sense-organs and through the exercise of memory, imagination, and reflective thinking; which is to say that the mind can operate in a variety of ways, or that it has a number of distinct powers or functions. These powers are known as faculties, such as the faculty of observation, of memory, of volition, and the like.

❉   ❉   ❉

According to this theory, the chief benefit of training lies in the development of power and not in the training of specific abilities.

60. Boyd H. Bode, *Conflicting Psychologies of Learning* (Boston: D. C. Heath and Company, 1929), pp. 15–16, 28, 35. Reprinted by special permission of the publishers.

Moreover, this development of power can be secured with a variety of materials. A muscle can be developed in various ways, and so can a faculty. It does not matter so much what we exercise our faculties on; the important thing is to exercise them. In fact it would not matter at all, except that some material serves the purpose of training better than others, just as some physical exercises develop the muscles more efficiently than others. Moreover, it is a fact that we do remember some things, even if the amount of what we remember is disappointingly small. Consequently, it is better to memorize useful facts than to exercise the memory on nonsense syllables. The choice of material, therefore, is not a matter of absolute indifference, but it seems fair to say that choice of material is of secondary importance.

61. Mind as Consciousness or Mental States

It is apparent even to the casual observer that the shift in position from belief in a substantive mind to the conception of mind as consciousness or an aggregate of mental states carries with it important implications for educational theory and practice. The repudiation of the substantive mind involves, as its implication, abandonment of the belief in faculty psychology and formal discipline. If there is no permanent and changeless entity, such as a doctrine of the substantive mind hypothecates, then the whole notion of formal discipline is clearly out of place. If the mind is made up of a collection of various experiences, the attention of the educator is necessarily directed toward content and toward the idea of the enrichment of experience.

This re-direction of attention, however, brings in its train certain difficulties. What is the teacher to do? These transitory mental states clearly cannot be trained. They do not continue in existence long enough to be trained, even if we knew how to train them or what to train them for. Moreover, the mental state, after it has had its few brief moments before the footlights of consciousness, passes away into the limbo of nothingness, so that training, if it could be applied, would be wasted. The mental states are as different from a substantive mind as can well be imagined. Instead of being unchanging and abiding, they are essentially fleeting and evanescent, like the lights and shadows on the waves on the sea-beach. If this is the sort of material with which the teacher has to work, what sort of educational program should be adopted?

61. Boyd H. Bode, *Conflicting Psychologies of Learning* (Boston: D. C. Heath and Company, 1929), pp. 88–89. Reprinted by special permission of the publishers.

62. Mind as *Tabula Rasa*

The mind of the new-born babe is a clean slate; little by little he writes on it the accumulated products of racial learning. If a child were to grow up in complete isolation, so that he had no opportunity to learn anything from social sources, he would be no better than a brute or an idiot.

63. Mind or Intelligence as a Course of Action

Mind is not a name for something complete by itself; it is a name for a course of action in so far as that is intelligently directed; in so far, that is to say, as aims, ends, enter into it, with selection of means to further the attainment of aims. Intelligence is not a peculiar possession which a person owns; but a person is intelligent in so far as the activities in which he plays a part have the qualities mentioned. Nor are the activities in which a person engages, whether intelligently or not, exclusive properties of himself; they are something in which he *engages and partakes*. Other things, the independent changes of other things and persons, cooperate and hinder. The individual's act may be initial in a course of events, but the outcome depends upon the interaction of his response with energies supplied by other agencies. Conceive mind as anything but one factor partaking along with others in the production of consequences, and it becomes meaningless.

The problem of instruction is thus that of finding material which will engage a person in specific activities having an aim or purpose of moment or interest to him, and dealing with things not as gymnastic appliances but as conditions for the attainment of ends . . . In short, the root of the error long prevalent in the conception of training of mind consists in leaving out of account movements of things to future results in which an individual shares, and in the direction of which observation, imagination, and memory are enlisted. It consists in regarding mind as complete in itself, ready to be directly applied to a present material.

62. Ross L. Finney, *A Sociological Philosophy of Education* (New York: The Macmillan Company, 1928), p. 64.

63. John Dewey, *Democracy and Education* (New York: The Macmillan Company, 1916), pp. 155–156.

64. Overemphasis on Biological Nature

Apparently there has been little change in the biological nature of man for thousands of years, and the biological unity of all human beings as a well established scientific fact. The findings of both biology and psychology clearly support the principle of the organic brotherhood of man. Biology affirms that all of the so-called "racial" or "nationality" groups must be viewed as members of the same human family since they can intermarry and bear fertile children, while the results of tests of mental ability show that there is no evidence in psychology to support the notion that we can divide human beings into "superior" and "inferior" groups on the basis of "racial" characteristics such as the color of skin, the texture of hair, the slant of eyes, or the structure of skull.

But the foregoing theory presupposes more than the mere biological unity of mankind; it also assumes that for the purposes of education, biological nature *is* human nature. Its conception of educational research is grounded in the faith that the scientific study of the human organism can give us all essential knowledge of human nature and behavior—that is, knowledge not simply of man's biophysiological equipment, but also of his basic needs and powers, his primary likes and aversions, his drives, his enduring interests, and his invariant principles of growth and learning. In other words, this whole approach to education is pervaded by the assumption that man is basically a creature of biology, not of human association and culture, and that the essential characteristics of human beings are given in the structure and the functioning of the biological organism.

❊ ❊ ❊

But the net outcome of these studies has not strengthened the notion that the prototypes for human conduct and the final norms for education are to be found in these sub-human or pre-social behaviors. On the contrary, these researches have vastly weakened, if indeed they have not destroyed, the very foundations of this assumption. The evidence which has been gathered does not support the preconception of those who hold that the simple and instinctive behaviors which appear earliest in the evolutionary sequence are more real and causally ef-

64. John L. Childs, *Education and Morals* (New York: Appleton-Century-Crofts, Inc., copyright 1950), pp. 57–60.

ficacious than the complex and purposeful behaviors which are characteristic of the life of man in human society. The search for an underlying and governing system of original or instinctive responses has resulted in quite unanticipated findings. The evidence which has been gathered supports the conception of a flexible native human endowment that can develop through experience and learning into a wide variety of human interests, drives and activities. Nor have these research studies confirmed the idealizations of the "nature romanticists." These findings do not show that the "spontaneous" occurrences at the pre-human or pre-reflective level of existence are all good, harmonious, and perfectly ordered for the well-being of living creatures; nor do they show that the life made possible by human art and culture is in any real sense artificial and inferior.

III. THE "WHOLE CHILD" AND INTEGRATION

65. Differentiation is Necessary to Integration

In an unchanging environment, the processes of differentiation and integration subside, life slows down and finally ceases. Complete adaptation to a static environment would be equivalent to death. Change is the source of action. Differentiation is the condition of life, the occasion for integration. If the universe is to offer endless creative opportunity to its creatures it must do so by providing endless differentiation, and hence with this principle of progressive differentiation one may well associate the concept of God. Logically, this is the ultimate principle, for the integration of a totality would be meaningless. Progressive integration implies progressive differentiation as its condition.

Human beings in their dealings with one another have failed to profit by an examination of the way things happen. They have attempted to induce in themselves and in those under their tutelage a type of integrative action which defeats its own object.

In sub-human animals, integration takes place automatically. It consists of the marshalling of all the animal's resources to meet each emergency as it arises. For each emergency a fairly stereotyped procedure is available and is brought into active play. In contrast with this relatively simple behavior, it has been supposed that children should be taught to organize their responses around some ethical

65. Hugh Hartshorne, *Character in Human Relations* (New York: Charles Scribner's Sons, 1932), pp. 217–218.

ideal, such as honesty, meeting even the most diverse and complex situations with conduct which would conform to the standard in question. At the same time, children have been placed in groups, the family, the school, the club, the gang, to each of which they are compelled to make satisfactory personal adjustments comparable to those which an animal makes to its physical and human environment. The result is, for the average child, an impasse. If he adjusts to his several groups, he falls down on his ideals. If he sticks to his ideals, he gets into trouble with his groups. When his ultimates are conceived in static terms while his real world offers variety and challenge, he tends to let the static ideal go, or else, in attempting to conform to a static ideal, he retires from active participation with his groups.

66. Integration of Conflicting Selves

Implicit in everything so far said has been a regard for "the whole child." Because some affect to find difficulty with this conception, a word or two of explanation seems called for. The conception of "the whole child" carries two implications which at bottom agree: one, that we wish at no time to disregard the varied aspects of child life; the other, that the child as organism properly responds as one unified whole . . .

To say that the biological organism acts as one unity is by no means to deny that persons do build varying and possibly opposed selves and that they act at one time from one self, and at a different time from another self. Still less is it to assert that all one's resources, all one's different habits, skills, knowledges, attitudes, etc., act simultaneously as the organism faces a situation. This would be so complete a denial of the proposition under consideration (i.e., that the organism acts as a unity) that one wonders how an intelligent critic could ever suggest such an objection . . .

The principle of the "whole child" and of the organism acting as a whole leads easily to the problem of the integration of personality. When a person faces a situation of one clearly defined type and learns to deal satisfactorily with it, he does, in some measure, reconstruct his personality on the basis of what is therein learned. If the situation recurs with ordinary variations, the personality may in time be appreciably rebuilt so that a characteristic attitude or set, corresponding to that type of situation, is readily assumed when such a situation

66. William H. Kilpatrick, "The Essentials of the Activity Movement," *Progressive Education*, 11:357–358, October 1934.

presents itself. It may, however, happen that one situation contains within itself contradictory demands which the person cannot harmonize. Under such conditions, he may accept one line of demand and reject the other. If he does so, and it works out acceptably, he will grow to be that kind of person. He might, however, so far as we see, have accepted the other line of demand and so built himself into *that* kind of person. In each case the organism has acted as a whole and built a pattern accordingly. But a third outcome is possible. The person, while recognizing the conflict between the two sets of demand, may still—especially under compulsion—try to meet both. A child will thus do one thing while the teacher is looking and another when the teacher does not see. In such case, the child's conduct is outwardly of one kind but inwardly of another. In this and other cases of reacting to conflicting stimuli, there results an internal conflict. Both lines of conduct call on the organism to act as a whole but in different ways. The two ways being incompatible with the person's efforts in either direction are interfered with by the demands from the other direction. His personality is thus distraught. He is on the road toward disintegration.

67. Integration is Something to Regain

If the child has no soul, then the aim of integration of personality evaporates. Without a soul, there is, in the first place, no principle of integration, and, in the second place, no person to be integrated.

The spiritual substantial soul is the principle of all our actions. In the language of modern psychology it is the principle of our behavior —a term which includes all internal processes as well as external behavior. The soul is that from which our behavior proceeds. Without such a substantial principle, our activities are a series of states or a stream of states in which each state becomes the actor and the thinker, so that even James himself is forced to slip in a bit of clandestine metaphysics in practically making each state a substance. Without this substantial principle there is nothing to unify our behavior. There is no principle of integration.

❈   ❈   ❈

According to Christian teaching, the lack of integration in the present order of things is the result of the fall of man. With the experi-

67. Sister Joseph Mary Raby, *A Critical Study of the New Education* (Washington, D.C.: The Catholic University of America Press, 1932), pp. 47–52.

mentalists, the integration has, quite simply, not yet been attained. With us, it has been lost.

In the state of original justice man was an integrated personality. His being was in order. The hierarchy of his powers was in perfect equilibrium, the lower in due subordination to the higher, and all subject to God. As a result of man's sin of pride, this original integration was lost. The will was no longer subject to God, as it had been in the state of innocence; and since the will, whose function it is to move all the other parts to their end, was turned away from God, all the other powers of the soul became inordinate. The inordinateness of the other powers of the soul consists chiefly in their turning inordinately to mutable good.

Thus the hierarchical order was lost. Man's will was no longer directed unerringly to its end. Each power tended inordinately to seek its own satisfaction, even when contrary to the dictates of reason. It is this lack of order within the self which makes integration necessary.

It scarcely needs mention that this explanation of the necessity for integration is not a popular one. In terms of modern evolutionism, integration, far from having been lost, is only now in the process of attainment. Organic evolution has practically ceased, but conscious, scientifically directed intellectual and moral evolution is only just beginning. Man is naturally perfectible and education is a kind of conscious evolution towards a greater perfection. . . .

What is the basis of integration of personality? Is it the "unification of the self through thoughtful purposing"? In part, and in the natural order, yes. But the matter transcends the natural order. The loss of integration through the fall of man was a loss of preternatural gifts, and the recovery of integration—never complete in this world—is a matter not of the natural only but of the supernatural. The possibility of integration lies in the fact of the Redemption. Integration of personality is an achievement; it is won only through personal struggle, with the help of God's grace in the Church, through prayer and the sacraments . . .

68. The Whole Child is a Myth

This leads me to speak of the assertion that the activity curriculum possesses the peculiar merit of educating "the whole child." In my opinion, the "whole child" is another psychological myth. Either

68. Guy M. Whipple, "The Activity Movement from an Adverse Point of View," *Progressive Education*, 11:342–343, October 1934.

that, or I am not psychologist enough to understand what the term means. One of the most obvious factors controlling mental organization is found in the selective operation of attention. Without the operation of this factor, mentality would be an impossible jumble of confusion. All that saves us as sane human beings is the reduction to a restricted few responses of the potentially enormous hook-up of impressions and reactions. In other words, we never operate as wholes; on the contrary, we focus upon the task before us. We can be efficient only by keeping *out* of the picture the elements of our psycho-physical organization that would be in the way. When we deal with a given situation, it is only a fragment of our mentality, only one of our numerous selves, that is concerned.

If educating the whole child, however, means educating some of him at one time and another part of him at another time, but seeking eventually completely to educate every part of him, even that is bad psychology. Take a simple case: It is well established that it is poor practice to try to make a child ambidextrous; the proper thing to do is to make one hand highly skilled and let the other be a helper. A like principle applies to mental training. Maximal all-round development is not a desirable educational goal.

IV. FREEDOM AND DETERMINISM

69. Nature and Operation of the Will

The term *will* as used by the Scholastics designates specifically *the controlling and sovereign faculty in man;* a faculty which is distinct from and superior to the sensory desires, the physical impulses, and the emotional cravings. The will is the *intellective appetite,* that is, it is the tendency to desire, to seek, and to *enjoy* that which is apprehended by the intellect as *good.* The will is man's rational appetitive power.

Man's will, more than any other of his faculties, has a direct practical bearing upon the problems of education. The will is the guiding force which molds and directs the life of man, and as such it is the chief integrating force in man's character. Without the function which the will contributes to his life, man would be not a person but merely an animated machine.

❋   ❋   ❋

Since the will is the rational appetitive power, it is by nature spiritual because the eliciting principle of the mental faculties is the spiritual

69. William A. Kelly, *Educational Psychology* (Milwaukee: The Bruce Publishing Company, 1946), pp. 188–199.

soul. However, like the intellect, the will can operate in this life only in conjunction with sensitive nature. Likewise, voluntary activity has an essential reference to the intellect. *Nothing is willed unless it is first known.* Thought must precede the deliberation of the will. An object is willed as it is known by the intellect and proposed to the will as desirable and good. Hence, the formal and *adequate object of the will is good as apprehended by the intellect.*

Acts of the will are performed under the influence of motives. A motive is that for which the act is performed. It is the reason why an act is performed and includes whatever influences the will in any degree. Since whatever is done voluntarily is done on account of some good to be derived from the action, the motive is always the idea of some good, that is, of something useful, noble, pleasurable, beneficial, advantageous, desirable, or gratifying which the individual wishes to obtain. The motive which impels the will to choose an object or to perform an action is the goodness of that object or action as presented to the will by the intellect, since motives may be effective only in so far as they are known. These motives may be highly diversified, ranging from the most fundamental sensory objects to the most lofty ethical ideals, but they all have the common character of goodness.

The motives actuating the will act upon it either as means or as ends. The reasons for choosing one end rather than another, and when the end has been selected, the reasons for using some means in preference to others are examined, weighed, and compared with one another. This examination of motives is termed *deliberation.* This deliberation is followed by *choice or decision* which is the acceptance or rejection by the mind of an object or a course of action after the motives for and against the selection of the object or course of action have been considered.

✿   ✿   ✿

The will is the only faculty for which freedom of choice is claimed. Hence, psychology is concerned with the genesis and the nature of this ability possessed by man to choose between conflicting motives, which choice determines how he will act in a specific situation. *Freedom means absence from restraint or compulsion.* Restraint may be either *internal or external. Freedom of the will is the capacity for self-determination,* implying the absence of external force and of internal necessity. The essential feature in freedom of the will is the *element of choice,* which is the culmination of the exercise of freedom. To will freely is to choose freely. However, since one cannot choose what he does not know, freedom of the will does not imply the power to act without motives. Freedom of the will does mean that after deliberation upon motives presented by the intellect a free choice is made between these motives. Freedom of the will is therefore the power of determining which motives will prevail in the mind to influence selection by the will, but without the will being necessitated by these motives. Therefore, freedom of the will means that when an individual is confronted by two or more possible motives, he may choose one and reject the others, after having weighed the motives for accomplishment and having considered the motives which militate against it. Even then, after having recognized the *good*, he may act or not act because he is free to determine his actions.

When it is stated that the will of man is free, it is by no means asserted that all the acts of man are free. The freedom of the will means only this, that when all the conditions for an act of the will are present, the will is endowed with the power to choose among various motives intellectually apprehended as good, to act or to abstain from action. Furthermore, there are actions which are not free, over which the individual has no control and for which he is not responsible. The doctrine of free will does not imply that man is constantly exerting this power. By far the larger part of man's life is administered by reflex acts, by the automatic working of the organism and by acquired habits. The Scholastics distinguish most carefully between spontaneous and deliberate acts of the will, designating the former as human acts and the latter as acts of man.

It is significant that the Catholic Church has also proclaimed the doctrine of the freedom of the will on the principle that God created man, commanded him to obey the moral law, and promised to reward observance and to punish violation of this law. By proclaiming this doctrine the Church recognizes as a point of Faith that man is justly held responsible for his actions because he possesses the genuine power of real choice and the true ability to determine the course of his thought and his actions; because he is endowed with the capacity to decide which motive shall prevail within his mind and to mold his own life and character accordingly.

The freedom of the will is proved by man's consciousness of his freedom in volition and by man's awareness of his responsibility for his voluntary acts.

The consideration of man's mental states by means of careful and repeated introspective analysis of consciousness testifies to the conclusions that man in the exercise of his volitional acts possesses freedom. Man when exercising voluntary activity considers that he is free.

70. Development of the Will

But why insist at all upon the reproducing of the old type? and why limit to "this extent" the scope of the liberty of choice? Why do we not display with complete equableness all views of the best way of life and say, "Now choose; think out your course for yourselves"? Instead of teaching our children our morality, why not teach them ethical science? instead of religion, metaphysical criticism? instead of our political faith, political philosophy? instead of our manners, the principles of aesthetics? In short, why not make thinkers of them rather than partisans? Why not abolish the last remnant of that ancestor-worship which dwarfs the new life by binding it to the passing life?

The answer is, we have no right to aim at any smaller degree of freedom than this, *nor, for the most part, do we:* but before a completely free will can be brought into being, it is first necessary to bring into being a will. The manifest absurdity of asking a child to choose his own moral code and the rest is due not alone to the fact that he lacks the materials to choose from, but still more to the fact that he does not know what he wants. The first task of education is to *bring his full will into existence.* And this can only be done by a process so intimate that in doing it the type is inevitably transmitted. The whole meaning of education is wrapped up in this process of evoking the will; and apart from it nothing in education can be either understood or placed.

The will can develop only as the several instincts wake up and supply examples of the goods and evils of experience. To bring instincts into action, all that any social environment need do (and almost all it can do) is to supply the right stimulus, together with an indication of what the stimulus means. A response cannot be compelled; for whatever is compelled is not a response. No behavior to which we might drive a child would be *play:* if playthings and playing comrades fail to bring out the play in him, we are all but helpless. A response can only be *e-duced.*

* * *

. . . And the first peril of education is not that the child's will will be overborne, but that through no exposure or inadequate exposure to

70. William E. Hocking, *Human Nature and Its Remaking* (New Haven, Conn.: Yale University Press, 1923), pp. 257–260.

the objects that would call out his best responses, he achieves only half a will instead of a whole one, a will partly-developed and therefore feebly-initiative, casual, spiritless, uninterested. If I were to name the chief defect of contemporary education, it would not be that it turns out persons who believe and behave as their fathers did—it does not: but that it produces so many stunted wills, wills prematurely grey and incapable of greatness, not because of lack of endowment, but because they have never been searchingly exposed to what is noble, generous, and faith-provoking.

71. An Existentialist View of Education

Thus, the end of education for an existentialist is making individuals aware of the meaning of homelessness, of being-at-home, and of the ways of returning. In the strict sense, this means that existentialism is concerned principally with liberal education, freeing man from his isolation and his anonymity, freeing his mind from the confusions that prevent him from seeing his situation and his powers. So much, it has in common with psychiatric therapy. No philosopher today is more concerned with education in this sense than an existential philosopher. Every existential philosopher is a doctor and a missionary, not for some esoteric doctrine called existentialism, but for the purpose of encouraging individuals of all kinds and conditions to understand their situation and themselves. And it is the starting-point of every existentialist that no other modern philosophy has taken the self and its situation seriously enough to make that situation the subject matter of inquiry. It is for this reason that one so often hears it said that if existentialism has any model in the past, it is in stoicism, in tragedy, or in the Christian religion. The existentialist has a view of man which varies less than is supposed from one existentialist to another. All existentialists start with the individual who chooses his course and who dies in disquietude. And all of them protest against the forces within man and in his contemporary situation that discourage him from being-at-home, or, worse, from seeing himself as both mortal and responsible. All are actively and specifically concerned with the limits of man's nature and the desolation of his contemporary frustrations or, more precisely, with homelessness.

71. Ralph Harper, "Significance of Existence and Recognition for Education," in 54th Yearbook of the National Society for the Study of Education, Part I, *Modern Philosophies and Education* (Published by the Society, Chicago, 1955), p. 227.

72. The Paradox of Intellectual Freedom

A "free mind" indeed! Are we men, or are we only liberals? Are not those right who tell us "intellectual freedom" is a contradiction in terms? Can it mean anything but freedom to impose our ideas on others? Speech, discussion, yes, even teaching—we can understand how by ceaseless care they may be made relatively free. But how can mind, how can what we think, how can knowledge of what is so, possibly be free? How can our thought hope to escape the passions and prejudices, the ignorance and the interests in which it is inevitably rooted? And does not any measure of success involve in turn a surrender to the compulsion of truth? Does not the very nature of thinking lie in bondage to its human origins and in submission to the rigorous conditions of its validity?

When we speak so hopefully of defending the mind against external and artificial restraints we are forgetting internal and natural bonds far more pervasive and inescapable. The wisdom of a century of psychologists, social scientists and historians might have taught us what slaves we are to our fellows and to our past. Our most daring thoughts, we know, ripen in the long tradition and accumulated knowledge of our society; our feelings and our opinions are rooted in the thousand social habits and attitudes that make us what we are. Our institutions, our class, our group, our profession—these limit and shape our mind at every turn. Our most original innovators are linked most closely with their predecessors; even our boasted pursuit of what we like to call "free inquiry" is so dependent on a fragile chain of scientific tradition, so exposed to every wave of popular feeling, that it is the first victim of any social shock. And then we fancy we are intellectually free—we who can so easily explain the historical sources, the emotional roots and the class bias of any man's ideas!

❋   ❋   ❋

"Ye shall know the truth and the truth shall make you free."

But despite the Evangelist we are not yet come to the end of our quest. We have rather arrived at the central paradox of intellectual freedom, with which the greatest minds have wrestled and failed to agree. For in its very nature, it has seemed, the last thing intellect is or can hope to be, is free. The fruit of intelligence and knowledge is

72. John Herman Randall, Jr., "The Paradox of Intellectual Freedom," *The American Scholar*, 9:9–11, 14, Winter, 1939–40. Reprinted by permission of the publishers.

not freedom. It is power, or it is understanding; and neither leaves the mind with any unfettered choice. For power is no liberator: it rather sets conditions and obligations of its own from which there is no escape. The more power we possess to do what we can the more we are bound to conform to those conditions and to observe those obligations —and the more inexorably intelligence is compelled to seek what they are, and how what that power can do must be done. And the compulsion of understanding, though less harsh, is no less ultimate. For to know what is, and why it must be so, may indeed win us release from the vain endeavor to do what cannot be done; but in abandoning the illusion of external power we are none the less bound to be what we are and to do what we must. Neither with the power to do, nor with the understanding why, can the mind find independence of circumstance or hope to legislate its own career. The knowledge that is power makes us slaves of the responsibilities of power. And the knowledge that is understanding can set us free only by convicting us of powerlessness to alter what we are and must be. We are caught in the cruel dilemma: if knowledge be power it brings no freedom; if knowledge bring freedom it is at the price of impotence.

❋   ❋   ❋

Knowledge is power, and power is bondage—that wisdom cannot be gainsaid. But our mistake has been to take all bondage as the utter destruction of freedom. And we have made the mistake because we have assumed that freedom is a single thing, one and undivided, which we must possess whole and entire or not at all. If that assumption be true, then intellectual freedom is indeed a paradox that drives us to make freedom and bondage, power and obligation, one and the same. This dialectic may satisfy our philosophies of freedom but it hardly fits our needs. But we can escape it if we realize that freedom is not general but specific and determinate: it is release from one kind of bondage the better to assume the yoke of another. It can never mean the escape from all obligation. Freedoms and obligations are both correlative and plural, and each is at once a freedom from this and a submission to that. Knowledge itself is both an emancipation and an exchange of bondages: it frees us from the slavery of ignorance for the service of the conditions and responsibilities of knowing. Without losing its determinate nature, thought can never be wholly free; nor can it be wholly bound without ceasing to be thought.

73. Free Will is Not Absolute

. . . If the will were transcendental in the extreme sense—i.e., if it were fully independent of all interests in the choice and performance of duties—the best instruction would not necessarily have any influence upon one's performance of duty. But very few persons, if any, believe that to be the case. While the will enjoys freedom of choice this freedom is not absolute, but is limited to the desires that have been awakened. Of conflicting desires it is possible for the will to choose those of the higher order. The relative intensity of these desires is, however, certainly a factor in this choice. Now since the scope, quality, and intensity of desire may be greatly affected by instruction, it is possible for the educator to exert a marked influence upon the will, and hence upon character. The ideal character is approached as the friction between desire, and actual duty is diminished; and the school, in awakening right desires through interest, is causing such an approach . . .

74. Freedom is Inherent in Reflective Conduct

In certain of its aspects, the problem of freedom of will has become so encumbered with the refuse and debris of all kinds of other matters as to be best "solved" by letting alone . . . Fortunately none of these difficulties seriously affects educational questions, while in those concrete matters with which education is concerned there is a general consensus of belief.

1. Freedom of will in the sense of motiveless choice is, even if it exists, of no importance for education, which is concerned with the formation of a character interested in ends that are valuable, and interested in a way that makes these ends stable and effective motives. Or, we can go farther, and say that such freedom, even if it exists, is of negative value to the educator; that is, it introduces a factor of arbitrariness, of caprice, of whimsical unaccountableness, that would be such an undesirable element of character that one of the aims of education would be to counteract it. The supposition that unmotivated choice would be of any positive worth is due to a false conception of

73. Frank M. McMurry, "Interest: Some Objections to It," *Educational Review*, 11:151, February 1896.
74. John Dewey, in Paul Monroe, editor, *Cyclopedia of Education* (New York: The Macmillan Company, 1911), Vol. 2, pp. 705–706.

motive; that is, to regarding it as a force which acts from without upon the self, as if the latter were passive or idle until externally appealed to. Since, however, the self is active on its own account . . . a motive has its origin and residence with the self, so that in acting in accord with motive it may still be expressing its own nature.

2. Plasticity, tendency to variation, to growth, to readjustment of habit, are also native to the self. This covers a large part of the practical meaning of "free will," viz., power to reform, to develop, to alter unfavorable tendencies, and to take on new and better habits. Absence of freedom suggests a rigid domination from without which is fatal to growth and reconstruction from within; while, as a matter of fact, it is only in cases so extreme as to be pathological that initiative and plasticity cease.

3. Preference, selective activity in a specific direction, is also a concrete trait of human action. It has been said that the chief defect of both the conventional upholders and opponents of freedom is that they try to get behind the fact of preference; the opponents, by denying it or reducing it to an illusion; the upholders, by regarding it not as a self-sufficing fact, but something to be accounted for by reference to a faculty which is its cause. Once recognize that all organic activity is partial, preferential, interested in some special direction or toward some end, and we have included a significant element of freedom, practically unordered.

4. Reflection presents and weighs alternatives. A thinking being is free in a sense in which no unthinking being could be free, even if fully endowed with "free will." For a reflecting agent can present to himself the consequences of a proposed act; he does not have to wait till the consequences are externally and irretrievably produced to see whether they are desirable or undesirable. If on reflection, the consequences are seen to be adverse, the proposed line of action, if dropped for preference or the bent of disposition, is shifted to some other alternative, which is then weighed. Just in the degree in which one is gifted with the habit of reflection, in that degree he is capable of acting in the light of a foreseen future instead of being pushed from behind by sheer instinct or habit.

With respect to freedom, then, the task of the educator is three-fold. First, to keep alive plasticity, initiative, capacity to vary; to prevent induration and fixation in fossilized automatic habits. Even a thoroughly good habit needs to be kept flexible, so that it may be adapted, when the need arises, to circumstances not previously experienced even by way of anticipation. Secondly, to confirm preferences; to build up and strengthen positive and constructive interests in specific directions. Nothing is more fatal practically than the growth of a spirit of indifference, of boredom, or of miscellaneous and easily diverted responsiveness. Thirdly, to make preferences *reasonable;* that is to say, to develop in individuals the habit of forecasting the consequences of acting upon a given preferential tendency, of comparing one set of results with another, and by these means enlightening preference as its own deeper and more abiding nature. Capacity transforms habit when required. Steady and specific interests, foresight, and deliberation,—given these factors of character, and purely speculative difficulties in the concept of freedom may be left serenely alone.

75. Kinds of Determinism

The theory which denies the freedom of the will is termed *determinism.* This doctrine maintains that there is no spiritual soul endowed with a will which is the eliciting principle of volitional acts, but that acts result from such conscious or unconscious processes as reflexes, instincts, sensation, feelings, associations, habits, judgments, and the like, which are the antecedents and the causes from which volitional acts proceed. There are various types of determinism, according to the nature of the antecedents which are held to account for man's actions. The first type is *mechanical determinism* or *fatalism* which maintains that whatever man does is predestined by the laws of nature. According to the various aspects of this theory, man's thoughts, his character, his external actions are merely the inevitable outcome of his circumstances. They are inexorably predetermined in every detail by events in the past over which he has no control. The second type is *psychological determinism,* which holds that the will is uniformly determined by the strongest motive; that choice invariably follows what is presented as the greatest good. Those who hold this never attempt to show how every action can be traced to its cause, which in turn relates to other preceding causes. The third type is *biological determinism* in which volition is likened to reflex action. Man is regarded not as a free agent but as a machine which is automatically adjusted to its environment and is therefore freed from blame for his unworthy acts as well as undeserving of praise for his good behavior.

75. William A. Kelly, *Educational Psychology* (Milwaukee: The Bruce Publishing Company, 1946), pp. 193–194.

76. Advantages of Determinism

To an understanding of the material of education, psychology is the chief contributor.

❋   ❋   ❋

A complete science of psychology would tell every fact about every one's intellect and character and behavior, would tell the cause of every change in human nature, would tell the result which every educational force—every act of every person that changed any other or the agent himself—would have. It would aid us to use human beings for the world's welfare with the same surety of the result that we now have when we use falling bodies or chemical elements. In proportion as we get such a science we shall become masters of our own souls as we now are masters of heat and light. Progress toward such a science is being made.

77. Determinism in Educational Psychology

Behaviorism Is Not the Only Deterministic Psychology. Many people have misunderstood modern psychology and have attributed this view, that no human activity occurs without a sufficient cause in the way of preceding activity or external physical stimulation, to that particular movement in psychology which is called "behaviorism." It should be pointed out that this view is not peculiar to behaviorism but is common to all modern systems of psychology. According to all the modern psychological systems, behavior could be predicted if we had sufficient knowledge of the stimulating conditions and of the nature of the person concerned. This predictability, which is the outgrowth of conformity with natural law, is not, however, incompatible with freedom of a certain kind. Whatever acts a person performs depend upon the internal nature of the person, as well as upon the external situation which is present at the time. Freedom may be taken to mean merely this dependence of activity upon our own internal nature. If freedom is defined in this way, then conformity to natural law does not mean

76. Edward L. Thorndike, "The Contribution of Psychology to Education," *Journal of Educational Psychology*, 1:6, January 1910.

77. Clarence Ragsdale, *Modern Psychologies and Education* (New York: The Macmillan Company, 1936), pp. 35–37. By permission of the author.

lack of freedom; it means rather lack of capriciousness, willfulness, or irresponsibility, it means the presence of constancy, responsibility, and dependability in human nature.

Determinism Is Commonly Assumed in Child Training. It would be a very disastrous thing for modern life if human behavior were not highly predictable. When a mother trains her child to tell the truth, she proceeds on the assumption that, after a certain amount of training, the child will no longer be free to tell the truth or to lie whenever an opportunity arises. She assumes, rather, that the result of her training will be the production of such an effect in the child's nature that it will no longer be free to lie, but can respond only by telling the truth. When in school we teach a child that four plus three is seven, and give it repeated opportunity to practice making this combination of numbers, we do so on the theory that after a certain amount of practice the child will no longer be free to obtain any other result from the addition of four and three than the one desirable result of seven. If in spite of all the training of the mother concerned with truth-telling, or the training of the teacher concerned with the addition of numbers, the child is still free to do as it pleases, home training and formal education have no meaning or value.

78. Mental Hygiene Approach is Consistent with Moral Responsibility

Mental hygiene contributes to religious education both a point of view and a methodology. Religion in the past has held bad conduct to be an evidence of sin. It has assumed that individuals have a tendency to do wrong because of the depravity of human nature. Consequently, it has sought to transform this sinful nature, to change the "hearts" of people, and thus to affect their conduct. People have been asked to repent of their conduct on the assumption of deliberate intent to do wrong and consequent moral responsibility.

✿   ✿   ✿

To summarize, the point of view of mental hygiene is (1) to look upon conduct as symptomatic; (2) to recognize that it has been learned in the experience of the individual and is important to the individual in some way; (3) to discover the origin of this conduct in the history

78. Harrison S. Elliott, "Mental Hygiene and Religious Education," *Religious Education,* 24:616–618, September 1929. Used with permission of the Religious Education Association.

and environment of the person; and (4) to treat these causal factors with the expectation that the conduct will change when the causes of it are removed . . .

This point of view does not waive the question of moral responsibility, but recognizes that the degree of moral responsibility of the individual depends upon his training. If a child has grown up in a home where he was completely looked after and had no chance to take responsibility, or even worse, where he was entirely spoiled; if he has had no opportunity to make decisions or to learn moral discriminations, then he may be as an adult, a morally irresponsible person because he learned to be irresponsible as a child. Under these circumstances it is not useful to punish him for his irresponsibility but much more desirable to take the steps which will enable him to become responsible. The ability to be morally responsible is one of the goals of education, and towards the achievement of this goal, mental hygiene brings a distinct contribution.

79. Responsibility is the Product of Education

Responsibility is no more originally given than is individuality. It is something to be developed. He is responsible who can be made to become responsible. The ground of responsibility in conduct is "not in antecedent conditions but in liability of future consequences." That which is done is done. The educator is concerned with that which has been done only in so far as it gives guidance to that which must still be done if an individual is to develop an adequate sense of responsibility for his conduct. Praise and blame, rewards and punishments can be justified only to the extent that they help and do not hinder the attainment of this end.

79. John L. Childs, *Education and the Philosophy of Experimentalism* (New York: Appleton-Century-Crofts, Inc., copyright 1931), p. 157.

4

Learning

Problems in the Philosophy of Education Discussed in this Section

1. Should learning be primarily conceived as an active or passive affair? As a matter of impression or expression?
2. Is learning an activity initiated by the learner, or is it a reaction of the learner to the impact of his environment?
3. Is learning growth? If learning is growth, does it occur according to some preconceived end? If so, how far is this end or pattern resident in biological structure? How far is it determined by the contingencies of the environment?
4. Can we study learning without regard to purpose? Without regard to self-consciousness?
5. *Should* children learn in the way that educational psychologists say they *do* learn? Or as a logician might say they ought to learn?
6. Assuming that one learns the new in terms of the old, just how does the new become the old?
7. To what extent is a child's I.Q. a function of his heredity? Of his environment? What are the ethical implications of this question?

80. Learning is Self-Active

Just as a person may be cured in a two fold manner, through the operation of nature alone or through nature with the aid of medicine, so there is a twofold manner of acquiring knowledge, the one when the natural reason of itself comes to a knowledge of the unknown, which is called "discovery," the other when someone extrinsically gives aid to the natural reason, which is called "instruction." Now, in those things which are done by nature and art, art works in the same way

80. St. Thomas Aquinas, *De Magistro*, in Mary Helen Mayer, *The Philosophy of Teaching of St. Thomas Aquinas* (Milwaukee: The Bruce Publishing Company, 1929), pp. 52–53.

and by the same means that nature does, for just as nature in one suffering from cold induces health by warming him, so does the doctor. Hence, art is said to imitate nature. Similarly, it happens in the acquisition of knowledge that the one teaching leads another to a knowledge of the unknown in the same way as he (the learner) would lead himself to a cognition of an unknown in discovery. Now, the process of reason in one who arrives at a cognition of an unknown in discovery is the application of general, self-evident principles to definite matters, and proceeding from them to particular conclusions and from these to others. Hence, and according to this, one man is said to teach another because the teacher proposes to another by means of symbols the discursive process which he himself goes through by natural reason, and thus the natural reason of the pupil comes to a cognition of the unknown through the aid of what is proposed to him as with the aid of instruments. As, then, a doctor is said to cause health in a sick person through the operation of nature, so man is said to cause knowledge in another through the operation of the learner's natural reason—and this is to teach. Hence, one man is said to teach another and to be his master . . .

81. Stimulus-Response Learning

All human activity is *reactivity*. For every action there is a definite incentive or cause. Activity is not the result of a sort of spontaneous combustion; it is the response to stimulation. The total state of affairs by which a man is at any time influenced is called the *stimulus* or the *situation* and whatever action results—attention, perception, thought, feeling, emotion, glandular secretion, or muscular movement—is called the *reaction* or the *response*.

82. Initiative in Learning Rests with the Organism

Considered from the more comprehensive point of view, the total process of adjustment and education may properly be regarded as a reaction between man and the environment which results in furnishing the conditions for his physical, intellectual, and moral growth. While

---

81. Edward L. Thorndike and A. I. Gates, *Elementary Principles of Education* (New York: The Macmillan Company, 1930), p. 62.

82. John C. Chapman and George S. Counts, *Principles of Education* (Boston: Houghton Mifflin Company, 1924), p. 8. Used by permission of the publishers.

common parlance speaks of the environment producing certain changes in the individual, interpreted too strictly this form of speech is in error. The environment can never produce an adjustment; adaptation is always the act of the organism in response to a certain stimulation. While it is conditioned by the environment, the initiative is always with the organism . . .

83. Learning as Connectionism

I read the facts which psychologists report about adjustments, configurations, drives, integrations, purposes, tensions, and the like, and all of these facts seem to me to be reducible, so far as concerns their powers to influence the course of thought or feeling or action, to connections and readinesses. Learning is connecting. The mind is man's connection-system. Purposes are as mechanical in their nature and action as anything else is.

84. Reasoning in Learning Is Naturalistic

Philosophically the question whether the idea or theory of drives and mechanisms can be extended to the so-called higher levels of learning is of great importance. Reasoning and thinking, some psychologists claim, are matters of an entirely different nature from learning on the motor level, and require for their explanation such additional principles or factors as insight and Gestalt. But, behavioristically investigated in the light of all the available evidence, there is no reason to suppose that any such powers or entities enter into reasoning. Reasoning, in short, is as natural and as determined as is any behavior act, and involves the same structural-functional relationships of organism and environment, in terms of present, past and future purposed experience, the latter two being present, symbolically, in terms of words, formulae and the like. This is important both educationally as well as philosophically. From the latter point of view the use of the same assumptions and methodology makes for greater unity and brings a larger field of experience into integration and relationship. To suppose that new and undetermined factors, not directly demonstrable

83. Edward L. Thorndike, *Human Learning* (New York: The Century Company, 1931), p. 122.
84. Daniel B. Leary, *Educational Psychology* (New York: The Ronald Press Company, 1934), pp. 349–350.

and assumed largely to avoid undesired conclusions, enter into the type of behavior we call reasoning is to abandon reason itself. That reasoning is more subtle, more detailed, more abstract and more complicated than reflex or motor behavior is one thing; but to assume it has no relationship to simpler processes is to draw lines for the sake of drawing them. The "wish" that reasoning be something apart from law and rule is part of the basis for so judging that it is. The desire to somehow free thought from the determinism of the flesh is partly responsible for those theories which make reasoning a will of the wisp. Yet, if reasoning is not determined and not related to experience and desire, why does it ever function and how does it ever reach cogent conclusions? Reasoning becomes a mystery in proportion as it becomes sacred. The more we divorce reason from a structural-organic background, from the play of past, present and purposed experience and of a mechanistic relationship to drives, urges and interests, the more we proclaim that reasoning is inconsequential, cannot be taught and is fundamentally a mystery of which we really know nothing.

85. Behaviorism Rejected as a Philosophy

. . . It is only as a methodology that we embrace behaviorism. As psychologists, writing an exact psychology, we champion it for its usefulness, but as philosophers, writing a theory of education, we reject it for its arrogance. A philosophy of education bound by rigid behaviorism, disregarding by definition the core of human experience, would be fatuous and futile.

*   *   *

The point cannot be overstressed that human purposes and values, and even attitudes and appreciations—the central concern of education —cannot be described in mechanistic terms without losing their meaning and significance. Behaviorism as a methodology for the scientific investigation of the habit processes in education is invaluable, and as a methodology we embrace it willingly. But, as a theory covering all aspects of human experience, especially the more intimate facts of consciousness, it must be vigorously rejected. Unless it is made to play the subsidiary role of an instrumentality for the achievement of educational purposes its influence on educational thinking will be

85. John C. Chapman and George S. Counts, *Principles of Education* (Boston: Houghton Mifflin Company, 1924), pp. 94–98. Used by permission of the publishers.

pernicious. A philosophy of education must not be held in bondage by its servant, behaviorism.

86. How We Learn and How We Ought to Learn

"People," you may say, "learn in other ways than by rational methods. Psychologists and sociologists have shown that men learn by irrational means. Look at the operation of stereotypes and prejudices in thinking and conduct. Look at the operation of unconscious mechanisms and impulses in men's thought and behavior. Look at the amount people learn by rote imitation and uncritical absorption from their culture." And I reply, "Of course, these are facts. There are ways of learning other than by methods of reasoning. But does a *description* of actual ways of learning ever decide the way people *ought to learn to learn* or the way we *ought to teach them to learn?* It would be easy for teachers if people learned only by rational methods. Teaching would then be unnecessary. But by what ways have men learned to learn dependably, so that the consequences of their learning are good, so that the results of their learning are deliberately controlled, public, and generalizable, so that men generally can agree on the results of their learning? The answer is through the methods of reasoning. Scientific method, logic, methodology are, from an educational standpoint, ways of learning. But they are ways to learn which men have devised with satisfactory, dependable, and generalizable results. Teachers who try to move directly from the psychologist's description of how men learn to a position on how men *ought to learn to learn* and try to derive educational method from a psychology of learning are showing a basic fallacy of judgment. The emphasis upon psychology and the relative absence of logical studies in the curricula of teacher training institutions furnish primary evidence that we as a profession have fallen into this error. For it is from logical studies, not from psychological ones, that we learn how we ought to learn."

87. Learning as Recollection

Learning is precisely not the wearing down of a pathway in the nervous system, the repetitive establishment of a routine. So far from

86. Kenneth D. Benne, "Some Fallacies in Current Educational Thinking," *Teachers College Record*, 48:135, December 1946.
87. James L. Mursell, "The Miracle of Learning," *Atlantic Monthly*, 155:735, June 1935.

being the formation of habit, it requires a breach with established ways of doing and thinking and the substitution of better ways. Improvement is in the truest and most accurate sense a creative process. Long ago Plato perceived this. "How," he asked himself, "can anything absolutely new come into our minds?" It seems to whenever we learn, whenever we recombine our ideas or improve our skills. He found this impossible and replied that indeed we never learn anything but only recollect what is already implicitly known.

88. Sharpening the Mind

I appeal to you, as practical teachers. With good discipline, it is always possible to pump into the minds of a class a certain quantity of inert knowledge. You take a text-book and make them learn it. So far, so good. The child then knows how to solve a quadratic equation. But what is the point of teaching a child to solve a quadratic equation? There is a traditional answer to this question. It runs thus: The mind is an instrument, you first sharpen it, and then use it; the acquisition of the power of solving a quadratic equation is part of the process of sharpening the mind. Now there is just enough truth in this answer to have made it live through the ages. But for all its half-truth, it embodies a radical error which bids fair to stifle the genius of the modern world. I do not know who was first responsible for this analogy of the mind to a dead instrument. For aught I know, it may have been one of the seven wise men of Greece, or a committee of the whole lot of them. Whoever was the originator, there can be no doubt of the authority which it has acquired by the continuous approval bestowed upon it by eminent persons. But whatever its weight of authority, whatever the high approval which it can quote, I have no hesitation in denouncing it as one of the most fatal, erroneous, and dangerous conceptions ever introduced into the theory of education. The mind is never passive; it is a perpetual activity, delicate, receptive, responsive to stimulus. You cannot postpone its life until you have sharpened it. Whatever interest attaches to your subject-matter must be evoked here and now; whatever powers you are strengthening in the pupil, must be exercised here and now; whatever possibilities of mental life your teaching should impart, must be exhibited here and now. That is the golden rule of education, and a very difficult rule to follow.

88. Alfred North Whitehead, *The Aims of Education and Other Essays* (New York: The Macmillan Company, 1929), pp. 8–9.

89. Learning as a Function of Novel Experience

All conduct seems to be an effort of the individual to restore some upset equilibrium. From this point of view, if the organism or the individual is upset, it will use whatever repertoire of behavior patterns it has to restore the equilibrium. If it has no old pattern available, then it must create anew—and *learn* means exactly creating a new pattern of behavior to meet a novel situation.

Do you see, then, that *learn* is exactly the correlative of the novelly developing experience; *learn* is essential in that kind of life; and *learn* is creative because we are dealing novelly with a novel situation. Learn is essentially creative from this point of view, and this is highly to be contrasted with that conception of learn which arose when life seemed so static as to make thinking unnecessary. According to this older conception of learn, learning meant accepting what was laid down to be learned; but learn, on this new basis, is active and creative.

90. Learning as Abstraction and Generalization

Experience, according to Dewey, is an active-passive affair in which something is done and something is undergone in consequence of what has been done; experience becomes reflective when the relation between what is done and what is undergone is perceived.

✳　　　✳　　　✳

Thomism places a similar emphasis upon the importance of both activity and passivity in learning which is readily seen in the concepts of the active intellect and the passive intellect. The process, however, is immaterial and is very specifically described. Man is a substantial union of soul and body, in which the body is the instrument the imperfect soul must use to discover its imperfection of knowledge and, by searching in the objects that surround it, to find the knowledge that will overcome this imperfection. To this end the soul has two powers of apprehension, a lower one, the sensitive, and a higher one, the intellectual. The sensitive power apprehends what are called "sensible species" (*species* is the Greek word for idea) from the objects

89. William H. Kilpatrick, "A Theory of Progressive Education to Fit the Times," *Progressive Education*, 8:288–289, April 1931.

90. William J. Sanders, "Thomism, Instrumentalism, and Education," *Harvard Educational Review*, 10:102–106, January 1940.

around it. Since the soul is immaterial, it cannot grasp matter, but it can grasp the species of the form with which every material object is endowed. It does this through the power it has of abstracting this form from the matter through the five particular senses, and referring these perceptions to the common sense which in turn apprehends the operations of the five senses, and distinguishes the perceptions of the five senses from one another. The sensible species thus abstracted are retained by the power of the sensitive soul called the "imagination," or "phantasy," and the species thus retained is called a "phantasm." Memory is the recalling of phantasms, or species previously apprehended and retained in the imagination. This sensible species, however, is a particular; it is not a universal. It is not "tree," but "this tree," it is not "man" but "this man." Yet before a species can be in the intellect as a universal, it must be in the senses as a particular.

The intellect, in both its aspects, the active and the passive, has for its object, not the sensible species, or particular forms that are the object of the sensitive power, but the intelligible species, or universal forms. The aspect of the intellect that learns is the passive intellect—at the beginning of learning it is a *tabula rasa*—yet it can know. The forms that will fill it and therefore bring about the realization of its nature, do not exist outside of the soul as intelligibles, for they are embedded in matter. Therefore, in order to become known, the form must be abstracted from the matter, it must be made intelligible, and this is achieved by the *active* intellect. The active intellect, therefore, abstracts the intelligible species, the form by which the thing is known, and presents it to the passive intellect, which takes the form into itself. In this process, the active intellect avails itself of the sensible species or phantasm that is present in the imagination, but it presents it to the passive intellect not in its particular form but in its universal form—not as "this tree" or "this man" but as "tree" or "man." When it is in possession of this true form, the intellect then creates a concept or word which truly represents the form. This entire process goes on without the consciousness of the learner; until a judgment is made, truth is present in the intellect, but it is not consciously present. When the intellect forms a judgment, it adds something of its own to the reality it has assimilated; it says, "this is a tree" or "this is a man," and thus brings about conformity between the concept and the object. Truth is the accord between the concept in the intellect that judges and the object, whereas error is the lack of accord between them.

It is important to understand that the active and passive intellects are not two different intellects, but powers or aspects of the same intellect; the sensitive and intellectual powers are likewise not compartments of the soul, but different modes of operation of the one soul. The distinction between the powers or faculties of the soul must not lead them to be mistaken for separate organs of the soul; in the entire procedure described above, it is a whole, undivided soul, seeking knowledge throughout the variety of operations necessary for its secure knowledge.

From this, the Thomistic explanation of learning, it should appear that the same teaching methods advocated by instrumentalism may be endorsed. Sense experience is of primary importance, and the curriculum by which a great amount of doing and sensing is afforded is that most likely to lead to the understandings that the intellect actively grasps and retains. It is well to remark also that there is no fixed limit in this life to the capacity of the intellect for understandings and for subsequent experiences, and that the more it learns and acts, the greater will be its future learning and activity. The growth of experience for the Thomist has a purpose to guide, but not to limit it, whereas for the instrumentalist there is no purpose save further growth. Again, although the Thomist proves that knowledge can be accurate and valid, he will readily admit that in many complicated situations, due to the multiplicity of accidents (that is, non-substantial phenomena), the conclusions reached may be erroneous and need correction in the light of later investigation; he therefore disagrees with Dewey, who, building upon this precariousness in the sphere of particular activity, denies validity to all knowledge, and goes so far in his latest book as to substitute for the word "knowledge," a term denoting the ultimate in flux, "warranted assertibility." Most important of all, Thomism offers an explanation accounting for the immateriality of knowledge which is philosophically sound, whereas the instrumentalist epistemology, building on a materialistic foundation, can not possibly explain satisfactorily how we can know anything. It is in the treatment of the problem of knowledge that the greatest gaps are apparent, and the awkward handling of this problem is the source of most of the embarrassment with which this system of naturalistic monism is met.

91. Mechanistic vs. Organismic Learning

In the opinion of mechanists, all reactions of the organism are forced, and substitution through juxtaposition is the sole means of acquiring a modification of response.

As an alternative to this view of original nature I suggest that the stimulus is never a discrete entity; that it operates only as a formal

91. Robert M. Ogden, "The Need of Some New Conceptions in Educational Theory and Practice," *School and Society,* 18:344–347, September 1923.

pattern whose configuration, though ill-defined in the early experience of the individual, is effective, nevertheless, as a pattern, rather than as a discrete stimulus or as an aggregate of stimuli. Accordingly, the nervous structure of the organism is thrown into similar patterns of stresses and strains, and these corresponding patterns of nervous energy eventuate in the overt response or manifest behavior of the organism.

The characteristic of behavior is therefore one of uniformity rather than one of chaotic multiple responses. Similarly, the characteristic of perception, or the stimulation of the organism, is a pattern rather than a summation of stimuli of the multiple-causation type.

It follows the instinct is more typical of original nature than the reflex. The reflex approaches, though it never quite attains, the independence of a mechanism. Similarly, voluntary action is more typical of the educated being than habit, though habit again approaches, though it never quite attains, the status of a mechanism.

*   *   *

Passing now to the conception of learning, it is obvious to students of this subject that current hypotheses are mostly of a mechanistic type. We are told that we learn by forming habits, and that the simplest way of learning is by repetition. Practice makes perfect because exercise "stamps in" the bonds of connection between the ultimate parts in any sequential performance or act. All is thus reduced to the law of association with its subordinate principles of frequency, recency, and innate or acquired readiness for response. The interpretation of learning as a conditioned reflex adds nothing, so far as I can see, to the older principles of association, except that it restates them in terms of behavior without reference to any mental content. But the crux of the problem lies in the learning of a new act, in the achievement of a new adjustment; and whether this be under the conditions of a blindly groping trial and error, or whether it be the sudden and forthright adoption of a means to an end, the mechanistic interpretation fails because it does not allow for the continuity and the dynamic unity of organic behavior. A hungry organism seeking food is dominated by its desire. It seeks with its whole being, and all its behavior is integrated, not only with reference to its desire, but also with reference to the fulfillment of this desire. Thus the selection of a new mode of response involves a transformation of the situation, and the new act which is thus acquired integrates with the animal's desire and with its achievement, whereas the abortive acts which do not accomplish this end are eliminated, because they do not participate in this integration. Any attempt to break up the continuity of learning into separate acts, and to conceive them as being associated together as so many different parts ignores the observed facts of behavior. Furthermore, the attempt leaves us with the insoluble problem of explaining the selection of an appropriate or "right" action by means of something that affects the organism only after the act has occurred, namely, by means of the satisfaction that comes only after a way has already been found to attain it.

One of the most fundamental aspects of the pattern of learning is the underlying rhythm of behavior which demands completion and is satisfied only by the appropriate filling-in of the gaps which occur whenever an obstacle to the attainment of an end is introduced. In this connection the rhythms of organic behavior, as well as the corresponding rhythms of consciousness, are subjects of study which demand much closer investigation than they have thus far obtained. We are too apt, I think, to regard rhythm as a mere matter of a uniform succession of beats, whereas the patterns of organic behavior are likely to evince typical configurations of an order that cannot be reduced to simple unilinear sequences of time.

※   ※   ※

The conception of school-work is likewise in need of reinterpretation, for here again the values of method and content are obviously relational and functional rather than static and structural. The theory of "identical elements," for instance, as being requisite for a transfer of training is in my opinion a perversion of the facts by its implication that study has to do with just so many counters which must be arranged in just such a sequence, in order to constitute knowledge and a basis of right action.

For my part, I believe that the instruments of knowledge and the instruments of conduct are both transitional media bridging gaps between perceived wholes, and thus creating new configurations of insight and intelligence. The perceived wholes first to be grasped are the orthogenic forms and figures to which we are predisposed by nature. In other words, these outstanding figures and patterns of response are the objects of experience and the types of behavior with which we begin our course through life. Education, then, is but the elaboration of these patterns, at first vague and crude, with which we are originally endowed.

92. The Field Theory of Learning

We see that the speeding automobile is "going to turn over," that the man is "angry and going to strike," that the couch is soft and

92. Boyd H. Bode, *How We Learn* (Boston: D. C. Heath and Company, 1940), pp. 224–228. Reprinted by special permission of the publishers.

comfortable. These things are not "in the mind"; they are as truly "objective" as the shape and size and weight of objects. They are not in the mind because the mind is not a thing—whether a substance or a collection of mental states—but a function. The *function* of pointing or leading is what is meant by mind. This function is not anything separate; it is something that things *do*. Through the medium of our responses future events or possibilities get themselves translated into present fact, and thus they become effective for the control of behavior.

✿   ✿   ✿

Mind, then, is a function of symbolizing or forecasting, or, as we sometimes say, of understanding or foreseeing. In order to complete the account it is necessary to indicate how this peculiar and distinctive function operates in the control of behavior. By way of contrast we may refer once more to the explanation of purposive behavior that is commonly offered by the soul-substance theory and the theory of mental states. According to these theories there is first a stimulation of some sense organ. This stimulation is transmitted to the cerebral cortex, where it arouses a perception. This perception marks the beginning of conscious experience and is identified as the stimulus. This stimulus directs the discharge of neural excitation from the cortex into the muscles. Everything that comes after the occurrence of the sensory experience which is called forth in the cortex is labelled response. The account given by Behaviorism is essentially the same, except that the sensory experience as a distinctive happening is omitted altogether. The stimulus is the physical process that operates on the sense organ or the cortex and from that point on everything is response.

In terms of the field concept the relation of stimulus and response is less simple. Since the field operates as a unit, we are bound to assume that the whole field, including the body, is active from the start. This is just another way of saying that the reflex-arc concept, in which the activity is a pure sequence, is all wrong. The "stimulus" does not precede the "response" but the two operate simultaneously. And this, in turn, is just a way of saying that both stimulus and response require redefinition.

✿   ✿   ✿

. . . Dewey argues that such events as seeing and hearing take place because there is already a response going on. This response is necessary if seeing or hearing is to occur; the response is not a consequence of the sensory experience but is an antecedent or condition of it.

There is a certain definite set of the motor apparatus involved in hearing just as much as there is in subsequent running away. The movement and posture of the head, the tension of the ear muscles, are required for the "reception" of the sound. It is just as true to say that the sensation of sound arises from a motor response as that the running away is a response to the sound.*

All this is obviously in entire accord with the requirements of the field concept. The perceiving body, as a part of the field, is in action from the start of the perceptual process; and so it is "just as true to say that the sensation of sound arises from a motor response as that the running away is a response to the sound." But if this be so, why speak of stimulus and response at all? In the case of gravitation, for example, these terms seem to have no appropriateness. The moon pulls on the earth and the earth pulls reciprocally on the moon. Neither moon nor earth can be designated usefully as the stimulus, just as there is no point in describing the action of either as a "response" to the other member of the team.

93. Modifiability of the I.Q.

The whole question of predestination of individuals, of classes, races or nations, whether this predestination is divine, biological or cultural is closely tied up with one's beliefs about human nature. The problem of the I.Q. is, therefore, one of the more crucial problems of our culture. Are individuals, classes or peoples destined to live within the limits prescribed by their genes, or are their futures dependent upon cultural factors over which they may have some measure of control themselves? If the latter, to what extent can they control these factors individually or collectively? What difference would it make if men not only could exercise some control over the conditions that shape their future, but likewise realized that fact?

*   *   *

We can more easily point out the significance of this inquiry if we outline two contrasting psychologies in order to note what difference they make in social and educational policy. We will take two theories

* John Dewey, *Philosophy and Civilization* (New York: G. P. Putnam's Sons, 1933), p. 239.

93. George E. Axtelle, "Significance of the Inquiry into the Nature and Constancy of the I.Q.," *Educational Method*, 19:99–104, November 1939.

as representative of two extreme positions although there are obviously many shades of psychological theory in between. On the one hand we have that general position which looks upon mind as an essence, spiritual substance or faculty of rather specific limitations of powers. Mind varies from individual to individual, class to class, and people to people in amount, quality or power. Its improvement is purely a function of exercise which, however, does not affect its original power or amount, but simply develops what is inherently present. Hence an adequate test would reveal its inherent power, quality or amount, because its limits are set in advance by nature, i.e., the genes.

"Backward" and "inferior" individuals, classes or peoples are backward or inferior because they lack the essential power to acquire and advance within their own culture as individuals, or to progress as cultures. Their amount of intelligence accounts for their status socially, economically and culturally. Dominant individuals, classes or peoples are so because of their natively superior inventiveness, originality or intelligence. Man's weaknesses, on the other hand, are to be attributed to his own inherent limitations, the "sinfulness" of his nature. War, poverty, disease, crime, injustice, superstition, greed, persecution, these are all expressions of his original sin, his natural limitations. According to this point of view it might be argued that modern civilization is confronted with the impasse of having become too complex and difficult, too involved for the intellectual and moral capacities of the masses of mankind.

According to this position human nature is relatively unchanging. Man inherits through his germ plasm a rather complete pattern of behaviour and personality. Learning is supplementary to this inherited equipment but scarcely touches its basic structure and pattern. Hence such institutions as war, imperialism, economic exploitation and struggle, sex, class and race differences and relationships are inherent in the original nature of man. Education may give a certain gloss and finish, strengthen some and inhibit other traits, add an equipment of skills and information. But basically what education can do is limited by the original equipment with which we begin.

Progress, therefore, from this point of view may consist in a continuous accretion to the cultural equipment and materials of a people, but has little meaning for human nature as such. In biological terms this point of view gives support to the doctrine of original sin. Man inherits natural limitations and deficiencies which render him ever liable to social and individual digressions and frailties. Crime and delinquency, poverty, injustice, war, ignorance, prejudice, intolerance, greed, and vice are his natural endowment. Education, religion and the state have as their primary responsibility therefore the subjection and control of these innate tendencies. Since these are natural, innate endowments, authority, discipline, and coercion must ever be relied upon to hold them in check, or society itself is undermined. Since man of necessity must live in society, obedience to authority is imperative to any form of human existence.

Those who are superior in any sense are in that respect stewards of the inferior. It is their moral obligation to maintain their authority and demand respect and obedience. Parent, teacher, priest, employer, official and expert must protect their status and dignity lest their subordinates take advantage of their laxity and evade their authority. Thus the exercise of authority is as much an obligation as is obedience to it. A certain cynicism with regard to human nature is therefore the beginning of wisdom, for without it authorities are in constant danger of relaxing their vigilance and control.

Since the masses are so deficient in intelligence society can be controlled or improved only by an élite. While this élite may engage in criticism it is exceedingly dangerous to permit this criticism to extend to the masses. On the contrary they must be controlled by fictions, myths and dogmas which are held incontrovertible. Education and learning for the masses must consist in the acquisition of the information, beliefs, attitudes and skills essential to their status and role in society, "to the position in life to which God has seen fit to call them." In education as elsewhere fear, reward, punishment and discpline play a central role. It will be seen that education and progress have very definite limitations. Democracy is a chimera, a false and dangerous ideal which may threaten the very foundations of civilized life.

The ultimate consequence of such a position is the necessity of turning to other sources of authority and control than human intelligence, for obviously this limitation and inherent sinfulness of man applies to all classes and persons. Man must, therefore, turn to divine guidance and inspiration. A religious institution is the obvious answer to this need. Its doctrine, its dogma of faith and morals, its infallibility based upon revelation and inspiration, give a sanction to authority which makes it an imperative guardian of human life and conduct. Without such access to authority and wisdom beyond the human, man lacks the ultimate sanctions essential to his own well-being. The church, therefore, has responsibility not only for the religious life of a people but equally for their education, training, and control in civic matters.

✻   ✻   ✻

A contrasting theory of human nature and intelligence sees man as biologically continuous with other animals, differing from them in possessing the anatomical and nervous structures basic to the use of tools and to speech. The biological variants basic to these two functions give an entirely new direction to the subsequent course of the evolutionary process. With speech and tools man developed material and social cultures. Survival is no longer a merely biological and individual affair, but becomes supra-organic, cultural as well as biological. Survival values and capacities belong to the culture and the group very much more than to the individual. Individuals are very largely fashioned by their status and role in their culture. Cultures themselves have their distinctive histories and physical settings which largely account for their survival values.

Another great distinction between the biological character of man and of other animals may be found in the differences underlying their inherited behaviours. Other animals seem to inherit relatively specific behaviour patterns, while in man we find great biological indetermination. The patterning of behaviour in man seems to be dependent more largely upon learning, habituation and the canalization of the culture. While man creates cultures, cultures as truly fashion men. What may be instinct in other animals seems in man to be a function of habit and learning in a social context which supplies the patterns.

According to this theory, intelligence, instead of being an original essence, entity or faculty, is a quality of learned behaviour. Everything we think, feel or do, leaves some trace in our behaviour, and as a consequence we think, feel and do differently. This difference in our behaviour we call learning or habit. By virtue of habit experience becomes cumulative and conserving. Habit may vary in quality from the extreme of routine, repetition, rigidity and automatism on the one hand to the other extreme of flexible adaptability, sensitivity and thoughtful responsibility. The quality of habit depends upon the circumstances under which it is developed. To the degree that learning and habit are the product of pure drill, repetition and authority, they are blind mechanisms. They possess man even more than man possesses them. On the other hand, to the degree that behaviour in a situation is thoughtful, sensitive and reflectively responsible, resultant habit, the learned increment of the situation will be correspondingly flexible and sensitive. In one instance there is response to a physical stimulus, in the other there is sensitive interaction with the meanings of a total situation. To the degree that habit is flexible, sensitive to meanings, behaviour is intelligent. We see this difference between intelligent and routine habit when we compare progressive experimental adaptive behaviour with behaviour that is set in a rut, old fogyish, the slave of routine and convention.

Intelligence grows with exercise. The growth is not like that of a muscle but is creative, continuously developing new powers and insights. It grows not by continuous accretion of new elements and factors but by continuous reconstruction and transformation of existing powers and tendencies. We could probably clarify the concept of intelligence if we were to discontinue the use of the noun and use only the verb, adverb and adjective forms of the word, since it is not a quantity or entity but rather a function and quality of a process. Such words as *thoughtful, reflective, experimental, intelligently, deliberately, thinking and experimenting* more nearly convey what is involved.

Intelligence in this sense is not only a function of problematic situations, it is also a function of social cultural situations. For all that mind is exploring and experimental, it explores and experiments within certain broad limits set by the group and cultural life. What a man may consider as problematic, the way he may attack a problem and the equipment he will bring with him in dealing with it depend to a very large measure upon the culture and group life of which he is a part. Thus man may expect to achieve increasing control over his own evolutionary process. As he discovers the influences of group life upon the character of individual development, as he learns how to control those elements in the culture that affect his own growth, he is increasingly able to direct his own subsequent development. The establishment of schools, the use of printed materials, control of radio and movies are most obvious instances. The character of instruction within the schools themselves is not so obvious but probably more important. If this point of view is correct we can vastly enhance the intelligence of our people by developing that *kind* of school that deliberately fosters the experimental, thoughtful, deliberate action, that sees learning as a group, active, creative function.

If this concept is correct it is not human nature that resists change but rather human institutions which resist. If human nature is flexible, deriving its pattern from its culture, then we might expect that a proper reconstruction of our culture might greatly affect our attitude and conduct with regards to war, poverty, disease, crime, ignorance and vice. Where the former theory counsels a conservative if not reactionary social outlook, this theory encourages a progressive, experimental, reconstructive attitude. Where the former sees progress as a precarious, superficial phenomenon, the latter sees progress as the natural consequence of the growth of intelligence and education. To the degree that we learn how to release the capacities of man and then deliberately reconstruct the conditions under which people live so as to permit this release to take place, man's destiny is in his own hands.

Faith in the possibilities of human nature and in its almost unlimited capacities for improvement, combined with the theory that intelligence is a function of freedom and responsibility in dealing with problems leads to an anti-authoritarian democratic outlook. The central problem both educationally and socially is one of how to initiate and develop such agencies of intercommunication that individuals and groups may adequately identify themselves with the larger culture and cope reflectively with its problems. Anything which tends to set up isolations and to clog the channels of communication from this point of view becomes a blasphemy against the human spirit. Coercion and arbitrary authority, circumventing a thoughtful, experimental and responsible behaviour truncate intelligence and stifle its growth.

Leadership whether that of parent, teacher, priest, lawgiver or expert has vastly greater responsibilities according to this position than in an authoritarian society. For they now not only are authorities in the sense of having more experience in a given area, but they must be skilled in releasing the creative powers of those to whom they are authorities. Guidance becomes the art and process of provoking a thoughtful responsible attitude toward situations and helping individuals and groups learn how best to make use of their own and the resources of their culture in dealing with them. The dogmatic and authoritarian attitude prevents the development of a critical intelligent capacity to make use of these resources in their fullest degree. On the contrary it tends toward the development of blind, routine, mechanical habits which can respond only to very narrow meanings, destroying a sensitive, flexible adaptability, a deliberate, thoughtful responsibility in the presence of novel situations.

If human nature is a function of social experiences, then the inequality of classes, races and cultures may be explained in terms of history and culture rather than biology. Inferiority is something to be studied and remedied rather than to be treated with cynicism or condescension. If we acknowledge the social character of personality, then inferiority of any individual or group becomes a liability to the larger group or society. Under the former theory inferiorities might appear necessary evils, since someone had to do the "dirty work" of the world. This is another way of saying that the "superiority" of individuals and groups demands those whom that "superiority" can exploit. It is possible that a measure of unconscious rationalization may be responsible for the assumption that this inferiority is irremediable, since to remedy it would remove the grounds for superiority and exploitation.

Since intelligence is a function of initiative, responsibility and freedom in group life, a cumulative growth of meaning resulting from deliberate action, democracy is imperative to man's fullest growth. Progress then means, not the accretion of cultural materials so much as the continuous cumulative, creative growth of intelligence both socially and individually. We must, therefore, cherish above all other values, those circumstances and conditions that liberate man's creative powers. We should similarly avoid as the pestilence those circumstances which stifle them. Authoritarianism, conventionality, "respectability" and persecution are the great Bads of human life, for they frustrate intelligence at its source.

Education according to this theory is a world and race building function. It means the creation of circumstances that call forth initiative, responsibility, conscientiousness, sensitivity, that cultivate judgment and refine sensibilities, that awaken and create identifications of the self with others, that build insight regarding the forces that impinge upon society and the individual and competence in their manipulation. Accordingly every institution, custom or practice must be continuously evaluated and reconstructed in terms of its educative influence, its consequences for personality, disposition and intelligence. Democracy and intelligence are therefore correlative terms. Progress is the cumulative growth of society in intelligence and democracy. Since the three terms refer to relative qualities of life—that is, qualities that exist in degree and not absolutely—we must think of them all in a dynamic sense. They exist together and vary each as the other.

5

The Nature of Knowledge

Problems in the Philosophy of Education Discussed in this Section

1. In a "real life" situation does the learner ever get to know his environment as it *really* is?
2. How can one decide whether the results of educational research are true? Is it enough that they "work"? That they are "relatively" true?
3. How should pupils and teachers conceive the truth? Is truth affected by the interest or purpose of pupils? Of the state?
4. May educational policy be theoretically sound but practically unsound?
5. Do educators ever have to make assumptions? When? How can they tell whether their assumptions are warranted? Should a thoroughgoing sceptic enter the teaching profession? Can a teacher teach without faith? If not, in what must he have faith?
6. Is learning primarily a matter of cognition or of judgment? May knowledge be learned intuitively? Does learning to know something in any way alter the thing known?
7. Can there be learning or knowing without doing in any field? In the realm of moral education? In geography? In history?
8. Is knowledge waiting in books and libraries to be learned? Will the learner get to know the world better through books or through experience? Is vicarious experience knowledge?
9. When is a student warranted in learning on authority?
10. What is the nature of the problematic in learning? Is it psychological? Metaphysical?
11. What is the role of intelligence in the world order?

I. TRUTH

94. Truth is Everywhere the Same

I shall not be attentive when you tell me that the plan of general education I am about to present is remote from real life, that real life

94. Robert M. Hutchins, *The Higher Learning in America* (New Haven, Conn: Yale University Press, 1936), pp. 64–67.

is in constant flux and change, and that education must be in constant flux and change as well. I do not deny that all things are in change. They have a beginning, and a middle, and an end. Nor will I deny that the history of the race reveals tremendous technological advances and great increases in our scientific knowledge. But we are so impressed with scientific and technological progress that we assume similar progress in every field. We renounce our intellectual heritage, read only the most recent books, discuss only current events, try to keep the schools abreast or even ahead of the times, and write elaborate addresses on Education and Social Change.

✻   ✻   ✻

Our erroneous notion of progress has thrown the classic and the liberal arts out of the curriculum, overemphasized the empirical sciences, and made education the servant of any contemporary movements in society, no matter how superficial. In recent years this attitude has been accentuated by the world-wide depression and the highly advertised political, social, and economic changes resulting from it. We have been very much upset by all these things. We have felt that it was our duty to educate the young so that they would be prepared for further political, social, and economic changes. Some of us have thought we should try to figure out what the impending changes would be and frame a curriculum that embodied them. Others have even thought that we should decide what changes are desirable and then educate our students not merely to anticipate them, but also to take part in bringing them about.

One purpose of education is to draw out the elements of our common human nature. These elements are the same in any time or place. The notion of educating a man to live in any particular time or place, to adjust him to any particular environment, is therefore foreign to a true conception of education.

Education implies teaching. Teaching implies knowledge. Knowledge is truth. The truth is everywhere the same. Hence education should be everywhere the same. I do not overlook the possibilities of differences in organization, in administration, in local habits and customs. These are details. I suggest that the heart of any course of study designed for the whole people will be, if education is rightly understood, the same at any time, in any place, under any political, social, or economic conditions. Even the administrative details are likely to be similar because all societies have generic similarity.

If education is rightly understood, it will be understood as the cultivation of the intellect. The cultivation of the intellect is the same good for all men in all societies. It is, moreover, the good for which all other goods are only means. Material prosperity, peace and civil order, justice and the moral virtues are means to the cultivation of the intellect.

95. Truth as Correspondence to Reality

. . . It is logical and defensible to hold with William James and common sense, that there is a difference between truth and reality. Reality is; truth is what it is said to be. Truth is a construction of the knowledge function, the intellectual function. Hence the primary function of intelligence is the discovery of the nature of reality, not its creation. The significance of this more realistic interpretation of nature for the educator is not far to seek. With the scientist he may admit that a process of transformation called evolution is taking place in the world, and yet not believe that the mind of man is the chief agency of this transformation. He may see that truth is a product of intelligence, but that reality is not created thereby. He may think of intelligence as a means of discovery, and of discoveries as a guide to life. The notion that things exist independent of knowledge puts him in tune with the world of science and of common sense, and broadens as well as solidifies the basis of his thought. The world may sometimes disappoint his expectancies, but its behavior has all the uniformities discovered by science, and probably many more. The knowledge of these uniformities, enabling him to predict and control events, will be his guide. At the same time he will deeply respect the intellectual function through which the ways of nature are revealed. Indeed he will train the younger generation how to think, as well as how to use the thoughts of others. He will not, however, expect the youth of today to rediscover the truth of yesterday . . .

96. Appearance and Reality

. . . we never dare assume that we human mortals have ever explored and apprehended our objective world exhaustively. Here the ancient distinction between appearance and reality becomes crucial. We know,

95. Frederick S. Breed, "Progressive Education," *School and Society*, 37:546–547, April 1933.
96. Theodore M. Greene, "A Liberal Christian Idealist Philosophy of Education," in 54th Yearbook of the National Society for the Study of Education, Part I, *Modern Philosophies and Education* (Published by the Society, Chicago, 1955), p. 103.

and we can know, objective reality only as it appears to us. *All* our knowledge of the real is, first of all, necessarily anthropomorphic in that all we can know of the real is what we men with our limited, finite, cognitive capacities, *can* know. This is as true of our scientific knowledge of nature as of our moral insights and our knowledge of God. But, secondly, as we probe deeper and deeper into reality and as our reconstructions of it progessively improve, we pass, as it were, from very distorted appearances of the real to more and more accurate and reliable appearances. "Appearance," in short, is essentially a function not of reality itself but of our knowledge of it; the more adequate our knowledge, in any area of inquiry, the more closely, we must assume, does its "appearance" resemble its actual nature *sub specie aeternitatis.*

97. The Role of Social Consensus

The principle of truth-seeking as social consensus may be defined, in preliminary fashion, as follows: the truth of those experiences most vital in the social life of any culture are determined, not merely by the needful satisfactions they produce, but also by the extent to which they are *agreed upon* by the largest possible number of the group concerned. Without this factor of agreement or consensus, the experience simply is not "true."

Reconstructionism is not interested in arguing that social consensus is *the* criterion of truth. We have repeatedly emphasized the progressivist method of truth-seeking through experimental intelligence as indispensable. Moreover, enthusiasts of that method may or may not wish to insist that truth-seeking as social consensus is already suggested by their own formulation. All the reconstructionist contends is that the criterion needs to be much more greatly emphasized and clearly explicated and that, *for those crucial purposes of goal-seeking* and *future-making* it should be his most important single criterion.

In various respects truth-seeking as social consensus rests upon the several principles of knowledge already analyzed. Let us summarize them. It assumes: with the *first* principle, that goal-seeking is a determinative characteristic of modern man and that the goals most fundamental to our culture can and should be specified; with the *second* principle, that goals sought are vital examples of prehension

97. Theodore Brameld, *Patterns of Educational Philosophy* (Yonkers, New York: World Book Company, 1950), pp. 465, 550–553, 556–557. Used by permission of the publishers.

in that each one not only possesses its own pattern of organic unity but each tends to fuse with others into still larger prehensions, which ultimately may become the counterpart of an entire cultural design; with the *third* principle, that all individual and social goals are profoundly motivated by unrational drives, which, however, are also capable of more or less accurate expression through conscious and organized channels; with the *fourth* principle, the cultures build ideological shells over their institutions and practices—shells that tend to harden and resist modification or reconstruction and thus to conceal changes occurring beneath them; and with the *fifth* principle, that such changes also tend to generate utopian conceptions, which sooner or later are more consonant with the direction a culture may, or should, be in process of taking, and, hence, which tend in varying degrees to clash with ideologies themselves. We shall see bit by bit how these principles are all involved in social consensus.

✻   ✻   ✻

Finally, social consensus helps to achieve a principle that guarantees positiveness, direction, and clear-cut commitment—qualities without which the experimental method in and of itself is likely to become weak and perhaps helpless. In this effort, the aim is to overcome the difficulties of the extreme *relativism* encouraged by such a philosophy as progressivism, which expresses the ideology of a *transitional* culture. The stress in social consensus is not merely on the continuous modifiability of the process as this is related to changing circumstances, but on the worldwide cultural design that can and should now be agreed upon. True, this is not a timeless, purely rational consensus of disembodied logic. But for our revolutionary age it is or should nevertheless become very definite and clear. In brief, the aim is to establish this positive objective by a procedure that escapes the pitfalls both of dogmatism and of overtentativeness—and so to avoid these and other frailties that permeate alternative levels of belief beckoning for our allegiance.

Thus our delineation of social consensus closes with two rhetorical questions. In searching for truths by which we can now be guided, can we resort any longer to a supernatural or metaphysical authority, or to belief in the pre-ordained fixity of mechanized or spiritual laws? Yet, can we any longer function effectively or primarily by means of a cautious and relative process of inquiry that, in any case, insufficiently analyzes or formulates into cultural arrangements the dominant goal-seeking interests of individuals and groups for our revolutionary age? If our reply to these questions is negative (as we believe it must be increasingly), then we are compelled to consider an alternative. Translated into cultural programs and objectives, *truth-seeking as social consensus is the attempt of an entire culture to rediscover and then to reconstruct itself*—a culture which, left unreconstructed, suffers chronically from conflicts and disintegrating pressures.

✦   ✦   ✦

While we have been discussing social consensus (now explicitly related to group dynamics) as a *general* principle of learning, its practicability in actual school programs has not been carefully considered. Obviously, as most schools are now organized its process and its product are impracticable, for the practices of most schools rest largely upon different premises and objectives.

But even in schools built more directly from a reconstructionist design, group agreement is neither a possible nor desirable outcome of every learning situation. A group may find itself too divided to reach satisfactory concurrence; the evidence may be too contradictory and inadequate, feelings too hostile, or communication too cloudy. Yet even this kind of experience is educative. It helps students to appreciate the importance, on occasion, of suspended judgment—the need of further factual investigation and group learning before making decisions. Also, teachers and students should recognize that group dynamics is itself in an exploratory stage, with a vast amount of experimentation still before it. Its own leaders need, for example, to consider much more thoroughly its philosophic assumptions, its relations to social reality, its ambiguities as to its own values, its tendency to stress descriptive psychological process at the expense of normative cultural product.

Meanwhile, it is important to remember also that learning by social consensus must provide for differentiation into *each* of its three integral aspects. Learning from evidence, for example, properly should occupy a substantial proportion of school time; both the indirect evidence of such fields as history and the direct evidence of individual or group interests are indispensable. Likewise, communication through the language arts, as well as the graphic and musical arts, requires sustained attention and therefore generous periods for practice. During these periods, as during the study of evidence, the role of agreement is subordinate though still implicit.

Finally, it should be reemphasized that the *reliability* of agreement as a test of truth and value ranges from major to minor among various fields of learning. As was explained earlier, not even the physicist can entirely avoid the assumption of consensus in his methods and results. But because of the greater objectivity of his subject matter and controls, it plays a less prominent role for him than for the axiologist, who cannot and should not avoid the factor of prehended and/or un-rational awareness of goal-seeking interests as fundamental to his own subject matter and controls. Hence, recall that consensus functions as a kind of spectrum—being of least importance to scientific truth-seeking, and of most importance to ethical or esthetic value-seeking. In actual human experience it is so essential to both of these as to obliterate wholly the hard-and-fast line that often separates epistemology from axiology.

Since, however, "actual human experience" is the very stuff of vital education, social consensus still remains an over-all principle of the school even when divisions are provided in the curriculum where the respective aspects of that principle are focused upon. Study in the natural sciences emphasizes the aspect of agreement least heavily, the aspect of communication moderately, the aspect of experimental evidence most heavily. Study of the social sciences follows the same order of emphasis where "objective" truth is being sought concerning, let us say, population trends or the distribution of wealth. More often, however, economics, political science, anthropology, psychology should seek to bring the three aspects of social consensus into fairer balance, thereby providing students with opportunity to experience how social consensus actively functions in the human sciences. Study of the arts and of philosophy itself might reverse the emphasis from that of the natural sciences in order to accent two important facts: first, the decisiveness of agreement in the determination of values, however difficult the determination may be; second, the fact that when agreement is attained it often possesses its own prehensive quality of esthetic harmony, its own unity of feeling and thought.

As a matter of fact, when any school is fully dedicated to the clarification and implementation of the governing purposes of national and international reconstruction, all of these distinctions become rather artificial. The study of evidence is then never carried on exclusively for its own sake—whether in history, or chemistry, or any other subject-matter area. Likewise, practice in the skills of communication and the group process is never completely segregated from the larger functions and goals to which these skills are instrumental. Public education becomes itself a kind of "group mind," a *means* of thinking and feeling its own way toward achievement of *ends* that bind its personnel as well as its curriculum together into an organic whole. And group dynamics, in this context, becomes a methodological key to the re-modelled school-community.

For this standard to be approximated, we must not forget that effective learning includes *every* aspect of social consensus. But since the first two (evidence and communication) are already more or less abundantly utilized by education—even though eclectically and often aimlessly—reconstructionism would place particular stress upon the third aspect (agreement). Continuous practice in group dynamics with the aim of reaching genuine consensuses, in respect for and action upon agreements reached, in appreciation of the need of strong cultural commitments—all should be provided from the earliest through the latest levels of learning.

Thus, in the larger perspective of the whole curriculum, study of evidence and of communication should always be correlated with study where agreement is directly effected. To illustrate, evidence about nuclear physics will properly carry over into communication of the political and economic effects of atomic energy and thus to majority agreements as to what should be done about it. In a word, social consensus, refined by the young science of group dynamics, is the symbol of an "integrated curriculum" integrated *for* something—for a powerful and encompassing social consensus, which, far from being *merely* educational, is culture-wide. Normatively, it is nothing less than the process and product of the majority of mankind seeking the social-self-realization now possible only through the reconstruction of culture on a planetary scale.

98. Truth and Social Clash

Since the school operates in a social medium, any advance in educational science, if it is to influence practice, must win its way in that medium. Certainly the relative futility of much of the pedagogical speculation of the past is due to the fact that it could not, or at least did not, gain a favorable hearing from the forces which condition and control the school. Plato, sensing this difficulty, insisted that "until philosophers are kings, or the kings and princes of this world have the spirit and power of philosophy, and wisdom and political leadership meet in the same man, cities will never cease from ill, nor the human race." Students of education today are too much inclined to attribute the failures of their predecessors to unsoundness of doctrine. They also tend to assume that their own thinking, because it is increasingly based on the methods and findings of science, will be acceptable to, and even welcomed by, those elements in society which actually determine the policies of public education. Clearly they assume too much . . . To any social group educational thinking is not

98. George S. Counts, *School and Society in Chicago* (New York: Harcourt, Bruce and Company, Inc., copyright 1928), pp. 343–344.

acceptable because of any claim to intrinsic validity, but rather because it serves that group in its struggles for rights, privileges, and "a place in the sun." Or perhaps we should say that in the world of living things, educational thinking is valid in the measure that it serves life-purposes. Toward truth in any abstract sense, social groups have no inclination; rather do they seek effective instruments for the winning of battles. If truth, however it may be defined, serves them, well and good; but if it does not, so much the worse for truth. Thus, whether the present scientific approach is to be more fruitful than the earlier approach of the philosopher will depend upon the ends to which it is put and its success in gaining social support.

99. The Pragmatic Test

In sum, for the experimentalist all ideas are hypotheses. They are possible ways of responding to the problematic as such. The test of hypotheses is their adequacy to resolve the confusion and ambiguity of the situation now in conflict. In other words, the ultimate test of all ideas, principles, and ethical intiutions is their ability *to make* good. They are judged by the concrete, public consequences to which they lead . . .

100. Truth is the Antecedent, Not Consequent, of Workability

Related to these two different views [idealism and pragmatism] of the center of reality are two corresponding and contrasting conceptions of the nature of truth. In the one case it is relative, a quality of the ideas that work successfully as hypotheses in guiding experience . . . Ideas are thus means whereby purposes to modify the environment become effective. In contrast, idealism holds that truth is absolute, a quality of ideas that correctly represent facts and their connections, the harmony between the finite and the infinite thought. From this standpoint ideas are not true because they work, but work, or will work when conditions are better, because they are true. Ideas thus have a representative as well as a controlling function, and knowl-

99. John L. Childs, *Education and the Philosophy of Experimentalism* (New York: Appleton-Century-Crofts, Inc., copyright 1931), p. 115.

100. Herman H. Horne, *The Philosophy of Education* (New York: The Macmillan Company, 1927), pp. 302–303.

edge is a mirror reflecting fact as well as a handle by which to control fact. Some knowledge may thus produce no physical change and control no environment, as our astronomical knowledge of how worlds are formed by spiral nebulae, and yet be true knowledge. And once true, always true. Truth does not change, though man's ideas of it may and do change.

101. Knowledge is the Outcome Only of Learning by Doing

The most direct blow at the traditional separation of doing and knowing and at the traditional prestige of purely "intellectual" studies, however, has been given by the progress of experimental science. If this progress has demonstrated anything, it is that there is no such thing as genuine knowledge and fruitful understanding except as the offspring of *doing*. The analysis and rearrangement of facts which is indispensable to the growth of knowledge and power of explanation and right classification cannot be attained purely mentally—just inside the head. Men have *to do* something to the things when they wish to find out something; they have to alter conditions. This is the lesson of the laboratory method, and the lesson which all education has to learn. The laboratory is a discovery of the conditions under which *labor* may become intellectually fruitful and not merely externally productive. If, in too many cases at present, it results only in the acquisition of an additional mode of technical skill, that is because it still remains too largely but an isolated resource, not resorted to until pupils are mostly too old to get the full advantage of it, and even then is surrounded by other studies where traditional methods isolate intellect from activity.

102. The Nature of the Problematic

In the more recent vocabulary of his *Logic*, Dewey speaks of the "indeterminate situation" instead of a "problematic" one. The change is not one concerned essentially with felicity of expression. Instead,

101. John Dewey, *Democracy and Education* (New York: The Macmillan Company, 1916), pp. 321–322.
102. George R. Geiger, "An Experimentalist Approach to Education," in 54th Yearbook of the National Society for the Study of Education, Part I, *Modern Philosophies and Education* (Published by the Society, Chicago, 1955), p. 156.

it is directed to pointing out that a doubtful situation is not simply doubtful in a psychological sense. The situation itself is not completely determinate. That is why there is a problem and why we have doubts. If subjective doubt were not in some way related to an existential situation, it would be to that degree pathological. It is the situation itself which is to be unified, integrated, resolved.

103. Education as the Constant Reconstruction of Experience

In its contrast with the ideas both of unfolding of latent powers from within, and of formation from without, whether by physical nature or by the cultural products of the past, the ideal of growth results in the conception that education is a constant reorganizing or reconstructing of experience. It has all the time an immediate end, and so far as activity is educative, it reaches that end—the direct transformation of the quality of experience. Infancy, youth, adult life,—all stand on the same educative level in the sense that what is really *learned* at any and every stage of experience constitutes the value of that experience, and in the sense that it is the chief business of life at every point to make living thus contribute to an enrichment of its own preceptible meaning.

We thus reach a technical definition of education: it is that reconstruction or reorganization of experience which adds to the meaning of experience, and which increases ability to direct the course of subsequent experience. (1) The increment of meaning corresponds to the increased perception of the connections and continuities of the activities in which we are engaged. The activity begins in an impulsive form; that is, it is blind. It does not know what it is about; that is to say, what are its interactions with other activities. An activity which brings education or instruction with it makes one aware of some of the connections which had been imperceptible. To recur to our simple example, a child who reaches for a bright light gets burned. Henceforth he *knows* that a certain act of touching in connection with a certain act of vision (and *vice-versa*) means heat and pain; or, a certain light means a source of heat. The acts by which a scientific man in his laboratory learns more about flame differ no whit in principle. By doing certain things, he makes perceptible certain con-

103. John Dewey, *Democracy and Education* (New York: The Macmillan Company, 1916), pp. 89–90.

nections of heat with other things, which had been previously ignored. Thus his acts in relation to these things get more meaning; he knows better what he is doing or "is about" when he has to do with them; he can *intend* consequences instead of just letting them happen—all synonymous ways of saying the same thing. At the same stroke, the flame has gained in meaning; all that is known about combustion, oxidation, about light and temperature, may become an intrinsic part of its intellectual content.

(2) The other side of an educative experience is an added power of subsequent direction or control. To say that one knows what he is about, or can intend certain consequences, is to say, of course, that he can better anticipate what is going to happen; that he can, therefore, get ready or prepare in advance so as to secure beneficial consequences and avert undesirable ones . . .

104. Difficulties of Pragmatism in Teaching History and Art

Since all knowledge is held to have a prospective reference, there is no knowledge of the past unless it is used. What then is the status of unused knowledge about the past? Of knowledge that enters into no hypothesis for controlling the present passing experience? It loses its status as knowledge. It is either forgotten or it becomes information. Losing its status as knowledge, it loses also its status as truth. No true statement can be made about the past unless thereby some problem is being solved. What happens to the status of unused truths about the past? They become dry records, the fossilized remains of truth. Since this view allows information as unused knowledge to remain, and allows the legitimacy of emotional satisfaction in unused knowledge, it may after all amount to no more than the sense in which the term knowledge is to be used. The contraction of knowledge to the field of use is the expansion of information in the field of art. But the information must have symmetrical and orderly arrangement. On this principle one could not cut out the "dead wood" in the curriculum unless it were first shown not to be an object of aesthetic contemplation. But this is not the intended conclusion of the argument for school reform. The root of the difficulty is that in logic Dr. Dewey is a pragmatist but in aesthetics he is not; truth must work but beauty need not.

104. Herman H. Horne, *The Democratic Philosophy of Education* (New York: The Macmillan Company, 1935), p. 499.

105. The Hierarchy of Knowledge

All men by nature desire to know . . . that which is desirable on its own account and for the sake of knowing it is more of the nature of wisdom than that which is desirable on account of its results, and the superior science is more of the nature of Wisdom than the ancillary; for the wise man must not be ordered but must order . . .

And these things, the most universal, are on the whole the hardest to know for they are farthest from the senses. . . . And understanding and knowledge pursued for their own sake are found most in the knowledge of that which is most knowable (for he who chooses to know for the sake of knowing will choose most readily that which is most truly knowledge, and such is the knowledge of that which is most knowable); and the first principles and the causes are most knowable; for by reason of these, and from these, all other things come to be known, and not these by means of the things subordinate to them. And the science which knows to what end each thing must be done is the most authoritative of the sciences, and more authoritative than any ancillary science; and this end is the good of that thing, and in general the supreme good in the whole of nature.

106. An Objective But Not Dogmatic Truth

In the perfect state there would be no discrepancy between the good citizen and the good man, and there would be no question of educational control, because the educator and the statesman would be one in their thinking. But in imperfect states, control must be split into two phases. On the one hand, the construction and maintenance of a school system is a function of the state. On the other hand, questions of curriculum and method cannot safely be left to politicians whose motives may be other than the love of truth and the desire to make men good.

The wise alternative is to give the educators, philosophers, and scientists authority in these matters on the ground that these groups are primarily interested in the discovery and the teaching of truth. Their authority would, therefore, be the authority of truth itself.

105. Aristotle, *Metaphysics*, Bk. I, chaps. 1–2.
106. Harry S. Broudy, *Implications of Classical Realism for Philosophy of Education*. The Association for Realistic Philosophy, *Proceedings*, 1949, pp. 13–14.

In natural science it can be said that scientific method and its results do exert a very powerful compulsion upon the public. Even the most corrupt politician does not try to bribe a chemical reaction. In other areas, unfortunately, there is no body of truth so compelling as to obviate wars of interpretation. Because philosophers cannot agree, and because religious leaders seem a little afraid of agreement, it is the state or the dominant group within a culture that determines what the "truth" in the debatable realm shall be.

It is an old dilemma. Either we commit ourselves to relativity in the field of value and surrender final authority to a power group, or we assert the objectivity of truth in these areas and immediately have twenty candidates for The Truth. For the Absolute and God never speak in public. The hope of reviving Classical Realism rests on the ability of its proponents to shake themselves loose from the countless dogmatists who feel themselves justified by it. Realists must make their claim to truth on philosophical grounds that all men as men can examine rationally. Otherwise intelligent and well-intentioned men will remain what they now regretfully are—the bedfellows of skepticism and relativism. If philosophers can rise above the particularity of race, creed, color, political habits, and cultural peculiarities, there is hope for an objective truth about man as man. Such a truth might well become authoritative for education and even for statesmanship. Once we discern the nature of the universal and essential and make provisions for that, we can allow full play to the peculiarities of the accidental, so that there will be room for a rich and stimulating cultural pluralism.

107. The Assumption of Relativity

Returning to the question of whether there is a cause-and-effect "order" in the universe independent of human intervention, a relativist readily and frankly admits that he does not know and that he sees no way ever of knowing. But, and this is a point seldom made explicit, *he assumes that there is.* The very fact that a thoughtful man, whether he be a philosopher or scientist, attempts to *read order into* the affairs of the world is, in itself, evidence that he is assuming the universe to be independently orderly. Else, he would be embarked on an almost hopeless task.

For example, a relativist—be he philosopher or scientist—assumes

107. Ernest E. Bayles, *Democratic Educational Theory* (New York: Harper Brothers, 1960), pp. 96–98.

a gravitational order of greater or lesser universality and designs the affairs of his life in accordance therewith. But the strictly relativistic position is always, without exception, that any order *which he takes to act upon* is an order *which he reads into* the universe; not one that is "really there." *He neither asserts nor denies that it is really there.* He assumes that it is, but this assumption is based on his experiences and will be changed as soon as, but not until, his experiences warrant. It has none whatsoever of the characteristics of a philosophic absolute. For him it has reality. He orders the affairs of his life by it. To him it makes a real difference. But for him it is not ultimate reality. It has all the ephemerality of his own brain processes, which produced it.

The Baconian-Newtonian science of the several centuries prior to the twentieth has been insistent on assignment of natural cause-and-effect relationships to processes and events. A "natural law" was presumed to be an ontological existent; a given cause directly and dependably responsible for a given effect. The epistemological function of science was, in consequence, that of discovering such independently existing, cause-and-effect relationships. Logically, therefore, nature is determinate. If one had complete knowledge of all natural laws, one could predict with certainty the course of a given line of events and, by logical projection, could plot the complete course of universal history. Thus, natural law is *the* fundamental, ontological existent; it causes electrons, protons, and neutrons to cause, in turn, atoms, molecules, substances, objects, and events. Natural law represents, in consequence, ultimate reality. This is philosophical and scientific realism. Nature is determinate, and natural law or order is the ultimate determinant.

The relativistic upheaval of the twentieth century, both in science and in philosophy, raised again the possibility of indeterminacy. Seemingly, one cannot have both complete clearness and complete coverage at one and the same time. The point is well illustrated by one's experience with a compound microscope; the more clearly one is able to focus upon a given stratum of an object under magnification, the more thoroughly the rest is out of focus. On the other hand, when one is able (perhaps with naked eyes) to see an object as a whole, one is by that very circumstance unable to see the minutiae which a powerful microscope can reveal. In other words, one cannot have everything at once.

The relativistic assumption that the "order" which a given individual reads into the universe is his own concoction avoids the dilemma of determinism. Whether nature is ultimately determinate or indeterminate is no longer a problem. It may be either way. In any case, however, as far as man's designs or plans are concerned, it is *man's interpretation of* what is "out there" which counts, and these interpretations are in no sense absolutely deterministic. They serve man's purposes of prediction, and via them he orders his life. He assumes his "laws" to be accurate until experience demonstrates them otherwise. They are what he has to work with, and all he has. But are these "laws" ultimately true? There is no assumption that they are. On the basis of man-made laws, man determines his plans for action. Subsequently, such laws and plans are subject to review and revision if and whenever experience so indicates.

II. WAYS OF KNOWING

108. School and the Teaching of Theory

First the school is the home of pure theory. Practical disciplines are also taught; we now have schools of engineering, architecture, business, law, medicine, etc. But in the school these procedures are taught not pragmatically but in relation to those pure theoretical principles which lie at their root. The student must learn to become detached from all special needs and interests and to examine things as they really are in themselves. . . .

The peculiar function of the school is to cherish and to cultivate pure knowledge. Hence, it must be detached from concrete life and practice. The scholar is a man of leisure (σχολή), not in the sense that he does nothing, but in the sense that he must be released from the immediate demands of concrete action. The practical man resents this. To him it seems like doing nothing. The academy, the home of pure theory and learning for its own sake, is an ivory tower playground, remote and impractical. As a matter of fact this is a terrible mistake. Of course, truth has a value of its own. It is good to know something as it really is. But in addition to this, it is directly relevant to human action. A practical procedure that is not grounded on the truth is never really practical. Pure theory is the unique possession of the academy. Its major aim is to cultivate such theory, to transmit the tools by which it is acquired, to preserve what has been gained, and to discover more. All other aims are derived from this.

A second aim that follows directly from this scholarly interest in pure theory is to extend our limited vision of the truth, to gain as

108. John Wild, "Education and Human Society: A Realistic View," in 54th Yearbook of the National Society for the Study of Education, Part I, *Modern Philosophies and Education* (Published by the Society, Chicago, 1955), pp. 28–30.

complete a view as possible. . . . The school is, therefore, the home of those integrative hypotheses and theories where an attempt is made to see things all together as they really are.

✻   ✻   ✻

In the third place, we must notice that the school is the source of that critical ferment and dynamism which is so characteristic of advanced civilizations and which distinguishes them from primitive societies. Such societies lack ivory-tower academies devoted to pure theory. . . .

So the school, when it is really detached and functioning in a healthy way, is ever the source of new ideas and social fermentation. The man of action has no time for long-range theoretical perspectives. His horizon is that of the *status quo*. No matter how irrational or avoidable they may be, the problems here are sufficient for him. To gain grounded vision for the future, men must be freed from this restricted perspective and the practical obsessions that attend it. They must have time to reflect and think . . . Men of affairs are never creative . . .

109. Thomist Views on Knowledge

It is an unfortunate mistake to define human thought as an organ of response to the stimuli and situations of the environment. . . . The truth of the matter is just the opposite. It is because human ideas attain being, or what things *are* (even if they do so in the most indirect manner, and in the symbols of physicomathematical science); it is because human thought is a vital energy of spiritual intuition grasping things in their intelligible consistency and universal values; it is because thinking begins, not with difficulties, but with *insights* and ends in insights whose truth is established by rational demonstration or experimental verification, not by pragmatic sanction—that human thought is able to illumine experience and to dominate, control, and refashion the world. At the beginning of human action, in so far as it is human, there is truth, grasped or believed to be grasped, for the sake of truth. Without trust in truth, there is no human effectiveness.

Thus, for Thomist philosophy, knowledge is a value in itself and an

109. Jacques Maritain, "Thomistic Views on Education," in 54th Yearbook of the National Society for the Study of Education, Part I, *Modern Philosophies and Education* (Published by the Society, Chicago, 1955), pp. 59–60.

end in itself; and truth consists in the conformity of the mind with reality—with what is or exists independently of the mind. The intellect tends to grasp and conquer being. Its aim and its joy are essentially disinterested. And "perfect" or "grown-up" knowledge ("science" in the broad Aristotelian sense) reaches certainties which are valid in their pure objectivity—whatever the bents and interests of the individual or collective man may be—and are unshakably established through the intuition of first principles and the logical necessity of the deductive or inductive process. Thus, that superior kind of knowledge which is wisdom, because it deals not only with mastering natural phenomena but with penetrating the primary and most universal *raisons d'être* and with enjoying, as a final fruition, the spiritual delight of truth and the sapidity of being, fulfils the supreme aspiration of the intellectual nature and its thirst for liberation.

There is no other foundation for the educational task than the eternal saying: It is truth which sets man free. It appears by the same token, that education is fully human education only when it is liberal education, preparing the youth to exercise his power to think in a genuinely free and liberating manner—that is to say when it equips him for truth and makes him capable of judging according to the worth of the evidence, of enjoying truth and beauty for their own sake, and advancing, when he has become a man, toward wisdom and some understanding of those things which bring him intimations of immortality.

110. Acquirement Through Inquiry

The theory that meaning is operational in nature, that the true is that which can be verified through public procedures, and that the locus of authority is within these experimental procedures by which conclusions are confirmed, has significant implications for education. As the pragmatists view it, the central implication of experimental method for education is that the program of the school should be so organized that it will provide opportunity for the young to engage in activities in actual life situations whose consequences will expand, revise, and test whatever ideas they develop. They are convinced that "acquiring" is best secured when it comes as a result of purposeful "inquiry" of this kind.

110. John L. Childs, *American Pragmatism and Education* (New York: Henry Holt & Co., 1956), p. 143.

111. Knowledge as Information

Probably the most conspicuous connotation of the word knowledge for most persons today is just the body of facts and truths ascertained by others; the material found in the rows and rows of atlases, cyclopedias, histories, biographies, books of travel, scientific treatises, on the shelves of libraries.

The imposing stupendous bulk of this material has unconsciously influenced men's notions of the nature of knowledge itself. The statements, the propositions, in which knowledge, the issue of active concern with problems, is deposited, are taken to be themselves knowledge. The record of knowledge, independent of its place as an outcome of inquiry and a resource in further inquiry, is taken to be knowledge. The mind of man is taken captive by the spoils of its prior victories; the spoils, not the weapons and the acts of waging the battle against the unknown, are used to fix the meaning of knowledge, of fact, and truth.

If this identification of knowledge with propositions stating information has fastened itself upon logicians and philosophers, it is not surprising that the same ideal has almost dominated instruction. The "course of study" consists largely of information distributed into various branches of study, each study being subdivided into lessons presenting in serial cut-off portions of the total store. In the seventeenth century, the store was still small enough so that men set up the ideal of a complete encyclopedic mastery of it. It is now so bulky that the impossibility of any one man's coming into possession of it all is obvious. But the educational ideal has not been much affected. Acquisition of a modicum of information in each branch of learning, or at least in a selected group, remains the principle by which the curriculum, from elementary school through college, is formed; the easier portions being assigned to the earlier years, the more difficult to the later.

The complaints of educators that learning does not enter into character and affect conduct; the protests against memoriter work, against cramming, against gradgrind pre-occupation with "facts," against devotion to wire-drawn distinctions and ill-understood rules and principles, all follow from this state of affairs. Knowledge which is mainly second-hand, other men's knowledge, tends to become merely verbal. It is no objection to information that it is clothed in words;

111. John Dewey, *Democracy and Education* (New York: The Macmillan Company, 1916), pp. 220–221.

communication necessarily takes place through words. But in the degree in which what is communicated cannot be organized into the existing experience of the learner, it becomes *mere* words: that is, pure sense-stimuli, lacking in meaning. Then it operates to call out mechanical reactions, ability to use the vocal organs to repeat statements, or the hand to write or to do "sums."

To be informed is to be posted; it is to have at command the subject matter needed for an effective dealing with a problem, and for giving added significance to the search for solution and to the solution itself. Informational knowledge is the material which can be fallen back upon as given, settled, established, assured in a doubtful situation. It is a kind of bridge for mind in its passage from doubt to discovery. It has the office of an intellectual middleman. It condenses and records in available form the net results of the prior experiences of mankind, as an agency of enhancing the meaning of new experiences.

112. Immediate and Vicarious Learning Contrasted

. . . There are beliefs about knowledge which are based upon the conviction that neither sense perception, conceptual thinking, nor intuitive insight are the sources of knowledge at its personally most significant levels, but that such knowledge is gained solely by *existence.* One *knows* most profoundly only what one *is.* On this view, knowledge is not *about* existence; it *is* existence. True knowledge is a state of being. This is not to deny that ordinary sense knowledge and the results of reflection and of intuitive perception have their place. But these sources of relatively objective knowledge do not have the personal power and relevance of knowledge by existence. Ordinary knowledge permits a degree of detachment of knower from the known. In contrast, knowledge by existence presupposes active involvement to the point of identification between knower and known. In fact, one criterion for this "existential" knowledge is that the distinction and separation of knower and known are overcome.

Two examples will help to clarify the meaning of existence as a source of knowledge. A person learns from books and conversations about the meaning of being poor, hungry, or fearful. He can even become an expert on the underprivileged. He can learn to feel their suffering and to predict in detail their attitudes and actions. But this

112. Philip Phenix, *Philosophy of Education* (New York: Henry Holt & Co., 1958), pp. 307–309.

knowledge is not the same as the knowledge of one who is actually himself in want and distress. To be poor is to know poverty in a far more profound way than the objective conception of poverty would permit. Again, one can claim to understand the rightness of personal integrity, but this knowledge is superficial until one wills and acts with honesty and sincerity and thus becomes an integral person. His knowledge of integrity as a moral virtue is then rooted in his very action and being.

It may be objected that this existential idea is too individualistic and subjective. If the most profound knowledge is only had through being, there must inevitably be severe limitations on what one can know because a person can only be himself and not any of the multitude of other different actual or possible selves. Does one have to be a criminal really to understand criminality? Is it not the unique power of mind that it can through imagination achieve cognitive identity with, and hence true understanding of, that which the knower has not embodied fully in his own existence? Reason or intuition may enable one to know poverty without being poor even more truly than the poor can know it, just as one can often understand what happens in a game better as a spectator than as a participating player.

When knowledge is identified with being, growth in knowledge becomes identical with personal becoming. Knowledge is conceived of as personal maturity or wisdom. The educational process from this standpoint requires the greatest patience and devotion, since there are no short cuts to knowledge by means of purely rational pursuits. True knowledge cannot be gained merely by observation, by the study of books, or by sustained reflection, but only by active participation in, personal identification with, and real embodiment of, that which is known. Learning is by doing, and nothing is considered learned until it becomes an expression of what the whole person is. Avoided are the spectator attitude, the development of an appearance of knowledge, sheer verbal cleverness, routine memorization of facts, and all other attainments which make of knowledge a veneer rather than a revelation of the depths of personal being.

113. Importance of Intuition

I hate the idea of a training of the subconscious—of the subconscious of the irrational—by means of I know not what yogism or techniques

---

113. Jacques Maritain, *Education at the Crossroads* (New Haven, Conn.: Yale University Press, 1943), pp. 42–43.

of suggestion. If the "neotechnic" age of education would proceed in this way, and deliver the child's soul over to be rifled by teachers transformed into modelers of the subconscious, it would be a bad omen for freedom and reason. But if we consider the other subconscious, the preconscious of the spirit, here we see that important and helpful changes might take place in our educational methods. Here it is not a question of techniques, nor of a training of the subconscious. It is rather a question of liberating the vital preconscious sources of the spirit's activity. Using Bergsonian language, I would say that in the education of the mind the emphasis should be shifted from that which is *pressure* (which, of course, remains somewhat necessary, but secondary) to that which awakens and frees the *aspirations* of spiritual nature in us. Thus creative imagination, and the very life of the intellect, would not be sacrificed to cramming memorization or to conventional rules of skill in making use of concepts or words, or to the honest and conscientious but mechanical and hopeless cultivation of overspecialized fields of learning.

With regard to the development of the human mind, neither the richest material facilities nor the richest equipment in methods, information, and erudition are the main point. The great thing is the awakening of the inner resources and creativity. The cult of technical means considered as improving the mind and producing science by their own virtue must give way to respect for the spirit and dawning intellect of man! Education thus calls for an intellectual sympathy and intuition on the part of the teacher, concern for the questions and difficulties with which the mind of the youth may be entangled without being able to give expression to them, a readiness to be at hand with the lessons of logic and reasoning that invite to action the unexercised reason of the youth. No tricks can do that, no set of techniques, but only personal attention to the inner blossoming of the rational nature and then confronting that budding reason with a system of rational knowledge.

What matters most in the life of reason is intellectual insight or intuition. There is no training or learning for that. Yet if the teacher keeps in view above all the inner center of vitality at work in the preconscious depths of the life of the intelligence, he may center the acquisition of knowledge and solid formation of the mind on the freeing of the child's and the youth's intuitive power. By what means? By moving forward along the paths of spontaneous interest and natural curiosity, by grounding the exercise of memory in intelligence, and primarily by giving courage, by listening a great deal, and by causing the youth to trust and give expression to those spontaneous poetic or noetic impulses of his own which seem to him fragile and bizarre, because they are not assured by any social sanction—and in fact any awkward gesture or rebuff or untimely advice on the part of the teacher can crush such timid sproutings and push them back into the shell of the unconscious.

114. Mysticism is Educationally Sterile

. . . After making allowance for all external influences, the mind that is in the mystical mood remains certain that the derivative elements in mystical experience are not the whole story. There is something here and now, it claims, that exists or is true on its own account, and not by the suffrage of anything else. Now, this hanging on like grim Death cannot be said to be derived; it is something more than a case of transmission; there is here some sort of original contribution by or through the individual. Whatever else mysticism is or is not, it is one way of asserting the finality of a person. It is also one way of asserting that the finality of the individual is a social finality, for the mystic always feels that he is in touch with something however undefined, that is akin to himself.

Let us endeavor to formulate this underived remainder in mystical experiences: One goes to the edge of all the good that is or ever has been actual; to the edge of all that oneself is and has been, and, looking over, says that there is still more to the good, and there is more to me, than ever has been actualized or expressed; that the truth of me lies in the beyond of me; that the goodness of the good lies in the beyond of the good; and that this "beyond" of the good and of me is one "beyond." The vagueness of this description is unavoidable. For the experience itself denies the adequacy of all terms that get their definition from past events and learnings. That mystics themselves, as a rule, affirm more than this must be admitted, but these other things, which are taken to be intuitions of specific truths, are demonstrably derived; and, moreover, the apparent confirmation of them by a present emotional glow can be wholly accounted for without reference to the truth of them.

But vagueness does not necessarily connote emptiness of meaning; it may connote meaning in process of being generated. In this possibility of "meaning in process of being generated" lies the crux of the problem of what is called the validity of the mystical experience . . . "Ineffability," which is non-communicability, was set down by William

114. George A. Coe, *What Is Christian Education?* (New York: Charles Scribner's Sons, 1930), pp. 277–281.

James as one of the prime marks of the mystic's experience. James was, in fact, much nearer the truth than those who resort to mysticism in defense of a particular set of beliefs already held. But in fact no mystical experience contains anything that is more ineffable than the constantly used notion of "I, myself," or the notion, "experienced good." The incommunicableness is, in fact, simply that of the personal reference of human experience as such.

Because mysticism so generally interprets itself in the terms of conventional beliefs, or else declares itself incommunicable, it is educationally sterile. Incommunicable knowledge (even if we could grant that it exists) cannot be taught, while traditional lore can be taught so much more effectively by systematic drill and habituation that any help from mysticism becomes superfluous.

At two points, however, efforts to weave mysticism into education have appeared in Protestantism. The first is the endeavor of evangelicalism to prepare pupils for a mystical conversion-experience by teaching about it, then to bring about the experience by non-educational methods (chiefly suggestion), and then to use it as confirmation of the antecedent teaching. The scheme broke down for several reasons. For one thing, the standard experience could not be produced except in a part of the pupils; for another thing, the fruits ascribed to conversion were produced by education without conversion; in the third place, the doctrine that underlay the whole discovered its own lack of historical, psychological, and ethical foundation.

The other attempt to weave mysticism into education is in the sphere of worship. The theory is that by putting a learner, young or old, into an attitude of contemplation within a fitting environment (as, a Gothic chapel), divine truth will breathe itself into him. It happens that this method employs, more or less, some of the conditions that favor original thinking. But this is not, as a rule, desired, or expected, or accomplished. Rather, the learner is surrounded by reminders of customary thoughts; he is under the influence of manifold and strong suggestion, the result of which, if it succeeds, is to endow a tradition with an emotion.

Yet mysticism might become educationally fruitful if it would only fix attention upon other phases of itself. In the first place, the mystic engages in implicit criticism of the actual, of the past, but he seems not to feel any responsibility for carrying this criticism explicitly through, nor for makng it effective at the points where it applies. Again, he is engaged in a process of active self-adjustment at the points where past experience does not yield him guidance, yet he does not carry this adjustment through—he either falls back into conventional ways or else seeks relief from them by a repeated flight into an almost objectless emotion. He affirms that there is more to him than his present self, yet he does not take possession of this more in any specific or systematic way. If, now, he would only take the next step, which would evoke out of the "beyond" something definite and critically approved to take the place of his present self and his present world, he might become creative, and he might show others the way of creation.

The history of mysticism justifies the judgment that its function is not the intuitive apprehension of truth. It commonly thirsts for absolute certainty, but in fact it leads to the edge of the uncertainties involved in the creation of a new self and a new world. It seeks rest in timeless being, but in fact it rests in the temporal practices, views, and standards of its environment.

What we have, then, as a net result, is the self-affirmation of a being that, though he resides in time and is subject to change, nevertheless participates in determining the content of time. He is in the future as truly as he is in the past and the present; that is, he is creative. This self-affirmation offers itself as participation; that is, the creativity of the person is a shared creativity.

If the direct personal realization of God to which the mystic aspires were understood by him as self-realization in and through moral creativity, he would become a leader in Christian education. For his whole attitude would be stimulating to others, and not least to the young—stimulating to analysis and criticism of the actual, stimulating to fellowship with all aspiring personalities, and stimulating to mutual action toward a better world, the Kingdom of the creative God.

115. Not Things But Experience of Things

And is it not necessary for the child to build up his notion of a space world by persistent efforts of the same sort as he must employ in making for himself a world whose parts are arranged according to a time order? In all of this we must remember that no matter what things are about him, nor what historical facts have preceded him, nor how widely the universe stretches out before the gaze of those who have already constructed a well-ordered image of it, that none of these things will avail him at all until he himself can experience them. Education concerns itself not with things but with our experience of things. If in any single case the learner fails to experience the thing which it sets before him as needful for him to know, the instruction has in so far been a failure.

115. Ernest C. Moore, *What Is Education?* (Boston: Ginn and Company, 1915), pp. 122–123.

116. Education as a Unique Experience

Education is another word for experience. School training and "real experience" are often contrasted to the disadvantage of the former, as in the hackneyed phrase, "Experience is the best teacher"; but experience in the last analysis is the only teacher. What the school attempts to do,—what, indeed, it is doing with increasing success as the art of teaching is refined,—is so to control the conditions of experience that the important lessons will be learned in the most economical and effective way.

The identification of education with experience, however, while clearly justified, is likely to obscure a very important service that education can be made to render,—a service, too, that "raw" experience, no matter how extended or how varied, cannot guarantee. The outstanding advantage of education as contrasted with raw experience lies in the fact that it enables the learner to transcend the limits of space and time within which the influence of raw experience is restricted.

✸   ✸   ✸

Even if "raw" experiences could be provided on a truly mammoth scale, then, they could not supplant the need for the vicarious experiences that the school with competent teachers can readily furnish. For the peculiar kind of experience which education represents, there is no substitute, because—

1. It transcends space in the sense that, through its influence, one may in effect live in far-distant lands, not infrequently gaining through vicarious experience a clearer conception of the conditions there prevailing than an untutored traveler could gain.

2. It transcends time in the sense that, through its influence, one may live in the past and gain a clearer conception of the conditions then prevailing than any persons actually living at the time could have gained.

3. It reduces to terms of individual experience the vast sweeps of race-experience. The individual, so to speak, personifies the group. The group's struggles, extending over generations, become his struggles; its triumphs become his triumphs;—a fact of tremendous significance in the development of the spirit of kinship or brotherhood, expressed in the past not always happily in a chauvinistic type of nationalism, but having within it, as Mr. Wells has so clearly pointed out, the possibilities of a common bond uniting all peoples.

116. William C. Bagley, "Education as a Unique Type of Experience," *Religious Education*, 18:35–37. February 1923.

4. It enables the insights, inferences, and interpretations of the keenest and cleverest minds to become the insights, inferences, and interpretations of all normal minds. Thus genius, rare and exotic though it be from the point of view of its actual appearance among human kind, becomes through its fruits in a very practical way in almost universal possession.

5. It is clearly both the condition and agent of progress, permitting the accumulation and consolidation of gains from individual to individual, from group to group, and from generation to generation, and insuring as well the perpetuation of the ideal of progress and of its method.

117. The Nature of Experience

The nature of experience can be understood only by noting that it includes an active and a passive element peculiarly combined. On the active hand, experience is *trying*—a meaning which is made explicit in the connected term experiment. On the passive, it is *undergoing*. When we experience something we act upon it, we do something with it; then we suffer or undergo the consequences. We do something to the thing and then it does something to us in return: such is the peculiar combination. The connection of these two phases of experience measures the fruitfulness or value of the experience. Mere activity does not constitute experience. It is dispersive, centrifugal, dissipating. Experience as trying involves change, but change is meaningless transition unless it is consciously connected with the return wave of consequences which flow from it. When an activity is continued *into* the undergoing of consequences, when the change made by action is reflected back into a change made in us, the mere flux is loaded with significance. We learn something.

❋   ❋   ❋

Two conclusions important for education follow. (1) Experience is primarily an active-passive affair; it is not primarily cognitive. But (2) the *measure of the value* of an experience lies in the perception of relationships or continuities to which it leads up. It includes cognition in the degree in which it is cumulative or amounts to something, or has meaning. In schools, those under instruction are too customarily looked upon as acquiring knowledge as theoretical spectators, minds which appropriate knowledge by direct energy of intellect. The very word pupil has almost come to mean one who is engaged not in having

117. John Dewey, *Democracy and Education* (New York: The Macmillan Company, 1916), pp. 163–165.

fruitful experiences but in absorbing knowledge directly. Something which is called mind or consciousness is severed from the physical organs of activity. The former is then thought to be purely intellectual and cognitive; the latter to be an irrelevant and intruding physical factor. The intimate union of activity and undergoing its consequences which leads to recognition of meaning is broken; instead we have two fragments: mere bodily action on one side, and meaning directly grasped by "spiritual" activity on the other.

118. Necessity of Activity in Theoretical Learning

. . . Much has been said about the importance of "self-activity" in education, but the conception has too frequently been restricted to something merely internal—something excluding the free use of sensory and motor organs. Those who are at the stage of learning from symbols, or who are engaged in elaborating the implications of a problem or idea preliminary to more carefully thought-out activity, may need little perceptible overt activity. But the whole cycle of self-activity demands an opportunity for investigation and experimentation, for trying out one's ideas upon things, discovering what can be done with materials and appliances. And this is incompatible with closely restricted physical activity.

119. Defect of Learning by Doing

A second matter is less metaphysical and more practical. It concerns the theory that we cannot appreciate what we have not experienced directly, that we must learn by doing, that without a basic direct experience we lack the organs for appreciating indirect experiences. Plato long ago taught that it might help a physician to have had the diseases he treats, but that it would not help a judge to have had the vices he must condemn, for, to have been vicious may leave the judgment blind.

The issue is, shall the teaching concerning vice depend upon the prior experience of its lack of worth? The theory advocated would seem to answer in the affirmative; or else, the realm of vice is not to be referred to at all. The issue puts the theory under a strain. The vices would be learned by initial experience, or else not learned at all. But it is objectionable that children should experience the wrong

118. John Dewey, *Democracy and Education* (New York: The Macmillan Company, 1916), p. 353.
119. Herman H. Horne, *The Democratic Philosophy of Education* (New York: The Macmillan Company, 1935), pp. 325–326.

before being warned against it. It is also objectionable that they should not be warned at all.

*   *   *

The rejection of the principle of learning the vices by direct experience does not mean that children will never fall into error and wrongdoing; but it means they will be prevented from doing so as much as possible, and, when they do so, the fact of such an unfortunate experience is to be properly utilized for instructional purposes. The theory works, not in providing the direct experience of wrong, but in using the unwelcome instances of it.

III. THE ROLE OF INTELLIGENCE

120. Intelligence as the Power To Grasp Essences

Intelligence is the power of the mind to form concepts; these latter are immaterial or spiritual entities existing in the mind, by means of which the mind grasps the innermost reasons or essences of things and understands that each essence may be realized in an unlimited number of individuals. Besides forming concepts, the intelligence combines them into judgments and reasoning processes; but these more complex operations are further elaborations of the concept, which is the fundamental function of the intelligence.

*   *   *

The concept is an immaterial or spiritual entity. In virtue of his power of forming concepts and thoughts man partakes of the spiritual world and is its member and citizen; by his power of thought man is in the natural order the image and likeness of God, the very child of God. It is one of the ends of education to give man from his earliest days of youth the firm conviction that by his nature he belongs to the spiritual world and has a familiarity, a kinship with God. *It is therefore the task and duty of our schools to bring out the spirtuality that is inherent in human nature from the early years of youth.* Where this end and purpose of education is defeated or neglected, that which is best and noblest in man remains dwarfed. Since it is the primary end and purpose of the Church to lead men to God, this same Church has the inherent right to the full opportunity of developing in man from his days of youth the spiritual nature which he has in common with God.

*   *   *

120. Gerard Esser, "The Meaning of Intelligence and Its Value for Education," *The Catholic Educational Review*, 33:262–269. May 1935.

The concept enables the mind of man to grasp what is deepest in things, *the ultimate reason of things*. The human mind when forming concepts and ordering them into thoughts, does not arrest itself at the surface of a thing, but it reaches down to its very bottom and apprehends its very essence or what the thing is. "The object of the intellect," says St. Thomas Aquinas, "is what the thing is. Hence the intellect will attain the more its perfect state, the more it grasps the essence of things."

Present-day educational methods are fond of recommending object lessons and of giving high praise to sensuous intuition; they borrow the aid of pictures and narrations. A magazine, a book, even an article finds favor if it contains apt illustrations. Indeed there is no doubt that sense intuition is a valuable aid for thought; but it should be borne in mind that it is a means to an end. If it aids in grasping the concept and thought, the thought should actually be grasped by its aid . . .

The concept enables the mind to detect in the particular thing a universal truth or a general law. The senses are interested in the particular; the eye enjoys this lily, that beautiful field of evergreens. The intellect looks at the universal truth: it perceives in the field of evergreens the cultivation of evergreens, the work of the mind which makes nature beautiful. You see the slowly running freight train. You are not interested in that train; but some reflection makes you realize that this train is running through one of the arteries through which life and comfort are brought to all parts of the country; this thought arrests your attention. Why are all of us so interested in the Pope? Certainly not because he is that particular person clothed in white robe; but we recognize in him a powerful and inspiring idea; for he represents the true religion of Christ, which binds together millions of Catholics all over the world and which has in the Pope its supreme leader.

121. The Learner Should Mirror the World

What constitutes the good of the individual? I will try to give my own answer without in any way suggesting that others should agree with me.

First and foremost, the individual, like Leibniz's monads, should mirror the world. Why? I cannot say why, except that knowledge and

121. Bertrand Russell, *Education and the Modern World* (New York: W.W. Norton & Company, 1932), pp. 10–11. Reprinted by permission of the publishers.

comprehensiveness appear to me glorious attributes, in virtue of which I prefer Newton to an oyster. The man who holds concentrated and sparkling within his own mind, as within a *camera obscura*, the depths of space, the evolution of the sun and planets, the geological ages of the earth, and the brief history of humanity, appears to me to be doing what is distinctly human and what adds most to the diversified spectacle of nature. I would not abate this view even if it should prove, as much of modern physics seems to suggest, that the depths of space and the "dark backward and abysm of time" were only coefficients in the mathematician's equations. For in that case man becomes even more remarkable as the inventor of the starry heavens and the ages of cosmic antiquity: what he loses in knowledge he gains in imagination.

But while the cognitive part of man is the basis of his excellence, it is far from being the whole of it. It is not enough to mirror the world. It should be mirrored with emotion: a specific emotion appropriate to the object, and a general joy in the mere act of knowing. But knowing and feeling together are still not enough for the complete human being. In this world of flux men bear their part as causes of change, and in the consciousness of themselves as causes they exercise will and become aware of power. Knowledge, emotion, and power, all these should be widened to the utmost in seeking the perfection of the human being. Power, Wisdom and Love, according to traditional theology, are the respective attributes of the Three Persons of the Trinity, and in this respect at any rate man made God in his own image.

122. "Copy" or "Spectator" Theory of Intelligence

But what sort of a thing is knowledge? And how do we come to have it? The easiest and at the same time the most dangerous answer is that knowledge is due to things making pictures of themselves upon our minds; that perfect knowledge or truth exists when this picturing is complete—when there is perfect agreement between the idea and the object or thing. According to this theory mind is only a rather intricate picture-making device—a kind of sensitive plate. It gets the images of things because they stamp images upon it. All knowledge is due to the impressions of things. Mind is a *tabula rasa*, upon which the senses write the images of the outer world. To be sure, it is dif-

122. Ernest C. Moore, *What is Education?* (Boston: Ginn and Company, 1915), pp. 31–33.

ferent from a camera with which we take photographs, in that it remembers its past photographs of things and is constantly combining them in strange new ways, so that it is sometimes difficult to tell just which of its pictures are due to the impressions of outer things and which are due to the liberties it has taken in combining them . . .

The essence of this theory is that knowledge is given to us by things. They are out there; mind is shut up in here. The senses are the apertures through which they communicate their images. Mind must be passive to get the clearest and truest pictures from outer things. It must present itself clean to the truth which comes to it from outside, or it will mix this truth up and blur it with its own past pictures. Strangely enough, both of the traditional schools of philosophy—realism and absolute idealism—define reality as eternally made existence, and for both of them knowledge-getting can be nothing more than the copying of the objects by the idea. Truth is something whose parts are eternally complete. Knowledge is its phantom, its shadow in our minds.

If we have copies only, how can we tell when they are true? Knowledge-getting is thus for these philosophies not a making but a receiving. Truth is an outer something which must come to us. The learner must simply hold the mirror up to the objective world.

123. The Mind is Conditioned by Culture

. . . If we accept the evolutionary point of view, we must recognize that *things* are prior to *symbols* or *words*, and that *activities* are prior to *meanings*. Nor is the priority merely chronological in nature; behavioral adjustments to surroundings not only come earlier than language and thought, they also constitute the matrix from within which all conceptions of relationships, or meanings, are developed. Conscious or cognitive experience is a derived mode of experiencing; it is sourced in the doing, the undergoings, the sufferings, and the enjoyments of primary experience, and its ultimate controls and tests are also provided by the events of primary experience. No matter how deep our respect for the life of reason, we do not serve the ends of reason when we attempt to make it a thing in and of itself. The life of reason has its vital continuities with the life of action and feeling, and although there is a sound basis for our high regard for the trans-

123. John L. Childs, *Education and Morals* (New York: Appleton-Century-Crofts, Inc., copyright 1950), pp. 141–143.

formations wrought in experience by the development in man of the capacity for reflective thought, we should never assume that reason can become the source of its own subject-matter. The process of human thought is indeed a distinctive kind of functioning, but it is nevertheless a form of human functioning, and like all other functionings of the living creature it is carried on by means of an environment. Apart from some context of ordinary human experience, the activity we designate as mind or reason does not occur.

This non-dualistic, functional theory of mind has important consequences for the work of education. Indeed, the evolutionary interpretation cuts the ground from beneath all of those educational practices that assume mind is an inborn essence that unfolds according to its own pre-formed and rational principles. The empirical evidence has never corroborated this doctrine of a universal, inborn mind; it has always supported the view that minds are the kind of affairs that are conditioned by particular cultures, and that they reflect the actual life experiences of the individuals who live in these different cultures. And with the development of an evolutionary, functional view of mind we are rapidly growing in the ability to provide an empirical explanation for those mental phenomena which were long supposed to demand a dualistic theory to account for them. Educators concerned to develop a program of education in harmony with modern thought and knowledge, will not continue to ground their activity in a view which assumes that mind is an inborn latency that unfolds in its own predetermined way irrespective of the life history of the individual human being. Fortunately there is a growing tendency in education to recognize that we can understand life and the mind of a child only as we understand the character of the surroundings in which he lives.

124. Intelligence is Shaped by Contingent World

There are certain commonplaces concerning intelligence which we must not weary of repeating. They have a significant bearing on indoctrination. Intelligence is possible only in a world which is plural, diversified, competitive, and changing. It is an activity which fuses the recognition of these traits with discernment of the variety and direction of their dynamic trends and with a choosing from among the alternatives these present. To intelligence, the grammar of assent is repugnant. Intelligence is born in doubt, it grows by inquiry, dis-

124. Horace M. Kallen, "Can We Be Saved by Indoctrination?" *Progressive Education*, 11:60–61, January-February 1934.

crimination, selection, and testing. To intelligence a doctrine is not a "truth" to rest in but a theory to work with, a tool justified not by what it is made of, or by how it looks, or by how it sounds, but by what it accomplishes. To prize doctrines on any other grounds is to practise hypostasis of the instrument, to turn the tool into an idol, as churches and states and schools persist in doing. Indeed, to prize it on any other grounds is to abort actuality; it is to make the end into a means, the means into an end. It is to confirm that man is made for the Sabbath—for the Church, for the State, for whatever institution. It is to affirm the conventional lie that individuals exist for "society," not for themselves and each other.

6

The Theory of Value

Problems in the Philosophy of Education Discussed in this Section

1. Does educational value inhere in the object of value—curriculum, text-book, laboratory, and the like—or does it depend on the preference of a valuer—student, teacher, or parent? What practical consequences follow a decision on this point?
2. What is the difference between educational values that are *desired* and those which are *desirable*? Which sort of value is *interest*?
3. How shall educational values be compared? Can they be organized into a hierarchy headed by a *summum bonum*? Are educational values ever incomparable? Are any educational values invaluable?
4. How will the progressive educator know whether innovations in education are superior to conventional or traditional practices? How will he know whether the child is "growing" in the *right* direction?
5. How are students' values changed? Are educational values ever obligatory? Can educational values be "assigned" to be learned?
6. Are all educational values in the last analysis instrumental? Can you name any that are not dependent on some other value, but are significant in and of themselves?
7. Can educational values be determined scientifically?

125. Semantic Analysis of Value

Language is used by man for a number of purposes of which the following are perhaps the most important:
(1) To communicate information.
(2) To arouse feelings (as in propaganda and some types of poetry).
(3) To direct people and animals (as in commands).
(4) To express feelings (as in some types of poetry and exclamations).

125. Charles D. Hardie, *Truth and Fallacy in Educational Theory* (Cambridge University Press, 1942), pp. 50, 123–127.

     ❉   ❉   ❉

We have assumed so far that in such a proposition as "knowledge of Greek literature is good" the intention is to convey information; that is, we have assumed that "good" is the name of a certain characteristic which we predicate of a number of things or mental states or what not, and we have been attempting to get clearer about the nature of this characteristic. Now I propose to deny this assumption. In other words I do not believe that when we make a proposition such as "knowledge of Greek literature is good," or any other proposition involving the word "good" or "valuable" in this sense of intrinsically good, our intention is to convey information about what it is like to know Greek literature. Our intention is rather to arouse a certain attitude in our audience. The use of language in the way we use it when we convey information is now generally called the *scientific use* of language; and the use of language in the way we use it when we try to arouse an emotional attitude in the hearer, or to influence him in some other way than by giving him information, is generally called the *emotive use* of language. Hence this third alternative about the nature of "good" is that when we make value judgments we are using language emotively rather than scientifically.

     ❉   ❉   ❉

But it is clear that value judgments must do more than merely express feelings. For we have seen that it is impossible to contradict a purely expressive utterance such as "Damn," but there is no doubt that people do disagree violently about value judgments, and if each person was merely expressing his own feelings such disagreement would be quite unjustified. This brings us to the second function of value judgments—namely, that they are persuasive. They are an attempt to arouse the same sort of feelings in the audience. Hence the judgment "knowledge of Greek literature is good" expresses roughly what is stated by "I like Greek literature and I want you to do so as well." When two people therefore disagree about the truth of a value judgment, each is attempting to arouse in the other the same sort of feeling which he himself experiences. This seems to me to explain the peculiar nature of controversy about value judgments and the difficulty (sometimes the impossibility) of securing agreement. Although most educationists have not interpreted value judgments in such a way, many parents in practice do accept the above account. Consider the case of a mother who says to her several children, "One thing is certain, we all like to be neat." If she really believed this, she wouldn't bother to say so. But she is not using the words descriptively. She is encouraging the children to like neatness. By telling them they like neatness, she will lead them to *make* her statement true, so to speak. If, instead of saying, "We all like to be neat" in this way, she had said "It's a good thing to be neat" the effect would have been approximately the same. If this account is correct, it follows that neither the ability to form a priori concepts, nor the ability to use intuitive induction is involved in learning the meaning of value judgments . . .

Again, if this account of the nature of value judgments is correct, it follows that the exercise of intelligence is not the only mental process necessary for their formation, but the ability to experience certain emotions is also necessary. A value judgment on this view does not assert that certain emotions are being experienced by an individual or a group of people, but expresses this fact, and clearly it cannot express the fact unless the fact occurs. This affords an explanation of the well-known fact that it is hopeless to teach a child to make value judgments about actions or objects unless the child is in such a situation that he is likely to experience the required emotions.

This account explains also, I think, why there has been so much disagreement among education theorists about what changes in be-havior are valuable, and why that disagreement has not been removed in the course of time in the way in which scientific disagreement is removed. The disagreement has not been in *what* has been said, but in the feelings which each educationist has had for the different activities of life, and each has attempted to persuade others to feel the same way as he does. If we realize this we can be tolerant to all their theories, for no one is right and no one is wrong. It is true that some may be said to be "better" than others, in the sense in which one poem may be better than another, but when we realize that we realize also that much of the sting has gone out of educational controversy.

126. Value as the Power to Satisfy Wants

Education seeks to secure for men things that are good instead of bad, conditions that satisfy instead of annoy, activities that are right and beneficial instead of wrong and harmful. Things are not good or bad in and of themselves; a man's acts are neither right nor wrong apart from their effects; no condition is either satisfying or annoying in isolation. Things, conditions, and acts can be classified as good or bad, beneficial or harmful, satisfying or annoying, or as otherwise

126. Edward L. Thorndike and Arthur I. Gates, *Elementary Principles of Education* (New York: The Macmillan Company, 1930), pp. 16–17.

possessing value and significance only when viewed from some point of view. In the last analysis, decisions as to the value and significance of things with which education is concerned are based on desires, wants, cravings, or urges.

    ❉   ❉   ❉

Value or worth or goodness means power to satisfy wants. One thing or condition or act is more valuable or more worthy or better than another because it satisfies wants more fully, or satisfies more wants, or causes less deprivation of wants.

127. The Objectivity of Values

I start with the major assumption that man is essentially a purposive being, with the capacity to approve or disapprove of everything that he encounters and does and is. Everything, therefore, is of actual or potential subjective significance (value or disvalue) to him. This assumption can also be stated objectively, in ontological terms. Reality makes its multiple impacts upon man for better and worse; his life and destiny are profoundly and inescapably affected by the complex reality which confronts him and of which he is a part. . . .

The value dimensions of reality are, therefore, just as "objective" as are its "factual" or nonvalue dimensions. They are objective in the same sense in which causality is objective; they present themselves to us with an orderly and coercive character of their own which we cannot ignore or misconstrue with impunity any more than we can ignore or misconstrue with impunity the complex pattern of spatio-temporal causality. Only on this assumption, in turn, can we take seriously man's age-old efforts to evaluate more validly and wisely. Significant evaluation is impossible if such evaluation has no appropriate referendum. If nothing is *in fact* more or less valuable, then no evaluation *can* be superior to any other; and if this is the case, then all man's purposive activities are, in the last analysis, mere "sound and fury, signifying nothing."

The distinction between appearance and reality is as valid, and as useful, in the realm of values as in the realm of fact. The only values that can concern us as men are the values which do, in fact, make a difference in our lives and which we can, in principle, progressively

127. Theodore M. Greene, "A Liberal Christian Idealist Philosophy of Education," in 54th Yearbook of the National Society for the Study of Education, Part I, *Modern Philosophies and Education* (Published by the Society, Chicago, 1955), pp. 103–104.

explore and apprehend. These values are what they are. But we dare not assume that our knowledge of them is ever wholly adequate or final. . . .

128. Instrumental and Intrinsic Values Contrasted

In answering the question of whether something desired is also desirable, one is involved in a *process* of *evaluation*—arrival at a value. Can this be other than completely arbitrary, "subject to individual will or judgment" alone? Seemingly, it can and doubtless should.

In dealing with the question of the further outcomes or ends to which a given object or event commits us, we are dealing with its instrumental or mediatory function. If we see it as promotive of a desired outcome or end, we regard it with favor or as having positive value. If we see it as obstructive to a desired outcome or end, we regard it with disfavor or as having negative value. Hence, this question has to do with *instrumental values*. And, as far as instrumental values are concerned, personal likes or dislikes, favor or disfavor, do not hold sway. It is in this sense that "the end justifies the means." If a given end is to be achieved, then means or instruments which further or promote that end *have* to be inaugurated—whether persons involved like it or not. And determination of means conducive to a given end under given circumstances is an epistemological—truth getting—matter, presumably to be by way of scientific investigation. Therefore, *instrumental values* are *scientifically verifiable*. To be arbitrary on a matter such as this is to court disaster.

There are, however, values of a different kind; values which in given contexts assume the status of ends in themselves, at least in the sense of the final ends in view. Note the contextual qualification; we are *not* thinking in terms of absolutes. Push a given matter back as far as you will, sooner or later an end-value is reached which, for the occasion, is consummatory, intrinsic, the stopping point beyond which (at least for the time being) one does not, possibly cannot, go. These we call *intrinsic values*, and it is these which are overpoweringly personal. It is to these that tradition applies the expression, *De gustibus non est disputandum*—there is no accounting for tastes. Therefore, intrinsic values are *not* scientifically verifiable. They are axiological, not epistemological. And in relativistic philosophy they are not determinable by epistemological pursuits.

128. Ernest Bayles, *Democratic Educational Theory* (New York: Harper & Brothers, 1960), pp. 106–107.

129. True Happiness

What is to be thought, therefore, of that cruel education which sacrifices the present to an uncertain future, that burdens a child with all sorts of restrictions and begins by making him miserable in order to prepare him for some far-off happiness he may never enjoy?

❀   ❀   ❀

Absolute good and evil are unknown to us. In this life they are blended together; we never enjoy any perfectly pure feeling, nor do we remain for more than a moment in the same state. The feelings of our minds, like the changes in our bodies, are in a continual flux . . .
Every feeling of hardship is inseparable from the desire to escape from it; every idea of pleasure from the desire to enjoy it. All desire implies a want, and all wants are painful; hence our wretchedness consists in the disproportion between our desires and our powers. A conscious being whose powers were equal to his desires would be perfectly happy.
What then is human wisdom? Where is the path of true happiness? The mere limitation of our desires is not enough, for if they were less than our powers, part of our faculties would be idle, and we should not enjoy our whole being; neither is the mere extension of our powers enough, for if our desires were also increased we should only be the more miserable. True happiness consists in decreasing the difference between our desires and our powers, in establishing a perfect equilibrium between the power and the will. Then only when all its forces are employed, will the soul be at rest and man will find himself in his true position.

130. Comparative and Incomparable Values

The theory of educational values involves not only an account of the nature of appreciation as fixing the measure of subsequent valuations, but an account of the specific directions in which these valuations occur. To value means primarily to prize, to esteem; but secondarily it means to appraise, to estimate. It means, that is, the act

129. Jean Jacques Rousseau, *Emile*, Barbara Foxley, translator (New York: E. P. Dutton & Co., 1911), pp. 42–44.
130. John Dewey, *Democracy and Education* (New York: The Macmillan Company, 1916), pp. 279–280.

of cherishing something, holding it dear, and also the act of passing judgment upon the nature and amount of its value as compared with something else. To value in the latter sense is to valuate or evaluate. The distinction coincides with that sometimes made between intrinsic and instrumental values. Intrinsic values are not objects of judgment, they cannot (as intrinsic) be compared, or regarded as greater and less, better or worse. They are invaluable; and if a thing is invaluable, it is neither more nor less so than any other invaluable. But occasions present themselves when it is necessary to choose, when we must let one thing go in order to take another. This establishes an order of preference, a greater and less, better and worse. Things judged or passed upon have to be estimated in relation to some third thing, some further end. With respect to that, they are means, or instrumental values.

❊   ❊   ❊

Certain conclusions follow with respect to educational values. We cannot establish a hierarchy of values among studies. It is futile to attempt to arrange them in an order, beginning with one having least worth and going on to that of maximum value. In so far as any study has a unique or irreplaceable function in experience, in so far as it marks a characteristic enrichment of life, its worth is intrinsic or incomparable. Since education is not a means to living, but is identical with the operation of living a life which is fruitful and inherently significant, the only ultimate value which can be set up is just the process of living itself. And this not an end to which studies and activities are subordinate means; it is the whole of which they are ingredients . . .

It equally follows that when we compare studies as to their values, that is, treat them as means to something beyond themselves, that which controls their proper valuation is found in the specific situation in which they are to be used. The way to enable a student to apprehend the instrumental value of arithmetic is not to lecture him upon the benefit it will be to him in some remote and uncertain future, but to let him discover that success in something he is interested in doing depends upon ability to use numbers.

131. The Progressive Validation of Values

At this point the classicist may acknowledge that he understands where the Progressive looks for the ends of an activity, how he relies

131. Lawrence G. Thomas, "The Meaning of 'Progress' in Progressive Education," *Educational Administration and Supervision,* 32:392–399, October 1946.

on the operations of group intelligence, and how he uses the generalizations from past experience as tools of analysis, but he may still ask: How is the validity or worthwhileness of such ends determined? If a desirable end is not merely any feasible end, how is its desirability established? It should be recalled that the classical solutions to this problem make the common assumption that the value of an object is inherent in that object, quite independently of its relations to other objects or of man's interest in that object. The highest values are spiritual and intellectual; the lowest values are material and physical. Thus, some objects or ends are inherently more valuable, more desirable than others, regardless of persons, places, or time. The only alternative to this view acknowledged by the classical philosophies is to consider values completely subjective and personal to each individual, so that one person's opinion or preference is as good as anyone else's and significant debate among persons on the selection of a desirable end is rendered impossible.

The Progressive, however, introduces a third point of view, usually called the instrumental theory of values. In outline, this view holds that values inhere neither in objects nor in the subject, but are relationships between persons and objects. An object must be desired in order to have value, but its being desired is only a necessary and not a sufficient condition of its being valuable. The key is the difference between "desired" and "desirable." That an object is desired is a simple question of fact. That an object is desirable means that it is worth being desired, and this involves more than an assertion of fact. Desirable objects are valuable objects, but merely desired objects may or may not be desirable or worth desiring, as everyone's experience will testify.

What makes desired objects desirable? The beginning point is to observe that any object is related to other things. It is related to the conditions out of which it grew, to the surrounding circumstances, and to the consequences which unescapably follow from its achievement or possession by a person. These other things are matters of interest to a person—they affect his efforts, his plans, his present enjoyments, and his anticipated satisfactions. The values of an object are its relationships to other matters of interest to the person or persons concerned.

✿   ✿   ✿

This is the process which the Progressive uses in determining the validity or worthwhileness of ends. First, the validity is determined intellectually, expressed in hypotheses. Implicit and fragmentary goods in the present situation are studied objectively to find how their essential conditions and probable consequences can be brought into some pattern of interdependent and mutually supporting relationships for projection as the end to be sought. The relationships in this pattern are the hypothecated values of the end. The end, so far, is an integrated value judgment, a value hypothesis to be acted on. The second stage in validating the end is acting upon it, to find out in experience whether the value-relationships hypothecated in the preliminary intellectual analysis and synthesis actually occur as anticipated. Since no act is undertaken so intelligently that all of its consequences are perceived beforehand, a reexamination of the new situation created by the action is almost always called for. What potential goods were overlooked in the first analysis but now appear more clearly? What unguessed consequences and new relationships have now appeared? What assumed relationships between current means and desired outcomes proved accurate? Which ones proved false? The answers to these questions usually demand a new definition and integration of the ends to be sought and of the means to be considered appropriate.

This process of validating ends is never final or complete. The validity of the ends can never be certain or guaranteed before action. Yet as this process of reflection and action followed by more reflection and action continues, our ends are constantly improved and we become more and more competent in making valid value judgments.

One final question of the classicists needs to be disposed of: Is there no ultimate end, no ultimate value from which one can gain secure direction? If not, how does the Progressive avoid the infinite regress of this being merely valuable for that, and that being merely valuable to something else, and so on? The danger of infinite regress exists only when one attempts to find ultimate certainty for one's value judgment before one acts. Logical analysis by itself has no stopping point. Since the classical view seeks ultimate certainty for its values independently of any action toward them, it had to postulate an ultimate or absolute end to avoid infinite regress.

This problem ceases to exist when one declines to require absolute certainty for a presumed value on merely logical grounds. The need for such certainty is eliminated when one's process of making evaluations includes an independent and objective way of testing and improving one's value judgments continuously. The Progressive's way of accomplishing this is to submit all his value judgments, when their intellectual formulization has proceeded as far as reflection on his experiences permits, to the verifying test of action upon them. As described above, this step gives him new experiences from which to criticize and recast his former value judgments in the direction of making a wider range of experienced goods more feasible and secure in the practical affairs of living. The Progressive method foregoes any merely logical certainty for value judgments but actually increases the certainty of achieving such values in human experience.

In the Progressive view, therefore, it is highly desirable that the ends of living, rather than being fixed and ultimate, be particular, relative, evolving and tentative.

✻   ✻   ✻

One practical consequence of the Progressive view is a heavy reliance on that kind of education which will promote this kind of growth. As would be expected, Progressive education differs radically in many respects from the educational implications of the classical view. The discussion may now be concluded by outlining some of the most important of these differences.

a) Both views seek valid aims for education, but they differ concerning the proper sources of valid aims. In the classical view, the ends of education are timelessly fixed and universal, quite independently of the status of our present knowledge about the nature of the educative process. The educative process is solely a means to these ends. This separation made it possible for Mortimer Adler to state in a public address that the scholastic philosophy had all the proper aims of education but that Progressive education had many of the best means. In the Progressive view, the ends of education are contextual and tentative, organically related to the resources of the existing situation and evolving in large part from the nature of the educative process itself.

b) Although the two views frequently subscribe to similar statements of the ends of education, their differing conceptions of the relation between ends and means produce significant differences in practice. In the classical view, ends and means are of different orders and are justified on different bases. The end justifies the means, so that the teacher is justified in using marks, gold stars, sugar-coated devices, and other types of external motivation just as long as the proper end is reached. In the Progressive view, ends and means are of the same order, distinguishable but continuous. The distinction between them is one of convenience rather than of necessity. Today's end becomes tomorrow's means. As described earlier, the means are to be justified on the same bases as the ends. Consequently, all motivation should be intrinsic, based on genuine interest in the present activity or in what it leads to.

c) Both views intend to prepare children for living more effectively and richly in the world of today. However, in the classical view, childhood is not an end in itself but is merely a means to better adult living. This often results in the teaching of adult values which have no meaning or significance for the child's present living. In the Progressive view, where there are no ultimate, fixed ends, childhood has its own valid ends. Part of their validity, according to the instrumental theory of values, is determined by the meaning of these childhood ends for the future living of the child. In other words, part of the validity of today's ends is determined by their significance as tomorrow's means, but today's ends are as "ultimate" as next year's ends; the best assurance for rich and effective living as an adult is the richest and most effective living possible as a child.

d) Both views recognize that the teacher is the most influential person in the classroom, but the teacher's rôle is conceived differently. In the classical view, the teacher is the sole source of the proper aims for classroom activities, and he in turn has obtained these aims from higher authority. Hence, his rôle is that of pre-established authority and oracle. In the Progressive view, the teacher merely has superior and richer experience to bring to bear on the analysis of the present situation, but the pupils need to participate in the construction of classroom aims, for their interests and experienced goods are valid parts of the process of setting up and testing the worthwhileness of the potential ends-means relationships existing in that situation. The teacher is vitally important as stage-setter, guide and coördinator, but he is not the sole source of authority.

e) Both views recognize that children need to learn the fundamental moral values of the culture, but the recommended methods of learning differ considerably. The classical view urges the achievement of an unquestioning acceptance of the fundamental moral values. These values have a validity and authority which is independent of human experience. Any method of learning them is satisfactory, even, on occasion, an apparently Progressive method, as long as they win unequivocal acceptance. In the Progressive view, the fundamental moral values of the culture are to be taught as the currently approved social policies, but they should be held subject to revision in the light of further experience. Hence, to a significant extent, the validity of these values is re-verified in the lives of the children in proportion to their growing competence to make such tests. The sanction for these values is found, not in external authority, but in continually criticized experience. Under these conditions and with this approach, children will never acquire an unquestioning acceptance of these values but will become increasingly more able to discover their genuine significance in the practical affairs of living and increasingly more eager to promote and preserve them.

f) The two views have different implications for the construction of the curriculum. In line with the classical view, the curriculum should be carefully and thoroughly laid out in advance. The curriculum, of course, should present truth. Truth is universal and absolute and should be studied for its own sake. Hence, insofar as the teacher knows the truth, he should present, in properly organized form, that part which the children are able to learn at this age, and that constitutes the curriculum. In the Progressive view, truths are relative and evolving. They are learned as the solutions of problems in the lives of the pupils. What these problems are depends on the present particular circumstances in the lives of the pupils and on the current stage of their development. In this matrix are found the unrealized potentialities from which the problems and goals of the class activities are constructed. Thus, a curriculum cannot be more than outlined broadly in advance by the teacher and will consist largely of an array of resources which the teacher anticipates may be called upon as the current activities of the class lead on to new interests and new problems. The actual details of the curriculum must be constructed coöperatively in the classroom from week to week. This approach involves neither dictation by the teacher nor the helpless inquiry, "What do you want to do today, children, if anything?" It requires a teacher of broad knowledge, great versatility, deep understanding of children, and much capacity for coöperative planning. The task of selecting and preparing such teachers should be neither underestimated nor ignored.

132. Relativity of Values Criticized

There have been, of course, a series of intellectual movements which have tended to bring about the present crisis [in value]. Some logical positivists, for instance, solemnly proclaim that the statement "thou shalt not kill" is meaningless. Wittgenstein says, "Ah, values—that is a terrible business. The best you can do is stammer when you talk about it." When statements of this kind, bearing some current prestige, are diffused among students and in the world at large, they make for untrammeled, completely rabid relativism. The Marxists, of course, have done their share to weaken the authority of traditional values—

132. Clyde K. Kluckhohn, *The Nature of Concepts, Their Interrelation and Role in Social Structure*, in Proceedings of the Stillwater Conference conducted by the Foundation for Integrated Education (Stillwater, Okla.: Oklahoma A. & M. College, 1950), pp. 84–86.

indeed, of any values except as sheer epiphenomena, verbal rationalizations after the fact. Psychoanalysts have also contributed to the confusion. Through a form of vulgarization of Freud's thought, popular opinion believes that his advice is something like this: "Conscience is a tyrant. It gets personalities mixed up and distorted. The best thing you can do is get as much freedom as you can from your conscience." Anthropologists too have talked about such things as "co-existing and equally valid forms of life." Of course, if such a statement is taken literally, it means that Nazism is justified and that slavery is legitimate because it is still practiced by a certain tribe in Africa. This untrammeled cultural relativity must take a good share of responsibility for the situation in which we find ourselves at present. In addition, the competition and disagreement among Christian sects has tended to weaken the authority of all churches, so that many modern men, at least in the Western world, tend either toward purposeless hedonism or toward an explicit or implicit theory of relativity as far as values are concerned . . .

Because of all this, general education, by and large, is neglecting its most important responsibility to society. It has avoided a consideration of values because they aren't scientific . . . Or have educators evaded the question of values or dealt with it half-heartedly for fear of stepping on someone's toes?

*   *   *

We not only have a clear practical duty as educators to give honestly what direction and persistency we can on matters of value, but also, as people engaged in research, we have a categorical imperative to make some exploration in this field. Why must we study values? It is because we cannot understand human behavior unless we study the basic conceptual assumptions of which values are a very important part. We must look at the human species from the point of view of the natural historian, in order to make certain propositions that will hold true for the whole species. One conclusion that is forced upon us by an examination of the human animal is the fact that he is an evaluating animal, always and everywhere. Moral standards may vary greatly among different cultures, but moral standards of some kind always exist. This is a fact that many of us seem to have overlooked.

*   *   *

There are thus some universal values, I must repeat, which are found in all cultures. It is a myth to say that morality is solely determined by each different culture . . .

133. Finality of the Criterion of Value

Closely related to modern man's assumption that reason is a neutral principle transcending the differences between competing systems is the conscious or unconscious allegiance to pragmatism. He has readily accepted the principle that we must test everything by the way in which it works but he has not seen that consequences can only be evaluated in terms of a criterion which transcends and yet is relevant to that which is being "tested." From any other standpoint such a criterion will be regarded—and rightly so—as arbitrary. John Dewey's writings on education are filled with illustrations of this tendency of the modern mind to absolutize his own criteria in the act of attacking others as arbitrary. Thus Dewey may be right in arguing that no tradition, be it that of a political party or a Church, can be accepted as the final criterion but he is certainly wrong in assuming that therefore man does not need any such criteria at all. In practice one inevitably enters. In Dewey's case it is that of early twentieth-century science, seen through the spectacles of an American middle-class liberal intellectual of an older generation.

134. The Good as Convertible with Being

Finally, let me say that in speaking of the ultimate ends of education I am restricting my view to education as one phase of human activity among many others. The ultimate end of every phase of human activity, considered without differentiation, is happiness. The reason, then, why I do not say that happiness is the ultimate end of education is because that would fail to discriminate educational activity from political activity, domestic activity, the activity of every other human art, for all these aim ultimately at happiness, though each has an end or ends peculiarly appropriate to itself. Hence we must regard the ultimate ends of education not as final ends, without qualification, but as final only with respect to education as a special

133. Arnold S. Nash, *The University and the Modern World* (New York: The Macmillan Company, 1943), p. 117.
134. Mortimer J. Adler, "In Defense of the Philosophy of Education," National Society for the Study of Education Forty-first Yearbook, Part I, *Philosophies of Education* (Chicago: University of Chicago Press, 1942), pp. 239–243.

process and activity distinct from government, domestic management, etc. It follows, of course, that the ends which are final specifically for education, like the ends which are final for other special activities, must in turn be means to that which is the ultimate end of every and all human activity, namely, happiness. And it should be understood, as well, that if the ends of education are absolute and universal, so is the ultimate end of human life. Human happiness, truly conceived, *is* the same for all men, which, as we have seen, is another way of saying that what all men *should* aim at, as the complete objective of their lives, is the same.

❋ ❋ ❋

We are now required to examine the premises which enter into this conclusion. The two crucial premises are definitions, one the definition of education in its minimum terms, the other the definition of *good* with respect to habit.

❋ ❋ ❋

What is to be proved here is the definition of a good habit as that development of a power or capacity which conforms to the natural tendency of that power or capacity. This proof depends upon the conception of the good of anything which can be perfected (which has potentialities capable of being actualized) as the actualization of its potencies. And this, in turn, depends upon the metaphysical conception of the good as convertible with being: Anything has as much goodness at it has being. Hence if a thing is naturally constituted by capacities to be developed, its ultimate good consists in their development, for thereby it has more actual being. Habits as developments of powers are perfections in so far as they increase and complete the being of the thing. But so far we can only say that whatever has powers subject to habituation is perfected by the formation of habits, without distinction among habits as good or bad, for any habit appears to be the actualization of a power, the development of a capacity. It is necessary, therefore, to go further and show that each power is itself a natural being, albeit an accident of the substance possessing it, and because it is natural can only be perfected by one mode of development. To do this, we must understand the metaphysical truth that every determinate potency is a tendency toward a certain actuality. Hence every natural power of man, being a determinate potency, tends toward a certain mode of actualization, a certain development. Now human habits without qualification are the development or actualization of human capacities for operation or activity, but habits are good only if they are developments conforming to the natural tendency of the power they develop.

This last point must be understood in a twofold manner. (a) In the case of the intellect itself, which, as a power of knowing, naturally tends toward the possession of truth as its perfection, the habit of knowledge is good by reason of conformity to the natural tendency of the cognitive power, and the habit of error is bad by reason of violation of that tendency. If the intellect were indifferently a power of knowing and not-knowing, possession of truth and possession by error would be indifferently good as actualizations of the cognitive power. Knowledge (possession of truth) is a good intellectual habit only because the intellect is a power of knowing, not a power of not-knowing. (b) In the case of every human power, other than the intellect itself, the natural tendency of the power is toward that actualization of itself which conforms to reason. This follows from the subordination of all human powers, in their exercised acts, to reason itself. Hence, in the case of every power there is a natural tendency which habit can violate or to which it can conform; and in conforming, the habit is good; in violating, it is bad. Clearly, then, a man is not bettered simply by habit formation, for if the habits be bad they impede the development of his total nature by violating the tendency of his powers to their own perfection. In short, human nature, partly constituted by its natural potencies at birth, is bettered or perfected in the course of life only through the formation of good habits.

135. Critique of Aims Based on Nature of Man

There are two generic ways of reaching what are sometimes called "the ultimate" ends of education. One relies on an immediate, self-certifying *intuition* of the nature of man; the other on the observation of the *consequences* of different proposals of treating man. The first is essentially theological and metaphysical; the second is experimental and scientific.

When they are intelligently formulated both approaches recognize that the ends of education are relevant to the nature of man. But a world of difference separates their conception of the nature of man. The religious or metaphysical approach seeks to deduce what men *should be* from what they *are*. And what they are can only be grasped by an intuition of their absolute "essential" nature. Whatever the differences between Aristotle, Aquinas, and Rousseau on other points —and they are vast—all assert that from the true nature of man the

135. Sidney Hook, "The Ends of Education," *The Journal of Educational Sociology*, 18:175–183, November 1944.

true nature of education follows logically. The scientific approach, on the other hand, is interested in discovering what the nature of man is, not in terms of an absolute essence, *but in terms of a developing career in time and in relation to other things.* It recognizes man's nature not as a premise from which to deduce the aims of education, but as a set of *conditions* which limit the range of possible educational aims in order to select the best or most desirable from among those for which man's nature provides a ground.

What aspects of man's nature are relevant to the formulation of valid educational ideals? At least three distinguishing, but not separable, aspects of human behavior. First, man as a physical organism is subject to definite laws of growth. Certain powers and capacities mature, flourish, and decline according to a definite cycle. Second, man as a member of society, is heir to a cultural heritage and social organization that determine the forms in which his biological impulses and needs find expression. Third, man as a personality or character exhibits a pattern of behavior, rooted in biological variation and influenced by a frame of social reference, which develops through a series of successive choices.

What ends of education should be stressed in the light of a survey of this threefold aspect of man's powers, and why? We say ends, rather than end, because an education that is relevant to at least these three aspects of human nature will have plural, even if related, ends.

*   *   *

On the level of character and personality, the aim of education is the development of intelligence. Here we reach the key value in the sense that it is both an end and the means of testing the validity of all other ends, moral, social, and educational. How is it to be justified? Why should we educate for intelligence? Again our answer is not because of the antecedent nature of man, but because of the *consequences* of intelligence in use. These consequences are many and desirable. Intelligence enables us to break the blind routines of habit when confronted by new difficulties, to discover alternatives when uniformed impulse would thrust us into action, to foresee what cannot be avoided and to control what can. Intelligence helps us to discern the means by which to enstate possibilities, to reckon costs before they are brought home, to order our community, our household, and our own moral economy. All this and more, in addition to the joy of understanding.

Whether man is intelligent, and how intelligent, are empirical questions, on which considerable evidence has accumulated. One might, of course, ask: What must the nature of man be in order for him to become intelligent? And if any one can derive from the answer more illumination than he had before, we can reply: Man must potentially have the nature of a rational creature in order to *become* intelligent. How little this tells us is apparent when we reflect that it is almost tautological to assert that a thing possesses potentially the qualities and relations it actually exhibits. Potentialities may not all be realized but everything realized is a potentiality. Men are and may become unintelligent, too. Unintelligence (or stupidity) is therefore also an antecedent potentiality. But since potentially man is both intelligent *and* unintelligent, what we select as the trait to encourage depends not merely on its potentiality but rather on its desirability. And desirability is an affair of fruits not of origins.

So far we have been attempting to justify the ends of education by their consequences. But there is another approach to the ends of education. This declares that we are dealing with a metaphysical question, which requires an answer based on the true metaphysics. Its chief exponents are Robert M. Hutchins, M. Maritain, and Monsignor Sheen. They hold to the belief that the appropriate end of education can be *deduced* from the true nature of man. The true nature of man is that which differentiates him from animals, on the one hand, and angels, on the other. It is expressed in the proposition: "Man is a rational animal." From which it is inferred that the end of human education should be the cultivation of reason.

I shall not stop to analyze the notion of reason and indicate how it differs from intelligence. What I want to point out is the fallacy in the presumed deduction of the ends of education from what uniquely differentiates man from other animals.

First of all, if what we have previously said is true, from what man *is* we can at best reach propositions only about what human education is, not what it *should* be. What man should be is undoubtedly related to what he is, for no man should be what he cannot be. Yet a proposition about what he is no more uniquely entails what he should be than the recognition of the nature of an egg necessitates our believing that an egg should become a chicken rather than an egg sandwich. A further assumption of the argument is the Aristotelian doctrine that the good of anything is the performance of its specific virtue or the realization of its potentiality. The "good" egg is one that becomes a chicken, the "good" man is one who realizes his natural capacity to think. This overlooks the obvious fact that the capacities of a thing limit the range of its fulfillments but do not determine any specific fulfillment.

Secondly, grant for the sake of the argument that animals other than man are incapable of any rationality. The question is an old and difficult one, handled satirically by Plutarch and experimentally by Kohler, both of whom disagree with the airy dogmatism of the neo-Thomists. Nonetheless, rationality is not the only feature which uniquely differentiates man from other animals. Man can be, and has been, defined as a "tool-making animal." By the same reasoning the neo-Thomists use, we can "deduce" that man's proper education should be vocational! Man is also the only animal that can commit suicide. Does it follow that education should therefore be a preparation for death?

Thirdly, even if man is a rational animal, he is not only that. He has many other traits, some noble, others ignoble, or, to put it more accurately, he has traits that in some contexts can acquire the character of nobility and, in others, ignobility. An education appropriate to man should take note of more than one of his traits and must take note of less than all. In either case some element of selection is involved.

What, after all, is meant by "the nature of man" whenever we speak of relating educational ends to it? The phrase masks a certain ambiguity that makes it difficult to tell whether its reference is empirical or metaphysical. A great deal of philosophical profundity consists in shifting back and forth between these two references and not being found out. When the neo-Thomists speak of *the* nature of man as the basis for educational ideals their concern is not primarily with biological, psychological, historical, and social features of human behavior. For since these terms designate specific processes of interaction between an organism and its environment, it would be risky to choose any set of traits as fixing forever *the* nature of human nature, and therefore *the* nature of education. But the neo-Thomists are concerned precisely with a conception of human nature which will permit the deduction that, in the words of Robert Hutchins, "education should everywhere be the same." Everywhere and at any time? Everywhere and at every time. In a weakened form, Mortimer Adler repeats this: "If man is a rational animal, constant in nature through history then there must be certain constant features in every sound educational program regardless of culture and epoch." And Mark Van Doren, who carries all of his teacher's ideas to recognizable absurdity, adds that because education and democracy have the same end—the making of men—they are one and the same. "So education is democracy and democracy is education." From man's nature we can apparently deduce not only that education should everywhere be the same, but the social system, too.

If education is determined by human nature, may not human nature change, and with it the nature of education? "We must insist," writes Hutchins, "that no matter how environments differ human nature is, always has been, and always will be the same everywhere."

This is truly a remarkable assertion. Before we ask Mr. Hutchins on what evidence he knows this to be true, let us see what it implies. For one thing it implies that human nature is completely independent of changes in the world of physical nature with which the human organism is in constant interaction. Now, certainly Mr. Hutchins cannot know that the world of nature "is, always has been, and always will be the same everywhere." He therefore must believe that no transformation of the physical basis of human life can possibly affect human nature. His assertion further implies that man's nature is completely independent of changes in the human body, particularly the brain and nervous system. This calls into question the whole evolutionary approach to the origin and development of the human species. It implies finally that the habitation of man's nature in a human body is unaffected by changes in society and social nurture.

There is only one entity that satisfies all of these conditions. It is the supernatural soul as conceived by theologians of the Christian tradition. It is not the Aristotelian concept of the soul because, for Aristotle, the soul was the form of the body, all forms were incarnate in matter, and the nature of man was construed from his behavior. The constancy of human nature in Aristotle was predicated on the notion of the constancy of the natural order as well. Were he, in the light of modern science, to abandon the latter notion, he would have surrendered the belief in the constancy of human nature, since it was integrally related to the behavior of the body in nature and society. But Mr. Hutchins admits all the facts of physical, biological, and social development in man's environment yet insists that man's nature cannot change. It is only when we realize that he is not talking about empirical, historical, suffering man that the peculiarities and ambiguities of his language are understandable.

This is the secret behind the talk of man's true and constant nature. M. Maritain and Monsignor Sheen are more frank with us than their epigoni at Chicago and St. John's. But all of them owe us a proof that the soul, as defined by them, exists. So far not a shred of valid evidence, experimental or rational, has been adduced to warrant belief in its existence. In fact, the achievements of genuine knowledge about human nature in medicine, biology, psychology, and history have been largely won by a bitter struggle against obstacles set in the path of scientific inquiry by believers in a supernatural soul.

136. Changing One's Values

The establishment of sound and lasting values, or the change from
trivial to serious values, necessarily involves the character of the person, those permanent traits and qualities which express what the person
is. The really serious question then is, can the modern university,
within the framework of its proper function and resources, actually
influence the student at that crucial point? May it not be the case
that the influence of the home, of the church and of the lower school
is much more powerful in this basic direction than the university, by
its very nature, could ever be? . . .

The university is both the preserver and transmitter of the intellectual
heritage of the culture in which it stands; its primary responsibility
is the informing of the mind and the orientation of the self in so far
as that can be achieved within the teaching and learning situation.
The university, above all, must not give the impression that it can accomplish more than is actually possible for an academic institution
and thus lead us to believe that it is training the self in ways that
transcend the academic situation. There are depths of personality
which the university cannot touch within the confines of regular
academic routine; if these depths are to be influenced at all within the
framework of higher education, it will be necessary for the university
not only to pay more attention to the total atmosphere within which
the student works but also to shift emphasis from the mass back to
the individual . . .

The interesting question is whether higher education by itself can reasonably be expected to bring about change at the core of the personality. In raising this question we are very close to the question posed
in other language by the ancient philosophers, can virtue be taught?
The answer must be the same one Plato gave, "no," if teaching means
what it means when the subject to be taught is physics, history or
mathematics . . .

*   *   *

Our Western religious and philosophical tradition has revealed in
the course of its development a certain basic difference of emphasis
within what we would call the value situation. And this contrast stands
behind the opposition between the Socratic and Kantian tradition on
one side and the teleological or utilitarian on the other. On the one

136. John E. Smith, *Value Convictions and Higher Education* (Edward W.
Hazen Foundation, New Haven, 1958), pp. 22–29.

hand, the person, his action, his motive and intention, have been made the primary subject of evaluation and judgment; value or worth attaches to the person and it is dependent upon the extent to which the will of the person is actually in conformity with a standard of honesty and sincerity in the performance of particular actions. The good self is, for example, the self drawn to and determined by the intrinsic nature of such values as truth, courage, humility and justice; these values are acknowledged and adhered to for their own intrinsic worth and not for some further end or consequence to which they may lead . . .

      ❂   ❂   ❂

The other side of the basic contrast previously mentioned is represented by the teleological or, more recently, the utilitarian tradition. Here the stress is laid not upon the person or self in its willing or its motive, but rather upon the public act and its consequences. Value on this view attaches almost exclusively to ends or goals and to the means whereby they can be realized. . . .

137. Need for an Unchanging Yardstick of Value

If man does not possess free will, then all his actions are determined; he has no more choice in the matter of good conduct than the circus horse, and it is nonsense to talk of character education at all. If there be no norm to determine what actions are good and what are bad, then indeed man is a weather-cock, carried now in this direction now in another, according as whim or the influence of his fellows or his environment is most prevalent. Even though he desire to be moral, unless he has a yardstick with which to measure the good and the bad, morality will be beyond his reach.

Scholastic philosophy teaches that there is such a yardstick, such a norm of morality, one eminently usable; namely, man's rational nature taken in its entirety. Consequently, the scholastic would hold that those actions are good that are in conformity with man's rational nature, those bad that are not in comformity with man's rational nature. What does reason teach us about man's nature? . . .

Difficult as it may be to indicate all the duties of man to God, his neighbor, and himself, this is nevertheless simplicity itself compared to the attempts made by some of the character educators who put before us a changing norm of morality. In the scholastic system there

137. William J. McGucken, *The Catholic Way in Education* (Milwaukee: The Bruce Publishing Company, 1937), pp. 142–143.

is a yardstick, fixed and unchanging, suitable for all ages and all countries. Granted that it may be hard in certain circumstances to determine what is lying, what is dishonesty, the fact remains that in the scholastic system lying and dishonesty are evil things. Further, there is a hierarchy of values. If there be a conflict between man's duties to God and to his neighbor, the inferior right must cede to the superior. First things come first . . .

7

Educational Aims

Problems in the Philosophy of Education Discussed in this Section

1. In practice, what gives rise to the need for educational aims? Are aims really means for solving problems? Can educational aims be considered independently from the available means for their achievement?
2. If an educational aim is not achieved, does the fault always lie with the means? Might failure ever indicate the necessity for reconstructing the aim itself?
3. Should educational aims arise out of an ongoing experience, or should they have a fixed character independent of experience?
4. Is the source of educational aims to be found in pupil impulses? In social demands? Can educational aims be determined scientifically?
5. Do present educational ends ever become future means to the achievement of later educational ends? Are there any educational aims which never become future means, but which are rather ends in and of themselves? What is the *ultimate* end of education?
6. What are the *proximate* aims of education? Should they emphasize the present life of the child, or his later adult life, or the life after death? How far in advance of the present can aims safely be projected? How long is the present?
7. If we evaluate educational practice in the light of its aims, how shall we evaluate the aims themselves?
8. Who should determine educational aims? Should education be autonomous in setting up its aims?
9. Does it matter which term is used: educational aims, ends, goals, objectives, purposes, results, or outcomes?

I. FUNCTION AND DETERMINATION OF AIMS

138. Education as Such Has No Aims

. . . Education as such has no aims. Only persons, parents and teachers, etc., have aims, not an abstract idea like education. And conse-

138. John Dewey, *Democracy and Education* (New York: The Macmillan Company, 1916), p. 125.

quently their purposes are indefinitely varied, differing with different children, changing as children grow and with the growth of experience on the part of the one who teaches. Even the most valid aims which can be put in words will, as words, do more harm than good unless one recognizes that they are not aims but rather suggestions to educators as to how to observe, how to look ahead, and how to choose in liberating and directing the energies of the concrete situations in which they find themselves . . .

139. Aim as Intelligent Foresight of Ends

To talk about an educational aim when approximately each act of a pupil is dictated by the teacher, when the only order in the sequence of his acts is that which comes from the assignment of lessons and the giving of directions by another, is to talk nonsense. It is equally fatal to an aim to permit capricious or discontinuous action in the name of spontaneous self-expression. An aim implies an orderly and ordered activity, one in which the order consists in the progressive completing of a process. Given an activity having a time span and cumulative growth within the time succession, an aim means foresight in advance of the end or possible termination. If bees anticipated the consequences of their activity, if they perceived their end in imaginative foresight, they would have the primary element in an aim. Hence it is nonsense to talk about the aim of education—or any other undertaking—where conditions do not permit of foresight of results, and do not stimulate a person to look ahead to see what the outcome of a given activity is to be.

In the next place the aim as a foreseen end gives direction to the activity; it is not an idle view of a mere spectator, but influences the steps taken to reach the end. The foresight functions in three ways. In the first place, it involves careful observation of the given conditions to see what are the means available for reaching the end, and to discover the hindrances in the way. In the second place, it suggests the proper order or sequence in the use of means. It facilitates an economical selection and arrangement. In the third place, it makes choice of alternatives possible . . .

*   *   *

The net conclusion is that acting with an aim is all one with acting intelligently . . .

139. John Dewey, *Democracy and Education* (New York: The Macmillan Company, 1916), pp. 118–120.

140. Perfect Ideals as Aims

An outline of a *Theory of Education* is a noble ideal, and does no harm even if we are not in a position to realize it immediately. But one should not consider the idea chimerical, and cry it down as a beautiful dream, simply because its execution meets with hindrances. An idea is nothing else than the concept of a perfection which has not yet been met with in experience; as, for example, the idea of a perfect republic governed according to the laws of righteousness. Is it for that reason impossible? Our idea must first be right, and then it is not at all impossible, even with all the hindrances which now stand in the way of its realization. If, for instance, every one should lie, would, merely for that reason, truthfulness be only a vagary? And the idea of an education which is to develop all the natural qualities in man is certainly truthful.

141. The Relation of Aims to Social Facts

Three problems are involved in a discussion of the aims and ideals of education.

I. The first concerns the nature of aims and ideals generally speaking. What is their nature in relation to actual conditions, to positive fact, to customary experience? It is quite clear that an aim, and still more, an ideal, involves dissatisfaction with existing conditions, and an effort to depart from them. But out of what material shall the aim and ideal be then constituted? Whence shall it be derived? What shall guarantee ideals against being mere products of fancy? An aim, in short, while it contrasts with the existing state of affairs must have sufficient contact with it to be practicable, to be capable of application to re-direction of existing conditions. An ideal, unless its value is to be purely emotional and inspirational, can differ from an aim only in possessing greater generality, greater scope and depth.

The problem has a definite bearing upon the discussion of educational aims. In general, they are divided into two classes: Those which find the ground of dissatisfaction simply in the ignorance, immaturity,

140. Immanuel Kant, in Edward F. Buchner, *The Educational Theory of Immanuel Kant* (Philadelphia: J. B. Lippincott Company, 1904), pp. 109–110.
141. John Dewey, in New Educator's Library, *Ideals, Aims and Methods in Education* (London: Sir Isaac Pitman & Sons, Ltd.), 1922, pp. 1–7.

lack of skill and control of the young; and those which draw the material of their ideals from dissatisfaction with existing social conditions. The first has the easier task. It derives its aims from the best achievements of existing adult life. Its essential aims are to reproduce these standards in the young; to bring the latter up to the level of what is best in the traditions and customs of the people to which those undergoing education belong. Education is conceived of as essentially a process of transmission and indoctrination.

The other school derives its aims and ideals from a consideration of the defects of existing society. Its dominating ideal is social reform, re-organization even on a large scale. It regards the period of immaturity not as something to be passed through on the way to reaching the adult level, but as an opportunity of progress to be taken advantage of in the process of creating a new and better society.

✻   ✻   ✻

If educationists are confined to a bare choice between the ideal of social transmission on one hand, and complete social transformation on the other, they are in a sad plight, and their choice will have to be made arbitrarily—not on educational grounds, but on grounds of general social and political preference. But the value of the opposition as it is presented by extreme thinkers is that it puts before us *factors* that must be reckoned with in forming all educational aims and ideals. The forces making in practice for the more conventional and conservative ideal are strong. They almost enforce themselves without any assistance from the side of philosophic principles. The most vehement educational reformer, if he attempts the definite work of concrete instruction and discipline, finds himself thrown back upon existing materials and habits. It is not possible to escape from them. He must employ transmitted material as the *means* of education. But that does not signify that the *ideal* shall be found in the means. The problem is to use existing knowledge, habits, institutions, as means of producing characters that, in being sensitive to what is best in existing civilization, shall also be critical of its defects, and equipped for its improvement. The radical or revolutionary school that has found its ideal in contrast with existing conditions has made a valuable contribution which must be included in every sound philosophy of education. Childhood and youth are not merely periods of immaturity. They are not chiefly negative. The period of special need of education is not one of defect or gap, of absence of adult achievements and standards. Plasticity does not signify a mere passivity to be shaped from without. Childhood and youth present something positive and active, the power of *growth*. They present, therefore, the maximum *possibilities* of social improvement and rectification with the minimum waste and friction.

Social reform that deals with adults whose habits of thought and feeling are more or less definitely set, and whose environment is more or less rigid, is working at a disadvantage.

II. *The Relation of Aims and Ideals to Existent Facts.* We find here the solution of the problem of the relation of aims and ideals to existent facts. Growth is itself the primary *fact* with which education deals. To protect, sustain, and direct growth is the chief *ideal* of education. It remains to make this general statement more definite by applying it to consideration of some of the chief aims about which educational discussion turns. The purpose will be to show that growth as an aim includes what is valuable in all of them. Our second chief problem concerns, then, aims and ideals which have obtained a certain vogue, such as preparation for life, discipline, natural development, culture, social efficiency, etc. How are they related to promotion of growth as an aim?

The ideal of preparation becomes self-contradictory when it is not secondary to the maintenance of the process of development. This is true, whether we take the half-formulated aims of preparation for promotion, for passing examinations, for entrance into some higher school, or the generalized conception of Spencer that education is adequate preparation for life. The end, if conceived merely as something delayed and postponed, something affecting exclusively a future time, has no intrinsic connection with the student's present activity. It fails to supply adequate motive power. A vaguely-discerned future disconnected from the present has little impelling power. It is so adventitious, that external stimuli have to be resorted to, such as threats of immediate penalties, promises of immediate rewards. A merely remote end also encourages procrastination. The present offers many attractions. These tend to crowd out an aim which can be realized only in some indefinite future. Making preparation the chief end fails, in other words, to secure good preparation. Continuous growth, on the other hand, effects a continuous re-organization of powers. Although it has an application in the present (since the pupil is to be growing here and now), it also leads continuously into new fields. The process of realizing present possibilities means a constant advance. It results in preparation, although preparation is not made the mainspring of effort.

The so-called individualistic aim, self-realization, or the full development of all powers, can be made definite and effective only when translated into terms of growth. As has often been stated, the ideal of complete development is only a species of the preparation ideal. Development is conceived as a product—not as a process. It is thought of emotionally rather than intelligently. It stands for something noble and sublime, but something projected into the mists of the unknown.

Development, on the other hand, as an active process means developing —something taking place, if it takes place at all, in the present. Hence, it is capable of observation and record; it can be made definite. Whether a pupil is now growing and in what direction, are matters of fact and not of blind aspiration for something far-away. Moreover, a purely future and remote development of all powers fails at the precise point where it makes its chief claim. It is not truly individual, but is a general formula whose exact application to individual pupils remains uncertain. Since no two pupils are duplicates of one another, complete development cannot signify for one person what it means for another. The quality of growing, on the other hand, is an individualized affair. The question is whether the particular person is living up to his own possibilities. He is judged on the basis of his own powers and his own environment. The test is whether he is taking full advantage of them. Complete development does not mean something abstract and absolute, but something relative to individual capacities and opportunities.

If the principle is clear, it is not necessary to apply it in detail to conceptions of culture, training or discipline of faculties, etc. Culture must mean a present refining, broadening, and fostering of processes of growing, if it is to be an aim available for guidance, and not a vague aspiration which can be rendered definite only by arbitrary translation into personal taste and preference. The idea of discipline through repeated exercise of faculties upon definite tasks has been founded upon a conception of faculties which present psychology holds to be mythological. It has also been used as a defence for all measures which make learning so difficult as to be obnoxious, while all outworn traditionary topics have protected themselves from examination by a claim to be disciplinary. Discipline can be substantiated as an aim only in so far as we fix our attention not upon vague so-called faculties, but upon actual instincts, impulses, habits, desires, and ask how these are to be so employed as to lead to increase of present *power*—of power to do, to accomplish. Only the incorporation of the idea of growth will render the idea of discipline positive and rational.

142. Proper Relation of Ends and Means

In contrast wtih fulfilling some process in order that activity may go on, stands the static character of an end which is imposed from without the activity. It is always conceived of as fixed; it is *something*

142. John Dewey, *Democracy and Education* (New York: The Macmillan Company, 1916), pp. 123–124.

to be attained and possessed. When one has such a notion, activity is a mere unavoidable means to something else; it is not significant or important on its own account. As compared with the end it is but a necessary evil; something which must be gone through before one can reach the object which is alone worth while. In other words, the external idea of the aim leads to a separation of means from end, while an end which grows up within an activity as plan for its direction is always both ends and means, the distinction being only one of convenience. Every means is a temporary end until we have attained it. Every end becomes a means of carrying activity further as soon as it is achieved. We call it end when it marks off the future direction of the activity in which we are engaged; means when it marks off the present direction. Every divorce of end from means diminishes by that much the significance of the activity and tends to reduce it to a drudgery from which one would escape if he could . . .

143. Sociological Determination of Aims

Now, the construction of a social ideal which deserves to win general acceptance is properly the work, not of education, but of sociology. Sociology usually professes to be a scientific study of what society is and has been, of the manner in which it has become what it now is, and of what it will become under given conditions. It studies not only the origin and growth of society and social institutions, but also their tendencies. Sociology is therefore the science from which we should naturally expect some expression of opinion in regard to what society ought to be. Out of its knowledge of social facts and possibilities it should be able to construct a social ideal to serve as the best presently possible standard for comparing and judging existing institutions, as a test for all proposals regarding social reform and for individual conduct, and as the ultimate aim of the school. This is one of the points at which education is dependent upon sociology.

144. "What Knowledge Is Of Most Worth?"

Before there can be a rational *curriculum*, we must settle which things it most concerns us to know; or, to use a word of Bacon's, now unfor-

143. Ira W. Howerth, *The Theory of Education* (New York: The Century Company, 1962), p. 376.
144. Herbert Spencer, *Education: Intellectual, Moral, and Physical* (London: G. Manwaring, 1861), pp. 7–9.

tunately obsolete—we must determine the relative values of knowledges.

To this end, a measure of value is the first requisite. And happily, respecting the true measure of value, as expressed in general terms, there can be no dispute . . .

How to live?—that is the essential question for us. Not how to live in the mere material sense only, but in the widest sense. The general problem which comprehends every special problem is—the right ruling of conduct in all directions under all circumstances . . .

. . . It behoves us to set before ourselves, and ever to keep clearly in view, complete living as the end to be achieved; so that in bringing up our children we may choose subjects and methods of instruction, with deliberate reference to this end. Not only ought we to cease from the mere unthinking adoption of the current fashion in education, which has no better warrant than any other fashion; but we must also rise above that rude, empirical style of judging displayed by those more intelligent people who do bestow some care in overseeing the cultivation of their children's minds. It must not suffice simply to *think* that such or such information will be useful in after life, or that this kind of knowledge is of more practical value that that; but we must seek out some process of estimating their respective values, so that as far as possible we may positively *know* which are most deserving of attention.

Doubtless the task is difficult—perhaps never to be more than approximately achieved. But, considering the vastness of the interests at stake, its difficulty is no reason for pusillanimously passing it by; but rather for devoting every energy to its mastery. And if we only proceed systematically, we may very soon get at results of no small moment.

Our first step must obviously be to classify, in the order of their importance, the leading kinds of activity which constitute human life. They may be naturally arranged into:—1. those activities which directly minister to self-preservation; 2. those activities which, by securing the necessaries of life, indirectly minister to self-preservation; 3. those activities which have for their end the rearing and discipline of offspring; 4. those activities which are involved in the maintenance of proper social and political relations; 5. those miscellaneous activities which fill up the leisure part of life, devoted to the gratification of the tastes and feelings.

That these stand in something like their true order of subordination, it needs no long consideration to show.

145. Insufficiency of Goals Based on Social Life Alone

Although the basic goals of the school curriculum can only be discovered by a thorough study of social life, these goals are not automatically revealed by such a study. The number and variety of activities
in which both children and adults engage may be enumerated and
catalogued, and social life and institutions may be analyzed in great
detail. Objective investigation may reveal the great common interests
and problems which grip the minds and release the energies of men.
A sound program for the school cannot be formulated in the absence
of the knowledge which such a study should give, but there are two
fundamental reasons why it will not by itself either fix the outlines or
determine the details of that program.

In the first place, in the absence of criteria of value, an objective
study of human activities will not reveal which activities are good and
worthy of perpetuation or which are evil and merit elimination from
social life. A particular activity, though universally practiced, might
be either lacking in positive worth or even definitely harmful to both
the individual and society. The materials of instruction should be
selected with a view to giving the child insight into society, the ability
to use its institutions, an apprecation of the value of its possessions,
a watchful regard for its welfare, and a compelling desire for its
improvement. The limitations of a mere objective study of society are
therefore obvious. It would fail to provide certain basic criteria of
value necessary to a definition of social welfare. It might, to be sure,
give us a consensus of popular opinion and show what men generally
regard as valuable. But criteria determined in this manner would
merely reflect the ends for which the society under study might at the
time be striving. These ends might include the merciless annihilation
of another people, the enslavement of a less favored race, the exaltation
of the mortification of the flesh, or the perpetuation of some religious,
economic, or political dogma. Many activities which are now far from
common should be accorded a place in the school curriculum. That
curriculum should be determined in the light of social needs, but a
study of the social situation will disclose those needs only to an intelligent and evaluating mind.

In the second place, a study of social practice will not reveal the

145. George S. Counts, in National Society for the Study of Education, Twenty-
Sixth Yearbook, Part II, *Foundations of Curriculum Making* (Chicago: University
of Chicago Press, 1927), pp. 83–85.

special function of the school. As we have already observed, the school is but one among many social institutions which discharge educational obligations. Let us assume that all of the activities in which men do, or might, engage are ranked from the most valuable to the least valuable or the most harmful according to some acceptable set of criteria. Should the school begin at the top of this list and include as many of the activities as its limited resources permit? The answer is clearly in the negative. Its resources are restricted. Consequently, those activities which are provided for elsewhere should not be permitted to burden the program of the school. In determining what should go into this program the curriculum-maker should recognize one negative and two positive principles.

The negative or limiting principle is the principle of the maturity of the learner. No activity should find its way into the curriculum if it is not suited to the level of maturity of the learner . . .

The two positive principles are the principle of difficulty of learning and the principle of social foresight. According to the first of these principles, the school should assume rather generally responsibility for the more difficult learning tasks. Since the facilitation of the process of learning is its distinctive function, the natural expectation is that the more difficult tasks would be allotted to it. While in its simpler forms learning may be guided successfully by incidental and informal instruction, in its more complex manifestations it requires the careful guidance of direct tuition.

According to the second of the two positive principles, the program of the school should seek to guard and promote the more permanent and far-reaching social interests. Since its all-controlling purpose is educational and since it is relieved from those pressing demands of the moment which commonly dominate other institutions, it may become a peculiarly effective instrument for giving expression to social foresight and wisdom. In fact, the school is about the only instrument of this kind that society possesses. The mature generation is always the victim of its own past. At any moment society is so caught in the meshes of its folkways that its behavior lags behind its knowledge. It is for this reason that a study of the frequency with which men engage in various activities oftentimes throws but little light on the problem of curriculum-construction. Even if a particular activity is regarded as desirable, a high frequency may not mean that it should be included in the school program. In fact, a high frequency may even suggest that it would be learned outside the school. The school is an instrument for doing the difficult educational tasks, for anticipating the problems of the future, and for directing the course of social behavior.

146. Biology as Source of Aims

In order to ascertain the relationship between education and life we must determine what life is. And to find a workable answer to the question what is life? we must ask not ethics which deals with ideals to be attained, but biology which tells of possibilities within reach. Education must seek guidance in what is, in order to attain a vision of what can be, and not put its faith in what ought to be, and condemn what is. What, then, is the function and meaning of life?

Biology answers that the function of life is to live and its meaning is to continue living. For all practical purposes, life is what life does, and what life does is to live and to persist in living. Beyond this we can not go and need not go to find what we are looking for, namely, a firm basis upon which to erect the superstructure of how life best can be served, which must ever be the paramount concern of education.

147. The Effect of Uncertain Future on Aims

. . . I do not refer here to the waste of energy and vitality that accrues when children, who live so largely in the immediate present, are appealed to in the name of a dim and uncertain future which means little or nothing to them. I have in mind rather the habitual procrastination that develops when the motive for work is future, not present; and the false standards of judgment that are created when work is estimated, not on the basis of present need and present responsibility, but by reference to an external result, like passing an examination, getting promoted, entering high school, getting into college, etc. Who can reckon up the loss of moral power that arises from the constant impression that nothing is worth doing in itself, but only as a preparation for something else, which in turn is only a getting ready for some genuinely serious end beyond?

146. Max Shoen, "Education and Life," *Education*, 47:321–322, February 1927.
147. John Dewey, *Moral Principles in Education* (Boston: Houghton Mifflin Company, 1909), pp. 25–26. Used by permission of the publishers.

148. The Vice of Externally Imposed Aims

The vice of externally imposed ends has deep roots. Teachers receive them from superior authorities; these authorities accept them from what is current in the community. The teachers impose them upon children. As a first consequence, the intelligence of the teacher is not free; it is confined to receiving the aims laid down from above. Too rarely is the individual teacher so free from the dictation of authoritative supervisor, textbook on methods, prescribed course of study, etc., that he can let his mind come to close quarters with the pupil's mind and the subject matter. This distrust of the teacher's experience is then reflected in lack of confidence in the responses of pupils. The latter receive their aims through a double or treble external imposition, and are constantly confused by the conflict between the aims which are natural to their own experience at the time and those in which they are taught to acquiesce. Until the democratic criterion of the intrinsic significance of every growing experience is recognized, we shall be intellectually confused by the demand for adaptation to external aims.

149. Education is Free to Determine its Own Aims

This matter opens up the field of educational values and objectives. How are they to be determined? From what are they derived? The assumption that gives rise to the procedures just criticized is the belief that social conditions determine educational objectives. This is a fallacy. Education is autonomous and should be free to determine its own ends, its own objectives. To go outside the educational function and to borrow objectives from an external source is to surrender the educational cause. Until educators get the independence and courage to insist that educational aims are to be formed as well as executed within the educative process, they will not come to consciousness of their own function. Others will then have no great respect for educators because educators do not respect their own social place and work.

Such a statement will seem to many persons both absurd and pre-

148. John Dewey, *Democracy and Education* (New York: The Macmillan Company, 1916), p. 127.
149. John Dewey, *The Sources of a Science of Education* (New York: Liveright Publishing Corporation, 1931), pp. 73–75.

sumptuous. It would be presumptuous if it had been said that educators should determine objectives. But the statement was that the educative process in its integrity and continuity should determine them. Educators have a place in this process, but they are not it, far from it. The notion that it is absurd springs from failure to view the function in its entirety. For education is itself a process of discovering what values are worth while and are to be pursued as objectives. To see what is going on and to observe the results of what goes on so as to see their further consequences in the process of growth, and so on indefinitely, is the only way in which the value of what takes place can be judged. To look to some outside source to provide aims is to fail to know what education is as an ongoing process. What a society is, it is, by and large, as a product of education, as far as its animating spirit and purpose are concerned. Hence it does not furnish a standard to which education is to conform. It supplies material by which to judge more clearly what education as it has been carried on has done to those who have been subjected to it. Another conclusion follows. There is no such thing as a fixed and final set of objectives, even for the time being or temporarily. Each day of teaching ought to enable a teacher to revise and better in some respect the objectives aimed at in previous work.

II. LEADING VALUES AS AIMS

150. General, Abstract Aims Are Not True Aims

It is of course possible to classify in a general way the various valuable phases of life. In order to get a survey of aims sufficiently wide . . . to give breadth and flexibility to the enterprise of education, there is some advantage in such a classification. But it is a great mistake to regard these values as ultimate ends to which the concrete satisfactions of experience are subordinate. They are nothing but generalizations, more or less adequate, of concrete goods. Health, wealth, efficiency, sociability, utility, culture, happiness itself are only abstract terms which sum up a multitude of particulars. To regard such things as standards for the valuation of concrete topics and process of education is to subordinate to an abstraction the concrete facts from which the abstraction is derived. They are not in any true sense standards of valuation; these are found, as we have previously seen, in the *specific*

150. John Dewey, *Democracy and Education* (New York: The Macmillan Company, 1916), pp. 285–286.

realizations which form tastes and habits of preference. They are, however, of significance as points of view elevated above the details of life whence to survey the field and see how its constituent details are distributed, and whether they are well proportioned.

No classification can have other than a provisional validity. The following may prove of some help. We may say that the kind of experience to which the work of the schools should contribute is one marked by executive competency in the management of resources and obstacles encountered (efficiency); by sociability, or interest in the direct companionship of others; by aesthetic taste or capacity to appreciate artistic excellence in at least some of its classic forms; by trained intellectual method, or interest in some mode of scientific achievement; and by sensitiveness to the rights and claims of others—conscientiousness. And while these considerations are not standards of value, they are useful criteria for survey, criticism, and better organization of existing methods and subject matter of instruction.

151. Social and Individual Aims

The sum of the matter is that at the present time education has no great directive aim. It grows, but it grows from specific pressure exerted here and there, not because of any large and inspiring social policy. It expands by piecemeal additions, not by the movement of a vital force within. The schools, like the nation, are in need of a central purpose which will create a new enthusiasm and devotion, and which will unify and guide all intellectual plans.

In earlier days there was an aim which worked throughout the whole system. Education was the key to individual success, to making one's way in life, to getting on and getting ahead. The aim corresponded with the realities of social life, for the national need was the material subjugation of a continent, the conquest of a wilderness. There was always a frontier just beyond, the pioneer advanced to take possession of it. It was enough for the school to equip the individual with the tools of learning and to fire him with ambition and zeal to get on. This real education came in contact with others and in struggles with the forces of nature. The aim was individualistic, but it was also in harmony with the needs of the nation.

This earlier purpose has lost its vitality and its meaning. It survives, but operates as an oppressive handicap. As President Hoover

151. John Dewey, "Some Aspects of Modern Education," *School and Society*, 34:583–584, October 1931.

said some time ago: "We are passing from a period of extremely individualistic action to one of associational activity." Except for a favored few, there is no longer any unbounded opportunity for advancement open to individuals. We live in an epoch of combination, consolidation, concentration. Unless these combinations are used democratically for the common good, the result will be an increasing insecurity and oppression for the mass of men and women. Education must cultivate the social spirit and the power to act socially even more assiduously than it cultivated individual ambition for material success in the past. Competitive motives and methods must be abandoned for cooperative. Desire to work, for mutual advantage, with others must be made the controlling force in school administration and instruction. Instead of imbuing individuals with the idea that the goal is to sharpen their powers so they can get on personally, they must be trained in capacity for intelligent organization so that they can unite with others in a common struggle against poverty, disease, ignorance, credulity, low standards of appreciation and enjoyment. There must be a purpose and methods which will carry over the earlier ideals of political democracy into industry and finance.

Only in respect to methods of thought and judgment should the earlier individualistic aim be retained; *there* it should be intensified. Democracy will be a farce unless individuals are trained to think for themselves, to judge independently, to be critical, to be able to detect subtle propaganda and the motives which inspire it. Mass production and uniform regimentation have been growing in the degree in which individual opportunity has waned. The current must be reversed. The motto must be: "Learn to *act* with and for others while you learn to *think* and to judge for yourself."

152. There is No Single Aim

Educational processes are many, and of varied type and content. The same is true of aims. There can be no *one* educational aim, however general and inclusive it may be. The variety of educational activities is productive of a multitude of aims, and one is justified in referring to *an* educational aim only to the extent that one views it as a general direction, or as a unifying outlook and a methodological basis of criticism. Educational aims may range from the most specific, such as the fostering of a certain habit or skill demanded by our society of

152. Hilda Taba, *The Dynamics of Education* (London: Kegan Paul, Trench, Trubner & Co., Ltd., 1932), p. 207.

today, to the most general, such as efficient citizenship, self realization of personality, effective sharing in life, depending on which particular process or particular body of processes of the total educational activity is singled out. The theoretical problem, in facing a multitude of aims, is not that of subordinating all specific aims to one single all unifying one, or of denying specific aims their right of functioning, but of weighing one aim against another, and of seeing every single one in the light of all the rest.

153. Satisfaction of Wants as Aim

Life is activity initiated and sustained to satisfy wants. Since this is the case, we may say provisionally that the ultimate aim of education for man is to secure the fullest satisfaction of human wants . . .

❋ ❋ ❋

In short, by attempting solely to fulfill the needs of a particular individual, family, community, nation, or even a league of nations, we shall not achieve the fullest satisfaction of the wants of individuals on the whole. On the contrary, by attempting to satisfy the wants of all human beings, the desires of each of us will be most fully satisfied.

154. A Buddhist View of Education

In the cycle of "becoming" . . . the instability and finiteness of whatever has had a beginning is inevitable. Life or "becoming" is a function of sensibility, of desire and ignorance . . . Every thing becomes, everything flows like a river . . . All that becomes is mortal; therefore to be immortal, it is necessary to put a stop to "becoming." This intimately concerns ourselves; the most dangerous aspect of ignorance—the original sin—is that which leads us to pin our faith that we, you and I, are this or that and that we can survive from moment to moment, day to day, life to life, as an identity.

❋ ❋ ❋

This "making become" of the self is an indispensable part of the Buddhist Pilgrim's Progress and equally important is the opposite task of putting a stop to all "becoming" and so build up the being that we

153. Edward L. Thorndike and Arthur I. Gates, *Elementary Principles of Education* (New York: The Macmillan Company, 1930), pp. 17–19.
154. Ratna Navaratnam, *New Frontiers in East-West Philosophies of Education* (Bombay: Orient Longmans, 1958), pp. 37–40.

are. This factor of becoming is an important question for the philosopher of education. The "becoming" that is merely a haphazard process of mechanical growth is entirely different from the "making become" which implies careful guidance and directed activity.

Education according to the Buddhist way of life, therefore, should concern itself with selective cultivation. The man who is liberated is one who is no more "becoming."

155. Intellectual Excellence Is Its Own End

Surely it is very intelligible to say, and that is what I say here, that Liberal Education, viewed in itself, is simply the cultivation of the intellect, as such, and its object is nothing more or less than intellectual excellence. Every thing has its own perfection, be it higher or lower in the scale of things; and the perfection of one is not the perfection of another . . .

156. Knowledge Is Its Own End

Knowledge is capable of being its own end. Such is the constitution of the human mind, that any kind of knowledge, if it be really such, is its own reward. And if this is true of all knowledge, it is true also of that special Philosophy, which I have made to consist in a comprehensive view of truth in all its branches, of the relations of science to science, of their mutual bearings, and their respective values. What the worth of such an acquirement is, compared with other objects which we seek,—wealth or power or honour or the conveniences and comforts of life, I do not profess here to discuss; but I would maintain . . . that it is an object, in its own nature so really and undeniably good, as to be the compensation of a great deal of thought in the compassing, and a great deal of trouble in the attaining.

157. Esoteric *Versus* Active Learning

As Christians we are specially concerned to maintain . . . balance. On the one hand we welcome an insistence that thinking should be

155. John Cardinal Newman, *The Idea of a University*, sixth edition (London: Longmans, Green & Company, 1886), p. 121.
156. *Ibid.*, p. 103.
157. Walter Moberley, *The Crisis in the University* (London: Student Christian Movement Press, 1949), p. 122.

responsible and should lead to action and engage the whole man rather than reflect a detached and merely speculative curiosity. On the other hand, the supreme Christian experience is not in action but in worship (which includes contemplation, and even, in a sense, enjoyment as well as action). For the Christian, truth is one aspect of the being of God, and to treat with contumely the cult of truth for its own sake comes near to repudiating the cult of God for his own sake.

158. The Highest End of Man

. . . that which is most proper to each thing is by nature best and most pleasant for each thing; for man, therefore, the life according to reason is best and pleasantest, since reason more than any thing else *is* man. This life therefore is also the happiest.

          ✿   ✿   ✿

Therefore the activity of God, which surpasses all others in blessedness, must be contemplative; and of human activities, therefore, that which is most akin to this must be most of the nature of happiness . . . Happiness extends, then, just so far as contemplation does, and those to whom contemplation more fully belongs are more truly happy, not as a mere concomitant but in virtue of the contemplation; for this is in itself precious. Happiness, therefore, must be some form of contemplation.

159. The Ivory Tower Decried

. . . Interest in truth for its own sake—the pure and undistracted purpose to know—is not the characteristic final purpose of knowing. Knowledge for its own sake, and the contemplative life, represent an esthetic or near-esthetic ideal rather than one normally attributable to cognition. It is merely a professional fallacy of the scholar to impute his own peculiar interest in finding out the truth to human cognizing in general, as if that were the aim which rules or should rule it. He who is disinterestedly interested in finding out and knowing; who subordinates the desires and interests of action to discovery

158. Aristotle, *Nichomachean Ethics*, Bk. X, chaps. 7–8.
159. Clarence Irving Lewis, *An Analysis of Knowledge and Valuation* (LaSalle, Ill: Open Court Publishing Company, 1945), p. 442.

of the truth, and to contemplation of it; likewise divests knowledge of its natural and pragmatic significance. By the same token, the ideal of the contemplative life is mildly abnormal, however valid and indubitable the values to which it is addressed. The ivory tower is characteristically the refuge of the practically defeated and of those who become disillusioned of the utilities of action.

160. Self-Realization as an Aim

Self-realization is the aim in ethics and education. The end of life must be a development in character—perfection rather than happiness. The true self can be realized only by sacrificing the lower self. The final problem in ethics and the ultimate aim in education must be tested in terms of the realization of the rational self. The supreme law of every educational process is to make the best of self possible. The pupil is to develop his own personality to the fullest extent and in doing so he is to assist in the development of other personalities associated with him. The duty to self and duty to others are coordinated by the profound world principle that each individual pupil is a part of the eternal consciousness and that pupils are fellows by virtue of a common relation to the Infinite Mind.

161. Social Institutions as Objectives

The ultimate aim of education is, of course, the self-realization of all persons. But, as we have seen, self-realization is to be achieved through a balanced participation in all the institutions of society. The immediate aim of education is, therefore, to prepare young people for effective participation in those institutions. *The institutions of society are the objectives of education.* It follows as a corollary that the curriculum must be composed of the intellectual resources used in operating those institutions.

*   *   *

To be exact, therefore, the objectives of education are not merely the institutions as they are, but as they are becoming. And not merely,

160. Arthur C. Fleshman, *The Educational Process* (Philadelphia: J. B. Lippincott Company, 1908), pp 125–126.
161. Ross L. Finney, *A Sociological Philosophy of Education* (New York: The Macmillan Company, 1928), pp. 93–95.

either, as they are likely to be, but as they *ought* to be. It is not enough that the educational program anticipate the social order of the future; it must anticipate what ought to be; and thereby help create it.

162. Specialization *Versus* Perfection of All One's Powers In Education

A generation ago one of the most popular statements of the aim of education was "The Perfection of All One's Powers," or, in Herbert Spencer's words, "Complete Living." These statements always needed qualification. For it is not desirable that life should complete itself by having all possible varieties of envy, jealousy, and cruelty; and it is certain that some features of the life process are more desirable than others. Completeness had to be interpreted as the fulfillment of certain selected features which would work together *harmoniously*— that is, without sacrificing worthy wants. Obviously, no one would advocate perfecting the power to worry or despair. Since certain powers conflict with others, it was necessary to change the phrasing to "harmonious development" or the like.

Specialization Is Necessary.—But even if the misleading character of the term *complete* and the vagueness of *perfection* are corrected by qualifying statements, the doctrine itself—that education's business is to make the best possible specimen of humanity out of each man— is faulty. The aim of life is not to stock the world as a museum with perfected specimens for man or deity to contemplate. It is to make men vital parts of an organized force for the welfare of the group. Powers are not for possession and display, but for use. This requires specialization rather than general perfection. Men have to live together and depend one upon another, not each trying to be the best possible creature in all ways, but each being taught to perform, and take pleasure in, those services in which by excelling he can do the most for the common good. Nor is it desirable, even from the point of view of individuals taken singly, that education should develop equally in every respect. Each individual, by sex, race, hereditary equipment, and the circumstances of time and place in which he is born, is more likely to meet certain situations than others during life, and it is to be competent and happy in those situations that he particularly needs to be trained . . .

162. Edward L. Thorndike and Arthur I. Gates, *Elementary Principles of Education* (New York: The Macmillan Company, 1930), pp. 24–25.

163. Individual vs. Citizen as Educational Goal

. . . The question arises whether education should train good individuals or good citizens. It may be said, and it would be said by any person of Hegelian tendencies, that there can be no antithesis between the good citizen and the good individual. The good individual is he who ministers to the good of the whole, and the good of the whole is a pattern made up of the goods of individuals. As an ultimate metaphysical truth I am not prepared either to combat or to support this thesis, but in practical daily life the education which results from regarding a child as an individual is very different from that which results from regarding him as a future citizen. The cultivation of the individual mind is not, on the face of it, the same thing as the production of a useful citizen . . .

164. The Aim of Christian Education

The proper and immediate end of Christian education is to cooperate with Divine grace in forming the true and perfect Christian, that is, to form Christ Himself in those regenerated by Baptism . . . For the true Christian must live a supernatural life in Christ . . .

❋   ❋   ❋

Hence the true Christian product of Christian education is the supernatural man who thinks, judges and acts constantly and consistently in accordance with right reason illumined by the supernatural light of the example and teaching of Christ; in other words, to use the current term, the true and finished man of character. For it is not every kind of consistency and firmness of conduct based on subjective principles that makes true character, but only constancy in following the eternal principles of justice . . .

The scope and aim of Christian education as here described, appears to the worldly as an abstraction, or rather as something that cannot be attained without the suppression or dwarfing of the natural faculties,

163. Bertrand Russell, *Education and the Modern World* (New York: W. W. Norton & Company, Inc., 1932), pp. 9–10. Reprinted by permission of the publishers.
164. Pius XI, "The Christian Education of Youth," *Catholic Educational Review*, 28:160–162, March 1930.

and without a renunciation of the activities of the present life, and hence inimical to social life and temporal prosperity, and contrary to all progress in letters, arts and sciences, and all the other elements of civilization . . .

❋   ❋   ❋

The true Christian does not renounce the activities of this life, he does not stunt his natural faculties; but he develops and perfects them, by coordinating them with the supernatural. He thus ennobles what is merely natural in life and secures for it new strength in the material and temporal order, no less than in the spiritual and eternal.

165. Natural and Supernatural Goals

The educational goals of the Thomist are of two orders, the supernatural and the natural, and they are approximated through the exercise of faith and reason. The highest end of man is beatitude, which is the knowledge of God. By its very nature, man's will tends toward this goal, and the will is aided towards its end by the intellect, the faculty the soul has for knowing. Theology, which is based upon revealed truth, is the sphere of faith, and philosophy is the sphere of reason. The knowledge of God is not a fixed ultimate goal, for the simple reason that it is approximated throughout eternity, but never attained; we can never exhaust God in our knowledge of Him as He exhausts us in His knowledge of us, therefore this ultimate end does not limit our activity as the instrumentalist fears. Furthermore, since man is an imperfect creature, his seeking must be done in the natural world—he is never confronted with the supreme good, but with the limited goods of here and now. This means that he must use reason, the discursive method of proceeding from self-evident facts and principles he has learned from experience (such as that the whole is greater than the part) to higher truths, which he then checks with the first principles. In this manner philosophy finds goals of action such as the virtues, that it can be sure are valid. The intellectual and moral virtues are indubitably valuable; they are patterns of behavior achieved through experiences that leave their mark upon the individual in the form of good habits, and as good habits, the intellectual virtues of intelligence, knowledge, wisdom, and prudence, and the moral virtues of justice, temperance, and fortitude are general enough

165. William J. Sanders, "Thomism, Instrumentalism, and Education," *Harvard Educational Review*, 10:100–101, January 1940.

not to limit and stultify experience. On the contrary, since they specify desired patterns of behavior, they are much more effective in guiding and enhancing experience than such amorphous instrumentalist virtues as single-mindedness, open-mindedness, and responsibility. Furthemore, their value is instrumental in that they lead man not only towards his supernatural goal, but also towards achieving the values he may come to choose, through deliberation, in his life here and now. Man, by the way, never chooses his end through deliberation—his end is the good, toward which he tends by his nature. The so-called ends he chooses deliberatively (and these are the only ends with which the instrumentalist is concerned) are merely means to further means, never ends of the will in the sense that beatitude is an end; they are means of instruments to his progress in virtuous experience in the world. Except for the fact that there is a supreme good and virtues that are constant guides to education, the immediate goals of education may be determined by the Thomist in precisely the same way they are determined by the instrumentalist; they emerge from deliberation as the fruit of experience. The Thomist, however, has the advantage of knowing where he is going, while the instrumentalist invites frustration and anarchy through the rapidly multiplying number of varied and opposed goals or immediate goods to which he finds himself offering allegiance.

166. The Moral and Intellectual Virtues as Goals

The question as to whether the intellectual virtues should receive more stress than the moral virtues, or vice versa, is very ancient . . .

The intellectual virtues fall into two groups, the speculative and the practical. The speculative are known as: (1) understanding, (2) science or knowledge, and (3) wisdom. The practical virtues are: (1) prudence, and (2) art. The moral virtues, commonly referred to as the cardinal virtues, are: (1) prudence, (2) justice, (3) temperance, and (4) fortitude. Note that prudence is both an intellectual and a moral virtue.

Certain educators, among them some eminent Catholics, would have the school stress almost exclusively the intellectual virtues. They hold that the primary purpose of the school is to transmit intellectual content . . .

   ✽   ✽   ✽

166. John D. Redden, and Francis A. Ryan, *A Catholic Philosophy of Education* (Milwaukee: The Bruce Publishing Company, 1955), pp. 232–234.

If, then, as Pius XI declared, the subject of Christian education is "man whole and entire," "soul united to body in unity of nature, with all his faculties natural and supernatural, such as right reason and revelation show him to be," it is evident that, for the needs of life, the moral virtues exceed in importance the intellectual virtues, and hence that the former ought to be stressed as much as, if not more than, the latter in the work of the school.

✻   ✻   ✻

The reason why some thinkers talk of "the intellectual *versus* the moral virtues" is that modern times have stressed out of all proportion the second intellectual virtue, namely knowledge (science) and have excluded the other two. Now the three speculative intellectual virtues are not separate and independent; they are, on the contrary, steps or gradations in perfection. Knowledge, for example, demands understanding; and wisdom presupposes and embraces both understanding and knowledge. The virtue of knowledge, like the other two speculative intellectual virtues, is concerned with truth; that is, it concerns itself with truth that can be known through demonstration. The truth spoken of here is that truth which is deduced from principles or facts (data).

The virtue of wisdom is concerned with *order*. It seeks beyond facts, beyond data, into *meanings*. It seeks relationship and meanings among facts. It demands ultimate explanations, and hence seeks the final truth, the ultimate goal . . .

The practical virtue that is directive of human action is prudence; the other is art. All the intellectual virtues are incomplete except prudence. Prudence is a complete or perfect virtue because, as Father Farrell points out, "it makes the whole man good." It is concerned with both the intellectual and the moral. "The interdependence of prudence and the moral virtues is complete: there is no moral virtue without prudence, and no prudence without moral virtues. Understanding, science, art, even wisdom can be had by a man who is thoroughly bad; but not prudence."

Prudence is vitally concerned with the specific acts of human life, with the elements which here and now affect a particular act. It is located in the intellect, but it deals specifically with human acts. Father Farrell designates it, "the chauffeur of human life that steers actions to right ends." Prudence is concerned not only with what is done, but also for what end a thing is done and especially by what means.

The intellectual virtues are insufficient in themselves for complete human living. They postulate reason as the supreme arbiter of human action. But reason, while supreme over the spiritual, is often disputed by the animal and vegetative aspects of man's nature.

The whole question of the intellectual and the moral virtues may be reduced to the following: is intellectual training or character formation the major purpose of the school?

It should be recognized that systematic intellectual training must be provided and adapted to the abilities of pupils; otherwise the school yields the right to be called a school. Mere training of the intellect, however, is not enough, especially from the viewpoint of Catholic philosophy. Since "man whole and entire" is the subject of Christian education, it is evident that moral training or character formation is also a vital concern of the school . . .

167. Ultimate Aims the Same Everywhere and Always

The *ultimate* ends of education are the same for all men at all times and everywhere. They are absolute and universal principles. This can be proved. If it could not be proved, there would be no philosophy of education at all, for philosophy does not exist unless it is absolute and universal knowledge—*absolute* in the sense that it is not relative to the contingent circumstances of time and place; *universal* in the sense that it is concerned with essentials and abstracts from every sort of merely accidental variation. Similarly, it must be said that educational means *in general* are the same for all men at all times and everywhere. If the *ultimate* ends of education are its first principles, the means *in general* are its secondary principles, and the scope of the philosophy of education goes no further than this—*to know these first and secondary principles in an absolute and universal manner.* To aim at knowing less than this, or to regard this as unknowable, is to deny that there is any philosophy of education; to aim at knowing more than this, without realizing that one ceases to function as a philosopher in so doing, is to confuse the philosophy of education with other subject matters and methods, or to confuse one's self by trying to solve, philosophically, problems which cannot be philosophically solved.

167. Mortimer J. Adler, "In Defense of the Philosophy of Education," National Society for the Study of Education, Forty-First Yearbook, Part I, *Philosophies of Education* (Chicago: University of Chicago Press, 1942), pp. 221–222.

168. Education for the Future, Not the Present

One *principle in the art of education,* which those men who devise educational plans should especially have in mind, is this: children should be educated, *not* with reference to their present condition, but rather with regard to a possibly improved future state of the human race,—that is, according to *the idea of humanity* and its entire destiny. This principle is of great moment. Parents usually educate their children for the present world, corrupt though it be. They should, however, educate them *better,* that an improved future condition be thereby realized.

But here we come upon two hindrances to this end: (a) Parents are usually anxious only that their children should prosper in the world, and (b) Princes regard their subjects as mere instruments for the accomplishment of their own purposes.

Parents exercise forethought for the home, princes for the state. Neither have for their ultimate aim the good of the world and the perfection for which man is intended, and for which he also has the capacity. But the plan of an educational scheme should be made cosmopolitan . . .

169. Education is Its Own Aim

According to general German opinion, education has in itself independent, ultimate values; our theory of education justifies this belief from the scientific point of view, and systematizes it; educational practice is based on it. Education is not linked with external purposes, nor is it a means to achieve these, which would, were this the case, become the final purposes. It is not the means of insuring the continuance of the German state or of its present form of government, nor of insuring Germany's power and position in the world; likewise, as in the past, it does not serve the state, nor aim to develop citizens, nor serve German imperialism and expansion. Its purpose is not the development of the social structure, not being a socializing influence, and it does not help in the selection of individuals, even during their

168. Immanuel Kant, in Edward F. Buchner, *The Educational Theory of Immanuel Kant* (Philadelphia: J. B. Lippincott Company, 1909), pp. 116–117.
169. Aloys Fischer, "Germany," *Educational Yearbook* (New York: Bureau of Publications, Teachers College, Columbia University, 1929), pp. 274–277.

childhood and youth, for places on the various rungs of the social ladder, and for a variety of dissimilar vocations, positions, and tasks. It is not its purpose to promote economic prosperity and the material welfare of the individual, nor to further general economic progress or even scientific progress, nor to advance artistic and mental production, that is, objective culture . . . To speak paradoxically, it is itself its sole aim. Education alone, and man's state of being educated, is its purpose apart from every application of education. Its end is the education of every human being regardless of his social or vocational status. "Development of all inner powers with which man has been blessed, into pure human wisdom, is the most general purpose of all education, even if only the humblest of human beings are concerned." The German believes that the mental state which follows the transformation of man in his natural condition into a worthy being, or more humbly put, a being whose life is determined by the desire for values, is the real aim, the meaning and purpose of education. Education is misinterpreted, if it is made a means to an end, a mere weapon, and it does not matter whether or not this weapon is used in the competitive struggle of individuals, or of social classes, or of nations . . . In this connection I need merely refer to the long prevalence of the ideal of "general education" . . . Of course, we are glad if a good, extended, and well organized education also enables the human being to become a good citizen and an able worker in his vocation, or prepares him for social responsibility. But education does not aim to develop a human being who is useful to the state, useful in his occupation and work, and useful to society and science. It does not aim to develop a human being whose usefulness is his only and his greatest asset; it aims to develop a person complete in himself and worth while, a person whose usefulness in different fields is a consequence of his inner worth. We are respecters of persons, and it is, therefore, impossible for our educational philosophy to conceive of education as a means of disposing of the individual, as a means of selecting and drilling, which is, in the end, always arbitrarily employed. We are inclined to leave ultimate decisions to the self-determination of those who are being educated, but, at the same time, try to see to it that they are excellently educated, and thus make use of their ability to determine their place by demanding of themselves all that they can give according to their individual situations, instead of accepting thoughtlessly what comes to them, or adapting themselves in the most comfortable manner, or devoting themselves to utilitarian speculations. To us, an educated person is one who is valuable in himself, and whose education is founded on his natural, personal assets, which may be presented without education and without being developed, and may manifest themselves in a rank growth. The state of being educated means to us that quality which enables one to turn to account the always accidental combination of natural gifts and natural weaknesses in creating a masterpiece of personality, a personality maintained in continuous self-development. Education is a prerequisite for the free manifestation of natural gitfs, and the force which determines the employment of those gifts for higher causes. It may be likened to the cut and setting of a precious stone whose natural brilliancy has been brought out to perfection by the cut and setting, while its imperfections have been removed.

170. Growth is Its Own End

Three ideas which have been criticized, namely, the merely privative nature of immaturity, static adjustment to a fixed environment, and rigidity of habit, are all connected with a false idea of growth or development,—that it is a movement toward a fixed goal. Growth is regarded as *having* an end, instead of *being* an end.

❋   ❋   ❋

Since in reality there is nothing to which growth is relative save more growth, there is nothing to which education is subordinate save more education. It is a commonplace to say that education should not cease when one leaves school. The point of this commonplace is that the purpose of school education is to insure the continuance of education by organizing the powers that insure growth. The inclination to learn from life itself and to make the conditions of life such that all will learn in the process of living is the finest product of schooling.

171. Critique of Growth as Its Own End

But the difficulty lies deeper. Growth aims at more growth, and education is subordinate only to education. This is the theory. Its weakness is, growth needs a goal. There is no need to mince words at all. Children must be directed in their growth toward something

170. John Dewey, *Democracy and Education* (New York: The Macmillan Company, 1916), pp. 60–61.
171. Herman H. Horne, *The Democratic Philosophy of Education* (New York: The Macmillan Company, 1935), p. 53.

worthwhile in personal and social relations. They must grow up to be something admirable by constantly having admirable models and patterns and associations. Growth must be toward an ideal of human character. This ideal is not the objectionable "idealizing of childhood," it is the unobjectionable idealizing of life itself as the embodiment of worthwhile purposes and patterns. We do not have to be afraid of the word goal. We need a goal to work toward. If it is really valuable, we rarely fully attain it. If we should attain it, another and higher goal should and would straightway take its place. There is no danger of the pursuit of a goal leading to a static life.

172. Growth is Not Toward a Fixed End

Growth as an Aim and Ideal. Does not, however, the conception of growth imply something final and remote toward which growth is directed? Must we not conceive of growth as approximation to a faraway goal? If so, growth cannot be an aim and ideal except in a secondary sense. This question raises some of the deepest issues of philosophy. Is the universe static or dynamic? Is rest superior to movement as a sign of true reality? Is change merely a falling away from or an approach to something fixed, changeless? Is evolution a positive thing, a reflex of power; or is it negative, due to defect and the effort to pass beyond it? An adequate discussion of such questions would take us far beyond the limits of this article. In addition to noting that the philosophy of education—here as elsewhere—finally leads into general philosophy, we must content ourselves with two remarks.

In the first place, the conception of growth as merely a means of reaching something which is superior to growth and beyond it, is a survival of theories of the universe as being essentially static. These theories have been expelled by the progress of science from our notions of Nature. Motion, change, process, are fundamental. In the last half century these same ideas have been successfully applied to the life and structure of living things, plants and animals. The moral sciences, to which education belongs, have become the last refuge of ideas which have lost their intellectual repute elsewhere. The scientific presumption is working against them everywhere.

In the second place, even if our ultimate philosophy accepts a static conception of reality to which growth is relative, yet the educator, if

172. John Dewey, in New Educator's Library, *Ideals, Aims, and Methods in Education* (London: Sir Isaac Pitman and Sons, Ltd., 1922), pp. 7–9.

his aims are to be at once definite and capable of support upon the basis of ascertained fact, must start from the process of growth. He must obtain from it clues and hints as to the nature of the final end, instead of trying to decide what is and what is not growth on the basis of a conception of an ultimate end. Opinions as to the latter differ widely. To start from that end is to involve education in disputes that cannot be decided except by personal taste or the acceptance of external authority. The physical growth of a child can, however, be decided by tests applied to present conditions—observable and recorded changes in height, weight, and other phenomena. These things, and not an ideal of an ultimate physical perfection, guide the wise physician and parent in estimating whether a child is growing, standing still, or retrograding. The problem of the educator is, likewise, to devise means of studying and discovering changes actually going on in the mental and moral disposition of pupils, and to construct criteria for determining what these changes signify with respect to growth. Only as the philosophy of education recognizes that for *its* purposes, at all events, growth is the chief aim and ideal, can philosophy be applied intelligently to the specific facts of education, instead of remaining a body of remote and inapplicable—even though lofty—conceptions.

8

Ethical Principles of Education

Problems in the Philosophy of Education Discussed in this Section

1. What is the motivation for socialized conduct? In rearing children do parents expect a *quid pro quo?* Does a teacher expect it for giving instruction? Does a student for paying university tuition? A citizen paying taxes? A purchasing agent buying textbooks?
2. What ethical criterion shall be set up to guide the teacher in his conduct toward pupils, supervisors, boards of education, parents, and colleagues? Can a decision be reached apart from some particular society?
3. What is the warrant for respecting the dignity of pupil personality?
4. Is it democratic for the present generation to fix the educational policies of future generations?
5. What is a profession? How is it distinguished from a vocation? Which of the two is education? Would an amateur status be preferable for teachers?
6. Should a higher type of ethical conduct be expected from a teacher toward a layman than would customarily be anticipated between laymen? Why?
7. Should a code of ethics cover the detail of daily teaching routine? If there were such a code, how would it differ from a statement of educational philosophy?
8. Do ethics require that an author of a work of educational research give public credit for any part of it that he has received from anyone, as a friend or relative or a paid employee, or as a student, or in the course of his own teaching, whether he received the information incidentally or on request?
9. Are social regulations, such as rules of a board of education, professional codes of ethics, and statutes on education, intended to repress individuals?
10. Is it ethical to enforce a code of ethics? If so, how should it be done?

173. Self-hood as an Ethical Concept

While, then, self-hood has a natural psychological basis, it is, in its realization, a social and a moral fact. This social and moral quality

173. John Dewey, in Paul Monroe, editor, *Cyclopedia of Education* (New York: The Macmillan Company, 1911), Vol. 5., pp. 318–319.

constitutes its importance from the educational point of view. In tribal societies, the well-being that constitutes the central point of reference in determining and judging conduct is to a large extent that of the group *en masse,* as over against other groups. Self-hood seems to belong to the tribe or clan, rather than to its members. There is correspondingly little sense of distinctive personality or subjectivity. The individual belongs, quite literally, to his group. With the rise of distinctions of superior and inferior, of chieftainship and kingship, a few, the rulers, think of themselves as having a special position, special ends, and a welfare which is to be specially, even uniquely, consulted. They achieve, in brief, a sense of self-hood. In the Greek city-state, each free citizen was treated, in his capacity of free citizen, as an individual, but self-hood was denied to slaves, serfs, and women, and, except in a latent sense, to children. Even with reference to free individuals, self-hood was not emphasized to much as the duty of subordination to the community interest. Early and medieval Christianity gave a powerful impetus to the sense of individuality, through the introduction of the notion of an eternal well-being or misery, depending upon the relation taken to God through the Church. The social organization remained such a fundamental factor in determining this relationship, however, that the conception of subjectivity still remained undeveloped. Instead of the idea of the self there appeared that of a "soul" which was possessed by all as an individual entity. In Protestantism, the individual became overt; the Church consisted of individuals who had, through direct relationship to God, found salvation, instead of its being the instrumentality by means of which the individual attained salvation. The growth of the principle of subjectivity was also emphasized by political conditions. The conception of the State underwent a change analogous to that of the Church. Instead of being, as in classic thought, prior to the individual, it was made by the free choice and voluntary compact of individuals. The formula of Kant, that every individual is to be treated morally as an end in himself, never as a means to others, is perhaps the first explicit and sweeping statement of the modern principle of the universality of self-hood.

This growth of the democratic spirit has modified the conception of childhood. The tendency is to conceive of children as already members of a social whole, in virtue of which they possess rights, instead of having rights merely potentially, in virtue of a future social membership. This conception corresponds to the extraordinarily rapid growth of interest in the education of the young characteristic of the last century. Education is conceived as a public duty which is owed to the young. The conception has also modified, almost transformed, in fact, the discipline of the young, and has affected, though less completely, the methods of teaching. The growing displacement of harsh and punitive discipline by milder methods and by greater regard for personal intelligence, and the disposition to use methods that throw more intellectual responsibility upon the pupil and less, comparatively, upon teacher and text, are practical expressions of the extension of the principle of self-hood or children. It is obvious that the revolution— for it is hardly less than that—brings new dangers and difficulties with its gains. When children are treated in external ways as full-fledged selves, while their power of reflection and the habit of judging from a social point of view are not cultivated, the result is a mere relaxation of external control, without the development of control from within through the formation of a genuine self-hood.

A marked characteristic of the modern conception of the self, as developed by psychologists, is the latitude given to diversity, in contrast with the rigid unity of the older notion. This extends not merely to recognition of specific and ineradicable differences of structure and function in different selves, but also to the coexistence of different and ununified tendencies, almost minor selves, in the same person. Because of the dependence of the self upon modes of social treatment, a person who enters into different sets of associations tends to develop selves that are only loosely connected with one another. A child is one person in family life, and another with his fellows upon the street, just as an adult may have one self in business and another at home or in the church. Unity of self is not an original datum, but an achievement. The responsibility of the school in coordinating into an orderly whole the diversity of social tendencies which, in the complexity of contemporary life, tend to dissipate and distract self-hood, is constantly increasing . . .

174. Uninhibited Self-Expression Unwarranted

The doctrine that the self is so sacred or complete or unique as to require absolute self-expression seems to rest on a false assumption as to the nature of the self, namely that the self is originally given complete and unique (though possibly at birth only potentially so in the germ). Such a theory does not accord with the facts. At birth so far as we can tell the self is practically non-existent. What there is would of itself fit with and allow an infinite number of infinitely different

174. William H. Kilpatrick, "Behavior Problems," *Childhood Education*, 5:122–123, November 1928.

possible selves. The self that actually comes into being is constructed under social direction and largely of socially supplied content. If the process be guided in one way one self results, guided another way another quite different self results.

The sacredness of the self may well be admitted as a postulate of ethics, but this sacredness is not of the kind to hold the educator away from the child, rather the contrary. The wise educator must continually guide in order that the child may increasingly achieve the kind of self that properly demands non-interference, namely the kind that does increasingly think adequately in terms of the pertinent facts and independently of interfering prejudices whether his own or of others. The child's self is at all times too sacred to allow anything to interfere with growth toward this consummation; but this very sacredness would demand that he be not the sole judge as to what shall happen.

The problem then in the end is practical, not theoretical. Granted the kind of self demanded by ethics, how shall we so act as best to help in growth toward this ideal? Since growing is learning and learning is strictly personal, the child must himself practice all the directions in which he should grow including exercise in judging and choosing. Our part then is to help this kind of learning creature to grow toward the ideal as set out. Increasing self-direction, decreasing control by us, but all during childhood our part is positive to help forward the process.

175. Sanction for Ethical Conduct in Experience

. . . The view of the good as that which corresponds to the fixed moral structure of "reality" is replaced by a conception of the good as that which satisfies the needs of flesh and blood human beings in their concrete relations with one another and with their natural environment. That is considered good which sustains and expands human activity. Activity, as stated above, is always *in* and *of* the environment, and is relative to that environment. Success and failure—satisfaction and dissatisfaction—in these ordinary interactions, which in their myriad forms constitute human experience, contribute the final criteria by which the good is measured.

Ethical behavior does not signify habitual obedience to fixed moral codes: it signifies the capacity to respond intelligently in actual life situations. In harmony with the conception of social democracy, that

175. John L. Childs, "Whither Progressive Education?" *Progressive Education,* 13:584, December 1936.

behavior is judged most ethical which, in terms of actual resources and limitations found within the situation, best promotes the greatest good of the greatest number. Ethical ideals, moral values, and all regulative principles grow from within this process of actual experience which is the ultimate test of both truth and value. Norms for human conduct have no other sanction than that which experience itself contributes.

176. Respect the Child

I believe that our own experience instructs us that the secret of Education lies in respecting the pupil. It is not for you to choose what he shall know, what he shall do. It is chosen and foreordained, and he only holds the key to his own secret. By your tampering and thwarting and too much governing he may be hindered from his end and kept out of his own. Respect the child. Wait and see the new product of Nature. Nature loves analogies, but not repetitions. Respect the child. Be not too much his parent. Trespass not on his solitude.

But I hear the outcry which replies to this suggestion:—Would you verily throw up the reins of public and private discipline; would you leave the young child to the mad career of his own passions and whimsies, and call this anarchy a respect for the child's nature? I answer,—Respect the child, respect him to the end, but also respect yourself. Be the companion of his thought, the friend of his friendship, the lover of his virtue,—but no kinsman of his sin. Let him find you so true to yourself that you are the irreconcilable hater of his vice and the imperturbable slighter of his trifling.

The two points in a boy's training are, to keep his *natural* and train off all but that:—to keep his *natural*, but stop off his uproar, fooling and horse-play;—keep his nature and arm it with knowledge in the very direction in which it points . . .

177. Need for Supernatural Guidance

Catholic philosophy and Catholic education share the fundamental conviction that man, being so inclined to what is beneath him, cannot properly understand, much less develop and perfect, his human nature

---

176. Ralph Waldo Emerson, *Education* (Boston: Houghton Mifflin Company, 1909), pp. 19–20. Used by permission of the publishers.

177. Franz DeHovre, *Catholicism in Education* (New York: Benziger Brothers, Inc., 1934), pp. 118–119. Reprinted by permission of the publishers, owners of the copyright.

unless he aspires to something outside and above himself. He must seek support and guidance in the supernatural. This principle is applicable to every phase of human activity properly so-called. Thanks to the supernatural, the natural man is prevented from degenerating into what is un-natural. Only a super-rational sanction for his acts prevents man from becoming irrational. His frail human wisdom is protected in its search for truth and preserved from error only when it is illumined by the light of Divine Wisdom and strengthened by the grace of Divine Power. Knowledge of oneself and of mankind is certain only when it is refined and clarified by the knowledge of God. Love of one's neighbor, desirable as it undoubtedly is, cannot be genuine unless it be purified by the love of God. Immaterial riches are preferred to material ones only when spiritual things are ranked as of first importance. Sensuality dominates man to such an extent that morality in the sense of an unchanging code, with its commandments, its prohibitions, its voice of conscience, its categorical imperative, cannot exist except it be rooted in religion . . .

178. Ethics of the Teachers' Strike

It is quite in order, therefore, for professionals to unite in political combinations for political action to secure material or social benefits that they cannot otherwise secure, just as they have a right to take political actions to insure the proper practice of their profession. Physicians are the proper judges of what good medical practice is, but only the political authority can adjudicate how much power to enforce their convictions it will permit the profession to have. And if the people deny them their plea for proper payment, what then?

At this point it has been argued that the only recourse left is a strike or the withholding of services in order to persuade the body politic to accede to one's requests . . .

It is at this point that teaching and teachers are caught in a quandry. Is it morally permissible for them to withhold their services in order to enforce economic or even professional demands that in the long run might benefit the pupils whom they temporarily refuse to teach?

       ❁   ❁   ❁

The moral principle to which the withholding of services as a means of collective bargaining is most repugnant is that which forbids the

178. Harry Broudy, *Paradox and Promise* (Englewood Cliffs, N. J.: Prentice-Hall, Inc., 1961), pp. 133–134.

willful injuring of the innocent for a good other than their own. Without some injury or threat thereof the strike as a weapon loses its edge. Therefore the injury to be morally defensible must be directed against those who had a voice in creating the evil situation; who can by their own action negotiate with the strikers; who can, therefore, act as moral agents. When such conditions obtain in schools, hospitals, and law courts strikes lose their moral awkwardness.

179. The Core of Professional Ethics

The central fact in any teacher's code of ethics, then, is the professional obligation to the pupil himself. The full realization of this ideal implies a change in educational methods which would rock our present school system to its foundations and wreck most of the vested interests now feeding on our schools and colleges. If teaching is a profession, then the pupil is the client; and professionalism requires that the treatment of the client be for his best interests . . . Again let us remind the reader that such considerations do form an important part of the philosophy or morals of education, its values and objectives. But ethics is concerned with a more matter-of-fact problem. No attempt is here being made to advance a general scheme of education. The point is simply this, that education requires from the professional point of view, the diagnosis and treatment of individual mental reactions in such a way as will serve the best interests of the pupil, the student, the scholar.

180. Professional Status

The academician participates with the members of all major professions in a behavior system distinguished by the following criteria:

1. Prolonged and specialized training based upon a systematized intellectual tradition that rarely can be acquired through mere apprenticeship.

2. Rigorous standards of licensure, fulfilment of which often confers upon the functionary a degree or title signifying specialized competence.

179. Carl F. Taeusch, *Professional Business Ethics* (New York: Henry Holt and Company, 1926), pp. 143–144. Used by permission of the publishers.
180. Logan Wilson, *Academic Man* (New York: Oxford University Press, 1942), pp. 113–116.

3. Application of techniques of such intricacy that competency tests cannot be deduced upon any simple continuum scale, nor can supervision be more than loosely applied.

4. Absence of precise contractual terms of work, which might otherwise imply a calculated limitation of output and an exploitative attitude toward productivity.

5. A limitation upon the self-interest of the practitioner, and a careful insulation of professional considerations from extraneous matters, such as private opinions, economic interests, and class position.

6. Certain positive obligations to the profession and its clientele.

Not every profession embodies all of these common elements, yet taken together they form a *Gestalt* or whole that enables one to differentiate the profession from other generic types of occupations. Professional work, unlike most business and industrial enterprise, has no simple unitary end such as the production of goods for profit. Common practices often fall short of ideals, and individuals have difficulty in drawing the line, but in economic enterprise, the professional aspect stresses service and the business aspect profits.

✿   ✿   ✿

Professional ideology supports the tradition of a body of equals, making corporate decisions (whenever enterprise is collaborative), and being judged in terms of individual competence. The relative non-interference on the part of society presupposes, in turn, self-imposed as well as professionally enforced duties and obligations. Though not isolated, the academic man is insulated—the assumption being that he will do his work disinterestedly or objectively. As men have known since the time of Francis Bacon, however, objectivity in scholarly enterprise is not simply a matter of writing in the third person singular. Higher education is ideally organized to minimize bias, careerism, and other factors injurious to the disinterestedness necessary for best professional performance, but the academic ethic is a result of the combination of certain positive factors and of the negation of others. Thus the scholar-scientist is not a person with no values, but one with disciplined values, and objectivity is a term that is always relative to wider values.

To insure the unfettered pursuit of learning, an optimum of free association must be maintained. The liberal tradition and the intellectual tradition are closely coupled, and disinterestedness as a normative pattern means that values must be universalized and divorced from contexts where they are distorted by prejudices and sentiments. The universalism of the academic world, as in that of ideal-experimental economic theory, assumes that actions shall be rational (most efficient in the choice of means). Any primacy of ulterior motives of personal gain and success is definitely dysfunctional. As one analyst of the professions has observed, 'In the professions and their great tradition is to be found one of the principal reserves against that false conception of utility, in its close connection with the love of money . . . encouragement of the professions is one of the most effective ways of promoting disinterestedness in contemporary society . . .'

Ethical codes are to some extent unenforceable in a legal sense, and their sanctions are usually non-legal. Laws in the main apply to territorial groups, whereas professional codes apply to functional groupings. Sanctions exist positively in the desire for approval and negatively in the sense of shame; tabus, publicity, education, and the effects of clarifying and interpreting individual cases all serve as sanctions of a sort.

Although moral aspects of professional behavior are regulated more by ethics than by law, professors, doctors, and lawyers are in no sense beyond economics and the ultimate value system of the community except when they become *déclassés*. Standards of licensure and ethical codes are not merely arbitrary in-group formulations, and must have a general social acceptance. Group opportunism, esoteric cultism, or monkish idealism in small, independent associations may be tolerated by society, but it is hardly conceivable that these tendencies would be allowed to develop unrestrained in the academic or any other major profession.

181. The Right to Stop Teaching

The code of ethics of the American Medical Association contains several sections pertaining to the rights and obligations of doctors to withdraw from a case. For present purposes, the most important of these sections is the one dealing with "Conditions of Medical Practice":

> A physician should not dispose of his services under conditions that make it impossible to render adequate service to his patients, except under circumstances in which the patients concerned might be deprived of immediately necessary care. (Section 2, Chapter VII).

This section is very similar in intent and meaning to Canon 44 of the Canons of Professional Ethics for lawyers. If a similar section were

181. Myron Lieberman, "Teachers Strikes," *Harvard Educational Review,* 26:50, 52, Winter, 1956.

to be adopted by teachers, teachers strikes would shut down ever public school in some communities, if not in whole states. Teachers would be justified in refusing to continue to work where community or state action so interfered with the teachers professional autonomy that they could not reasonably accept responsibility for their work. For example, some communities have forced teachers to stop teaching about the United Nations. Teachers in other communities are under compulsion to avoid any realistic discussion of racial myths and prejudices. In still other communities, the beliefs of certain religious sects cannot be questioned no matter how much they conflict with well established scientific laws. Teachers should not accept professional responsibility for the intellectual and civic development of children where such restrictions are enforced. In line with the legal and medical codes of ethics which forbid professional work under conditions which do not permit the exercise of professional skill and judgment, teachers should be *obligated* not to work in communities and states which refuse to provide professional conditions of service. If doctors and lawyers must refuse to practice under unprofessional conditions of employment, why should teachers render service "under conditions that make it impossible to render adequate service"?

❊   ❊   ❊

The contention that *all* strikes by teachers would be "strikes against children" bears some scrutiny. There is no doubt that it is harmful for children to be deprived of adequate educational services. On the other hand, the contention is misleading because it misstates the issues. It overlooks the possibility that teaching under unprofessional conditions serves the interest of children less well than no teaching at all would —in short, that a strike may be "for" as well as "against" children. Formal schooling can be carried on under conditions which make it more harmful than no formal schooling at all. It cannot be assumed that every strike would be to the detriment of the students. But even the detriment to the students *immediately* deprived of educational services is not to be the ultimate consideration. It might be noted that the legal code of ethics expressly recognizes the right of the lawyer to withdraw *even when it is to the detriment of the client:* "The lawyer should not throw up the unfinished task to the detriment of the client except for reasons of honor or self-respect." In other words, if we rely upon the ethical codes of the established professions, there is no basis for the belief that a devotion to professionalism obligates teachers to continue to render their services no matter what the conditions of such service. Withdrawal, even after agreement to serve is justified, even obligatory, under certain conditions, *and even if it is to the detriment of the client.*

182. The Teacher Strike In An Interdependent Society

The right of teachers to strike and the wisdom of exercising that right are closely tied to the acceptance of the strike in other areas of employment, both public and private. Looking at the picture as a whole, there are conflicting trends which rule out any dogmatic predictions about the future role of teachers strikes. It may turn out that there will be an increase in the kinds of government employees who have the *legal right* to strike while at the same time there will be a declining *exercise* of that right. This possibility is not as contradictory as it may appear. Teachers with the legal right to strike would have far less need to exercise that right than teachers who had no such right. Put in another way, the added bargaining power gained by having the right to strike helps to prevent conditions of employment from deteriorating to the point where strikes are necessary.

As our society has become increasingly interdependent, it has become necessary to place an increasing number of restrictions on the right to strike. The effects of strikes in a highly interdependent industrialized society cannot be confined to the employers and employees involved in the disputes. A careful analysis of the trends in labor legislation shows that recent legislation is making it more difficult for either employers or employees to initiate a work stoppage. If, as appears likely, our society grows in interdependence, the right to strike will probably be hedged in by even more restrictions than it is at the present time. In this connection, it is interesting to note that the Taft-Hartley Act does not prohibit strikes even when they create a national emergency. It merely sets forth a procedure which must be followed before such strikes can be called. There is not much consistency in holding that workers in transportation, communication, and power industries can strike for higher wages even if such action creates a national emergency but that the first grade teacher in the country school cannot strike even for back pay.

If our society becomes increasingly interdependent, and if as a result of increasing interdependence it becomes necessary to place more restrictions upon the right to strike, what happens to the bargaining

182. Myron Lieberman, "Teachers Strikes," *Harvard Educational Review,* 26:66–67, Winter, 1956.

power of employees? Even if employees seldom strike to achieve their goals, their right to do so may be essential to them at the bargaining table. Eliminating the right to strike weakens the bargaining power of employees to dangerously low levels; permitting employees in an interdependent society to strike runs the risk of interruptions of vital services, thereby endangering the community or even the nation. The dilemma is real and it is growing in importance.

9

Political Basis of Education

Problems in the Philosophy of Education Discussed in this Section

1. What similarities and differences are to be noted in a comparison of the processes of socialization and education? From a social point of view when may an individual be said to have "learned" a society's culture?
2. What would be the educational consequences of the theory that society is a contract entered into by its members? Of the theory that society is an organism? That social relationships are based on "social status"?
3. To what extent is the individual "self-made"? Self-educated? In social terms what does it mean to teach him to be self-reliant? To think independently for himself? To be self-appraising?
4. Should schools be divorced from politics?
5. By what ethical criteria should we judge the social dimensions of an educational system?
   a. *Liberté?* How do you explain the paradox that both communist and democratic countries claim to be exponents of freedom?
   b. *Égalité?* Is it paradoxical for a democratic country to cultivate an aristocracy of talent? Would educational opportunities be more just and efficiently provided under a benevolent despotism? How is the distribution of political power in a society reflected in the distribution of educational opportunities?
   c. *Fraternité?* What are the implications of Dewey's concept of "sharing" for private schools? For homogenous grouping? For coeducation? For desegregation? For fraternities and sororities?
7. What is to be done with the educational interests of minorities—communists, fascists, religious and racial groups?
8. Should educational administration be modeled to give teachers an opportunity to determine educational policies? To share responsibility for these policies? How far should power be shared with students in the classroom? In a scheme of student government?

183. The Political and Ethical Bases of Education

Education is at all times concerned with men-living-in-societies and its ends cannot be defined apart from a direct consideration of the

183. Isaac B. Berkson, *The Ideal and the Community* (New York: Harper & Brothers, 1958), pp. 279–280.

character of the society into which the individual is to live. This approach stands at variance with the view that the purposes of education can be derived from metaphysics in the sense of an *a priori* conception of the nature of being. It is equally opposed to the contrary position that the aims of education are to be sought in biological process, in the natural history of man as a product of evolution. Some idea of man's relation to the cosmic order lies in the background of every educational philosophy; and the biological drives require attention in the analysis of the methods and objectives of education. But neither the former view of the nature and destiny of man which we may call the supernatural, or the latter, which we may term the subhuman, can be taken as the basis of major educational policy. Only a study of the history of man as creator and creature of civilization can give us a clue to man's distinctive nature, and provide us with the educational principles needed to bring about a progressive fulfilment of man's deepest and highest purposes and thus achieve self-realization.

Philosophy of education is an aspect of social philosophy. As such, it revolves around two opposing but complementary poles of reference. In classical parlance, we may designate the one as "ethics," the other as "politics." In the context of the present discussion, the former may be termed "the ideal," the latter, "the community." The one is reminiscent of the Platonist Idea of the Good—a unity of truth with a rational good that includes beauty. It points to a way of life consonant with man's highest nature, to a pattern of enduring universal values. The second refers to the Aristotelian proposition that man is a political animal, or civic creature. It draws attention to the fact that men naturally live in societies. A corollary is, men live not in society in general, but in definite communities, under specific types of government, institutional structures, and economic systems.

These two concepts—ideal and community—are distinct but not disparate. The ethical life can be lived only within a society and the communal life is impossible without a communion of ideas and values. In all societies—except the primitive perhaps—there is a distance between the ideally conceived way of life and the existing social order. In some instances the gap is so great that the idea of the good can be pursued only outside the political frame—in the monastery or in the Epicurean garden, in the ivory tower of contemplative philosophy or in the mystical communion with a transcendent reality. In the favorable situation—as in the democratic society—the opposition between the actual and the ideal creates a tension which impels toward the ever-greater embodiment of the ideal in the life of the individual and of the nation.

184. The Social Contract

Every citizen promises in the civil compact to promote with all his might all the conditions of the possibility of the State . . . This he can best do by educating children to skill and usefulness for all sorts of reasonable purposes. The State has the right to make this education of children a condition of the State-compact; thus education becomes an *external* compulsory duty owed directly not to the child but to the State. It is the State which acquires in the civil compact the right to require education.

185. General or Social Will

There is, however, lurking in what I have said, an assumption which many students of society and of education will challenge. It is the assumption that social groups have "General Wills," that communities have purposes, that a society has intentions, which underlie such institutions as the school. Are there, as a matter of sober fact, such social wills and intentions? Or are they mere fictions, ideas which exist only as the sounding of words, without usable meanings? I need hardly say that Rousseau's General Will, after which we are here following, has been violently attacked as just such a fiction. All "wills," we are told, are individual. A social will is a myth. To accept Rousseau as one's guide is evidently not to escape from controversy but rather to be plunged into the midst of it. And yet the presupposition of "the will of the community" seems to me so essential to the understanding of teaching that I cannot give it up. We must rather try to find what clear and defensible meaning it can be made to have.

The term which in our own current discussion seems to come nearest to Rousseau's General Will is that of a "culture" or a "pattern of culture." I propose, therefore, that we examine this term and see where it may lead us.

✻   ✻   ✻

If now we apply to the field of education the idea which our figure of speech suggests we are brought to a first, preliminary definition of

184. Johann G. Fichte, in George H. Turnbull, *The Educational Theory of J. G. Fichte* (Liverpool: The University Press of Liverpool, 1926), pp. 134–135.
185. Alexander Meiklejohn, *Education Between Two Worlds* (New York: Harper & Brothers, 1942), pp. 86–95. Reprinted by permission of the publishers.

the social intention of teaching. It is a dangerous definition to give in the present state of political theory and practice. And yet, fundamentally, it seems to me valid. The purpose of all teaching is to *express the cultural authority of the group by which the teaching is given.* In the words of our figure, a school intends so to mold and inspire a pupil that at every moment of his experience he will, both in thought and in action, strike the right note in the composition which his community is playing. The society wills that the pupil shall be, in terms of its intentions, a good member—rather than a bad one—of its social order. It commissions the teacher to bring that about. It has work to do. It, therefore, wishes the pupil to be fitted to do that work. It has values to interpret and to maintain. It wishes him, therefore, to be sensitive to those values, to devote his life to their service. Every social group, as such, draws its own distinction between "good" and "bad" behavior and builds its system of teaching on that distinction.

186. Society Found in Communication

Society not only continues to exist *by* transmission, *by* communication, but it may fairly be said to exist *in* transmission, *in* communication. There is more than a verbal tie between the words common, community, and communication. Men live in a community in virtue of the things which they have in common; and communication is the way in which they come to possess things in common.

❊   ❊   ❊

Not only is social life identical with communication, but all communication (and hence all genuine social life) is educative.

187. Subordination of the Individual to the Group

. . . One ought not to estimate individuality too highly. Rather must we consider as mere empty words and wide of the mark, the assertion that the teacher should devote himself carefully to the individuality of the pupil and study and cultivate it. He has no time for this. In

186. John Dewey, *Democracy and Education* (New York: The Macmillan Company, 1916), pp. 5–6.

187. George W. F. Hegel, in Millicent Mackenzie, *Hegel's Educational Theory and Practice* (London: Swan Sonnenschein & Co., 1909), p. 94.

the family circle the child's idiosyncrasies are tolerated; but with the school begins a life according to general law and order, under arrangements common to all. There the mind must be brought to relinquish its peculiarities and to make his own what is common (or well known) knowledge, and the will of the majority; and to submit himself to the usual mode of instruction. This transformation of the mind and this alone is worthy of the name of education. The more cultivated a man is the less does one see in his behaviour anything peculiar or out of the way.

188. Individual and Social Interests Antithetic

Between individual and social interests there is a fundamental antithesis. This antithesis is like that in the biological world between feeling and function. Of the many individual powers, and of the infinitude of possible pleasurable individual activities some are helpful, some are harmful, to society. The task of education is to aid the social evolutionary process in eliminating the harmful interests and tendencies, and to stimulate and develop the activities and powers which are of special advantage to society at the given stage of its development. The completion of the individual is from one point of view necessarily limited by his social life. It must be sacrificed in the interests of society, not primarily because his own highest good demands it, but because society, the external educating power and agency, believes such a sacrifice essential to its own preservation and improvement.

This antithesis between individual and social interests is an actual but not an ideal one. The development of the individual and of society should lead to a harmony of interests. In such harmony alone is there perfect individual freedom. The school must synthesize the life of the individual and the social life. It must cultivate the disposition and the habit of striving for the attainment of social ends. This means that the school must be consciously organized and directed to promote the spirit of social service. Inasmuch as social service leads, from well known psychological laws, to the identification of the interests of the individual with those of society, social service, or assistance in the realization of an ideal humanity, is in the highest degree rational. It is the pathway to individual freedom . . .

188. Ira W. Howerth, *The Theory of Education* (New York: The Century Company, 1926), pp. 372–373.

189. Catholic Stress on the Individual

Catholic education tends to be individualistic. Society, the state, the church—all exist ultimately for the individual. Legislation and organization of education merely for the sake of society or the state is opposed. The relationship of the individual to God is the primary consideration. The individual may have his duties to society, but his duties toward God are primary. Majorities may not interfere to make the individual a means rather than an end.

190. Absolute Value of the Individual

The social philosophy of our democracy, and undoubtedly of all democracy, is based on the principle of claiming the absolute value of the human individual . . .

To grasp thoroughly its application to education, it is not without interest to recall the objection raised against this principle in France by political parties and by such philosophers as Auguste Comte, for example. It is destructive, they say, of all moral education. By conferring a right, sacred as it were, on the individual it grants him no other end than himself and allows him to set himself up against society; the principle is, accordingly, anarchical, antisocial, in short, immoral.

It is impossible to overcome this objection without thoroughly grasping the idea of democracy. Naturally the individual has as his purpose the duties that follow from his diverse functions in society. That is undeniable. But the philosophy of democracy aims at a higher value, namely, that he devote himself to these duties of his own accord, just as it wishes that he judge for himself in his own conscience the bases and foundations of the truths that he ought to believe. In a word, the idea of the right of the human being is the affirmation of the incomparable value of autonomy.

189. Maurice S. Sheehy, "Catholic Education in the United States," in P. Henry Lotz and L. W. Crawford, editors, *Studies in Religious Education* (Nashville: copyright 1931 by Lamar and Whitmore), p. 474. By permission of Abingdon-Cokesbury Press.

190. Félix Pécaut, "France," in *International Institute, Educational Yearbook*, (New York: Bureau of Publications, Teachers College, Columbia University, 1929), pp. 140–141.

191. Education to Will What the State Wills

. . . When is it that my will really is effective, really *wills?* I am a citizen of a state which has power; this power, this will of the state expresses itself to me in laws which I must obey. The transgression of laws, if the state is in existence, bears with it the inevitable punishment of the transgressor, that is, the application of that law which the offender has refused to recognize. The state is supported by the inviolability of laws, of those sacred laws of the land which Socrates, as Plato tells us, taught his pupils to revere. I, then, as a citizen of my country, am bound by its Law in such a manner that to will its transgression is to aim at the impossible. If I did so, I should be indulging in vain velleities, in which my personality, far from realizing itself, would on the contrary be disintegrated and scattered. I then want what the law wants me to will.

It makes no difference that, from a material and explicit point of view, a system of positive law does not coincide throughout with the sphere of my activity, and that therefore the major part of the standards of my conduct must be determined by the inner dictates of my particular conscience. For it is the Will of the State that determines the limits between the moral and the juridical, between what is imposed by the law of the land and what is demanded by the ethical conscience of the individual. And there is no limit which pre-exists to the line by which the constituent and legislative power of the State delimits the sphere subject to its sanctions. So that positively or negatively, either by command or by permission, our whole conduct is subject to that will by which the State establishes its reality.

But the Will of the State does not manifest itself solely by the enactment of positive legislation. It opens to private initiative such courses of action as may presumably be carried on satisfactorily without the impulse and the direct control of the sovereign power. But this concession has a temporary character, and the State is ever ready to intervene as soon as the private management ceases to be effective. So that even in the exercise of what seems the untrammelled will of the individual we discern the power of the State; and the individual is free to will something only because the sovereign power wants him to. So that in reality this apparently autonomous particular will is the will of the

191. Giovanni Gentile, *The Reform of Education,* D. Bigongiari, translater (New York: Harcourt, Brace, and Company, Inc., copyright 1922), pp. 27–32.

State not expressed in terms of positive legislation, there being no need of such an expression. But since the essence of law is not in the expression of it, but in the will which dictates it, or observes it, or enforces the observance of it, in the will, in short, that wills it, it follows that the law exists even though unwritten . . .

             *   *   *

So then, I exercise my true volition whenever the will of my state acts in my personal will, or rather when my will is the realization of the will of a super-national group in which my state co-exists with other states, acting upon them, and being re-acted upon in reciprocal determinations. Or perhaps better still, when the entire world wills in me. For my will, I shall say it once again, is not individual but universal, and in the political community by which individuals are united into a higher individuality, historically distinct from other similar ones, we must see a form of universality.

For this reason, then, we are justified in saying that our personality is particular when we consider it abstractly, but that concretely it realizes itself as a universal and therefore also as a national personality. This conception is of fundamental importance for those of us who live in the class-room and have made of teaching our life's occupation, our ultimate end, and the real purpose of our existence.

192. State the End, Individual the Means

Fascism seeks to provide this ideal in a new concept of the national State which is at the same time a challenge to the modern development of democracy. It is in fact a protest against the ideals of democratic government and of individualism which had their roots in the Protestant Reformation and the French Revolution. These ideals, since they placed the individual on a pedestal, imply a mechanical and atomistic concept of the State and of society and are based on the view that the sum of individual interests is the same as the collective interest of the State, and the general will or the ends of the State merely represent the aggregation of individual wills. From this point of view, the State and society exist for the sake of the individuals who compose them and the ends of both are determined by the ends, purposes, and interests of the individuals. Government is merely a mechanical device to hold the balance or "maintain justice" between the conflicting interests of individuals or groups. Representative government and rule by majori-

192. Isaac L. Kandel, *Comparative Education* (Boston: Houghton Mifflin Company, 1933), pp. 66–68. Used by permission of the publishers.

ties promote the selfish interests of an aggregate of individuals rather than the interests of the State which are directed to the well-being of all. Democratic forms of society are purely materialistic, are dominated by no fixed or stable ideals, and are subject to the whims of changing majorities; the present is isolated from the past, and the spiritual inheritances of the past, which make for the spiritual union of society, are rejected. The State or society exists merely as a means for promoting the happiness of individuals and the essence of social, economic and political life is liberty in an absolute sense, not sacrifice, or discipline, or duty.

Against this ideology Fascism opposes the view that society or the State is something more than the sum of the individuals who compose it, that it is the link between succeeding generations, and that it has ends of its own which may even be in conflict, but are always superior, because more far-seeing and unselfish, to those of the individual. These ends are moral and spiritual and involve language, culture, religion, customs, feelings and volition, economic interests, living conditions, and territory, all dominated by moral values of universal validity which serve to guide progress towards a national ideal. As opposed to the atomistic and mechanistic concept of the State, Fascism sets up an organic and historic concept of a State with a life and purposes of its own over and above those of the individual. The State thus becomes an end; the individuals are at once the means or instruments which may be employed to attain the end and find their happiness as they attain to a complete understanding of the end proposed by the State. Liberty in such a State does not mean self-realization or self-expression of the individual, but rather conquest of oneself in the interests of the State; liberty is not an absolute right, but is contingent upon the purposes of the State, which may concede it to or withdraw it from the individual. The highest ethical value lies not in liberty but in the preeminence of duty; liberty is not a natural right but a concession of the State. Hence sovereignty rests not with the individual members of the nation or their elected representatives, chosen more often than not on the basis of the selfish interests of a party or of the voters, but with the men capable of rising above their immediate private interests and of realizing the aspirations of the State as a unity in relation to its past, present, and future. The leaders are those who are better fitted to govern than others; their authority is derived not from below, from the masses ignorant of anything but their own interests, but from above. Hence government is organized as hierarchy exercising authority and bearing responsibility. The bases of government are authority, order, and discipline.

   *   *   *

Education thus becomes the most important means of enlightening the masses in the ideals of the Fascist State; until it could become universally organized in accordance with these ideals, other means, more forceful and less intellectual, had to be employed. Repression, it was recognized, was the only method by which ignorant opponents could be controlled; the future lay with the younger generation with whom education was to take the place of repression. Since the State is a moral and spiritual affair conscious of moral truths of universal validity, it alone has the right to control education which may be provided by public or other organizations, but always subject to state control which is exercised by a hierarchical administration, in which as little as possible is left to local representative committees . . .

193. Democratic Education is That Which is Good for All Men Everywhere

The question, "What is a good education?" can be answered in two ways: either in terms of what is good for men at any time and place because they are men, or in terms of what is good for men considered only as members of a particular social and political order. My thesis is that the best society is the one in which the two answers are the same; and that one society is better than another in so far as it approximates this ideal . . . If there is anyone who would say that this principle is merely a matter of opinion—and, *a fortiori*, that there are no objective and universal political truths—that person, whether he knows it or not, is as vicious as his fascist adversary, for he is ultimately reduced to the same position, that only might makes right. This is the suicide of the false liberal . . .

If, however, we affirm this principle as a clear truth, a corollary would appear to follow from it. We must affirm this principle. It is a basic tenet of American democracy that men have sacred rights above the State. While admitting that its present forms and operations may be far from perfect, we are, nevertheless, compelled to honor the institutions and practices of our government as abiding by this principle of justice. The corollary which would seem to follow is that American education is fundamentally sound, because we seek to solve the problem of education in our democracy only by determining what is good education for all men everywhere . . . Public education in a democracy serves the State not simply by making children into faithful

193. Mortimer J. Adler, "Liberalism and Liberal Education," *The Educational Record,* 20: 426–427, July 1939.

democrats, but primarily through serving the welfare of its citizens, not merely as subjects of the State, but as free men. In fact, unless education makes men free it cannot serve democracy at all.

194. Universal Education Rooted in a Self-Realizing Universe

Universal education is a recognition by all people of the world that every child shall be educated not so much from the standpoint of economic and commercial success in life, nor because it is a fundamental governmental principle of self-protection and self-preservation, but because it is an inherent principle in the very nature of mind itself in that it seeks to realize itself in and through the instrumentalities of education. Why should every mundane being be educated? Why should education be universal? There is a tendency in nature, in plant and animal life and in human existence to strive for the highest good. Universal education has its explanation and roots in a self-realizing universe. There is an energy in the world which is seeking its highest perfection and which requires universal education as a means to the attainment of this ultimate aim. That every individual in the world should be educated may be explained from the fact, that in man and in the world there is a spiritual principle seeking for perfection . . .

195. The Purpose of Equal Opportunity is to Develop Individuality

If the phrase be understood rightly the aim of education is the *development and enjoyment of individuality*. It is the realization, in the fullest measure possible under the conditions of human existence, of comprehensive and harmonious self-activity. It is self-realization, through self-expression, self-control, self-direction; always as a member of the community . . .

*   *   *

The true distinction, with reference to social ends, is between a good and a bad individualism. A bad individualism is one in which many

194. Arthur C. Fleshman, *The Metaphysics of Education* (Boston: Mayhew Publishing Company, 1914), pp. 63–64.
195. Joseph A. Leighton, *Individuality and Education* (New York: D. Appleton and Company, 1928), pp. 13–15.

or some individuals are not respected and treated as having any inherent worth in themselves, but are used merely as tools to serve the special interests of other individuals. The good individualism in social practice is one in which all the members of society are given equal opportunties to realize and enjoy their own capacities and aptitudes. This is the difference between oligarchic and democratic individualism. All so-called- and miscalled-aristocratic societies are those in which the many are sacrificed to the few. Democracy, as a social ideal, simply means that every one shall have a fair chance. And the prime condition of a fair chance is equalization of educational opportunities; which implies, of course, that the pupil shall have food, shelter, and clothing sufficient to enable him to take advantage of the opportunities.

On the other hand, equalization of opportunity does not mean the obliteration of distinctions, the filing down of differences between individuals. Individuals are born not only different in the sense of having a variety of capacities and aptitudes. They are born unequal, with respect to the same capacities and aptitudes. Until we have learned to standardize the production of babies, as we now do automobile parts, this will continue to be so. That is, in all probability, so long as the human race endures. It is just as well that it is so. Human life would lose most of its interest, if all human beings were alike. Nature seems to have been aiming, throughout the evolutionary process, at the production of the greatest possible development of various individualities. Certainly the scale on which we measure evolution is individuality. What we mean by "lower" is an organism possessing less initiative, less varied power of adaptation to, and control of, the environment. What we mean by "higher" is an organism possessing greater wealth of impulse, activity, adaptiveness, initiative, inventiveness, capacity to control its environment and to build up a life of its own.

196. Educational Opportunity Under Communism

What is the problem of authority during the period of dictatorship? Obviously, it is to destroy the remnant of the capitalistic order, to create new organs of proletarian dictatorship, and to destroy the old and construct a new ideology in all fields of thought. Undoubtedly during this period the school and the other educational institutions will attract the liveliest interest of the proletarian power. The aim of all workers in the sphere of public education will be to instill into the growing generation socialistic (communistic) ideas and thereby to in-

196. Albert P. Pinkevitch, *The New Education in the Soviet Republic* (New York: John Day Company, 1929), pp. 29–30.

crease the ranks of those who are fighting for the establishment of the socialistic (communistic) state. The aim is, so to speak, the indoctrination of the youth in the proletarian philosophy . . .

By what methods can this be accomplished? In the first place, by placing the control of education in the republic in the hands of communists and socialists sympathizing with the proletarian upheaval; in the second place, by a wide dissemination of communistic ideas through the press and children's literature; and, finally, through a corresponding organization of all the institutions of public education . . .

. . . Under a socialistic regime, that is, under a condition of perfect economic equality, everybody will receive the opportunity of a complete education which now even in the epoch of proletarian dictatorship is limited to the few; in a socialistic order the only deciding factor will be the ability of the individual . . .

197. Quantitative Equality In Education

Now the irreducible minimum of equality that a philosophy can demand and still call itself "democratic" is the sharing by men up to the level of their ability of the ends for which they must work and fight. Nor must their ability be considered to be justly represented by what it is at any given time, by the *status quo*, but rather by what it may become under favorable opportunities. That is, as a fundamental prerequisite of justice the chance at education must be passed around. Fairness in passing it around will probably be best guaranteed by demanding that the chance be made quantitatively equal, for the single reason that any judgment before actual trial that persons cannot profit equally from the same opportunity lends itself too obviously to prejudice and unfairness.

198. "Minimal" is Different from "Identical" Education

Citizenship has been defined as the contribution of one's instructed judgment to the public good. It follows therefore that the citizen has the right to such education as will fit him for the tasks of citizenship.

197. Thomas V. Smith, *The American Philosohpy of Equality* (Chicago: University of Chicago Press, 1927), pp. 308–309. Copyright 1927 by the University of Chicago.
198. Harold J. Laski, *A Grammar of Politics* (London: George Allen & Unwin, Ltd., 1925), pp. 113–114.

He must be provided with the instruments which make possible the understanding of life. He must be able to give articulate expression to the wants he has, the meaning of the experience he has encountered. There is no more fundamental division in the modern State than that between those who have the control of knowledge and those who lack such control. In the long run, power belongs to those who can formulate and grasp ideas. Granted that such ability exists in a wide range of inequality there is yet, once more, a minimum basis of education below which no one of average intelligence can be permitted to fall. For unless I can follow with understanding the processes of politics, those things which affect my life will be effected without my having the opportunity to make my will enter into the result. "First of all things," said Antiphon the Sophist, "I place education"; certainly in the modern world the citizen who lacks it is bound to be the slave of others. He will not be able to convince his fellows. He will not be able to restrain his nature into those paths along which it is best fitted to travel. He will not rise to the full height of his personality. He will go through life a stunted being whose impulses have never been ordered by reason into creative experiment.

The right to education does not mean the right to an identical intellectual training for all citizens. It involves the discovery of capacity and the fitting of the discipline conferred to the type of capacity made known. Obviously, it would be foolish waste to give an identical training to Meredith and Clerk-Maxwell. But obviously, also, there is a minimum level below which no citizen can fall if he is to use the necessary intellectual instruments of our civilization. He must be trained to make judgments. He must learn to weigh evidence. He must learn to choose between the alternatives between which he is called to decide. He must be made to feel that this is a world in which he can, by the use of his mind and will, shape outline and substance.

199. Opportunity Must Be Proportioned to Ability

All men struggle to secure those goods that will increase their happiness, but, as the supply is limited, the desire of every one cannot be fully gratified. Now, give all the right to strive after them and one man will obtain more than his fellows. He has been endowed by nature with greater physical strength, it may be, or a sharper mind, so that he can discern how he must conduct himself in order to obtain what he wants. Or he may have greater self-control, or talents which enable him to

199. Michael V. O'Shea, *Education as Adjustment* (New York: Longmans, Green & Company, 1906), pp. 123–124.

serve men in such a way that they will reward him with a larger portion of the world's goods than they themselves possess. And when one thinks of it he wonders that people do not differ more than they do in capacity; for when there are so many individuals, the characteristics of each being determined by different environmental influences, and a long line of forces acting through heredity, we should expect still greater variation in their powers than seems actually to exist. And it will be granted, surely, that in a democracy it is just as unfair, just as undemocratic, just as great a crime to prevent a man, strong in mind or character or body, from accomplishing what nature gave him the power to do, as to prevent the weak man from exerting his powers to their fullest extent in competition or cooperation with his fellows.

The practice, though (or perhaps one would be nearer right in saying the *theory*), in the schools of our own country tends rather towards the suppression of the exceptional individual, keeping him down to the level of mediocrity. We interpret the doctrine of equality to refer to the attainment of the same deserts by all instead of to the granting of equal opportunity. We have not carried the doctrine out to its logical conclusions yet, it is true, nor, on the other hand, have we adopted the opposite view. We stand confused in thought and vacillating in action between the interpretation of the doctrine of equality given by tradition and that given by ethics and science. What is needed to vitalize our education is an explicit recognition of the fact that *every* pupil in the schools must be given an opportunity to do his best, to achieve the most that he can in any direction. If there be one who excels the others by reason of native endowment or parental training or anything else, the school must be organized so that it can minister to his needs as fully as to the needs of his less fortunate fellows. To fail to do this is a crime alike against the individual and against society; for social well-being depends more largely upon the conservation of the strong, though they be but few, than upon the perpetuation of the weak, though their number be unlimited, just as the welfare of the human body is advanced more by two keen eyes than it would be by a hundred dull ones, and by two skilful hands than by dozens of clumsy tentacles.

200. The Few Preferred to the Masses

I have long accustomed myself to look with caution upon those who are ardent in the cause of the so-called "education of the people" in

200. Friedrich Nietzsche, *The Future of Our Educational Institutions*, J. M. Kennedy, translator (Edinburgh: T. N. Foulis, 1909), pp. 74–76.

the common meaning of the phrase; since for the most part they desire for themselves, consciously or unconsciously, absolutely unlimited freedom, which must inevitably degenerate into something resembling the saturnalia of barbaric times, and which the sacred hierarchy of nature will never grant them. They were born to serve and to obey; and every moment in which their limping or crawling or broken-winded thoughts are at work shows us clearly out of which clay nature moulded them, and what trade mark she branded thereon. The education of the masses cannot, therefore, be our aim; but rather the education of a few picked men for great and lasting works . . .

We know, however, what the aspiration is of those who would disturb the healthy slumber of the people, and continually call out to them: "Keep your eyes open! Be sensible! Be wise!" We know the aim of those who profess to satisfy excessive educational requirements by means of an extraordinary increase in the number of educational institutions and the conceited tribe of teachers originated thereby. These very people, using these very means, are fighting against the natural hierarchy in the realm of the intellect, and destroying the roots of all those noble and sublime plastic forces which have their material origin in the unconsciousness of the people, and which fittingly terminate in the procreation of genius and its due guidance and proper training . . .

201. Fascism and Education of the Élite

Education accentuates rather than levels out inequalities of natural endowment. Intelligence tests made of the same persons before, during, and at the end of either the four-year college course or a seven-or-eight-year combined college and professional course, show that the inequalities between different persons increase rather than diminish after undergoing the same course of training.

There is great social significance in the fact that the élite of exceptional natural endowment, who, as a matter of course, become the élite of power and influence, actual or potential, are a fairly constant percentage of the total population. From this fact it follows that no social system can long survive, once it tends strongly to declass more and more of the élite. In other words, the élite are more vital or resistant to suppression as wielders of power and influence than any social system. Civilizations come and go, but the élite go on forever. . . .

201. Lawrence Dennis, *The Coming American Fascism* (New York: Harper & Brothers, 1936), pp. 237–238. Reprinted by permission of the publishers.

There is nothing really depressing about these facts concerning the élite. Nor is there to be deduced from these facts any good argument against more and better education for everyone.

202. Education as a Tool of the Dominant Élite

The school must be one of the instruments of government of the group culture. The group culture should be the expression of the will of the dominant element of the élite whose values are validated by the power to enforce them. This method of validating values is the only one by which an argument can ever be ended and cooperative activity made possible . . . Education does not make or unmake the élite. It equips them and increases their social distance from the masses. It raises their potentialities as instruments of creation, destruction, and combat, processes which make up the mysterious drama of life.

203. The Élite and Higher Standards

It follows from what has been said in an earlier chapter about classes and élites, that education should help to preserve the class and to select the élite. It is right that the exceptional individual should have the opportunity to elevate himself in the social scale and attain a position in which he can exercise his talents to the greatest benefit of himself and of society. But the ideal of an educational system which would automatically sort out every one according to his native capacities is unattainable in practice: and if we made it our chief aim, would disorganize society and debase education. It would disorganize society, by substituting for classes, élites of brains, or perhaps only of sharp wits. Any educational system aiming at a complete adjustment between education and society will tend both to restrict education to what will lead to success in the world, and to restrict success in the world to those persons who have been good pupils of the system. The prospect of a society ruled and directed only by those who have passed certain examinations or satisfied tests devised by psychologists is not reassuring: while it might give scope to talents

202. Lawrence Dennis, "Education—the Tool of the Dominant Élite," *The Social Frontier*, Vol. I, No. 4, p. 14, January 1935.

203. From *Notes Towards the Definition of Culture*, copyright 1949 by T. S. Eliot. Reprinted by permission of Harcourt, Brace & World Publishing Co., Inc., pp. 103–104.

hitherto obscured, it would probably obscure others, and reduce to impotence some who should have rendered high service. Furthermore, the ideal of a uniform system such that no one capable of receiving higher education could fail to get it, leads imperceptibly to the education of too many people, and consequently to the lowering of standards to whatever this swollen number of candidates is able to reach.

204. Environmentalists More Democratic than Geneticists

The proportion of heredity and environment in forming an adult human character is very differently estimated by different authorities. Among men of science, there is a natural tendency for heredity to be emphasized by geneticists, while environment is emphasized by psychologists. There is, however, another line of cleavage on this question, not scientific, but political. Conservatives and imperialists lay stress on heredity, because they belong to the white race but are rather uneducated. Radicals lay stress on education, because it is potentially democratic, and because it gives a reason for ignoring difference of colour. This political cleavage on the whole overrides that of geneticist and psychologist.

205. Catholicism Both Authoritarian and Democratic

Authority is essential to the concept of Catholicism. The Church is hierarchical in her organization; her power is centralized; she proclaims the doctrine of infallibility; and Unity is one of her marks. All these features are identified with an aristocratic form of government. Indeed, it has been truly said that if the aristocratic form of society were to disappear from every other institution it would still be found intact in the Church, so essential is it to her very organization.

Yet, the Church is the Mother of all true democracy. She recognizes no system of castes and tolerates no distinction of slave and free. She has created the atmosphere in which the spirit of democracy has thrived and her teaching has been the soil in which the principle of the equality of men and of races has taken root . . .

204. Bertrand Russell, *Education and the Modern World* (New York: W. W. Norton & Company, Inc., 1932), p. 43. Reprinted by permission of the publishers.
205. Franz DeHovre, *Catholicism in Education* (New York: Benziger Brothers, 1934), p. 82. Used by permission of the publishers, owners of the copyright.

206. Education for Followership

. . . Nothing can be more clear than that the humbler economic functions are destined not only to remain, but to claim large percentages
of the population. If these people are to achieve self-realization it must
be *in* those humbler functions, not by getting out of them. Somebody
must remain in them; and for an honest democracy it does not so much
matter who; the real question is what will be their opportunity for a
satisfying life in them. The central problem of the new regime is
whether the men with the hoe, the pick, and the shovel are to be
brutalized or humanized. If the former, then the hope of democracy—
not to say of Christianity—is a delusion and a dream; but if the latter,
it will come through an education that enables them to utilize the
sciences, the fine arts, and the new humanities as copiously and effectively as do any other class of society. Only thus can the so-called open
class society be superseded by a real democracy; otherwise it will
revert gradually to caste.

✿   ✿   ✿

The truth seems to be that a mere echo is the best that can ever be
expected from the duller half of the population; and the vital question
is who secures them as a sounding board. In the present crisis the race
is between those who would selfishly exploit the masses and those who
would teach and thereby liberate them. The competing means are
education and propaganda—enlightenment and illusion. If the exploiters should win, the outward forms, even of democracy, could
hardly last a century, after which there would probably evolve some
sort of an industrial feudalism quite inimical to the objectives themselves of democracy. To load the dice of popular beliefs with the enlightened beliefs of enlightened leaders is the only preventive.

207. Liberty and Equality at Odds

The selective function of education is salutary and inherent. Salutary
because to give an instruction which is not assimilated, like eating

206. Ross L. Finney, *A Sociological Philosophy of Education* (New York: The
Macmillan Company, 1928), pp. 282–283, 289.
207. A. Lawrence Lowell, "Democracy, Equality, and Education," *Harvard
Teachers Record*, 1:98, November 1931.

food that is not digested, is not nutritive but positively injurious. Salutary also for the better students who are otherwise kept back by the attempt to teach with them those who cannot keep up. Salutary for the community, because more than any other form of government democracy needs the recruiting and perfecting of its best brains wherever found. The selective process is inherent because no form of schooling has yet been, or ever will be, devised that does not involve it. The diverse curricula in the American public schools do not exclude it, but on the contrary provide for it, and make it systematic. Under the old rigid academic program the less capable and less ambitious eliminated themselves by falling out, mainly at the end of the elementary period. Now they are virtually steered into courses that lead to much the same result . . .

To say this is not to criticize the plan of a variety of curricula in our public schools. They are desirable and necessary in any system of universal and compulsory education carried beyond the elementary stage; but it is worth while to consider frankly their results and their significance. They are not, and can not be, administered so as to promote equality among men; for while they provide opportunity for all to develop their natural abilities in the way they prefer, and thus foster individual liberty, they tend in so doing to increase, rather than reduce, diversity and inequality.

208. Opportunity Regulated by Abstraction Differential

It would seem to follow from the principle that all men are rational, that all have a natural right to the education that will allow them to perfect themselves as human beings. It is unfortunately true that the chief propounders of Classical Realism (Plato and Aristotle) proposed and sanctioned social practices that contradict this principle. The principle does, nevertheless, follow from the premises of Classical Realism, and it does not logically entail the three grades of intellect assumed by Plato nor any finite number of such grades. It, therefore, does not commit us to a caste system of education on the one hand, nor to quantitative or qualitative equality of education on the other. Who shall be educated and at what level is a question that can better be answered on empirical grounds than on speculative ones. The individual's right to education is limited only by his capacity to learn and the group's ability to provide opportunity to learn.

208. Harry S. Broudy, *Implications of Classical Realism for Philosophy of Education,* The Association for Realistic Philosophy, *Proceedings,* 1949, pp. 12–13.

Pupils vary with respect to the level of abstraction at which they can learn efficiently. Some can understand calculus; others must stop at applied geometry, and still others cannot go beyond rote arithmetic. In history, some cannot apprehend more than the isolated historical event simply or dramatically described; others can understand sequences of cause and effect; still others can comprehend theories of causation; and a few (mostly candidates for the doctorate) like to discuss the theories about theories of causation.

This abstraction differential, or differences in power to deal with abstractions, is evident on every level of instruction where symbols and ideas, i.e., the noetic skills, are involved. It means that even in general education this differential will determine just what will be taught and on what level. It is also the rational determinant of who should go to high school, college, or university. It is an important factor in the choice of an occupation.

Now since the abstraction differential can be determined empirically, albeit not with perfect precision by intelligence tests, a philosophy of education need not commit itself to either a caste system of education or to a mechanical equalitarianism. The ideal educational system recognizes the individual as a *unique* pattern of value potentials and tries to exploit these to their *maxima*. This uniqueness does not mean that individuals determine the truth nor that there is no truth that everybody ought to apprehend. Rather it is all one truth, but we do vary in the level at which we can assimilate it. By adhering to capacity for learning as a criterion, we can avoid the demand that everyone learn exactly the same thing in the same way, and likewise the notion that the whims of children are true guides for curriculum and organization.

209. Responsibility for Directing Things in Common

If British liberal social philosophy tended, true to the spirit of its atomistic empiricism, to make freedom and the exercise of rights ends in themselves, the remedy is not to be found in recourse to a philosophy of fixed obligations and authoritative law such as characterized German political thinking. The latter, as events have demonstrated, is dangerous because of its implicit menace to the free self-determination of other social groups. But it is also weak internally when put to the final test. In its hostility to the free experimentation

209. John Dewey, *Reconstruction in Philosophy* (New York: Henry Holt and Company, 1920), pp. 208–210. Used by permission of the publishers.

and power of choice of the individual in determining social affairs, it limits the capacity of many or most individuals to share effectively in social operations, and thereby deprives society of the full contribution of all its members. The best guarantee of collective efficiency and power is liberation and use of the diversity of individual capacities in initiative, planning, foresight, vigor and endurance. Personality must be educated, and personality cannot be educated by confining its operations to technical and specialized things, or to the less important relationships of life. Full education comes only when there is a responsible share on the part of each person, in proportion to capacity, in shaping the aims and policies of the social groups to which he belongs. This fact fixes the significance of democracy. It cannot be conceived as a sectarian or racial thing nor as a consecration of some form of government which has already attained constitutional sanction. It is but a name for the fact that human nature is developed only when its elements take part in directing things which are common, things for the sake of which men and women form groups—families, industrial companies, governments, churches, scientific associations and so on. The principle holds as much of one form of association, say in industry and commerce, as it does in government. The identification of democracy with political democracy which is responsible for most of its failures is, however, based upon the traditional ideas which make the individual and the state ready-made entities in themselves.

210. Number and Variety of Shared Interests

Now in any social group whatever, even in a gang of thieves, we find some interest held in common, and we find a certain amount of interaction and cooperative intercourse with other groups. From these two traits we derive our standard. How numerous and varied are the interests which are consciously shared? How full and free is the interplay with other forms of association? If we apply these considerations to, say, a criminal band, we find that the ties which consciously hold the members together are few in number, reducible almost to a common interest in plunder; and that they are of such a nature as to isolate the group from other groups with respect to give and take of the values of life. Hence, the education such a society gives is partial and distorted. If we take, on the other hand, the kind of family life which illustrates the standard, we find that there are material, intellectual, and aesthetic interests in which all participate and that the prog-

210. John Dewey, *Democracy and Education* (New York: The Macmillan Company, 1916), pp. 96–102.

ress of one member has worth for the experience of other members—it is readily communicable—and that the family is not an isolated whole, but enters intimately into relationships with business groups, with schools, with all the agencies of culture, as well as with other similar groups, and that it plays a due part in the political organization and in return receives support from it. In short, there are many interests consciously communicated and shared; and there are varied and free points of contact with other modes of association.

✿   ✿   ✿

The two elements in our criterion both point to democracy. The first signifies not only more numerous and more varied points of shared common interests, but greater reliance upon the recognition of mutual interests as a factor in social control. The second means not only freer interaction between social groups (once isolated so far as intention could keep up a separation) but change in social habit—its continuous readjustment through meeting the new situations produced by varied intercourse. And these two traits are precisely what characterize the democratically constituted society.

Upon the educational side, we note first that the realization of a form of social life in which interests are mutually interpenetrating, and where progress, or readjustment, is an important consideration, makes a democratic community more interested than other communities have cause to be in deliberate and systematic education. The devotion of democracy to education is a familiar fact. The superficial explanation is that a government resting upon popular suffrage cannot be successful unless those who elect and who obey their governors are educated. Since a democratic society repudiates the principle of external authority, it must find a substitute in voluntary disposition and interest; these can be created only by education. But there is a deeper explanation. A democracy is more than a form of government; it is primarily a mode of associated living, of conjoint communicated experience. The extension in space of the number of individuals who participate in an interest so that each has to refer his own action to that of others, and to consider the action of others to give point and direction to his own, is equivalent to the breaking down of those barriers of class, race, and national territory which kept men from perceiving the full import of their activity. These more numerous and more varied points of contact denote a greater diversity of stimuli to which an individual has to respond; they consequently put a premium on variation in his action. They secure a liberation of powers which remain suppressed as long as the incitations to action are partial, as they must be in a group which in its exclusiveness shuts out many interests.

The widening of the area of shared concerns, and the liberation of a greater diversity of personal capacities which characterize a democracy, are not of course the product of deliberation and conscious effort. On the contrary, they were caused by the development of modes of manufacture and commerce, travel, migration, and intercommunication which flowed from the command of science over natural energy. But after greater individualization on one hand, and a broader community of interest on the other have come into existence, it is a matter of deliberate effort to sustain and extend them. Obviously a society to which stratification into separate classes would be fatal, must see to it that intellectual opportunities are accessible to all on equable and easy terms. A society marked off into classes need be specially attentive only to the education of its ruling elements. A society which is mobile, which is full of channels for the distribution of a change occurring anywhere, must see to it that its members are educated to personal initiative and adaptability. Otherwise, they will be overwhelmed by the changes in which they are caught and whose significance or connections they do not perceive. The result will be a confusion in which a few will appropriate to themselves the results of the blind and externally directed activities of others.

211. Democracy in School Administration

. . . Until the public-school system is organized in such a way that every teacher has some regular and representative way in which he or she can register judgment upon matters of educational importance, with the assurance that this judgment will somehow affect the school system, the assertion that the present system is not, from the internal standpoint, democratic seems to be justified. Either we come here upon some fixed and inherent limitation of the democratic principle, or else we find in this fact an obvious discrepancy between the conduct of the school and the conduct of social life—a discrepancy so great as to demand immediate and persistent effort at reform.

Unfortunately, those who have noted this undemocratic condition of affairs, and who have striven to change it, have, as a rule, conceived of but one remedy, namely the transfer of authority to the school superintendent. In their zeal to place the center of gravity inside the school system, in their zeal to decrease the prerogatives of a non-expert school board, and to lessen the opportunities for corruption and private pull which go with that, they have tried to remedy one of the evils of

211. John Dewey, "Democracy in Education," *The Elementary School Teacher,* 4:195–197, December 1903.

democracy by adopting the principle of autocracy. For no matter how wise, expert, or benevolent the head of the school system, the one-man principle is autocracy.

The logic of the argument goes farther, very much farther, than the reformer of this type sees. The logic which commits him to the idea that the management of the school system must be in the hands of an expert commits him also to the idea that every member of the school system, from the first-grade teacher to the principal of the high school, must have some share in the exercise of educational power. The remedy is not to have one expert dictating educational methods and subject-matter to a body of passive, recipient teachers, but the adoption of intellectual initiative, discussion, and decision throughout the entire school corps. The remedy of the partial evils of democracy, the implication of the school system in municipal politics, is an appeal to a more thoroughgoing democracy.

The dictation, in theory at least, of the subject-matter to be taught, to the teacher who is to engage in the actual work of instruction, and frequently under the name of close supervision, the attempt to determine the methods which are to be used in teaching, mean nothing more or less than the deliberate restriction of intelligence, the imprisoning of the spirit. . .

*   *   *

I know it will be said that this state of things, while an evil, is a necessary one; that without it confusion and chaos would reign; that such regulations are the inevitable accompaniments of any graded system. It is said that the average teacher is incompetent to take any part in laying out the course of study or in initiating methods of instruction or discipline. Is not this the type of argument which has been used from time immemorial, and in every department of life, against the advance of democracy? What does democracy mean save that the individual is to have a share in determining the conditions and the aims of his own work; and that, upon the whole, through the free and mutual harmonizing of different individuals, the work of the world is better done than when planned, arranged, and directed by a few, no matter how wise or of how good intent that few? . . .

212. Democracy Through Consent, Not Coercion

The education of the whole people, in a republican government, can never be attained without the consent of the whole people. Com-

212. Horace Mann, in Paul Monroe, *Founding of the American Public School System* (New York: The Macmillan Company, 1940), p. 247.

pulsion, even if it were desirable, is not an available instrument. Enlightenment, not coercion, is our resource. The nature of education must be explained. The whole mass of men must be instructed in regard to its comprehension and enduring interests. We can not drive our people up a dark avenue, even though it be the right one; but we must hang the starry lights of knowledge about it, and show them not only the directness of its course to the goal of prosperity and honor, but the beauty of the way that leads to it.

10

Education and the Production and Ownership of Wealth

Problems in the Philosophy of Education Discussed in this Section

1. How is educational opportunity related to the standard of living? Could there be overproduction in education as well as in industry?
2. How are educational values conditioned by the way a person earns his living? Can we account in this manner for the difference in prestige value between cultural and vocational education?
3. Should the school be a vestibule to production and job placement? Or should agricultural and industrial activities be the means of getting an education?
4. When does *work* become *toil* or *drudgery*? When is it an engrossing occupation? How can the school capitalize on the difference?
5. What is the educational counterpart of an economic system advocating free competition for profits? How does this system condition school morality? What would be the educational consequences of an economic system where production is collectivized for use rather than individualized for profits?
6. Is the profit motive a safe guide to the selection of educational material in the movies and the press and on the radio? Should the school accept from commercial agencies free educational materials that include a certain amount of advertising?
7. Should teachers' salaries depend on the supply and demand of teachers, or on a "just" wage? Is a single salary schedule just? Are teachers ever the victims of exploitation?
8. On what theory is it justifiable to take the private wealth of one person to educate the child of another who is propertyless?

213. Social Infancy

The meaning of infancy is . . . economic leisure—freedom from the responsibilities of food-getting and self-support—and organic plasticity.

213. William C. Bagley, *The Educative Process* (New York: The Macmillan Company, 1905), p. 31.

Curiously enough, the Greek equivalent of the English word "school"
—*schole*—also means leisure. Because the child *must* be supported by
the labor of others during this period, he can utilize his time and
energy for remote rather than immediate ends; he can store up experiences for future years . . .

214. How Education Affects Economic Life

The prosperity and welfare of the laborer in modern industrial society is primarily dependent upon his money or nominal wages, which
in turn depend upon the relative supply of labor and of the other
factors of production. The supply of the other factors indicates the
demand for labor. If the number of workers is small relative to the
amount of available land, capital, and enterprise, wages will be high;
otherwise they will be low. Welfare demands that wages be high,
and, therefore, that the supply of land, capital, and enterprise be as
great as possible.

Education can do but little to increase the total amount of actual
land area in the world. Education has done much and can do more
to increase the amount of land available for agriculture and other
purposes. The draining of areas too wet for use, the "dry farming" and
irrigation of semi-arid and arid regions, and the adaptation of crops
to unclaimed lands, whatever their nature, are all examples of what
education can do in reclaiming waste land. To the extent the schools
assist in thus increasing the amount of usable land, they are playing
a part in raising the wages of labor.

Concerning the supply of capital and its increase, education can
do much more than in the case of land. The schools are doing much
and could do more in cultivating habits of thrift and restraint. Increased savings made available for investors means a lower interest
rate, the encouragement of enterprise, a consequent increase in the
demand for labor, and hence, higher wages. An essential element in
thrift is habits of industry without which, of course, little would be
available for saving. A pressing need in the schools and the home
is more attention to the matter of cultivating habits of industry. Industry, in turn, is unarmed without efficiency. Education, therefore, by
promoting technical efficiency, by cultivating habits of industry, of
rational spending, and of saving, and by stimulating invention, can do
much to increase the total supply of capital goods, which means higher
pay for labor.

214. J. Frank Day, "Education and Labor's Reward," *Journal of Educational
Sociology*, 4:626–629, June 1931.

Of course, capital is of no avail if not used. Putting capital to use is called investment and is the function of the entrepreneur. Useless is capital without enterprise, and feeble is enterprise without capital. The two are correlatives, each stimulating the supply and functioning of the other. What education can do directly to increase enterprise may be indicated in a few words. First, much might be done to stimulate the birth rate on the higher intellectual levels. Secondly, youth with money and brains or merely with brains could be encouraged and trained for industrial service and leadership. America has been more fortunate than have the older countries in attracting men of high ability into business service. However, much yet remains to be done in showing that opportunity for real social service exists as fully in the industrial field as in the so-called higher professions, and in stimulating the attitude not only among potential and actual entrepreneurs but also among the population generally that business and industrial service is worthy of the highest ability, and in demonstrating that fair profits are incidentally necessary yet subordinate to that service.

The supply of labor can also be considerably influenced by education. In the interest of welfare in general and of high wages in particular, the supply of labor ought to be increased on the higher levels and decreased on the lower levels. The duties, opportunities, and social responsibility of parenthood taught to all levels will have the desired effects of stimulating the birth rate among those whose ability and income qualify them properly to take care of a family and of repressing the birth rate among others with less ability and income. Any training or instruction that has the effect of raising the standard of living will result in the postponement of marriage and fewer children. Education ought, therefore, to be especially concerned with rationalizing the standard of living among those whose standard is already sufficiently high quantitatively, and with stimulating a higher standard among the poorer classes.

* * *

Industry works primarily upon goods; education works primarily upon users; neither industry nor education should, however, neglect the primary function of the other. An education resulting in mere technical efficiency in producing goods thought of as yards and pounds with little ability to find enjoyment or benefit in their use not only starves the souls of the workers by giving a one-course intellectual diet, but greatly limits the product of their subsequent labor measured in terms of utility. Such an education misses its primary function. The ultimate end of education is persons, all of whom should be workers. Uppermost in the minds of school administrators and teachers ought to be the producers and consumers. Organic income, both subjective and objective, may be derived from production as well as from consumption activities, in work as well as in leisure. To promote enjoyment and benefit in both labor activities and utilizing activities ought to be the primary economic aim in education.

215. Education and Economic Bounty

Nature has distributed resources very unequally over the earth. Owing to the whims of the gods of biology, geology, climatology, hydrology, and other natural realms, some countries received few resources; others were richly endowed. The United States was more liberally endowed than any other country on earth, and hence we have become richer than any other nation, possess the highest standard of living, use more luxury goods than all other nations put together, and transact one-half of the world's business.

Most Americans, including many educators, have attributed this to the profitableness of democracy and to the superiority of the "American way." They have assured us that all we have to do is to hold fast to the "American way," and we will continue to enjoy these things. Democracy is pleasant, but it so happens that it is usually not particularly profitable. We may preserve and hold fast to the "American way" forever, but this will not in itself perpetuate our prosperity. The two are simply not related to each other. Iceland is a wonderful country with unusually able people living under a democracy better than our own. It can never be rich, populous, nor important; its resources are too slim. In one-fourth the national lifetime of Iceland, the less democratic United States has become the wealthiest nation on earth. This is true for the same reason that if one has wood, iron, copper, gypsum, and cement materials he can build a house; but if one does not have these, he cannot. If one once had resources, but has used them up in building a house or has wasted them, he cannot build another, nor can he sell products and buy the materials for one. If a people have resources they can build an opulent social order; if they waste their substance they cannot maintain or replace that social order. Nor can they, without resources, secure them through foreign trade. Even *ersatz* commodities require basic source materials.

Why has not this dependence of society upon resources been made the center of popular attention, or received educational emphasis? The answer would seem to be twofold. First, the student of social

215. George T. Renner, "Education and the Conservation of Resources," *The Social Frontier*, 5:203–205, April 1939.

science has been engrossed by the study of institutions and ideologies in society to the extent of overlooking the fact that the whole structure is made from natural resources. A Rockefeller church in New York is only the profits from vast oil fields, just as a European cathedral is the sum total of the sous or kopecks wrung from the cabbage, potato, and beet fields of the peasantry. A Carnegie library in Cleveland represents the profitable combination of Pennsylvania coal and Minnesota iron ore. A great university in Seattle is the distillate of fish, saw logs, Yakima apples, and Palouse wheat. But little attention has been paid to these facts. Second, the original resources of our continent were so abundant as to stagger the imagination. The early settlers quickly evaluated these as inexhaustible and let the matter go at that. Ten generations of Americans have continued to regard their resources as so essentially limitless as to merit no attention. But they are not limitless—a fact which is fraught with considerable significance . . .

✦   ✦   ✦

It is commonly believed that if we use up certain materials, the scientists and inventors will provide new substances. Almost universally this is regarded as an axiomatic truth by all ranks of men from unskilled laborers to university students. It is suggestive to note that while the layman thus puts his trust in the bounty of science, the scientist himself has no such conviction. Instead, he will probably point out that such a belief is perhaps the greatest single hindrance to the conservation movement today.

Science has substituted kerosene for whale oil, and steel for many uses of wood, but this means only substituting exhaustible and irreplaceable materials for replaceable ones . . .

216. Education above the Bare Subsistence Level

If opportunity alone were enough, hereditary wealth, which vastly enlarges opportunity, ought to increase intellectual productiveness. There ought to be no place "where wealth accumulates and men decay." But there is too much truth in the common belief that abundant means usually lessens the output of creative work; and even Shakespeare, when rich enough to retire as a country gentleman, wrote no more. The mere opportunity for self-development, and for the free exercise of one's faculties, the mere desire for self-expression, are

216. A. Lawrence Lowell, *At War with Academic Traditions in America* (Cambridge, Mass.: Harvard University Press, 1934), p. 51. Reprinted by permission of the publishers.

not enough with most men to bring out all their latent powers. This is because in civilized life we are seeking to foster an activity far above the normal; we are striving to evoke a mental energy much greater than that required for a bare subsistence, and unless education can effect this it is a failure. In addition to opportunity, there must be a stimulus of some kind.

217. Education for Consumption as Well as Production

I need not labor the point that we are moving toward a social ethics in which the fundamental categories will be leisure rather than work, consumption, not production, expenditure, not saving. The machine civilization we are approaching cannot operate at all on any other bases. No longer can it be said—if a man will not work neither shall he eat. Today, many a man who does not work is more assured of eating than many who do. The capture of the tools, the materials, and the products of work by the large owner has completely destroyed the old concepts. And whether this ownership be continued or be changed, the fact of machine production, with its assurance of adequate products with relatively little labor, overthrows completely the old ideas of economic employment. This is not a radical social theory. It is a rapidly emerging fact to which the schools can no longer remain blind. Education has been becoming increasingly vocational in late years— motivated by the economic advantage of the individual, on the one hand, and concerned with meeting the conditions of employment set up by business and industry, on the other. For the masses of the people who will not require technical preparation for the professions, economic advantage through education will have less and less significance as their leisure increases. Even now, vast numbers have been long without employment and, because of their education, without occupation. Some of these have lost jobs once held and others have never had a job. A large proportion of the former will never work again, and as our schools pour forth their annual flood of new workers, these will be compelled to face the fact that they have been trained in thought and attitude for what can never be and have not been trained for what must be. The focus of education must shift to meet this condition but it must needs shift gladly and with a shout, for now at last may educa-

217. Hugh Hartshorne, "Character Education and School Administration," in C. M. Hill (ed.), *Educational Progress and School Administration* (New Haven, Conn.: Yale University Press, 1936), pp. 326–327.

tion, emancipated from the pressure to produce workers only, legitimately expand its program so as to develop the creative capacities
of the pupils for the free use of abundant leisure. Art, music, dancing,
handicraft, homemaking, and social science are no longer frills and
fads, but central in the curriculum of the school of tomorrow. We
shall educate not for work primarily, though this we shall not neglect,
but for play. For free creative play—the use of one's abilities in the
production of beauty, and the quest for knowledge and the untrammeled pursuit of the good—this is our main job as human beings. And
to learn how to spend ourselves in the remaking of our world into a
realm of beauty and an instrument of happiness to all is the great
task which now confronts us.

218. Education as Human Investment

. . . I should like, . . . with no ambition to be memorable, to deal
with the relation of education to economic and social change.

The problem begins with the curious and complex duality of the
role of man. Man is a goal—an end himself. We need look no further
for justification for his intellectual development or his intellectual
adventure. It is for these, or such as these, that he lives. A great many
intellectuals, including many educators, have declined to look further
for a rationale. If the ultimate purpose of education is agreed, why
search for a lesser one?

Yet there is a more vulgar view of man, and it is idle to deny its
hold. This regards him as an instrument of production—as a converter
of energy, or as a servomechanism, or in a more dignified role as a
directing force in productive activity. If the society sets great store
by production, as ours so obviously does, then it will set great store
by man as an agent of production. And this our society does. We are
not at all tolerant of the individual or group whose pursuit of happiness
brings him or them into conflict with production. We have no praise
for the idle or easygoing workman and certainly none for the feather-
bedding union.

❊   ❊   ❊

To say that investment in people has yet to establish itself in
comparison with investment in material capital would be a remark-

218. John K. Galbraith, "Social Balance" in *Current Issues in Higher Education*, 1959, Association for Higher Education (Washington, D.C.: National Education Association, 1959), pp. 45–48.

able understatement. For ages, the road company philosophers have been making the point that people are just as important in their own way as things—and just as worthy as objects of expenditure. And the poets in their audience have been nodding their agreement. The operative consequences have been remarkably slight. On weekdays wealth is still measured by physical capital and progress by the additions thereto.

Part of this can be attributed to the force of tradition. Part must again be credited to our old friend the practical man. That which is inconsistent with established belief is not only untrue but vaguely foolish. And you can see capital and you can't see learning. Only the impractical theorist reacts to what he cannot see.

Investment in human capital as opposed to material capital has also been damaged, I think, by the fact that the material calculation is not the only and not the primary justification. Man, to repeat, is an end in himself. We eat for the purposes of improving our productive efficiency. But with even more enthusiasm, we eat to avoid hunger and enjoy the food. Education increases our productivity. It is also a nourishing alternative to ignorance which, like food, has its own enjoyments and rewards. Like food, it is not only an aid to production but a prime object of consumption.

But the very attitudes which caused us to set such store by capital cause us also to accord an inferior role to consumption. It is by saving —refraining from consumption—that the capital stock is increased. Anything that interferes with saving is inferior. Expenditures on education, because they are consumption, get in the way of the higher claims of saving and capital investment.

And let no one suppose for a moment that this is a theoretical argument without operative content. Outlays for education are regularly opposed on the grounds that the community cannot afford them. Even more explicitly, it is said that the high taxes interfere with saving and investment and thus with enterprise and economic health. Education is agreeable and even worthy, but it is not a utilitarian or productive employment of resources. The taxes for the new high school, a consumption good, may cost the community a new brewery which is a capital good. This is a horrendous prospect, so the community must proceed warily. Those who speak for education have rightly and, I think, wisely insisted that education is both a means and an end. But this has handicapped them in arguing what is ordinarily a superior case on purely economic criteria.

I come now to the final problem in asserting the economic claims of education. It is the most serious. And were I writing a memorable paper, I might even claim that it is the one that will eventually ruin us.

This concerns the profound structural difference in our type of economy between the machinery which provides for material investment and that which provides for investment in human beings. In a private capitalist or market economy, the provision for investment in material capital is integral to the system. When there is a prospect for gain from a particular capital outlay—when the marginal return from an investment exceeds the going return on savings—the investment proceeds more or less automatically. No public decision is ordinarily required. It is not necessary to arrange a specific transfer of funds from some other employment. A very large part of modern investment occurs within the business firm. The latter has a ready-made supply of investment funds from its own earnings.

In contrast, investment in human beings is very largely undertaken by the state. And quite a bit of the remainder is in the domain of private conscience and charity. The return to the investment accrues partly to the individual and partly to the community. It is not, as in the case of a public utility, something on which the investor can levy a claim. Hence support for this investment is dependent on a decision to transfer funds from other uses. If there is an increased need for investment in people or an increased opportunity, there is no automatic process by which it will be recognized or exploited. The need or opportunity must be seen and then a decision must be taken to raise and apply public revenues to the purpose.

We should expect serious faults in machinery so designed. Since the estimate of return from investment in people, unlike the estimate of return in investment in capital, is almost completely subjective, we should expect, or anyhow fear, serious underestimation. The diversion of revenues from other purposes raises the question of who is to supply them. It is also entangled with the question of using taxes to promote greater equality. This would lead us to expect that underestimation would be coupled with underappropriation. And let me remind you that the criterion here is a strictly economic one. The test is whether we are keeping a parity of investment as between people and material capital.

This is a problem that Socialist-Communist countries do not have. In the nature of their organization, resources are in the public sector. They have, I would imagine, grave problems of education but they do not have this problem of subtraction and transfer . . . I do not have in mind the combination of prayer, incantation and higher interest rates on which the present administration relies. . . .

219. Educational Consequences of Two Conceptions of Industry

Let me now point out some of the particular educational differences which will be made according as one or other idea of industry in education prevails. In the first place, as to administration, those who wish, whether they wish it knowingly or unknowingly, an education which will enable employees to fit better into the existing economic scheme will strive for a dual or divided system of administration. That is to say, they will attempt to have a separate system of funds, of supervisory authorities, and, as far as possible, of schools to carry on industrial education. If they don't go so far as this, they will at least constantly harp on the difference between a liberal or cultural and a money-earning education, and will endeavor to narrow the latter down to those forms of industrial skill which will enable the future workers to fall docilely into the subodinate ranks of the industrial army.

In the second place, the conception that the primary object of industrial education is merely to prepare more skilled workers for the present system, instead of developing human beings who are equipped to reconstruct that scheme, will strive to identify it with trade education—that is, with training for certain specific callings. It assumes that the needs of industrial education are met if girls are trained to be skilled in millinery, cooking and garment-making, and boys to be plumbers, electric wirers, etc. . . .

In the third place, the curriculum on this narrow trade plan will neglect as useless for its ends the topics in history and civics which make future workers aware of their rightful claims as citizens in a democracy, alert to the fact that the present economic struggle is but the present-day phase taken by the age-long battle for human liberties. So far as it takes in civic and social studies at all, it will emphasize those things which emphasize duties to the established order and a blind patriotism which accounts it a great privilege to defend things in which the workers themselves have little or no share. The studies which fit the individual for the reasonable enjoyment of leisure time, which develop good taste in reading and appreciation of the arts, will be passed over as good for those who belong by wealth to the leisure class, but quite useless in the training of skilled employees.

219. John Dewey, "Learning to Earn," *School and Society*, 5:333–334, March 1917.

In the fourth place, so far as the method and spirit of its work is concerned, it will emphasize all that is most routine and automatic in our present system. Drill to secure skill in the performance of tasks under the direction of others will be its chief reliance. It will insist that the limits of time and pressure for immediate results are so great that there is no room for understanding the scientific facts and principles or the social bearings of what is done. Such an enlarged education would develop personal intelligence and thereby develop also an intellectual ambition and initiative which might be fatal to contentment in routine subordinate clerical and shop jobs.

Finally, so far as such a training concerns itself with what is called vocational guidance, it will conceive guidance as a method of placement —a method of finding jobs. It will measure its achievements by the number of children taking out working papers for whom it succeeds in finding places, instead of by the number whom it succeeds in keeping in school till they become equipped to seek and find their own congenial occupations.

The other idea of industrial education aims at preparing every individual to render service of a useful sort to the community, while at the same time it equips him to secure by his own initiative whatever place his natural capacities fit him for. It will proceed in an opposite way in every respect. Instead of trying to split schools into two kinds, one of a trade type for children whom it is assumed are to be employees and one of a liberal type for the children of the well-to-do, it will aim at such a reorganization of existing schools as will give all pupils a genuine respect for useful work, an ability to render service, and a contempt for social parasites whether they are called tramps or leaders of "society." Instead of assuming that the problem is to add vocational training to an existing cultural elementary education, it will recognize frankly that the traditional elementary education is largely vocational, but that the vocations which it has in mind are too exclusively clerical, and too much of a kind which implies merely ability to take positions in which to carry out the plans of others. It will indeed make much of developing motor and manual skill, but not of a routine or automatic type. It will rather utilize active and manual pursuits as the means of developing constructive, inventive and creative power of mind. It will select the materials and the technique of the trades not for the sake of producing skilled workers for hire in definite trades, but for the sake of securing industrial intelligence—a knowledge of the conditions and processes of present manufacturing, transportation and commerce so that the individual may be able to make his own choices and his own adjustments, and be master, so far as in him lies, of his own economic fate. It will be recognized that, for this purpose, a broad acquaintance with science and skill in the laboratory control of materials and processes is more important than skill in trade operations. It will remember that the future employee is a consumer as well as a producer, that the whole tendency of society, so far as it is intelligent and wholesome, is to an increase of the hours of leisure, and that an education which does nothing to enable individuals to consume wisely and to utilize leisure wisely is a fraud on democracy. So far as method is concerned, such a conception of industrial education will prize freedom more than docility; initiative more than automatic skills; insight and understanding more than capacity to recite lessons or to execute tasks under the direction of others.

220. Opportunity and the Point of Diminishing Returns

There are certain tests, however, which may be used in discovering whether a nation is approaching the point of diminishing returns in extending educational opportunity, so far as its economic effects are concerned.

One test would be the development of a situation where additional schooling would no longer tend to reduce extremes in income. This would mean that differences in incomes of workers were due to differences in capacity and diligence, rather than to differences in educational opportunity. When all persons are given the same opportunity to obtain the schooling and training essential to occupational efficiency, then differences in earnings are not accentuated by unequal opportunity. Under conditions existing in the United States at present equal educational opportunity does not exist. All persons do not have the same opportunity to capitalize their talents. Therefore we should continue to expand educational opportunity until differences in earnings of individuals due to the factor of scarcity of workers in certain callings, except as this scarcity is an outcome of differences in capacity and diligence, have been greatly modified. One role of education in a democracy is to remove factors, other than those named above, which result in differences in income.

220. Educational Policies Commission, *Education and Economic Well-Being in American Democracy* (Washington, D. C.: National Education Association, 1940), p. 114.

221. Education Under Individualistic and Collectivistic Economies

What are the old and now discredited principles and forces?

The economic life has thus far been built around the profit motive. Production takes place in the hope of securing a profit and only when this hope is realized. Now it may be true that profits indicate social approval. Yet it cannot be claimed that profits are a correct measure of social usefulness. But the individual is not concerned with this. His sole aim is profits and thus the entire economic life has been built with isolated individual interests at the center.

This economic importance of the individual, recognized and protected by law, was rationalized by the theory that the welfare and success of the individual would ultimately result in the greatest benefit to society. This theory, based upon a deep faith in the efficient and automatic operation of natural forces, therefore placed man, the individual, in the center of the stage. Private initiative, rugged individualism, free and effective competition, these were the catchwords of our economic thinking. To give stability to this structure, the laws were drawn to protect, above all, the rights of the individual. The unquestioned right to freedom of activity, except when obvious and unreasonable or unfair injury to others resulted from this activity, was guaranteed by constitutions and statutes.

Translated into political terms, this high value placed upon the individual formed the basis of our democratic institutions. Selected by the simple process of counting hands, those who were to lead the nations and to direct their policies were drawn from the mass and entrusted with powers requiring great knowledge and insight. And public faith rested entirely upon the assumption that anyone once given the opportunity could readily acquire such knowledge and vision.

Education in its content and method reflects these principles.

More and more, education has become subjective. To develop to the utmost the individual—to allow the greatest freedom of self expression—has become the ideal, and educational method has been adjusted to this ideal. Not outside authority, not objective necessity, but the individual's interests and desires are given greatest weight. Pupil

221. J. Anton De Haas, "Economic Nationalism and Education," *Harvard Teachers Record*, 4:64–69, April 1934.

initiative, not teacher planning, freedom of choice rather than adult needs, more and more control the learning process.

*   *   *

Out of the old, the new is born.

What world, economic and cultural, will be built by those nations which have turned away from the old? The new economic nationalism calls for a national life run along more efficient lines, directed not by amateurs, but by experts, and motivated not by the profits to be secured by individuals, but by social needs, by the welfare of the national group.

*   *   *

If the profit motive is no longer to be regarded as the reliable guide for economic action, a new guide must be substituted. No longer self-seeking, but social usefulness becomes the criterion. But this means that some authority other than the individual must be established to determine the social usefulness of his activities. Now in principle it makes little difference whether this authority is the authority of an absolute ruler or dictator or whether it is constituted by the cooperative machinery of the group to which the individual belongs. In both cases an authority outside the individual dictates and becomes the channel through which the social will expresses itself.

The new economic nationalism implies, therefore, a planned economy, and a planned economy is impossible unless we change our economic motives from self-seeking to social service. Private capital will find its justification in the contribution which it makes to social well-being. But this means that the individual is no longer monarch in his own domain. He produces, invests, sells, and buys, not in the process of experimentation and only in the hope of profits, but principally, if not entirely, according to the national plan. He will no longer build new skyscrapers which will make surrounding buildings obsolete before their time and will place additional traffic burdens upon an already over-taxed transportation system—the Empire State Building stands as the most impressive single monument of the old, a monument to the uncontrolled, undirected, antisocial profit motive.

The legal concepts will change accordingly. Already we can recognize in this country a willingness on the part of the courts to interpret the New Deal in its various legal forms in terms of the new concepts. In Germany and Italy where the process of reorganization is more advanced, we hear no more of the "rights of man," but a good deal about the "duties of man."

Obviously, we shall have to change our form of government. This does not mean that we shall have to abandon the democratic form of government altogether. But in the words of President Roosevelt, "The real truth of the matter is that for a number of years in our country the machinery of democracy had failed to function." The answer to this can only be a reorganization of our government and a method of selecting those who will direct its affairs, in which votes will not merely be counted, but weighed.

In the face of such fundamental changes in our economic, legal, and political concepts, the task of the educational system will be different from any thus far imposed. It will require an entirely different emphasis.

Now understand me well. I am not passing judgment. I am not advocating any economic or social system, neither am I presuming to advise you as to your duties as teachers. I am merely trying to examine current happenings and trends and to interpret them in my own way. In other words, I am just thinking aloud—I am not outlining a program. It seems to me that, when preparing children to fit into the new world, we shall have to reexamine our old principles. And I should not be surprised if we discovered that the emphasis upon the developing of personality does not seem to fit into the picture.

The subjective approach to education was perhaps justified when the world was a free-for-all arena in which almost limitless opportunities for self-expression in terms of economic activity existed. The new world will have an entirely new set of rules. If not one's personal wishes and desires, but one's duty to society becomes the ruling motive, then society will demand that the schools prepare the pupils primarily for coordinated activity within the national group. The first demand will be to have the children taught to work systematically, conscientiously and accurately in the face of the desire to do something else.

Not child interest but social necessity will rule. There are certain fundamental activities which must be performed—each requiring certain readily determined bits of mental equipment. It shall be the function of the schools to give this equipment. In this program it will be necessary first of all to determine to whom and to how many certain specific training will be given, and then how this training may be most effectively imparted.

The children will have to discover that there is a difference between work and play. Schools built primarily and even exclusively upon pupil initiative and interest and upon the development of personality may well come to be regarded in years to come as the Empire State Buildings of education.

※ ※ ※

The practical reason why the demand for a planned national economy has arisen is that the period of unlimited economic expansion is probably at an end. The geographic frontiers are gone, but so are probably most of the industrial frontiers. We may expect new inventions, but in all probability the changes to come will be largely in the nature of learning to do better things we are already doing. We have conquered the air, have annihilated distance, we may build faster autos, and of different design, but we already possess means of mechanical locomotion.

Our system of education thus far has assumed the existence of unlimited and ever-expanding possibilities, and the potential capacity of each individual to reach the top. We are now discovering that there is little if any room at the top—that most of the room is at the bottom of the social scale. We have thus far interpreted equality of opportunity to mean opportunities for all, and have thus made a fetish of giving educational opportunities to the largest possible number. Like the bulbous growth of business in our period of so-called prosperity, the inflated numbers in our institutions of learning have been regarded as the surest indication of the nation's greatness. But we can't all be lawyers or doctors, we can't all hold whitecollar jobs, and in a society in which men are valued not for their acquisitive abilities, but for their contribution to the common welfare, a good carpenter will be as much respected as a good bookkeeper.

If we have had uncontrolled overproduction in industry, education has no less been lacking in self-restraint. More and more copying the methods of big business, our educational system is similarly infected with the virus of mass production and overburdened with administrative overhead, until many of our universities are no longer free companies of scholars, but high-pressure factories of learning, under the autocratic rule of super-executives. We have sought salvation in system and in greater and greater output.

If social usefulness becomes the criterion of capital and labor alike, labor, work of all kinds, acquires new dignity and meaning. No work is shameful except slipshod work, and no educational system is socially useful which, through undirected mass production, fills the ranks of one group of occupations to overflowing, while unfitting the children for the making of a social contribution in less spectacular pursuits.

In the new world self-discipline, or discipline enforced from the outside, will restrain business activity within socially profitable limits. Education will be similarly put under restraint.

It will probably express itself in a much greater differentiation in training than we have thus far known. It will probably mean a very careful selection of candidates for various pursuits, while admission to the training for the various occupations will be largely controlled on the basis of nation-wide employment statistics . . .

222. The "Get-by" Attitude in School

Another tendency of American education will need correction if the schools are adequately to aid society in its adjustment to the machine-slave civilization. The "profit motive" will, of necessity, be greatly modified, and the present is a good time to re-emphasize ideals of fine workmanship as a driving force in human achievement. It happens, however, that both educational theory and school practice in this country have increasingly belittled this ideal during the past two decades. Our dominant educational theory is based upon the philosophy of pragmatism. What works passing well is not necessarily good but what works well enough is good enough. The "get-by" attitude is distinctly encouraged in many American schools. How good should a pupil's handwriting be? As good as he can make it? By no means. It should be good enough to "get by," that is to meet a standard on one of the handwriting "scales"—a standard that is recognized as "good enough" for most people. It is difficult to conceive of an attitude more fatal to ideals of fine workmanship than that which is developed in the practical implications of such a theory when spread over from eight to sixteen of the most impressionable years of life.

223. Competitive and Socialized Schoolroom Morality

The mere absorption of facts and truths is so exclusively individual an affair that it tends very naturally to pass into selfishness. There is no obvious social motive for the acquirement of mere learning, there is no clear social gain in success thereat. Indeed, almost the only measure for success is a competitive one, in the bad sense of that term—a comparison of results in the recitation or in the examination to see which child has succeeded in getting ahead of others in storing up, in accumulating the maximum of information. So thoroughly is this the prevalent atmosphere that for one child to help another in his task

222. William C. Bagley, *Education and Emergent Man* (New York: The Ronald Press Company, copyright 1934), pp. 171–172.
223. John Dewey, *The School and Society* (Chicago: The University of Chicago Press, 1900), pp. 29–30.

has become a school crime. Where the school work consists in simply learning lessons, mutual assistance, instead of being the most natural form of cooperation and association, becomes a clandestine effort to relieve one's neighbor of his proper duties. Where active work is going on all this is changed. Helping others, instead of being a form of charity which impoverishes the recipient, is simply an aid in setting free the powers and furthering the impulse of the one helped. A spirit of free communication, of interchange of ideas, suggestions, results, both successes and failures of previous experiences, becomes the dominating note of the recitation. So far as emulation enters in, it is in the comparison of individuals, not with regard to the quantity of information personally absorbed, but with reference to the quality of work done—the genuine community standard of value. In an informal but all the more pervasive way, the school life organizes itself on a social basis.

224. Educational Options for Humanizing Industry

In times past a conflict in the experience of the common man has usually existed between the economic and the intellectual and moral life. The gaining of a livelihood has been regarded as having nothing in common with the more humane interests of mankind. Work has been looked upon as evil, as something to be escaped, as always involving drudgery and the negation of freedom and spontaneity. The unfavorable connotation which this short word carries is clearly suggested by the fact that the three words offered by Webster as synonyms of *work* are *labor, toil,* and *drudgery.*

This attitude toward work goes far back into antiquity. In the third chapter of the first book of the Hebrew sacred scripture it finds perfect expression. "In the sweat of thy face shalt thou eat bread"; so runs the ancient curse laid upon man as he was driven from paradise. Here is a most interesting and illuminating effort on the part of man to account for the fact that work is well-nigh universally a disagreeable experience. The necessity of work is clearly looked upon as a great misfortune, that can be explained only in terms of divine wrath. It is regarded as punishment for some early transgression of the race. And interestingly enough one of the most powerful dogmas of the Christian Church postulates the return of a purified race to a

224. John C. Chapman and George S. Counts, *Principles of Education* (Boston: Houghton Mifflin Company, 1934), pp. 255–259. Used by permission of the publishers.

paradise from which all toil is banished, and in which the redeemed enjoy eternal rest. The hard conditions of life through which the race has passed, rather than any inherent quality of work, is reflected in this tradition. While the lot of the masses of the people has usually included much drudgery, many occupations in every age have furthered the growth of personality. These callings the privileged and fortunate classes have ever sought to monopolize for themselves and their children; and not improbably these favored groups have had much to do with the perpetuation, if not with the origin, of the tradition which they rigorously and even conscientiously apply to other classes, that man is condemned to degrading toil because of ancestral sins.

❀   ❀   ❀

For the purpose of meeting this situation two divergent proposals have appeared in the Great Society. The one we may style the doctrine of leisure, the other the doctrine of work. Those who adhere to the former doctrine are many and are found in positions of power and influence. Perhaps rationalizing their own desires that the present industrial system will remain substantially as it is, they assume that this tendency toward the degradation of labor is an inevitable consequence of mechanical invention, and suggest that the only salvation of the common man is to be found in shorter hours of labor and a compensating leisure life. They would deny to him the possibility of expressing himself in his work, but would be willing to pay him well for it. They would insist that he sell his birthright for a slightly gilded bowl of pottage. This view implies no fundamental social change, but recognizes as final the apparently inexorable logic of the industrial revolution.

The other doctrine would seek salvation through work rather than leisure, and consequently implies a radical reconstruction of the economic order. The champions of this view maintain that, if we care to give to the problem the time and energy and the heart and mind which are so freely given to the increase of profits, the economic life can be so reorganized as to foster the growth of personality. Their argument assumes the following form. In modern industry, with its inventions and its countless applications of science, this elevation of work is most easily possible. The very diversity of the economic life should make possible a cultivation of individual aptitude, capacity, and interest not conceivable in the past. In a more primitive age it would have been difficult to make of industry a great educational enterprise, for the foundations upon which it rested were little understood. In that day there was some basis in necessity for the interpretation given in the third chapter of Genesis, but the conditions of life to-day make possible a more humane philosophy of work. The situation is greatly changed. There is no longer need of continuing the cruel paradox of civilization that the very activities in which men engage for the purpose of maintaining physical existence must tend to impoverish the spiritual life. For such a condition there is small excuse, since through mechanical invention, so it is suggested, man can dominate nature and compel it to do the drudgery involved in the support of human life. The machine may be made the slave rather than the master of man.

Which solution must education champion? As to the relative merits of these two doctrines there is much dispute. That the second is the more attractive must be admitted. It should therefore be supported in so far as the native equipment of men makes it possible and the conditions of productive efficiency permit. In the field of industry the greatest educational task of this generation is that of so organizing our economic life that the area of conflict between the demands of productive efficiency and the personal growth of the worker will be reduced to the minimum. The existing economic order in its concern for profits has shown such a ruthless disregard for the lives of the workers that in the long run it would undermine its own foundations. That monotonous work, however, can be wholly eliminated from industry is probably an idle dream. By giving to each individual the knowledge underlying the process in which he is engaged, much that is now the most meaningless routine can be made significant; by rotation from task to task, where the work of industry has become minutely differentiated, the monotony may be relieved and the adaptability of the worker preserved; and by participation in the management of the enterprise the highly specialized operative can be given some feeling of his own worth and an opportunity to give expression to his creative and social impulses.' In a word, even the simplest of callings can be made to take on complexity and meaning to the degree that its relations to the rest of life are appreciated.

225. Educational Significance of Work

Industry is to-day our only real school of experience, drawing on the most potent motives of life for the learning and pursuing of the activities which constitute the industry. A large proportion of all the workers

225. Hugh Hartshorne, *Character in Human Relations* (New York: Charles Scribner's Sons, 1932), p. 288.

are minors in their most formative years. What are they learning in this school? The futility of effort, the discouragement of defeat, the cynicism which is bred by the hypocrisy of those in power, the hopelessness that foresees inevitable unemployment at forty or fifty, the indigence of dependence—the concrete attitudes which we lightly refer to as "social unrest." Is there no remedy for such a condition? There is one, and that is to recover for work its educational and cultural significance, stripping it of its sordid absorption in mere things and mere rewards, and so organizing it that children may have their happy place in it. This would mean slowing it down to the point where overproduction would not result from the employment of half the people half the time. And this in turn would mean the translation of profits into earnings. Better a technically less perfect industrial scheme than one which destroys itself because of its single-minded devotion to financial gain.

226. Work and Education Contrasted

. . . I hope I step on nobody's toes too hard when I say, as I must say, that therefore it is an absolute misuse of school to include any vocational training at all. School is a place of learning for the sake of learning, not for the sake of earning. It is as simple as that. Please understand that I do not mean vocational training can be totally dispensed with; I mean only that it should be done on the job. It should be done as preparatory to work; and as preparatory to work, it should be compensated. No one should have to take vocational training without compensation, because it is not self-rewarding. To include vocational training in school *without compensation* is to suppose that it is education, which it is not at all. In contrast to vocational training, liberal education is learning for its own sake or for the sake of further education. It is learning for the sake of all those self-rewarding activities which include the political, aesthetic, and speculative.

There are three further comments I should like to make on this distinction. First, professional education can be both vocational and liberal, because the kind of work for which it is the preliminary training is essentially liberal work. The work of a lawyer is liberal, not servile, work. In Greece free men who were citizens were all lawyers; there education for legal practice was liberal education. Professional

226. Mortimer J. Adler, "Labor, Leisure, and Liberal Education," *Journal of General Education*, 6:43, October-July, 1951.

education is vocational only in so far as this kind of leisure activity happens to be a way that some men, in our division of labor, earn their compensation.

Second, liberal education can involve work simply because we find it necessary to compel children to begin, and for some years to continue, their educations. Whenever you find an adult, a chronological adult, who thinks that learning or study is work, let me say that you have met a child. One sign that you are grown up, that you are no longer a child, is that you never regard any part of study or learning as work. As long as learning or study has anything compulsory about it, you are still in the condition of childhood. The mark of truly adult learning is that it is done with no thought of labor or work at all, with no sense of the compulsory. It is entirely voluntary. Liberal education at the adult level can, therefore, be superior to liberal education in school, where learning is identified with work.

Third, if schooling is equivalent to the proper use of leisure time in youth, then the proper use of leisure time in adult life should obviously include the continuation of schooling—without teachers, without compulsion, without assignments . . .

227. The Christian Role of Work in Education

To see how technical culture fits into a scheme of general liberal education one must draw together various insights. For if Marx's sweeping philosophy of labor suggests that work life is entitled to academic representation, Dewey has indicated the precise formality under which it is to be represented and the traditional humanists keep us from forgetting that it is a matter of proportionate representation. It is not now a question of vocational institutes and professional schools whose purposes unfold after or apart from the period of general schooling. It is rather a question of the role to be played by work experience in the development, not of the specialist, but of the normally mature —the liberally educated—man or woman. For if the demands of craftsmanship challenge any workman to reflect, plan, choose, and endure, then they too are liberalizing, for they nurture the uniquely human powers of thought and free choice.

✣   ✣   ✣

To begin with, the school has some concern for the students' selection of their future occupations, since it certainly has some influence

227. John W. Donohue, *Work and Education* (Chicago: Loyola University Press, 1959), pp. 204–209.

on that choice. It was once commonly claimed that the liberal college prepared for life, not for making a living. Yet the curriculum of this college did condition occupational choice, since it was understood to be the usual prerequisite for certain professional and managerial careers from which those who had not gone through this course were effectively barred. In any event, the high school and college cannot ignore a question which its students are actually deciding during the years they spend in these schools. Such decisions are clearly crucial. A man's entire personal history and even his achievement of greater or less moral stature may depend to a considerable extent upon the character of his experience at work. It will make a great deal of difference whether he realizes therein some success and the satisfaction of feeling himself contribute to the human heritage or whether he knows only boredom, frustration, and failure. Since the critical selection is often made in terms of the alternatives with which education has acquainted young people, the school has to do more than administer a few vocational-preference tests. Serious damage may result if schools not only fail to awaken students to the possibility of careers in science, technology, or the arts but actually render these careers forever beyond their reach because the academic program never acknowledges their existence. It is neither necessary nor possible for the high school to examine in detail all occupations. It should be possible, however, for it to instill an appreciation of work in its fullness and to suggest something of its enormous contemporary variety: the mechanical and fine arts, theoretical and applied science, the professions, business, and service occupations.

Such an education for work would ideally prepare for wise occupational choice by developing a philosophical and theological understanding of work itself. This wide view of technical enterprise might constitute a unit in long-established curricular divisions. In the secondary school, for instance, it could be inserted into the social sciences or religion classes. At the collegiate level it could find a point of departure in philosophy or theology. Since it is something of an interdisciplinary venture, the study of work might also be comfortably housed in a niche of its own. On the other hand, the idea of integration appears very logically when theology or philosophy are drawn into the problem of work or when the social studies are drawn upward to the point where wider vistas open. To be sure, a school disbarred by law or custom from developing the resources of religion could go only part of the way here.

This theoretical phase must also include some reflection on the current social questions touching labor. We know that there are still people who oppose the principles of free unionism, governmental safeguards against wide-open markets, more equitable distribution of the national income, and federal insistence upon worker insurance against the hazards of old age and unemployment. Yet these are measures which go a long way toward humanizing work for masses of people. A school will do a great deal if it helps young persons appreciate worthwhile social advance of this sort and prepares them to continue the work of social purification and progress.

This sort of education is doubtless rather glancing in the lower grades. It is struck off briefly in social studies and religion classes and reflected from the personal attitudes of the teacher. It is to the high school and college that one must look for a consistent and explicit treatment of those questions in history, sociology, ethics, and theology. This is a moment of theory which may be supplemented by firsthand observation of plants, farms, and offices as well as by readings and informed discussions. Not many novelties are needed, though, for this is also an emphasis which can be introduced into the existing academic regime without any sharp transformations.

The school's second contribution to a humanism of work lies in the area of practical, concrete experience. Somewhere in its program it should find place for education *through* work, for a savoring of the actual rewards of craftsmanship as an exercise of pragmatic intelligence and the source of special creative and social satisfactions. This would supplement the work education given by the family or compensate for its neglect. Its aim, as Dewey knew, is to exploit those cultural virtualities which industry in its mechanized stages is not easily prepared to do. Later on, the technical and professional schools can train marketable skills. But the shops and hobby clubs of our lower schools should have in view work simply as one moment and means of a child's intellectual and moral growth. It is not necessary, therefore, for these shops to match the equipment and procedures of contemporary industry. On the contrary, the specific pattern of technical culture can be better learned, perhaps, through making by hand products currently machine-produced. The detailed division of labor, so fruitful for mass output, is pointless when the workman's own development is the aim. In the school workshop, then, the students set their own goals and plan their own strategy so far as this is feasible. Then they carry the project faithfully through to completion as well and honestly as they can. Thus they will discover both the rewards and the price of this sort of work, this making of things *well*. In that discovery lies a humanistic benefit as young craftsmen learn, not only the character and possibilities of matter, but something also of their own human condition. They taste in their work the actuality both of its law and its joy.

Christian educators will not require work projects to carry so large a share of the task of character education as Dewey would commit to them. They will not make social situations and conflicts the actual generators of moral rules and values, nor will they explain social ethics in strictly pragmatic terms. At the same time, they know very well that there is a vast difference between the speculative grasp of the nature, norms, and content of the morally good life and that life actually possessed. Moral education has a necessary instructional moment, but it can no more stop there than building can stop at the drawing board. The moment of practice must follow if ethical principles are to be transmuted into living fonts of action and if behavior is to correspond with belief. Aristotle and St. Thomas did not agree with Plato that virtue could be taught in the strict sense of the word. In the geometry class, indeed, the student is "taught" when he is brought to see for himself that two parallel lines never meet in an Euclidean universe. When he understands as much, the specific work of the teacher is done, for the student is, in this respect, a "geometer." The teacher can also conduct the same pupil to a theoretical appreciation of the meaning, necessity, and beauty of truthfulness, but that does not insure his being honest. When speaking of moral training, therefore, St. Thomas did not use *docere* (to teach) but, making a significant change of verbs, remarked that the child should be accustomed, *assuescere*, to acting virtuously; should be taught, as it were, through the practice of personal action. A great deal of such ethical action, however, is altruistic and is unfolded in interpersonal relationships. It is quite true, therefore, that work projects during or after school or school-sponsored in the community can offer splendid opportunities for young people to discover those values of fraternity, generosity, and cooperation which are elsewhere taught rather abstractly.

228. Labor as the Core of the Communist School

In the case of the Soviet Republic . . . the question of enlisting the widest masses of the people in the work of cultural and economic construction is a question of life and death. Consequently before leaving school the child must receive a clear understanding, in theory and practice, of how to build a state for those who labor. "The unified school therefore places the labor of the people at the center of its attention. This basic theme penetrates the program of the school in all of its stages, and the approach to labor is not from the point of

228. Albert P. Pinkevitch, *The New Education in the Soviet Republic* (New York: John Day Company, 1929), pp. 152–155.

view of a specialist but rather from the point of view of a builder of a new life who regardless of his profession must have a clear comprehension of the relations and interdependences of the various forms of labor. Such a comprehension we call general education."

＊   ＊   ＊

The reader should be reminded at this point of the tremendous social and political role of labor in the school. To us this labor does not mean "labor processes," nor "self-service," nor "school workshops," but the central axis of the entire school. As long as labor is looked upon as something utilitarian or valuable from the point of view of motor training we shall not have a school which merits the name of socialistic or communistic. Our pupil must feel himself a member of and a worker in a laboring society; and the attainment of this result marks the first step toward an understanding of the interests of the proletariat and of the mutual struggle for the social revolution. Some four or five hours a week in a manual training class will achieve nothing in this direction. What is needed is an ideological concentration about this axis, an organic integraton of labor with the scientific, artistic, and social work of the school. Corresponding organizational norms are also necessary to the fulfillment of the given aim . . .

229. Capitalist and Communist Motivation

Perhaps the most striking difference between education in capitalistic America and the Soviet Union is in *objective*. In general, American education tends to train for individual achievement usually in the business world, and the acquisition of wealth is lauded as a high achievement. In the Soviet Union education trains for collective achievement on behalf of group welfare. Individual business achievement for private gain and the acquisition of wealth is considered to be almost on a par with theft. The aim is the development of socially minded human beings in accordance with Communist ideology.

230. Ghandi's Craft Centered Education

According to Gandhiji, the creative element in work can be properly utilized to educate man to grow to the full stature he is capable of.

229. Jerome Davis, "Education under Communism Contrasted with that under Capitalism," *Journal of Educational Sociology*, 9:166, November 1935.
230. M. S. Patel, *The Educational Philosophy of Mahatma Gandhi* (Ahmendabad: Navajivan Publishing House, 1953), pp. 195–196.

Here we have the roots of Gandhiji's craft-centered education, which "aims at harnessing the educative possibilities of man's normal activities to satisfy his everyday needs to the chariot of progress from the cradle to the grave."

The difference between Gandhiji and his precursors in the realm of education is that, whereas the latter recognized the need of an activity or manual work as an indispensable accompaniment of the educational process, Gandhiji laid down that "the whole of general education should come through the craft." This is perhaps Gandhiji's most notable contribution to the philosophy of education. He believes that "the craft chosen should be so learnt that its produce may have economic value sufficient to defray the tuition expense of the pupil." This is a sound educational principle, because, if the work done has no economic value, it would be cut off from reality and life. "For Gandhiji, craft-work is not merely a means of literary education; it is also an end in itself. Unless craft-work is treated as an end in itself, it will lose progressively its economic value, efficiency and significance."

231. Individual and Group Competition

Is competition wholly bad and is it going to disappear altogether from these new schools? The old forms of competitive examinations, marks, and prizes do produce activity from some individuals. That competition is efficient as a motive force to a certain extent cannot be denied, nor that there are dangers in depending too uncritically on the spirit of cooperation. That cooperation is preferable morally is accepted by anyone who prefers love to hate; the man you work with in real sympathy is your brother; the man you work against is your enemy. It is also generally more economical to make use of everybody's work fitted into a pattern, than, as so often happens in a competition, to use the best or even merely the cheapest labour, while the efforts of the rest are scrapped. But men and women, and children particularly, do find a satisfaction in beating their neighbours in a race, as well as in working with them in a common activity; the older type of educationalist had some justification for his dependence on competition though he drove it to death. In relegating the competitive motive to the second place, there is no need to aim at its complete suppression; the Russians have a very practical solution to the problem in Soviet society, whereby competition is made a group matter; socialist com-

231. Beryl Pring, *Education, Capitalist and Socialist* (London: Methuen and Company, Limited, 1937), pp. 230–232. By permission of the publishers.

petition means that type that occurs between two groups, two factories, farms, or schools, for instance, to see who can first complete their portion of a planned cooperative enterprise . . .

If cooperation is to be the main motive of activity in socialist schools, we must consider certain dangers in that motive, for, like every other good thing, it is not wholly good and may be applied to bad ends. The dangers are at once apparent when it is remembered that the fascist state is a corporate one, which is proof enough that the spirit of cooperation can be used for widely different ends. What better example is there of cooperation than a battleship or a well-disciplined army? The capitalist can use the cooperative spirit and the socialist the competitive. These are ultimately motives, not aims; the ends which they are used to achieve decide their ultimate value . . .

232. The School as Bulwark of Private Property

I believe that the greatest security which is thrown about the institution of property lies not in the laws and constitutions passed at our national and state capitals but in the laws which the teachers of America are enacting in the hearts and minds of the oncoming generation every day and week and year; those laws that are caught up in the emotions, that get fixed in the imagination and ideals of a people, which make them respect the property of another in order that the other may respect their property. I have not a drop of communistic blood in my veins. I believe that the institution of individual and corporate property, the right to have and to hold, lies at the very basis of the character and the happiness of the individual, the home and the community. I know that much of grief and bitterness comes from its abuse, but it seems that no great institution exists without some attendant harm. But the greatest security that comes to the institution of private and corporate property resides in the right education of all the youth of the nation . . .

232. Francis G. Blair, "Education in Relation to Material Values," *School and Society*, 31:422–423, March 1930.

11

Education and Socio-Economic
Class Structure

Problems in the Philosophy of Education Discussed in this Section

1. Should the educational expectation of children be measured by the socio-economic status of their parents? Should economic opportunities to gain an education be proportioned to children's talents regardless of their family origins? Can current educational injustices be cured as long as society remains capitalistic?
2. Are ill effects to be feared from educating a person beyond his social class or economic expectations?
3. Is it possible for the public school to be neutral or equitable in trying to serve at one and the same time the class interests of the proletariat and of the bourgeoisie?
4. Is the superior education of the few to be considered as a right or a privilege? As a reward for superior services rendered?
5. Should the dominant curriculum pattern be based on the culture of the working class or on that of the middle and upper classes? What are the pros and cons of either position?
6. With what class should teachers cast their lot? Should teachers organize along academic and professional lines or along lines of economic class interest? Should they advocate the class struggle for the solution of social problems?

233. Universal Education: A Product of
Middle-class Democracy

The movements for universal education and general suffrage in the nineteenth century offer perfect illustration of both the limits and the potentialities of growing rationality and moral idealism in the equalization of privilege and power. The principle of universal education

233. Reinhold Niebuhr, *Moral Man and Immoral Society* (New York: Charles Scribner's Sons, 1936), pp. 120–121.

was a product of the democratic movement, initiated by middle-class idealists. While this movement in general was exploited and appropriated by the middle classes, without giving the industrial classes the full share of it, which democratic principles demanded, the idea of universal education redounded, nevertheless, to the benefit of all classes and gave the industrial classes the self-reliance and intelligence by which they could resist the middle-class effort to exploit the democratic movement for class purposes. While genuine idealism contributed to the extension of educational privileges to all classes, it must be noted that it was easier to establish universal education than universal suffrage, because the former represents only privilege and the latter both privilege and power. Dominant classes are always slowest to yield power because it is the source of privilege. As long as they hold it, they may dispense and share privilege, enjoying the moral pleasure of giving what does not belong to them and the practical advantage of withholding enough to preserve their eminence and superiority in society. While education is potential power, because it enables the disinherited to protect their own interests by organised and effective methods, the dominant classes have suppressed their fears of this effect of education by the thought that education could be used as a means for inculcating submissiveness . . .

234. Educational Opportunity under Aristocracy and Plutocracy

The system of distribution determines the division of the community into classes, and wherever there are classes, different classes will receive different kinds of education. In a capitalist society, wage-earners get least education, and those who aim at entering a learned profession get most, while an intermediate amount is considered suitable for those who are going to be "gentlemen" or business men. As a general rule, a boy or girl belongs to the same social class as his or her parents. But those who win scholarships by exceptional ability can rise from the wage-earning class into the professional class. By this means, in England, the best brains born into the wage-earning class are politically sterilized, and cease, as a rule, to be on the side to which their birth would have assigned them. In this fluidity of classes, a plutocratic society differs from an aristocratic one; that is one reason why revolutions are less apt to occur under plutocracies than under aristocracies.

234. Bertrand Russell, *Education and the Modern World* (New York: W. W. Norton & Company, Inc., 1932), pp. 196–197. Reprinted by permission of the publishers.

235. Benefit of a Leisure Class to Education

Every civilization requires a certain amount of economic burden to steady it; a leisure class is as necessary as are the various industrial classes. This leisure class, however, must be a working and not an idling class. Every leisure class is always perilously near its own destruction. The true leisure class is a reservoir, often a well-spring, of true culture. It makes scholarship possible. It protects ethics. It standardizes morals. It reflects, criticizes, evaluates, appreciates, and encourages whatever is good in the world. It knows sympathy and has time and disposition to manifest the graces of social and personal life. It works, though indeed it may work upon things at present invisible. Many an economic parasite is a moral or cultural paragon: many such a parasite has built for the economic life of future society.

This is a hard doctrine, resented in many quarters, resented by nearly every economic worker who hears it and has time to think of it. Because of their resentment against those who may give their whole life to leisure, there is a defensive and reactionary disposition in certain quarters to declare that economic laborers shall have no leisure at all. But this conclusion is distinctly a *non sequitur*. The familiar notion of such as Tolstoi, that in an ideal society all will work as producers of economic goods or as servants of such producers part of the time, and have leisure for the rest, is a merely mechanical view. This view ignores one of the great qualities of a civilized society,—its power to store up goods, scholarship, traditions, arts, culture, against the future. A civilized society does not live from hand to mouth, no, nor by a year at a time; but it lives centuries beyond its economic working period, as Rome and France lived. If a man may work mornings and enjoy economic leisure afternoons; if he may work six days and rest the seventh; if he may work winters and rest summers or work summers and rest winters; if he may support his children in the economic idleness of school-going; if he may, and indeed ought to, lay up a store "against the rainy days" of invalidism, old age, accident, and illness; if he can ever earn the right to travel for recreation and for intellectual and moral improvement; if he has a right to the mere society of his fellow men in hours, days, and seasons when neither he nor they are bearing the burdens of active labor,—and all these things are part and parcel of civilization,—then of right the man is entitled

235. William E. Chancellor, *Motives, Ideals, and Values in Education* (Boston: Houghton Mifflin Company, 1907), pp. 11–13. Used by permission of the publishers.

to leisure. The other questions—how he is to be supported in his leisure; whether a child may or may not be rightfully or wisely given, by inheritance or by other social favor, a leisure that he (or she) has not earned; whether the leisure class is or is not too large, too secure, too luxurious—do not concern us here as critics of education . . . But we must recognize the fact that in every civilized society there must be some who eat bread in the sweat of other men's faces; whose obligation is to return tenfold to their souls. Education must prepare for the noblest social services of leisure, deserved or justified, if not actually earned.

236. Education as Equalizer of Class Antagonism

Now surely nothing but universal education can counterwork this tendency to the domination of capital and the servility of labor. If one class possesses all the wealth and the education, while the residue of society is ignorant and poor, it matters not by what name the relation between them may be called: the latter, in fact and in truth, will be the servile dependants and subjects of the former. But, if education be equally diffused, it will draw property after it by the strongest of all attractions; for such a thing never did happen, and never can happen, as that an intelligent and practical body of men should be permanently poor. Property and labor in different classes are essentially antagonistic; but property and labor in the same class are essentially fraternal. The people of Massachusetts have, in some degree, appreciated the truth that the unexampled prosperity of the State—its comfort, its competence, its general intelligence and virtue—is attributable to the education, more or less perfect, which all its people have received; but are they sensible of a fact equally important—namely, that it is to this same education that two-thirds of the people are indebted for not being today the vassals of as severe a tyranny, in the form of capital, as the lower classes of Europe are bound to in the form of brute force?

Education, then, beyond all other devices of human origin, is the great equalizer of the conditions of men—the balance-wheel of the social machinery. I do not here mean that it so elevates the moral nature as to make men disdain and abhor the oppression of their fellow-men. This idea pertains to another of its attributes. But I mean that it gives each man the independence and the means by which he can

236. Horace Mann, Twelfth Annual Report as Secretary of the Massachusetts State Board of Education, in Mary Mann, *Life and Works of Horace Mann* (Boston: Horace B. Fuller, 1868), Vol. 3, pp. 668–670.

resist the selfishness of other men. It does better than to disarm the poor of their hostility towards the rich: it prevents being poor. Agrarianism is the revenge of poverty against wealth. The wanton destruction of the property of others—the burning of hay-ricks and corn-ricks, the demolition of machinery because it supersedes hand-labor, the sprinkling of vitriol on rich dresses—is only agrarianism run mad. Education prevents both the revenge and the madness. On the other hand, a fellow-feeling for one's class or caste is the common instinct of hearts not wholly sunk in selfish regards for person or for family. The spread of education, by enlarging the cultivated class or caste, will open a wider area over which the social feelings will expand; and, if this education should be universal and complete, it would do more than all things else to obliterate factitious distinctions in society.

The main idea set forth in the creeds of some political reformers, or revolutionizers, is that some people are poor *because* others are rich. This idea supposes a fixed amount of property in the community, which by fraud or force, or arbitrary law, is unequally divided among men; and the problem presented for solution is how to transfer a portion of this property from those who are supposed to have too much to those who feel and know that they have too little. At this point, both their theory and their expectation of reform stop. But the beneficent power of education would not be exhausted, even though it should peaceably abolish all the miseries that spring from the co-existence, side by side, of enormous wealth and squalid want. It has a higher function. Beyond the power of diffusing old wealth it has the prerogative of creating new. It is a thousand times more lucrative than fraud, and adds a thousand-fold more to a nation's resources than the most successful conquests. Knaves and robbers can obtain only what was before possessed by others. But education creates or develops new treasures,—treasures not before possessed or dreamed of by any one.

237. Limitations of Middle-Class Progressive Education

The weakness of Progressive Education thus lies in the fact that it has elaborated no theory of social welfare, unless it be that of anarchy or extreme individualism. In this, of course, it is but reflecting the viewpoint of the members of the liberal-minded upper middle class who send their children to the Progressive schools—persons who are fairly well-off, who have abandoned the faiths of their fathers, who

237. George S. Counts, *Dare the School Build a New Social Order?* (New York: John Day Company, 1932), pp. 7–10.

assume an agnostic attitude towards all important questions, who pride themselves on their open-mindedness and tolerance, who favor in a mild sort of way fairly liberal programs of social reconstruction, who are full of good will and humane sentiment, who have vague aspirations for world peace and human brotherhood, who can be counted upon to respond moderately to any appeal made in the name of charity, who are genuinely distressed at the sight of *unwonted* forms of cruelty, misery, and suffering, and who perhaps serve to soften somewhat the bitter clashes of those real forces that govern the world; but who, in spite of all their good qualities, have no deep and abiding loyalties, possess no convictions for which they would sacrifice overmuch, would find it hard to live without their customary material comforts, are rather insensitive to the accepted forms of social injustice, are content to play the role of interested spectator in the drama of human history, refuse to see reality in its harsher and more disagreeable forms, rarely move outside the pleasant circles of the class to which they belong, and in the day of severe trial will follow the lead of the most powerful and respectable forces in society and at the same time find good reasons for so doing. These people have shown themselves entirely incapable of dealing with any of the great crises of our time—war, prosperity, or depression. At bottom they are romantic sentimentalists, but with a sharp eye on the main chance. That they can be trusted to write our educational theories and shape our educational programs is highly improbable.

*   *   *

If Progressive Education is to be genuinely progressive, it must emancipate itself from the influence of this class, face squarely and courageously every social issue, come to grips with life in all of its stark reality, establish an organic relation with the community, develop a realistic and comprehensive theory of welfare, fashion a compelling and challenging vision of human destiny, and become less frightened than it is today at the bogies of *imposition* and *indoctrination*. In a word, Progressive Education cannot place its trust in a child centered school.

238. Education in Open Class Society

The so-called open class society of the present is a sort of impossible compromise based upon fundamental principles that are self-contra-

238. Ross L. Finney, *A Sociologicl Philosophy of Education* (New York: The Macmillan Company, 1928), pp. 376–377.

dictory. It assumes equal opportunity for all; but as a matter of fact the very class distinctions that furnish its motivation are themselves the result of artificial privileges and handicaps arising chiefly out of the organization of our economic system. Without discounting the reasons for private property and the inheritance thereof, one need be no socialist to realize that the children of the prosperous classes have opportunities for getting a start in life that the children of the poor do not have. Nor need one attribute unemployment and the perennial poverty of the unskilled to the profits system and its automatic necessity for employing just less than all of the available supply of labor, to see that the children of that class lack opportunities for getting a start in life which are enjoyed by children of the more prosperous classes. We subconsciously dread to recognize private property and the profits system as artificial social arrangements lest we be forced to abandon the sustaining illusion of equal opportunities for all. But the fact remains that *children*—who have done nothing to merit handicaps or deserve privileges—do inherit the successes and defeats of the parental generation. Our system is a class system based upon economic achievement; but a system in which one's achievements—except in exceptional cases—are predetermined only in part by innate abilities, but in part also by artificially inherited handicaps and advantages. It is an open class system in which the classes are *not* really open to all alike. It contains within it the remnants of caste. It is, therefore, a compromise of inherent contradictions.

239. Educational Hypocrisy of Privileged Classes

The most common form of hypocrisy among the privileged classes is to assume that their privileges are the just payments with which society rewards specially useful or meritorious functions. As long as society regards special rewards for important services as ethically just and socially necessary (and the reversion of equalitarian Russia to this principle of unequal rewards suggests that it will not be easily abrogated), it is always possible for social privilege to justify itself, at least in its own eyes, in terms of the social function which it renders. If the argument is to be plausible, when used by privileged classes who possess hereditary advantages, it must be proved or assumed that the underprivileged classes would not have the capacity of rendering the same service if given the same opportunity. This assumption is invariably made by privileged classes. The educational advantages which

239. Reinhold Niebuhr, *Moral Man and Immoral Society* (New York: Charles Scribner's Sons, 1936), pp. 117–118.

privilege buys, and the opportunities for the exercise of authority which come with privileged social position, develop capacities which are easily attributed to innate endowment. The presence of able men among the privileged is allowed to obscure the number of instances in which hereditary privilege is associated with knavery and incompetence. On the other hand it has always been the habit of privileged groups to deny the oppressed classes every opportunity for the cultivation of innate capacities and then to accuse them of lacking what they have been denied the right to acquire. The struggle for universal education in the nineteenth century prompted the same kind of arguments from the privileged in every country. The poor were incapable of enjoying the benefits of education, and if they secured it they would make too good use of it by resisting the exactions of their oppressors more successfully . . .

240. Communist Indictment of Middle-Class Control of Schools

The development of machine production has decreased the significance of the workers' trade knowledge; by successfully substituting mechanical for hand power the machine has rendered obsolescent many vocational skills. Man consequently has become an appendage to the machine, and is no longer the master of the machine as he was in the days of the reign of handicraft. In many cases all that is required of the worker is the execution of simple manipulations whose significance for the most part he does not understand; his only need is for elementary literacy, for the ability to read and write. The ruling bourgeoisie therefore have quite naturally apportioned to the "people" the most insignificant crumbs of education, and even this minimum of opportunity has been provided only where the industrial capitalistic classes have occupied the seats of power. The land-owning nobility, the clergy, and the backward groups of the merchant bourgeoisie have never exhibited the least concern over the education of the proletariat and the peasantry. Why universal literacy is therefore confined to countries with a highly developed capitalism is altogether clear.

❊   ❊   ❊

Of course no bourgeois educator ever admits that he represents merely the interests of his class. Always and everywhere the reference

240. Albert P. Pinkevitch, *The New Education in the Soviet Republic* (New York: John Day Company, 1929), pp. 150–151.

is to universal human aims, to serving society as a whole, and so on . . .
Yet when they spoke about the middle and higher schools these apolo-
gists of capitalism were more or less sincere. Only rarely did representatives of the people reach these institutions, and for the most part the
few who did get this far broke every tie that bound them to their own
class. The student population of the secondary schools and the universities was composed almost entirely of children of the bourgeoisie, the
intelligentzia, the clergy, and the nobility. After receiving the benefits
of the higher education they with few exceptions served jealously the
interests of their class.

241. Communist Basis for Education

We return to the analysis of industrial man. The outstanding feature
of his *objective* life in the main, is that he has become a factory worker.
The disturbing aspect of his *subjective* life is his emotional divorce
from what is so distinctively human, the use of labor to make his world.
As a sound basis for education it would be necessary to have a sound
social relation to the labor process. The meaningful and educative
value of labor must be reexamined, and yet this is only possible when
society is reconstructed. A society which harmonizes its productive
forces with the human relations involved with productive technology
is alone able to practice the social harmony of all its people. Likewise,
only in a genuinely equalitarian and co-operative society can education become a constructive force and the equal development of all
potential abilities be realized. Only then can the breach between
intellectualism, abstraction, ideals, and theory, on the one hand, and
practice, technology, science, and realities, on the other, be healed.

In a society in which work is honored and none live without labor,
education will be linked with the actual master of the material environment. . . .

*   *   *

Hence we can understand why Soviet theory has stressed the role
of the workshop, the laboratory, and the relations of the school to the
local community, to the local factory, to the nearest cooperative farm,
to the larger provincial and even national industrialization projects,
and to the vast agricultural and reforestation schemes. There is no

241. Robert S. Cohen, "On the Marxist Philosophy of Education," in 54th
Yearbook of the National Society for the Study of Education, Part I, *Modern
Philosophies and Education* (Published by the Society, Chicago, 1955), pp.
198–201.

conflict between the understanding of the principles of science and an immersion in the problems of the local manufacturing plant; on the contrary, the latter (or its reflection in the problems of the school situation) are the basis for the pupil's personal involvement in scientific understanding. . . . And he will have the teachers who break decisively with all purely verbal methods of passive education. The twin evils of pure verbalism and pure vocationalism will, in this manner, be avoided. They are so evident in American schools, appearing now as the shop course, or as the vocational trades or secretarial curriculum, now as the college preparatory but technologically illiterate high school or private preparatory-school curriculum, now as the Great Books program in adult education, now as the technical improvement program for adults in one trade or other. It is necessary that these evils be avoided by denying the values of neither practical nor theoretical education, of neither practical citizenship nor liberal and humane arts.

To the maxim that all teaching be organized about the recognition and practice of human labor is added the principle that education should be based on the purposive, creative, and independent act of the pupil. It is necessary, in utilizing the creativeness of each boy and girl, to avoid any idealization, and in particular to avoid the creation of a sentimental utopian school community, unattached to the world for which all education is a preparation. . . .

242. Impossibility of an Impartial State

The liberal educator's implicit conception of the nature of our existing state and its role and function in the social process provides us with further proof that he does not conceive of the structure of American society as a class structure. His conception of our state is typically liberal. He assumes that our state is a neutral entity, an independent entity. It has no interests of its own; its aim is to serve every individual without discrimination or prejudice. It is the instrument of each individual, by which he protects his rights and interests; it is not, as the Marxist sees it, a class instrument, but the instrument of any group or collection of individuals which can make itself into a majority; and every individual is free to become a part of that majority. It stands above the rights of any single individual or group. Its function is not that of defending the rights and interests of any single individual or

242. Zalmon Slesinger, *Education and the Class Struggle* (New York: Govici Friede, Inc.), 1937, pp. 49–52.

group as against the interests of any other single individual or group; and its role is that of arbiter and judge whenever conflict arises.

✿   ✿   ✿

Clearly, such a conception of the state does not take account of a class-structured society. A neutral and impartial state, in the mind of the Marxist, is imaginable and possible only in a non-class-structured society in which the basic interests, rights and powers of all individuals are relatively mutual. He does not view it as conceivable in a class-structured society. In such a society, the Marxist claims, the state cannot be impartial and unbiased in its distribution of rights and powers to both classes. For in a class society the interests of the propertied class are in irreconcilable conflict with those of the propertyless and, assuming the state's responsibility to protect property rights, it becomes impossible for the state to function impartially. How can the state in such a society, asks the Marxist, protect the opposing interests of both classes? How can the state be true to its own basic function, the protection of property rights, and, at the same time, protect the interests of the propertyless?

243. Educational Limitations of a Dominant Social Class

The laboring classes are becoming interested in the social and economic order in which they live and work; they are convinced that they are the objects of exploitation by the favored classes; they desire the power which comes from clear insight into the forces which surround them; and they do not trust the instruction which society provides for them through schools controlled by boards of education composed, for the most part, of persons representing the employers' point of view. In no other way can the establishment and support of schools of their own on the part of organized labor be understood. Throughout the history of labor's struggle for freedom this fear of an education provided by the favored classes has found continuous expression . . .

✿   ✿   ✿

The argument may be advanced that these board members, though drawn from a restricted class, will, because of the superior educational opportunities which they have enjoyed, rise above a narrow loyalty to their own group and formulate educational policies in terms of the common interest. We all wish that this were so, but there is little

243. George S. Counts, *The Social Composition of Boards of Education* (Chicago: University of Chicago Press), 1927, pp. 87–92.

evidence from the human past to support it. The rare individual will strive earnestly to have regard for the best interests of all classes, but no one can transcend the limits set by his own experience. The best of us are warped and biased by the very processes of living . . .

In shaping educational policy, the peculiar limitations of any dominant social class should be noted. Whether that class is a priesthood, a holy order, a military aristocracy, the bourgeoisie, or the proletariat matters not. They all suffer from the same affliction. A dominant class is a privileged class, a class that is favored by the existing social arrangement. It therefore tends to be conservative, to exaggerate the merits of the prevailing order, and to fear any agitation favoring fundamental changes in the social structure. It represents the past rather than the future; its creative period lies in a preceding age; its genius has already found expression. As a consequence, it is content to enjoy and conserve the fruits of its period of struggle. On the other hand, the forces which represent the future, the forces which will fashion the civilization of tomorrow, are not now in the seats of power. In fact, just what these forces are can scarcely be discerned with surety even by the wisest of men, for they exist today only in embryo. They consequently do not appear significant, and they are significant only in potentiality. The latent strength of any social movement is not to be measured by its present vitality nor by any mark of identification. History tells us that the dominant forces of any age rarely extend the hand of welcome to their successors. To the degree, therefore, that the school is under the control of these forces, however benevolent they may appear, the chances are that its face will be turned toward the past. Its function will be defensive and conservative rather than creative and progressive.

244. Teachers Should Avoid Narrow Class Consciousness

The answer to the question as to whether or not unionism is desirable must be found in the motives that prompt teachers to join any group, whether it be a union, a fraternity or a federation. To the extent that such groupings are prompted primarily by selfish interests, and are based upon class appeal and concepts of economic and national life that run counter to those for which our government stands, such groups, whether you call them by one name or another, are vicious and undemocratic. We cannot ignore the bald fact that the

244. William L. Ettinger, "Democratized School Administration," *School and Society*, 12:267, October 1920.

schools of a democracy are the schools of the whole people, and not the schools of a particular class. Moreover, let me affirm with great emphasis that nothing can be more detrimental to our schools than the assumption that the classroom teachers constitute a laboring class, a sort of intellectual proletariat who differ both in kind and degree from supervisors and administrators who, by analogy, are classed as a sort of pedagogical capitalistic class, constituting the sworn oppressors of the teachers with whom they live and labor day by day, and from whose ranks they are chosen. Any appeal to gross prejudices or to narrow class consciousness, whether labelled unionism or what not, contains the germs common to anarchism or bolshevism. A teachers' union and the general union movement among teachers are just as good or just as evil as teachers make them. It is therefore the bounden duty of teachers in such organizations to be active to prevent the use of such groups for personal, political, or professional exploitation, and, above all, to maintain and promote those fine conceptions of service to our children and to our city which have always distinguished the teaching profession.

245. Social Amelioration through Education, Not Class Struggle

I find myself confused by the articles that have appeared . . . urging that educators adopt the class concept as their intellectual guide and practical dynamic. I do not know just what is meant by the class concept; what its implications are, intellectual and practical. The arguments, when boiled down, seem to amount to the following:

A radical reconstruction of the existing social order is demanded. The needed reconstruction is opposed by the powerful class now in control of social affairs, whose property, power, and prestige are threatened by the reconstruction that is required. On the other side are the workers who suffer in countless ways from the present social order and who will be the gainers in security, freedom, and opportunity, by basic change. Teachers are workers and their own class interest is with fellow-workers. Moreover, social consciousness and social conscience should lead them to side with the workers; they belong on that side of the struggle that is going on.

Now my confusion arises because I do not see the bearing of these considerations, even if they are admitted, upon the conclusion drawn;

245. John Dewey, "Class Struggle and the Democratic Way," *The Social Frontier*, 2:241–242, May 1936.

namely, that the concept of the class struggle is the one which will give educators the intellectual and practical direction they need. In fact, this conclusion seems to me to be of the nature of a *non-sequitur*. At least it seems to be a *non-sequitur* except upon the basis of an un-expressed premise. This premise, made explicit, would be to the effect that recognition of certain facts, namely, those of class struggle, is sufficient to give direction to the thinking and activity that are to be brought to bear upon the facts. I can see that the empirical facts, as far as they are admitted to be facts, constitute a most serious problem. I do not see how the terms of a social problem are identical with the method of its solution, certainly not with a solution by any experimental method. I do not see how they constitute the leading ideas that will give direction to the efforts of educators. To know the empirical facts is one condition of experimental method; but the question of what to do about the facts and how to do it is another matter.

When the importance of the concept of class and class war is urged by those who have no use for the experimental point of view, I do not experience the confusion I have spoken of. For example, I do not find the gap I have mentioned in the position of communists of the current Marxist-Leninist type. For their premise is that class struggle is and always has been the source of social change; that class struggle by means of the forces of material productivity conditions the nature, the rise, and the fall of all social and cultural institutions; that at present the war is between the capitalist bourgeoisie and the proletariat; that the irrepressible conflict now going on will finally break out into overt civil war; that the end of the struggle will be the dictatorship of the proletariat as the means of final transition to a classless society. There is no ambiguity in this view. It is clear-cut and simple, for it rests upon the assumption that the class struggle determines of itself the course of events and their issue, either automatically or else because a sufficient number of persons become aware of the class struggle and become class conscious.

If this is the point of view of those who urge upon educators the importance of the class concept, it is free from the confusion to which I have referred. But such does not seem to be the case . . .

The further difference that follows is of even greater significance. It concerns the nature of the educational process. If the essential facts are all in, and if these facts in and of themselves decide the nature of educational policy, then, when the essential facts are said to be those of class struggle, it follows that education becomes simply a matter of inculcation—in short, of agitation and propaganda. But some at least of those who urge the importance of the class concept do not seem to draw this conclusion. Yet what is the point of the class concept as a determining factor in educational procedure unless it is to have such a controlling influence on the latter that education becomes a special form of constant indoctrination? And in that case what becomes of the plea for freedom in teaching? Is it a plea merely for freedom to inculcate a certain view of society, logically entailing lack of freedom for presentation of other views?

The point may be made clearer by supposing that one adopts the position implied in the following question of Dr. Childs: "Is it not highly probable that they (a myriad of interest groups) will merge into large classes and that American society *ultimately* will be divided into those who advocate and those who oppose this drastic reconstruction?" If one believes that this is likely to happen, what then? Shall the educator as an educator endeavor to hasten and intensify the division? And what attitude shall he take toward the problem of *how* drastic social reconstruction is to be effected? Does education have anything to do with development of the attitudes and convictions that influence the *manner* of the transition? Putting the question in an extreme form, is it the task of educators, because of acceptance of the class concept, to intensify a consciousness of class division and class war, or is it to help determine the kind of social awareness that is to exist so that the transformation may be accomplished, as far as possible, by educational means instead of by conflict? What kind of classes are we to have, as far as education has anything to say on that matter, whether its influence be light or great? Is it enough, for the purpose of effecting the needed social transformation, that the exploited class become conscious that it is an exploited group and then try to gain the physical or even the political power to become the dominant class? From the standpoint of those who put their faith in the idea that a violent revolution is the solution, and that subsequent dictatorship by a class is the best or only means to effect the transformation, it is quite possible that this *is* enough, that anything else would tend to hinder the day of reconstruction. But I have difficulty in imagining any educator taking this point of view unless he has abandoned in advance all faith in education.

I hope the point of these questions is clear. What does the acceptance of the class concept *mean* for the work of the educators? I cannot but think that the acceptance of a *social* point of view rather than that of a special class has led those who have advocated the class concept to adopt the convictions they hold about the place of education in social transformation. If this is so, it would seem as if this broader and more inclusive point of view is the one from which they should carry on their educational work. The acceptance of this point of view does not mean that they should close their minds to the injustices and inequities of the present order, to their effects—impoverishment and insecurity—or to the disastrous effect of these tragic evils upon the culture of all groups in society. But certainly those who believe that education in the schools has some part to play in bringing about social transformation have a greater responsibility than any others to consider the *means* by which the transformation is to be brought about and the especial place of educational means among the total means . . .

The issue of whether educators shall stay out of the process of social transformation or shall participate in it is quite another question from that of whether their participation shall be controlled by the class concept. To see this point seems to me the beginning of clarity of thought upon the whole matter. And there need be no fear that honest adoption of the democratic idea and criterion will lead to apathy and complacency—save in the case of those so intellectually dishonest that they would find some evasion in any case. The democratic frame of reference is capable of energizing action as well as of directing critical reflection and educational thought.

As far as I can see, the ambiguity in the concept of class orientation arises from confusing orientation *toward* a class, the class of workers, with orientation *by* a class interest. One's sympathies and, as occasion presents itself, one's efforts may well be with workers as against an exploiting class. But one's frame of values and one's controlling framework of ideas may nevertheless be derived from a sense of a comprehensive social interest. As I read the articles to which reference has been made, this larger sense is in fact their animating spirit. The writers urge teachers to recognize that they too are workers and that their function and their success in performing it, are bound up with the struggle in which workers are engaged. I am not taking exception to this point of view nor am I urging that teachers should be "neutral"—an impossibility in any case. It is possible to be alert and active in the struggle for social reorganization and yet recognize that it is *social* reorganization that is required, and that it must be undertaken in the social, rather than a class interest. Because I am persuaded the writers recognize that educational means and methods, rather than those of brute force, should play as large a part as possible in bringing about the reorganization, I am concerned lest they urge their plea from the standpoint of a class rather than from that of our democratic tradition and its methods.

12

Public and Private Education

Problems in the Philosophy of Education Discussed in this Section

1. Should the civil state concern itself with education (socialism)? Should the state leave education to the attention of other social agencies such as the family and the church (laissez-faire)? Or can education be managed without any civil state (anarchy)? According to what principle do you decide?
2. Up to what point of development does a child have a right to be educated by the public? Is he entitled to free tuition, textbooks, transportation, medical service, meals, and so on? If so, will these services encourage parasitism? At what point does education become a privilege?
3. In view of the great inequalities among families, would it be more democratic if the state would supplant the family as educator?
4. When you think of school and society, do you think of society as a definite entity? As a single all-inclusive social group?
5. Should the civil state have a right to exercise a monopoly in providing and maintaining schools? Is it wise to grant perpetual charters to private schools, as was done with Dartmouth College?
6. Is the civil state identical or coterminous with society conceived as single and all-inclusive, or is it just one among many social groupings? What significant educational consequences flow from these alternatives?
7. Do private schools perform any worthwhile social functions which justify their existence? If so, should not the government subsidize them for doing so? Who would judge the worth of private educational achievements?
8. Is it democratic to coerce minorities? How about compulsory attendance laws? Do youth have a duty to develop their potentialities?
9. To whom does the child belong? To the family, the state, or himself?

246. Natural and Absolute Right to Education

I believe in the existence of a great, immortal, immutable principle of natural law, or natural ethics—a principle antecedent to all human

246. Horace Mann, Tenth Annual Report as Secretary of the Massachusetts State Board of Education, in Mary Mann, *Life and Works of Horace Mann* (Boston: Horace B. Fuller, 1868), Vol. 3, p. 533.

institutions, and incapable of being abrogated by any ordinance of man; a principle of divine origin, clearly legible in the ways of Providence as those ways are manifested in the order of nature and in the history of the race, which proves the *absolute right* to an education of every human being that comes into the world; and which, of course, proves the correlative duty of every government to see that the means of that education are provided for all.

247. Education a Privilege, Not a Right

A man who does not work for the improvement of society is not an educated man. For education is a privilege given by society; it is not a right taken by the individual. It is the community that educates a man for its purposes and its purposes alone . . .

248. Three Possible Relations of Government to Education

There are three main points of view concerning the relations of the State and the individual.

The first point of view may be called *anarcho-individualistic*. In political economy this point of view was represented by the Manchester school with its motto "laissez faire, laissez passer," and in education by the old English policy, which gave full freedom to private voluntary efforts, but did not spend a penny on education. According to this doctrine every individual had the full right to decide the kind and scope of education which he wished to receive. No authority, whether clerical or secular, could compel any child to attend any school. Before the child attained maturity this problem was dealt with by his natural guardians—his parents. In practice this led to a great abuse of children. Not only were thousands of children left uneducated by their illiterate parents, but they were even deprived of their childhood and had to work for their living from an early age . . .

The second point of view can be called *communistic*. Plato elaborated this doctrine in his communistic State. In the twentieth century this ancient theory was revived as an outgrowth of Hegelian philosophy

247. Isaiah Bowman, "A Design for Scholarship," *School and Society*, 43:379, March 1936.

248. Nicholas A. Hans, *The Principles of Educational Policy* (London: P. S. King and Son, Ltd., 1933), pp. 2–5.

in two opposite forms. One is represented by the communistic government of Soviet Russia and the other by the fascist government of Italy. As the Soviet policy is a more extreme and logical form of this doctrine it will be more useful to take it as an example. The State represents the common interests of the nation and its central government knows best of all the needs and requirements of the whole. The State regulates the output of educated specialists in accordance with its needs. The individual citizen has no right to decide his future profession or occupation; it is decided by authorities. Private schools or classes are prohibited by law and all education which is available is State education. All children are educated for the State, by the State and in the State institutions. The curriculum and every detail is prescribed by the central authorities. To what final results this policy will lead in Russia is difficult to predict. At present it is an undisputed fact, however, that all private initiative is suppressed, the general standard of education lowered and the rising generation dogmatic and intolerant.

The third point of view may be called *democratic*. This point of view lies just between the two extremes, although it should not be considered as a compromise since it is based on its own principles. This policy is pursued by many modern democracies, has various forms and is in constant evolution. We might here distinguish two main traditions in common progress towards democracy. In English-speaking countries the adjustment between the individual and the State started from the individual. The Anglo-Saxon tradition maintains that the private agency is the stimulating element in social work whereas the State is the staying element. It was always considered that the province of the individual and of private agency was to initiate the policy and that of the State to take over the proven work and to make it general. Thus in these countries the progressive movements were usually started by private initiative and State intervention followed much later. The more the extension of educational service grew, the wider it embraced the whole nation, the more grew the intervention of the State. The goal of this evolution is a perfect balance of both factors—of private initiative and of the State. In the continental countries the evolution towards democracy began from the other end. The enlightened State was the initiator of progressive social and educational reforms and the individual had to submit to centralized and sometimes rigid legislation. It tended often to a State monopoly and regulation from the centre of all sides of school life. The twentieth century and especially the post war years brought a change into these countries as well. The right of the individual to private initiative is more recognized and the local communities are given more freedom in differentiating their school curriculum. Both traditions are approaching each other in their endeavor to reach the common goal. It is not yet attained; some States are nearer, some further from it, but general features are common to all . . .

249. Education under Anarchism

The Anarchist supports his indictment of the State as superfluous by concrete illustrations. He asks, for example, "Is the State necessary for education?" and answers that it is not. If the mass of the workers are only given enough leisure to instruct themselves, those among them who are fond of tuition will be only too eager to instruct the others, and numbers of voluntary educational societies will spring up anxious to outrival each other in excellence of teaching.

250. The Welfare State

The major doubts and fears the critics have about welfare legislation in general . . . boil down to three main points.

They say, first, that if Washington does everything *for* the people, it will soon be in a position to do everything *to* the people. And when that happens history will say a long good-bye to the uniquely American idea of limited government, where all power rises from the people and where the primary purpose of government is to create a stable society in which the individual is free to pursue his own ends. In its stead, we will have a strong-arm central government with all its by-products; bureaucracy, rigidity, humorlessness.

✻   ✻   ✻

Now in all this, I recognize one underlying line of argument that goes as follows: Freedom of the individual is our most prized possession; welfare measures mean greater activity by government, often the Federal Government; "therefore," the adoption of any such measures must entail a loss of freedom for the individual.

✻   ✻   ✻

What is the individual freedom we cherish? It is not an abstract principle, not a set of phrases to be chanted in hushed tones. It is the

249. C. E. M. Joad, *Introduction to Modern Political Theory* (Oxford University Press, 1924), p. 106.

250. Abraham Ribicoff, "To Promote the General Welfare," *New York Times Magazine,* July 9, 1961, p. 9.

bundle of rights that are ours to enjoy—the right to live where we choose, to worship where we wish, to work at whatever trade or profession we prefer, to become educated wherever we please in schools and colleges we select, to decide for ourselves how we will enjoy our leisure time; in short to live productive and creative lives to the limit of our capacities.

One must be free to do these things. But being free is no assurance that these things can be done.

With freedom there must be opportunity. And this is what we seek —the creation of opportunity to become educated, to find employment, to earn decent wages, to enjoy good health. With these opportunities established and strengthened, each individual can enjoy a free life and make his utmost contribution to our free society.

251. Public Education an Invasion of Freedom

1. In the same way that our definition of state-duty forbids the state to administer religion or charity, so likewise does it forbid the state to administer education. Inasmuch as the taking away, by government, of more of a man's property than is needful for maintaining his rights, is an infringement of his rights, and therefore a reversal of the government's function toward him; and inasmuch as the taking away of his property to educate his own or other people's children is not needful for the maintaining of his rights; the taking away of his property for such a purpose is wrong.

Should it be said that the rights of the children are involved, and that state-interposition is required to maintain these, the reply is that no cause for such interposition can be shown until the children's rights have been violated, and that their rights are not violated by a neglect of their education. For, as repeatedly explained, what we call rights are merely arbitrary subdivisions of the general liberty to exercise the faculties; and that only can be called an infringement of rights which actually diminishes this liberty—cuts off a previously existing power to pursue the objects of desire. Now the parent who is careless of a child's education does not do this. The liberty to exercise the faculties is left intact. Omiting instruction in no way takes from a child's freedom to do whatsoever it wills in the best way it can; and this freedom is all that equity demands. Every aggression, be it remembered—every infraction of rights, is necessarily *active;* whilst every neglect, careless-

251. Herbert Spencer, *Social Statics* (New York: D. Appleton Co., 1886), pp. 360–362.

ness, omission, is as necessarily *passive*. Consequently, however wrong the non-performance of a parental duty may be—however much it is condemned by that secondary morality—the morality of beneficence (pp. 83 and 84)—it does not amount to a breach of the law of equal freedom, and cannot therefore be taken cognizance of by the state.

2. Were there no direct disproof of the frequently alleged right to education at the hands of the state, the absurdities in which it entangles its assertors would sufficiently show its invalidity. Conceding for a moment that the government is bound to educate a man's children, then, what kind of logic will demonstrate that it is not bound to feed and clothe them? If there should be an act-of-parliament provision for the development of their minds, why should there not be an act-of-parliament provision for the development of their bodies? If the mental wants of the rising generation ought to be satisfied by the state, why not their physical ones? The reasoning which is held to establish the right to intellectual food, will equally well establish the right to material food: nay, will do more—will prove that children should be altogether cared for by government. For if the benefit, importance, or necessity of education be assigned as a sufficient reason why government should educate, then may the benefit, importance, or necessity of food, clothing, shelter, and warmth be assigned as a sufficient reason why government should administer these also. So that the alleged right cannot be established without annulling all parental responsibility whatever.

252. Parent Paramount to State in Education of Child

"Considering natural law only, parents cannot be compelled by the civil authority to send their children to an elementary school. But they may be obliged in particular cases." . . . Let us state briefly the reasons of Rosetti.

First, parents alone are judges of the material and intellectual wants of their children; the control is due to them in strict justice: an obligation of that kind is an abridgment of their control; and therefore a violation of justice. Secondly, the only reason why the State could interfere would be the violation of the right of the child; but all the child is strictly entitled to is to receive the education necessary to live in comfort in the condition of his parents. On the other hand,

252. René I. Holaind, "The Parent First: An Answer to Dr. Bouquillon's *Query*," *Pamphlets on Education* (New York: Benziger Bros., 1891), p. 20.

it is not universally true that the three R's are necessary to live in comfort; hence it cannot be proved by natural law alone that the parents can be compelled to give their children a knowledge of the three R's. The author adds, that ignorance, though itself an evil, often saves men from great dangers which result from the reading of bad books, etc., etc.

In point of fact, neither Rosetti nor any other Catholic writer objects to knowledge: they object to State programmes and to compulsion. They object to State interference in domestic affairs, and whenever the government leaves its imperial duties to cross the family threshold, Catholic writers resent the intrusion and bid the rulers halt. Moreover, they fully know that he who can make and unmake programmes of studies can crush competition and rule the social forces for his own private ends.

253. Child Belongs to the State

Again, since the state as a whole has a single end, it is plain that the education of all must be one and the same, and that the supervision of this education must be public and not private, as it is on the present system, under which everyone looks after his own children privately and gives them any private instruction he thinks proper. Public training is wanted in all things that are of public interest. Besides, it is wrong for any citizen to think that he belongs to himself. All must be regarded as belonging to the state: for each man is a part of the state, and the treatment of the part is naturally determined by that of the whole . . .

254. Dominance of Proletarian Interests in Communism

Every state naturally strives to dominate completely the education of the young. The contemporary state as an organization of class interests constantly struggles for supremacy, that is, for the supremacy of the class which for the time is in power. Public education aiming, as it does, to mold the future citizen is a mighty instrument which the

253. Aristotle, "Politics," in *Aristotle on Education*, John Burnet, translator (Cambridge University Press, 1913), p. 106.

254. Albert P. Pinkevitch, *The New Education in the Soviet Republic* (New York: John Day Company), 1929, pp. 24–25.

government cannot pass on to others. In other words, regardless of the clamor which bourgeois educators may raise regarding the matter, the school and the other educational institutions cannot be outside of politics. The slogan "down with politics in the school" is an hypocrisy, for its realization is possible to a certain extent only in the socialistic society of the future. If we cast the eye back over the history of public education, we shall see that at no time and at no place has the school been outside of politics. In ancient Greece, and particularly in Sparta, the education of the citizens was entirely in the hands of the state. The same practice, although in a somewhat less well-defined form, prevailed throughout the Middle Ages. The French Revolution in its demand for the definite subordination of education to the political aims of the new state faced this question in a remarkably direct and frank manner. Moreover, do we not observe the same tendency in all countries in both Europe and America during the nineteenth century? And our great Russian Revolution pursues an identical policy, but with greater clarity and with greater honesty than the capitalistic nations. The present Russian state, which is transitional between capitalism and socialism, places political power in the hands of the workers and the peasants. The Revolution was made, and its principles are now being enforced, by the proletariat. It is quite natural, therefore, that the authorities should bring into the foreground the cultural problems of the laboring classes and the working peasantry. Communists are least of all inclined to appeal to moral principles; but even if we adopt the point of view which is hypocritically advanced by the contemporary capitalistic regime, the point of view of formal democracy and Christian morality, we can only welcome the sincerity of the existing power in Russia, because it does strive to represent the interests of an overwhelming majority of the population.

255. Liberalism and Education

We can now approach a consideration of liberalism from the positive side. Liberalism is essentially based upon a faith in the worth and dignity of the individual; it does not believe that the state is a philosophical figment existing outside of and above the individuals who make it up, but that these individuals have both a right and a duty to determine its conduct and progress. This means then that the individual must enjoy the rights to freedom of oral and written ex-

255. Isaac L. Kandel, "Liberalism and Education," *The Educational Forum,* 1:266–268, March 1937.

pression, freedom of association, freedom of worship, and freedom to exercise his initiative and energy. Liberalism is not a plan but an attitude of mind. As far as progress is concerned the liberal believes that social evolution is slow because he believes in the process of free discussion rather than violent revolution. And this gradualism is one of the causes of opposition from those who are disappointed at the slow adaptation of modern society to the rapidly developing changes of our era.

The definition of liberalism here given is the one that is usually accepted as the complete definition and is always identified with the doctrine of *laissez faire*. While it cannot be denied that this doctrine may have been cradled in the same philosophy as liberalism, it is not synonymous with it. And it is too often forgotten by those who talk of rugged individualism and the *laissez faire* doctrine in the same breath, that *laissez faire* as a practical policy would mean "administrative nihilism." Liberalism does not mean that the state is to refrain from action, nor that the function of the state is that of a policeman to maintain conditions under which rugged individualism may express itself freely. Liberalism—and its history in England may be cited— came toward the close of the nineteenth century to imply that the state has positive powers for the creation of conditions for social, political, and economic security.

It is at this point that the American interpretation of the liberal philosophy has fallen short; it has emphasized freedom and liberty, but it has failed to stress duty and obligation; the American will stand for his rights; he is not equally sensitive about his responsibilities. There has developed a confused concept of freedom as absence of restraint and discipline, as though freedom has any meaning except in constituted society. And this concept has been transferred into our educational philosophy with its emphasis on the primacy of the individual's interests, drives and urges, and of a theory of growth without anything fixed in advance. Freedom, the heart of the concept of liberalism, has no meaning unless it is balanced by a sensitiveness to responsibility, to the ideal of *noblesse oblige*, to the moral and social implications of its exercise. If liberalism has been and is interpreted as opposed to social or state action, the fault lies with the interpreters and not with its philosophy. Essentially, however, liberalism differs from totalitarianism in its opposition to the imposition of decisions by force and in its insistence upon argument and discussion based upon knowledge as the method of social progress. Liberalism is not a doctrine of individualism unrestrained but of freedom for the individual as a member of society.

The implications of such a philosophy affect every aspect of education. We have tended too much in recent years to consider education almost wholly from the point of view of the individual. We have in other words followed in education only the partial definition of liberalism and education no less than the social scheme has catered to rugged individualism. Your student of education will talk today more glibly about the individual's drives, interests and urges, about individual differences, and about a variety of methods, all of which increase differences between individuals, than he can about social values and the social culture in which the individual is to take his place. Even our system of defining education in quantitative terms was developed in the interests of the individual. But where in American educational theory can one find the moral equivalent for a democracy such as ours of the all-pervasive influences of the various totalitarian concepts? We pay tribute in our professions to the theory that education is a social process but fail to give this process any meaning. American education originated in and was built upon the philosophy of liberalism. Even before formal systems of government administration were established two very important ideals of liberalism had already received universal acceptance—the first of these was faith in the worth and dignity of the individual; the second was that organized society must enable the individual to rise to his full worth by the provision of as full and varied educational opportunities as possible. Not only have these ideals been accepted but they have been in large measure realized.

To insist, however, on the importance of education as a social process functioning in a group culture does not from the liberal point of view mean that this culture can be defined in a detailed doxology like Fascism, Nazism and Communism. To do this is to expose education to the disease of orthodoxy with all the consequences that such a disease implies in the form of espionage, oaths, heresy-hunting, curbs on free inquiry, and, perhaps worse than all, intellectual hypocrisy on the part of teachers which must in the long run undermine their educative influence in a democracy such as ours. This danger cannot be minimized; it confronts American education already. If American ideals of democracy and free government are sound, they have nothing to fear from criticism. If American culture is to be free, flexible, varied and progressive in response to changing conditions, it cannot be cribbed, cabined, and confined at the behest of a minority, whether that minority is dubbed reactionary or progressive. The sign of a healthy culture is that variety which comes from the spontaneous interaction of individuals or groups of individuals; a pluralistic and not a totalitarian interpretation of that culture is implicit in the free institutions and ideals which are the common foundations of social stability in American democracy.

256. Equality of Opportunity Requires State Action

The implications for the problem under consideration,-*Who shall have control of the education of the child?*-are obvious. If the progress of society depends upon the trained initiative of responsible individuals, the burden of providing facilities for their education devolves upon society. The new note of the twentieth century is the recognition of individual worth and of the importance of encouraging its fullest development. Equality of opportunity can only be provided by the concerted efforts of society. Education thus becomes not a police measure of the State established in the interests of its own security and stability, but the right of every individual for the attainment of the fullest development of his abilities, irrespective of his social origin . . . If equality of opportunity is accepted as the essential principle of the modern State, then there can be no question but that educational facilities must be provided by the State. If the interests of the State are best served by the fullest development of the individual, and by the promotion of variety of experience rather than by uniformity, then the task of the State is to create the best machinery for their encouragement, and its concern is not that all shall be educated alike in the same institutions, but that all shall have equal opportunities for education accessible to them. Accordingly, the State on these principles does not establish a monopoly to the exclusion of private schools, if there are groups which desire to maintain them, but exercises such supervision as will guarantee adequate standards in all schools.

257. Compulsory Education Must Be Free and Vice-Versa

Compulsory attendance is logically connected with gratuitous education, otherwise it would be unjust towards the poorer groups and unworkable. On the other hand free education if introduced without

256. Isaac L. Kandel, *Comparative Education* (Boston: Houghton Mifflin Company, 1933), p. 54. Used by permission of the publishers.
257. Nicholas A. Hans, *The Principles of Educational Policy* (London: P. S. King and Son, Ltd., 1933), p. 11.

compulsory attendance would become a new privilege of the wealthy classes as the poorer and uneducated parents would not send their children to the school. Both principles must be introduced simultaneously. Strangely enough compulsory attendance and free education have seldom been connected in the history of legislation. Usually compulsory attendance has preceded free education . . .

258. Justification of Tax for Public Schools

Hereditary distinctions of rank are sufficiently odious; but that which is founded on poverty is infinitely more so. Such a law should be entitled 'An act for branding and marking the poor, so that they may be known from the rich and proud.' Many complain of this tax, not so much on account of its amount, as because it is for the benefit of others and not themselves. This is a mistake; it is for their own benefit, inasmuch as it perpetuates the government and insures the due administration of the laws under which they live, and by which their lives and property are protected. Why do they not urge the same objection against all other taxes? The industrious, thrifty, rich farmer pays a heavy county tax to support criminal courts, build jails, and pay sheriffs and jail keepers, and yet probably he never has, and never will have, any direct personal use of either. He never gets the worth of his money by being tried for a crime before the court, by being allowed the privilege of the jail on conviction, or receiving an equivalent from the sheriff or his hangman officers! He cheerfully pays the tax which is necessary to support and punish convicts, but loudly complains of that which goes to prevent his fellow-being from becoming a criminal, and to obviate the necessity of those humiliating institutions.

This law is often objected to, because its benefits are shared by the children of the profligate spendthrift equally with those of the most industrious and economical habits. It ought to be remembered that the benefit is bestowed, not upon the erring parents, but the innocent children. Carry out this objection and you punish children for the crimes or misfortunes of their parents. You virtually establish cases and grades founded on no merit of the particular generation, but on the demerits of their ancestors; an aristocracy of the most odious and insolent kind—the aristocracy of wealth and pride.

258. Thaddeus Stevens, speech in behalf of the Pennsylvania free school act of 1834, reproduced in United States Commissioner of Education, Annual Report, 1898–99, Vol. 1, 520.

259. The Reason for Social Services in the Public School

The dangers of forming parasitic habits, great and real as these are in both the home and the school, should not lead us to deny to the child that help and support which are necessary to his normal development. Such a procedure would mean grave loss both to the individual and to society. As far as circumstances will permit, all the help that will be profitably used by the child in the development of his body, of his mind, and of his character, should be given, and in the giving the best interests of society are served. When the poverty of the family makes it necessary to use the efforts of the immature child for family support instead of for the child's own development there is loss not to the child alone but to the family and to the state. In this consideration free schools find their justification, and in the same consideration it is sought to justify the growing practice of supplying the child's need through the school in other than educative directions. The children are sometimes fed in the school. Their eyes are examined and glasses provided by the school. Adenoids are removed by the school surgeon and district nurses furnished by the school seek to assuage many of the ills to which flesh is heir. The wisdom of supplying the children with these helps is scarcely open to question, even though the wisdom of supplying this help through the school instead of through the home may be seriously questioned.

260. Socialism a Dangerous Tendency in Education

The socialistic idea of education destroys completely all necessity for sacrifice on the part of the parent, and all motive, therefore, for gratitude on the part of the child, and in time, all motive for that child, grown to maturity in ignorance of filial gratitude, to interest himself, much less to sacrifice himself, in the matter of his children's education. The tendency of the modern school is to restrict the duty of the parent to that of feeding and clothing the child . . . If the State, that nonentity for which each one of us, and therefore, none of us,

259. Thomas E. Shields, *Philosophy of Education* (Washington, D. C.: The Catholic Education Press, 1921), pp. 218–219.

260. James P. Munroe, "Certain Dangerous Tendencies in Education," *Educational Review*, 3:147–149, February 1892.

is responsible, is to bring up my children for me; if morality, good manners, and the domestic virtues are to be taught by someone else while I am but to provide the material things of life; then, forsooth, I will lay aside such sums as may meet these temporal wants, and with the balance, large or small, will eat, drink, and be merry; for surely I have no better use in the world. The fact that in a few generations the State will fall to pieces is not for me to consider, since I am credibly informed that the sacred duty of maintaining it is taught in the schools. This wicked and absurd result of socialism is, of course, extreme. There are, fortunately, human tendencies retarding such a mad career as this. Of these are avarice, making us save even where there is no direct motive for saving; family pride, unwilling to resign the task of shaping its heirs; and, above all, parental love, refusing to deny itself to its offspring.

Socialism in school matters is, beyond its narrowest interpretation, wholly without warrant. Once having established the machinery of free schools, once having placed proper safeguards for its maintenance and protection, the State should determine the least that it must do to preserve its integrity and provide for its healthy growth. It should then rigidly exclude from the school all that belongs to the parent, as well as all that, being non-essential to the life of the State, ought to be left to individual effort . . .

The socialistic tendency has brought about, in many of the United States, the passage of laws not warranted by such a view as this. Chief among these are the laws establishing high schools and those providing free text-books. The first are wrong in so far only as they make the high school absolutely free; the second, while justifiable in theory, are wrong in practice.

The maintenance of free high schools is unwise, first, because it obliges a whole community to pay for what only a limited number can enjoy; second, because, necessarily expensive it robs the lower schools of funds essential to them; and, third, because it offers to boys and girls wholly unfit for secondary education, a temptation to exchange the actual benefit of remunerative work at 15 years of age for the doubtful advantage of a training that can have no direct bearing upon their life work, and which, at the time of life it occurs, may do decided harm . . .

The provision for free text-books is logical. If teachers and school-buildings are to be furnished at the public cost, why not books also? This position can be disputed only on the ground of expediency. It is well for the parent to feel at some point the immediate money responsibility of his children's education. It is desirable that the child, at the close of his course, should have some tangible evidence of his school life, especially in those homes where text-books are almost the only literature. But these are minor things; there is greater danger lest, in the providing of text-books, there should be a neglect of more important provisions; for example, proper books of reference, good maps and similar aids, and above all, proper teachers . . .

261. State to Have No Monopoly in Education

The fundamental theory of liberty upon which all governments in this Union repose excludes any general power of the State to standardize its children by forcing them to accept instruction from public teachers only. The child is not the mere creature of the State; those who nurture him and direct his destiny have the right, coupled with the high duty, to recognize and prepare him for additional obligations.

262. Public and Private Schools as Stimulus to Each Other

That the whole or any large part of the education of the people should be in State hands, I go as far as anyone in deprecating. All that has been said of the importance of individuality of character, and diversity in opinions and modes of conduct, involves, as of the same unspeakable importance, diversity of education. A general State education is a mere contrivance for molding people to be exactly like one another: and as the mold in which it cases them is that which pleases the predominant power in the government, whether this be a monarch, a priesthood, an aristocracy, or the majority of the existing generation, in proportion as it is efficient and successful, it establishes a despotism over the mind, leading by natural tendency to one over the body. An education established and controlled by the State, should only exist, if at all, as one among many competing experiments, carried on for the purpose of example and stimulus, to keep the others up to a certain standard of excellence.

261. U. S. Supreme Court Justice James C. McReynolds, speaking for the Court in *Pierce v. Society of Sisters*, 268 U.S. 510, 535 (1924).
262. John Stuart Mill, *On Liberty* (London: J. W. Parker & Sons, 1859), pp. 190–191.

263. Types of Private School and Reasons for Them

Private schools may be divided into three large classes. First, there are those which are frankly experimental in their purpose and are being maintained largely for the purpose of testing educational theory and advancing educational science. The worth of this type of school is so generally recognized that it needs no defense. A wiser disposition of wealth which has accumulated in private hands would be difficult to imagine.

Second, there are many private schools, often of college grade, which are animated by a broad social spirit and which aim to provide superior educational opportunities of the conventional type. Such institutions, although usually drawing their students from the favored classes, relieve the public of certain educational burdens. Few would argue that these schools should be abolished.

Third, there are schools, usually supported and controlled by sects and classes, whose primary object is the perpetuation of some philosophy of life or attitude towards the world which is not taught in the public schools. In this group would fall all denominational and parochial schools, most of the great private preparatory schools for children of wealthy parentage, and finally such institutions as the labor colleges which receive their support from labor organizations and aim to develop leadership for the working class. From many quarters today come sharp criticisms of these institutions and bills are being presented before state legislatures, sometimes with success, providing for their abolition. The sectarian schools are attacked in some instances on the grounds of promoting a foreign culture; the schools for the wealthy are said to be undemocratic in their sympathies; and the labor colleges are accused of spreading radical social and economic doctrine. With the purposes of some of these institutions we are not in accord, but we feel it would be a grave mistake to attempt to legislate them out of existence. Our attitude is much like that expressed by Voltaire in writing to his adversary Helvetius; "I wholly disapprove of what you say—and will defend to the death your right to say it." The most pernicious of the existing educational agencies merely reflect the class organization of an undemocratic society and are but symptoms of conditions that can be altered only by

263. John C. Chapman and George S. Counts, *Principles of Education* (Boston: Houghton Mifflin Company, 1924), pp. 621–623. Used by permission of the publishers.

striking at those forces which lead to social stratification. We would further contend that liberty of thought and of conscience requires the granting of practically complete freedom to any group of citizens to establish schools for the perpetuation of any set of doctrines sincerely held. That the teachings in such institutions are not anti-social in their character and are in accord with the spirit of the fundamental law of the land is of course assumed. Except to make certain minimum requirements regarding the teaching of those basic subjects which are necessary to life in a complex society, the state should not proceed in regulating the conduct of these schools. The passing of private enterprise from the field of educational effort should not be forced by legislative enactment but should be the natural outcome of the improvement of the public school and the unification of the social order.

264. Divisiveness of Private Schools

Equally influential is church or sectarian isolation, the education of children of adherents of one sect in separate schools. No one can disclaim the right of parents to educate their children; but the effect of sectarian isolation in school, no matter what the religion taught may be, is mistrust, contempt, and too often, hatred, of all other sects. The creed does not rely upon its intrinsic value, but upon its method of isolation; upon the keeping of the children of its peculiar sect separate, that they may be inoculated with prejudices, instead of being filled with love for all mankind. It is true that a few come together from all schools into the universities, but there is no actual union. The class or the sectarian feeling by this time has become so strong, that mutual sympathy is well-nigh impossible.

Isolation is the most effective method of aristocracy . . .

265. Priority of State over the Family in Communism

In bourgeois society, the child is regarded as the property of its parents —if not wholly, at least to a major degree. When parents say, "My daughter," "My son," the words do not simply imply the existence of

264. Francis W. Parker, *Talks on Pedagogics* (New York: John Day Company, 1937), p. 307.

265. Nikolai I. Bukharin and Eugenii A. Preobrazhensky, *The A. B. C. of Communism*, Eden and Cedar Paul, translators (New York: Lyceum Literature Department, Workers Party of America, 1921), pp. 233–235.

a parental relationship, they also give expression to the parents' view that they have a right to educate their own children. From the socialist outlook, no such right exists. The individual human being does not belong to himself, but to society, to the human race. The individual can only live and thrive owing to the existence of society. The child, therefore, belongs to the society in which it lives, and thanks to which it came into being—and this society is something wider than the "society" of its own parents. To society, likewise, belongs the primary and basic right of educating children. From this point of view, the parents' claim to bring up their own children and thereby to impress upon the children's psychology their own limitations, must not merely be rejected, but must be absolutely laughed out of court. Society may entrust the education of children to the parents; but it may refuse to do anything of the kind; and there is all the more reason why society should refuse to entrust education to the parents, seeing that the faculty of educating children is far more rarely encountered than the faculty of begetting them. Of one hundred mothers, we shall perhaps find one or two who are competent educators. The future belongs to social education. Social education will make it possible for socialist society to train the coming generation most successfully, at lowest cost, and with the least expenditure of energy.

The social education of children, therefore, must be realized for other reasons besides those of pedagogy. It has enormous economic advantages. Hundreds of thousands, millions of mothers will thereby be freed for productive work and for self-culture. They will be freed from the soul-destroying routine of housework, and from the endless round of petty duties which are involved in the education of children in their own homes.

. . . By intensified propaganda among parents, the party must overcome bourgeois and petty-bourgeois prejudices concerning the necessity and superiority of home education . . .

266. Educational Importance of the Home

The question of home versus school is difficult to argue in the abstract. If ideal homes are contrasted with actual schools, the balance tips one way; if ideal schools are contrasted with actual homes, the balance tips the other way. I have no doubt in my own mind that the

266. Bertrand Russell, *Education and the Modern World* (New York: W. W. Norton & Company, Inc., 1932), pp. 65–71. Reprinted by permission of the publishers.

ideal school is better than the ideal home, at any rate the ideal urban home, because it allows more light and air, more freedom of movement, and more companionship of contemporaries. But it by no means follows that the actual school will be better than the actual home. The majority of parents feel affection for their children, and this sets limits to the harm they do them. But education authorities have no affection for the children concerned: at best, they are actuated by public spirit, which is directed towards the community as a whole, and not merely towards the children; at worst, they are politicians engaged in squabbles for plums. At present, the home plays an important part in forming the mentality of the young, a part by no means wholly good, but perhaps better than that which would be played by the State if it were in sole control of children. Home gives the child experience of affection, and of a small community in which he is important; also of relations with people of both sexes and different ages, and of the multifarious business of adult life. In this way it is useful as a corrective of the artificial simplification of school.

Another merit of home is that it preserves the diversity between individuals. If we were all alike, it might be convenient for the bureaucrat and the statistician, but it would be very dull, and would lead to a very unprogressive society. At present, the differences between individuals are greatly accentuated by the differences between their homes. Too much difference is a barrier to social solidarity, but some difference is essential to the best form of cooperation. An orchestra requires men with different talents and, within certain limits, different tastes; if all men insisted upon playing the trombone, orchestral music would be impossible. Social cooperation, in like manner, requires differences of taste and aptitude, which are less likely to exist if all children are exposed to exactly the same influences than if parental differences are allowed to affect them. This is to my mind an important argument against the Platonic doctrine that children should be wholly reared by the State.

✿   ✿   ✿

It is therefore dangerous to diminish the influence of home in education until we know what is going to take its place. Given a world State emancipated from theology, it is probable that the home would cease to be of value to young people, and that they would, on the average, become both happier and more intelligent through the removal of parental influences. But at present, except in Russia, all progress has to be won in opposition to Church and State, and anything that increases their hold over men's minds is to be viewed with alarm.

The question whether children should be removed from parents and brought up by the State must be considered, not only in relation to children, but also in relation to parents. The parental sentiment has a powerful influence upon behaviour, not only in women, but also in men. We have not the data to enable us to judge what men and women would be like if this sentiment were removed, but we may safely conjecture that they would be greatly changed. It is probable that most women would feel little desire for children in such circumstances, and that child-bearing would have to become a paid profession, adopted as a branch of the civic service. It is probable that the relations of men and women would grow trivial, and that serious conjugal affection would become rare. It is probable that men would become less inclined to work hard, since at present, in middle life, the chief incentive of many men is desire to provide for their families. This is proved by the heavy payments men make for life insurance, which show that they care what happens to their families after they are dead. It may be doubted whether, in a world where the family did not exist, ordinary men would concern themselves with events occurring after their death. It is possible that a kind of paralysis would descend upon the community, such as descends upon a hive of bees when the queen is removed. As to this, only experience can decide, and as yet experience is lacking.

There is, however, a great deal to be said on the other side. All possessive emotions are dangerous, and not least those of parents for their children. The feelings of parents for their children are intensely individualistic and competitive; many men who, while they are childless, are full of public spirit, become absorbed in the welfare of their own family as soon as they become fathers. The passion for private property is largely bound up with the family, and communists, from Plato downwards, are right in thinking that their economic system demands the cessation of private property in children. It is possible that whatever is admirable and useful in the parental sentiment could be transferred to the children in a given school, or, in exceptional individuals, to children in general. This, if it could be done, would be a definite moral advance. The parental sentiment is, I believe, the chief source of altruism, and many childless women have shown how valuable it can become when it is universalized. Perhaps, if it could be freed from the possessive taint which it must have while it is associated with actual physical parenthood, the world might lose some of its fierceness, and men might come to wish well to the generality of mankind. All this is conjectural, but it is a hypothesis which should be borne in mind.

The question of home versus school is one which, up to a certain point, can be decided on a basis of common sense, without raising fundamental issues. But when we try to pass beyond that point, we are met by our ignorance of human psychology: we do not know how much in our sentiments is instinctive, or how vigorous our sentiments could be if they were trained to be quite other than they are at present . . .

13

Church and State in Education

Problems in the Philosophy of Education Discussed in this Section

1. Should the civil state possess ethical as well as political sovereignty in matters educational? To what extent are pupils and teachers, as such, private individuals?
2. What are the respective spheres of influence in education of family, church, and state? In case of conflict, whose interest is paramount? Why?
3. Should the divine mandate of the Catholic Church over education be considered to extend to the secular curriculum as well as to the religious and moral? What are the democratic implications of an infallible teaching agency?
4. Are the educational interests of children more in peril from tyranny of the state or from the orthodoxy of the church? Is educational freedom to be gained by divorcing church and state and setting their absolutisms over against each other?

267. Educational Spheres of Family, Church, and State

Education is essentially a social and not a mere individual activity. Now there are three necessary societies, distinct from one another and yet harmoniously combined by God, into which man is born: two, namely the family and civil society, belong to the natural order; the third, the Church, to the supernatural order.

In the first place comes the family, instituted directly by God for its peculiar purpose, the generation and formation of offspring; for this reason it has priority of nature and therefore of rights over civil society. Nevertheless, the family is an imperfect society, since it has not in itself all the means for its own complete development; whereas civil society is a perfect society, having in itself all the means for its

---

267. Pius XI, "Christian Education of Youth," *Catholic Educational Review*, 28:132–157, March 1930.

peculiar end, which is the temporal well-being of the community; and so, in this respect, that is, in view of the common good, it has pre-eminence over the family, which finds its own suitable temporal perfection precisely in civil society.

The third society, into which man is born when through Baptism he receives the Divine life of grace, is the Church; a society of the supernatural order and of universal extent; a perfect society, because it has in itself all the means required for its own end, which is the eternal salvation of mankind; hence it is supreme in its own domain.

Consequently, education, which is concerned with man as a whole, individually and socially, in the order of nature and in the order of grace, necessarily belongs to all these three societies, in due proportion, corresponding, according to the disposition of Divine Providence, to the coordination of their respective ends.

And first of all education belongs pre-eminently to the Church, by reason of a double title in the supernatural order conferred exclusively upon her by God Himself; absolutely superior therefore to any other title in the natural order.

      ✿   ✿   ✿

In the first place the Church's mission of education is in wonderful agreement with that of the family, for both proceed from God, and in a remarkably similar manner. God directly communicates to the family, in the natural order, fecundity, which is the principle of life, and hence also the principle of education to life, together with authority, the principle of order.

      ✿   ✿   ✿

The family therefore holds directly from the Creator the mission and hence the right to educate the offspring, a right inalienable because inseparably joined to the strict obligation, a right anterior to any right whatever of civil society and of the State, and therefore inviolable on the part of any power on earth.

      ✿   ✿   ✿

On this point the common sense of mankind is in such complete accord, that they would be in open contradiction with it who dared maintain that the children belong to the State before they belong to the family, and that the State has an absolute right over their education. Untenable is the reason they adduce, namely, that man is born a citizen and hence belongs primarily to the State, not bearing in mind that before being a citizen man must exist; and existence does not come from the State, but from the parents . . . It does not however follow from this that the parents' right to educate their children is absolute and despotic; for it is necessarily subordinated to the last end and to natural and Divine Law . . .

❂   ❂   ❂

These rights have been conferred upon civil society by the Author of nature Himself, not by title of fatherhood, as in the case of the Church and of the family, but in virtue of the authority which it possesses to promote the common temporal welfare, which is precisely the purpose of its existence. Consequently education cannot pertain to civil society in the same way in which it pertains to the Church and to the family, but in a different way corresponding to its own particular end and object.

Now this end and object, the common welfare in the temporal order, consists in that peace and security in which families and individual citizens have the free exercise of their rights, and at the same time enjoy the greatest spiritual and temporal prosperity possible in this life, by the mutual union and coordination of the work of all. The function therefore of the civil authority residing in the State is twofold, to protect and to foster, but by no means to absorb the family and the individual, or to substitute itself for them.

Accordingly in the matter of education, it is the right, or to speak more correctly, it is the duty of the State to protect, in its legislation, because the prior rights, already described, of the family as regards the Christian education of its offspring and, consequently, also to respect the supernatural rights of the Church in this same realm of Christian education.

It also belongs to the State to protect the rights of the child itself when the parents are found wanting either physically or morally in this respect, whether by default, incapacity or misconduct, since, as has been shown, their right to educate is not an absolute and despotic one, but dependent on the natural and Divine law, and therefore subject alike to the authority and jurisdiction of the Church, and to the vigilance and administrative care of the State in view of the common good. Besides, the family is not a perfect society, that is, it has not in itself all the means necessary for its full development. In such cases, exceptional no doubt, the State does not put itself in the place of the family, but merely supplies deficiencies, and provides suitable means, always in conformity with the natural rights of the child and the supernatural rights of the Church.

In general then it is the right and duty of the State to protect, according to the rules of right reason and faith, the moral and religious education of youth, by removing public impediments that stand in the way.

In the first place it pertains to the State, in view of the common good, to promote in various ways the education and instruction of youth. It should begin by encouraging and assisting, of its own accord, the initiative and activity of the Church and the family, whose successes in this field have been clearly demonstrated by history and experience. It should moreover supplement their work whenever this falls short of what is necessary, even by means of its own schools and institutions. For the State more than any other society is provided with the means put at its disposal for the needs of all, and it is only right that it use these means to the advantage of those who have contributed them.

❃   ❃   ❃

Accordingly unjust and unlawful is any monopoly, educational or scholastic, which, physically or morally, forces families to make use of government schools, contrary to the dictates of their Christian conscience, or contrary even to their legitimate preferences.

This does not prevent the State from making due provision for the right administration of public affairs and for the protection of its peace, within or without the realm. These are things which directly concern the public good and call for special aptitudes and special preparation. The State may therefore reserve to itself the establishment and direction of schools intended to prepare for certain civic duties and especially for military service, provided it be careful not to injure the rights of the Church or of the family in what pertains to them. It is well to repeat this warning here; for in these days there is spreading a spirit of nationalism which is false and exaggerated, as well as dangerous to true peace and prosperity.

❃   ❃   ❃

Since however the younger generation must be trained in the arts and sciences for the advantage and prosperity of civil society, and since the family of itself is unequal to this task, it was necessary to create that social institution, the school. But let it be borne in mind that this institution owes its existence to the initiative of the family and of the Church, long before it was undertaken by the State. Hence, considered in its historical origin, the school is by its very nature an institution subsidiary and complementary to the family and to the Church. It follows logically and necessarily that it must not be in opposition to, but in positive accord with those other two elements, and form with them a perfect moral union, constituting one sanctuary of education, as it were, with the family and the Church. Otherwise it is doomed to fail of its purpose, and to become instead an agent of destruction.

❃   ❃   ❃

. . . The so-called "neutral" or "lay" school, from which religion is excluded is contrary to the fundamental principles of education. Such a school moreover cannot exist in practice; it is bound to become irreligious . . .

For the mere fact that a school gives some religious instruction (often extremely stinted), does not bring it into accord with the rights of the Church and of the Christian family, or make it a fit place for Catholic students. To be this, it is necessary that all the teaching and the whole organization of the school, and its teachers, syllabus and textbooks in every branch, be regulated by the Christian spirit, under the direction and maternal supervision of the Church; so that Religion may be in a very truth the foundation and crown of the youth's entire training; and this in every grade of school, not only the elementary, but the intermediate and the higher institutions of learning as well.

*   *   *

Let it be loudly proclaimed and well understood and recognized by all, that Catholics, no matter what their nationality, in agitating for Catholic schools for their children, are not mixing in party politics, but are engaged in a religious enterprise demanded by conscience. They do not intend to separate their children either from the body of the nation or its spirit, but to educate them in a perfect manner, most conducive to the prosperity of the nation. Indeed a good Catholic, precisely because of his Catholic principles, makes the better citizen, attached to his country, and loyally submissive to constituted civil authority in every legitimate form of government.

268. Catholic Church as Infallible Teaching Agency

. . . In this proper object of her mission, that is, "in faith and morals, God Himself has made the Church sharer in the Divine Magisterium and, by a special privilege, granted her immunity from error; hence she is the mistress of men, supreme and absolutely sure, and she has inherent in herself an inviolable right to freedom in teaching." By necessary consequence the Church is independent of any sort of earthly power in the origin as well as in the exercise of her mission as educator, not merely in regard to her proper end and object, but also in regard to the means necessary and suitable to attain that end. Hence with regard to every other kind of human learning and instruction,

268. Pope Pius XI, "The Christian Education of Youth," *The Catholic Educational Review*, 28:133–134, March 1930.

which is the common patrimony of individuals and society, the Church has an independent right to make use of it, and above all to decide what may help or harm Christian education. And this must be so, because the Church as a perfect society has an independent right to the means conducive to its end, and because every form of instruction, no less than every human action, has a necessary connection with man's last end, and therefore cannot be withdrawn from the dictates of the Divine law, of which the Church is guardian, interpreter and infallible mistress.

269. The State to Teach Prudence, the Church Piety

On the whole, learning is, for Locke and for his fellows, a servant of prudence rather than of virtue. Great knowledge is not needed to make a man acceptable to God. "Simple piety" will do—in fact it may be preferred. But if one wishes to get on in the world, to advance one's own self-interest, then one must study men and the world to see how they may be used for the realization of one's purposes. Education becomes deeply vocational in intention. Learning is no longer a following after the Divine reason. It is an instrument of worldly success . . .

Locke's apostasy has also had a profound effect in starting the drift which has carried the school out of the hands of the church and into the hands of the state. If the division of human conduct into two distinct fields be accepted then it inevitably follows that neither church nor state is fitted to take charge of education as a whole. The church, representing God, may well undertake to teach piety and virtue. The government, if it can teach at all, may instruct young people in the ways of prudence, the customs and habits suitable to the social contract which guards their interests. But neither institution is fitted to give guidance in both realms. An unworldly church cannot teach common sense. Nor can a state, whose motivations go no deeper than self-interested prudence, be expected to impart private virtue, generous sentiment, human aspiration. If Locke's moral dualism is accepted, then, at one stroke, both church and state are found to be unfitted to take charge of education as a whole. As one searches out the motives which have prompted the transferring of the control of the schools from one institution to another, it is that double unfitness which seems to be the most powerful influence. "Neither of them can do

269. Alexander Meiklejohn, *Education between Two Worlds* (New York: Harper & Brothers, 1942), pp. 67, 68. Reprinted by permission of the publishers.

it," we have said; "therefore turn it over to the state."—It is little wonder that our Protestant-capitalist education has collapsed. It is little wonder that the civilization which gives and receives that education is now involved in desperate self-destroying strife.

270. State and Church in the Natural and Supernatural Order

Those who do not understand the teachings of the Catholic Church sometimes labor under the mistaken notion that there is a conflict, according to the teaching of the Church, between the natural and the supernatural, but in her teachings we find instead of conflict an insistence upon the natural as presupposed by the supernatural. The Church's ultimate aim is, indeed, the development of the supernatural virtues of faith, hope and charity, of poverty, obedience and chastity, but she demands as a prerequisite the development of the corresponding natural virtues and she lends to the teacher all the wealth of her supernatural treasures for the attainment of these ends. His efforts are to be reenforced by divine grace; his knowledge is to be strengthened by revealed truth; his motives are to be transfigured by supernatural sanction.

While the Church demands and secures the development of the supernatural virtues as a prerequisite and as a means to the securing of her own specific aim in the supernatural order, the State's aim does not reach beyond the natural. The virtues of faith, hope and charity, of disinterestedness, obedience and self-conquest as taught in the State schools neither presuppose nor secure the development of the corresponding supernatural virtues and for this reason the teaching in the State schools is, and must remain, inadequate in the eyes of the Church.

The Church cannot consent to such a division of the work of education as would commit to the State schools the development of the natural virtues and reserve to the Catholic school the development of the supernatural virtues. The unitary character of life and the inseparable relations of nature and grace demand that the natural and the supernatural unfold in the child's consciousness simultaneously and in their true relations. The natural and the supernatural in the virtues which she inculcates must function as one indivisibly vital entity. The supernatural must ever strengthen and invigorate the natural. It must

270. Thomas E. Shields, "Relations between Catholic and Public Schools," *Catholic Educational Review*, 12:140–141, September 1916.

supply to the natural virtues an enriched course, a wider vision and a more efficient sanction.

Experience has abundantly shown that moral qualities cannot be taught after the manner in which the ordinary branches of the curriculum, such as mathematics, or physics, or literature, are taught. Moral qualities are not begotten of mere knowledge. Their absence may coexist with the widest knowledge, and they may be present in a preeminent degree where knowledge is meager. Moral qualities are vital entities and their production is subject to the law of homogenesis. Like begets like; virtue is lit at the lamp of virtue in the natural as well as the supernatural order . . .

271. Necessity for Divorce of Church and State

. . . It seems important to point out that though the separation of church and state has its good and more than sufficient reasons, it is often advocated for reasons that can be harmful in their consequences for both religion and democratic society. To suppose, for instance, that church and state must be separated in order to divorce religion and politics is to entertain an illusion that this can really be done. Furthermore, one motive underlying the attempted divorce has been to defend an absolute authority for the church at least in some sphere of "faith and morals" and for the state in the sphere of legal adjustment. This should be considered a bad motive by all who are opposed to institutional absolutism in either sphere. Personally I should not want to grant absolute authority over faith and morals to any institution, nor to depart from that federalism in government which involves the denial of absolute legal authority to any single system of laws. Absolutism departmentalized tends towards something lifeless and mechanical in both the secular and the religious spheres.

The good reason for a separation of church and state is not to divorce religion and politics, but to prevent either church or state from obtaining an actual monopoly in either sphere. It is an interest in freedom. To the extent that church and state are persuaded to relinquish their absolutistic, not to say totalitarian, tendencies, there is much less need of their separation. The remark has its bearing on the politics of "Establishment" in England, for example. But seeing

271. Second Conference on the Scientific Spirit and Democratic Faith, *The Authoritarian Attempt to Capture Education* (New York: King's Crown Press, 1945), pp. 138–139.

that church and state are not so thoroughly persuaded to relinquish absolutistic claims, and perhaps never can be, what resources has a democratic society in the interest of freedom? It has two. The first consists in checking one absolutism by the other, hence their separation. A second consists in seeing to it that many religious and many legal functions are actually performed by groups and organizations that are not making absolutistic claims. Continued vigorous and flourishing development along this second line is of great importance, I think, to democratic society.

272. Secularism Explained

In religion, the secular method bears both a cause and effect relation to the principle of separation of church and state. Separation has as its purpose the freeing of the religious conscience from governmental control. It guarantees to religious organizations and individuals the privilege of formulating and propagating their faiths without interference by the state. To assure this freedom, it removes religion completely from the sphere of public control; but, in exchange, it imposes upon religious organizations the responsibility of self-support, and, within the sphere of public education, procedures that are scrupulously objective and fair.

Secular education is thus a method of thinking and a way of living that strives for mutual understanding and good will in a realm where, as Justice Frankfurter has said, "conflicts are most easily and most bitterly engendered." It is neither identical with naturalism nor is it "materialistic" or "atheistic." Rather it is a logic and a discipline designed to further community of thought and action within an heterogenous people. By means of this logic men can raise themselves above the battle of religious sects and the conflicts of interests in all the relationships of life. It is a method that strives to alleviate and to reconcile these interests, and, on occasion, to attain a vision of a new heaven and a new earth. While not an exclusive invention of the American people, it is born of America's unique experience with diversity. It is a method, finally, that gave birth to the American secular public school and now looks to that school for the education of American youth in a way of life that may well constitute the most distinctive contribution of American civilization to the creation of one world out of many cultures.

272. Vivian T. Thayer, "Sectarian Attacks on Public Education," *Educational Theory,* 3:125, April, 1953.

273. No Church School Control under Communism

To state that there is no place in our school for any kind of religious influence is hardly necessary. Clearly the church, which has always been a powerful agency for clouding the social consciousness of the workers, should not be admitted into the school.

274. Neither God nor Metaphysics to be Core of State Schools

Whatever "educational" functions the state may undertake, the Christian Church must resist any and every attempt by the state to mold the souls of its citizens at the depths where education touches them. The state must not be allowed to put either God or metaphysical first principles at the center of its educational system—not because God does not belong there, but because no state can be trusted to administer that kind of educational system. That way lies either the fascist or communist abyss. It spells the end of democracy.

273. Albert P. Pinkevitch, *The New Education in the Soviet Republic* (New York: John Day Company, 1929), p. 153.
274. "God Centered Education," editorial in *Christian Century,* 54:543, April 1937.

14

Nationalism and Education

Problems in the Philosophy of Education Discussed in this Section

1. What educational values are involved in nationalism? Do they differ from the values in patriotic education?
2. Is nationalism in education incompatible with democratic education? With religious education?
3. Should national unity be enforced through compulsory patriotic education?
4. What are the relative ethical values of centralized national educational administration as against local educational administration?
5. Is education for national loyalty incompatible with education for loyalty to some world political unit like the United Nations?
6. In order to have "one world," is it necessary to have one educational philosophy? If so, how will this philosophy transcend the multiplicity of educational philosophies now predicated on diverse conceptions of religion, politics, economics, and the like?

275. Patriotism in Education

The devolopment of nationalism has forced men out of narrow sectionalism into membership in larger social units, and has cultivated loyalty to a state which rises above petty and selfish interests. But it has also raised the problem whether nationalism implies the cult of docility and uniformity in public matters; it has also brought into the foreground the question of the meaning of patriotism and the place of propaganda and indoctrination in the development of men's minds. If patriotism is defined in the spirit of jingoism and imperialism, in terms of pride in the strength, the power, and the superiority of one's nation, the world is in constant danger . . . If, however, patriotism is

275. Isaac L. Kandel, *Comparative Education* (Boston: Houghton Mifflin Company, 1933), pp. 9–10. Used by permission of the publishers.

defined as loyalty to the moral and spiritual ideals of one's nation, confidence in what it can contribute to the progressive civilization of the world and to the well-being of humanity, acceptance of the right of other nations to embark on a similar mission, and faith that more can be gained for national as well as international progress from cooperation and the pooling of resources than from the pursuit of selfish interests, the world as well as each nation will benefit. If the first view of patriotism is accepted, propaganda and indoctrination in education mean the exploitation of prejudices, bigotry, and human weaknesses, which colors not only the teaching of patriotism but the whole educative process. If the second definition is adopted, propaganda and indoctrination do not cease to have their place in education, but they imply the cultivation of human intelligence to criticize what is demoralizing and to honor what is choice-worthy. In the one method the emphasis is on dictation, on authority; in the other, the growth of free personality in ability to reach decisions on the basis of knowledge and inquiry is stressed. The danger is as imminent today as it was in the nineteenth century that, because nations have grown up through conflicts, dislike and hostility without, the cult of nationalism and its expression as patriotism may have inherent in it intolerance and hatred of other nations. There are signs, however, that in education at any rate, no matter what the facts may be in politics, it is being recognized that a spirit of nationalism can be cultivated which is ready to play its part in the development of world-mindedness.

276. Patriotism and General Welfare

It is important to note from the standpoint of philosophy that important truths discoverable by human reason bear directly upon the teaching and the practice of patriotism. Among these truths the following can be presented briefly:

1. All human beings are entitled to our love, in a certain degree, because they are like ourselves and there should be a special affinity between those realities that are specifically the same. The members of our own nation are more like ourselves than are other human beings and consequently they have a special right to call upon our love and service. Real patriotism profits from this affinity.

2. The human individual is not entirely material. It is a person

276. Ignatius Smith, "Education for Patriotism," in Roy J. Deferrari, editor, *Essays on Catholic Education in the United States* (Washington, D.C.: The Catholic University of America Press, 1942), pp. 55–57.

composed of a soul which is independent of matter in its operation and consequently in its origin, but which is united with matter to form an individual of rational nature. The individual and immortal soul created by God gives to our fellow citizens, as to ourselves, a value that makes them worth living for, worth protecting, and sometimes worth fighting for even unto death. The nation is not a vague abstraction and not the unwarranted hypostasizing of a name. The nation is the collection of the persons and the homes which compose it. Each of these persons is important because of its spiritual nature and its eternal destiny, and their collective importance makes the nation sacred and worthy of the patriotic devotion of its citizens.

3. The nation and its government must be concerned about the welfare and the development of the entire personality, material and spiritual, of all of its citizens. It must provide opportunities for the physical, mental, moral, and spiritual development of all its people and it must see that opportunities for such development are not jeopardized either by sedition at home or by war from abroad. The government will help to earn the patriotic devotion of its people in the degree to which it provides for the development of the entire personality of all the people. Upon the citizens rests the obligation to honor the right of their fellow men to such complete development and to promote this development with patriotic fidelity. No correct idea of patriotism can be given philosophically without teaching the young the value of the home and the sanctity of marriage. Many of our youth are the victims of homes shattered by divorce. They are forced into society without the training in the virtues of citizenship which can be given only in homes that are permanent and in families that are large. With the value of an unbroken marriage and of marital relations that are generous with God and nation our citizens must be familiarized if real patriotism is to be developed.

4. The concept of patriotism philosophically is based on the relation of an individual in a community to the common weal of the group. The common good is not isolated from the welfare of the individuals, as it is sometimes conceived to be in totalitarian states. Neither is the common good the sum total of the welfare of the individuals. Individual welfare must not be achieved at the cost of the welfare of associates in the community or by injury to the state through which fellow citizens might suffer. Neither may the good of the state be advanced in an isolated way by disastrous infringement on the rights of the citizens. The individual good, the development of the individuals and the common weal, advance or lag together. Social living is a partnership which places on every individual responsibility for the

progress of his neighbor and for the progress of government through which the benefits of the common weal are distributed to all. The philosophical reasoning is important in the education of our young and old in patriotic love and service. Citizens must advance together through patriotic service to their nation or eventually they will fail together. The burdens of patriotic service for the common weal must be distributed to all according to their ability to carry the load.

5. Another philosophical principle of tremendous importance in the teaching of patriotism is the need of authority in the preservation of the common weal. Were all the citizens of a nation totally unselfish and altruistically devoted to the common weal, authority and law would not be necessary. Unfortunately, individuals are more concerned about their own good than about the welfare of the community and of its members. This means that authority and law have got to decide what should be done by individual citizens, in this particular situation, for the advancement of the common weal. Naturally the self-will which makes law and authority necessary will create opposition to authority on the part of those whose desires have been frustrated. Public authority in a democracy is elected by the people with the understanding that the recipient of the power will have the right, under the limitations of the Constitution, to decide what is and what is not for the common weal. One of the prime conditions of patriotism is the recognition of the relation of authority and law to the common weal. There can be little real patriotism in a democracy where there is no recognition of this basic philosophy of the importance of authority.

6. Integrated with the recognition of the function of authority and law in the development of patriotism is the concept of the importance of reverence for authority and obedience to law. Democracy differs from totalitarian government in this respect at least, that it gives its citizens wide opportunity to render *voluntary* and *intelligent* obedience to the laws which they have established through their elected representatives. Submission to the law of a tyrant is often a matter of endurance and compulsion. Submission to law and authority in a democracy ought to be a matter of intelligent appraisal of the need of obedience for the solidarity and perpetuity of social organization and of political society. The teaching of patriotism will meet with nothing but failure unless the habit of intelligent submission and reverence is made basic in the formation of character. Otherwise democracy will be nothing more than a concatenation of independently seditious mobs masking their discontent under the guise of republicanism and protected by the very liberties which their disobedience will help to make impossible. It is not going too far to say that the basic truths, well

within the realm of philosophy, can be explained without difficulty to students, and that without the teaching of them both patriotism and democracy are idle dreams.

277. Democracy and Decentralization of Control

The second safeguard against the exercise of arbitrary and short-sighted authority on the part of the state is the decentralization of control. If each of the forty-eight states is allowed that complete freedom of action in educational matters which is provided by the federal constitution, ideas of promise which are given a hostile reception in one state may be granted a favorable hearing in another. From the standpoint of the development of a democratic system of education this is without doubt the great merit of our federal system. Somewhere, sooner or later, advanced educational and social theories are almost certain of a trial. In this limited setting before they are given a wide adoption their worth may be proved. A richer field for educational experimentation than exists in the American commonwealth would be difficult to find. Much freedom should also be allowed the local authorities, the cities, the counties, the towns, and the villages, in the control of education. The work of the state organization should be confined very largely to that of stimulating and harmonizing the growth of education within the state. At certain points, where the essence of the educative process is not at stake, standardization is desirable, but the bureaucracy which is the curse of many governments must be rigorously avoided.

278. Compulsory National Unity

The Board of Education . . . adopted a resolution . . . ordering that the salute to the flag become "a regular part of the program of activities in the public schools," that all teachers and pupils "shall be required to participate in the salute honoring the Nation represented by the Flag; provided, however, that refusal to salute the Flag be

277. John C. Chapman and George S. Counts, *Principles of Education* (Boston: Houghton Mifflin Company, 1942), pp. 623–624. Used by permission of the publishers.

278. U. S. Supreme Court Justice Robert A. Jackson, speaking for the Court in *Board of Education v. Barnette*, 319 U.S. 626, 640–642 (1942).

regarded as an act of insubordination, and shall be dealt with accordingly."

*   *   *

National unity as an end which officials may foster by persuasion and example is not in question. The problem is whether under our Constitution compulsion as here employed is a permissible means for its achievement.

Struggles to coerce uniformity of sentiment in support of some end thought essential to their time and country have been waged by many good as well as by evil men. Nationalism is a relatively recent phenomenon but at other times and places the ends have been racial or territorial security, support of a dynasty or regime, and particular plans for saving souls. As first and moderate methods to attain unity have failed, those bent on its accomplishment must resort to an ever-increasing severity. As governmental pressure toward unity becomes greater, so strife becomes more bitter as to whose unity it shall be. Probably no deeper division of our people could proceed from any provocation than from finding it necessary to choose what doctrine and whose program public educational officials shall compel youth to unite in embracing. Ultimate futility of such attempts to compel coherence is the lesson of every such effort from the Roman drive to stamp out Christianity as a disturber of its pagan unity, the Inquisition, as a means to religious and dynastic unity, the Siberian exiles as a means to Russian unity, down to the fast-failing efforts of our present totalitarian enemies. Those who begin coercive elimination of dissent soon find themselves exterminating dissenters. Compulsory unification of opinion achieves only the unanimity of the graveyard.

It seems trite but necessary to say that the First Amendment to our Constitution was designed to avoid these ends by avoiding these beginnings. There is no mysticism in the American concept of the State or of the nature or origin of its authority. We set up government by consent of the governed, and the Bill of Rights denies those in power any legal opportunity to coerce that consent. Authority here is to be controlled by public opinion, not public opinion by authority.

The case is made difficult not because the principles of its decision are obscure but because the flag involved is our own. Nevertheless, we apply the limitations of the Constitution with no fear that freedom to be intellectually and spiritually diverse or even contrary will disintegrate the social organization. To believe that patriotism will not flourish if patriotic ceremonies are voluntary and spontaneous instead of a compulsory routine is to make an unflattering estimate of the appeal of our institutions to free minds. We can have intellectual individualism and the rich cultural diversities that we owe to exceptional minds only at the price of occasional eccentricity and abnormal attitudes. When they are so harmless to others or to the state as those we deal with here, the price is not too great. But freedom to differ is not limited to things that do not matter much. That would be a mere shadow of freedom. The test of its substance is the right to differ as to things that touch the heart of the existing order.

If there is any fixed star in our constitutional constellation, it is that no official, high or petty, can prescribe what shall be orthodox in politics, nationalism, religion, or other matters of opinion or force citizens to confess by word or act their faith therein. If there are any circumstances which permit an exception, they do not now occur to us.

We think the action of the local authorities in compelling the flag salute and pledge transcends constitutional limitations on their power and invades the sphere of intellect and spirit which it is the purpose of the First Amendment to our Constitution to reserve from all official control.

279. Education for World Citizenship

Apart from national cohesion within the State, which is all that State education attempts to achieve at present, international cohesion, and a sense of the whole human race as one co-operative unit, is becoming increasingly necessary, if our scientific civilization is to survive. I think this survival will demand, as a minimum condition, the establishment of a world State, and the subsequent institution of a worldwide system of education designed to produce loyalty to the world State. No doubt such a system of education will entail, at any rate for a century or two, certain crudities which will militate against the development of the individual. But if the alternative is chaos and the death of civilization, the price will be worth paying. Modern communities are more closely knit than those of past times in their economic and political structure; and if they are to be successful there must be a corresponding increase in the sense of citizenship on the part of individual men and women. Loyalty to a world State would not, of course, entail the worst feature of loyalty to one of the existing States, namely, the encouragement of war. But it might entail considerable curtailment of the intellectual and of the aesthetic impulses. I think, nevertheless, that the most vital need of the near

279. Bertrand Russell, *Education and the Modern World* (New York: W. W. Norton & Company, 1932), pp. 26–27. Reprinted by permission of the publishers.

future will be the cultivation of a vivid sense of citizenship of the world. When once the world as a single economic and political unit has become secure, it will be possible for individual culture to revive. But until that time our whole civilization remains in jeopardy. Considered *sub specie aeternitatis*, the education of the individual is to my mind a finer thing than the education of the citizen; but considered politically, in relation to the needs of the time, the education of the citizen must, I fear, take the first place.

280. A Philosophy of Education for UNESCO

From acceptance of certain principles or philosophies, UNESCO is obviously debarred. Thus, while fully recognizing the contribution made to thought by many of their thinkers, it cannot base its outlook on one of the competing theologies of the world as against the others, whether Islam, Roman Catholicism, Protestant Christianity, Buddhism, Unitarianism, Judaism, or Hinduism. Neither can it espouse one of the politico-economic doctrines competing in the world to-day to the exclusion of the others—the present versions of capitalistic free enterprise, Marxist communism, semi-socialist planning, and so on. It cannot do so, partly because it is contrary to its charter and essence to be sectarian, partly for the very practical reason that any such attempt would immediately incur the active hostility of large and influential groups, and the non-cooperation or even withdrawal of a number of nations.

For somewhat similar reasons it cannot base itself exclusively on any special or particular philosophy or outlook, whether existentialism or *élan vital,* rationalism or spiritualism, an economic-determinist or a rigid cyclical theory of human history. Nor, with its stress on democracy and the principles of human dignity, equality and mutual respect, can it adopt the view that the state is a higher or more important end than the individual; or any rigid class theory of society. And in the preamble to its constitution it expressly repudiates racialism and any belief in superior or inferior "races," nations, or ethnic groups.

And finally, with its stress on the concrete tasks of education, science and culture, on the need for mutual understanding by the peoples of the world, and on the objectives of peace and human welfare on this planet, it would seem debarred from an exclusively or primarily other-worldly outlook.

280. Julian Huxley, *UNESCO: Its Purpose and Its Philosophy* (Washington, D.C.: Public Affairs Press, 1948), pp. 4–6.

So much for what UNESCO cannot or should not adopt in the way of philosophies or guiding principle. Now for the positive side. Its main concern is with peace and security and with human welfare, in so far as they can be subserved by the educational and scientific and cultural relations of the peoples of the world. Accordingly its outlook must, it seems, be based on some form of humanism. Further, that humanism must clearly be a world humanism, both in the sense of seeking to bring in all the peoples of the world, and of treating all peoples and all individuals within each people as equals in terms of human dignity, mutual respect, and educational opportunity. It must also be a scientific humanism, in the sense that the application of science provides most of the material basis for human culture, and also that the practice and the understanding of science need to be integrated with that of other human activities. It cannot, however, be materialistic, but must embrace the spiritual and mental as well as the material aspects of existence, and must attempt to do so on a truly monistic, unitary philosophic basis.

Finally, it must be an evolutionary as opposed to a static or ideal humanism. It is essential for UNESCO to adopt an evolutionary approach. If it does not do so, its philosophy will be a false one, its humanism at best partial, at worst misleading. We will justify this assertion in detail later. Here it is only necessary to recall that in the last few decades it has been possible to develop an extended or general theory of evolution which can provide the necessary intellectual scaffolding for modern humanism. It not only shows us man's place in nature and his relations to the rest of the phenomenal universe, not only gives us a description of the various types of evolution and the various trends and directions within them, but allows us to distinguish desirable and undesirable trends, and to demonstrate the existence of progress in the cosmos. And finally it shows us man as now the sole trustee of further evolutionary progress, and gives us important guidance as to the courses he should avoid and those he should pursue if he is to achieve that progress.

An evolutionary approach provides the link between natural science and human history; it teaches us the need to think in the dynamic terms of speed and direction rather than in the static ones of momentary position or quantitative achievement; it not only shows us the origin and biological roots of our human values, but gives us some basis and external standards for them among the apparently neutral mass of natural phenomena; and it is indispensable in enabling us to pick out, among the chaotic welter of conflicting tendencies today, those trends and activities and methods which UNESCO should emphasize and facilitate.

15

The School and Social Progress

Problems in the Philosophy of Education Discussed in this Section

1. Is it the duty of the school to conserve the social heritage? Does an existing social order have the right to use the school in the maintenance of its own existence?
2. Does the school have a normative function to perform in relation to the social heritage? Would this function necessarily be at variance with the conservative one?
3. Does the normative function of the school warrant its attempting to lead in the construction of a new social order? Who shall decide what kind of social order? Shall the teachers decide?
4. In attempting to point the way to a new social order, would the school be encroaching on the prerogatives of the legislature? Would this be true if, as Dewey says, education is its own end?
5. Can the school hope to be an independent critic of the social order? Can the school be free from politics and yet be secure when criticizing them?
6. Do the foregoing considerations apply equally to public and to private schools? To secondary and to higher schools?
7. Should the posture of the school alter when evolutionary change accelerates to a revolutionary pace?

281. Interaction of Education and Social Change

It is possible to put the processes of social change and of education in opposition to one another, and then debate whether desirable social change would follow education, or whether radical social change must come before marked improvements in education can take place. We hold that the two are correlative and interactive. No social modification, slight or revolutionary, can edure except as it enters into the action of a people through their desires and purposes. This introduc-

281. John Dewey and John L. Childs, in *The Educational Frontier*, William H. Kilpatrick, editor (New York: The Century Company, 1933), p. 318.

317

tion and perpetuation are effected by education. But every improvement in the social structure and its operations releases the educative resources of mankind and gives them a better opportunity to enter into normal social processes so that the latter become themselves more truly educative.

The process of interaction is circular and never-ending. We plead for a better, a more just, a more open and straight-forward, a more publicsociety, in which free and all-round communication and participation occur as a matter of course in order that education may be bettered . . .

282. Education Should Conform to the Constitution

No one will doubt that the legislator should direct his attention above all to the education of youth; for the neglect of education does harm to the constitution. The citizen should be moulded to suit the form of government under which he lives. For each government has a peculiar character which originally formed and which continues to preserve it. The character of democracy creates democracy, and the character of oligarchy creates oligarchy; and always the better the character, the better the government.

283. School Should Take Initiative for New Social Order

If we may now assume that the child will be imposed upon in some fashion by the various elements in his environment, the real question is not whether imposition will take place, but rather from what source it will come. If we were to answer this question in terms of the past, there could, I think, be but one answer: on all genuinely crucial matters the school follows the wishes of the groups or classes that actually rule society; on minor matters the school is sometimes allowed a certain measure of freedom. But the future may be unlike the past. Or perhaps I should say that teachers, if they could increase sufficiently their stock of courage, intelligence, and vision, might become a social force of some magnitude. About this eventuality I am not over sanguine, but a society lacking leadership as ours does, might even accept the guidance of teachers. Through powerful organizations they might at

282. Aristotle, *Politics*, Bk. VIII. chap. 1.
283. George S. Counts, *Dare the School Build a New Social Order?* (New York: John Day Company, 1932), pp. 27–31.

least reach the public conscience and come to exercise a larger measure of control over the schools than hitherto. They would then have to assume some responsibility for the more fundamental forms of imposition which, according to my argument, cannot be avoided.

That the teachers should deliberately reach for power and then make the most of their conquest is my firm conviction. To the extent that they are permited to fashion the curriculum and the procedures of the school they will definitely and positively influence the social attitudes, ideals, and behavior of the coming generation. In doing this they should resort to no subterfuge or false modesty. They should say neither that they are merely teaching the truth nor that they are unwilling to wield power in their own right. The first position is false and the second is a confession of incompetence. It is my observation that the men and women who have affected the course of human events are those who have not hesitated to use the power that has come to them. Representing as they do, not the interests of the moment or of any special class, but rather the common and abiding interests of the people, teachers are under heavy social obligation to protect and further those interests. In this they occupy a relatively unique position in society. Also since the profession should embrace scientists and scholars of the highest rank, as well as teachers working at all levels of the educational system, it has at its disposal, as no other group, the knowledge and wisdom of the ages. It is scarcely thinkable that these men and women would ever act as selfishly or bungle as badly as have the so-called "practical" men of our generation—the politicians, the financiers, the industrialists. If all of these facts are taken into account, instead of shunning power, the profession should rather seek power and then strive to use that power fully and wisely and in the interests of the great masses of the people.

The point should be emphasized that teachers possess no magic secret to power. While their work should give them a certain moral advantage, they must expect to encounter the usual obstacles blocking the road to leadership. They should not be deceived by the pious humbug with which public men commonly flatter the members of the profession. To expect ruling groups or classes to give precedence to teachers on important matters, because of age or sex or sentiment, is to refuse to face realities. It was one of the proverbs of the agrarian order that a spring never rises higher than its source. So the power that teachers exercise in the schools can be no greater than the power they wield in society. Moreover, while organization is necessary, teachers should not think of their problem primarily in terms of organizing and presenting a united front to the world, the flesh, and the devil. In order to be effective they must throw off completely the slave psychology that has dominated the mind of the pedagogue more or less since the days of ancient Greece. They must be prepared to stand on their own feet and win for their ideas the support of the masses of the people. Education as a force for social regeneration must march hand in hand with the living and creative forces of the social order. In their own lives teachers must bridge the gap between school and society and play some part in the fashioning of those great common purposes which should bind the two together.

284. An Independent School-State Advocated

As a matter of political theory, a school-state wholly independent of a political-state lies within the realm of possibility. Both the school-state and the political-state would rest upon the same base of the general electorate. An argument in favor of these two distinct entities is that the political-state has to deal with material things of a somewhat ephemeral nature. The school-state, on the other hand, would maintain an educational system that would be free to develop educational programs without reference to political consequences that might ensue from the interferences of the political state. A further argument in favor of this kind of separation is that in all cases where political authorities have certain ends to accomplish, either immediate or remote, the schools are the first object of control. They become the most vital forces in the determination of new political principles. In reality, school systems should not be used for furthering any political aims whatsoever. They should deal with children as human beings whose chief problem in life is to develop individuality and to find opportunities for release of inherent powers which later may be used either in support of existing institutions or, if need be, in their reorganization.

285. School and Politics in the Bourgeois State

The more cultured the bourgeois state, the more subtly did it lie when it declared that the school could stand above politics and serve society

284. Department of Superintendence, Twelfth Yearbook, *Critical Problems of School Administration* (Washington, D.C.: National Education Association, 1934), pp. 65–66.

285. Nikolai Lenin, *Collected Works*, English translation (New York: International Publishers Company, Inc., 1945), Vol. XXIII, p. 215.

as a whole. As a matter of fact, the school was turned into nothing but an instrument of the class rule of the bourgeoisie. Its purpose was to supply the capitalists with obedient lackeys and intelligent workers . . . We publicly declare that education divorced from life and politics is a lie and hypocrisy.

286. Overconfidence in School as an Agency of Social Reform

The most persistent error of modern educators and moralists is the assumption that our social difficulties are due to the failure of the social sciences to keep pace with the physical sciences which have created our technological civilization. The invariable implication of this assumption is that, with a little more time, a little more adequate moral and social pedagogy and a generally higher development of human intelligence, our social problems will approach solution . . . On the whole, social conservatism is ascribed to ignorance, a viewpoint which states only part of the truth and reveals the natural bias of the educator. The suggestion that we will only make a beginning in intelligent thought when we "cease mouthing platitudes," is itself so platitudinous that it rather betrays the confusion of an analyst who has no clear counsels about the way to overcome social inertia. The idea that we cannot be socially intelligent until we begin experimentation in social problems in the way that the physical scientists experimented fails to take account of an important difference between the physical and the social sciences. The physical sciences gained their freedom when they overcame the traditionalism based on ignorance, but the traditionalism which the social sciences face is based upon the economic interest of the dominant social classes who are trying to maintain their special privileges in society. Nor can the difference between the very character of social and physical sciences be overlooked. Complete rational objectivity in a social situation is impossible. The very social scientists who are so anxious to offer our generation counsels of salvation and are disappointed that an ignorant and slothful people are so slow to accept their wisdom, betray middle-class prejudices in almost everything they write. Since reason is always, to some degree, the servant of interest in a social situation, social injustice cannot be resolved by moral and rational suasion alone, as the educator and

286. Reinhold Niebuhr, *Moral Man and Immoral Society* (New York: Charles Scribner's Sons, 1936), pp. xiii–xvi.

social scientist usually believes. Conflict is inevitable, and in this conflict power must be challenged by power. That fact is not recognized by most of the educators, and only very grudgingly admitted by most of the social scientists. . . .

Modern educators are, like rationalists of all the ages, too enamored of the function of reason in life. The world of history, particularly in man's collective behavior, will never be conquered by reason, unless reason uses tools, and is itself driven by forces which are not rational.

287. School Cannot Be New Social Order in Embryo

We are not supporters of the thesis that an existing society can be changed through the school. To make the school the embryo of a future socialistic order is impossible for the simple reason that the school cannot be independent of its environment. Moreover, the school should be most intimately related to the contemporary life; it should study, observe, and participate in an organized way in that life.

288. Burden of Proof on Social Innovator

Due . . . to the importance of social order, and the consequent necessity for social control, the argument ventures to lay down the following principle, namely, that *the burden of proof is on the innovator and the disobedient.* And at this principle we arrive not only from the facts of social organization and social control, but also from the phenomena of random motion, as involved in any new coordination. It is safe to assume that ninety per cent of disobedience and innovation is but random motion; and if random motions had the right of way in social life social order would be impossible . . . It is only from the rarely exceptional recalcitrant that moral progress may result. Recalcitrance is always the object of suspicion, therefore; and rightly so. Only posterity can tell whether Joan of Arc is a criminal or a martyr; the representatives of the established order can wisely do no other than to assume that her freakish recalcitrance is criminal. We conclude, therefore, that until, with respect to any particular rule of conduct,

287. Albert P. Pinkevitch, *The New Education in the Soviet Republic* (New York: John Day Company, 1929), pp. 153–154.
288. Ross L. Finney, *A Sociological Philosophy of Education* (New York: The Macmillan Company, 1928), pp. 485–486.

there develops a new consensus of social opinion, the agents of social control are obligated to maintain the existing order.

289. Gradualism of Education Ineffective to Produce Fundamental Social Change

The democratic technique assumes gradualism as its procedure in social change. For if fundamental social change is urgent, if a legal majority is a pre-requisite to the realization of social change, if the building and organization of a majority opinion in favor of fundamental social change is most unlikely to be realized within the near future, and if these changes cannot possibly be brought about in the absence of a legal majority in its favor, gradualism remains the only logical way out. If social change must result only from cooperative effort brought about by means of education, such change must inevitably be evolutionary. Education is an instrument which functions in an evolutionary manner and which repeatedly calls for compromise if it is to be at all functional and forward-moving. Thus, until an organized majority opinion in favor of fundamental social change is attained, social change must, according to the proponents of this technique, be piecemeal and gradual, and accomplished by means of collaboration and compromise with the dominant economic class.

Such an approach to social reconstruction seems to be based upon either a quantitative and atomistic conception of our social mentality or upon the assumption that qualitative social changes are realizable by quantitative means. It may be questioned whether this is possible, seeing that the difference between capitalism and collectivism is a qualitative one, which cannot be reduced to quantitative units, serially arranged and serially reconstructed. Capitalism and collectivism are not continuous; they are not points at different positions on the same scale. The difference is indivisible and immeasurable and cannot, therefore, be achieved by quantitative procedures, i.e., by a series of partial, fractional and piecemeal changes. So long as a society is based upon private ownership of the means of production, it remains individualistic, even if certain aspects of its economy are socialized. One society is not more collectivistic than another merely because more phases of its economy are socialized. So long as the profit-motive remains undisturbed and private ownership remains unrestricted, these socialized reforms do not move our economy nearer to collectivism.

289. Zalmon Slesinger, *Education and the Class Struggle* (New York: Covici Friede, Inc., 1937), pp. 243–245.

290. Possible Implications of Marxism for Education

Where they [teachers] may learn the most from Marx is precisely at that point which, at least by those who go along with him in both his analysis of capitalism and in his solution—collectivism,—has been most neglected. This is the crucial point of method—of how, on the one hand, the present system is to be combated, and how, on the other, the new system is to be instituted in its place.

What actual means should the teacher, who is peculiarly concerned with this question, use in the task which in no small way is his? The most obvious means is, of course, that of persuasion . . .

* * *

Where Marx had less faith than the great majority of liberal educators, however, was in the efficacy of democratic deliberation to solve by itself our deepest social problem. In this he was more tough-minded than those of our contemporaries who, despite fifty odd years of additional experience with capitalist civilization, still cringe before the painful facts Marx pointed out. For "It is true," he wrote to his friend Kugelmann, "the solution cannot proceed along pleasant lines."

These facts are embodied in two principles:

1. The opposition of the class in control of capitalist society is so tremendous that nothing short of counter-opposition frequently bordering upon, indeed crystallizing into, illegality will suffice to defeat it.
2. When the ruling class is once replaced a period of oppression will continue to be necessary until gradually the citizenry honestly comes to agree that collectivism is a better solution of our troubles than capitalism.

Both principles assume that logical persuasion alone is an inadequate technique. It follows that teachers who confine their attention to it not only follow a wrong road, Marx would probably declare, but so obscure the issue as to betray the common goal.

* * *

Marx believed in the modifiability of human nature. He suggested that in the course of a generation or two, education patterned after the indoctrination of capitalist schools and colleges but orientated from different premises would work great changes in citizens of the new order. He hinted that the old habits of self-interest, motivated

290. Theodore B. Brameld, "Karl Marx and the American Teacher," *The Social Frontier*, 2:54–56, November 1935.

by lust for profit, could be sublimated beneath fresh habits of self-interest, motivated instead by social acclamation, creative achievement, and economic rewards justly proportional to work done. But he did not believe for a moment that human nature can be changed over night. Until it is changed a greater or lesser degree of coercion will continue to be necessary—greater perhaps in countries like Russia where industrial development and literacy were low; lesser perhaps in countries where technics and literacy are already high.

The two principles of class struggle and workers' dictatorship are for Marx really aspects of the same problem. Either before or after the breakdown of capitalism we must not delude ourselves by too much trust in the merely deliberative, peaceful, or evolutionary. Marx would insist accordingly that teachers cannot grapple with the problems of capitalist society by polite docility or timid criticism. At the same time he would be frank to admit that, so long as teachers live and work as they must within institutions like public schools, they cannot face these problems by wholesale flaunting of entrenched authority.

The question of method, therefore, becomes for the teacher a difficult and serious one. No single formula can altogether solve the dilemma of participation which is effective and not merely reckless.

This much, at any rate, seems clear from Marx's standpoint. The teacher who wishes to conduct his activity—within the school and without—in behalf of the collectivist ideal must free himself from the fallacy that the choice before him is naught or all. The question is not whether he as citizen and as worker can or cannot direct his energies along lines indicated by Marxian tactics. The question is rather in what degree can he. The answer would of course vary within the individual school and community, and it would include activities not always immediate in their results but broad in scope and future in aim. At least three ways, however, are implied in the Marxian approach by which progressive teachers can to some extent be effective while living in the midst of a capitalist society.

Teachers, first, should recognize that unless they choose to follow the older educational philosophy of neutrality they must accept a point of view consonant with the requirements of the new America. They must then influence their students, subtly if necessary, frankly if possible, toward acceptance of the same position. This does not mean that fair and intelligent analysis of "the other side" should be avoided; on the contrary it becomes an indispensable means in the teacher's hands. Such analysis, however, if really fair is bound to be far more scrutinizing and challenging than heretofore . . .

Second, implicit in Marx's theory is the call to teachers to analyze afresh the moral issues involved in opposition to capitalism. That disobedience of law is under certain conditions ethical is precisely the view of any labor sympathizer who ignores an injunction forbidding strike pickets. Marx almost admits that successful insurrection against the capitalist class is the highest moral act possible in our society . . . Let us avoid violence when at all feasible, Marx would assert. Let us never resort to it indiscriminately. Meanwhile, let us achieve by the vote all the rights we can. But let us not characterize violence categorically as immoral under all circumstances.

And finally, teachers need to move much farther in the direction of "class consciousness," so Marxism infers. Not only must they organize strongly and independently among themselves—an accomplishment which still lies almost wholly ahead of them. They must clarify their position as having much in common with both other professionals like newspaper reporters or engineers, and with non-professionals like factory workers. In economic status the teacher's position is much closer to the ditch-digger than to the college trustee. And it was Marx's firm belief that one's economic status after all determines, more than anything else, the condition of one's life.

291. Indispensable Role of Education in Revolution

But suppose it is admitted for the sake of argument that a social revolution is going on, and that it will culminate in a transfer of power effected by violent action. The notion that schools are completely impotent under existing conditions then has disastrous consequences. The schools, according to the theory, are engaged in shaping as far as in them lies a mentality, a type of belief, desire, and purpose that is consonant with the present class-capitalist system. It is evident that if such be the case, any revolution that is brought about is going to be badly compromised and even undermined. It will carry with it the seeds, the vital seeds, of counter-revolutions. There is no basis whatever, save doctrinate absolutism, for the belief that a complete economic change will produce of itself the mental, moral, and cultural changes that are necessary for its enduring success. The fact is practically recognized by the school of thought under discussion in that part of their doctrine which asserts that no genuine revolution can occur until the old system has passed away in everything but external political power, while within its shell a new economic system has grown to maturity. What is ignored is that the new system cannot grow

291. John Dewey, "Education and Social Change," *The Social Frontier*, 3:237, May 1937.

to maturity without an accompanying widespread change of habits of belief, desire, and purpose.

292. Teacher, Servant of the Status Quo

The prime purpose of the public educational system is to prepare students in the public schools to assume the obligations and duties of citizenship in this State. The public school teacher is a representative and officer of the State *as it now exists*. He is employed by that State to teach loyalty to its institutions and obedience to its laws. He is not employed to explore the controversial fields of political economy with the view of championing Utopian schemes of reform or change.

In entering the public school system the teacher assumes certain obligations and must of necessity surrender some of his intellectual freedom. If he does not approve of the present social system or the structure of our government he is at liberty to entertain those ideas, but must surrender his public office. If a change in our social system or in the structure of our government is at any time demanded by the people of this State or of the United States, the mandate must be disclosed by the verdict of the polls. The public school must not be employed as a rostrum for distinctive propaganda of any character. Its teaching staff must not be allowed to spread the gospel of discontent among the people. No person who is not eager to combat the theories of social change should be entrusted with the task of fitting the young and old of this State for the responsibilities of citizenship.

293. Educational Issues as Political Decisions

There is no point in arguing facts and still less in arguing suppositions of fact. The preliminary problem in controversy is to discriminate between issues of fact—issues which are ultimately controlled and resolved by the accumulation and analysis of all the relevant circumstances and conditions—and issues of principle. Issues of fact settle themselves when the facts are known and faced. Many of the bitterest disputes in American education would yield to the facts without further

292. *Revolutionary Radicalism,* Report of the Joint Legislative Committee of the State of New York Investigating Seditious Activities, Clayton Lusk, Chairman (Albany, 1920), Vol. 3, p. 2, 343.

293. Mortimer J. Adler and Milton Mayer, *The Revolution in Education* (Chicago: University of Chicago Press, 1958), pp. 185–186.

effort, if the facts were known. In so far as they are accessible, educators have only themselves to blame for continued confusion; but it may not be amiss to observe that the confusion itself, the disorganization (or unorganization) of education in America, perhaps precludes making a start.

Facing the facts is something else. On the whole, and certainly in so far as the issues are controversial, this is a political and not an educational problem. Education in the United States is controlled by the citizenry, and it is they who will decide whether or not to accept the reforms indicated by the facts, once the facts are before them. Here, in the realm of political decision, the educator can perhaps educate the public, but, again, the public will decide whether or not it is willing to listen to the educator, or, indeed, whether or not he is to have a voice.

294. Confidence in the Next Generation

A system of general instruction which shall reach every description of our citizens from the richest to the poorest, as it was the earliest, so will it be the latest of all the public concerns in which I shall permit myself to take an interest. Nor am I tenacious of the form in which it shall be introduced. Be that what it may, our descendants will be as wise as we are, and will know how to amend, and amend it until it shall suit their circumstances.

295. School Builds Social Order Wanted by Society

If the question is asked, Can the school build a social order? the answer is that it can do nothing else, since the only content which education has at its disposal is made up of the cultural and material environment of the school and of life. It can fail in its task if it is carried away by sentimental claims for the rights of the child or the individual and by superficial manifestations of activities and creative arts without a solid background. It can succeed only if it becomes deliberately conscious of the meaning and significance of the social

294. Thomas Jefferson, letter to Joseph C. Cabell, Jan. 14, 1818, in *Writings of Thomas Jefferson* (New York: G. P. Putnam's Sons, 1899), Vol. X, p. 102.
295. Isaac L. Kandel, "Can the School Build a New Social Order?" *Kadelpian Review*, 12:147–152, January 1933.

order which it serves. This has been the history of education in the past; it is the story of education today . . .

❊   ❊   ❊

The school is the instrument for maintaining existing social orders and for helping to build new social orders when the public has decided on them; but it does not create them. In the same sense that society is prior to the individual, the social order is prior to the school. As a profession we may have ambitions to do more than this—to criticise the existing order, to help to build a better future, but the fact is inescapable that the school is the servant of society . . .

This fact gives the educator his opportunity but it serves at the same time as an element of restraint. The American school can do more, far more, than it has yet done in building the American social order, but it cannot go any more rapidly than the public will allow . . .

❊   ❊   ❊

The school, then, cannot build a new social order nor should teachers combine as a group to penetrate from within. This is not a matter of courage or cowardice; it is a question of fact which all history of education has proved and which the study of any educational system, even the most radical and revoltionary, confirms. The school can only build the social order which society desires and derives its coloring from the social scene; it does not create or modify it but strengthens and gives reality to it. This condition does not detract from the task which teachers can perform and that is to devote more attention to the meaning of the culture and ideals, the hopes and ambitions which society expects to attain through the school, to discover the reasons for the break in gauge between school and society, to analyze the causes for the failure of the school to fulfil the duties which it has professedly assumed, in a word, to make the public more conscious of the ideals which it fundamentally does desire for its children, to dignify and ennoble them.

296. Advantage of Teachers Withdrawn from Life

The state, through her educational system, seeks to transmit to the rising generation the institutions and spiritual treasures built up by the present and past generations. All advance of society is to be

296. Thomas E. Shields, *Philosophy of Education* (Washington, D.C.: Catholic Education Press, 1921), pp. 424–425.

looked for in the activities of the adult population. In the Catholic system, on the contrary, the deliberate purpose is to lift adult society to a higher level through the Catholic school. This purpose she seeks to accomplish through her teaching communities. The secular teacher brings with him into the school, daily, the atmosphere of the world in which he lives; the women who form such an overwhelming majority of the public school teachers are an integral part of the social and economic world of their day and they share its spirit and its progress.

The teacher, however, is seldom in the forefront of social or economic progress; her professional duties withdraw her during her working hours from the actual strife, hence she cannot transmit the latest achievements of society, the things that are actually growing where the struggle is intense, and no other source of inspiration and guidance is provided for her. The religious teacher, on the contrary, is withdrawn from the world and lifted above its strife and turmoil. Through daily religious exercises and the practice of the rules of the community and the virtues enjoined, she brings the redeeming influence of Jesus Christ and of His saving teachings to bear upon the children who come under her influence, thus implanting high ideals and thus shaping their lives to standards that far outrun the highest achievements of the world.

297. Role of School to Stabilize

Paradoxical as it may seem, it is the conservative functions of education that are most significant in a period of profound change. Of the conservation of well established fact and principle there can be no reasonable question, but the sum-total of this knowledge (if all departments of human inquiry are included and if hypotheses generally agreed upon by competent scholars as reasonably true and worthy of provisional acceptance as guides to conduct are also included) is literally staggering in its dimensions as compared with the learning-capacity of even gifted individuals . . .

A second function of education in eras of rapid change may be called a stabilizing function. The very time to avoid chaos in the schools is when something akin to chaos characterizes the social environment. The very time to emphasize in the schools the values that are relatively certain and stable is when the social environment is full of uncertainty and when standards are crumbling. In the Golden

297. William Bagley, *Education and Emergent Man* (New York: The Ronald Press Company, copyright 1934), pp. 154–156.

Decade, which ended with the financial crash of 1929, American education, instead of being a stabilizing force, persisted in following the *Zeitgeist*. It seems always to be thus; education follows, it does not lead. And, curiously enough the very leaders who were pleading that education lead instead of follow were doing their best throughout the decade to encourage education in the "following" habit! They even boasted of the unstable program that was so rapidly developing in the schools; only they called it a "fluid" or an "adjustable" program. Words do make a difference after all!

If education is to be a stabilizing force it means that the school must discharge what is in effect a disciplinary function. The materials of instruction, the methods of teaching, and the life of the school as a social organization must exemplify *and idealize* consideration, cooperation, cheerfulness, fidelity to duty and to trust, courage, and perseverance in the face of disappointment, aggressive effort toward doing the task that one's hand finds to do and doing it as well as one can, loyalty to friend and family and those for whom one is responsible, a sense of fact and a willingness to face facts, clear and honest thinking. These may not be eternal values, but one may venture a fairly confident prediction that they will be just as significant a thousand years from now as they have ever been in the past.

298. Oneness of Education and Politics

Our schooling does not educate, if by education be meant a trained habit of discriminating inquiry and discriminating belief, the ability to look beneath a floating surface to detect the conditions that fix the contour of the surface, and the forces which create its waves and drifts. We dupe ourselves and others because we have not that inward protection against sensation, excitement, credulity and conventionally stereotyped opinion which is found only in a trained mind.

This fact determines the fundamental criticism to be levelled against current schooling, against what passes as an educational system. It not only does little to make discriminating intelligence a safeguard against surrender to the invasion of bunk, especially in its most dangerous form—social and political bunk—but it does much to favor susceptibility to a welcoming reception of it. There appear to be two chief causes for this ineptitude. One is the persistence, in the body of what is taught, of traditional material which is irrelevant to present conditions

298. John Dewey, "Education as Politics," *The New Republic*, 32:140–141, October 1922.

—subject-matter of instruction which though valuable in some past period is so remote from the perplexities and issues of present life that its mastery, even if fairly adequate, affords no resource for discriminating insight, no protection against being duped in facing the emergencies of today. From the standpoint of this criterion of education, a large portion of current material of instruction is simply aside from the mark. The specialist in any one of the traditional lines is as likely to fall for social bunk even in its extreme forms of economic and nationalistic propaganda as the unschooled person; in fact his credulity is the more dangerous because he is so much more vociferous in its proclamation and so much more dogmatic in its assertion. Our schools send out men meeting the exigencies of contemporary life clothed in the chain-armor of antiquity, and priding themselves on the awkwardness of their movements as evidences of deep wrought, time tested convictions.

The other way in which schooling fosters an undiscriminating gulping mental habit, eager to be duped, is positive. It consists in a systematic, almost deliberate, avoidance of the spirit of criticism in dealing with history, politics and economics. There is an implicit belief that this avoidance is the only way by which to produce good citizens. The more undiscriminatingly the history and institutions of one's own nation are idealized, the greater is the likelihood, so it is assumed, that the school product will be a loyal patriot, a well equipped good citizen. If the average boy and girl could be walled off from all ideas and information about social affairs save those acquired in school, they would enter upon the responsibilities of social membership in complete ignorance that there are any social problems, any political evils, any industrial defects. They would go forth with a supreme confidence that the way lies open to all, and that the sole cause of failure in business, family life or citizenship lies in some personal deficiency in character. The school is even more indurated from a frank acknowledgment of social ills than the pulpit—which is saying a good deal. And like the pulpit it compensates for its avoidance of discussion of social difficulties by a sentimental dwelling upon personal vices.

The effect is to send students out into actual life in a condition of acquired and artificial innocence. Such perceptions as they may have of the realities of social struggles and problems they have derived incidentally, by the way, and without the safeguards of intelligent acquaintance with facts and impartially conducted discussion. It is no wonder that they are ripe to be gulled, or that their attitude is one which merely perpetuates existing confusion, ignorance, prejudice, and credulity. Reaction from this impossibly naive idealization of institutions as they are produces indifference and cynicism. It is astonishing that the professed conservative moulders of public opinion take so little notice of the widespread cynicism of the mass at the present time. They are even more credulous than those whom they appear, superficially, to dupe. This attitude of indifference and opposition is now passive and unorganized. But it exists as a direct result of the disillusionment caused by the contrast between things as they are actually found to be and things as they had been taught in the schools. Some day some more or less accidental event will crystallize the scattered indifference and discontent into an active form, and all the carefully built up bulwarks of social reactions will be washed out. But unfortunately there is little likelihood that the reaction against reaction will be more discriminating than the previous state of things. It too will be blind, credulous, fatalistic, confused.

It seems almost hopeless to name the remedy, for it is only a greater confidence in intelligence, in scientific method. But the "only" marks something infinitely difficult of realization. What will happen if teachers become sufficiently courageous and emancipated to insist that education means the creation of a discriminating mind, a mind that prefers not to dupe itself or to be the dupe of others? Clearly they will have to cultivate the habit of suspended judgment, of scepticism, of desire for evidence, of appeal to observation rather than sentiment, discussion rather than bias, inquiry rather than conventional idealizations. When this happens schools will be the dangerous outposts of a humane civilization. But they will also begin to be supremely interesting places. For it will then have come about that education and politics are one and the same thing because politics will have to be in fact what it now pretends to be, the intelligent management of social affairs.

16

Teaching Controversial Issues

Problems in the Philosophy of Education Discussed in this Section

1. What does the infinitive *to teach* mean?
2. Should the school be neutral on controversial issues? Can it be? If not, can it be fair in giving instruction related to such issues?
3. Is teaching as indoctrination sometimes inevitable? For example, to save time in the teaching of well-established facts of science? Of well-established morals? Of Democracy?
4. Can there be "defensible partiality" in the teaching of political concepts?
5. Is it ever proper to expurgate the classics that children read?
6. Should controversial issues be taught differently to students with high and low I.Q.'s?

299. Censorship of the Curriculum

. . . Least of all should we tell them [children] stories and paint them pictures of battles between gods and giants, and other hostilities, many and various, of gods and heroes with their kinsfolk and families. But if in any way we are likely to convince them, that never yet was any citizen at feud with his fellow, and that to be so is a sin, this is rather what must be told them from earliest childhood by old men and women, and as they grow older we must compel the poets who compose tales for them to keep pretty near to this. But bindings of Hera by her son, and hurlings into space of Hephaestus by his father because he was going to defend his mother when beaten, and battles between gods which Homer has composed, we must not receive into the city, whether the poet had an allegorical meaning or had not. For the

299. Plato, *The Republic,* in Bernard Bosanquet, translator, *The Education of the Young in The Republic of Plato* (Cambridge University Press, 1917), pp. 53–54.

young are not capable of judging what is an allegory and what is not, but whatever one of that age has received among his impressions is wont to become indelible and immutable. For which reason, perhaps, it should be treated of the first importance that the earliest tales they hear should be invented most beautifully in their bearing upon goodness.

300. Limitations on Freedom of Teaching

Moderation in Refuting—In those questions in which he [the teacher] is free to hold either side, he shall defend his view in such a way as to allow moderate and kindly consideration for the opposite view, especially if the previous teacher has held that view. But if writers can be reconciled, he must be careful not to neglect to do so. Finally, he shall conduct himself with moderation in citing and refuting authorities.

Avoiding New Opinions—Even in matters where there is no risk to faith and devotion, no one shall introduce new questions in matters of great moment, or any opinion which does not have suitable authority, without first consulting his superiors; he shall not teach anything opposed to the axioms of learned men or the general belief of scholars. Rather, all should follow closely the approved doctors and, as far as local custom permits, the views accepted in Catholic schools.

301. Indoctrination in Science and Religion Endorsed

Every educational institution makes use of indoctrination. Children are indoctrinated with the multiplication table; they are indoctrinated with love of country; they are indoctrinated with the principles of chemistry and physics and mathematics and biology, and nobody finds fault with indoctrination in these fields. Yet these are of small concern in the great business of life by contrast with ideas concerning God and man's relation to God, his duties to God, his neighbor and himself, man's nature and his supernatural destiny. The Catholic educator makes no apology for indoctrinating his students in these essential

300. *Ratio Studiorum* (1599), quoted in Edward A. Fitzpatrick, *St. Ignatius and the Ratio Studiorum* (New York: McGraw-Hill Book Company, Inc., 1933), p. 151. Used by permission of the publishers.
301. William J. McGucken, *The Catholic Way in Education* (Milwaukee: The Bruce Publishing Company, 1937), p. 60.

matters. To instruction in the arts and sciences, the Catholic university adds the notion of an unchanging standard of morality, the ideas of duty and responsibility to a personal and omnipotent God . . .

302. Strengthening Sound Doctrine by False

In such a [Catholic parochial] school, in harmony with the Church and the Christian family, the various branches of secular learning will not enter into conflict with religious instruction to the manifest detriment of education. And if, when occasion arises, it be deemed necessary to have the students read authors propounding false doctrine, for the purpose of refuting it, this will be done after due preparation and with such an antidote of sound doctrine, that it will not only do no harm, but will be an aid to the Christian formation of youth.

303. Teach Duller Half to Be Right Rather than Original

. . . It is principally through the schools that this new coinage of the collective intellect should be paid into general circulation. It is not enough that we teach children to think, we must actually force-feed them with the concentrated results of expert thinking. To this end there is immense occasion for memoriter training and sheer drill. Ours are the schools of a democracy, which all the children attend. At least half of them never had an original idea of any general nature, and never will. But they must behave as if they had sound ideas. Whether those ideas are original or not matters not in the least. It is better to be right than to be original. What the duller half of the population needs, therefore, is to have their reflexes conditioned into behavior that is socially suitable. And the wholesale memorizing of catchwords —provided they are sound ones—is the only practical means of establishing bonds in the duller intellects between the findings of social scientists and the corresponding social behavior of the masses. Instead of trying to teach dullards to think for themselves, the intellectual leaders must think for them, and drill the results, memoriter, into their synapses. For the dullards it is that or nothing.

✿   ✿   ✿

302. Pius XI, "The Christian Education of Youth," *Catholic Education Review*, 28:157, March 1930.
303. Ross L. Finney, *A Sociological Philosophy of Education* (New York: The Macmillan Company, 1928), pp. 394–395, 409–410.

Two things appear: first, that the best minds are capable of gradually inventing a far better civilization than we now possess; and, second, that the masses are capable of negotiating by imitation any culture system that the brightest can invent provided they are given opportunity for memoriter learning of, and imitative participation in, all the intellectual resources of which that culture system is constituted. There is unlimited hope, therefore, for the uncultured classes of society, and for the now backward races of mankind, *provided they be not segregated.* Similarly, to select the duller children, who seem obviously predestined for the simpler economic functions only, segregate them from the brighter half, and deprive them of imitative participation in the study of the arts, the sciences, and the new humanities, is a formula for creating a caste-stratified society. And the more scientifically accurate the selection the more deadly the social results. Dr. Bagley is right, therefore, in calling such a procedure an educational determinism. But the way out is not through discrediting the findings of the tests, nor in the claim that the dull can compensate for their limitations by extra effort. The way out is rather through the insights of a *social* psychology. For social psychology reveals the fact that similar behavior can be secured in dull and bright alike by having them learn the same subject matter, but in different ways—a difference that always results normally when persons of different intelligences participate together in the same group activities.

304. Indoctrinating Democracy

. . . The schools of a democracy should create in the pupils a devotion to the political and social practices of democracy. It is perhaps a little strange that in setting forth this proposition I am introducing a controversial issue. To be sure in Russia today there would be no question but that the schools should inculcate the principles of Marxian socialism . . . But in our own country there seems to be an assumption that to go all out for democracy would be undemocratic.

Under the guarantees of our Bill of Rights any citizen may advocate the overthrow of democracy. He may propose the substitution of a fascist dictatorship or of a proletarian autocracy. Therefore, say some, it is not logical that the schools of a democracy should be committed in advance to the superiority of its own system of social administration. They should be impartial. They should adopt the problem-solving

304. Edward H. Reisner, "The Quality of School Experience Appropriate to a Democracy," *Teachers College Record*, 40:700–702, May 1939.

attitude. They should admit as a possibility the hypothesis that the United States might be a better and a happier country if the Bill of Rights were abolished and a dictatorship established. They should not advocate and support too wholeheartedly the superiority of democratic institutions because in so doing they would be indulging in a process of "indoctrination."

There is a story told of a medieval scholar who put a pretty puzzle up to his contemporaries. A donkey, he said, is standing at a mathematically equal distance from two equally desirable bundles of hay. In the absence of any advantage which would favor the donkey's moving either to the right or to the left to reach either bundle of hay, would it not stand still and starve to death? It is to be assumed that the donkey, being neither a mathematician nor a philosopher, would find a way to his feed.

Does the force of logic compel us to keep our schools indecisive in this matter of inculcating devotion on the part of pupils to the democratic way of life? Many among us would say that if it did, so much the worse for logic. They would disregard fine-drawn dialetic for what seems to be the obvious dictate of social necessity. However, even in terms of logic, the way to an enthusiastic and decisive support of democracy for our schools does not seem to be denied.

Our preference for democracy does not come as a purely intellectual process of problem solving, although undoubtedly the presentation to consciousness of the conditions of existence under autocracies as compared with those of a democracy is involved in the decision. Rather do we prefer democracy for ourselves and our children because we like better the realities of the democratic way of life. We favor a government in which public policy is based on the widest possible consultation of the public will. We demand the full and free operation of those conditions which foster the dissemination of facts and which lead to as intelligent and voluntary choices of the people as are possible. We favor the development of individuals to their fullest potentialities. We desire the broadest possible spread and the highest possible level of welfare and security and of enjoyment of the goods of life for all our citizens. We work for the elimination of divisive prejudices and hates and for the development of understanding and good will among all our citizens. We believe that nations may live and work together in cooperative ways and that war as an instrument of policy is self-defeating in the long run and may ultimately pass out of the international picture. We believe in peace and strive for peace in face of a world that has gone mad with the spirit of war. Such, by and large, are the values which our nation lives by and for. Being for those values, we are for democracy as the form of social organization which embodies and fosters them.

If we are for those values, why should we hesitate to place them in the forefront of the purposes and objectives of instruction? We do not hesitate to pass on to children the most authoritative scientific knowledge of our times. We do not apologize for giving them the most authentic picture of the past which we can discover. We do not hold back when it is a matter of equipping them with such habits of conduct as will make for their easy adjustment with their fellows. And why should we hesitate to represent to them our profound conviction that the best values of social existence are those which are bound up with the ideal and the practice of democracy?

There is probably justification for raising the question, now and again, as to whether democracy can and will survive in the United States, particularly so if such examination of our common life makes us aware of the tendencies and practices which are inimical to democracy and which need to be corrected if democracy is to live on. But the quality which should be dominant in our schools is not one of fearful doubt in this matter, but one of devotion to the values of the democratic form of social existence and of determination to make those values prevail more richly and more extensively.

There is every reason to hold that the schools of a democracy should inculcate the same devotion to the values of the democratic way of life as authoritarian states are doing for the systems which they favor. And by that is not meant partisan and chauvinistic adherence to a label, but deepseated appreciation of the values of democracy and enlistment in the long struggle to make those values ever more and more a reality in American life. In making such a commitment for our public schools we are embodying in their program the highest social values which we, as aspiring, stumbling human beings, know. To do less would show us recreant to our opportunity and our duty.

305. Arguments Against Indoctrination

(1) Indoctrination is unfair to the child. During the period of education he has a right to see all sides of each question, he has a right to have each side clearly and fairly presented, he has a right to expect from the schools the unvarnished truth. He early learns

305. Carleton Washburne, "Indoctrination Versus Education," *The Social Frontier*, 2:213, April 1936.

that his parents have certain prejudices. He makes certain allowances for these. But if he cannot count on his teachers' objectivity and honesty, where shall he turn?

(2) Indoctrination is the antithesis of education. Education involves the drawing out of the child, the developing of his own capacities and thought. Indoctrination involves the imposing upon the child of one set of ideas, to the exclusion of his own thought. Education is the freeing of the individual. Indoctrination is the binding of the individual to the views of some group of adults. Education should lead toward growth. Indoctrination stultifies growth.

(3) Anyone who supposes that he has the one and final solution to any problem is inexcusably bigoted and is, therefore, unfit to educate children. Any intelligent person must recognize that however probable he thinks it is that his particular solution to a controversial issue is the best one, there are other persons of equal intelligence who have equal certainty that their solution is right, and that there is always the possibility that either one or both of them may be wrong and that still another solution may be better. The growth of society depends upon our free exploration of all possible avenues of escape from our present evils, of all possible avenues toward our ultimate ideals. Indoctrination shuts off all avenues but one.

(4) The strongest arguments against indoctrination are perhaps the practical ones. If one group can use the schools to indoctrinate the children toward its particular answers to controversial questions, so can another group. After any School Board election the new Board can, if indoctrination is to be allowed, change textbooks, curriculum, and teachers to fit its pet ideas, while after the next School Board election the whole thing may be reversed. The schools become, in a country which is not yet under a dictatorship, footballs of politics in the worst sense; and, in a country where there is a dictatorship, the way is paved for inculcating the dictator's ideas in all growing young minds.

Those in the educational profession who consciously advocate indoctrination in the schools are almost without exception those who would use it to change the existing social order. Yet from a practical standpoint they would completely defeat their own purpose were they successful in getting an acceptance of the idea that the schools may be used to indoctrinate. For, of necessity, majority opinion favors that which is—were it not so, what is would be changed. If the schools are to be used to indoctrinate, obviously they will be used to indoctrinate toward that which the majority desires. To advocate indoctrination is therefore, not a way to bring about a new social order but a way to perpetuate the old.

306. Defensible Partiality

Under certain conditions the use of propaganda is indispensable to other types of teaching than indoctrination. Whatever his philosophy, no instructor can avoid the occasional need to take short cuts by omitting some of the evidence or some of the possible ways of communicating that would enter into a given learning situation were it to be treated as exhaustively as possible. Moreover, propaganda often impresses a fact, rule, or value upon students much more effectively than would a neutrally analytical approach. There is no reason why learning for worthwhile ends should not be warmed with the persuasive qualities that advertisers so often exploit for their own purposes. Reconstructionism, more forthrightly than other philosophies, with the possible exception of perennialism, believes that if education is to be a great cultural force—if it is to shape attitudes and inspire action—it should make use of the colorful and dramatic qualities possessed by propaganda.

Let it be clearly understood that in uttering this "heresy" we do not imply that propaganda and education are synonymous. Education in its totality, as we have said, encompasses the fullest possible consideration of evidence, the most thorough effort at clear communication, and the most scrupulous respect for disagreements as well as agreements. Hence the legitimate role of propaganda in education should be determined by the extent to which it is helpful yet always subordinate to the complete process and product of learning for social-self-realization. Hence, also, its role should be determined by the extent to which both students and teachers realize it is being so utilized in the school.

The teacher's duty thus includes two chief responsibilities relating to propaganda: (1) to label propaganda for what it is, meanwhile giving students practice in the detection of its techniques; and (2) to develop, even in very young students, the clear realization that they often learn facts, rules, attitudes, and beliefs by short cuts which, although necessary at certain times, should nevertheless be investigated for their accuracy or desirability at other times. Only thus can propaganda be transformed into education proper. For example, a rule of health that is learned by the child through propaganda (from an illustrated poster on the wall of a classroom, for example) is genuinely relearned and incorporated into the habits of the adult through education in the causes of disease.

306. Theodore Brameld, *Toward a Reconstructed Philosophy of Education* (New York: Dryden Press, 1956), pp. 204–205.

The more successfully this practice of continuous criticism and active revaluation develops in children the less likely are they to be victimized by propaganda at any time, the less likely are they to assume naively that propaganda and education are completely opposed in practice, and the less likely, too, are both children and adults to assume that all propaganda is bad and should as far as possible be eliminated—an undertaking that would not only be undesirable but one in which success would be impossible.

307. Method for Teaching Controversial Issues

. . . What should be the pattern according to which controversial issues shall be handled in the schools?

I should say let us make them the nuclear subject matter of education. Being controversial, they will of themselves have the spirit and figure of life. Being momentous to the community, they cannot fail to be momentous also to those members of the community who are teachers and pupils. The options they present are urgent.

✿   ✿   ✿

But how choose? We hear a good deal about the judicial process with its law of evidence, its "impartial judgment" according to "the weight of the evidence." And one way to define the technique of choice and decision is on the analogy of a court of justice weighing the evidence. To me, the concepts of "the weight of evidence," "the impartial judge," are simply legal fictions with a place among the other illusions.

I prefer the scientific and democratic process of attaining a consensus, through free untrammeled discussion in which all differences are confronted, thrashed out, and thereby integrated with one another. There is no social issue, let it be public ownership as against private, Communism as against the present form of American government, Fascism as against Communism or anything else you like, concerning which a consensus cannot be attained in the same manner as by the sciences.

The method of the schools should be the method of open, free discussion aiming at consensus—the method of the sciences applied to social issues . . .

This calls for treating students as responsible individuals, able to look after themselves, to manage their own affairs and to maintain

307. Horace M. Kallen, "Controversial Social Issues," *Progressive Education,* 10:187–188, April 1933.

their own standards. It means that students must have at least the freedom of self-government, self-management, and self-instruction which their elders have. And this means that our conception of the function of the teacher must be revised, and his relations to his pupil redefined. For teaching is one thing, learning is another. Teaching is something teachers do to pupils. Learning is something pupils can do only for themselves. As things stand today, a sizeable obstacle to learning by the pupil is teaching by the teacher. It is an obstacle because the teacher's function is a police-function, disciplinary, directive, controlling. It focalizes the pupil's passions and prejudices upon the person of the teacher instead of upon the theme of the lesson. The deadness of the theme reenforces this focalization. The result is that school life involves a real class war between pupils and teachers. Where the central theme is alive this cannot happen, for a live theme is one which of itself engages the pupil's passions and prejudices. Now, only controversial issues are living ones, and the more social such issues are, the more living. Once a pupil's loves and hates are engaged, and drained, by such issues, the teacher becomes a source of aid and comfort, guiding the heart to the informations and ideas that will sustain its cause; the curse of irrelevancy is lifted from the schools; the educational establishment is reunited with the processes of the common life from which it is now cut off, and education, being now concerned with living issues, makes good its claim to be a preparation for life.

308. Method of Problem-Solving Bound to Be in Arrears

. . . The problems of the modern world appear and change faster than any set of teachers can grasp them, much faster than they can convey their substance to a population of children. If the schools attempt to teach children how to solve the problems of the day, they are bound always to be in arrears. The most they can conceivably attempt is the teaching of a pattern of thought and feeling which will enable the citizen to approach a new problem in some useful fashion. But that pattern cannot be invented by the pedagogue. It is the political theorist's business to trace out that pattern. In that task he must not assume that the mass has political genius, but that men, even if they had genius, would give only a little time and attention to public affairs.

308. Walter Lippmann, *The Phantom Public* (New York: Harcourt, Brace and Company, Inc., 1925), p. 27.

309. Moral Consequences of Neutrality

In the sphere of moral decision the very refusal to choose, since refusal has specific consequences, is itself a moral act. The fact is now generally realized that a declaration to do nothing is itself a statement of policy. In so far as the commitments of educators, scholars, and citizens have consequences for the determination of social issues, moral responsibility for things left undone, as well as for things done, cannot be escaped . . .

310. A Definition of Impartiality

It is the business of a philosophy of education to make clear what is involved in the action which is carried on within the educational field, to transform a preference which is blind, based on custom rather than thought, into an intelligent choice—one made, that is, with consciousness of what is aimed at, the reasons why it is preferred, and the fitness of the means used. Nevertheless intelligent choice is still choice. It still involves preference for one kind of end rather than another one which might have been worked for. It involves a conviction that such and such an end is valuable, worthwhile, rather than another. Sincerity demands a maximum of impartiality in seeking and stating the reasons for the aims and the values which are chosen and rejected. But the scheme of education itself cannot be impartial in the sense of not involving a preference for some values over others. The obligation to be impartial is the obligation to state as clearly as possible what is chosen and why it is chosen . . .

311. The Teacher's Personal Point of View

What shall I . . . do about my own convictions? Shall I use them in teaching these young people or shall I teach quite independently of what I think? If I really have convictions that matter to me I cannot

309. American Historical Association, Commission on Social Studies, *Conclusions and Recommendations* (New York: Charles Scribner's Sons, 1934), pp. 28–29.
310. John Dewey and John L. Childs in *The Educational Frontier*, William Kilpatrick, editor (New York: The Century Company, 1933), p. 288.
311. William H. Kilpatrick, *Education and the Social Crisis* (New York: Liveright Publishing Corporation, 1932), pp. 76–78.

possibly teach independently of them. They are an essential part of me. Does this mean that I shall set up my convictions as formulations which my pupils should accept and so "teach" them? It does not. That would not be education. I must know that there are difficulties here and I must guard against the dangers involved. I must use the best knowledge I have in helping my pupils to survey the field and to weigh the arguments. But I must be careful that my superior knowledge does not keep them from searching and thinking and concluding for themselves. Probably I must at some stage tell openly what I think, but I must so tell it and so couple other possibilities with it that my pupils are not unduly influenced to accept my position on any basis of authority. Otherwise, I am not making them independent and capable in thinking, or, more exactly, I am keeping them from really thinking and so from growing as they should.

❋   ❋   ❋

This way of utilizing my best knowledge, yet so as not to indoctrinate my pupils, gives me my just defense when others would charge me with using my school access to foster in partisan fashion my own position. I have not "taught" my position. I have made my pupils study not so much it as an area. My position will be considered as one of the possible hypotheses, but always in comparison with other positions. I may even present the argument that influenced my own decision, but in such fashion that through it all my pupils have been helped to learn to think and decide for themselves. This, and not that they reach my decision, has been my aim. That I shall not entirely succeed in maintaining my intended fairness is but probable, but I must make the effort.

Some may ask whether this care to keep the teacher's conviction from affecting unduly the thought processes of the pupils may not deprive them of possibly the best part of an education, namely vision and zeal, vision of a worthy cause and zeal to pursue it. That there is danger need not be denied, but is it not fairer to charge the possible loss here rather to the attitude within the community than to the teacher? It is this which makes it a partisan matter. Because the parents feel as they do, the teacher cannot speak freely. His long-run effectual influence demands that he make manifest his fairness on the partisan question, even at some loss elsewhere. Even so he can present his position with its vision as one hypothesis for consideration, so that, even at the worst, there need be no total loss. Of course, if the parents were united in sharing the teacher's conviction, or if they were indifferent, he could work more effectually on the vision and zeal, though even then he should have to guard the pupils' thinking lest his position interfere there. The teacher's task in the face of partisan opposition is simply the common situation involving contradictory values. Do what he will, he cannot get all. He must act for the largest whole as best he can see it.

17

Academic Freedom

Problems in the Philosophy of Education Discussed in this Section

1. What is the justification for academic freedom? Is it an inalienable right?
2. Should academic freedom be unconditional? If so, can it exist in a sectarian college or state university? Should it permit teaching of subversive doctrines?
3. Should academic freedom be limited to the field of the teacher's specialization? To utterances in the classroom? To any particular rungs of the educational ladder?
4. Should academic freedom be conditioned by the existing state of law and order? Are loyalty oaths an infringement of academic freedom? Is a teacher justified in "taking" the fifth amendment?
5. Who should judge whether a teacher's academic freedom has been abridged?
6. Should teachers openly join and participate in political parties? Parties of the extreme left? Are teachers' religious affiliations to be involved in academic freedom? Are their personal habits to be involved?
7. Does academic freedom stand on a different footing from a teacher's civil liberties? Should it?
8. Are the enemies of academic freedom entitled to its protection?

312. Unlimited Independence of Instruction

. . . The independence of instruction is, in a manner, a part of the rights of the human race. Since man has received from Nature a perfectibility whose unknown limits extend—if they even exist—much beyond what we can yet perceive, and the knowledge of new truths is for him the only means of developing this happy faculty—the source

312. Francois Condorcet, *Report on the General Organization of Public Instruction*, in F. de la Fontainerie, *French Liberalism and Education in the Eighteenth Century* (New York: McGraw-Hill Book Company, Inc., copyright 1932), pp. 374–375. Used by permission of the publishers.

of his happiness and of his glory, what power could have the right to say to him: "This is what you need know; this is as far as you may go"? Since truth alone is useful, since every error is an evil, by what right would any power, whatever it be, dare to determine wherein lies truth, wherein lies error?

Besides, any power which would forbid the teaching of an opinion contrary to that which has served as a basis for the established laws, would attack directly the freedom of thought, would frustrate the aim of every social institution: the perfecting of the laws, which is the necessary consequence of the combat of opinions and the progress of knowledge.

313. Subordination, Not Freedom, the Source of Culture

All culture begins with the very opposite of that which is now so highly esteemed as "academical freedom": with obedience, with subordination, with discipline, with subjection. And as leaders must have followers so also must the followers have a leader—here a certain reciprocal predisposition prevails in the hierarchy of spirits: yea, a kind of pre-established harmony. This eternal hierarchy, towards which all things naturally tend, is always threatened by that pseudo-culture which now sits on the throne of the present . . .

314. A Durable Basis for Academic Freedom

Let us return, momentarily, to the business of tentative definition. Academic freedom is a security against hazards to the pursuit of truth by those persons whose lives are dedicated to conserving the intellectual heritage of the ages and to extending the realm of knowledge. It is the right, or group of rights, intended to make it possible for certain persons (always very few in number, in any society, when compared with the bulk of the population) to teach truthfully and to employ their reason to the full extent of their intellectual powers. We will not find these rights guaranteed by any article of the federal or state constitutions, or described in any legislative enactment, here in Amer-

313. Friedrich Nietzsche, *The Future of Our Educational Institutions*, J. M. Kennedy, translator (Edinburgh: T. N. Foulis, 1909), p. 140.
314. Russell Kirk, *Academic Freedom* (Chicago: Henry Regnery Co., 1955), pp. 3–4, 17–18.

ica; and, with some small exceptions, throughout the civilized world these liberties are the product of custom and moral prescription, rather than of positive law. Nor do these rights have any easily ascertainable sanction of force behind them. Juridical thinkers of the school of Austin, then, scarcely can admit that academic freedom is a right at all; for in the Utilitarian view of rights, a right has reality only when it is expressly asserted by the authority of the state, or when (whether through the agency of the state or of some other coherent group) it has positive force—in the final resort, *physical* force—to assert its claim. Nor is it easy to see how academic freedom can be anything more than a phrase for pragmatic thinkers, however much they may praise it; for to the pragmatist, the impulse of the present generation is everything, and what Burke called "the contract of eternal society" is nothing: in other words, rights have no origin in the laws of God or of nature, but are simply the products of social convention, to be obliterated when the experience or interest of the present generation ceases to approve them.

Academic freedom, in short, belongs to that category of rights called "natural rights," and is expressed in custom, not in statute.

❀   ❀   ❀

My point is this: in the Middle Ages, as in classical times, the academy possessed freedom unknown to other bodies and persons because the philosopher, the scholar, and the student were looked upon as men consecrated to the service of Truth; and that Truth was not simply a purposeless groping after miscellaneous information, but a wisdom to be obtained, however imperfectly, from a teleological search. The community did not create these privileges of the Academy, any more than the community created wisdom; rather, the community simply recognized the justice of the Academy's claim to privilege. The community did not expect to be served, except in the sense that it might be so fortunate as to gather some crumbs that fell from the academic table. Like Socrates and like Aquinas, the learned man, the teacher, was a servant of God wholly, and of God only. His freedom was sanctioned by an authority more than human. Now and then that freedom was violated, just as anointed kings were murdered or reverend priests were robbed, on occasion; yet it scarcely occurred to anyone to attempt to regulate or to suppress the freedom of the Academy; it was regarded almost as a part of the natural and unalterable order of things. . . .

315. Freedom Subject to Divine and Natural Law

Human liberty necessarily stands in need of light and strength to direct its actions to good and to restrain them from evil. Without this, the freedom of our will would be our ruin. First of all there must be law; that is, a fixed rule of teaching what is to be done and what is to be left undone . . . In other words, the reason prescribes to the will what it should seek after or shun, in order to [gain] the eventual attainment of man's last end, for the sake of which all his actions ought to be performed. This ordination of reason is called law. In man's free will, therefore, or in the moral necessity of our voluntary acts being in accordance with reason, lies the very root of the necessity of law. Nothing more foolish can be uttered or conceived than the notion that because man is free by nature, he is therefore exempt from law. Were this the case, it would follow that to become free we must be deprived of reason; whereas the truth is that we are bound to submit to law precisely because we are free by our very nature. For law is the guide of man's actions; it turns him towards good by its rewards, and deters him from evil by its punishments.

*   *   *

From this it is manifest that the eternal law of God is the sole standard and rule of human liberty, not only in each individual man, but also in the community and civil society which men constitute when united. Therefore, the true liberty of human society does not consist in every man doing what he pleases, for this would simply end in turmoil and confusion, and bring on the overthrow of the State; but rather in this, that through the injunctions of the civil law all may more easily conform to the prescriptions of the eternal law. Likewise the liberty of those who are in authority does not consist in the power to lay unreasonable and capricious commands upon their subjects, which would equally be criminal and would lead to the ruin of the commonwealth; but the binding force of human laws is in this, that they are to be regarded as applications of the eternal law, and incapable of sanctioning anything which is not contained in the eternal law, as in the principle of all law . . .

*   *   *

315. Leo XIII, *Libertas Praestantissimum*, quoted in John A. Ryan and Francis J. Boland, *Catholic Principles of Politics* (New York: The Macmillan Company, 1940), pp. 169–178.

Moreover, the highest duty is to respect authority and obediently to submit to just law; and by this the members of a community are effectually protected from the wrongdoing of evil men. Lawful power is from God, and whosoever resisteth authority resisteth the ordinance of God; wherefore obedience is greatly ennobled when subject to an authority which is the most just and supreme of all. But where the power to command is wanting, or where a law is enacted contrary to reason, or to the eternal law, or to some ordinance of God, obedience is unlawful, lest, while obeying man, we become disobedient to God. Thus, an effectual barrier being opposed to tyranny, the authority in the State will not have all its own way, but the interests and rights of all will be safeguarded—the rights of individuals, of domestic society, and of all the members of the commonwealth; all being free to live according to law and right reason; and in this, as we have shown, true liberty really consists.

*   *   *

A like judgment must be passed upon what is called liberty of teaching. There can be no doubt that truth alone should imbue the minds of men; for in it are found the well-being, the end, and the perfection of every intelligent nature, and therefore nothing but truth should be taught both to the ignorant and to the educated, so as to bring knowledge to those who have it not, and to preserve it in those who possess it. For this reason it is plainly the duty of all who teach to banish error from the mind, and by sure safeguards to close the entry to all false convictions. From this it follows, as is evident, that the liberty of which we have been speaking,* is greatly opposed to reason, and tends absolutely to pervert men's minds, in as much as it claims for itself the right of teaching whatever it pleases—a liberty which the State cannot grant without failing in its duty. And the more so, because the authority of teachers has great weight with their hearers, who can rarely decide for themselves as to the truth or falsehood of the instruction given to them.

Wherefore, this liberty also, in order that it may deserve the name, must be kept within certain limits, lest the office of teaching be turned with impunity into an instrument of corruption. Now truth, which should be the only subject-matter of those who teach, is of two kinds, natural and supernatural. Of natural truths, such as the principles of nature and whatever is derived from them immediately by our reason, there is a kind of common patrimony in the human race.

* The Pope earlier in this encyclical letter had been inveighing against the sort of nineteenth century liberalism denounced by his predecessor, Pius IX, in his *Syllabus of Errors.*

On this, as on a firm basis, morality, justice, religion, and the very bonds of human society rest; and to allow people to go unharmed who violate or destroy it would be most impious, most foolish, and most inhuman. But with no less religious care must we preserve that great and sacred treasure of the truths which God Himself has taught us. By many and convincing arguments, often used by defenders of Christianity, certain leading truths have been laid down: Namely, that some things have been revealed by God; that the only begotten Son of God was made flesh, to bear witness to the truth; that a perfect society was founded by Him—The Church, namely, of which He is the head, and with which He has promised to abide till the end of the world. To this society He entrusted all the truths which he had taught, in order that it might keep and guard them and with lawful authority explain them; and at the same time He commanded all nations to hear the voice of the Church as if it were His own, threatening those who would not hear it with everlasting perdition. Thus, it is manifest that man's best and surest teacher is God, the source and principle of all truth; and the only-begotten Son, who is in the bosom of the Father, the Way, the Truth, and the Life, the true Light which enlightens every man and to whose teaching all must submit: *And they shall all be taught of God.* In faith and in teaching of morality, God Himself made the Church a partaker of His divine authority, and through His heavenly gift she cannot be deceived. She is therefore the greatest and most reliable teacher of mankind, and in her dwells an inviolable right to teach them. Sustained by the truth received from her divine Founder, the Church has ever sought to fulfill holily the mission entrusted to her by God; unconquered by the difficulties on all sides surrounding her, she has never ceased to assert her liberty of teaching, and in this way the wretched superstition of Paganism being dispelled, the wide world was renewed unto Christian wisdom. Now reason itself clearly teaches that the truths of divine revelation and those of nature cannot really be opposed to one another, and that whatever is at variance with them must necessarily be false. Therefore, the divine teaching of the Church, so far from being an obstacle to the pursuit of learning and the progress of science or in any way retarding the advance of civilization, in reality brings to them the sure guidance of shining light. And for the same reason, it is of no small advantage for the perfecting of human liberty, since our Savior Jesus Christ has said that by truth is man made free: *You shall know the truth, and the truth shall make you free.* Therefore, there is no reason why genuine liberty should grow indignant, or true science feel aggrieved, at having to bear the just and necessary restraint of laws by which, in the judgment of the Church and of Reason itself, human teaching has to be controlled. The Church indeed—as facts have everywhere proved—looks chiefly and above all to the defense of the Christian faith, while careful at the same time to foster and promote every kind of human learning. For learning is in itself good, and praiseworthy, and desirable; and further, all erudition which is the outgrowth of sound reason, and in conformity with the truth of things, serves not a little to confirm what we believe on the authority of God. The Church truly, to our great benefit, has carefully preserved the monuments of ancient wisdom; has opened everywhere homes of science, and has urged on intellectual progress by fostering most diligently the arts by which the culture of our age is so much advanced. Lastly, we must not forget that a vast field lies freely open to man's industry and genius, containing all those things which have no necessary connection with Christian faith and morals, or as to which the Church exercising no authority leaves the judgment of the learned free and unconstrained. From all this may be understood the nature and character of that liberty which the followers of Liberalism so eagerly advocate and proclaim. On the one hand, they demand for themselves and for the State a license which opens the way to every perversity of opinion; and on the other, they hamper the Church in diverse ways, restricting her liberty within narrowest limits, although from her teaching not only is there nothing to be feared, but in every respect very much to be gained.

316. Freedom Is to Teach Truth, Not Error

Rooted as it is in a deeper liberty, academic freedom in its largest and best sense is an instance of those fundamental and inalienable rights which belong to us because of our very nature as men. A basic human right is not a bare physical power, nor is it a mere brute fact. A man's right to life continues even though he cannot defend himself against an unjust aggressor. An innocent man's right to freedom of movement remains even when the walls of the concentration camp are too high to scale. Our natural right to the truth survives even if the truth is kept from us by superior force or by a cunning so subtle that we do not recognize its existence. Nor is a basic human right something of which it may be said, "The State giveth and the State taketh away." It is essentially an inviolable moral power to perform a certain act, to have a certain thing, or to receive something from

316. John K. Ryan, "Truth and Freedom," *The Journal of Higher Education*, 20:350–354, October 1949.

others. Because we are what we are, something more than "the horse and the mule that have not understanding," we are endowed with a body of natural rights. Among those that are most pertinent to the present discussion are the right to freedom of expression, of information, of communication in accordance with truth and justice; the right to education suitable for the maintenance and development of man's dignity as a human being; the right to religious formation through education and association.

*   *   *

We are all familiar with such statements as that which is so approvingly put upon Voltaire's lips: "I disapprove of what you say, but I will defend to the death your right to say it." But if what I disagree with be something destructive of all that is good, should I then "defend to the death" this asserted right to propagate error? Must I hold in the name of tolerance and academic freedom that a man has "a right to be wrong" and to draw himself and others into disaster?

*   *   *

Error has no rights. To teach in the classroom or elsewhere what one knows to be false is to violate the dignity of one's nature as a man and to destroy the special virtue that belongs to the teacher. To put forth mere personal opinion as final doctrine can amount in certain instances to the same thing. To do this is not to exercise academic freedom, but rather to abuse it and to work toward its destruction. Upon the teacher, even more than upon other men, rests an obligation to tell the truth. This obligation grows with the weight of the subject that he teaches and with the consequences that his words may have for his students and for society.

Because of this duty to tell the truth, along with the correlative right to speak out, the teacher must be in some degree the philosopher, the lover of wisdom and the searcher after it. As such, he cannot fall victim to certain sophistries that are sometimes advanced and defended. Thus it has been said that the search for the truth is better than its discovery, that final truths can never be established, and that the truth can be a disadvantage or danger to us, darkening our minds, weakening our wills, and restricting our freedom. Like the true philosopher, the true teacher will avoid misology, that belief that there is no soundness or health in reasoning, against which Socrates once warned his friends. He will likewise keep himself clear of the intellectual and moral disease that is skepticism. If the doubting question is put to him, What is truth? he will have an adequate answer, stating the nature of truth, its kinds, and the obligations that it imposes upon himself and others.

317. The Basis for Academic Freedom

I have argued on many occasions that *one* of the justifications of academic freedom is that it helps us to win new knowledge. But I am not satisfied that the case for academic freedom rests on the assumption or presupposition that all truth is not yet discovered in the sense that it is a necessary condition for belief in academic freedom. Mr. Boas writes that "if everything which could be known were known, then the Augustinian dictum that man is not free to err would force itself upon us as an ultimate truth." I do not see why. Augustine, of course, did not believe that everything knowable was already known, yet he held that no man is free to err about anything known to be true. And there are others who, differing with Augustine about what it is we know to be true, agree with him that men are not free to err concerning it. In such cases we could defend the right to err, even about what is known to be true, among other reasons, on the ground that freedom to err is part of freedom of inquiry, and that the habits of free inquiry will lead to new truths.

But suppose everything were known. I still would disagree with Augustine and Mr. Boas. I would hold that to find out things for oneself is often morally more important than being right, and that a certain violence is done to the mature human personality if it is compelled to yield to the compulsions of any authority except the luminous coercions of logic and scientific method. Morally, a society in which mature human beings are free to err about truths seems to me superior to one in which they are compelled to accept as truths what they do not understand as truths. This is not the same thing as Lessing's preference for the striving for truth to the possession of it.

I go further than Mr. Boas here in denying the statement that "all truth has not yet been discovered" is a necessary presupposition of a belief in academic freedom. I believe that we should permit a scholar whose competence has been established to challenge *any* proposition in his field even in elementary mathematics and logic, and I would not define his competence in terms of the acceptance or rejection of

317. George Boas and Sidney Hook, "The Ethics of Academic Freedom" in *Academic Freedom, Logic, and Religion* (Philadelphia: University of Pennsylvania Press, 1951).

the proposition disputed. At any definite time there are certain tests of competence; and it is wiser to take the risk that the investigator will not urge absurdities than to insist that any particular statement is beyond challenge. Competence is best defined in terms of the *methods* by which a conclusion is reached rather than in terms of any particular proposition believed. . . . I admit that one has to win the *academic* right, as distinct from his civil or constitutional right, to say things which his colleagues regard as absurd. But I am convinced that it is important to defend the right of those who are properly qualified in their field to talk what seems like nonsense, especially in an age when the very foundations of science are shifting and the claims of parapsychology are becoming more insistent.

318. Misconceptions of Academic Freedom

VIII. Freedom beyond the scholar's area of competence?

It has been said that academic freedom should be confined to the recognized area of the individual scholar's competence and must not be extended to writings or utterances "outside his field."

This view, formulated in the definitions or pronouncements of many sincere advocates of freedom of teaching and research, was perhaps suggested by the fact that competence is the chief factor in the selection of scholars for academic posts, and incompetence the chief ground on which separation from academic posts can be justified. But what this means is that no one should be appointed unless he is competent in the field in which he is expected to search and teach, and that no one should be allowed to hold a post in a field in which he is clearly incompetent. It does not follow, however, that a scholar must be silent on questions pertaining to fields for which he was not appointed, or that he must avoid expressing himself on matters which even he himself may consider outside his area of competence. Still less does it follow that a professor should be reprimanded or dismissed if he expresses his opinions in fields that lie beyond the area assigned to him by the terms of his academic appointment.

Recognition of incompetence as a cause for separation—recognition that the dismissal of a teacher incompetent in his specialty does not violate academic freedom—implies absolutely nothing regarding the freedom of a teacher, whose competence in his specialty is not ques-

318. Fritz Machlup, "Misconceptions Concerning Academic Freedom," *American Association of University Professors, Bulletin*, 41:768–781, Winter, 1955.

tioned, to expound on matters outside his specialty. Is it perhaps possible to deduce from the "presuppositions" of the principles of academic freedom whether that freedom should be confined by the boundaries of a scholar's area of competence or should have no such boundaries?

There are at least five different ways in which professors engage in "extra-curricular" speech:

1. Although appointed as a teacher or researcher in a particular subject, a professor may have scholarly interests in one or more other fields of learning, cognate or quite apart, and may engage in research, lecturing, and writing in these fields.

2. Although thoroughly trained only in particular fields, a professor may have intellectual curiosity about matters in other disciplines and may freely express his views on these matters in and out of his classroom and in and out of his university.

3. A professor may be interested in political or religious issues and hold forth on them without inhibitions, both in the classroom and on the public platform.

4. A professor may find it necessary or desirable in his lectures to expatiate on ramifications of the problems he discusses which lie outside his field of competence.

5. As a counsellor and adviser to his students, a professor may discuss their personal problems with them and may take positions on questions for which he has no special qualifications.

Should any of these "invasions of foreign areas" be condemned as improper? All have been so regarded at one time or another. The first of the five kinds of "transgression," incidentally, is different from the other four in that the trespassing scholar would not consider himself as unqualified in the areas into which he has expanded; if some professors in the invaded fields call for "border control" to keep out the men from other university departments, we may suspect that professional jealousy is behind their complaints. The other four kinds of professorial sorties are admittedly into territories which they do not master; thus, if professors warn their colleagues against such sorties, their caution can be attributed to the modesty and conscientiousness which are typical of most scholars. Typically, scholars have serious inhibitions against talking about things of which they know little, inhibitions they acquired when they realized how hard it is to achieve valid generalizations in their own specialty. Not all scholars, of course, have these inhibitions. The question with which we are concerned, however, is not whether professors should be encouraged to overcome their scholarly inhibitions—we believe that they should not—but rather whether areas other than those of certified competence should be considered "out of bounds" and whether a "transgressing" professor should be dismissed.

Against the restrictionist view, let us recall that almost all great thinkers, originators, and developers of great ideas were polyhistors, not narrow specialists. Will anyone seriously contend that Leibnitz should have "specialized" instead of freely holding forth on philosophy, mathematics, law and theology? that Newton should not have been free to lecture and write on theological problems? that Kant should have stayed away from law and politics? that the mathematician Cournot, the logician Jevons, the astronomer Newcomb, should not have felt free to expound the principles of economics?

It is not only difficult but dangerous to define a scholar's "area" of competence, because such an area ought not to be a static but a continually enlarging one. Interdisciplinary thinking and discussion, on problems for which perhaps no one has a satisfactory answer, is precisely what is most needed in our time, if not at all times. Progress is chiefly made by those who continually press forward to enlarge their areas of competence and to question all certified competences.

All this, perhaps, will be thought by many to be beside the point, for what the limitists nowadays really have in mind when they object to extensions of academic freedom beyond the area of competence is the scholar's taking part in public discussions of current political problems. For several centuries it was the area of religious controversy which many wanted to declare as "out of bounds"; now it is chiefly the area of social, economic and political controversies from which the professors are to be scared away. And for professors not in the fields of social, economic, or political science, this would be achieved through the area-of-competence clause in the definition of academic freedom.

From its very beginning the American Association of University Professors has rejected such limitations of academic freedom. The Association's 1915 *Declaration of Principles* stated that it was not desirable

> that scholars should be debarred from giving expression to their judgments upon controversial questions, or that their freedom of speech, outside the university, should be limited to questions falling within their own specialties. It is clearly not proper that they should be prohibited from lending their active support to organized movements which they believe to be in the public interest.

In other words, while the recognition of academic freedom entails academic responsibilities, particularly a moral obligation of the professor to refrain from "intemperate and sensational modes of expression," it does not entail a reduction of his civil liberties. It is possible, of course, that there is a point of view from which it can be argued that a professor who exercises his freedom of speech as a citizen in discussing political questions thereby foregoes his tenure rights, and that the trustees, if they dislike his ideas, may dismiss him from his post; but this point of view can hardly be reconciled with the fundamental principles on which academic freedom rests.

A definition of academic freedom which tends to discourage the academic scholar from discussing controversial questions is not consistent with the objectives of academic freedom. The restriction of academic freedom to "areas of competence" is obviously designed to act as such a discouragement.

IX. Freedom to teach subversive ideas?

It has been said that academic freedom must not include the right to advocate or teach "subversive ideas."

Any one informed about the history of academic freedom knows that the most serious interferences with the freedom of teaching have been interferences on the part of authorities fearful of what they regarded as subversion. While in the past many of the ideas condemned as subversive were in the fields of religion or in the natural sciences, where new ideas challenged religious dogma, it is now in the fields of politics and economics that "subversive" ideas are most feared.

In the past, it was exactly the teaching of allegedly subversive ideas in the universities that needed protection from interference. It was exactly the issue of subversion which demonstrated the need for academic freedom. Free enterprise and free markets for the products of the human mind required immunity for the writer and teacher who tried to overturn religious dogma or economic orthodoxy or the belief in a particular form of government. It was through the overturn—i.e., the subversion—of accepted dogmas that we have progressed as far as we have; and it was through subversion of an accepted government that we established the one under which we now live.

That society approves almost all past subversions of doctrine and many past subversions of government need not mean that it should always welcome new subversions and grant immunity to those who promote them. But in any case, confusion must be avoided between the overthrow of doctrines or beliefs—even beliefs in a form of government—and the actual overthrow of a government; the one is in the sphere of thought, the other in the sphere of action.

A discussion of "subversive teaching" must appear rather unrealistic, inasmuch as substantiated charges that a particular professor has been teaching subversive ideas are extremely rare in our times. The facts usually established are the past associations of the professor; from this his accusers deduce his beliefs; from this they deduce that his teaching may have reflected his beliefs; and from this they deduce that he has taught subversive ideas. Obviously, on the basis of such conjectures no charges of subversive teaching can be brought. But the issue, however hypothetical, merits examination. In view of the fact that vigilantes are inclined to mark as "subversive" what others would consider only as radical, is it possible to draw a line where real subversiveness begins? And should some degree of subversiveness be regarded as definitely outside the protection of academic freedom?

Speaking first of the subversion or violent overthrow of government, it may be worth remembering the position of the founding fathers of our republic. Thomas Jefferson, in his Inaugural Address in 1801 said:

> If there be any among us who would wish to dissolve this Union or to change its republican form, let them stand undisturbed as monuments of the safety with which error of opinion may be tolerated where reason is left free to combat it.

Others went further and recognized a basic "right to revolt." Indeed, the right to subvert the government was written into several state constitutions. And this principle was reaffirmed by Abraham Lincoln when he said:

> Whenever [the people] shall grow weary of the existing government, they can exercise their constitutional right of amending it or their revolutionary right to dismember or otherthrow it.

But if we should have lost this confidence, if a majority of us should feel insecure under a freedom to overthrow the government, we should at least be intelligent enough to make some significant distinctions. There are important differences among (1) a teacher who organizes a violent uprising, tells his students what actions they should take, what weapons wield, what buildings occupy at an appointed time or signal; (2) a teacher who harangues his students, urging them to participate in a revolutionary conspiracy; (3) a teacher who presents to his students the "need" or "desirability" of a violent overthrow of the government; (4) a teacher who, in his comparative description of alternative social, political, and economic systems, is disparagingly critical of the present system and full of praise for a substitute system; (5) a teacher who, in his comparative description of social, political, and economic institutions within the present system, shows a decided preference for radical changes.

Can the term "subversive" be legitimately applied to all these cases? With due respect for differences in semantic taste, the indiscriminate use of the term for such different situations would be misleading, to say the least. Most for us would probably propose a demarcation line before or after the third of these cases. Should some or all of them be beyond the protection of academic freedom? Some of us may propose the same demarcation line; others, though inclined to draw the line to include the third case among those of "subversive teaching," may prefer not to regard it as a revolutionary act, but as an "error of opinion" which "may be tolerated where reason is left free to combat it."

Concerning hostile criticism of our present systems and institutions, there should be no doubt that such teaching can be offset by the more objective or contrarily biased presentation of other teachers. Indeed, the teachers who understand the operations of the capitalistic system will be more effective in their exposition if they can take issue with the "subversive" views to which their students may have been exposed in the lectures of its enemies.

To say that teachers must be "scientifically objective" is well enough; but it is neither possible nor desirable for a good teacher always to be "neutral" and to suppress his value judgments. Perhaps "objectivity" in teaching is always a matter of degree. Commitment is always present, at least as regards premises. Almost all our teachers in the social sciences share the preference of the American people for democracy and for capitalism. It would be hypocrisy to call a favorable appraisal "objective" and an adverse one "biased." We all condemn communist countries for suppressing academic freedom when they silence the critics of communism and the friends of capitalism. In any case, academic freedom does not stop this side of "dangerous" beliefs. We must not, as cowards, allow ourselves to brand as "conspiracy violently to overthrow the government" the teaching of ideas that can be answered by reasoned argument.

✿   ✿   ✿

XI. Freedom for those without independence of thought?

It has been said that academic freedom does not include the freedom to teach—or even to hold—doctrines dictated by some outside authority and slavishly accepted by a teacher who has surrendered his own independence of thinking.

We agree with this rejection of propagandists who follow the party line or preach the articles of faith of a political or ecclesiastical authority, inasmuch as they may hold the doctrines in question not as a result of an honest search for truth but in blind submission to authority. Rarely, however, will a practical course of action follow from this point of view; for it is hardly possible to ascertain whether or not a teacher is truly convinced of the validity of the conclusions which he presents to his students or on what grounds his convictions are based.

There are those who take a scholar's membership in an organization devoted to the propaganda for a certain faith as evidence of a lack of integrity and independence of his thought. While some may regard such evidence as persuasive with regard to a member of the Communist Party, one can quickly realize the iniquity of this procedure when one applies it to other organizations or associations, professional, political, or religious. And we must not apply to one group a principle which we would reject for another. We must not impugn the motives of anyone merely on the ground of his associations. Even if we knew with absolute certainty that most members of a certain association or party have in effect surrendered their freedom of thought, we have no right to conclude that all members have done so.

Of course, if manifest untruths and patent distortions of firmly established facts were presented to students or the public in conformance with orders emanating from notorious sources of propaganda, it would be possible to prove that a propagandizing teacher or researcher was deliberately disseminating what he knew to be untrue. Where such proof is conclusive, action by the faculty against the offender is called for. But rarely will a case be that simple. For as a rule the teacher cannot himself verify the truth or falsity of all that he teaches. No scholar could possibly have tested personally all the findings and conclusions in his own field of competence, let alone those in other fields. He must needs accept a large amount of findings and conclusions reached by other specialists; indeed, he must accept probably the bulk of his knowledge on the authority of others. Who can say that his faith in such authority is not genuine, not honest? Who can prove that a scholar's acceptance of truths pronounced by others indicates a surrender of his independence?

Since a scholar's affiliation or association is not acceptable as conclusive evidence and since confession will hardly be obtained without intolerable inquisition, there is, apart from proofs of deliberate distortions of verifiable facts, no simple and acceptable way of establishing that a professor lacks independence of thought; where such lack cannot be established, it is useless as a criterion for judging his continued fitness as a college or university teacher.

XII. Freedom for those who would destroy freedom?

It has been said that academic freedom must be denied to those who conspire to destroy it.

It is cogently argued that, if we treasure freedom, we must not grant freedom to work for the abolition of freedom. There are at least four categories of persons to whom this argument may apply: those who openly denounce unrestricted intellectual freedom as "license," unwholesome to a good society; those who are members of a group or party known to be hostile to the free institutions of democratic-capitalist nations; those who advocate the adoption of institutions or policies incompatible with the maintenance of intellectual freedom, but who deny this incompatibility; and those who advocate these institutions or policies while frankly admitting their incompatibility with full freedom of speech.

The debate about the distinction between liberty and license, and about the alleged need for limits to intellectual freedom in a good society, has been going on for at least 2500 years. Although several conspiracies to restrict intellectual freedom have had temporary success, champions of unrestricted freedom refuse to be inconsistent and to silence their opponents. He who believes in full freedom of speech cannot consistently restrict the freedom of those who disparage such liberty by calling it license, and ask for the imposition of restrictions.

The question of "implied advocacy of the destruction of freedom," inferred from party membership, is most controversial at the present time. The argument runs as follows: It is an established fact that the Communists have abolished academic freedom wherever they are in political power; it is reported on good authority that members of the Communist party are pledged to support its objectives by fair means or foul; it follows that membership in the Communist party is sufficient evidence of conspiracy to destroy freedom, and that such membership "extinguishes the right to a university position."

The logic of this argument is obviously faulty if we accept the fundamental principle of American justice, that guilt is personal and cannot be established by opinion and association; we cannot make party membership a decisive criterion. The number of known exceptions is too large to permit us to generalize even for purposes of presumptive evidence. There are many who joined the Communist party and left it again, disillusioned. Thus there must have been, at any given time, members of the party who did not believe in the supposed objectives of the party, but had to "find out"; many members may be finding out at present, experiencing their enlightenment and disillusionment. There may be others who joined the party and signed all sorts of pledges without intending to serve its revolutionary aims, or without recognizing that such aims are pursued or, if pursued, are incompatible with the maintenance of intellectual freedom. One may blame such people for being shockingly naïve; but one cannot honestly make safe inference from membership to belief in the destruction of freedom. (Indeed, there are those who joined the party in order to report its activities to the security agencies of our government.) Thus, party membership, past or present, does not prove that a member is a participant in a conspiracy to destroy freedom.

The third category of implicit foes of intellectual freedom consists of those who advocate the adoption of institutions or policies incompatible with the maintenance of intellectual freedom but who deny this incompatibility. If we, on empirical and analytical grounds, are convinced of this incompatibility while they deny it, we are bound to conclude that they are either naïve or dishonest. The toleration of honest error, however naïve, is surely the essence of intellectual freedom. If we can prove that they are dishonest, we can and should eliminate them from their academic positions. But the proof, as has been explained before, is difficult, because evidence that some one speaks and writes what he knows to be untrue is hard to come by.

There remain—if they exist in colleges and universities—the avowed totalitarian communists about whose beliefs one need not make any questionable inferences. They frankly admire the political institutions of the Soviet Union, and openly advocate the adoption in our country of these institutions, including the abolition or restriction of most political freedoms. If such a man can be found in an academic position, trying to impart his honest convictions to his students, should we let him go on teaching? Before we give in to an impulse, let us be conscious of one clear fact: if we silence him, *we* have *actually* abrogated freedom of speech, whereas *he* has merely talked about doing so.

319. Freedom the Product of a Positive Rather than a *Laissez-Faire* State

As a matter of fact, the attainment of liberty of thought and of conscience, of speech and of the press, which the eighteenth century conceived as fundamental among the rights of men, was coupled with a notion of *laissez faire* in government, which left the school in dependence upon private agencies, and so a mere expression of family ambitions or denominational views. Thus we have the "freedom of teaching" of the France of the Revolution and of the United States during much of its history. The state simply lets education alone. Such an arrangement theorists like Herbert Spencer conceive to be the one most conducive to the welfare of the individual and the progress of society. Consequently, they oppose any attempt on the part of the state to assume control of the school.

❖   ❖   ❖

319. Ernest N. Henderson, *A Textbook in the Principles of Education* (New York: The Macmillan Company, 1910), pp. 459–462.

According to this view,—the *laissez-faire* theory of education—the school will be freest to investigate, to teach, and so to progress in case it is left to private agencies which are protected in their freedom of teaching. A national system is supposed to mean paternalism, the suppression of variation, and so of progress, in a word, absolutism with all its attendant evils. What we need is freedom on the part of the individual to study what he chooses. Let the laws of demand and supply operate as freely as human contrivances can permit. The school, made dependent on the demands of its patrons, will supply whatever their ambitions and intelligence require. Thus, it is assumed, each will get the kind and the amount of education that he deserves. We will have justice in giving to each what he earns and values, freedom in forcing upon none what they do not want, and progress in providing the greatest freedom for the development of individual differences and for their struggle for existence.

The believer in *laissez faire* holds that freedom of teaching involves no interference on the part of the state in the work of education. But such an arrangement leaves it a mere servile flunky upon the tastes and prejudices of its patrons. It must give that which will insure it pupils. Under such conditions there is no freedom to teach, for if the school does not teach what the parents want,—that is, if it does not give up its freedom,—it cannot teach at all, since it will have no patronage. Hence, genuine academic freedom requires that the state should protect the school in determining the content and method of education. Without this privilege and responsibility academic freedom is left ineffectual.

The two issues, that of control of education by the school and that of control and support of the school by the state, have gone hand in hand. If it be admitted that there should be complete academic freedom, one must at the same time grant that the school can be placed in this position only by the generous support and protection of a democratic state. Historically it is true that national education has been both conservative and calculated to favor the welfare of the nation or that of a dominant class rather than that of the individual. However, this result sprang from the fact that the state has been under the control of classes or of conservatives. When once this institution has become imbued with the spirit of progress, there is no reason why it should not favor intellectual investigation and reform through education. Moreover, the democratic state is pledged to secure, so far as possible, equality of opportunity. Hence, it cannot favor education in the interests of classes. The event has proved that national education tends toward both the most exact justice to the child and the largest efficiency in the school.

But while it may be agreed that national education means the greatest measure of academic freedom for the school, many may question the wisdom of permitting such power to come into the hands of the teaching class. It remains to show that the greatest efficiency in education springs from giving to the school the power to determine what and how it shall teach. There are two fundamental reasons for this complete academic freedom. These are the growth of education into a profession involving special knowledge and skill, and the fact that education deals with individuals who are incapable, without direction, of knowing or getting what they should have . . .

320. Pupils Primary Beneficiaries of Academic Freedom

It should be recognized first and held in mind constantly that the issue of academic freedom relates primarily to pupils rather than to teachers. The issue is whether children and youth shall have freedom to learn, to go through the educative process of fashioning the pattern of their minds so that they will recognize evidence, weigh facts, and draw useful conclusions. The denial of academic liberty is the denial of intellectual opportunities to youth. It is upon this ground that the battle must be waged. It almost always happens that when a question of freedom of teaching arises, the discussion centers about the teacher, as if the infringement of his rights and liberties were the important stake. This tendency always throws the emphasis in the wrong place and the whole issue out of clear focus. Attention should be kept where it belongs, upon the interests of students. Shall they be denied the processes of educational experience?

321. Phases of Academic Freedom

The teaching by the professor in his class-room on the subjects within the scope of his chair ought to be absolutely free. He must teach the truth as he has found it and sees it. This is the primary condition of academic freedom, and any violation of it endangers intellectual progress. In order to make it secure it is essential that the teaching in the class-room should be confidential. This does not mean

320. Melvin E. Haggerty, "The Paramount Service of Education to Society," *The Annals of the American Academy of Political and Social Science*, 182:18–19, November 1935.

321. A. Lawrence Lowell, *At War with Academic Traditions in America* (Cambridge, Mass.: Harvard University Press, 1934), pp. 267–271. Reprinted by permission of the publishers.

that it is secret, but that what is said there should not be published. If the remarks of the instructor were repeated by the pupils in the public press, he would be subjected to constant criticism by people, not familiar with the subject, who misunderstood his teaching; and, what is more important, he would certainly be misquoted, because his remarks would be reported by the student without their context or the qualifications that give them their accuracy. Moreover, if the rule that remarks in the class-room shall not be reported for publication elsewhere is to be maintained, the professor himself must not report them. Lectures open to the public stand on a different footing; but lectures in a private class-room must not be given by the instructor to the newspapers. That principle is, I believe, observed in all reputable institutions.

This brings us to the next subdivision of the inquiry, the freedom of the professor within his field of study, but outside of his class-room. It has been pointed out that he ought not to publish his class-room lectures as such in the daily press. That does not mean a denial of the right to publish them in a book, or their substance in a learned periodical. On the contrary, the object of institutions of learning is not only the acquisition but the diffusion of knowledge. Every professor must, therefore, be wholly unrestrained in publishing the results of his study in the field of his professorship. It is needless to add that for the dignity of his profession, for the maintenance of its privileges, as well as for his own reputation among his fellows, whatever he writes or says on his own subject should be uttered as a scholar, in a scholarly tone and form. This is a matter of decorum, not of discipline; to be remedied by a suggestion, not by a penalty.

In troublous times much more serious difficulty, and much more confusion of thought, arise from the other half of our subject, the right of a professor to express his views without restraint on matters lying outside the sphere of his professorship. This is not a question of academic freedom in its true sense, but of the personal liberty of the citizen. It has nothing to do with liberty of research and instruction in the subject for which the professor occupies the chair that makes him a member of the university. The fact that a man fills a chair of astronomy, for example, confers on him no special knowledge of, and no peculiar right to speak upon, the protective tariff. His right to speak about a subject on which he is not an authority is simply the right of any other man, and the question is simply whether the university or college by employing him as a professor acquires a right to restrict his freedom as a citizen. It seems to me that this question can be answered only by again considering his position in his class-room and outside of it.

The university or college is under certain obligations to its students. It compels them to attend courses of instruction, and on their side they have a right not to be compelled to listen to remarks offensive or injurious to them on subjects of which the instructor is not a master,—a right which the teacher is bound to respect. A professor of Greek, for example, is not at liberty to harangue his pupils on the futility and harmfulness of vaccination; a professor of economics, on Bacon's authorship of Shakespeare; or a professor of bacteriology, on the tenets of the Catholic Church. Everyone will admit this when stated in such extreme forms; and the reason is that the professor speaks to his class as a professor, not as a citizen. He speaks from his chair and must speak from that alone. The difficulty lies in drawing the line between that which does and does not fall properly within the professor's subject; and where the line ought to be drawn the professor can hardly claim an arbitrary power to judge, since the question affects the rights both of himself and his students. But serious friction rarely arises, I believe, from this cause; and a word of caution would ordinarily be enough.

The gravest questions, and the strongest feelings, arise from action by a professor beyond his chosen field and outside of his class-room. Here he speaks only as a citizen. By appointment to a professorship he acquires no rights that he did not possess before; but there is a real difference of opinion today on the question whether he loses any rights that he would otherwise enjoy. The argument in favor of a restraining power on the part of the governing boards of universities and colleges is based upon the fact that by extreme, or injudicious, remarks that shock public sentiment a professor can do great harm to the institution with which he is connected. That is true, and sometimes a professor thoughtlessly does an injury that is without justification. If he publishes an article on the futility and harmfulness of vaccination, and signs it as a professor in a certain university, he leads the public to believe that his views are those of an authority on the subject, approved by the institution and taught to its students. If he is really a professor of Greek, he is misleading the public and misrepresenting his university, which he would not do if he gave his title in full.

In spite, however, of the risk of injury to the institution, the objections to restraint upon what professors may say as citizens seem to me far greater than the harm done by leaving them free. In the first place, to impose upon the teacher in a university restrictions to which the members of other professions, lawyers, physicians, engineers, and so forth are not subjected would produce a sense of irritation and humiliation. In accepting a chair under such conditions a man would surrender a part of his liberty; what he might say would be submitted to the censorship of a board of trustees, and he would cease to be a free citizen. The lawyer, physician, or engineer may express his views as he likes on the subject of the protective tariff; shall the professor of astronomy not be free to do the same? Such a policy would tend seriously to discourage some of the best men from taking up the scholar's life. It is not a question of academic freedom, but of personal liberty from constraint, yet it touches the dignity of the academic career.

That is an objection to restraint on freedom of speech from the standpoint of the teacher. There is another, not less weighty, from that of the institution itself. If a university or college censors what its professors may say, if it restrains them from uttering something that it does not approve, it thereby assumes responsibility for that which it permits them to say. This is logical and inevitable, but it is a responsibility which an institution of learning would be very unwise in assuming. It is sometimes suggested that the principles are different in time of war; that the governing boards are then justified in restraining unpatriotic expressions injurious to the country. But the same problem is presented in war time as in time of peace. If the university is right in restraining its professors, it has a duty to do so, and it is responsible for whatever it permits. There is no middle ground. Either the university assumes full responsibility for permitting its professors to express certain opinions in public, or it assumes no responsibility whatever, and leaves them to be dealt with like other citizens by the public authorities according to the laws of the land.

322. Academic Freedom in a Sectarian College

Coming directly to the subject in hand, I will state my position. It is this, that the Christian college possesses the right to control its teaching and that it is duty bound to do so, in order that it may fulfil the intention of its founders and the purpose of those who have sacrificed for it. It must be able to give assurance to parents and friends as well as students themselves that the influences which prevail shall be truly Christian. It is my starting-point, and I wish to point out that in dealing with this subject the starting-point is most important. Suppose we begin with academic freedom as the final and determinative factor, to which all else must bend; it is quite evident that we can

322. Edmund D. Soper, "Academic Freedom in a Christian College," *School and Society*, 30:524–527, October 1929.

not travel in a very definite direction towards a very definite goal. There is a kind of inevitability about it. But suppose we take our start with the proposition that the maintenance of the Christian character of the college is primary, the result is very different. It is so different, some would say, that academic freedom has completely disappeared. A defensible attitude may have taken its place, but it is not academic freedom. I am not so particular about terms, but I do believe that if academic freedom be defined as something absolutely complete, without any qualifications at all, there is room for the question just raised. Yet, as a believer in freedom, I hope to show that we have not done away with it in taking this stand, but that something very noble and satisfying, which can with justice be called by no other name than freedom itself, still remains . . .

※　　　　　※　　　　　※

What I have in mind is the freedom of a Christian teacher. When his fundamental attitude to Christ is assured I can see no limit to his freedom. It is the freedom of the man who has come to himself and has reached his basal attitudes in life. To him the acceptance of the Christian position is the most liberating experience of his life. He feels rightly related to the universe and its Creator and Sustainer. The way of Jesus is the way of life to him. He has broken with other philosophies of life as less satisfying and now experiences what great and noble men have felt down through the ages, that Christianity is not primarily a problem, but is what it was intended to be, the solution of a problem. His freedom is based on the most reasonable view of life there is, so far as he can see, and thus has a content not known by those who have never realized what the universe and its God may mean when seen in the face of Jesus Christ . . .

323. Political Unity Compatible with Metaphysical Differences

Now there has certainly been much loose talk about "tolerance" in and out of academic circles. But the issue with which we are here concerned is a fairly simple one. The "tolerance" that is essential to political democracy is the civil liberty which permits men of various faiths and doctrines to cooperate *politically* as members of the *political* community without prejudice to these further faiths and doctrines,

323. Arthur E. Murphy, "Sectarian Absolutes and Faith in Democracy," *The Humanist*, 1:110–111, Autumn 1941.

whatever they may be, so long as they do not impair the security of the state or infringe on the civil rights of others to a similar immunity. The assumption on which it is based is that political unity is compatible with diversity on these further issues, and that it is therefore not the business of the state to impose any such doctrine, e.g., through the public schools, or to exclude others as detrimental to the public welfare. These doctrines may be *in other respects* extremely important, and neither scepticism nor indifference with respect to their truth is implied, though there may well be some toward which a reasonable man will be well advised to be either sceptical or indifferent. That is not within the province of the state to determine and the attempt on its part to lay down sectarian requirements for good citizenship should for that reason be opposed by free men as an infringement of their civil rights.

The justification of this position is two-fold. First, these doctrines, whatever their *de jure* universality in the opinion of their devotees, cannot *de facto* command the unforced assent of considerable bodies of men who are, in *other* respects, reasonable individuals and good citizens. To insist upon their acceptance as prerequisite for "democracy" would be to impose a sectarian test for citizenship and thus to narrow the area within which political cooperation and good will are genuinely possible. Professor Adler thinks that the acceptance of metaphysics as "public knowledge" is essential if we are to be saved from positivism—"the central corruption of modern culture." But the plain fact is that metaphysics is *not* public knowledge in the sense that its Adlerian truths are accessible to all otherwise reasonable men who give their attention to this subject, or even to the majority of them. Professor Maritain, whose "authority" on this subject Adler would hardly question, makes this abundantly clear in a revealing statement: "Metaphysical widsom is in its essence a pure natural wisdom." But it involves "The mystery of abstractive intuition," an intuition in which, at the summit of abstraction, being itself, insofar as it is being, is disclosed. "It is this intuition which makes the metaphysician. *Everybody does not have it.* And if we ask why positivism, old and new, and Kantism ignore this intuition, we shall be bound finally to say that it is because *there are philosophers who see, and philosophers who do not see.*" If we recall that what this intuition discloses to Maritain and Adler is the first principles of scholastic metaphysics, we shall have to add that the philosophers who have *not* seen are the overwhelming majority of those who, since the fifteenth century, have been generally recognized as the leaders in this field. To dignify such esoteric insights as "public knowledge" to which the findings of the sciences are subordinated seems an odd and arbitrary procedure. But that is not the issue here. These privileged "seers" *may* be right and the rest of us wrong, though I do not for a moment believe it. But since in fact we do not see and cannot, on the level of free inquiry be made to do so, the demand that we accept the "authority" of these principles is in fact a demand that we accept them *on* the authority of Professors Maritain, Adler, and others who tell us that they see them. *That* is the kind of "authority" against which the professorial mind has been, and is, in rebellion. The resurrection of such "authority" as a necessary basis for the "rational" defense of democracy, and hence for our political security, is an attack upon the principle of tolerance in its plainest and most elementary sense.

324. Teacher Oaths Qualified

. . . The loyalty and competence of teachers are attacked by special legislation impossing oaths on them and forbidding them to "teach" certain topics. As far as the oath to support the Constitution of the United States and the State is concerned, little objection seems to lie on the surface of things. Are not the employees of the schools public officers? Are not public officers required to take an oath of office? If resort is had to technicalities, then note must be taken of the fact that most employees in the schools are not public officers in the legal sense. They belong to the great body of civil servants of whom oaths are not ordinarily required. Subordinate employees in engineering, health, and other professional services are employees, not public officers, and oaths are not exacted of them. Thus to impose oaths on all teachers, and to forbid the teaching of subjects belonging of right to education, is in fact to single teachers out as a class and to assume the existence of disloyalty to country and to knowledge in their ranks. It also assumes that anyone who is disloyal in fact will be deterred from taking the oath, or will be transformed by the oath into a loyal citizen.

                     ✻   ✻   ✻

The Constitution of the United States and the fundamental law of each state guarantee the freedom of inquiry and discussion which education is under obligation to preserve and cherish. That is not all. These constitutions also make provisions for changes which eventuate from freedom of inquiry and discussion; besides giving a wide latitude for operations of policy within the limits of existing constitutional

324. Educational Policies Commission, *The Unique Function of Education in American Democracy* (Washington, D.C.: National Educational Association, 1937), pp. 119–123.

law. In common with all other citizens, teachers are under obligation to respect the law; but in common with all other citizens they must recognize that changes in the law are constantly before the public for consideration. If they observe the dictates of truth when they teach the subjects touching government, economy, and society, they are compelled to present fairly and squarely changes which have been made, great issues of change now pending, and the underlying assumptions by which they are to be determined. An oath to support a constitution does not impose an obligation to condemn and resist changes in it; such an oath carries with it an express obligation to support provisions which authorize alterations. This is obvious enough to seem banal, but confusion in public opinion requires restatement.

325. Freedom Requires Tact as well as Courage

Teachers must learn that self-restraints, wisdom, and judicial attitudes as well as freedom are virtues. The teacher not only owes obligations to society, to students, and to his own professional standards, but to the community in which he lives and works. Unfortunate results ensue when a community tries to ignore a teacher's individuality and convictions. It is just as unfortunate, though, for a teacher to ignore the individuality and attitudes of the community. To free a teacher from repressions of an unsympathetic community only to have an unsympathetic teacher scoff at all the community's deepest convictions is not to create freedom but to transform one brand of intolerance into another. Freedom for the teacher must be accompanied by freedom for the community, so that teacher and community together may work out mutual problems with good will toward each other, sympathy for one another's motives, reciprocal attempts to understand conflicting points of view, and willingness to let each retain his own convictions in circumstances where teacher and community continue to disagree. The community will be liberalized and educated to freedom much more speedily by persuasion than by defiance. Many teachers are bad boys, who have never ceased to enjoy smashing things, and what is more fun to smash than the ideals of a "backward" community? Others have reached the adolescent stage of delight in shocking people and gaining notoriety. Still others are just plain fools. Such teachers work more damage than any number of avowed enemies of freedom. This problem of adjustment of teacher and community is difficult indeed . . .

325. Howard K. Beale, *Are American Teachers Free?* (New York: Charles Scribner's Sons, 1936), pp. 767–768.

18

Method of Instruction

Problems in the Philosophy of Education Discussed in this Section

1. Does method in teaching differ essentially from method in learning? From method of inquiry in research? Should the teacher's method ever be based on authority?
2. Is it more important to teach children how to think rather than what to think? Should thinking or problem-solving be postponed until a backlog of experience has been accumulated?
3. What metaphysical presuppositions are most favorable to encouraging the student to think critically? Within what limits can the student be told to puzzle problems out independently?
4. What is the importance of making provision for pupil "activities"? For drill?
5. What does it mean to "study" one's lesson?
6. Is education primarily a matter of manipulation of the pupil's environment in order to direct his activities? If so, how can instruction escape being mechanical?
7. To what extent should method involve actual participation in economic production and political administration? Should these social enterprises be slowed down and simplified to a point where they can be educationally significant to the young?
8. What ethical considerations are involved in the homogeneous grouping of children?

326. Method Independent of Aim

Dynamite explodes in the same way,—according to the same laws,— whether it is used as a harmless blast in a mine or to deal death and destruction at the will of an anarchist. Similarly, the principles of educational method work in the same way whether they are to produce a theologian or a thief.

326. William C. Bagley, *The Educative Process* (New York: The Macmillan Company, 1926), pp. 41–42.

327. How and What to Think Inseparable Pedagogically

It is often said that the schools should teach how to think rather than what to think. From such an ideal no one can dissent. Lay critics often assume that when they have enunciated such a principle they are taking issue with educators. But indeed they are not. Hardly a treatise on education but has argued for the same ideal; scarcely a teacher but writes it as Arcticle One of the professional creed. But the practical challenge of the classroom reveals to the teacher, as reflection should reveal to any intelligent layman, that the how and the what are inextricably interwoven. The best teachers—in the formal school, in the home, or on the platform—may aim at the ideal of independent thinking; but at the same time they profoundly influence thinking toward results that they have accepted. This is due largely, of course, to the fact that such thinking as they themselves have done, thinking which they correctly or incorrectly consider independent, has led them to conclusions which seem sound; and immature minds are easily influenced to follow the same patterns to similar results . . .

328. How to Make Pupils Think

When one stimulus tends to evoke one response, while another stimulus is acting in another and incomplete direction, or when inconsistent aims present themselves simultaneously, reflective thought is demanded in order to discover a new single stimulus which will coordinate the conflicting ones, or to project a comprehensive aim which will reconcile those opposing each other. The natural cue and occasion of thinking seems always to be found in some such situation. The lesson to be drawn as regards methods of teaching is obvious. The instructor stimulates thinking most successfully either by presenting the old or familiar under such conditions that unexpected discrepancies and incompatibilities appear in it, or by presenting the new in such a way that it both excites and resists assimilation by the old . . .

327. Thomas H. Briggs, *The Great Investment* (Cambridge, Mass.: Harvard University Press, 1930), p. 30. Reprinted by permission of the publishers.

328. John Dewey, in Paul Monroe, editor, *Cyclopedia of Education* (New York: The Macmillan Company, 1911), Vol. 2, p. 175.

329. Importance of Discussion

There is no way to make the problem a common possession save by making the school a talking school. As soon as one can be brought to say something upon the subject under discussion, he has committed himself to think about it further. He has defined his own views and become responsible for them to his group. Now he must either support them or renounce them . . .

330. Teacher Operates Principally on Environment

Continuity and interaction in their active union with each other provide the measure of the educative significance and value of an experience. The immediate and direct concern of an educator is then with the situations in which interaction takes place. The individual, who enters as a factor into it, is what he is at a given time. It is the other factor, that of objective conditions, which lies to some extent within the possibility of regulation by the educator. As has already been noted, the phrase "objective conditions" covers a wide range. It includes what is done by the educator and the way in which it is done, not only words spoken but the tone of voice in which they are spoken. It includes equipment, books, apparatus, toys, games played. It includes the materials with which an individual interacts, and, most important of all, the total *social* set-up of the situations in which a person is engaged.

331. Twofold Nature of the Art of Teaching

Now the art of teaching is like to knowledge, namely, the intellect and those things which are naturally understood, namely, first principles. Wherefore knowledge is acquired in two ways, both by discovery without teaching, and by teaching. Consequently the teacher begins to teach in the same way as the discoverer begins to discover, namely, by

329. Ernest C. Moore, *What Is Education?* (Boston: Ginn and Company, 1915), p. 259.
330. John Dewey, *Experience and Education* (New York: The Macmillan Company, 1938), pp. 43–44.
331. St. Thomas Aquinas, *Contra Gentiles,* in Mary H. Mayer, *The Philosophy of Teaching of St. Thomas Aquinas* (Milwaukee: The Bruce Publishing Company, 1929), pp. 145–146.

offering to the disciple's consideration principles known by him, since *all learning results from preexisting knowledge;* and by drawing conclusions from those principles; and again by proposing sensible examples, from which there result, in the disciple's mind, the phantasms which are necessary that he may understand. And since the outward action of the teacher would have no effect, without the inward principle of knowledge, which is in us from God, hence among theologians it is said that *man teaches by outward ministration, but God by inward operation:* even so the physician is said *to minister to nature* when he heals. Accordingly knowledge is caused in the disciple by his master, not by way of natural action, but after the manner of art, as stated.

332. Teacher's Knowledge Must Be Perfect

. . . Without doubt a man can, through his implanted light of reason and without a teacher or aid of outside instruction, come to a knowledge of many unknown things, as is evident in everyone who acquires knowledge by discovery. A man is thus in a way a cause of his own knowledge; he cannot, however, be called his own teacher or be said to teach himself.

. . . Instruction implies perfect action of knowledge in the teacher or master. Hence, he who is the teacher must have explicitly and perfectly the knowledge which he causes in another, as in one learning through instruction. But when knowledge is acquired through the intrinsic principle, that which is the active cause of knowledge does not have the knowledge to be acquired except partially, that is, as much as is understood by the germinal capacities or potentialities for knowledge, which are the general principles; and, therefore, from such causality the name of teacher or master, properly speaking, cannot be assumed.

333. Problems and Solutions

Aquinas acknowledges God as man's Head Teacher. He, in His wisdom, arranged the universe so that man would sense problems. He ordered the universe so that it would suggest a solution. He allowed

332. St. Thomas Aquinas, *De Magistro,* in Mary H. Mayer, *The Philosophy of Teaching of St. Thomas Aquinas* (Milwaukee: The Bruce Publishing Company, 1929), pp. 64–65.
333. Mary H. Mayer, *The Philosophy of Teaching of Thomas Aquinas* (Milwaukee: The Bruce Publishing Company, 1929), p. 90.

man to reflect upon the problem, but as a prudent Teacher, made it easy for man to distinguish error from truth by speaking to man in revelation and by establishing a teaching Church.

334. Herbart and Dewey Compared on Method

This brings us to note the contrast between the Herbartian and the Dewey steps. Teachers are so constituted that they like to think the new way is not so different from the old after all; thus, they can be loyal to the old and accept the new at the same time; and so not much change after all will be necessary. Teachers are not alone in making such complacent adjustments. Really, the contrast between Herbart and Dewey is fundamental. Herbart is an intellectualist and Dewey is a pragmatist. Herbart believes the idea is primary and Dewey believes the act is primary. Herbart begins teaching by awakening old ideas in the mind of the child; Dewey by noting the activity which engages the child. Herbart teaches by presenting new ideas to the child similar to the old ones; Dewey by assisting the child in defining his problem, if he requires it. Herbart leads the mind on to a comparison of ideas, ending in a generalization; Dewey leads the child on to study the data of his problem and to form hypotheses. Finally, Herbart seeks an application of a truth already found, Dewey seeks the testing of the validity of the hypothesis by a trial application. In Herbart we think and then act; in Dewey we think between acts. Parallel columns showing these contrasts would be as follows:

Herbart	*Dewey*
1. Preparation	1. Activity
2. Presentation	2. Problem
3. Comparison	3. Data
4. Generalization	4. Hypothesis
5. Application	5. Testing

Students of Herbart will recall he himself had but four steps, named by him, somewhat clumsily, Clearness, Association, System, and Method, corresponding to the last four in the list given above, and that his followers divided the first into two and re-named the others.

These two methods admirably supplement each other; they are usable in different fields. Herbart is effective in the linguistic, literary, historical, and ideational fields; Dewey in the fields of the manual

334. Herman H. Horne, *The Democratic Philosophy of Education* (New York: The Macmillan Company, 1935), pp. 206–207.

arts and the sciences. Wherever the content of books is taught, Herbart is useful; wherever the manipulation of things is primary, Dewey is useful. Of course, Herbart does not regard the practical as really educative, and Dewey does not regard the theoretical as really educative. Herbart regards the practical as the field for the use of true ideas, Dewey regards the theoretical as a phase of the practical.

335. Teaching and Learning Best When Adventurous

On the dynamic position, however, as a rule, the more educative an experience proves in the end to be, the more truly was it for the learner an adventure into the unknown. To be sure, the proportion of known and unknown will vary from occasion to occasion and from person to person. Too much unknown would mean failure and possible discouragement. Too little would mean fooling and vain repetition. It may surprise some to think that the same holds also for the teacher. Each experience of the class is also an experience for him. If there be too much unknown to him in what the class (and he) undertake, failure and discouragement for him threaten. If too little, then no learning and drudgery are consequently probable. Moreover, he will teach better, be more sympathetic, be more interesting, more inspiring—and his students will learn more—if he himself consciously feels that he does not know all that will come out of the experience, either to the pupils or to himself. The dynamic point of view which approves "adventure" and respects personality seems the best road to interest and learning to all concerned. In fact so significant is this for democracy, both ethically and psychologically, that we seem warranted in asserting that a consistent democracy will accept no other kind of learning as typical.

336. Teaching as Joint Inquiry by Pupils and Teacher

What kind of teaching would fit into such a democratic society? Evidently only one in which there was a high degree of openmindedness among teachers and ultimately among pupils. Teachers would not

335. William Kilpatrick, in National Society for the Study of Education, Twenty-sixth Yearbook, Part II, *Foundations of Curriculum Making* (Chicago: University of Chicago Press, 1927), pp. 144–145.

336. Charles C. Peters, "Understanding the Nature and Operation of the Mores," *The Social Frontier*, 4:284, June 1938.

be *telling*, but teachers and pupils would be jointly *inquiring*. Indeed *all* good teaching *is* cooperative inquiring rather than imparting or even guiding. In a democratic situation teacher and pupils sit down to learn from one another. Jointly they seek the truth, the teacher just as expectant to learn something new from the pupils as they are expectant to learn from him. Together they are trying to envisage what will go in the world of reality, and all test each other's proposals in terms of what they know from experience about reality. If the teacher carries more authority than pupils it is only because he has seen more of life and can make more proposals of hypotheses and of consequences that the pupils recognize as true than any one of them can make.

337. Critique of Method as Inquiry

. . . In his logical studies Dewey has developed the implications of scientific procedure for our view of the nature of reflective thought, and in his educational writings he has declared that the essentials of educational method are "identical with the essentials of reflection." Following the lead of Dewey, the pragmatists in education have made the pattern of experimental inquiry foundational in the program of the school. Two basic assumptions are thus inherent in the pragmatic method of education. The first is that all thinking is in the nature of research, and is, therefore, concerned with the resolution of problematic situations. The second is that the best provision is made for learning when the *acquiring* of habits, knowledge, appreciations, and attitudes is a function of the process of *inquiring*. . . .

❖   ❖   ❖

Of the great strengths in this conception of the learning process the writer is fully convinced. But as here formulated, and as often expounded in the writings of eminent pragmatic leaders in the field of education, there are certain ambiguities and difficulties in this interpretation. Any valid discussion of it must, of course, take account of the other writings on education of those who espouse it. The above statement that "*acquiring* is always secondary, and instrumental to the act of *inquiring*" tends to suggest that the formation of habits and attitudes is necessarily a *conscious* process. This is very far from the view of the pragmatists who have constantly emphasized that in both

337. John L. Childs, *American Pragmatism and Education* (New York: Henry Holt & Co., 1956), pp. 353–357.

the home and the school the child may acquire habits and attitudes of which neither he nor his parents and teachers are aware. What Dewey is, therefore, actually affirming is that so far as possible the acquisition of skills, techniques, meanings, and beliefs should be made a conscious process, so that the learner will grasp the conections—the life significance and relevance—of that which he is learning. One of the important contributions of the pragmatic theory of education is its insistence that the young are not to be conditioned as robots, nor trained as animals, but that they should rather be educated as human beings possessed of the potentialities of intelligence.

Experience has shown, however, that even when thus interpreted, there are difficulties associated with the effort to make the research pattern of experimental inquiry the foundational and the inclusive pattern for educational method and teaching. One of these difficulties is that the research pattern focuses educational attention, as Dewey states, upon those situations in which things are fluid because they have become "uncertain or doubtful or problematic." Certainly there is great vitality in this conception, and wherever it has been employed it has brought new intellectual life into the school because it has tended to make education a frontier activity concerned with those aspects of civilization where new meanings and new institutional arrangements are in the process of reconstruction and development. As Dewey has stated, the function of intelligence is to detect those situations in which received patterns of living and thinking are being challenged by scientific discoveries, technological inventions, and altered modes of living.

But can it be maintained that the *educational* function is synonymous with the *research* function? Obviously the two have much in common, but the writer is convinced that education suffers whenever the two are identified. The reason is that there are many things in a human civilization that are functioning so well that they are not problematical in any vital sense, and yet they need to be communicated to the young. In other words, the educator concerned with the introduction of the young to the ways of life and thought of his people must take account of all that the young need to learn in order to become competent members of their civilization. Even in our period of cultural transition and transformation there is much that is so stable in our culture that it presents no significant problem of reconstruction, and yet is an indispensable part of that which the young should learn. The school in its survey of cultural affairs cannot afford to ignore or slight all of those basic human relationships and processes of a civilization which are functioning well and yet are required of all who are to participate effectually in it. In other words, the body of subject matter which should be transmitted to the young is broader than that which is involved in the tensional, disturbed, life situations of a human group.

In the second place, as Dewey's own statement suggests, there are two kinds of "inquiry" and they need to be distinguished. Indeed, it is possible that they are so different in nature that it is misleading to contend that the pattern of education which holds for the one can adequately cover the other. On the one hand, we have what is commonly known as a genuine research situation. Here inquiry is for the purpose of discovering ways of dealing with problematical situations or subject matters in which no one has or knows the answer. The pattern of Dewey's analysis of the steps in the complete act of thought is derived from the study of situations of this kind. Inquiry begins in a *problem;* the aim of those engaged in it is the *discovery* of a way of resolving it.

But the typical educational situation is somewhat different from this. The inquiries of the young for the most part relate to areas in which the teachers are already in possession of most of the meanings which the young are struggling to acquire. A basic problem of the teacher is that of the best means of communicating to the young that which is already known. Undoubtedly, all that the pragmatists have emphasized about the importance of the young acquiring these meanings through purposeful undertakings carried on in a context of felt need and recognized significance is critically important, but it does not seem to the author that, when all these factors are taken into account, the problem of the *communication* and the *acquisition* of meaning can be *equated* with the problem of the *discovery* of meaning in the sense in which the achievement of knowledge through research is ordinarily interpreted. In research the problem to be resolved is paramount and controls the whole process. The supreme test of a research project is what has been discovered as a result of the investigation. In education the meanings already known and which are to be communicated to the young necessarily occupy a central place. The supreme test of an educational experience is not primarily what new knowledge has been uncovered, but rather what changes have taken place in the habits, appreciations, meanings, and attitudes of the young. That many of these changes can best take place through activities in which the interests and the purposes of the young play a dominant role has been shown to be the case, but it has not been shown that this is equally true for all age levels. Particularly at the secondary and junior college level, as well as in the fields of occupational or vocational specialization, the skills, techniques, and meanings which are to be learned probably have to play a larger part in the planning and the administration of the curriculum than many of the adherents of the new education have been willing to admit. Their wholesale attacks on "subjects" have somewhat diverted them from giving the attention to the problem of the selection and the organization of subject matter in the school which it deserves.

All of which calls attention to a third lack or ambiguity in the functional theory of the curriculum, namely, just what is meant by a "problem." Dewey has declared that a problem is not an assignment, and in his classical summary of the essentials of educational method he has said that in order to have an authentic problem the pupil must be involved in a genuine situation of experience—there must "be a continuous activity in which he is interested for its own sake"—and, second, a real problem must "develop within this situation as a stimulus to thought." Unfortunately, experience shows that Dewey's fellow pragmatists have derived different educational directives from this formulation.

For some, the statement points to the primacy of what has been described as "incidental learning"—the view that "the connection between studying and carrying on the job must be sufficiently close so that the job determines directly what is to be studied," and provides opportunity for the pupil to try out in practical projects whatever meanings are developed during the course of the inquiry. On this basis learning is simply a "means to an end and not an end in itself."

Other pragmatists have contended that when problem-solving activities are thus narrowly conceived they cannot provide for much that should be learned. They contend that at certain stages in the development of the child central attention must be given to systematic study of important bodies of subject matter, for all subsequent intellectual development requires the mastery of these fundamental processes and bodies of knowledge. They admit that we have much to learn about what should be included in these disciplinary studies, as well as about the way in which they should be organized so that the experience of learning will be one of desirable growth through meaningful reconstruction of experience. They contend, however, that the task of developing satisfactory answers to these problems must be confronted, and the new education movement will be legitimately open to criticism until it demonstrates that its respect for the child, its respect for learning through purposeful activity, and its respect for learning in the context of actual life situations is compatible with rigorous and progressive intellectual undertakings on the part of the young.

338. Pupil Experience Used Deductively Rather than Inductively

Given sympathy and understanding between the mature and the immature, direct personal guidance requiring obedience, quickly and without floundering experimentation, puts the experience of the race at the disposition of its young members. The experience of the young then becomes a deductive proof of the things taught instead of an inductive discovery. In view of the vast amount of knowledge the race already has acquired and the relatively slight amount of it that any individual can re-discover for himself, and the likelihood that he will make no valuable addition to it at all, direct personal control will probably continue to hold the major, but not the exclusive, place in the educative process. As a test let the reader recall the greater influences that have shaped his life; are they not persons rather than things controlled by persons?

339. Activity as Vital Part of Learning

This discussion rejects the doctrine that students should first learn passively, and then, having learned, should apply knowledge. It is a psychological error. In the process of learning there should be present, in some sense or other, a subordinate activity of application. In fact, the applications are part of the knowledge. For the very meaning of the things known is wrapped up in their relationships beyond themselves. Thus unapplied knowledge is knowledge shorn of its meaning.

The careful shielding of a university from the activities of the world around is the best way to chill interest and to defeat progress. Celibacy does not suit a university. It must mate itself with action.

340. Communist Conception of Activity Program

The attempt to make the pupil an active and independent worker in the process of the acquisition of information is characteristic of the

338. Herman H. Horne, *The Democratic Philosophy of Education* (New York: The Macmillan Company, 1935), pp. 30–31.
339. Alfred N. Whitehead, "Harvard: The Future," *Atlantic Monthly,* 158:267, September 1936.
340. Albert P. Pinkevitch, *The New Education in the Soviet Republic* (New York: John Day Company, 1929), pp. 238–239.

entire soviet educational program. Moreover, in its emphasis on activity and self-activity our school has practically nothing in common
with the school of old Russia and with the overwhelming majority of
the contemporary West European or even American schools. Our aim
is to develop an active warrior and builder. We assume therefore that
the only school capable of achieving this aim is one which places upon
the pupil from the day of his entrance the responsibility of building
his own life. The best bourgeois schools, when introducing the idea of
activity and self-activity, confine the child within the narrow bounds
of the school and thus bar him from active participation in life. As a
consequence the winged phrases that we prepare for life in school and
that school and life must be intimately related remain but empty words.
Our school, in accordance with the general aims of education, seeks
to create a sturdy and stalwart warrior against capitalistic society. It
aims to form this warrior through the process of direct participation in
life. This basic tendency, even if not altogether realized, is the outstanding characteristic of the soviet school.

From the standpoint of method our teaching is characterized, first
of all, by the most intimate relation with problems of practical life.
Under our conditions this means the establishment of the closest possible association with the task of building a socialistic state and of
participating in socially useful work . . .

341. Importance of Applied Learning

Knowledge should never be familiar. It should always be contem-
plated either under the aspect of novel application, or under the aspect
of skepticism as to the extent of its application, or under the aspect of
development of its consequences, or under the aspect of eliciting the
fundamental meanings which it presupposes, or under the aspect of
a guide in the adventures of life, or under the aspect of the aesthetic
of its interwoven relationships, or under the aspect of the miraculous
history of its discovery. . . .

In the first place: Develop intellectual activities by a knowledge of
the certain truths, so far as they are largely applicable to human life.
In the second place: Train the understanding of each student to assess
probable knowledge in respect to those types of occurrences which
for any reason will be of major importance in the exercise of his activities. In the third place: Give him adequate knowledge of the pos-

341. Alfred N. Whitehead, *Essays in Science and Philosophy* (New York:
Philosophical Library, 1947), pp. 155, 161.

sibilities of aesthetic and moral satisfaction which are open to a human being, under conditions relevant to his future life. . . .

342. Problem-Solving Must Await Acquisition of Facts

The acquiring and storing up of information is in itself a worthy aim for junior high school courses; the House of Thought is not worthily to be built until there are brought together in one place all the materials for the building. A pathetic and disgraceful amount of time and energy has been wasted by conscientious teachers in trying to force immature children to think deeply about the things of which they have but just begun to learn, because of the insistence of misguided education that children must apply everything they find out at once. Let the time in the junior high school rather be given to the acquisition of facts, thoroughly learned, arranged in orderly sequences, clearly understood in their concrete narrative aspects; but, except when clearly demanded by the children themselves, let the theoretical, abstract, controversial, and application aspects be left until the students are more mature and more broadly prepared to go surely in those more difficult paths.

343. Making Drill Meaningful

Because meaningless drill has proved so repellent, many teachers fear any sharing of decisions regarding this with pupils. The crux lies in the word "meaningless." Let the actual situation of any child call to him for drill and there seems no lack of willingness to engage in it, as we see in the case of small boys with their first roller skates or of larger boys with their catching and batting. Even clearer, perhaps, is the case of very young children with their repetition of words and phrases and noise-making operations, often to the great annoyance of unsympathetic adults. One could without difficulty make out a good case that the child is a "natural" repeater. But learning is far from being mere repetition. Let but the experiences of the child arouse sufficient interest in and regard for consequences, and repetition as

342. Frances M. I. Morehouse, "Principles Governing the Differentiation Between Junior and Senior High School History," *Historical Outlook*, 15:157, April 1927.
343. William H. Kilpatrick, "The Essentials of the Activity Movement," *Progressive Education*, 11:357, October 1934.

such retires into the background. Felt connection is the best basis of acquisition. We used to think that much mechanically repetitive drill was necessary to learning such things as spelling, writing, and number combinations. Now it appears that bare repetition, without any supporting connection or check, carries no learning effect; while, for the normal child, a sufficiently varied and interesting school life will by its inherent use of spelling, for example, teach ninety per cent of what may be needed . . .

344. The Social Control of Method

There are . . . various ways of accepting the social conception of education in name and denying it in fact. One way is that of the academic intellectualist. He is sufficiently impressed with the vogue of the social concept to desire to attach himself to it; but in substance he remains a traditionalist. So he calls attention to the fact—and it is a fact—that number, linguistic forms, words, history, etc., the material of the accepted curriculum, are social tools, such important social instrumentalities that social life could not be carried on without them. Every other consideration and subject is, upon this educational philosophy, an "extra"; the school may be obliged to take it up, but that is only because some other institution is failing in its duty, not because it belongs in school. In principle the school is a fenced-off sanctuary devoted exclusively to "teaching" and "learning" the great intellectual means by which civilized society is maintained. Of course society would relapse into barbarism without the transmission of the arts, skills, and understandings which make up the traditional curriculum. The essential point of a social conception of education, however, is that these subjects be taught *in* and with definite reference to their social context and use; taken out of their social bearing, they cease to have a social meaning, they become wholly technical and abstract. It is then a mere matter of accident for what ends they are used outside of the conscious educational system. There is nothing to protect them from being tools of private advantage and material success, or even being put to anti-social use. Moreover, apart from reference to their place and function in social life, the educator has no guide to help decide what parts and aspects of the great complex of intellectual subject-matter shall be selected nor any guide in choosing the methods of instruction and discipline which build up atti-

344. John Dewey and John L. Childs, in *The Educational Frontier* (William H. Kilpatrick, editor (New York: The Century Company, 1933), pp. 51–52.

tudes in the pupils. The inevitable effect is conformity to and dupli-
cation of the existent order with all its limitations and evils.

345. When Method of Authority Is Warranted

. . . It is urged that the process of education should run parallel as
far as possible to the way in which the race has developed. In practice
this means two things: (1) Education at each stage of a child's life
should make use of those conceptions which were current at the
corresponding stage of the race's evolution. (2) Education should
ensure that each child is, as far as possible, placed in the attitude of a
discoverer, that is, he should be left to find things out for himself
instead of accepting results on the authority of the teacher.

❋   ❋   ❋

Those people who have made discoveries in the history of the race
have been in a position very different from the child. The actual discoverer, before his discovery, has a great deal of knowledge, knows
exactly what gaps have to be filled in, and arranges his experiment in
such a way that, so far as he is aware, the gap will be filled in. That
is, he knows what facts to pay attention to and what facts to ignore, he
knows what hypotheses are worth considering and what hypotheses
are not worth considering, and he knows how to test those hypotheses
which are. But the child has none of all this, and it is the function
of the teacher to provide it. This function is fulfilled if the teacher
provides and arranges the facts and sets the pupil to derive conclusions from them. That is, the teacher should not set the child to do
certain experiments and see if he gets the right results. Rather he
should provide the child with adequate information and set him
to devise the experiments which will enable conclusions to be drawn.

Some of those educationists, however, who consider (2) to be true
do so not only because they hold that there is a correspondence between the stages of child development and the stages of human evolution, but also because they hold that authority should have no place in
education. The child, they argue, ought not to accept anything because he is told to accept it, but ought only to accept what he has
found out for himself. This raises a point of some difficulty. The
opinion has gained ground that it is somehow more "hard-headed" and
"scientific" not to accept anything on authority, and this has made some

345. Charles D. Hardie, *Truth and Fallacy in Educational Theory* (Cambridge
University Press, 1942), pp. 20–23.

educationists feel that if children are to be educated on "scientific" lines then they must be taught to find things out for themselves.

It should be remembered, however, that the actual practice of scientists is very different, for they are continually accepting results as true which are published by fellow-scientists and I think, by consideration of this fact, we can arrive at some criteria which will decide when it is reasonable to accept anything on authority. I think there are two cases in which it is reasonable.

(1) When our authority is in a position to observe facts which we are not in a position to observe, *provided that in addition* (a) other authorities who have been in a position to observe the facts agree, and (b) the conclusions which our authority states do not conflict with facts which we are able to observe. For example, we accept certain geographical facts on the authority of travellers if they have been in a position to observe these facts and we have not, and if in addition (a) other travellers who have been in a position to observe these facts agree, and (b) the conclusions which may be drawn from the facts do not conflict with facts which we are able to observe, such as weather conditions.

(2) The second case in which it is reasonable to accept results on authority is when they are stated as conclusions to an argument which we are unable to follow, *provided that in addition* (a) the argument follows from premises which we know to be true, or if we do not know them to be true, we know are accepted by other authorities, and (b) the argument is considered to be valid by other authorities . . .

Hence I think it is quite clear that far from it being "unscientific" to accept results on authority, it may be extremely scientific, and it certainly seems to me that education would be quite impossible unless it is done. If that is so, then it follows that there is no ground for the view that the child ought to be placed as far as possible in the attitude of a discoverer and left to find things out for himself.

346. Docility

We come back to the fact that individuals begin their career as infants. For the plasticity of the young presents a temptation to those having greater experience and hence greater power which they rarely resist. It seems putty to be molded according to current designs. That plasticity also means power to change prevailing custom is ignored.

346. John Dewey, *Human Nature and Conduct* (New York: Henry Holt and Company, 1922), p. 64. Used by permission of the publishers.

Docility is looked upon not as ability to learn whatever the world has to teach, but as subjection to those instructions of others which reflect *their* current habits. To be truly docile is to be eager to learn all the lessons of active, inquiring, expanding experience. The inert, stupid quality of current customs perverts learning into a willingness to follow where others point the way, into conformity, constriction, surrender of scepticism and experiment. When we think of the docility of the young we first think of the stocks of information adults wish to impose and the ways of acting they want to reproduce. Then we think of the insolent coercions, the insinuating briberies, the pedagogic solemnities by which the freshness of youth can be faded and its vivid curiosities dulled. Education becomes the art of taking advantage of the helplessness of the young; the forming of habits becomes a guarantee for the maintenance of hedges of custom.

19

Logic and the Order of Instruction

Problems in the Philosophy of Education Discussed in this Section

1. Is it possible to be sure what is *the* logical way in which to teach? In order to take this view, what basic assumption must be made?
2. Must both teacher and pupil conform to the same logic? If not, what different assumption is made as to the nature of logic? Is there one logic for learning and another for remembering?
3. Does the psychological organization of the lesson differ at all from the logical? If so, is it therefore illogical?
4. Can a teacher transmit his logical organization of experience to a pupil?
5. Can organization be imposed on activities or subject matter, or must it be found in them? Or must it be found in the learner's purpose?
6. Do subject-matter divisions have any logical justification?

347. The Logic of Teaching

Teaching involves logic as well as language. This is the case because reasoned discourse leads to conclusions. It begins somewhere and ends somewhere. And logic, in its deductive sense, is a way of clarifying our linguistic expressions and of ordering sentences in such a way that we can decide upon the truth of our conclusions.

Just as we have neglected the role of language in teaching, so have we disregarded logic. This neglect of logic has resulted partly from our erroneous notion that the research which dislodged faculty psychology and its theory of formal discipline also discredited the study of logic, and partly from our erroneous ideas of what logic was supposed to do for us. The overthrow of formal discipine had no bearing upon the uses of logic when properly perceived. Logic does not purport to tell us how we do in fact think. It has nothing to do with the pondering

347. B. Othanel Smith, "The Anatomy of Teaching," *Journal of Teacher Education,* 7:344–345, December, 1956.

processes, whatever they are, by which ideas occur to us and by which we reach conclusions. The principles of logic describe neither thinking nor thought. Nor do they tell us how our thinking ought to proceed. They are not norms to which the thinking process should conform. Rather logic is useful to us when we scan our thinking to tell whether or not the conclusions we have reached follow necessarily from our premises, or, as in inductive thinking, to decide the probable truth of our conclusions.

Seen in this light, logic plays an important role in the process of teaching. For one thing, a statement becomes clear to us either when its key words are adequately defined or when it is fixed in the chain of sentences to which it is logically linked, or when both of these obtain. Now, teaching in its didactic sense embraces both of these performances. For, as we have already said, such teaching includes the activities of defining, explaining, justifying, proving, and the like. And these without exception are logical operations.

The fact that these activities are logical activities is seldom recognized. We have failed to recognize their logical nature because of our tendency in education to psychologize everything. In pedagogical discussion we use two sets of concepts, both of which we believe to be psychological, when in fact only one set is so. One of these sets consists of such concepts as inferring, perceiving, conceiving, generalizing, thinking, and judging. We use these in talking about psychological processes. And we are correct in doing so. Of course, there is a legitimate question as to whether there are internal processes corresponding to these names, but that question is one which we leave to the psychologists. The other set of concepts are identified by such terms as define, interpret, explain, justify, and prove. These are logical rather than psychological. They are operations which we perform with words and sentences and which we cannot perform without words and sentences. And these operations are found in the domain of logic.

For purposes of illustration we shall consider definition and explanation. It hardly need be said that a great deal of school learning consists of definitions. Our books and discussions are filled with definitions. Now in logic we are told that there are different ways of defining words. To define a word is to tell how it is to be used. We can define the word "seed" by saying that "a seed is that part of a flowering plant that holds the embryo and associated structures." What we have done is to tell the class of things to which a seed belongs, by saying that it belongs to the class of things called "parts of a flowering plant." Then we have told how a seed differs from other members of the class of things to which it belongs such as leaves, roots, and stem. Wherever the expression "part of a flowering plant which holds the embryo and associated structures" appears in our discussion we can substitute the word "seed" without changing the meaning. This is what we do when we define a word. Thus a definition represents a decision; for it lays down the rules for the use of a word. Since they are decisions, definitions are neither true nor false.

The amount of time used inefficiently in the classroom because the teacher does not know how to deal with questions involving definitions is greater, I fear, than we like to think. Classroom discussion is often snarled up by disagreements about the meaning of words, as though words somehow had meanings in the same way that dogs have fleas. Many fruitless discussions might be avoided were the teacher capable of handling definitions through a knowledge of logic and its operations.

Similarly, the logic of explanation is appropriate when the teacher is called upon to explain either statements or events, or to evaluate explanations given by students. Suppose the teacher is called upon to explain the fact that in the early morning the wind blows from the land toward the sea. What must he do? The answer is that he must try to find the premises from which the factual conclusion—the wind blows from the land toward the sea in the early morning—can be drawn. Now any number of premises may be chosen, depending upon the teacher's knowledge. But if he is trained in physics, he will reason from the general law that heated bodies expand and thus become lighter per unit of volume. It is not necessary here to follow the logical steps the teacher must take to get from the general law to the particular event to be explained. But he will go on to show that the air over the ocean becomes warmer at night than the air over the land, and that the cold, heavier air over the land then displaces the ocean air which is warmer and lighter. An explanation thus consists in showing that the fact to be explained can be taken as an instance of the general law which has been used as the explanatory principle.

Failure to understand what an explanation is leads to all sorts of entanglements in the classroom. Sometimes the discussion centers in the question of whether or not an explanation is a true one. To answer the question it is necessary that the truth of the premises be tested. But unfortunately the teacher often lacks the knowledge of logic necessary to test the truth of statements used as premises. Then, too, teachers sometimes mistake the mere recounting of events for explanation. A student is asked to tell why the French Revolution happened. So he relates events leading up to the revolution as an explanation of why the revolution occurred. Now, the mere recounting of events is not an explanation in the logical sense, for there is no general principle from which to derive the event to be explained. Sometimes, however, a student, or even a teacher, uses a general principle without making it explicit. Consequently it is subjected neither to critical appraisal nor to the test of fact. Partly for this reason, instruction in history often lacks rigor and thus fails to engage the higher mental processes of students.

348. Realistic Logic of Teaching

Supposing, now, we inquire as to *how* facts "express themselves." We find, if we listen to a realist teacher in his own classroom, just as we find when we read textbooks written with a realist outlook, that facts seem to have been well trained in realist logic. They are extremely clear and extremely distinct. They are interrelated in external ways which do not detract from their essential distinctness as the realist proceeds to build up structures which are marvels of precision. They fall into classes which can be defined in terms of classificatory logic, and always obey all the rules of definition and classification. They fall into systems of which each part implies every other part, in a way which not only resembles the neat patterns of mathematics, but completely coincides with certain of those patterns.

✻   ✻   ✻

If we ask a realist whether such coincidence between the laws of facts and the laws of realist logic is not a little too much for our credulity, he gravely reassures us. Logic is natural. The laws of thought are not something different from, and independent of, the laws of nature. In fact, the laws of thought are laws for thought, because they are the laws of the things which thought thinks. Two and two do, in point of fact, make four. They cannot do otherwise. Their logical necessity is, ultimately, a factual necessity. The logical consequences of true premises are themselves true because, ultimately, that is the way things are. The logical methods of arrangement of material for presentation in the classroom thus are not some particular human being's reading of a subjective longing for order and system into what is, perhaps, not in itself so ordered and systematized, but are, strictly, the submission of the individual teacher's mind to the invincible logic of facts. Facts have their laws, and their laws dictate our logic. Nature is like that; and, in obeying logic, both teacher and pupil are con-

348. Rupert C. Lodge, *Philosophy of Education* (New York: Harper & Brothers, 1937), pp. 252–254. Reprinted by permission of the publishers.

forming to nature and are attaining to genuine objectivity. From the standpoint of realism, the teacher's method is nature's way.

349. Method of Inquiry as Logic of Teaching

Curiously enough, the internal and necessary connection between the actual process of thinking and its intellectual product is overlooked by two opposite educational schools.

One of these schools thinks that the mind is naturally so illogical in its processes that logical form must be impressed upon it from without. It assumes that logical quality belongs only to organized knowledge and that the operations of the mind become logical only through absorption of logically formulated, ready-made material. In this case, the logical formulations are not the outcome of any process of thinking that is personally undertaken and carried out; the formulation has been made by another mind and is presented in a finished form, apart from the processes by which it was arrived at. Then it is assumed that by some magic its logical character will be transferred into the minds of pupils . . .

It is evident from these examples that in such a scheme of instruction, the logical is identified exclusively with certain formal properties of subject matter; with subject matter defined, refined, subdivided, classified, organized according to certain principles of connection that have been worked out by persons who are expert in that particular field. It conceives the method of instruction to be the devices by which similar traits are imported into the mind by careful reproduction of the given material in arithmetic, geography, grammar, physics, biology, or whatnot. The natural operations of the mind are supposed to be indifferent or even averse to all logical achievement. Hence the mottoes of this school are "discipline," "restraint," "conscious effort," "the necessity of tasks," and so on. From this point of view studies, rather than attitudes and habits, embody the logical factor in education. The mind becomes logical only by learning to conform to an external subject matter. To produce this conformity, the study should first be analyzed (by textbook or teacher) into its logical elements; then each of these elements should be defined; finally, all the elements should be arranged in series or classes according to logical formulae or general principles. Then the pupil learns the definitions one by one and, progressively adding one to another, builds up the logical

349. John Dewey, *How We Think* (Boston: D. C. Heath and Company, 1933), pp. 79–84. Reprinted by special permission of the publishers.

system, and thereby is himself gradually imbued, from without, with logical quality.

A reaction inevitably occurs from the poor results that accrue from these professedly "logical" methods. Lack of interest in study, habits of inattention and procrastination, positive aversion to intellectual application, dependence upon sheer memorizing and mechanical routine with only a modicum of understanding by the pupil of what he is about, show that the theory of logical definition, division, gradation, and system does not work out practically as it is theoretically supposed to do. The consequent disposition—as in every reaction—is to go to the opposite extreme. The "logical" is thought to be wholly artificial and extraneous; teacher and pupil alike are to turn their backs upon it, and to give free rein to the expression of existing aptitudes and tastes. Emphasis upon natural tendencies and powers as the only possible starting point of development is indeed wholesome. But the reaction is false, and hence misleading, in what it ignores and denies: the presence of genuinely intellectual factors in existing powers and interests.

The other type of school really accepts the underlying premise of the opposite educational theory. It also assumes that the mind is naturally averse to logical form; it grounds this conviction upon the fact that many minds *are* rebellious to the particular logical forms in which a certain type of textbook presents its material. From this fact it is inferred that logical order is so foreign to the natural operations of the mind that it is of slight importance in education, at least in that of the young, and that the main thing is just to give free play to impulses and desires without regard to any definitely *intellectual* growth. Hence the mottoes of this school are "freedom," "self-expression," "individuality," spontaneity," "play," "interest," "natural unfolding," and so on. In its emphasis upon individual attitude and activity, it sets slight store upon organized subject matter. It conceives *method* to consist of various devices for stimulating and evoking, in their natural order of growth, the native potentialities of individuals.

Thus the basic error of the two schools is the same. Both ignore and virtually deny the fact that tendencies toward a reflective and truly logical activity are native to the mind, and that they show themselves at an early period, since they are demanded by outer conditions and stimulated by native curiosity. There is an innate disposition to draw inferences, and an inherent desire to experiment and test. The mind at every stage of growth has its own logic. It entertains suggestions, tests them by observation of objects and events, reaches conclusions, tries them in action, finds them confirmed or in need of correction or rejection. A baby, even at a comparatively early period, makes inferences in the way of expectations from what is observed, interpreting what it sees as a sign or evidence of something it does not observe with the senses. The school of so-called "free self-expression" thus fails to note that one thing that is urgent for expression in the spontaneous activity of the young is *intellectual* in character. Since this factor is predominantly the *educative* one, as far as instruction is concerned, other aspects of activity should be made means to its effective operation.

Any teacher who is alive to the modes of thought operative in the natural experience of the normal child will have no difficulty in avoiding the identification of the logical with a ready-made organization of subject matter, as well as the notion that the way to escape this error is to pay no attention to logical considerations. Such a teacher will have no difficulty in seeing that the real problem of intellectual education is the *transformation* of natural powers into expert, tested powers: the transformation of more or less casual curiosity and sporadic suggestion into attitudes of alert, cautious, and thorough inquiry. He will see that the *psychological* and the *logical*, instead of being opposed to each other (or even independent of each other), are connected as the earlier and the terminal, or concluding, stages of the same process. He will recognize, moreover, that the kind of logical arrangement that marks subject matter at the stage of maturity is not the only kind possible; that the kind found in scientifically organized material is actually undesirable until the mind has reached a point of maturity where it is capable of understanding just *why* this form, rather than some other, is adopted.

350. Logical and Psychological Methods of Teaching

It may be of use to distinguish and to relate to each other the logical and the psychological aspects of experience—the former standing for subject-matter in itself, the latter for it in relation to the child. A psychological statement of experience follows its actual growth; it is historic; it notes steps actually taken, the uncertain and tortuous, as well as the efficient and successful. The logical point of view, on the other hand, assumes that the development has reached a certain positive stage of fulfilment. It neglects the process and considers the outcome. It summarizes and arranges, and thus separates the achieved results from the actual steps by which they were forthcoming in the

350. John Dewey, *The Child and the Curriculum* (Chicago: University of Chicago Press, 1902), pp. 25–30.

first instance. We may compare the difference between the logical and the psychological to the difference between the notes which an explorer makes in a new country, blazing a trail and finding his way along as best he may, and the finished map that is constructed after the country has been thoroughly explored. The two are mutually dependent.

*   *   *

There is, then, nothing final about a logical rendering of experience. Its value is not contained in itself; its significance is that of standpoint, outlook, method. It intervenes between the more casual, tentative, and roundabout experiences of the past, and more controlled and orderly experiences of the future. It gives past experience in that net form which renders it most available and most significant, most fecund for future experience. The abstractions, generalizations, and classifications which it introduces all have prospective meaning.

The formulated result is then not to be opposed to the process of growth. The logical is not set over against the psychological. The surveyed and arranged result occupies a critical position in the process of growth. It marks a turning-point. It shows how we may get the benefit of past effort in controlling future endeavor. In the largest sense the logical standpoint is itself psychological; it has its meaning as a point in the development of experience, and its justification is in its functioning in the future growth which it insures.

*   *   *

Every study or subject thus has two aspects: one for the scientist as a scientist; the other for the teacher as a teacher. These two aspects are in no sense opposed or conflicting. But neither are they immediately identical. For the scientist, the subject-matter represents simply a given body of truth to be employed in locating new problems, instituting new researches, and carrying them through to a verified outcome. To him the subject-matter or the science is self-contained. He refers various portions of it to each other; he connects new facts with it. He is not, as a scientist, called upon to travel outside its particular bounds; if he does, it is only to get more facts of the same general sort. The problem of the teacher is a different one. As a teacher he is not concerned with adding new facts to the science he teaches; in propounding new hypotheses or in verifying them. He is concerned with the subject-matter of the science as *representing a given stage and phase of the development of experience*. His problem is that of inducing a vital and personal experiencing. Hence, what concerns him, as a teacher, is the ways in which that subject may become a part of experience; what there is in the child's present that is usable with reference to it; how much elements are to be used; how his own knowledge of the subject-matter may assist in interpreting the child's needs and doings, and determine the medium in which the child should be placed in order that his growth may be properly directed. He is concerned, not with the subject-matter as such, but with the subject-matter as a related factor in a total and growing experience. Thus to see it is to psychologize it.

351. Order of Knowledge and Order of Learning

Here I have two fundamental points to make, which I shall try to make briefly. The first concerns the *objective order* of the subject-matters themselves; the second concerns the *methods of teaching* the subject-matters, with reference to the distinction between the order of knowledge and the order of learning.

By the objective order of the subject-matters I mean, of course, the order of the objects of knowledge *secundum se*—the order of things known according to their intrinsic knowability, rather than their relative knowability, that is, their knowability to us.

       ❈   ❈   ❈

If we apply these principles to all the fundamental theoretic subject-matters, we will find that, just as in the objective order, theology precedes metaphysics, and metaphysics, the philosophy of nature, and the philosophy of nature, the philosophy of man, which is one of its parts, and the whole of philosophy, as dealing with essences, the whole of science, as dealing with phenomenal accidents; so in the subjective order, the members of this series are perfectly reversed: science should be studied before philosophy, and the philosophy of man before the philosophy of nature, and these before metaphysics and theology.

       ❈   ❈   ❈

But, certainly, one thing is already clear: the objective order of subject-matters,—of objects as knowable in themselves and apart from us,—does not and cannot determine the right subjective order of teaching and learning.

       ❈   ❈   ❈

The second principle is the basic distinction between discovery and instruction as types of learning. Discovery is learning without a

351. Mortimer J. Adler, "The Order of Learning," *The Philosophy of Christian Education*, American Catholic Philosophical Association, Proceedings of the Western Division, 1941, pp. 117–122.

teacher; instruction is learning with a teacher's aid. But both are, *as learning,* essentially the same, and the order of learning must be essentially the same, therefore, whether the learner proceeds by discovery or by instruction. Furthermore, what is most important of all, since the teacher is always only a cooperative cause, and never a primary or sole cause, of learning, the intellectual activities which occur without aid in the case of discovery must be going on also in the case of instruction.

From these two principles, we can conclude that the order of teaching must follow the order of learning, and that this order is primarily the order of discovery, for, as we have seen, even in learning by instruction, the primary causes of learning are the same sort of acts which cause discovery, when the learning goes on without a teacher's aid. The significance of this point—which I think is of the greatest importance—may not be grasped unless it is put into contrast with the now prevalent error. Today, in most cases, teaching proceeds as if the order of teaching should follow the order of knowledge, the objective order of knowledge itself, even though we know that this objective order cannot be followed in the process of discovery. In fact, it is completely reversed. Instruction which departs from the order of discovery also departs from the order of learning, for the way of discovery is the primary way of the mind to truth, and instruction merely imitates nature in imitating discovery. The objective structure of knowledge in no way indicates the processes of the mind in growth.

Now the order of discovery is primarily inductive and dialectical, not deductive and scientific. Let me explain. The usual distinction between induction and deduction—going from particulars to universals or universals to particulars—has always seemed to be somewhat superficial, if, in fact, it is correct at all. Rather, it seems to me, the deductive order is going from what is more knowable in itself to what is less knowable in itself; and thus there is an objective foundation for less intelligible truths in more intelligible ones—the intelligibility being intrinsic to the object known, being *secundum se,* not *quoad nos.* In contrast, the inductive order is going from what is more knowable to us to what is less knowable to us. Thus, the deductive order is the demonstration of conclusions from prior principles, or, where demonstration does not take place, the analytical expansion of prior truths in terms of their consequences; whereas the inductive order is the discovery of self-evident principles, on the one hand, and, on the other, it is the inferential procedure whereby every basic existential proposition is known—*for no existential proposition (concerning God, or substance, or the diversity of essences) can be demonstrated deductively.* All *a posteriori* inferences are inductive, not deductive, and these are among the most fundamental inferences of the mind in the discovery of truth about the things. The other fundamental step is the intuitive induction of first principles.

Therefore, the methods of teaching any subject-matter should be primarily inductive and dialectical, rather than deductive and simply expository, for the former method is a conformity of teaching to the order of learning, as that is naturally exhibited in the order of discovery, which teaching must imitate as a cooperative art; whereas the latter method is a conformity of teaching to the order of knowledge itself, and this is an order which should not determine teaching, for it does not determine learning.

20

Interest, Effort, and Discipline

Problems in the Philosophy of Education Discussed in this Section

1. How is interest related to educational aims? Aims to value theory?
2. Should interest motivate instruction by appealing to pupil desire or to what is desirable?
3. Should interest be viewed as the result of instruction, or is it a condition precedent to good teaching?
4. Will interest best be enlisted where learning occurs in real life situations? What is a *real life* situation?
5. Should all instruction be interesting? When it is not should it be "made" so? If this is done, what danger is there of "soft pedagogy"? Of reducing what is good and true in the curriculum to the mere level of expediency?
6. When interest is lacking, should the student nonetheless make an effort to learn? Is there added moral value in putting forth effort in the face of the uninteresting?
7. When is education good discipline?
8. Where the pupil is not interested and will not put forth effort, is it justifiable to use compulsion to insure learning? Is it justifiable to offer rewards and prizes?

352. Interest as Instrumental

The word interest, in its ordinary usage, expresses (i) the whole state of active development, (ii) the objective results that are foreseen and wanted, and (iii) the personal emotional inclination . . .

When the place of interest in education is spoken of in a depreciatory way, it will be found that the second of the meanings mentioned is first exaggerated and then isolated. Interest is taken to mean merely the effect of an object upon personal advantage or disadvan-

352. John Dewey, *Democracy and Education* (New York: The Macmillan Company, 1916), pp. 148–150.

tage, success or failure. Separated from any objective development of affairs, these are reduced to mere personal states of pleasure or pain. Educationally, it then follows that to attach importance to interest means to attach some feature of seductiveness to material otherwise indifferent; to secure attention and effort by offering a bribe of pleasure. This procedure is properly stigmatized as "soft" pedagogy; as a "soup-kitchen" theory of education.

But the objection is based upon the fact—or assumption—that the forms of skill to be acquired and the subject matter to be appropriated have no interest on their own account: in other words, they are supposed to be irrelevant to the normal activities of the pupils. The remedy is not in finding fault with the doctrine of interest, any more than it is to search for some pleasant bait that may be hitched to the alien material. It is to discover objects and modes of action, which are connected with present powers. The function of this material in engaging activity and carrying it on consistently and continuously *is* its interest. If the material operates in this way, there is no call either to hunt for devices which will make it interesting or to appeal to arbitrary, semicoerced effort.

The word interest suggests, etymologically, what is *between,*—that which connects two things otherwise distant. In education, the distance covered may be looked at as temporal. The fact that a process takes time to mature is so obvious a fact that we rarely make it explicit. We overlook the fact that in growth there is ground to be covered between an initial stage of process and the completing period; that there is something intervening. In learning, the present powers of the pupil are the initial stage; the aim of the teacher represents the remote limit. Between the two lie *means*—that is middle conditions:—acts to be performed; difficulties to be overcome; appliances to be used. Only *through* them, in the literal time sense, will the initial activities reach a satisfactory consummation.

These intermediate conditions are of interest precisely because the development of existing activities into the foreseen and desired end depends upon them. To be means for the achieving of present tendencies, to be "between" the agent and his end, to be of interest, are different names for the same thing. When material has to be made interesting, it signifies that as presented, it lacks connection with purposes and present power: or that if the connection be there, it is not perceived. To make it interesting by leading one to realize the connection that exists is simply good sense; to make it interesting by extraneous and artificial inducements deserves all the bad names which have been applied to the doctrine of interest in education.

353. Hedonism of Interest Criticized

There is the same difficulty with the term "interest" that there has been with the term *pleasure* or *happiness,* taken as a technical term for the highest end of man. Hedonism is a doctrine which has played a greater part in the history of ethics. It is not of any use to attack hedonism by asserting that the true end of man is not happiness or pleasure. Any end that you may name, other than happiness or pleasure, will be at once cunningly seized upon by the Epicurean. He will inquire with a smile whether your highest object and aim in life does not secure the greatest sum of pleasure and happiness in the long run? Your affirmative answer seems to him a fatal admission of the triumph of his principle. So, with regard to the doctrine of interest which affirms that the pupil should be developed through his interest; that interest in short should be the first principle of the teacher; that he must make it his first and foremost endeavor to interest his pupils in what they are studying. If you point out a higher or highest object in studies—namely the acquaintance of the pupil with the rational order of the universe in which he lives: the attainment of wisdom and holiness—the advocate of interest will inquire with the same covert sarcasm whether this is not to be made interesting to the pupil—in fact whether it is not really the most interesting of all things, if rightly taught? The refutation of hedonism is not to be found in setting up an antithetic principle. It is not happiness, nor non-happiness, that should be regarded as the highest aim of man— "happiness is not," although Mr. Pope supposed it to be, "our being's end and aim."

The refutation of hedonism may be made without the fear of self-contradiction, if one approaches the subject by considering the undetermined character of the term "happiness" taking note of the fact that happiness includes all grades and kinds, namely a temporary happiness which is followed by a permanent injury to the soul as well as a highest happiness which leads through manifold trial and suffering to eternal blessedness. It is evident that happiness does not contain within it the determining principle: it demands a higher principle in order to correct its own indefiniteness and vagueness . . . In order to define his chosen field of happiness, he must bring in a higher principle which relates to man's origin and destiny and to his realization of the Divine will in holiness and in the knowledge of truth. Then he will have introduced and justified his term "happi-

353. William T. Harris, "Professor Dewey's Doctrine of Interest as Related to Will," *Educational Review,* 11:490–492, May 1896.

ness," but at the same time will have subordinated it. Happiness is in this way proved to be a secondary principle by its own advocates.

Just so the principle of interest is a subordinate principle and it is shown to be such by its advocates, who attempt to point out what realm or sphere of interest is proper and to be encouraged. They make a study of the child's interest, and looking out upon the universe toward the careers which will arise from different species of interest, They select the kind of interest that leads in the surest manner toward human perfection in will and intellect. They also study the other kinds of interest and find out which of them will tend wholly toward the bad, and likewise which of them will lead by circuitous paths toward the good. In this way the Herbartians, and other advocates of interest as a principle of education, subordinate the principle of interest to a higher principle, namely the rational perfection of man, the attainment of full self-expression; the realization of the reasonable in this universe and the attainment of full self-consciousness; the discovery of the Divine as the final end of human endeavor.

354. Interest as Acceptance

Now one very significant conclusion appears. Whatever of an experience we accept to act on now or later, that we learn and it becomes part of us. And we learn it *as* and *only so far as* we accept it. If we accept it as a fact, albeit a disagreeable one, we learn it as a fact and we learn at the same time the attitude which counts it disagreeable. The standards of action which we accept to act on we learn, and they become part of us. If those I accept be high, I become a person of high standards. If low, I become a person of low standards. Whatever I accept to act on, that I learn and it becomes part of me. Moreover, I learn these things as holding under the conditions and reservations with which I accepted them. If, as a child, I accept a certain thing to act on when mother is at hand but not to act on if no grown persons is about to enforce it—if I do so accept it with these limitations, then I do so learn it.

This restatement of the law of effect reaches down to the heart of the activity program. What the proponents of this movement wish is such activity as *does* call out wholeheartedly the best that is in the child . . . We are particularly concerned with the standards he accepts to act on, for out of these his moral character as well as his everyday proficiency is largely built. It is then evident that we must stress

354. William H. Kilpatrick, "The Essentials of the Activity Movement," *Progressive Education,* 11:352–353, October 1934.

pupil purposing because attitude more than anything else determines what the learner will accept, what standards he will act on as he weighs and accepts or rejects.

To say of such considerations as the foregoing that they "intensify individualism" or "enthrone a glorified hedonism" becomes an assertion beyond understanding. That child life holds the possibility of individualism and of hedonism is true (as later adult life too often and too painfully shows) but child life holds just as truly the opposites as any teacher or parent well knows. What shall be called into play and accepted depends largely on the opportunity granted and the encouragement accorded. A program which consciously bases itself on thus calling out the best, as does the activity movement, would seem on the face of it to have a somewhat better chance at success than an alternative which concerns itself rather with the learning of subject matter than with the growth of the child.

355. Knowledge as a Basis of Interest

In brief, it may be suggested that interest begets interest, that interest accompanies natural mental growth, that interest is felt in any unified variety, and that interest appears in the novel that is similar to the familiar.

❋   ❋   ❋

Knowledge is the basis of interest,—one is interested in that concerning which he knows something, and wants to know more . . . That teacher is interesting who can make new things seem old, and old things new.

356. What Interest Is and Is Not

Interest is not a form of knowledge, though knowledge may be interesting; neither is it a kind of action, though action too may be interesting. But interest is primarily a feeling . . . Every one knows that when he is interested something is proving attractive to him, is catching and holding the mind's attention, and that to this something it is no effort to attend . . .

❋   ❋   ❋

355. Herman H. Horne, *The Philosophy of Education* (New York: The Macmillan Company, 1927), pp. 194–196.
356. *Op. cit.*, pp. 189–191.

Interest in education is not ease, it is effortless activity; it is not a classroom vaudeville, with the teacher as chief performer, it is engrossing occupation; it is not an amusing entertainment of the pupils, it is a joyous attainment by the pupils; it is not play, it is attractive and compelling work; it is not pursuing the line of least resistance, it is discovering the line of greatest attraction. And the true opposite of interest is not hard work, but drudgery . . .

    ✻   ✻   ✻

As soon as an object of endeavor becomes interesting in itself, like the learning of a lesson, like the recitation of a class, or the solving of a problem, this object becomes an end of action in itself. It is no longer done as a disagreeable means to an agreeable ultimate end. It is done for its own sake. The way has become attractive and worth while as well as the goal.

357. Attention and Interest Differentiated

True motivation is based upon *interest* rather than upon *attention*. It is true that when attention is secured through some artificial means such, for example, as telling the pupil that a certain thing to be done is very important, when really it is not, or, telling him that *you* want him to do this for *you*, when really all you are trying to do is to keep the pupil busy, a genuine interest will *sometimes* be aroused. Or, even if attention is coerced through the exercise of the will, a genuine interest is sometimes aroused. But obviously, the only proper motivation is to arouse a genuine interest through *real* and not artificial means. When interest is aroused attention will take care of itself and under no other circumstances is a teacher assured of the continued attention of her pupils.

358. Flexibility of Interest

According to some, an activity program must grow directly out of the existing attitudes and contacts of those under instruction. To others, this course appears to be antagonistic not only to acquisition of subject

357. Robert A. Cummins, "Safe Steps Toward the Project Method—II," *Educational Method*, 3:207, January 1924.

358. John Dewey in National Society for the Study of Education, Thirty-third Yearbook, Part II, *The Activity Movement* (Chicago: University of Chicago Press, 1934), pp. 84–85.

matter in any organized way but also to preparation for meeting the inevitable requirements of later life. Others still evade the idea by setting up forms of activity that are practically uniform for all, so that the habit of conforming individual activity to that of others is established.

This problem, as far as theory is concerned, arises because a false antithesis is set up. There are multitudes of active tendencies in the young and a multitude of nascent preferences and dawning interests. There is a great deal of elasticity within an individual; individuality is rather a *direction of movement* than anything definitely formed. Selection and arrangement have to occur anyway unless everything is carried on at haphazard according to the caprice or pressure of the moment. The problem is therefore to discover *within* present experience those values that are akin to those which the community prizes, and to cultivate those tendencies that lead in the direction that social demands will take. If emphasis is put upon these points of community, not all clashes of personal desire and social claim will be avoided, but in the main there will be growth toward harmony . . .

❊   ❊   ❊

Much of the practical difficulty and conflict that exist is due to a false idea of the definiteness and fixity of the desires and interests of childhood. When children are asked in an overt way what they want or what they would like to do, they are usually forced into a purely artificial state and the result is the deliberate creation of an undesirable habit. It is the business of the educator to study the tendencies of the young so as to be more consciously aware than are the children themselves what the latter need and want. Any other course transfers the responsibility of the teacher to those taught. Arbitrary "dictation" is not a matter of words or of form, but consists in imposing actions that do not correspond with tendencies that can be discovered within the experience of those who are growing up. The pupil also makes an arbitrary imposition on himself when, in response to an inquiry as to what he would like, he, because of ignorance of underlying and enduring tendencies and interest, snatches at some accidental affair. On the other side, those who strongly insist upon the priority of social claims and values to present experience usually overlook the leverage they might find in the latter for an uncoerced approach to their end, and they also exaggerate the fixity of social demands. There is nothing that society itself needs more than self-reliant personalities with habits of initiative, re-adaptability, and inherent decisiveness.

359. Method as Rhetorical

. . . it is the duty of the school to teach . . . theoretical and practical principles and procedures in such a way as to elicit zeal and devotion. The teacher as an authority exercises a mediating, communicating function. His first duty is to gain firm ground, to have something sound and true to communicate. But this does not exhaust the matter. His next duty is really to communicate it, to see that it is presented in such a way as to take possession of the student. Even though the truth is known, if it cannot be transmitted and maintained, culture will die . . . At the mature level where it is largely a matter of transmitting ideas and theories, clarity, economy of words, and dialectical ability are more important. At every level deep conviction, rhetoric, and persuasive force are required of the genuine teacher. Education is the art of communicating truth. It has not been fully achieved until this truth not only lies within, but actually possesses, the mind and heart of the student.

360. What Makes a "Life Situation" Real

One is forced to the conclusion, therefore, that he cannot arrive at a definition of "life situations" through any objective description of the situations themselves. The real crux of the matter lies in a different direction. It is not the objective features of the situation which really make the difference, it is the subjective; we must try to define the phrase under discussion from the standpoint of the attitude of the child who is doing the studying.

Let us assume tentatively as a definition the following: A life situation is one of which the child recognizes the significance and meaning to him. This definition is in accord with the philosophy which prompted the adoption of the phrase we are discussing, for that philosophy is consistently opposed to the process of keeping children busy on academic tasks which are meaningless and useless to them. Such a procedure is different from the situation in adult life where most of

359. John Wild, "Education and Human Society: A Realistic View," in the 54th Yearbook of the National Society for the Study of Education, Part I, *Modern Philosophies and Education* (Published by the Society, Chicago, 1955), p. 30–31.

360. Edwin H. Reeder, "What are Life Situations?" *Teachers College Record* (Bureau of Publications, Teachers College, Columbia University), 29:411, February, 1928.

the things we do make a definite pecuniary, social, or recreational contribution to our needs and are therefore meaningful to us.

361. Interest as an Artificial Product of the School

Take the problem of motivation. We have filled the earth with debates over the problem of interest. In the rural environment to which I have referred there was no such problem. Whoever heard of a farm being run on the basis of interest? Milking the cows and feeding the pigs were not projects; they were just plain chores. They were done, not in response to "felt needs," but in conformity to a schedule. These chores were bound up with the whole way of life on the farm. This way of life was the natural and normal outlet for energy and ambition. The average boy on the farm, in his eagerness to be rated as a man, was willing to endure a great deal of strenuous work and monotonous drudgery in order to secure recognition. There was no conscious attempt to relate the work of the farm to interest, because this relation was already established.

Now contrast this with the situation that is presented in a modern progressive school. The latter is an *artificial* situation, not in any insidious sense, but in the sense that it is a substitute for the life outside of the school. To provide such a substitute was an inescapable necessity. But the fact that it is a substitute introduces certain important differences. There is not the same practical reason for doing things. There is not the incentive that comes from direct participation in the activities of adults. There is, in short, no complete continuity between the school and what may, by contrast, be called "real life." Yet incentives must be present in order to prevent school work from degenerating into meaningless routine. Consequently it was found necessary to appeal to more immediate interests, to felt needs, and the like. Under the circumstances, the emphasis on interest was natural and inevitable. Yet the doctrine of interest is, in a sense, a school doctrine; we have a doctrine of interest because we have schools.

To put it differently, we emphasize interest in the school because we cannot be sure that the incentives which normally spring from the larger community life are present and operative. We utilize immediate interests for the purpose of reaching more remote incentives. The whole justification for the appeal to interest is that this wider range of incentives must be brought into play. In other words, we utilize

361. Boyd H. Bode, "Education and Social Change," *Progressive Education,* 11:46–47, January-February 1934.

immediate interests in order to secure a large measure of participation in the life of the community.

362. Individualistic Competition in the School

Imagine forty children all engaged in reading the same books, and in preparing and reciting the same lessons day after day. Suppose that this constitutes by far the larger part of their work, and that they are continually judged from the standpoint of what they are able to take in in a study hour, and to reproduce in a recitation hour. There is next to no opportunity here for any social or moral division of labor. There is no opportunity for each child to work out something specifically his own, which he may contribute to the common stock, while he, in turn, participates in the productions of others. All are set to do exactly the same work and turn out of the same results. The social spirit is not cultivated—in fact, in so far as this method gets in its work, it gradually atrophies for lack of use . . .

✻   ✻   ✻

The children are judged with reference to their capacity to present the same external set of facts and ideas. As a consequence they must be placed in the hierarchy on the basis of this purely objective standard. The weaker gradually lose their sense of capacity, and accept a position of continuous and persistent inferiority. The effect of this upon both self-respect and respect for work need not be dwelt upon. The stronger grow to glory, not in their strength, but in the fact that they are stronger. The child is prematurely launched into the region of individualistic competition, and this in a direction where competition is least applicable, viz., in intellectual and spiritual matters, whose law is cooperation and participation.

363. No Lasting Interest Without Difficulty

Lack of interest in any subject depends, for children, far less on the nature of the subject than on a persistent thwarting of the will to power in dealing with it; *interest accompanies any task in which a*

---

362. John Dewey, *Ethical Principles Underlying Education* (Chicago: University of Chicago Press, 1903), pp. 15–17.
363. William E. Hocking, *Human Nature and Its Remaking* (New Haven, Conn.: Yale University Press, 1918), 1929, p. 271.

mental momentum is established. But momentum can be gained only when difficulty can be indefinitely increased, so that the very conditions which may discourage, drive away interest, and even induce loathing of a subject, are conditions which make great interest possible when the will to power is called into lively action. We may put it down as a maxim of education, so far as interest is concerned,— *Without difficulty, no lasting interest.*

364. Educational Implications of Existentialism

We come now to a consideration of the role of education in an existential world. What does all this mean for the education of man?

At the outset, it seems probable that the existential school will be a place where man's non-rational, i.e., his aesthetic, moral, and emotional self will be much more in evidence than his scientific, rational self. Experimentalists have envisioned a school where youngsters learn by using the scientific method to solve real, genuine problems, by using their reflective intelligence to explore and test possible alternative solutions to the perplexities their environment poses. Existentialists, while no doubt providing room for this kind of teaching, will be more interested in developing the effective side of man, his capacity to love, to appreciate, to respond emotionally to the world about him.

This seems probable because of the Existentialist Imperative—the necessity for personal "involvement" in human situations and the consequent requirement for unguided, unjustifiable but nevertheless responsible choice on the part of the individual person. Existentialists are not so concerned about gathering factual evidence on a problem; science can do that. They are more concerned with what man does with the evidence. Science does not prescribe answers; it only gathers data. It is the individual who selects the answers, and he does so with no help from anyone. He is not compelled by nature to select any one answer; he can select any. His selection is therefore his alone, and he is responsible for it. He cannot justify it except in terms of himself. He may of course choose in a way in which the majority chooses. But the company of a majority does not make his choice right. He is condemned to live in constant anguish and doubt as to whether his choice was the right one.

Although there is no easy escape from this anguish, it is presumed

364. VanCleve Morris, "Existentialism and Education," *Educational Theory,* 4:255–256, October, 1956.

that the development of the affective dimension of human personality would better prepare the individual for this kind of existence than would the development of his rational and scientific faculties which are after all supposed to be kept objective, neutral, and therefore free of personal preference.

For better or worse, therefore, the Existentialist educator would seem to be committed to the task of developing the choice-making power in the individual, and it seems probable that in working to this end, he will move away from the sciences, including the social sciences, and increasingly turn to the humanities and the arts. For it is here where man's aesthetic, emotional, and moral proclivities are exercised.

By way of paradox, however, the opposite point of view might easily be developed. If the business of living is to be, at least in part, an effort to escape from this anguish, the *deadening* of the affective centers might emerge as a suitable educational objective. In this event, the more dull and insensitive a person became, the more satisfying and certain a life he would presumably lead. I take it however that Existentialists do not consider the amelioration of anguish as either possible or desirable. It is in the very nature of things that we are free; being free we are committed to live in anguish, and we must make the best of a very difficult situation.

As for pedagogy, it seems inevitable that the existential school will become more individual-centered. In a way, it will have to be, since its prime consideration is the individual living unattached in a friendless world. The "group method," so long a friend of democratic Experimentalism, will have to be discarded. You cannot teach the individual the true significance of his unique individualism with group dynamics; the very function of group dynamics is to illustrate the superiority of group decision over individual decision.

In fact, it would seem likely that all forms of cooperative endeavor would atrophy, at least all those in which decisions were sought (as distinguished from those in which factual information is shared). And we would likely find boys and girls working individually with their teachers, assessing the material before them and learning the necessity for making existential choices.

To an Experimentalist, this would of course be an intolerable kind of school, one in which the social and gregarious qualities of human experience would certainly atrophy and die. But the Existentialist does not value gregariousness. Gregariousness is only a transparent excuse for the loss of man's unique existential individuality, only a pretty word for explaining man's unhappy capitulation to the cosmic forces trying to make him a mass animal. If man is to regain that which makes him human, he must be willing once again to stand alone, willing to withstand the pressures of history and culture, and to chart the course of his own life, not only for himself but on behalf of Man.

365. Effort and Discipline

Another contrast in the two philosophies [idealism and pragmatism] is afforded in their respective attitudes toward discipline and effort. In the one they are the children of interest. An interest is that which *lies between* where one is and where one wants to be. Having an interest thus identifies the person with his activity realizing a purpose. His effort is put forth because he is interested in what he has to do, and his discipline comes as the effect of his effort following his interest. The evidence of becoming disciplined is the continued attention to the object desired and continued persistence in attaining it. The ideal is to be immediately interested in the thing that is being done; if not, the next desirable thing is to be interested in the end to be attained which sheds an interest mediately upon the unwelcome means necessary to attain it. This is said to be not the old hard pedagogy of doing what you don't like, nor the soft pedagogy of doing what you like, but the new pedagogy of liking what you do . . .

In contrast, as the body of this text indicates, idealism accepts the view of interest leading to effort and discipline as far as it goes but recognizes that it may not go far enough. By way of supplement it is pointed out that some obligations are binding, that duties must be done, that right must be obeyed, that voluntary attention to the uninteresting but important is possible, that effort at times can and must be put forth, that discipline in doing the disagreeable that is necessary is worth while, that so effort may lead to interest, that even if interest never comes as a result of effort in such cases, still the obligatory thing must be done. In this way children set gently but firmly to doing what they should do, may develop an interest that continues to carry them on; if not, they have done their duty just the same; and some duties they have, felt or unfelt as such. The sense of *ought* remains. Emphasis is placed in the one philosophy on the interest that leads to effort; in the other, in addition, on the effort that leads to interest, or, *in extremis,* to doing right without interest. The latter may involve coercion and obedience in moral issues . . .

365. Herman H. Horne, *The Philosophy of Education* (New York: The Macmillan Company, 1927), pp. 312–314.

366. Discipline as Self-Mortification

The other question involved in the understanding of the situation which we are considering is that of effort. The acceptance of the validity of intrinsic motivation seems to imply a belief that it is better to do a thing because we want to do it than because we do not want to do it. There is a fairly prevalent notion that quite the contrary is true. Is there not a greater value to the child in sitting down and attacking the geography lesson which he does not want to study than in working on the airplane? This view proceeds from the principle that it is better to do what we do not want to do than what we do want to do. In the thinking of many both without the Church and within it this notion is somehow vaguely considered to be truly Catholic and in some manner bound up with Christian asceticism.

Self-denial, even in things lawful, is a part of the life of every true Christian. We deliberately do things which we do not want to do; and, what is more, we expect thereby to further the attainment of an ordered self. It must be remembered, however, that we do not perform the act of mortification simply *because* we do not want to do it. We do it to show our love for our Lord or to order one or more of our inordinate appetites which, as we have seen, in slipping the leash of the will as the result of the fall, turn inordinately to mutable good, to the detriment of the whole man. Thus, even on the supernatural level we really perform the act of self-denial because, as a means to an end, we do want to do it.

If this is true even in the supernatural order, it is more true in the natural order. As human beings we always act for a purpose. If we can present the child with an environment in which he will engage in purposeful activities which he recognizes as valuable and which he thereby wants to undertake, we are merely leading the child to act in accord with his nature as a human being.

367. Compulsion as a Supplement to Motivation

Social relationships range from complete, voluntary mutuality to absolutely coercive exploitation. Normally they compromise these two

366. Sister Joseph Mary Raby, *A Critical Study of the New Education* (Washington, D.C.: The Catholic University of America Press, 1932), p. 89.
367. Ross L. Finney, *A Sociological Philosophy of Education* (New York: The Macmillan Company, 1928), pp. 157–159.

extremes. This overemphasis upon the voluntary in school practice is an inference from the individualistic obsession of the *Zeitgeist*. Moreover, it is based upon a misreading of the facts of social life, in which contraint of one sort or another always has played an important part. No sociologist would assert that the world could be run without compulsion. Artificial incentives, however liable to abuse, are indispensable in such a world as ours, where division of labor is complexly organized, where the objectives of effort are often very remote, and where the restraints imposed upon the natural instincts are often so irksome. If the learning situation in school were exactly similar to the learning situation outside the school, incentives, devices, and compulsions would still have a very considerable place in the learning process. There would be hard tasks to do; and they would be done under duress, if necessary. To omit this element makes the school *unlike* the social process, instead of like it; and therefore deprives young people of a discipline that is very important as preparation for life.

❉   ❁   ❉

For it is in the very nature of formal schooling that these features can never be completely dispensed with; and teachers are entitled to the comfort of realizing that that is so—the fashionable pedagogical theories of the hour to the contrary notwithstanding. For, after all, *preparation* for life is exactly what that formal schooling is upon which civilization depends for its survival. Necessarily its objectives are more or less remote; necessarily its motivation is more or less artificial. The thing to do, therefore, is to select the material that really is relevant to life, graduating the pupils to their several stages of development as well as possible, explaining to the older children the reasons for learning it, and sugar-coating it within reason for the younger ones. It is legitimate to humbug the children, and especially the younger ones, into imagining that the artificial situations and motivation which the teacher invents are natural; but it is poor policy for the teacher to humbug himself in these matters. For such artificial motivation can never, in the very nature of the case, be one hundred per cent successful; there almost always will remain some necessity for compelling children to learn their lessons, and in extreme cases it is quite proper to motivate them with a whip. Then we shall have a school practice that parallels the social practice as it really is, and that can be justified by a well-balanced sociological theory. Moreover, it will train efficient, law-abiding citizens; whereas it is to be feared that our soft, degenerate pedagogy does not.

368. Shortcomings of Stern Discipline

A still popular belief, once entertained by the generality of teachers, is that rigorous imposition of tasks and stern discipline—telling and compelling—take the wildness out of "little savages," making them tractable members of society. The fact is that such schooling does not make pupils into tractable members of the school itself; instead, it makes them into adepts at evasion. It trains them to use their wits to circumvent authority. If from the discipline of such a school any transfer to after-school life takes place—and some transfer is likely—it will be in the direction of the individualism that gets around laws by secrecy, lawyer's tricks, and collusion with officials; the individualism that then goes on to acquire control of legislation and of the courts on behalf of special interests. The sovereignty of the state, in such a case, is first set at naught, and then used as a tool for the exploitation of one's fellows.

369. Fallacy of Opposing Interest and Effort

It is a common, though somewhat surprising, fact that there is generally a common principle unconsciously assumed at the basis of two theories which to all outward appearances are the extreme opposites of each other. Such a common principle is presupposed by the theories of effort and interest in the one-sided forms in which they have already been stated.

This identical assumption is the externality of the object or idea to be mastered, the end to be reached, the act to be performed, to the self. It is because the object or end is assumed to be outside self that it has to be *made* interesting, that it has to be surrounded with artificial stimuli and with fictitious inducements to attention. It is equally because the object lies outside the sphere of self that the sheer power of "will," the putting forth of effort without interest, has to be appealed to. The genuine principle of interest is the principle of the recognized identity of the fact or proposed line of action with the self; that it lies in the direction of the agent's own growth, and is, therefore,

368. George Coe, *Educating for Citizenship* (New York: Charles Scribner's Sons, 1932), p. 23.
369. John Dewey, "Interest in Relation to Training of the Will," Second supplement to *First Yearbook of the National Herbart Society*, 1895–1900, pp. 8–11.

imperiously demanded, if the agent is to be himself. Let this condition of identification once be secured, and we neither have to appeal to sheer strength of will, nor do we have to occupy ourselves with making things interesting to the child.

The theory of effort, as already stated, means a virtual division of attention and the correponding disintegration of character, intellectually and morally. The great fallacy of the so-called effort theory is that it identifies the exercise and training of will with certain external activities and certain external results. It is supposed that, because a child is occupied at some outward task and because he succeeds in exhibiting the required product, that he is really putting forth will, and that definite intellectual and moral habits are in process of formation. But, as a matter of fact, the moral exercise of the will is not found in the external assumption of any posture, and the formation of moral habit cannot be identified with the ability to show up results at the demand of another. The exercise of the will is manifest in the direction of attention, and depends upon the spirit, the motive, the disposition in which work is carried on.

*   *   *

The principle of making objects and ideas interesting implies the same divorce between object and self as does the theory of "effort." When things have to be *made* interesting, it is because interest itself is wanting. Moreover, the phrase is a misnomer. The thing, the object, is no more interesting than it was before. The appeal is simply made to the child's love of pleasure. He is excited in a given direction, with the hope that somehow or other during this excitation he will assimilate something otherwise repulsive.

370. Discipline as Persistent Pursuit of an Intelligently Chosen End

A person who is trained to consider his actions, to undertake them deliberately, is in so far forth disciplined. Add to this ability a power to endure in an intelligently chosen course in face of distraction, confusion, and difficulty, and you have the essence of discipline. Discipline means power at command; mastery of the resources available for carrying through the action undertaken. To know what one is to do and to move to do it promptly and by use of the requisite means is to be dis-

370. John Dewey, *Democracy and Education* (New York: The Macmillan Company, 1916), pp. 151–152.

ciplined, whether we are thinking of an army or a mind. Discipline is positive. To cow the spirit, to subdue inclination, to compel obedience, to mortify the flesh, and to make a subordinate perform an uncongenial task—these things are or are not disciplinary according as they do or do not tend to the development of power to recognize what one is about and to persistence in accomplishment.

21

Freedom As Method

Problems in the Philosophy of Education Discussed in this Section

1. What is the justification for pupil freedom in the classroom? Should freedom be a means or an end of instruction?
2. When should children be taught to seek freedom "under" or "through" social convention, and when "from" social convention?
3. Is freedom for the teacher as well as for the pupil? Is the amount of freedom limited, so that the more the pupil has, the less the teacher has?
4. To what extent are freedom and intelligence correlated in education? Freedom and creativity? Can genuine creativity be expected from the immature?
5. Is freedom to be conceived negatively, like *laissez-faire*, as an absence of control or restraint? What then happens to authority?
6. When can teachers and parents depend on the moral autonomy of children?

371. Meanings Associated with Freedom

The complexity of the conception of freedom is shown in the great variety of descriptive terms used in reference to human manifestations of freedom. Consider, for example, the following words, all somewhat closely associated with one or more aspects of freedom: lax, spontaneous, easy-going, undisciplined, cantankerous, ill-mannered, vulgar, intolerant, irresponsible, insubordinate, enslaved, unruly, lawless, orderly, conventional, business-like, formal, disobedient, self-controlled. The traits are readily distinguished on the basis of their desirability or undesirability, but each, in a certain sense, suggests freedom.

By grouping certain of these words, we can describe what would seem to be a desirable type of child. Thus, we want a pupil to be will-

371. Ernest Horn, "Educating for Freedom and Responsibility," *Religious Education,* 25:631, September 1930.

ing but not wilful; we want him to be free but not irresponsible; spontaneous rather than compelled; determined but not cantankerous; tractable rather than obstinate; rational rather than prejudiced; steady rather than erratic. We like his attitude to be that of a person scrupulously fulfilling a contract which he has made rather than that of a person obeying an arbitrary demand.

All these illustrations show how slippery is the word freedom. This very slipperiness makes it necessary to formulate principles which will help us to an adequate concept of freedom as a school problem.

372. Further Meanings of Freedom

It would therefore seem that freedom has played many parts in the history of education. It appears as a synonym of anarchy, as an aid to the process of learning, as a means of escape from the limitations of the self, as a determinant of the content of education, as an equilibrant of conflicting elements in the pupil's nature, as the operation of individual judgment, intelligence, and reason, as the development of all the faculties, as obedience to the moral, or social law, as a principle of "directness" or "nearness," as an internal formation of personality, as creative or pleasurable, or self-activity, as a "third term" between teacher and pupil, as a principle of experimental education, as a designation of free persons or of auto-education, as a characteristic of various "circles" of behaviour, or of specific stages of development, and finally as a right of children as well as of adults. It has passed through a stage of denial, through a stage in which it is a means to an end, through a stage in which it acts as a control upon the pupil, through a stage in which it states a principle of partnership with the teacher, through a stage in which it is recognized to be a right of the pupil's life. Finally, it has the distinction of being considered as the animating aim and guiding principle of education.

373. Child Liberty under Anarchism

What is the duty of the parent toward the child? The position of the Anarchist is that there are no such things as rights and duties

372. W. J. McCallister, *The Growth of Freedom in Education* (New York: R. R. Smith, Inc., 1931), p. 543.
373. Benjamin R. Tucker, "Some Social and Anarchist Views of Education," *Educational Review*, 15:8–9, January 1898.

except so far as they are a matter of contract; and, as there can be no contract between a parent and an unborn child, and as a mere infant is incapable of making a contract, it is obivous that there can be no duty to an unborn child or an infant. Until they are able to assert themselves, until they are able to contract, they are the property of their creators (I mean, of course, their human creators), and such creators should have sole control of them, and neither the state nor anybody should be allowed to step in between the creator and his property. If the creator sees fit not to give his child an education, that is his business. It is to be added, however, that the Anarchist holds that the motive of parental affection is all-sufficient to insure the care of children by their parents.

The only ethical teaching that the Anarchist believes in, for either public or domestic purposes, is the inculcation of the doctrine of equal liberty. The child is more amenable than anybody else to this teaching if taken in hand in the beginning. If his own liberties are respected by his parents; if there is no attempt to interfere with him; if, whenever he wishes to do a thing, he is allowed to do it, simply with an explanation of the consequences that will follow, and if no compulsion is exercised upon him except as it would be exercised upon an invasive adult,—i.e., if the compulsion exercised upon a child was a purely defensive compulsion against any invasive act which the child was going to commit,—the child, then, from its very treatment, would acquire an idea of his own liberties and of the liberties of others, and would learn to insist upon the one and respect the other. Such ideas are carried out by all Anarchistic parents who understand their own ideas and have themselves sufficient strength of character to live up to them.

It is said that all children are naturally disposed to take property belonging to others. A child should be early taught the idea of property. He should be given something as his own, and, as early as possible, should be allowed to earn something as his own, and then care should be taken that his enjoyment of the property should never be interfered with, and the same care taken that he never interferes with others in the enjoyment of their property. In that way he would, at a very early age, get a very clear idea of the sanctity of the individual, of his earnings, and his personal property. And that idea covers all there is in ethics.

374. Freedom of Action as a Means to Free Use of Intelligence

The only freedom that is of enduring importance is freedom of intelligence, that is to say, freedom of observation and of judgment exercised in behalf of purposes that are intrinsically worth while. The commonest mistake made about freedom is, I think, to identify it with freedom of movement, or with the external or physical side of activity. Now, this external and physical side of activity cannot be separated from the internal side of activity; from freedom of thought, desire, and purpose. The limitation that was put upon outward action by the fixed arrangements of the typical traditional school-room, with its fixed rows of desks and its military regiment of pupils who were permitted to move only at certain fixed signals, put a great restriction upon intellectual and moral freedom . . .

But the fact still remains that an increased measure of freedom of outer movement is a *means*, not an end. The educational problem is not solved when this aspect of freedom is obtained. Everything then depends, so far as education is concerned, upon what is done with this added liberty. What end does it serve? What consequences flow from it? Let me speak first of the advantages which reside potentially in increase of outward freedom. In the first place, without its existence it is practically impossible for a teacher to gain knowledge of the individuals with whom he is concerned. Enforced quiet and acquiescence prevent pupils from disclosing their real natures . . .

The other important advantage of increased outward freedom is found in the very nature of the learning process. That the older methods set a premium upon passivity and receptivity has been pointed out. Physical quiescence puts a tremendous premium upon these traits. The only escape from them in the standardized school is an activity which is irregular and perhaps disobedient. There cannot be complete quietude in a laboratory or workshop. The non-social character of the traditional school is seen in the fact that it erected silence into one of its prime virtues. There is, of course, such a thing as intense intellectual activity without overt bodily activity. But capacity for such intellectual activity marks a comparatively late achievement when it is continued for a long period. There should be brief intervals of time for quiet reflection provided for even the young. But they are

374. John Dewey, *Experience and Education* (New York: The Macmillan Company, 1938), pp. 69–76.

periods of genuine reflection only when they follow after times of more overt action and are used to organize what has been gained in periods of activity in which the hands and other parts of the body besides the brain are used. Freedom of movement is also important as a means of maintaining normal physical and mental health. We have still to learn from the example of the Greeks who saw clearly the relation between a sound body and a sound mind. But in all the respects mentioned freedom of outward action is a means to freedom of judgment and of power to carry deliberately chosen ends into execution. The amount of external freedom which is needed varies from individual to individual. It naturally tends to decrease with increasing maturity, though its complete absence prevents even a mature individual from having the contacts which will provide him with new materials upon which his intelligence may exercise itself. The amount and the quality of this kind of free activity as a means of growth is a problem that must engage the thought of the educator at every stage of development.

There can be no greater mistake, however, than to treat such freedom as an end in itself. It then tends to be destructive of the shared cooperative activities which are the normal source of order. But, on the other hand, it turns freedom which should be positive into something negative. For freedom from restriction, the negative side, is to be prized only as a means to a freedom which is power: power to frame purposes, to judge wisely, to evaluate desires by the consequences which will result from acting upon them; power to select and order means to carry chosen ends into operation.

Natural impulses and desires constitute in any case the starting point. But there is no intellectual growth without some reconstruction, some remaking, of impulses and desires in the form in which they first show themselves. This remaking involves inhibition of impulse in its first estate. The alternative to externally imposed inhibition is inhibition through an individual's own reflection and judgment. The old phrase "stop and think" is sound psychology. For thinking is stoppage of the immediate manifestation of impulse until that impulse has been brought into connection with other possible tendencies to action so that a more comprehensive and coherent plan of activity is formed. Some of the other tendencies to action lead to use of eye, ear, and hand to observe objective conditions; others result in recall of what has happened in the past. Thinking is thus a postponement of immediate action, while it effects internal control of impulse through a union of observation and memory, this union being the heart of reflection. What has been said explains the meaning of the well-worn phrase "self-control." The ideal aim of education is creation of power of self-control. But the mere removal of external control is no guarantee for the production of self-control. It is easy to jump out of the frying-pan into the fire. It is easy, in other words, to escape one form of external control only to find oneself in another and more dangerous form of external control. Impulses and desires that are not ordered by intelligence are under the control of accidental circumstances. It may be a loss rather than a gain to escape from the control of another person only to find one's conduct dictated by immediate whim and caprice; that is, at the mercy of impulse into whose formation intelligent judgment has not entered. A person whose conduct is controlled in this way has at most only the illusion of freedom. Actually he is directed by forces over which he has no command.

375. Teacher Guidance is Compatible with Pupil Freedom

There is a present tendency in so-called advanced schools of educational thought (by no means confined to art classes like those of Cizek) to say, in effect, let us surround pupils with certain materials, tools, appliances, etc., and then let pupils respond to these things according to their own desires. Above all let us not suggest any end or plan to the students; let us not suggest to them what they shall do, for that is an unwarranted trespass upon their sacred intellectual individuality since the essence of such individuality is to set up ends and aims.

Now such a method is really stupid. For it attempts the impossible, which is always stupid; and it misconceives the conditions of independent thinking. There are a multitude of ways of reacting to surrounding conditions, and without some guidance from experience these reactions are almost sure to be casual, sporadic and ultimately fatiguing, accompanied by nervous strain. Since the teacher has presumably a greater background of experience, there is the same presumption of the right of a teacher to make suggestions as to what to do, as there is on the part of the head carpenter to suggest to apprentices something of what they are to do. Moreover, the theory literally carried out would be obliged to banish all artificial materials, tools and appliances. Being the product of the skill, thought and matured experience of others, they would also, by the theory, "interfere" with personal freedom.

Moreover, when the child proposes or suggests what to do, some

375. John Dewey in *Art and Education: A Series of Essays by Members of the Staff of the Barnes Foundation* (Merion, Penn.: The Barnes Foundation Press, 1947), pp. 37–38.

consequence to be attained, whence is the suggestion supposed to spring from? There is no spontaneous germination in the mental life. If he does not get the suggestion from the teacher, he gets it from somebody or something in the home or the street or from what some more vigorous fellow pupil is doing. Hence the chances are great of its being a passing and superficial suggestion, without much depth and range—in other words, not specially conducive to the developing of freedom. If the teacher is really a teacher, and not just a master or "authority," he should know enough about his pupils, their needs, experiences, degrees of skill and knowledge, etc., to be able (not to dictate aims and plans) to share in a discussion regarding what is to be done and be as free to make suggestions as anyone else. (The implication that the teacher is the one and only person who has no "individuality" or "freedom" to "express" would be funny if it were not often so sad in its out-workings.) And his contribution, given the conditions stated, will presumably do more to getting something started which will really secure and increase the development of strictly individual capacities than will suggestions springing from uncontrolled haphazard sources.

376. Education as a Precondition of Freedom

We sometimes mistake the nature of freedom by thinking of it as the absence of control. The free individual is taken to be the person who has thrown off the brakes, who allows his impulses full sway, who indulges in unrestricted "self-expression." This is one kind of freedom, to be sure, but it is not the kind that has been fought for by the wise men of the world. Worthy freedom is that in which internal control has taken place of external control. Responsibility takes the place of compulsion. The individual no longer needs to be controlled by society because he governs his own conduct in conformity with the welfare and needs of society and of himself alike.

The study of children has shown unmistakably that they advance gradually from an egocentric to a relatively objective and disinterested attitude toward the world and the people in it. To the infant and the young child the persons and things about him are means to the satisfaction of his own desires. He manipulates them so far as he is able to serve his own ends. He interprets what goes on about him as centered in himself. The very heavenly bodies follow him and do his

376. Frank N. Freeman, "Education as a Prerequisite to Freedom," *School and Society*, 45:594–596, May 1937.

bidding. His thoughts, imaginings and dreams have an unquestioned validity and reality. The distinction between what is and what he believes has not occurred to him.

The child's attitude toward law and authority also undergoes marked change. While he seeks to impose his will on others he also accepts the authority of adults over him, and unquestioningly recognizes rules even when they are arbitrarily applied. With the absence of responsibility or internal control goes the acceptance of authority or external control.

As the child matures in mind he gradually comes to recognize various kinds of reality outside himself with which he must square his own thoughts and actions. One type of this external reality is represented in science and another type in ethics. As he becomes acquainted with the body of facts and laws which have accumulated in the experience of mankind in its search after truth, he gradually comes to see that he can not hold as true whatever he may think. Truth is something which is independent of his individual fancy. It must be patiently sought after and respected when it is found. He is not free to believe anything he chooses; he must subject himself to the truth.

The same is true of conduct. To the young child, as has been said, egoistic behavior is checked only by external authority. In time, however, and first in his dealings with other children, he recognizes that others have wishes also and that this implies a mutuality in the recognition of rights. Thus there grows the recognition of rules or principles governing the conduct of persons in relation to each other, and he learns to control his conduct in relation to them. He has learned to exercise self-direction and self-control in place of submitting mainly to the direction and control of others.

Has the individual who has thus learned to recognize and abide by the facts of science and the principles of ethics merely substituted one form of bondage for another? Confusion of thought often arises at this point and blurs the idea of freedom. The seeming paradox that a person may be free and yet bow to a reality beyond himself has its classic solution in the religious attitude of willing acceptance of this reality, and identification of oneself with it. But this is somewhat beside our immediate problem.

✻ ✻ ✻

We have seen that the attainment of freedom is reached through the substitution of internal control for external control. In science and conduct, and even in art and play, freedom is not exemption from the necessity of conforming to reality; it is rather the development of the ability and the disposition to so conform without external direction or authority. Freedom without such ability and disposition is a mere hollow shell because it does not provide the person with the means by which he can reach any desired goal.

The place of education in the attainment of freedom now seems clear. It is to promote the development by which the individual becomes capable of self-direction and self-control. This development is a positive attainment which is not to be gained by any such simple and easy means as merely removing external control. External control must gradually be removed, to be sure, but such removal must run parallel and keep pace with the intellectual and moral development of the child. Relaxed too rapidly it produces disorganization and demoralization; retained too long it brings dependence or rebellion.

What, then, are the conditions of self-control and self-direction? They may be summed up as knowledge, ability to think, discipline and goodwill. Doubtless the necessity of these will not be questioned. A wise decision can hardly be made if one is ignorant of the facts on which such a decision is based. Perhaps knowledge may be regarded as an out-of-date term and experience proposed as a substitute. But if knowledge suggests too much information gained at second hand, experience seems to imply too exclusive reliance on the limited knowledge which is gained at first hand. In any case, ignorance must be overcome, and both types of knowledge must be employed.

                                    *   *   *

The whole process of education—learning to recognize reality in the shape of persons and things, to take direction, to acquire the knowledge and ability to fit one to assume self-direction—all this requires discipline. Discipline is . . . first imposed from without and then self-imposed, but it is discipline in either case. There is a kind of sentimental notion abroad that if we follow nature closely enough mental growth will take place automatically with no trace of stress or strain. Most honest students of human nature know better. The psychiatrist in particular, whose business it is to deal with persons in whom development has gone awry, knows better. He knows that the mentally sick are those who for one reason or another have not learned to face reality and adjust to it and have folded up under the stress and strain which it imposes. Frequently, of course, the external stress is unduly great and a breakdown might have been avoided by reducing it. But it can not be eliminated, and every person must learn how to meet it. This requires discipline . . .

After the child has been educated in the ways I have indicated, he is ready for freedom because he has acquired the necessary means to self-direction and self-control. He reaches this condition by gradual steps and by different degrees in different areas. But he does not himself direct the process of his own education from the outset, for the simple reason that only one who knows the process can direct it. The purpose of the whole process is to bring him to self-direction and freedom, but this is the final and not the initial step. In fact, freedom is possible only to one who has the skill and knowledge to direct his own course. It is the positive power to accomplish one's ends and not mere absence of restrictions. To give the child this freedom the school must assume direction of his development. In order for the child to direct his own course of education he would have to be educated before he began.

377. Learning Obedience Before Exercising Freedom

The *first* epoch in the pupil's life is that in which he must show submissiveness and positive obedience; the *second* is that in which he is permitted to make use of his powers of reflection and of his freedom, but under laws. In the former there obtains a mechanical, in the latter a moral constraint.

The submissiveness of the pupil is either *positive* or *negative*. It is *positive* when he must do that which he is commanded, because he himself cannot judge, and the mere capacity for imitation still exists in him. It is *negative* when he must do that which others desire, if he wishes others to do things to please him. In the first instance he risks being punished; in the second, not obtaining what he wishes. In the latter instance, although he is able to think, he is still dependent upon others for his pleasures.

One of the greatest problems in education is, How can subjection to lawful constraint be combined with the ability to make use of one's freedom? For constraint is necessary. How shall I cultivate freedom under conditions of compulsion? I ought to accustom my pupil to tolerate a restraint upon his freedom, and at the same time lead him to make good use of his freedom. Without this all is mere mechanism, and he who is released from education does not know how to make use of his freedom. At an early age he must feel the inevitable opposition of society, in order to learn the difficulty of self-support, economy, and acquisition, so as to be independent.

Here the following must be observed:

(a) The child should be left perfectly free, from earliest childhood,

377. Immanuel Kant, in Edward F. Buchner, *The Educational Theory of Immanuel Kant* (Philadelphia: J. B. Lippincott Company, 1904), pp. 130–133.

in everything (except in such instances where he might injure himself; as, for example, when he reaches for an open knife), unless the
manner of his freedom interferes with that of others; as, for example,
when he screams, or is merry in too noisy a way, he discommodes
others.

(b) The child must be shown that he can attain his aims only as he
permits others to reach theirs; as, for example, he will be granted no
pleasure if he does not do what others desire, that he must learn, etc.

(c) It must also be shown to the child that he is under such constraint as will lead him to the use of his own freedom; that he is cultivated, so that one day he may be free, that is, not dependent upon
the foresight of others . . .

Here public education has the most evident advantage, since in it
one learns to measure his powers and the limitations which the rights
of others impose upon him. In this form of education no one has prerogatives, since opposition is felt everywhere, and merit becomes the
only standard of preferment. This education produces the best pro-
totype of the future citizen.

22

Measurement and Evaluation

Problems in the Philosophy of Education Discussed in this Section

1. How can the teacher make sure that his method has resulted in learning by the pupil? What is the difference between measuring and evaluating learning?
2. What does the measurement of learning assume as to the nature of learning? When measurement is expressed in cardinal numbers, what further assumptions are made as to the nature of learning? Are these assumptions sound?
3. With which is educational philosophy most concerned: the objectivity, reliability, or validity of educational measurement?
4. What theory of learning is implicit where learning is checked by evaluation? How does one evaluate pupil learning? How does one evaluate a teacher's instruction?
5. Should there be formal examinations? If so, what kind would be consistent with the philosophy you have developed so far? Does society have a stake in the examination system? Should examinations be used for motivation? As aims?
6. What do marks, diplomas, and degrees signify? Could they be dispensed with? Should anyone ever "fail" in school?

378. Science Should Relieve Philosophy of Measurement and Evaluation

In sum it is the business of measurement to evaluate, refine, and select subordinate goals. Heretofore this function has been almost wholly within the province of the philosophy of education. From time immemorial philosophy has had two functions: (1) to receive from the hands of science the threads of knowledge and to weave them into a consistent pattern and (2) to patch temporarily with old scraps the

378. William A. McCall, "My Philosophy of Life and Education," *Teachers College Record* (Bureau of Publications, Teachers College, Columbia University), 36:309, January 1935.

holes where thread is lacking or too slender for use. The evaluation of goals in a hierarchy is an illustration of this temporary functioning of philosophy. As quickly as possible this function should be taken over by the most exact scientific technicians, whether they be psychologists, statisticians, or scientific philosophers.

379. Measurement is Predicated on the Correspondence Theory of Truth

Modern educational measurement is a thorn in the side of the instrumentalist because it is the product of a different philosophy. It rests on a realistic foundation. Its basic assumptions are consistent with those of natural science and of common sense, but contradict certain assumptions of pragmatism. Its procedure is more consistent with the assumption of the existence of independent reals, the assumption that things can be without being known. It accepts the general experience approach in philosophy just as pragmatism does, but holds that knowledge consists, first, in the prehension of pre-existent entities, and second, in the discovery of their interrelationships. It proceeds on the assumption that intellectual analysis is a key to an understanding of the world and successful adjustment thereto; that, indeed, this is the most essential outcome of intellectual procedure and the intellectual life.

The method of analysis is bitterly resisted by our opponents, even though it explains the most impressive chapter in the history of human intelligence, the remarkable contribution of science to an understanding of the world. The whole, it is contended by the "progressive" thinker, is greater than the sum of its parts. Measurement based on the method of analysis is, therefore, said to deal with relatively insignificant pieces of personality, and neglects that latest fetish of the legions of educational light, the integrated individual. If, however, measurement today is on a false scent, if it seems wrongly to be looking backward for light instead of forward with the pupil's active purposes, why has natural science found the method of analysis so significant? Science analyzes common salt into its components, sodium and chlorine, and has found that knowledge of the parts contributes to control of the whole. The scientist has no hesitancy in admitting that the qualities of the separate components differ markedly from the qualities of the compound. This means merely that two things in a given relation may exhibit qualities that are not exhibited by either

379. Frederick S. Breed, "Fundamental Assumptions in Educational Measurement," *Phi Delta Kappan*, 20:120, December 1937.

when not in this relation, which is simply the principle underlying emergent evolution.

The realist now urges that no description of the intellectual function, of scientific method, or of educational procedure, can be adequate without the recognition of selective response to parts of the world that explains perception at the basis of knowing, and the acts of conception involving similar selectivity at its apex. On this assumption modern measurement can safely rest its case.

380. Borrowing of Educational Measurement from Physical Science

Education is an art rather than a science. That, in concrete operation, education is an art, either a mechanical art or a fine art, is unquestionable. If there were an opposition between science and art, I should be compelled to side with those who assert that education is an art. But there is no opposition, although there is a distinction . . .

     ❁   ❁   ❁

Educational science cannot be constructed simply by borrowing the techniques of experiment and measurement found in physical science. This could happen only if some way had been found by which mental or psychological phenomena are capable of statement in terms of units of space, time, motion, and mass. It is unnecessary to state that this condition has not been fulfilled. Nor have we as yet any *other* general hypotheses in the light of which to know *what* we are measuring and by which we can interpret results, place them in a system and lead on to fruitful indirect measurements. This principle is practically important at the present time. There is a tendency to assume that we are getting the material of a science of education merely because the techniques of older, better established sciences are borrowed and used.

It is no reproach to a would-be science that in early stages it makes experiments and measurements the results of which lack generalized significance. A period of groping is inevitable. But the lack of an intellectually coherent and inclusive system is a positive warning against attributing scientific value to results merely because they are reached by means of recognized techniques borrowed from sciences already established and are capable of being stated in quantitative formulae. Quantity is not even the fundamental idea of mathematics.

380. John Dewey, *The Sources of a Science of Education* (New York: Liveright Publishing Corporation, 1931), pp. 13–27.

381. Critique of Quantitative Assumption in Measurement

Nor need the progressive educator be unduly scared by the idea that science is constituted by quantitative results, and, as it is often said, that whatever exists can be measured, for all subjects pass through a qualitative stage before they arrive at a quantitative one; and if this were the place it could be shown that even in the mathematical sciences quantity occupies a secondary place as compared with ideas of order which verge on the qualitative. At all events, *quality* of activity and of consequence is more important for the teacher than any quantitative element. If this fact prevents the development of a certain kind of science, it may be unfortunate. But the educator cannot sit down and wait till there are methods by which quality may be reduced to quantity; he must operate here and now. If he can organize his qualitative processes and results into some connected intellectual form, he is really advancing scientific method much more than if, ignoring what is actually most important, he devotes his energies to such unimportant by-products as may now be measured.

Moreover, even if it be true that everything which exists could be measured—if only we knew how—that which does *not* exist cannot be measured. And it is no paradox to say that the teacher is deeply concerned with what does not exist. For a progressive school is primarily concerned with growth, with a moving and changing process, with *transforming* existing capacities and experiences; what already exists by way of native endowment and past achievement is subordinate to what it may become. Possibilities are more important than what already exists, and knowledge of the latter counts only in its bearing upon possibilities. The place of measurement of achievements as a theory of education is very different in a static educational system from what it is in one which is dynamic, or in which the ongoing process of growing is the important thing.

382. Theory of Equal Units in Measurement

In the effort to reduce learning to a quantitative scale, much misunderstanding has arisen in regard to the meaning of units. This misun-

381. John Dewey, "Progressive Education and the Science of Education," *Progressive Education*, 5:199–200, July-September 1928.

382. B. Othanel Smith, *Logical Aspects of Educational Measurement* (New York: Columbia University Press, copyright 1938), pp. 138–142.

derstanding has resulted largely from the failure to recognize that units can be classified into two distinct types. It is fairly evident that in educational literature little or no distinction is made between units that are equal by definition and units that are equal by experimental demonstration . . .

❊   ❊   ❊

It may be that some of the qualities dealt with in educational measurement will turn out to be capable of expression in really equal units. If this occurs, no one can predict what the particular procedure of obtaining them will be. But it can be asserted that whatever it is, it will be experimental and will publicly demonstrate that such qualities have a structure consonant to that of the axioms of addition. For in the process of satisfying the conditions of addition, equal units are derived. Failure to recognize this point has led educational and psychological measurement astray in the quest for truly equal units. In these fields it has been assumed that addition is made possible by the derivation of equal units, whereas equal units are established by addition. As a result, units equal only by definition have been advanced as though they were equal in a quantitative sense. When we have changed our guiding question from "How to find equal units?" to "How can we satisfy experimentally the axioms of addition?" we shall have cleared up much of our confusion, and, what is of even more importance, opened the way for the formulation of experimental operations in keeping with the end we seek. Until such operations have been made a matter of history, the contention that truly equal units have been established in educational measurement must remain an empty affirmation.

383. Danger of Overlooking the Individual in Group Measurement

It is all too frequently assumed that by narrowing the limits within which prediction is unreliable we can actually predict. Reduce the probability of error as we may, what we "know" about any tested individual as to his subsequent behavior or achievement in some correlated activity is either not "knowledge" at all but a guess, or a meagre generality. This of course is not true of groups. We can predict for a group because of the nature of chance distributions. But the group

383. Hugh Hartshorne, "Can Growth in Religion Be Measured?" *Religious Education*, 17:228, June 1922.

standard or equation or curve only by rare chance ever fits the individual not yet tested. A bad guess as to a child's probable school achievement based on his I.Q. is bad enough. But a bad guess as to his character is tragedy. There can be no substitution for direct knowledge of the individual's own social will.

384. Isolation and Control in Measurement

Interdependence determines the limits of quantitative measurements for educational science. That which can be measured is the specific, and that which is specific is that which can be isolated. The prestige of measurements in physical science should not be permitted to blind us to a fundamental educational issue: How far is education a matter of forming specific skills and acquiring special bodies of information which are capable of isolated treatment? It is no answer to say that a human being is always occupied in acquiring a special skill or a special body of facts, if he is learning anything at all. This is true. But the *educational* issue is what *other* things in the way of desires, tastes, aversions, abilities and disabilities he is learning along with his specific acquisitions.

The control of conditions demanded by laboratory work leads to a maximum of isolation of a few factors from other conditions. The scientific result is rigidly limited to what is established with these other conditions excluded. In educating individualities, no such exclusion can be had. The number of variables that enter in is enormous. The intelligence of the teacher is dependent upon the extent in which he takes into account the variables that are not obviously involved in his immediate special task. Judgment in such matter is of qualitative situations and must itself be qualitative.

The parent and educator deal with situations that never repeat one another. Exact quantitative determinations are far from meeting the demands of such situations, for they presuppose repetitions and exact uniformities. Exaggeration of their importance tends to cramp judgment, to substitute uniform rules for the free play of thought, and to emphasize the mechanical factors that also exist in schools. They contribute at most to the more efficient workings of present practices in some subjects. They have already been fruitful in securing eliminations, especially in the more routine skills, such as the three R's. But they do not give any help in larger questions of reconstruction of

384. John Dewey, *The Sources of a Science of Education* (New York: Liveright Publishing Corporation, 1931), pp. 64–66.

curriculum and methods. What is worse, they divert attention and energy from the need of reconstructions due to change of social conditions and to the inertia of traditions of the school system.

385. Measurement and Evaluation Distinguished

The movement away from measurement to evaluation is a long step in promoting better integration. Measurement has always stood for uniformity, external control, statistical methods, academic situations, and other devices of the subject curriculum. The centers of attention in evaluation are *value* to the learner and how he *behaves* as a result of such value. Since these pupil values are not amenable to statistical quantitative measurement and since pupil behavior is only slightly determined by present quantitative-measurement results, the movement toward a greater consideration of values and behavior means evaluation and not measurement. Since the underlying conceptions of evaluation are closer to those considered important in promoting integrating behavior, the change of emphasis in courses of study must be considered significant.

386. The Validity of Validity

We are . . . confronted with the fact that the logic of validity is polar in character. That is, we set out with the principle that learning is quantitative and that responses to the items of a test bear a proportional relation to a person's total achievement. Then we devise instruments on the basis of this principle, and thereafter justify the principle by the consequences which issue from acting upon it. By recourse to the principle, we construct instruments that free our observations of error; and then we turn about and justify the principle, because it is in agreement with observations made by the instruments.

❋   ❋   ❋

If the procedure of validating instruments is polar, is it not possible to deny its guiding principle and, by making other assumptions, to set up another procedure in opposition to the one we have? In other

385. L. Thomas Hopkins, *Integration: Its Meaning and Application* (New York: Appleton-Century-Crofts, Inc., copyright 1937), p. 299.
386. B. Othanel Smith, *Logical Aspects of Educational Measurement* (New York: Columbia University Press, copyright 1938), pp. 86–88.

words, if the argument is polar, the selection of guiding principles would appear to be an arbitrary matter. We would thus be able to shift from one guiding principle to another, depending upon the preferences of the test-constructor. The validity of achievement tests is therefore not guaranteed on some absolute, logical ground. Apparently there is a choice of ways by which an independent criterion of learning may be confirmed.

❋   ❋   ❋

Complete skepticism may be avoided if we keep in mind that any guiding principle may depend for support upon connections beyond its own context. A particular principle would be of little value to science without transitive aspects. If we cannot directly and objectively establish proof of any guiding principle, at least its correctness may be explored in two indirect ways: first, by an examination of its interconnections with other principles whose values have already been accepted; and, second, by taking account of the direct consequences which flow from its application . . .

387. Long- and Short-Range Measurement

Activity may be judged and evaluated according to its concrete and tangible results or according to the contribution it makes to a relatively intangible personal development. In theory, it may be measured by both without their conflicting with one another. In practice, one or the other so tends to predominate that different, almost opposed, types of educational procedure may result. Measurement in its quantitative, statistical form fixes attention upon near-by, fairly direct results of action. Personal development is a thing of much longer time-span and lends itself to qualitative rather than quantitative judgment. It is open to the objection that it is "subjective." On the other hand, the more mature and experienced the teacher, the less will he or she be dependent upon tangible, directly applicable, external tests, and will use them, not as final, but as guides to judgment of the direction in which development is taking place. The more fully the processes of long-term growth are studied, the more objective will be the estimates of what is going on in particular individuals, while too much reliance upon special tangible tests tends to prevent attention to the conditions and laws of general growth.

387. John Dewey in the National Society for the Study of Education, Thirty-third Yearbook, Part II, *The Activity Movement* (Chicago: University of Chicago Press, 1934), pp. 84–85.

What has been said applies directly to the mooted question of educational "ends" and "objectives." The valuation of activity on the basis of close-by, tangible results tends toward formation of one type of ends and objectives; namely, those that are specific and externally definable and measurable. Consequently, acceptance of this view will dictate a program that will, although it is an activity program, differ radically from the activity program in which concrete tangible results are subordinated to an enduring long-span growth. While my own philosophy leans decidedly in the latter direction, I am here concerned more with pointing the distinction that will explain differences in so-called activity programs and aid in clarifying thinking and decision on the subject than in settling the question.

388. The Social Bearing of Examinations

It must be borne in mind that all tests and examinations are artificial; whereas life itself is the only real and natural test of educational results. . . . The artificial test is a device for forecasting the normal test of social life; and that is its essential function. That is a social, rather than a pedagogical, function; the findings constitute a criterion by which society estimates the fitness of a candidate for a given social function. The state bar and medical examinations, for example: their purpose is to determine whether the candidate is fit to function as a lawyer or a doctor. Similarly, [of] the granting of a certificate to teach. . . .

389. A Marking System Geared to Social Ideal

Competition among human beings does not necessarily nor generally mean a bitter hand to hand struggle for existence in which the weak are ruthlessly pushed aside and left to perish. It rather means a more or less conscious attempt of the individual to achieve certain ends that have been set up as social ideals. Of course it is true that in the striving for this end some will outstrip others in the race; some will arrive at the goal, or at least get reasonably near it, while others will be left far behind. However, the emphasis is not on getting the best

388. Ross L. Finney, *A Sociological Philosophy of Education* (New York: The Macmillan Company, 1928), pp. 371–372.

389. Stephen S. Colvin, "Marks and the Marking System as an Incentive to Study," *Education*, 32:563, May 1912.

of somebody else, but on the attainment of the goal. It is this socializing of the competitive instinct that has taken away from it its brutal
character and has made it one of the most valuable of humanizing
forces. In the form of the social ideal, it assures a progress that would
be impossible without it. It is a question merely of having definite
and well-recognized standards. Now, for the majority of pupils a
mark is just such a standard. It is an objectified social ideal, one
that the child can comprehend. In striving to attain this standard
he is usually thinking of the standard, not of surpassing someone else.
Such an attitude is entirely as it should be. It would be unwise to have
it otherwise.

390. Maintaining Standards

. . . it would seem evident that traditional views of education (and
philosophy) limit change to means only. This seems clearly indicated
by familiar talk about "closing the gap," "holding up standards,"
"going back to fundamentals." But experimentalism cannot see this
clean dichotomy between ends and means . . . "Ends in view" that
can *never* be reached but function only as absolute, unattainable ideals
would seem at best Pickwickian. Change can be controlled and meaningful only if ends, like means, are free to change. Any other interpretation is but reaffirmation of the very discontinuity that experimentalism is pledged to challenge.

391. Complete Accuracy of Test Results Impossible

There is no good reason for expecting tests of persons to yield the
constant results found in physical measures. Exactly the same situation can never recur and can never be presented to two different persons. We deal in human life with a series of events having common
elements but always distinguished by unique features and having thus
unique totalities. The attempt to measure one trait after another,
eventually to be summed into a total character, is doomed for two

390. George R. Geiger, "An Experimentalist Approach to Education," in the
54th Yearbook of the National Society for the Study of Education, Part I,
Modern Philosophies and Education (Published by the Society, Chicago, 1955),
p. 149.

391. Department of Superintendence, Tenth Yearbook, *Character Education*
(Washington, D.C.: National Education Association, 1932), p. 404.

reasons. One is the very simple fact that before we can get to the last traits in the series the individual will have changed in some of the aspects earlier measured. We cannot measure fast enough. Even our measuring does something to change the person we would measure. Moreover, if we could bid the sun and all events in time to stand still for our measuring, we still would have the impossible task of combining a series of rigid abstractions into an integrated whole, the parts of which interact, supplement, and compensate.

392. Democratic Significance of Statistics

Developments in government, in social philosophy, in economic organization, and in educational goals since the time of Quételet have enormously heightened our sense of the importance of all the people. More and more the modern temper relies upon statistical method in its attempts to understand and to chart the workings of the world in which we live. Particularly in those sciences which deal with human beings, whether in their physical and biological aspects or in their social, economic, and psychological relations, the spirit of our time asks that its conclusions be based not so much on the distinctive reactions of one or two individuals as upon the observation of large numbers of individuals, the measurement of their common likenesses and the extent of their diversity . . .

    ✿   ✿   ✿

The object of a statistical study is not a single event or individual but a group of events or individuals, and the outcome of a statistical investigation can never be stated as a single immutable law which is invariably true for all members of the group, but its conclusions must be stated as a tendency which is true in the main for the group but not necessarily true for any given individual in the group. Therefore the statistician speaks of trends rather than laws, of probability rather than certainty. Maxwell concluded that most research in physics is primarily statistical and on this basis he developed his kinetic theory of gases.

Clearly the majority of educational problems are concerned with groups, their main trends and the variability of individuals away from the trend of the group. Schools are not administered for a single

392. Helen M. Walker, "Democracy and Statistical Method," *Teachers College Record* (Bureau of Publications, Teachers College, Columbia University), 32:600–603, April 1931.

child but to give maximum advantages to all children. Educational philosophy is not developed by studying one child intensively, but by envisioning the common needs and problems of the many. Curricula are built for thousands of children. The laws of learning were not developed by studying isolated individuals. Even the student of the history of education likes to generalize.

✿   ✿   ✿

Fundamental and pervasive as statistical thinking is in education, it must not be supposed to be an end in itself. Statistical method is a tool for organizing facts so as to render them available for the study of the philosopher, the historian, the psychologist, the curriculum builder, the sociologist, the economist, the administrator. A statistical study can only describe what is, it cannot determine what ought to be except in so far as it may throw light upon the probable concomitants and consequences of certain situations. It is fatuous to suppose that statistical method can provide mechanical substitutes for thinking, although it is an indispensable aid to thinking in an age which wants to embrace all the people in its plans.

23

The Curriculum

Problems in the Philosophy of Education Discussed in this Section

1. What relation does the curriculum bear to race experience? To child experience? Should the curriculum be child-centered? Should the child ever have to undergo the curriculum simply because it is race experience? Can the teacher ever assume certain experiences on the part of the pupil?
2. Should the student have to learn facts? What are facts? Can facts be learned and stored away against the day of use?
3. Does the *activity* curriculum necessarily imply physical activities?
4. How far from their natural setting can curriculum materials be removed if conditions of efficient learning are to be maintained?
5. Should the curriculum be made out in advance? *Ex tempore?* How reliably can teachers foresee the kinds of problems their pupils will meet in the future?
6. Should there be a curriculum for each pupil? Should pupils help to make it?
7. Should the lay public, in the form of boards of education or legislatures, ever determine courses of instruction?

393. Common Ground of Method and Curriculum

In propagating interest in the control of ideals it is evident that the curriculum consists of methods of achieving objectives, but it is not so evident, though equally true, that all the content of the curriculum is methodic. Everything taught or discovered, recorded or achieved, has been a method . . .

In like manner facts are methods of control . . .

If we consider painting, sculpture, architecture, or literature, the same principle holds . . .

❀   ❀   ❀

393. Werrett W. Charters, *Curriculum Construction* (New York: The Macmillan Company, 1929), pp. 74–77.

443

Until quite recent years the school has been chiefly concerned with a statement of methods and only incidentally with putting the methods into practice. This distinction has been partially described in the aims of education by the terms "information" and "conduct." As a matter of common procedure the schools have sought to give information upon the assumption that the mere giving of information will influence conduct. But a different idea is now gaining ground: that in practice as well as in theory, the function of instruction is not fulfilled until the information has actually modified conduct.

394. Culture and Subject Matter

Subject matter and culture, however, are not equivalent. As noted in an earlier chapter, the culture of a people is the man-made part of the environment. The culture consists not only of facts, principles, social norms, and an infinitude of meanings, all of which comprise subject matter, but also of tools and machines, institutions, and modes of individual and social action. Subject matter is, therefore, only a part of the total culture. . . . Tools and machines are not subject matter; however, knowledge about tools and machines—about their construction, their operation, and their various uses—is subject matter.

395. A Dynamic Conception of Subject Matter

A renaming of the sciences is needed. They are noun substantives, they should be nouns participial. Reading, writing, spelling, numbering, drawing, forging, weaving, cooking, painting, when we study them, have an immense advantage over physics, chemistry, mathematics, history, logic, ethics, and literature, just because their names end in *-ing*, leaving no doubt as to their nature and the kind of service which they undertake to perform for us. The other studies do not invite us to take them by the hand. Their *-ic* and *-ry* endings intimate to us that they are not of our world and that their perfection has long since been accomplished . . .

394. B. Othanel Smith, William O. Stanley, and J. Harlan Shores, *Fundamentals of Curriculum Development* (Yonkers, N.Y.: World Book Company, copyright 1951), pp. 273–274. Quoted by permission.
    395. Ernest C. Moore, *What is Education?* (Boston: Ginn and Company, 1915), p. 344.

396. Child and Curriculum Not Opposed to Each Other

This fundamental opposition of child and curriculum . . . can be duplicated in a series of other terms. "Discipline" is the watchword of those who magnify the course of study; "interest" that of those who blazon "The Child" upon their banner. The standpoint of the former is logical; that of the latter psychological. The first emphasizes the necessity of adequate training and scholarship on the part of the teacher; the latter that of need of sympathy with the child, and knowledge of his natural instincts. "Guidance and control" are the catchwords of one school; "freedom and initiative" of the other. Law is asserted here; spontaneity proclaimed there. The old, the conservation of what has been achieved in the pain and toil of the ages, is dear to the one; the new, change, progress, wins the affection of the other. Inertness and routine, chaos and anarchism, are accusations bandied back and forth. Neglect of the sacred authority of duty is charged by one side, only to be met by counter-charges of suppression of individuality through tyrannical despotism.

❀   ❀   ❀

What, then, is the problem? It is just to get rid of the prejudicial notion that there is some gap in kind (as distinct from degree) between the child's experience and the various forms of subject-matter that make up the course of study. From the side of the child, it is a question of seeing how his experience already contains within itself elements —facts and truths—of just the same sort as those entering into the formulated study; and, what is of more importance, of how it contains within itself the attitudes, the motives, and the interests which have operated in developing and organizing the subject-matter to the plane which it now occupies. From the side of the studies, it is a question of interpreting them as outgrowths of forces operating in the child's life, and of discovering the steps that intervene between the child's present experience and their richer maturity.

Abandon the notion of subject-matter as something fixed and ready-made in itself, outside the child's experience; cease thinking of the child's experience as also something hard and fast; see it as something fluent, embryonic, vital; and we realize that the child and the curriculum are simply two limits which define a single process. Just as two

396. John Dewey, *The Child and the Curriculum* (Chicago: University of Chicago Press, 1902), pp. 14–17.

points define a straight line, so the present standpoint of the child and the facts and truths of studies define instruction. It is continuous reconstruction, moving from the child's present experience out into that represented by the organized bodies of truth that we call studies.

*   *   *

Hence, the facts and truths that enter into the child's present experience, and those contained in the subject-matter of studies, are the initial and final terms of one reality. To oppose one to the other is to set the moving tendency and the final result of the same process over against each other; it is to hold that the nature and the destiny of the child war with each other.

397. How to View the Culture of the Past

The theory that the proper subject matter of instruction is found in the culture-products of past ages (either in general, or more specifically in the particular literatures which were produced in the culture epoch which is supposed to correspond with the stage of development of those taught) affords another instance of that divorce between the process and product of growth which has been criticized. To keep the process alive, to keep it alive in ways which make it easier to keep it alive in the future, is the function of educational subject matter. But an individual can live only in the present. The present is not just something which comes after the past; much less something produced by it. It is what life is in leaving the past behind it. The study of past *products* will not help us understand the present, because the present is not due to the products, but to the life of which they were the products. A knowledge of the past and its heritage is of great significance when it enters into the present, but not otherwise. And the mistake of making the records and remains of the past the main material of education is that it cuts the vital connection of present and past, and tends to make the past a rival of the present and the present a more or less futile imitation of the past. Under such circumstances, culture becomes an ornament and solace; a refuge and an asylum. Men escape from the crudities of the present to live in its imagined refinements, instead of using what the past offers as an agency for ripening these crudities.

The present, in short, generates the problems which lead us to search the past for suggestion, and which supplies meaning to what

397. John Dewey, *Democracy and Education* (New York: The Macmillan Company, 1916), pp. 88–89.

we find when we search. The past is the past precisely because it does not include what is characteristic in the present. The moving present includes the past on condition that it uses the past to direct its own movement. The past is a great resource for the imagaination; it adds a new dimension to life, but on condition that it be seen as the past *of* the present, and not as another and disconnected world. The principle which makes little of the present act of living and operation of growing, the only thing *always* present, naturally looks to the past because the future goal which it sets up is remote and empty. But having turned its back upon the present, it has no way of returning to it laden with the spoils of the past. A mind that is adequately sensitive to the needs and occasions of the present actuality will have the liveliest of motives for interest in the background of the present, and will never have to hunt for a way back because it will never have lost connection.

398. Organization of Subjects in the Curriculum

It does not follow that the sequence appropriate to the problems of the research specialist is necessarily identical with the sequence appropriate to the citizen. The organizational pattern adopted by the research disciplines was designed for a definite and highly specialized purpose. The scholar's problem is primarily intellectual, the discovery and verification of further knowledge. He has accordingly organized his material in a way calculated to promote inquiry in a particular area of human knowledge—that is to say, in such a way that each proposition is derived from other propositions and leads to still other propositions. The very existence of subjects is due to this enterprise; there are no subjects save as scholarly abstractions useful in inquiry. For the purposes for which it was intended, this organization, especially in the physical sciences, is unquestionably one of the most brilliant achievements of man. The fact remains that it is an organization adapted to the specialized problems of the research scholar.

The problems of the man and the citizen, on the other hand, are practical problems. As such they are primarily concerned, not with the discovery of knowledge but with the making of decisions and the formulation of policy. Accordingly, material must be organized on the basis of the relationship between ends and means, rather than on the basis of the logical relationships between propositions. This does

398. B. Othanel Smith, William O. Stanley, and J. Harlan Shores, *Fundamentals of Curriculum Development* (Yonkers, N.Y.: World Book Company, copyright 1951), pp. 218–219. Quoted by permission.

not mean, of course, that practical judgments do not involve the use of propositions or that they can ignore with impunity the demands of logic. But the focus of the practical judgment is the working out of a solution of a practical problem. The difference, therefore, is that between the organization of material appropriate to the development of a systematic body of theoretical knowledge and the organization of material appropriate to the application of knowledge to the control of some practical human enterprise. In the first case, the logical relationship between propositions properly supplies the basic principle of organization; whereas, in the second case, it is the end or purpose that provides the controlling principle.

Moreover, largely as a result of the difference in focus, the issues arising in the exercise of the practical judgment almost invariably cut across the boundaries of the research disciplines. Thus the control of atomic energy, to take a single example, is a moral, economic, and political as well as a physical and chemical problem . . .

399. An Ideal-Centered Curriculum

It is better to center education in *ideals* for children and the race rather than in children themselves. After all, children are immature, dependent, and plastic members of the race. They are often irrational in their individuality. As Socrates said in effect to the Sophists, not man, but reason is the measure of all things; not individuality, but universality; not percepts, but concepts. Ideals are the norms for all human experience, including that of children. After all, it is still true that obedience to just law is a virtue, that following physical laws leads to health, that truth is something to be discovered, rather than made, that conformity is a large element even in creativity, that repression is a necessary phase of expression. Under the influence of paidocentricism (what a hybrid!) self-expression may easily become self-explosion.

400. Curriculum Not to Be Made Up Wholly of Principles

President Hutchins' proposals have two outstanding merits. They emphasize the truth too often neglected or denied in recent years that

399. Herman H. Horne, *This New Education* (New York: Abingdon Press, 1931), p. 82.

400. Charner Perry, "Education: Ideas or Knowledge?", *International Journal of Ethics*, 47:355–357, April, 1937. Copyright 1937 by the University of Chicago.

principles of order and abstract conceptual systems are logically the foundation for knowledge of particulars; and they set a confused world the good example of attempting uncompromisingly to place first in educational practice what is basic in logic.

The immediate issue is this: Does putting first in educational practice what is logically basic mean putting it first in chronological order in the curriculum? Apprehension of principles of order and clarification of conceptual systems and of general principles based thereon should be, we may grant, placed first in order of importance among the goals of education; but this does not imply that study of principles of order should come first in time, study of most abstract systems second, study of less abstract systems third, and the application of concepts to concrete material last of all. Resolution of this issue depends, however, upon examination of the relation between conceptual systems and the subject matter to which they are applied. President Hutchins' curriculum presupposes, apparently, the doctrine that principles of order may be learned, taught, or known in separation from the conceptual systems in which they are exemplified, and that conceptual systems may be apprehended and clarified in separation from the general knowledge in which they are exemplified. This doctrine, unless very carefully qualified, amounts to the assumption that concepts and principles of order are objects of knowledge in the same way particulars are.

✿   ✿   ✿

In considering how concepts are known, one must keep clearly in mind that concepts are not initially or primarily objects of knowledge. They are ordinarily and primarily ways of knowing reality and means of organizing a subject matter into orderly and systematic knowledge. Biologists do not discover a system of classification and then look around for objects to be classified. . . .

Concepts are ways of knowing reality; and to know a concept is to think about or know reality in a certain way and to be conscious of what one knows. Consequently the place to find concepts is in knowledge. One does not, to be sure, complete one's knowledge and then examine the concepts. On the contrary, attention to and clarification of concepts is essential to the development of knowledge and to the establishment of knowledge on a rational foundation. But neither can one complete his structure of concepts and then apply this structure to reality or existence. The development of knowledge of reality and the apprehension and systematization of concepts must proceed in close relation to each other. Logic cannot fruitfully either precede or follow knowledge. Logical analysis should accompany and pervade all stages of both the development and the transmission of knowledge.

✿   ✿   ✿

No conceptual systems and no general principles can be presented or understood without the use of examples. . . .

401. Formal and Instrumental Knowledge in the Curriculum

It may be remarked here that with the disappearance of the distinction between training and education, another distinction of great importance also disappeared, necessarily disappeared. I refer to the distinction between formative knowledge and instrumental knowledge. The discipline set by the Great Tradition concerned itself exclusively with formative knowledge. To justify replacing this discipline with another procedure which concerned itself chiefly with instrumental knowledge, as the procedure of training must obviously do, it became convenient to maintain that the distinction between these two orders of knowledge was quite artificial, that instrumental studies were in themselves formative, as much so as any, and altogether to be preferred on this account as well as on all others. Nothing worth having was to be gained by the intensive study of Greek and Roman literature, classical history, mathematics and formal logic, that could not be gained to better purpose by the study, say, of modern languages, English and the sciences. The revolutionary spirit had its way so completely that this distinction at once faded out of sight, and at present, probably, most of the younger spirits among us are quite unaware that it was ever drawn.

402. In Defense of Facts

It is customary among the élite of educational reformers to disparage these particular, small, specialized items of achievement in favor of higher and more far-reaching powers, such as the ability to discover and organize and apply knowledge, versatility, readiness to change to fit a changing world, and creativeness. And probably a certain amount of such disparagement is healthy. But some of it seems to me to deserve attack as uninformed, ill advised, and misleading. In any case, it is only fair that someone should defend the hum-drum details of knowledge, behavior, skill and taste. This I shall try to do.

401. Albert J. Nock, *The Theory of Education in the United States* (New York: Harcourt, Brace and Company, Inc.), 1932, pp. 60–61.

402. Edward L. Thorndike, "Facts as Objectives of Education," from "In Defense of Facts," *Journal of Adult Education*, 7:381–383, October 1935.

Limits of space confine me to the case of knowledge, but the arguments will in general apply throughout.

Mere knowledge is out of favor for many reasons. One is that the schools were indiscriminate, heaping up task after task for learning just because the task was something that could be learned, and neglecting training in organizing and using what had been learned already. Another is that where the schools did exercise discrimination, it was too often in favor of facts valuable only or chiefly as preparation for later advanced study. So the beginner in physics was taught methods of making exact measurements; the beginner in zoology learned elaborate details about the frog, the earthworm, or the grasshopper. A third reason is that much of the supposed factual information was not factual but verbal and, hence, as learned, carried very little information about reality. For example, at the tender age of five, according to traditions of the Thorndike family, I was taught in school to reel off a list of a hundred or more words naming the bones of the human body. But such achievements are not factual; they are of the nature of liturgy or incantation. These unfortunate associations of pedantry, propaedeutic exercises, and verbalism with factual knowledge have prejudiced us illogically against it.

It is also customary to contrast mere knowledge, habit, skill, and the like, unfavorably with intellectual power, character, and personality. What we should do, it is said, is to give men and women power to think, not a package of ideas; to make their characters good and strong and benevolent, not to improve petty habits; to develop healthy, integrated personalities adjusted to the real world of things and men, not to work piecemeal at this, that, and the other detail of behavior and attitude.

This contrast of general or total powers, qualities, and tendencies with particular detailed facts, habits, and attitudes, and derogation of the latter, is guilty of three cardinal errors. It assumes that such general or total powers exist as unitary traits or entities which can be changed throughout in something the same way that a man's skin can be made black all over by dipping him into a vat of ink, or that his entire blood stream can be influenced by certain drugs. The evidence goes to show that, on the contrary, specificity is the rule, and that the words naming general or total powers, qualities, and tendencies usually refer really to statistical averages and summations of particulars . . .

The contempt for mere knowledge assumes that the general or total powers, traits, and the like are easily amenable to educational influences. On the contrary, the more unitary they are, the more they are rooted in the person's original constitution, given to him by nature as

is the color of his eyes, or the type of his blood, or the number of neu-
rons in his brain, and the less amenable they are to educational influence. The general intellectual factor just mentioned—the general
intellectual ability of ordinary educational discussion—resists efforts
to increase it so obdurately that some of the most competent investi-
gators of the matter deny that it can be increased at all. It is idle to
argue that we should give men power to think, in so far as that power
is given or withheld by biological causes that are beyond our control.

The third error is neglect of the fact that whatever general total
powers, quantities, and tendencies there may be, either as unities or
as aggregates, they are modifiable only by specific ideas, habits, attitudes, and the like.

An educational reformer can talk about improving a man's character as a whole, but the only way he can do the job or any fraction of
it is by improving the actual responses the man makes to the situations
of life. The only holds he can get on character are by way of ideas,
ideals, acts, and desires, and their connections one with another and
with the events of the physical and social world.

403. Moral Quality of the Curriculum

The present curriculum emphasizes descriptive knowledge and facts
and all but neglects the moral content of the culture. Everywhere the
individual is encouraged to understand things and to perform certain
skills. He is continually asked in school such questions as: What is
this? Can you describe so and so? Can you explain this? What causes
this? Who did thus and so? Where and when did such a thing happen?
Why did it happen? Seldom, if ever, is the individual asked whether
or not a particular course of action or an event is good or bad, or by
what principle he considers it to be good or bad. These questions are
thought to be mere matters of opinion about which one person's judgment is as good as another's. Consequently, it is thought that nothing
can be gained by studying such matters.

Thus the school has followed a *laissez faire* policy with respect to
moral principles, or the rules of the game of democracy. The school
must now do an about-face on the place of moral principles in the
curriculum. It must no longer shrink from taking a clear stand when
it comes to questions of value; it must not tolerate the notion that

403. B. Othanel Smith, William O. Stanley, and J. Harlan Shores, *Fundamentals of Curriculum Development* (Yonkers, N.Y.: World Book Company, copyright
1951), pp. 111–112. Quoted by permission.

agreement on values is neither important nor feasible in a democracy. The fundamental principles comprising the core of American culture must become objects of study in the same sense and to the same degree that the principles of science are now studied. Only then can democracy as a value-system be understood and used in social action at the level of deliberate acceptance and criticism.

The heart of a culture is its universals. The heart of the universals is the values or, in other words, the rules by which people order their social existence. These rules, when built into the personalities of the individuals comprising the society, create the personality type peculiar to the culture. Hence, the heart of any satisfactory educational program consists of those basic values that give meaning to the purposes, plans, and activities of the individual.

404. Predicting Future Problems for the Curriculum

In more specific detail, by a proper study of society, its ways and its resources, we must look as far into the future as we can to catch its problems. This practice must permeate our curriculum. While we cannot be sure of the precise details of future social problems—and for real education it is better so—we can within limits foretell that certain unsolved problems will press for solution. These with proper care for age and interest will furnish excellent subject-matter for the kind of study demanded above for the unknown future. Here methods of attack upon that shifting future can be worked out and learned. That teachers do not know the answers to the problems will help, not hurt, the work. In this realm also the why of right and wrong on the big social scale may well receive an attention now too much overlooked. That vested interests will object is reason for the study rather than argument against it, but this opposition illustrates the added difficulties that emerge as soon as we take education seriously.

405. Improvising the Curriculum

An experimental school is under the temptation to improvise its subject-matter. It must take advantage of unexpected events and turn

404. William H. Kilpatrick, *Education for a Changing Civilization* (New York: The Macmillan Company, 1926), pp. 110–111.
405. John Dewey, "Progressive Education and the Science of Education," *Progressive Education*, 5:201, July–September 1928.

to account unexpected questions and interests. Yet if it permits improvisation to dictate its course, the result is a jerky, discontinuous movement which works against the possibility of making any important contribution to educational subject-matter. Incidents are momentary, but the use made of them should not be momentary or short-lived. They are to be brought within the scope of a developing whole of content and purpose, which is a whole because it has continuity and consecutiveness in its parts. There is no single subject-matter which all schools must adopt, but in every school there should be some significant subject-matters undergoing growth and formulation.

406. The Experience-Centered Curriculum

The question is sometimes raised as to whether a curriculum based upon the experience of the learner will not be fragmentary and unrelated. The answer to this problem is to be found in the size and organization of the units. If the units are small, not significant, and unrelated, atomism is certain to result. Many of the earliest experiments in what their authors conceived to be an experience-centered curriculum undoubtedly show this result. But this weakness by no means inheres in the concept of an experience-centered curriculum. Dealing with the experience of growing persons requires the facing of long, integrated units that carry with them large masses of racial experience.

In the matter of atomism, the experience-centered curriculum is under no greater danger than a subject-matter curriculum, or a curriculum built upon isolated traits and habits. It would be impossible to conceive of a more atomistic result than has followed from a course credit system which, on the whole, has assumed the form of a ledger account of "things taken." Such attempts as have been made to secure integration through correlation of subjects seek the basis of integration in subject-matter—in something entirely external to the learner's experience. It by no means follows that because subject-matter is logically integrated wthin itself it is genetically and vitally integrated in the experience of the learner.

406. William C. Bower, "The Nature, Concept and Form of the Curriculum," in Philip H. Lotz and Leonidas W. Crawford, editors, *Studies in Religious Education*. Copyright 1931 by Lamar and Whitmore. By permission of Abingdon-Cokesbury Press, Nashville, Tenn.

407. Legislative Prescription of the Curriculum

We respectfully suggest that it is not the function of legislative bodies to prescribe the detailed contents of the school curriculum. The people, through their legislative representatives, may properly formulate a general statement of the aims and purposes of education. The task, however, of discovering appropriate materials of instruction through which to achieve those aims and purposes, is a technical one of great difficulty, demanding special professional preparation. Neither the general statement of the aims and purposes of education nor the task of discovering appropriate materials can safely be left to organizations which represent minority interests. The propaganda and interference of these minority groups in school matters constitutes one of the greatest menaces in modern education.

407. National Society for the Study of Education, Twenty-sixth Yearbook, Part II, *Foundations of Curriculum Making* (Chicago: University of Chicago Press, 1927), p. 16.

24

Play and Art in Education

Problems in the Philosophy of Education Discussed in this Section

1. What is the educational significance of work and play? How do these two activities differ? When does play become fooling? When does work become drudgery?
2. Is art education a frill? Or does all education succeed or fail in proportion as it results in being artistic?
3. What is an *art?* What is the difference between the fine, industrial, and liberal arts? What kind of art is teaching?
4. Do all subjects in the curriculum have aesthetic values? Are these values always ends in themselves? Are they ever instrumental?
5. Is art as a form of self-activity in the school necessarily expressionistic? Should art work seek to approach the universal?
6. May the educational outcomes of art education be ineffable, or must they be communicable as other educational products are?
7. Is artistic education creative? Does the artistic, creative attitude to be cultivated in the child differ essentially from the problem-solving attitude? Is it necessary in art education to produce works of art?
8. Should art education serve a moral purpose?

408. The Confusion of Work and Play

It is the writer's contention . . . that a fundamental fallacy of the Progressive movement lies in its assumption that work and play can be identified under the same psychological rubric . . .

Now, quite obviously, every adult is likely to find some phases of his work enjoyable; some people find many phases of their work enjoyable. In a certain sense enjoyable work may seem like play. But no matter how enjoyable one's work, the moment that one confuses the work attitude with the play attitude one is in danger. The danger

408. William C. Bagley, *Education, Crime and Social Progress* (New York: The Macmillan Company, 1931), pp. 98–99.

lies in the quite human temptation to avoid tasks which do not make
an immediate appeal. Try as it may, the Progressive theory of education has not as yet managed to escape the fallacies of the doctrine of
immediate interest. It may use other names, but the fundamental
fallacy cannot be camouflaged by terminology; it is inherent in any
educational theory that confuses work and play. From this point of
view, its grave peril lies in the fact that in the last analysis (and very
quickly in school practice) it reduces to opportunism pure and simple.

409. Work and Play Sharply Distinguished

This activity of the mind in allowing itself to be absorbed, and
consciously so, in an object with the purpose of making it his own,
or of producing it, is *Work*. But when the mind gives itself up to
its objects as chance may present them or through arbitrariness, careless as to whether they have any result, such activity is *Play*. Work is
laid out for the pupil by his teacher by authority, but in his play he
is left to himself.

Thus work and play must be sharply distinguished from each other.
If one has not respect for work as an important and substantial activity, he not only spoils play for his pupil, for this loses all its charm
when deprived of the antithesis of an earnest, set task, but he under-
mines his respect for real existence. On the other hand, if he does not
give him space, time, and opportunity, for play, he prevents the
peculiarities of his pupil from developing freely through the exercise
of his creative ingenuity. Play sends the pupil back refreshed to his
work, since in play he forgets himself in his own way, while in work
he is required to forget himself in a manner prescribed for him by
another.

Play is of great importance in helping one to discover the true
individualities of children, because in play they may betray thoughtlessly their inclinations. This antithesis of work and play runs through
the entire life. Children anticipate in their play the earnest work of
[later] life; thus the little girl plays with her doll, and the boy pretends
he is a soldier and in battle.

Work should never be treated as if it were play, nor play as if it
were work. In general, the arts, the sciences, and productions, stand
in this relation to each other: the accumulation of stores of knowledge is the recreation of the mind which is engaged in independent

409. Karl Rosenkranz, *Pedagogics as a System*, Anna C. Brackett, translator (St.
Louis: R. P. Studley Company, 1872), pp. 14–15.

creation, and the practice of art fills the same office to those whose work is to collect knowledge.

410. Occasions for Work and Play

When fairly remote results of a definite character are foreseen and enlist persistent effort for their accomplishment, play passes into work. Like play, it signifies purposeful activity and differs *not* in that activity is subordinated to an external result, but in the fact that a longer course of activity is occasioned by the idea of a result. The demand for continuous attention is greater, and more intelligence must be shown in selecting and shaping means. To extend this account would be to repeat what has been said under the caption of aim, interest, and thinking. It is pertinent, however, to inquire why the idea is so current that work involves subordination of an activity to an ulterior material result.

The extreme form of this subordination, namely drudgery, offers a clew. Activity carried on under conditions of external pressure or coercion is not carried on for any significance attached to the doing. The course of action is not intrinsically satisfying; it is a mere means for avoiding some penalty, or for gaining some reward at its conclusion. What is inherently repulsive is endured for the sake of averting something still more repulsive or of securing a gain hitched on by others. Under unfree economic conditions, this state of affairs is bound to exist. Work or industry offers little to engage the emotions and the imagination; it is a more or less mechanical series of strains. Only the hold which the completion of the work has upon a person will keep him going. But the end should be intrinsic to the action; it should be *its* end—a part of its own course. Then it affords a stimulus to effort very different from that arising from the thought of results which have nothing to do with the intervening action. As already mentioned, the absence of economic pressure in schools supplies an opportunity for reproducing industrial situations of mature life under conditions where the occupation can be carried on for its own sake. If in some cases, pecuniary recognition is *also* a result of an action, though not the chief motive for it, that fact may well increase the significance of the occupation.

Where something approaching drudgery or the need of fulfilling externally imposed tasks exists, the demand for play persists, but tends

410. John Dewey, *Democracy and Education* (New York: The Macmillan Company, 1916), pp. 239–241.

to be perverted. The ordinary course of action fails to give adequate stimulus to emotion and imagination. So in leisure time, there is an imperious demand for their stimulation by any kind of means; gambling, drink, etc., may be resorted to. Or, in less extreme cases, there is recourse to idle amusement; to anything which passes time with immediate agreeableness. Recreation, as the word indicates, is recuperation of energy. No demand of human nature is more urgent or less to be escaped. The idea that the need can be suppressed is absolutely fallacious, and the Puritanic tradition which disallows the need has entailed an enormous crop of evils. If education does not afford opportunity for wholesome recreation and train capacity for seeking and finding it, the suppressed instincts find all sorts of illicit outlets, sometimes overt, sometimes confined to indulgence of the imagination. Education has no more serious responsibility than making adequate provision for enjoyment of recreative leisure; not only for the sake of immediate health, but still more if possible for the sake of its lasting effect upon habits of mind. Art is again the answer to this demand.

411. Neither Play at Work nor Work at Play

Play stands in contrast with work. The subjection of the individual to the demands that the environment makes on him is work. The spontaneous physical expression of individuality is play. Work is always for some ulterior end to be attained; play is always for its own sake. Work may or may not be agreeable; play is always pleasant. Work is serious; play is light. In work the universal self dominates; in play the particular private self.

❊   ❊   ❊

In the school the place of play is fundamental beside work. It affords the necessary reaction from work and preserves the individuality of the pupil. It, and not calisthenics, is the true rest from work. Without it, a return to work with zest is impossible. Its educational effects in the way of unintended preparation for later living are incalculable . . .

But as the school must not work at play, so must it be said that it must not play at work. To do everything playfully is to remain a child. The school must teach the child to do his duty, even if it is

411. Herman H. Horne, *The Philosophy of Education* (New York: The Macmillan Company, 1927), pp. 74–80.

against his inclination. Nor must children be deceived into working under the guise of play, which confusedly mixes opposite elements in life. Yet the work, as work, may be made so attractive that they will love to do it. Indeed the highest and noblest kind of work has this element of play in it, this element of joy in the activity for its own sake. Play in work is very different from play at work. Hence it is not desirable to have the school run on the sense of duty alone. The work itself should be so compelling in interest that it is freely willed, and that the element of drudgery is largely lacking . . .

412. Importance of Art in Education

The ultimate motive power, alike in science, in morality, and in religion, is the sense of value, the sense of importance. It takes the various forms of wonder, of curiosity, of reverence, of worship, of tumultuous desire for merging personality in something beyond itself. This sense of value imposes on life incredible labours, and apart from it life sinks back into the passivity of its lower types. The most penetrating exhibition of this force is the sense of beauty, the aesthetic sense of realized perfection. This thought leads me to ask, whether in our modern education we emphasize sufficiently the functions of art.

413. Creativity in School

It is an easy next step to the much disputed question of creative ability. How many have this ability? Is it widespread or is it rare? And in what does it show itself? Only in music, literature, and the fine arts? Or in all lines of human endeavor? All these questions have already been implicitly answered in the discussion on creative thinking, but it will perhaps again be well to make some specific statements. First, we cannot here limit the term "creation" to a contribution to the world's stock; that is, to those few outputs which constitute in worth positive additions to the world stock over and above anything previously existing. Psychologically speaking, any one creates who devises a response that is new to *him*. But no such creation is entirely new. Always, even with the utmost genius, there enters the factor of sug-

412. Alfred N. Whitehead, *The Aims of Education* (London: Williams and Norgate, Ltd., 1929), pp. 62–63.
413. William H. Kilpatrick, "The Essentials of the Activity Movement," *Progressive Education*, 11:354, October 1934.

gestion from some prior form or source. Thus, along any chosen line, we may form an imitation-creation scale: at the upper end, the highest known proportion of creation to the prior existing model or suggestion; at the lower end, the least of this creation and the greatest known amount of mere adoption and imitation. On such a scale we can readily arrange that all men should somewhere fall, thus forming probably an approximation to the normal distribution curve. We all create in greater or less degree. Specifically, there appears no just reason for limiting creation to music, literature, and the fine arts. Statesmanship can show its scale and so can cooking, plowing, generalship, and science. There is no line of human activity that does not so distribute itself.

414. The Role of Appreciation

In one of its meanings, appreciation is opposed to depreciation. It denotes an enlarged, an *intensified* prizing, not merely a prizing, much less—like depreciation—a lowered and degraded prizing. This enhancement of the qualities which make any ordinary experience appealing, appropriable—capable of full assimilation—and enjoyable, constitutes the prime function of literature, music, drawing, painting, etc., in education. They are not the exclusive agencies of appreciation in the most general sense of that word; but they are the chief agencies of an intensified, enhanced appreciation. As such, they are not only intrinsically and directly enjoyable, but they serve a purpose beyond themselves. They have the office, in increased degree, of all appreciation in fixing taste, in forming standards for the worth of later experiences. They arouse discontent with conditions which fall below their measure; they create a demand for surroundings coming up to their own level. They reveal a depth and range of meaning in experiences which otherwise might be mediocre and trivial. They supply, that is, organs of vision. Moreover, in their fullness they represent the concentration and consummation of elements of good which are otherwise scattered and incomplete. They select and focus the elements of enjoyable worth which make any experience directly enjoyable. They are not luxuries of education, but emphatic expressions of that which makes any education worth while.

✸   ✸   ✸

414. John Dewey, *Democracy and Education* (New York: The Macmillan Company, 1916), pp. 278–281.

And what has been said about appreciation means that every study in one of its aspects ought to have just such ultimate significance. It is as true of arithmetic as it is of poetry that in some place and at some time it ought to be a good to be appreciated on its own account— just as an enjoyable experience, in short. If it is not, then when the time and place come for it to be used as a means or instrumentality, it will be in just that much handicapped. Never having been realized or appreciated for itself, one will miss something of its capacity as a resource for other ends.

415. The Creative and Problem-Solving Attitudes Contrasted

Students of the creative act maintain that there is a difference between the process of problem-solving (in which assimilation plays the leading role) and that of creative self-expression and contemplative awareness. The instrumentalists deny this. They maintain that the assimilative act and the creative act are merely differing aspects of the same general procedure of learning. Always protagonists of the unity of experience, they maintain that those who distinguish between "assimilation" and "creation" are resorting to a dualism.

*   *   *

Consider, first, the attitudes orienting the act of problem-solving. In confronting a problem, the worker is oriented outward . . .

In the creative attitude, however, the orientation is inward. It is subjective, not objective as in problem-solving. The creating process is propelled by an inner urge to objectify moods, to portray overtly personal integrations of meaning, generalization, and emotion . . .

There is also a second distinction. Whereas the "problem" of the problem-solver is external to the individual, the "problem" of the artist is internal. There is a difference in definiteness.

*   *   *

Now compare the appreciative attitude with that of problem-solving and creating. The former has resemblance to both of them, but it is much more like the creative attitude than that of problem-solving. What are its elements? Although it is stimulated by external condi-

415. Harold Rugg, *Culture and Education in America* (New York: Harcourt, Brace and Company, Inc., copyright 1931), pp. 364–370.

tions, it is not really oriented externally. It is oriented by the internal personal gathering-together of the self . . .

In all three of these attitudes there is of course meaning, generalization, physical adjustment, and emotional content, but there are distinctive differences in their amount and integration. The appreciative and creative attitudes are effective only to the degree to which they are highly charged with emotion. The problem-solving attitude is effective only to the degree that the worker maintains emotion at a low ebb. This does not mean that the problem-solver is not also gathered together emotionally. He is concentrated intently on his task. Sometimes a thrilling orientation is perhaps essential to success. On the other hand it is frequently the emotional intensity of concentration that inhibits the making of appropriate generalizations.

416. A Taste for the Discipline of Studies

If we need to be sustained in our educational planning, as no doubt we do, by some principle of high generality, we might do well, accordingly, to turn to the relatively neglected field of *aesthetic* experience. In speaking of "the creative nature of learning" or "the art of getting an education," we often assume, in a casual way, the existence of some parallel between the activity of a learner and that of an artist. Taken sufficiently seriously, the experience of the artist might be expected to provide some valuable clues to the purposes of higher education.

Let us begin, then, by reflecting upon the circumstances attending genuine artistic creativity. We shall, of course, not be so romantic or simple-minded as to conceive of the artist as impressing upon his chosen material a vision which forms and completes itself in the seclusion of his imagination. The relation between the artist and his material is a great deal more complex and more interesting; no work of art springs fully formed from its creator, and the process of externalizing a design in the sensuous medium is an essential aid to self-criticism and self-correction. But the material is not merely a medium for the tentative embodiment of the artist's design—a mode of expression and nothing more. There is, rather, in all artistic creation a characteristic *tension* between the man and the material in which he works. The artist will not gladly think of material as wholly passive; it has for him "a kind of life of its own."

416. Max Black, "Education as Art and Discipline," *Ethics*, 54:290–293, July 1944. Copyright 1944 by the University of Chicago.

Thus the relation between artist and material, far from being that of active agent to passive substance, tends rather to resemble human contest. As in all social interaction (but in combat most conspicuously), the tentative purpose and actions of the participant are constantly modified and determined by awareness of and adaptations to the protagonist, so also in the practice of the arts, the artist literally *wrestles* with his material, while it both resists and nourishes his intention.

It is not hard to see why this should be so. To create a work of art having a determinate form is to reveal a potentiality of the material used. Now the form is not a kind of rubber stamp pressed upon the material; the artist must *learn*, by repeated and endless experiment, what the material can do and how far it can satisfy his creative intention. Such knowledge does not lie on the surface; the creation of a work of art is likely to proceed, not by some smooth manipulative adaptation, but far more often by a process of stubborn interaction, for the term "conflict" is not too strong a description. The incidental difficulty of the process (and it may be considerable) is unimportant: there is a kind of difficulty, often experienced by the ungifted, which arises from a sheer failure to understand or master the medium. But the gifted artist meets with a different and educative resistance, which is one of the sources of that energy of artistic creation so striking to the onlooker. He finds himself constantly excited by the qualities objectively present in the material which it is his aim progressively to discover. All art is, in an important sense, a process of education of the artist in the possibilities of the medium.

So important is this "resistance" of the material, as a necessary condition for aesthetic tension, that the artist will resent any attempt, by the use of mechanical aids, to blur or muffle those objective and resistant qualities by whose mastery his own intention becomes evident to himself and visibly manifest in the final work of art. Artistic creation demands respect for the materials of creation. At its best, such respect merges into a love for the intrinsic nature of the material upon which all artistic integrity is founded.

The sacrifices and renunciations, the schooling in self-criticism which such a love demands, make it proper to speak of the practice of an art as a "discipline." But the discipline of art must not be confused with that of a drill sergeant or taskmaster. Inasmuch as mastery of the material means for an artist the molding of it into an expression of himself, there can be no question of subjection to alien authority, and the tension of all creation comes increasingly to be felt as an *internal* struggle, joyfully accepted, for self realization.

How far do these considerations apply to the process of learning?

There are some obvious differences, to be sure. The student is not expected to make original contributions to knowledge. . . .

        ❅   ❅   ❅

Education so conceived is very far from being a performance in which the learner is a mere passive spectator. If the subject is to detain him, fix his thought, and feed his interest, "giving a colour to his excitement which would be different with a different subject matter," his attitude toward the subject must resemble very closely that of an artist toward his material. He, too, must respect his subject matter in a manner which depends essentially upon his belief in the independent existence of its potentiality for value; he, too, must be prepared to enter into that complex relation of submission and mastery from which the *discipline* of the art emerges.

        ❅   ❅   ❅

Certainly, the nature of what consitutes objectivity varies from one subject to another. . . . But what is here being evoked in general terms is familiar in the experience of ordinary men and women no less than of scholars. Respect for a material, recognition of objectivity, submission to the conditions limiting and forming creative activity, self-discipline in the service of an ideal, are admirable qualities displayed by most people at some times and in some occupations—in household skills, sports, and personal relations. The problem of any university is to arouse and foster such qualities in the more remote fields of intellectual and aesthetic activity—to provide the conditions in which the student will be inspired by a passion for truth and beauty which will shrink from no extremes of self-discipline to achieve its ends.

I am inclined to believe that the aesthetic aspects of the learning process have in general been too much underrated and neglected by educational theorists. It may be that the fascination exercised upon immature minds by Marxist dialectic or the pretentious classifications of our contemporary pseudo-Thomists arises from some groping desire for simplicity and harmony. There is an aesthetic satisfaction in finding data marshalling themselves in order—provided one can forget that the order has been predetermined and the facts selected to fit. The patterns and the orders which reveal themslves in the more objective pursuit of truth are inevitably more complex and so, for the cultivated taste, less agreeable. It should be a prime object of higher education, in so far as it is committed to the cultivation of the intellectual virtues, to encourage and develop a taste for the more austere but, in the end, more satisfying aesthetic progressively to be discovered in the realms of objective facts and values.

417. Stages in a Child's Aesthetic Development

There seem to be three general stages in the child's aesthetic development. First is a period of undifferentiated aesthetic response, when any experience may be a thrilling affair—the dabbling in sounds, color, and social responses—without any understanding of its general significance. The happy expectant attitude of children as they explore all the elements of their surroundings without any practical purpose, and with complete disregard of their significance, is a pure, unmediated, aesthetic attitude. We do the child injustice when we attribute a purpose other than that of pure experiencing to these activities. If we smile at the romanticists who thought the child in his pensive moods was remembering heaven, we should be dismayed at the sentimentalism of the psychologist who thinks the child is consciously trying to make a practical adjustment. It is this pure interest in experience for its own sake that Dewey has called the "childlike" attitude, and in which he sees so much merit for learning.

The transition to the second stage of development takes place with the emergence of significance attaching to those previously purposeless responses. Some responses naturally result in pain, others with a moral bearing bring punishment; but most important of all, the child learns that he has power as an agent to bring about consequences. As this relation between acts and consequences dawns on him, he is aware of purpose, and may be aware of its correlate, responsibility. At the same time, the aesthetic or feeling phase of the experience becomes mediated, differentiated. His experiences bring pleasure in so far as his purposes are fulfilled, and frustration in so far as they are not realized. It is during this stage that the child enters the public school and engages in the planned activities of that institution. The second stage supersedes the first, but naturally the aesthetic content is not superseded unless through instructional perversion. Experiences may be practical or for pleasure, as one may play a game in order to return to a necessary task relaxed and refreshed, or merely for the pleasure of playing it. In the first case the game is a means to an end, in the second it is an end in itself. In both cases the pleasure may be the same, and one cannot differentiate between the aesthetic quality in either case. If, however, the "recreational" purpose of games is stressed, if one is told to play so that he can work better, or because he will be regarded

417. William J. Sanders, in *The Public School and Spiritual Values,* Seventh Yearbook, John Dewey Society (New York: Harper & Brothers, 1944), pp. 182–189.

as a good fellow, or because it is required, or because when he grows up he will make better business or professional contacts through skill in playing games, the aesthetic quality will probably be lost; in such cases we say the "pleasure has been taken out of it." This reaction does not so frequently occur because the emphasis in physical education today is largely on playing the game for the fun there is in it.

*   *   *

Arrested development may be caused in school when the practical is emphasized at the expense of the aesthetic. When art is regarded as skill in communication through words, painting, and music, for example, it is subordinated to something external to itself and is maintained on the level of a means. This tendency is the tendency of the new philistinism that sees social significance in all activities to the exclusion of beauty; it is an evangelical puritanism, the only spiritual interest of which is moral. Those with this point of view take upon themselves the responsibility of using all arts as techniques for ameliorative social organization—a very good purpose in its place, but unfortunate when it overrides the aesthetic development of children or adults.

The third stage is reached when the person is mature and cultivated sufficiently to feel the aesthetic experience as a mediated whole. In the first stage there is unmediated experience—just experience without apparent relation of means and ends except of the vaguest sort. In the second stage mediation takes place; means are differentiated from ends, and the relation between them is understood. But the stress is on the ends—on accomplishment, mastery of what is external to the experience itself. If development is not arrested at the second stage, means and ends become identified within a whole pattern, although the distinction between them is not lost. There is greater unity. The end is not beyond and outside of the means, nor is the means inferior to the end, but merely subordinated to it in the unified whole.

Aesthetics is not mere feling, but feelings induced by insight into the perfect pattern of means and ends. The aesthetic response, then, requires cultivation. It is not an intellectual matter in the sense of being exclusively intellectual. It is an affair involving the intellect, de-desires, and emotions in such a perfect totality of pattern that the cultivated intellect does not appear to be important in the response, although it could not be achieved without intellectual insight. It is from this perfectly clear unity of means and ends, made possible by the act of insight, that the intense feeling of enjoyment arises.

Can practical arts give such satisfaction? Indeed they can, but the satisfaction is not so lasting or so bountifully recurrent. The craftsman delights in making a perfect object, but the perfection of the object is measured by its success in fulfilling the purpose for which it was designed, not by the delight it gives . . .

The question may be asked, "Does not art have a moral purpose, and should not the work of art make a man better morally?" Fine art does not have a moral purpose expressly, for if it did, it would have an end beyond itself to which it is subordinated. If music, painting, literature, or drama stimulate licentiousness or immorality, or were created for the purpose of doing so, the particular art product is not fine art, because it was designed for an end beyond itself. Yet true works of art (and art will mean hereafter fine arts; the practical arts will be so designated) will be good in the moral sense. Art does not preach moral lessons, in other words, but moral lessons may be drawn from it.

*   *   *

Dewey criticizes the tendency to distinguish the fine arts as something beyond and superior to the practical arts because they are objects of pursuit by an esoteric, leisured few; but this does not mean that the distinction between them can be ignored. What Dewey is attacking is the attitude that deprives the practical arts of aesthetic value and would exclude the aesthetic experience from the lives of people in general who had little opportunity for contact with the fine arts. There is nothing in his writings that would identify the fine and practical arts without distinction; but this, unfortunately, has been overlooked by some of his interpreters. The aesthetic quality of practical experience should be exploited to its utmost, and the child should be given every opportunity to enjoy what might be called "pure" experience, a term used here simply for the purpose of distinction. The applied sciences are distinguished from the pure sciences on the same basis that practical art is distinguished from fine art, and in philosophy there is a similar distinction generally made between practical reason or ethics, and pure reason, or metaphysics. Our concern here is with the spiritual, or aesthetic, values that reside in the experiences of the curriculum, whether they come under the guise of fine or practical arts, and the manner in which these values can be realized through instruction.

418. Detractors of Art Education Answered

To me, the fundamental detractors of the arts in America today may be classified loosely as the "Philistines," the "Puritans," the "Pro-

418. Kenneth D. Benne, "Art Education as the Development of Human Resources," *Art Education Today* (New York: Columbia University Press, 1948), pp. 2–4.

fessors," and the "Patriots." (I am putting these in quotation marks to indicate that they represent typical points of view prominent in each class of people named, not the viewpoint of all members of each class.) I hope we can find, in discussing these detractors, what the justification of art education cannot properly be and thus clear away the underbrush which hides an adequate positive justification.

The "Philistine" is inveterately the foe of the arts. And, while the boundaries of the United States seem today less nearly coincident with the boundaries of "Philistia" than they seemed to many in the late 1920's, the "Philistine" is still prominent among us. The arts, the "Philistine" is likely to say, bake no bread; the arts meet no payrolls; the arts make no direct contribution to the practical, pecuniary life of our economy. The "Philistine" is likely to be airily generous, if well-to-do, toward the arts as a woman's pastime, as evidence of conspicuous and wasteful "culture." He will admit that leisure, when the important work of the day is done, needs the arts for relaxation, for getting distracted minds off the cares and worries of practical life.

We cannot accept the "Philistine's" dismissal of the arts from any influence or consequence in the *processes* of practical production of goods and services. We know, after William Morris and Thorstein Veblen, that much of the disease of modern production is its abolition of the instinct of workmanship from processes of production and its glorification of pecuniary, extrinsic profit as the central motivation of practical life. We know further that artistic motivation and aesthetic sensitivity must be restored to the work life of men and women if health is to be restored to our body politic. If art experience is to have its full effect in freeing and sensitizing the qualitative choices of men in practical life, the controls and motivations of production, which the "Philistine" accepts and condones, must be basically changed.

Art education should not compromise with the "Philistine" by relegating the arts to the periphery of life or of education, to leisure-time "therapy" for the enervating character of "practical" industrial and business pursuits. Nor should the art educator promise the "Philistine" that the products of an education imbued with the sensitivity and spirit of art experience will furnish docile and efficient cogs in a humanly stultifying industrial machine. Good art education will rather make good rebels against unaesthetic or anaesthetic conditions in practical life.

No more can the art educator properly compromise with the "Puritan." "Puritans," whether in Plato's *Republic*, in Massachusetts Bay Colony, or in our country today have always feared the arts for endearing the potential qualitative richness of life in this world to those who experience the arts deeply. "Puritans" always urge some absolute principles of morality, based often on dubious revelation, against the disorder and chaos, as it seems to them, of human life and experience. The artist whose choices of action are determined by the possibilities of the most satisfying qualitative experience in any situation continually threatens the arbitrary power of the "Puritan's" absolute morality over the wills and hearts of men. The "Puritan" will accept the arts only if they lend their power to propagandizing for his preconceived pattern of life and morals.

Now, the educator who promises that art education will underwrite any absolute scheme of morals, will exalt thrift or fidelity or abstinence or whatnot as guides to life, is false to the spirit of art and artist deeply realized. It is not that experience in the arts is amoral or immoral. Far from it. It is rather that experience in the arts, properly interpreted, teaches a morality counter to all absolute moralities. The ultimate guide of the artist-moralist is a freed and sensitive qualitative intelligence. The moral goal of a society in which the arts flourish near its center is an aesthetically rich and satisfying experience for all men. We must oppose the "Puritan's" view of life and art if we are to advance art education in the education of the public.

Nor is the positivist "Professor" an advocate of an integral place for the arts in life and education. The "Professor's" view of the proper end of life and education is the growth and accumulation of factual knowledge. The "Professor" often argues rightly that the growth of intelligence is the prime condition of the release and development of human resources in our day. But the positivist "Professor" has a far too limited view of intelligence. He identifies the method of intelligence with the method of science, with the method of validating factual knowledge. Sensitivity to the qualities of human experience, discrimination among these qualities, emotional identification with the course of action which promises to lead to the optimum qualitative richness in the lives of people—these have little or no place in the "Professor's" scheme of intelligence. The artist as artist has no quarrel with science and factual knowledge unless he happens also to be an obscurantist. He knows that factual knowledge is a necessary condition to the full development of human potentialities for ordered and richly satisfying experience. But he knows too that knowledge must be imagined if it is to be employed sensitively and wisely for human development. He knows that emotionally starved or distraught and qualitatively blind people are the more dangerous for having the skill and cunning which science gives alike to whole men or to part men. And he must insist that any adequate conception of human intelligence should be nurtured at once by the sensitivity and discrimination of the artist and by the accurate knowledge of the possibilities and limitations of human action which the method of the scientist provides.

The art educator who justifies art experience in the curriculum by the positive knowledge it helps students to acquire, whether knowledge of biology, physics, or social science, has found only a "Professor's" justification for art activity. The art educator who strives to make his subject academically respectable in the eyes of his positivist brethren by developing a factual content to be memorized, a content blended of art history, time-honored critical judgments, and statistics, about the arts, and by testing growth in his program by measures of the mastery of this content has sold his soul to the positivistic "Professor." He is no firm friend of art education as the development of human resources.

Nor can we let the "Patriot" seduce us as art educators if we are seeking to build art experience deeply into the process of developing a sane and ordered and humanly satisfying world. It is easy to purchase support in certain quarters today, when a dying nationalism attempts frantically to involve an infant world order in its own death agony, by asserting the pure and essential "Americanism" of our intent and of our craft. A declaration of independence from our old colonial status in European art may degenerate from a valid critique of the evils of any dependent colonialism into a tasteless exaltation of American arts *qua* American. The cultivation of native themes and the use of native subjects may lose the innocent character of working with and out of the materials of our own present experience to shape a more adequate experience and may acquire the quality of chauvinistic propaganda. If we condemn our nationalistic art critics for being hobbled by the "Patriots," we must also condemn the judgment of the art educator who makes the propagation of American modes and styles, current or "antique," his touchstone of criticism. We must equally deplore the judgment of the art educator who seeks a complete "correlation" of art activity with American history.

It is right that we use the materials of our experience, our American experience, in attempts to find a more adequate articulation of that experience. But we are false to the potentially universal humanity of art experience if we seek to mold this experience in support of exclusive nationalistic shibboleths and attitudes. At the best, such attitudes are less than human in their intent and scope of communication; in our day, when world cooperation is a pressing practical need and not a remote theory, such attitudes have become downright antihuman.

If we try now to state the positive impact of our critique of fundamental detractors of the arts and of attempts by art educators to appease these detractors, it boils down to something like this. We should insist that the influence of the arts must permeate the practical choices of men, must help to provide a critique of current processes of organizing and motivating the pursuits of men. We cannot limit the arts to a leisure-time compartment of our lives, much as the "Philistine" may urge such a role for art. We must insist that the arts are not irrelevant to morality but that they offer an experimenal, humanist morality counter to all preordained, absolute systems of morality. We must see that the arts are no foe of science and knowledge but that they are supremely pertinent to the determination of the uses to which we put our knowledge. The sciences must be completed by the arts if sensitive and humane judgment concerning the uses of our technology are to be achieved. And artistic activity should today be dedicated to improvement of universal humanity, not of Americans or any other nationals only.

25

Student Discipline and Government

Problems in the Philosophy of Education Discussed in this Section

1. Is good discipline a prerequisite to good instruction or a product thereof? Why is society by and large law-abiding? Under what circumstances is it least so? What corollaries can be drawn for the school?
2. Is school discipline sometimes necessary at any price? Should the nature of the inner response of the pupil ever be sacrificed for the outward appearance of law and order?
3. Is a teacher ever justified in gaining social control through the use of ridicule or coercion? Can a teacher use these means and yet treat the child as an end? Are state laws wise that prohibit corporal punishment?
4. If the teacher resorts to punishment, on what theory should it be administered?
5. In student self-government, should children exercise actual power or should power only be loaned to them subject to recall or review?

419. Spare the Rod and Spoil the Child

He that loveth his son will continue to lay stripes upon him, that he may have joy of him in the end. He that chastiseth his son shall have profit of him, and shall glorify of him among his acquaintance . . . He that maketh too much of his son shall bind up his wounds; and his heart will be troubled at every cry. An unbroken horse becometh stubborn; and a son left at large becometh headstrong. Cocker thy child, and he shall make thee afraid; play with him, and he will grieve thee. Laugh not with him, lest thou have sorrow with him; and thou shalt gnash thy teeth in the end. Give him no liberty in his youth, and wink not at his follies. Bow down his neck in his youth, and beat him on the sides while he is a child, lest he wax stubborn, and be disobedient unto thee; and there shall be sorrow to thy soul. Chastise

419. *Ecclesiasticus*, II, xxi.

thy son, and take pains with him, lest his shameless behaviour be an offense unto thee.

420. On Obedience and Punishment

Obedience, above all things, is an essential trait in the character of a child, particularly that of a pupil. It is twofold: first, it is an obedience to the *absolute* will of him who directs; but it is, secondly, an obedience to a *will regarded as rational and good.* Obedience can be derived from constraint, and then it is *absolute,* or from confidence, and then it is of the other kind. This *voluntary* obedience is very important; but the former is also externally necessary, since it prepares the child for the accomplishment of such laws as he will have to fulfil later as a citizen, even if they do not please him.

Children must, therefore, be under a certain law of necessity; but this law must be a universal one which is to be especially observed in schools. The teacher must show no predilection, no preference for one child; for otherwise the law ceases to be universal. As soon as the child sees that all others are not subjected to the same law as he, he becomes presumptuous.

It is always said that everything should be presented to children in such a manner that they will do it from *inclination.* Without doubt this is good in many cases, but there is also much that must be prescribed for them as *duty.* This will be of very great value during their whole life; for, in public duties, in the labors of an office, and in many other instances, duty alone, not inclination, can guide us. Even if we suppose that the child does not perceive the duty, it is none the less better if he be given the idea of it; and, while he can easily see his duty as a child, it is much more difficult to perceive that something is his duty as a man. If he could see this also, which is not possible before maturer years, his obedience would be more perfect.

All transgression of a command by a child is a lack of obedience, and this entails punishment. Even if the transgression is due simply to negligence, correction is not useless. This punishment is either *physical* or *moral.*

Moral punishment is that which affects our desire to be honored and loved, this being auxiliary to morality; for example, when the child is shamed and treated coldly and reservedly. These inclinations should be preserved as far as possible. This kind of punishment, there-

420. Immanuel Kant, quoted in Edward F. Buchner, *The Educational Theory of Immanual Kant* (Philadelphia: J. B. Lippincott Company, 1904), pp. 188–192.

fore, is the best, since it comes to the aid of morality; for example, if a child lies, a look of scorn is sufficient and most suitable.

Physical punishment consists either in the refusal of that which the child desires or in the infliction of chastisement . . .

Disobedience entails punishment. This is either really *natural,* brought by man upon himself by his own conduct; for example, the child falls ill if he eats too much; and these forms of punishment are the best, for man experiences them, not only in his childhood, but throughout his whole life; or it is *artificial.* The desire to be esteemed and loved is a sure means of making chastisements durable. Physical means should serve merely to supplement the insufficiency of moral punishments. When the latter are of no avail, and recourse is had to the former, the formation of a good character ceases. But in the beginning physical constraint supplies the deficiency of reflection in the child.

421. Responsibility and Freedom

Having enumerated these four cardinal duties in the schoolroom— regularity, punctuality, silence, and industry—let us now note their higher significance reaching beyond the schoolroom into the building of character for life. The general form of all school work is that of obedience. The will of the pupil comes into relation with the will of the teacher and yields to its sway. The will of the pupil inhibits its own wayward impulses, suppresses them, and supplants them by a higher rational will. In the act of obedience to a higher will the pupil becomes conscious of responsibility. Responsibility implies a sense of freedom. The child becomes conscious of its ability to accept or refuse —to obey or disobey. It becomes conscious of its power to originate actions and to give a new form to the chain of causation in which it finds itself. The great fact in the schoolroom is that the pupil is held responsible at each and every moment for all that he does. If he forgets himself and uses his voice, if he whispers, if he moves from his seat, if he pushes a book off his desk by accident, all these things are brought back to him at once by the presiding teacher. He is responsible not only for positive acts but also for neglect. Whatever he does or whatever he leaves undone is his business; this is justly regarded as the most potent means of ethical instruction. To use the language of the founder of the great system of ethics in modern times, Immanuel

421. W. T. Harris, "School Discipline," *The Third Yearbook of the National Herbart Society* (Chicago: The University of Chicago Press, 1908), pp. 65–66.

Kant, the child learns in the school to have a sense of his "transcendental freedom." He learns that he and not his environment is responsible for what he does or leaves undone. He regards himself as the author of his deed; he recognizes it as true that he is in the midst of a flowing stream of causation; he is the focus of innumerable influences, all tending to move him in this or that direction or hold him in this or that position. But he recognizes himself as an original cause, a will power that can react on any and all the influences that are flowing inwards towards himself. He can modify this stream of causation; he can hold back and inhibit the several influences which flow towards him; he can shape all of these so as to conform them to the ideals of his freedom; he can act in such a way as to extend his influence upon the external world and upon his fellow human beings; he can act so as to realize his ethical ideals. This is the sense of transcendental freedom. Transcendental freedom does not mean that any person can do or perform anything that he wishes upon the external world, for that would be not merely transcendental freedom but absolute omnipotence. Transcendental freedom is not omnipotence, but the power to originate some modifications upon the stream of causality within which one finds himself. Freedom means self-determination instead of the determination of something else. The fact that a person could not modify anything in the world would not prevent him from having a transcendent freedom in case he could inhibit the influence flowing in upon him; if he could resist external influence he would thereby prove his freedom.

422. Breaking the Child's Will

This brings me to the particular matter of "breaking a child's will." This usually means compelling him to follow the parent's choice rather than his own. It is better not to join this issue, not to conquer a child. Anticipate the issue; if the matter be important, decide it yourself in advance before allowing the child to reach or state his decision; if the matter is not over-important, leave him to decide for himself; even at some risk. If in an important matter the child's will is fixed, do not so much cross as circumvent him. Children raised in abject submission to parents become tyrants as adults; those whose wills were never broken, whose spirits were never crushed within them,

422. Herman H. Horne, *Idealism in Education* (New York: The Macmillan Company, 1923), p. 139.

make forceful and resolute characters. If you would make weak and irresolute men and women, break their wills as children.

423. The Social Basis of Discipline

I do not wish to refer to the traditional school in ways which set up a caricature in lieu of a picture. But I think it is fair to say that one reason the personal commands of the teacher so often played an undue role and a reason why the order which existed was so much a matter of sheer obedience to the will of an adult was because the situation almost forced it upon the teacher. The school was not a group or community held together by participation in common activities. Consequently, the normal, proper conditions of control were lacking. Their absence was made up for, and to a considerable extent had to be made up for, by the direct intervention of the teacher, who, as the saying went, "*kept* order." He kept it because order was in the teacher's keeping, instead of residing in the shared work being done.

424. Discipline Born of Active Work

Of course, order is simply a thing which is relative to an end. If you have the end in view of forty or fifty children learning certain set lessons, to be recited to a teacher, your discipline must be devoted to securing that result. But if the end in view is the development of a spirit of social cooperation and community life, discipline must grow out of and be relative to this. There is little order of one sort where things are in process of construction; there is a certain disorder in any busy workship; there is not silence; persons are not engaged in maintaining certain fixed physical postures; their arms are not folded; they are not holding their books thus and so. They are doing a variety of things, and there is the confusion, the bustle, that results from activity. But out of occupation, out of doing things that are to produce results, and out of doing these in a social and cooperative way, there is born a discipline of its own kind and type.

423. John Dewey, *Experience and Education* (New York: The Macmillan Company, 1938), pp. 60–61.
424. John Dewey, *The School and Society* (Chicago: University of Chicago Press, 1900), pp. 30–31.

425. Discipline in the Progressive School

In the matter of discipline the progressive school is even more subject to attack. If a child misbehaves in an old-fashioned school, he is naughty and his parents meekly undertake to see that he stops giving trouble. If he misbehaves in a modern school, the school is spoiling him, it has no standards of conduct, it sets no store by those sterling qualities obedience and orderliness. It is probably true that a progressive school seems disorderly to visitors who cannot imagine a school except as a place where rows of silent children sit quietly at desks until told to do something by a teacher. But modern education does not aim at this kind of order. Its aim is the kind of order that exists in a roomful of people, each one of whom is working at a common task. There will be talking, consulting, moving about in such a group whether the workers are adults or children. The standard for order and discipline of a group is not how silent is the room, or how few and uniform the kinds of tools and materials that are being used, but the quality and amount of work done by the individuals and the group. A different technique is required of the teacher in such a room from that required by a teacher in a room where each pupil sits at a screweddown desk and studies the same part of the same lesson from the same textbook at the same time.

*   *   *

Many others who grew up under the stern old adage, "Spare the rod and spoil the child," cannot bear, apparently, to believe that any more pleasant or congenial method of learning can possibly be good for the young. They cherish many vestiges of the old idea that children are little limbs of Satan and that the only way to bend them to the uses of civilization is force and long training in doing things just because they are told to do them, regardless of whether or not the work is of any immediate use or interest. Without this training, they claim, one will never be able to see a difficult or dull job through to completion in later life. The strong moralistic bias that colors these views seems to make it impossible for their holders to see that in giving meaning, in his own daily life, to the work a child does, there is actually a gain in the disciplinary value of the work, rather than a loss. There is gain because the work is immediately valuable and satis-

425. John Dewey, *Education Today*, pp. 276–279. Copyright 1940 by John Dewey. Courtesy of G. P. Putnam's Sons.

factory to the child. Therefore his best effort goes into it and his critical powers and initiative are exercised and developed. Moral and intellectual powers increase in vigor when the force of the worker's spontaneous interest and desire to accomplish something are behind them. This is as true of children as of adults. It is these powers that the progressive schools seek to release. If they sometimes fail, if they sometimes make mistakes, it must be remembered that their techniques are still being developed, that they are new. We should remember, too, that the time-honored and hoary techniques of the traditional school do not always succeed in teaching every pupil to extract square roots fluently, or to be able to push every difficult and wearisome task through to a triumphant conclusion. How much shirking and bluffing goes on in old-fashioned schools?

426. Some Physical Coercion is Inescapable

Discipline by force is not direct education; but it is, at times, and with a minority of the children, a condition of education. Such discipline in school is precisely what the policeman and the jail are in the community. You must have your policeman and jailer to protect the community against the two per cent of its citizens who lack the normal domestic, economic, social, and civic interests in life. In the same way, there must be a policeman and jailer quality in every teacher; and, figuratively speaking, there must be a billy, a pair of hand-cuffs, and a cell in every school. No school is any more safe without them, than a community. They are essential to the prosecution of its work; and they check bad habits, and induce good habits in the obstreperous individual.

Furthermore, this background of inexorable, impartial discipline must win on every issue it joins, and fight every battle, if need be, to the bitter end . . .

427. Punishment by State and School Contrasted

Punishment as an educational means is nevertheless essentially corrective, since, by leading the youth to a proper estimation of his fault

426. William D. Hyde, *The Teacher's Philosophy* (Boston: Houghton Mifflin Company, 1910), pp. 10–11. Used by permission of the publishers.

427. Karl Rosenkranz, *Pedagogics as a System*, Anna C. Brackett, translator (St. Louis: R. P. Studley Company, 1872), p. 20.

and a positive change in his behavior, it seeks to improve him. At the same time it stands as a sad indication of the insufficiency of the means previously used . . .

In the statute-laws, punishment has the opposite office. It must first of all satisfy justice, and only after this is done can it attempt to improve the guilty. If a government should proceed on the same basis as the educator it would mistake its task, because it has to deal with adults, whom it elevates to the honorable position of responsibility for their own acts. The state must not go back to the psychological ethical genesis of a negative deed. It must assign to a secondary rank of importance the biographical moment which contains the deed in process and the circumstances of a mitigating character, and it must consider first of all the deed in itself. It is quite otherwise with the educator; for he deals with human beings who are relatively undeveloped, and who are only growing toward responsibility. So long as they are still under the care of a teacher, the responsibility of their deed belongs in part to him. If we confound the standpoint in which punishment is administered in the state with that in education, we work much evil.

428. Inflexible School Discipline

The inevitable consequence is the lowering of our standards, a nonchalant contempt upon the part of the pupils for properly constituted authority, and, in extreme cases, the prevalence of disgraceful morals. The only remedy is the very thing the *Zeitgeist* most abhors, namely, a system of school discipline as inflexible and final as that which obtains in the army. It should be kept out of sight for the most part, to be sure. On the surface of things the school should present the appearance of voluntary self-government by the students themselves, under the supervision of the finest social idealism. But the student body should understand perfectly that absolutely irresistible compulsion is closeted with the faculty and the board, to be used to the uttermost if necessary. And it should be brought to bear upon the lessons as well as upon school decorum and ordinary morals. Without such discipline it is hard to see how the schools of a democracy can conserve the necessary orderliness and the fundamental institutions of civilization.

428. Ross L. Finney, *A Sociological Philosophy of Education* (New York: The Macmillan Company, 1928), p. 480.

429. Discipline by Consent and by Imposition Contrasted

Which method is socialist education to adopt? There can be only one answer when it is fully realized that a discipline based on fear must be imposed from above; a socialist state should be a democratic state, where the ruled are also the rulers, where the state has no welfare apart from that of its citizens, where the discipline does not appear to be imposed by any power that is impervious to the claims of the individual. Therefore, if we are to breed citizens who are not afraid to rule themselves and to accept the discipline of active participation in creative labour, fear must be banished from the schools; and with fear go hatred and cruelty . . . Disobedience and inattention in schools are usually ultimately due to boredom; a discipline that results from interest in a project is positive, and does away with the state of mental and emotional undernourishment that is the cause of anti-social behaviour. Similarly crime in society grows out of poverty, unemployment, and bad social environment; a state which can provide work with a real importance to society for all its citizens, will go a long way towards the reduction of crime. In the same way a school that can satisfy the particular interests of the children and focus their attention through some work that appeals positively to them, will have solved its major disciplinary problem. What remains of crime when this form of discipline is applied in school and state will probably be due to pathological causes and should be treated as a doctor would prescribe for a sick man.

430. Adults Have Interests Too

It is important that the matter of jurisdiction be kept continually in mind. Children may not be permitted, of course, to damage or destroy school property wantonly or unnecessarily, for the reason that a larger-group concern is at stake. Children's wishes and desires should, indeed when they wish it, be expressed to the jurisdictional group and given serious consideration by that group. But there is nothing undemocratic

429. Beryl Pring, *Education, Capitalist and Socialist* (London: Methuen and Company, Ltd., 1937), pp. 219–220. Used by permission of the publishers.
430. Ernest Bayles, *Democratic Educational Theory* (New York: Harper & Brothers, 1960), p. 111.

in denying to any group within a democracy the opportunity to flout enactments of the jurisdictional group of which it is only a part. Such smaller groups should *participate* in decision-making, but not decide by and for themselves.

On matters over which they have jurisdiction, however, school children's considered decisions should stand even though a teacher may consider them wrong. Children may not be permitted to jeopardize life, health, property, or the integrity of the educational process, for those are matters of larger-group concern. Short of such, even "wrong" decisions should hold sway until experience convinces the group that a change should be made. A teacher will, of course, call the children's attention to the manner in which their decisions are working out—*good decisions as well as bad ones,* and never in an I-told-you-so manner.

431. Teacher Personality as Disciplinary Force

The real teacher, the naturally gifted teacher, never bothers about these puzzling questions of pedagogical discipline. He teaches with such devotion; he is so close spiritually to his pupils, so sympathetic with their views; his work is so serious, so sincere, so eager, so full of life, that he is never compelled to face a recalcitrant, rebellious personality that could only be reduced by resorting to the peculiar means of discipline. The docility of the pupils in the eyes of the able teacher is neither an antecedent nor a consequent of his teachings; it is an aspect of it. It originates with the very act by which he begins to teach, and ceases with the end of his teaching. Concretely, the discipline which good teachers enforce in the classroom is the natural behaviour of the spirit which adheres to itself in the seriousness and inwardness of its own work. Discipline, authority, and respect for authority are absent whenever it is impossible to establish that unique superior personality, in which the spiritual life of the pupils and of the teachers are together fused and united. Whenever the students fail to find their ideal in the teacher; when they are disappointed by his aspect, his gaze, his words, in the complex concreteness of his spiritual personality, which does not rise to the ideal which at every moment is present in their expectations, then the order of discipline is lacking. But when this actual unity obtains—this unity which is the task of the teacher,

431. Giovanni Gentile, *The Reform of Education,* D. Bigongiari, translator (New York: Harcourt, Brace and Company, copyright 1922), pp. 175–176.

and the aim of all education—then discipline, authority, and respect are present as never failing elements.

432. Reward and Punishment in the Communist School

Rewards and punishments, praise and blame also constitute forms of direct influence. In contemporary educational theory the first of these is considered almost entirely superfluous. As a stimulus for emulation rewards are admissible only in imperfect societies. To be sure, certain types of distinctions, such as tokens and badges, not having a purely material character, may occupy some place in a soviet state which is remote from the fetishism of bourgeois monarchies and republics. However, by destroying much of this exterior tinsel the Great Russian Revolution has already made tremendous forward strides. In all probability a socialist society will in time stamp out of existence the last vestiges of this system of artificial distinctions. The chief reward for the accomplishment of any kind of creative work, aside from the feeling of satisfaction which comes as a result of fruitful effort, will then be the recognition of its worth by contemporaries and perhaps even by posterity.

✿   ✿   ✿

How then should we react to punishment in general and to corporal punishment in particular? First of all, let us establish quite definitely the following condition. If resort to punishment can be avoided and if the desired results can be accomplished by other means, we must repudiate it altogether. We are convinced that the time will come in society when the use of punishment will not be necessary. But to us this is not a question of principle. For a revolutionary Marxist even the question of capital punishment itself is not a question of principle. There are moments when the communistic power resorts to this means as a measure of terror, not because it "craves blood," as its enemies love to represent, but because the revolting proletariat, in order to retain power, must employ it as a protective measure. According to our view there are no absolute truths; "truth is always concrete."

432. Albert P. Pinkevitch, *The New Education in the Soviet Republic* (New York: John Day Company, 1929), pp. 41–44.

433. Levels of Discipline

We have been stressing throughout this presentation that "discipline" is a basic concept in the Catholic theory of education. This fact has its theological foundations in the Catholic theory of the nature of man. Again we repeat that the Catholic theory here is not that of the Protestant reformers who brought forth the theory of "total depravity" as a result of the fall of our first parents. If man's nature is totally depraved his every action is sinful. Therefore he can be saved by faith alone (Luther) or he is saved by being among the predestined (Calvin). Not so the Catholic theory. Rather man's nature was wounded by the fall. His intellect was darkened and his will weakened, but offsetting this fact is the redeeming power of Christ's grace which makes it possible for man not merely to regain what was lost but to climb to heights beyond nature and live a life truly supernatural. In this interpretation of the nature of man, discipline is a basic concept . . . And since man, a unitary organism, functions as a whole, moral discipline (of the will) as well as mental discipline (of the intellect) are at the very center of the Catholic theory of education.

We must remember, however, that just as in the case of the mental disciplines, the ideal to be aimed at is the development of the ability to carry on self-dependent study whereby the individual reaches his full development in the intellectual life; so too in the moral disciplines, their end and aim is the power of self-control in all the vicissitudes of life. If this outcome is achieved, the moral virtues will characterize the life of the student who has been submitted to this discipline.

With this interpretation of the principle *self-development through self-discipline* the "new freedom" takes on intelligent meaning. The student cannot be expected to develop the power of self-control if he never has an opportunity to practice self-control . . . When the child is sufficiently mature to have any realization of his obligations toward others, toward God, his Father in heaven, and toward his fellows on earth, his brothers in Christ; and as soon as he manifests the ability and the desire to conduct his life in conformity with the laws of God and of society, he should be free to do so. He will grow in this power and he will develop this attitude only insofar as he is free to make his own choices, to feel the sting of regret when they are blunders and gain

433. William F. Cunningham, *The Pivotal Problems of Education* (New York: The Macmillan Company, 1940), pp. 469–472.

the respect and confidence of his associates, when they are wise. As he grows older, as his understanding of his obligations deepens and his attitude of respect for others strengthens, he should enjoy a constantly enlarging liberty, until in late adolescence he is practically on his own, subject only to the rules and regulations that society must impose to preserve peace and order in any large community. If by prayer and self-discipline the student spiritualizes his constantly enlarging liberty and brings under control his impulses and his passions, he will enjoy the freedom of which St. Paul speaks, "the freedom wherewith Christ has made us free."

What can the teacher do in his own classroom and in his administrations throughout the school, particularly when he is functioning as the director of any co-curricular activity where freedom is the condition of success, to bring about the realization of the ideal discipline, *liberty under the law?* First of all, the teacher must understand what we may call the "planes" of discipline. There are two of these, the natural and the supernatural, but the natural plane admits of three levels. The lowest level is the level of *compulsion.* Here discipine is imposed from above down. It is external to those who are subject to it. It rules by force and when the force is removed the only residue is a feeling of resentment, not the establishment of habits of proper behavior. The second level we may call *personal* discipline. It is centered in the personality of the one who administers it. Some times it has its origin in respect for that personality, possibly in affection, but there is always a certain admixture of fear; fear lest this person holding the respect or the affection of the one subject to this discipline, be offended. Herein lies its weakness as an educative influence. When the person who exercises this type of discipline is no longer present to enforce it, its restraining influence may disappear. The behavior habits which function when he is present may not carry over into life at large as controls of conduct, and this is the very purpose of discipline in the educative process. The third level of discipline on the natural plane we may call *social* discipline. Its basis is respect for the group, not for one person within the group. For this reason it is the discipline of democracy. The ideal of democracy is liberty for all but it must be *liberty under the law,* and the law is the welfare of all. The individual shares in the communal life. But if he is to share this communal life in a way that will not infringe on the rights of the community as a whole, he must exercise self-control. In a dictatorship, control is imposed from above down. In a democracy the only adequate basis for social control is self-control exercised by the larger group under intelligent leaders. "The best-governed people is the least governed,"— if they govern themselves.

The second plane of discipline is the supernatural. This is the fourth level. It brings God into the picture not merely as the source of all authority with the right to impose discipline but also as the source of power to the people, lifting them up to the plane of the supernatural through the influence of divine grace. Social discipline is founded in the brotherhood of man. But supernatural discipline gives real meaning to that brotherhood since it makes all human beings brothers in Christ through the fatherhood of God. This is the discipline that should always be the aim of the Christian teacher. It is the new law that Christ brought to a pagan world. It is founded in his two commandments "Love God" and "Love your neighbor." Its fruition is peace and order in the society in which it holds sway.

434. Punishment as Re-education

Punishment was formerly regarded as the securing of vengeance against the offender and as a warning to others. It is doubtful whether we can justify, from the standpoint of ethics, punishment of an individual for the sake of the effect of the punishment upon other people. If we center our thinking about the effect of punishment upon the person who has committed an offense, we may turn our thinking in either of two directions. We may believe that he has committed a crime because he "wanted to," that is, we may believe that he has a nonmaterial mind, which is free to choose either the good or the bad thing, but that in this particular instance it has chosen wrongly. When we proceed to imprison him, and make his body uncomfortable for the sake of reforming his mind or soul, we are guilty of absurdity, for we have supposed that his mind is free either to commit a crime or to refrain, regardless of what happens to his body. Punishment, then, degenerates into needless torture, or the securing of revenge. From such a viewpoint, the more cruel and inhuman the punishment, the better it attains its purpose. Much of the opposition to prison reform of the present day is based upon such a view. This attitude seems to be inherent in the popular and teleological conception of human activity. If, on the other hand, we regard criminal activity as the result of physical causes, existing within the nervous and other bodily structure of the criminal and in his environment, we have only to discover the proper physical remedies and apply them, to bring about a reformation of the criminal. Punishment, from this point of view,

434. Clarence E. Ragsdale, *Modern Psychologies and Education* (New York: The Macmillan Company, 1936), pp. 39–40. Used by permission of the author.

consists of re-education, that is, the breaking of bad habits, and the replacing of these bad habits with habits which are socially useful . . .

435. A Sound Basis for Fear

The current individualism has led to much superficial sentimentality about breaking a child's will, the unnatural monstrosity of an appeal to fear, the nobility of independent self-direction, and the like. The facts of life are quite to the contrary. The struggle for existence is always motivated by fear; while group integration and social control are always based on ultimate coercion of some sort . . . Hence, respect is seven-tenths fear; and a flippant person is he who does not realize what things a sensible person is bound to be afraid of.

❀   ❀   ❀

Thus compulsory obedience is often a most effective type of moral education—provided the code enforced is intrinsically good. Moral education needs a reinstatement of discipline.

436. Role of Fear Qualified

To say, as some do today with Pestalozzi, that fear has no place in school life is going from one extreme to another; as long as human nature is what it is, fear will have its place in school life as it has in the larger community life. It will act as a restraint from wrongdoing, which is the first step on the path of duty; "The fear of the Lord is the beginning of wisdom" is as true and wholesome a maxim today as it was thousands of years ago. Fear, however, is a poor incentive to intellectual activity. It may induce the child to perform the task assigned to him, but the intellectual gain that may be realized through this method will be negligible. Intellectual education should ever be a work of free will.

The question of the fear "incentive" leads us on to the related topic of punishment and its use in the school. That there is and ever will be occasion for punishment in school no one would seriously deny. The question, then, is not whether or not punishment should be used

435. Ross L. Finney, *A Sociological Philosophy of Education* (New York: The Macmillan Company, 1928), pp. 306–307.

436. Pierre J. Marique, *The Philosophy of Christian Education* (Englewood Cliffs, N. J.: Prentice-Hall, Inc., 1939), pp. 299–300.

in the school, but to what purpose it should be used and what characteristics it should possess. The purpose of punishment becomes at once evident by considering the essential function of the school, which is to make children, boys and girls, morally better. There may be other purposes for punishment in civil and military life, but in the school, as in the family, it should have one purpose: to prevent wrongdoing, to secure obedience to law.

437. Punishment as Social Hope of Reformation

It is a prevalent sentiment that the treatment of crime should aim only at the future, heal the disturbed mind, and drop all thought of retribution, which looks vengefully to the past. As if we could deal with the future of a human mind except by dealing with its maxims; and could deal with its maxims except by dealing with the deeds which those maxims have produced! It is only when we give up a person as hopeless that we cease to take issue with the decisions that reveal him; he then becomes to us, in fact, a determined *thing*, and is excluded from our society as effectually as if by some magic curse we had transformed him into an automaton. By such self-contradictions false sentiment never fails to reveal its own unreality. Punishment, I repeat, is an expression of social hope—the hope of remaking or saving the man, by revealing to him in the language of deeds the meaning of his own deed. Thus the typical punishment of crime takes the form of stimulating the treatment of the rebel, the rightless man: it is an exclusion from society, within society—an incarceration—an exclusion that may be revoked when the argument has its effect. The argument is clearer in proportion as the element of physical suffering is minimized. The suffering of punishment should reveal the worth of what the criminal has ignored; his liberty, his free companionship and friendship, his political powers, his ability to make and execute plans in the community at large, his right to build continuously on an achieved degree of power and station, however modest. Discontinuity is a sufficient argument, if any argument is sufficient. And if none is sufficient, the criminal is indeed the rebel; and must be so treated. The exclusion must be as permanent as the unconvinced will.

The truth is that society cannot punish unless it can create a "conviction." For as long as the criminal retains the maxim of his deed,

437. William E. Hocking, *Human Nature and its Remaking* (New Haven, Conn.: Yale University Press, 1918), 1929, pp. 284–285.

his suffering is a mere hardship, not an argument. The hardship becomes punishment only in so far as he perceives and accepts its meaning. *There can be no retribution without reformation;* this is the true principle underlying modern changes in the treatment of delinquency and crime . . .

438. Training in Democratic Citizenship

At present, though our political philosophy declares that there is no just government without the consent of the governed, all minors are ruled without their consent, even in matters that are universally recognized as within their capacity. *Degrees of capacity to govern* are utterly unrecognized in our constitutional law. In a single instant, when the hands of the clock touch the midnight hour, our young people pass from zero right of franchise to maximum right.

The scheme is almost incredibly crude. It is in no wise geared into our educational system. The state trains its children for citizenship for eight years in the elementary school, then for four years in the high school, and often for four years more in the college—*trains them for citizenship*—yet at no point in the process does the state satisfy itself, or certify to pupil or parent, whether or not any degree of competence as a citizen has been achieved. Graduation from the course of study prescribed by the state is not graduation into any function or right of the citizen whatsoever. Yet we wonder why adolescents show so little sense of social responsibility, so little respect for law, and why educated Americans do not feel the weighty import of the ballot!

Most persons who think about the problem at all would agree, without doubt, that the only really good school government is that in which the pupils themselves achieve reflective, social self-control, and that training *for* democracy must be, in the nature of the case, training *in* democracy. Yet, under our present laws, every scheme of pupil self-government is inevitably infected with a certain untruth. For pupils have no right to self-government; they are merely permitted to run their own affairs by a teacher, a principal, or a superintendent who, as far as pupil self-government is concerned, is an irresponsible ruler.

438. George A. Coe, *Law and Freedom in the School* (Chicago: University of Chicago Press, 1924), pp. 70–71.

439. Student Self-Government

Democracy applied to school-management, or self-government as it is usually called, has a great deal in its favour from many points of view. In the first place it uses the co-operative spirit for purposes that can also be served by the intellect, and that we have already seen to be a desirable mixture. It is this side of school-life that emphasizes the communal spirit, making plain to children that co-operation is an absolute necessity in some form for the smooth running of society if the rights of the individual to choose his own work and recreation are not to be trespassed upon . . . But—and this needs saying with emphasis—the democracy must be real; there must be no suggestion of play, no feeling that the staff can step in and alter the decisions of the community if their judgment disagrees with that of the children. Even where the contemporary schools have in force the system of prefects, a form of oligarchy, as in the public schools, there is this fatal atmosphere of play, of apprenticeship about the authority of the older boy, an atmosphere that breeds irresponsibility . . . There can be no educational value in such authority, which is dangled before the young as a toy and, anyway, is only lent them. Real democracy means that the school council, which makes the laws and punishes offenders, is all-powerful, for its term of office, though it may be criticized openly and fearlessly. That council must be elected by an equal vote from all members of the community, staff and children, old and young; on the council, a staff vote should count as much as, but no more than, a child's vote. The staff will come under the same laws as the children and must treat them as seriously. Will this mean riot, irresponsibility, disrespect or the appearance of any other bogey, that so frightens the school teacher now? . . . Self-government needs a new orientation of mind and cannot be successful unless applied whole-heartedly; the democracy must be complete and utterly serious. At present, the game of defying an authority that is an absurdity, is much more amusing than the game of playing at democracy; the petty officials of a tyranny have always been the objects of the intense scorn and hatred of the populace.

Psychologically will it work? There are some, even among the progressive educationalists, who consider that self-government puts too great a strain on the individual child, especially at the early stages

439. Beryl Pring, *Education, Capitalist and Socialist* (London: Methuen and Company, Ltd., 1937), pp. 237–241. Used by permission of the publishers.

of education. This does not seem to be the case where it has been tried; the child can easily bear a collective responsibility, whereas an individual one, such as is involved in the office of form-leader or prefect, would worry him or make him precocious. Nor need any of the problems that arise for his consideration be beyond his powers, as long as they are not related too soon to wider theoretical issues of morality or politics, as they will all be closely connected with his own life and his immediate needs and ideas. We do not debar a man from the political vote because he has not studied political economy; we depend on his judgment of his own requirements. Why debar a child from his share of school government on the plea that he is too young to understand such things? If the atmosphere of the proceedings is serious, self-government will not mean chaos. On the whole a child resents assaults on his property as much as, if not more so, than an adult; bullying is usually a matter of individual maladjustment, and in the mass children have a strict sense of justice; to-day nothing arouses more enmity against a teacher than "favouritism." But the greatest revolution that such a system demands, is in the attitude of the teacher to the child, and vice versa. A new humility is necessary in this sphere; we school-marms and pedagogues must cease to be demi-gods. We are no better in ourselves than many of the children we teach. That we know more, even that we are sometimes in greater control of ourselves, is due to our age. Meanwhile we have probably lost something in spontaneity, energy, and generosity. Is there anything that is disgraceful or unseemly in being the equal of a child? I might quote the Gospels at this point, but no one takes them seriously these days. As for teaching, as Xenophon said: "How shall a man learn except from one who be his friend?" and of what value is the friendship in which one party demands the constant recognition of his supposed superiority? Self-government, with its necessary condition that the teacher lose an artificial dignity, to ask for a new one dependent on his merits alone, is the only form of discipline that will fit into a school that is based on sympathy and mutual understanding, and not on fear and hatred. But this last change is perhaps the most difficult to achieve of all the reforms I have been advocating; it is easier to build fifty new schools, to evolve a totally new curriculum and time-table with new methods of teaching, than to eradicate the tone of command from the voice of a school-mistress, or to drag a school-master from his pedestal of superiority. All we can do is to find comfort in the idea that in a society where unemployment is unknown, no one need become a teacher for any reason but love of children (love of teaching is no qualification), and that love breeds humility.

440. Learning from Anarchy

The case for self-government in schools is put by some strenuous advocates in a form whose consequences it is important to face clearly. Starting from the sound position that boys and girls can best learn the significance and value of the moral order by building it up for themselves, they proceed to argue that the process, if it is to be genuine, or at least complete, must start from the beginning. As one of the leaders in the new way has said, it is only when young people have had the "searching experience" of a moral chaos that the craving for something better is powerfully aroused in them. We must accept the evidence which has now been offered from many quarters that the moral activity thus initiated and supported may have the happiest and most striking results upon the character of those who share in it. But we are bound to ask what happens to those who come after them and find the foundations of a decent common life already laid and a fair building already erected upon them. Deprived of the "searching experience" of moral anarchy, will they not also miss the educative experience of fashioning a moral order to replace it? There are uncompromising spirits who do not shrink from what seems to be the inevitable answer. They agree that as soon as a stable rule of life has been established the community has exhausted its usefulness; it must be broken up and a fresh start made for the benefit of the next generation of citizens.

Reformers of a less heroic cast may well shrink from accepting so drastic a deduction from their principles, and will turn back to re-examine the premises from which it follows. They will then observe that their intransigeant colleague has eliminated from his educational scheme one element which the world in general holds to be of prime importance—namely, the influence of tradition. The methods used in the upbringing of children have varied widely from age to age, and even from one family or school to another at the same epoch; but from the dawn of civilization the elder generation has conceived its task to be to form the younger generation in the tradition in which itself was formed, modified in such directions as its experience may have suggested to be desirable. Conservative reformers are content to seek improvements in the practice based on this ancient faith; our revolutionaries would have us reject the basis altogether, and build education anew on some form of the dogma of natural goodness.

440. T. Percy Nunn, *Education, Its Data and First Principles* (London: Edward Arnold & Co., 1920), pp. 101–103. Used by permission of the publishers.

26

Moral Education

Problems in the Philosophy of Education Discussed in this Section

1. How do you recognize a moral situation when it occurs in school? Would you distinguish moral from ethical instruction?
2. Can moral character be gained by training in such specific traits as honesty, courage, temperance, and the like?
3. Does the normal curve of learning hold for moral education as it does in other skills?
4. Does moral knowledge stand on any different footing from knowledge in the secular branches?
5. Is there any sound difference between a student's making an error and committing an immoral or a sinful act?
6. How can the parent or teacher insure that right knowledge will issue in right conduct? If the child has the right attitude, if he means well, should he be relieved in some degree from responsibility for any untoward consequences of his conduct?
7. On what sanctions should the school rely to insure right conduct? How should "oughtness" be taught? Do the standards here differ at all from those in general value theory? Do they differ further according to political or economic ideology?
8. Is it ethical to conduct research in moral education by deliberately setting up a situation which tempts wrongdoing, in order to test what the pupil has learned about right conduct?

441. Error and Sin Distinguished

Education which denies evil must be abandoned because it fails to make a distinction between an intellectual error and bad behavior. If I add ten and ten to make thirty, I err, and an eraser can correct it; but if I tell a falsehood about my neighbor and ruin his reputation,

441. Fulton J. Sheen, "Anti-Christ," the twelfth in a series of nineteen addresses on guilt, delivered on *The Catholic Hour*, March 2, 1941. Washington, D.C.: National Council of Catholic Men.

I sin. Modern education makes no distinction between error and sin; it teaches that what we call evil is only an intellectual error. That is why it preaches that crime and anti-social behavior are due to mental immaturity. Only the ignorant sin; the intelligentsia can't sin—they *know*. Hence, educate everyone and evil will disappear.

The fact is, education does not take away evil because the training of the reason is quite distinct from the training of the will; knowing is not doing. Modern education which trains only the mind takes away error—sometimes; but it does not train the will or take away sin. Nothing is so destructive of our national life than this fallacy that the educated are sinless because they have an A.B. . . . The truth is rather the contrary, the uneducated in this country have less evil in them than the intelligentsia; they may make errors, but they commit less sin. And on the day of Judgment it will be far better to be ignorant before the face of Almighty God than worldly wise but sinful.

442. Importance of Teaching Ethics

In our country, where the truths of religion cannot be taught systematically in the public schools, for good and sufficient reasons, as we think, it is the more important that ethics be taught. But this recommendation is no simple matter. The fact that we are discussing it so late in this series shows it is not the thing to begin with in developing character. Furthermore, we cannot rely upon it implicitly; if pupils have been rightly trained before studying ethics, they will hardly need ethics to make them do right; on the other hand, if pupils are not good, ethics will hardly make them so. The fact is that ethics is a science; it reaches the intellect, but the springs of character are the emotions and the will. If ethics degenerates into exhortation, the net is being spread in the sight of the bird; Christianity has discovered how hard it is to reform the world by preaching . . .

Why then teach ethics? Because, though knowledge does not insure right action, there can be no right action without knowledge. Because, too, knowing the right, through the motor-tendency of ideas, is at least a temptation to do it. That man is actively bad, morally depraved, who sins against the light he has. Ethics turns the light on; it cannot make men prefer darkness to light.

442. Herman H. Horne, *Idealism in Education* (New York: The Macmillan Company, 1923), pp. 136–137.

443. Teach Children Morals, Not Ethics

Now what is asked of us teachers is that we invite our pupils to direct study of the principles of right conduct, that we awaken their consciousness about their modes of life, and so by degrees impart to them a science of righteousness. This is theory, ethics; not morals, practice; and in my judgment it is dangerous business, with the slenderest chance of success. Useless is it to say that the aim of such instruction need not be ethical, but moral. Whatever the ultimate aim, the procedure of instruction is of necessity scientific. It operates through intelligence, and only gets into life so far as the instructed intelligence afterward becomes a director. This is the work of books and teachers everywhere: they discipline the knowing act, and so bring within its influence that multitude of matters which depend for excellent adjustment on clear and ordered knowledge. Such a work, however, is evidently but partial. Many matters do not take their rise in knowledge at all. Morality does not. The boy as soon as born is adopted unconsciously into some sort of moral world. While he is growing up and is thinking of other things, habits of character are seizing him. By the time he comes to school he is incrusted with customs. The idea that his moral education can be fashioned by his teacher in the same way as his education in geography is fantastic. It is only his ethical training which may now begin . . .

Nor indeed is performance likely to be improved by ethical enlightenment if, as I maintain, the whole business of self-criticism in the child is unwholesome. By a course of ethical training a young person will, in my view, much more probably become demoralized than invigorated. What we ought to desire, if we would have a boy grow morally sturdy, is that introspection should not set in early and that he should not become accustomed to watch his conduct. And the reason is obvious. Much as we incline to laud our prerogative of consciousness and to assert that it is precisely what distinguishes us from our poor relations, the brutes, we still must acknowledge that consciousness has certain grave defects when exalted into the position of a guide. Large tracts of life lie altogether beyond its control, and the conduct which can be affected by it is apt—especially in the initial stages—to be rendered vague, slow, vacillating, and distorted. Only

443. George H. Palmer, *Ethical and Moral Instruction in the Schools* (Boston: Houghton Mifflin Company, 1909), pp. 8–13. Used by permission of the publishers.

instinctive action is swift, sure, and firm. For this reason we distrust
the man who calculates his goodness. We find him vulgar and repellent. We are far from sure that he will keep that goodness long. If
I offer to shake hands with a man with precisely that degree of warmth
which I have decided it is well to express, will he willingly take my
hand? . . .

This, then, is the inexpugnable objection to the ethical instruction
of children: the end which should be sought is performance, not
knowledge, and we cannot by supplying the latter induce the former.
But do not these considerations cut the ground from under practical
teaching of every kind? Instruction is given in other subjects in the
hope that it may finally issue in strengthened action, and I have acknowledged that as a fact this hope is repeatedly justified. Why may
not a similar result appear in ethics? What puts a difference between
that study and electricity, social science, or manual training? This:
according as the work studied includes a creative element and is intended to give expression to a personal life, consciousness becomes
an increasingly dangerous dependence. Why are there no classes and
textbooks for the study of deportment? Is it because manners are
unimportant? No, but because they make the man, and to be of any
worth must be an expression of his very nature. Conscious study would
tend to distort rather than to fashion them. Their practice cannot
be learned in the same way as carpentry.

444. Virtue and the Virtues

The trouble with formal moral instruction *as it has been understood*
lies deeper than most of its critics have realized. Times without number we have insisted that a pupil who understands the virtues may not
practice them. Yes, but the incurably radical fault of such instruction
is its lack of truth. For it has falsely assumed that a pupil who does
practice the virtues of the schedule will attain to virtue. There are
two reasons why this is untrue. The first is that most of the virtues in
the catalogue are abstract qualities of will, not concrete social purposes; they describe some of the conditions of an efficient will, but
they leave out the social mark of a good will. The second reason is
that moral character is represented as made up of a combination of
qualities or virtues. Socrates declared truly that virtue is one and
indivisible, not a collection of virtues. Now, the unity of a good char-

444. George A. Coe, "Virtue and the Virtues," *Religious Education*, 6:487,
January 1912.

acter consists in holding to a social end or purpose through a period
of time, and making the details of conduct all contribute to this end.

It follows that the material for moral instruction is the functions
of men and of institutions in society. Let us stop studying virtues,
and study instead what actual men do, and why they do it.

445. The Connection of Knowledge and Morals

A noteworthy paradox often accompanies discussions of morals. On
the one hand, there is an identification of the moral with the rational.
Reason is set up as a faculty from which proceed ultimate moral
intuitions, and sometimes, as in the Kantian theory, it is said to supply
the only proper moral motive. On the other hand, the value of concrete, everyday intelligence is constantly underestimated, and even
deliberately depreciated. Morals is often thought to be an affair
with which ordinary knowledge has nothing to do. Moral knowledge
is thought to be a thing apart, and conscience is thought of as something radically different from consciousness. This separation, if valid,
is of especial significance for education. Moral education in school
is practically hopeless when we set up the development of character as
a supreme end, and at the same time treat the acquiring of knowledge
and the development of understanding, which of necessity occupy the
chief part of school time, as having nothing to do with character. On
such a basis, moral education is inevitably reduced to some kind of
catechetical instruction, or lessons about morals. Lessons "about morals" signify as matter of course lessons in what other people think
about virtues and duties. It amounts to something only in the degree
in which pupils happen to be already animated by a sympathetic and
dignified regard for the sentiments of others. Without such a regard,
it has no more influence on character than information about the
mountains of Asia; with a servile regard, it increases dependence upon
others, and throws upon those in authority the responsibility for
conduct. As a matter of fact, direct instruction in morals has been
effective only in social groups where it was a part of the authoritative
control of the many by the few. Not the teaching as such but the
re-enforcement of it by the whole regime of which it was an incident
made it effective. To attempt to get similar results from lessons about
morals in a democratic society is to rely upon sentimental magic.

At the other end of the scale stands the Socratic-Platonic teaching

445. John Dewey, *Democracy and Education* (New York: The Macmillan
Company, 1916), pp. 410–414.

which identifies knowledge and virtue—which holds that no man does evil knowingly but only because of ignorance of the good. This doctrine is commonly attacked on the ground that nothing is more common than for a man to know the good and yet do the bad: not knowledge, but habituation or practice, and motive are what is required . . .

It is not necessary, accordingly, to dispute about the proper meaning of the term knowledge. It is enough for educational purposes to note the different qualities covered by the one name, to realize that it is knowledge gained at first hand through the exigencies of experience which affects conduct in significant ways. If a pupil learns things from books simply in connection with school lessons and for the sake of reciting what he has learned when called upon, then knowledge will have effect upon *some* conduct—namely upon that of reproducing statements at the demand of others. There is nothing surprising that such "knowledge" should not have much influence in the life out of school. But this is not a reason for making a divorce between knowledge and conduct, but for holding in low esteem this kind of knowledge. The same thing may be said of knowledge which relates merely to an isolated and technical specialty; it modifies action but only in its own narrow line. In truth, the problem of moral education in the schools is one with the problem of securing knowledge—the knowledge connected with the system of impulses and habits. For the use to which any known fact is put depends upon its connections. The knowledge of dynamite of a safecracker may be identical in verbal form with that of a chemist; in fact, it is different, for it is knit into connection with different aims and habits, and thus has a different import.

Just because the studies of the curriculum represent standard factors in social life they are organs of initiation into social values. As mere school studies, their acquisition has only a technical worth. Acquired under conditions where their social significance is realized, they feed moral interest and develop moral insight. Moreover, the qualities of mind discussed under the topic of method of learning are all of them intrinsically moral qualities. Open-mindedness, singlemindedness, sincerity, breadth of outlook, thoroughness, assumption of responsibility for developing the consequences of ideas which are accepted, are moral traits. The habit of identifying moral characteristics with external conformity to authoritative prescriptions may lead us to ignore the ethical value of these intellectual attitudes, but the same habit tends to reduce morals to a dead and machine-like routine. Consequently while such an attitude has moral results, the results are morally undesirable

—above all in a democratic society where so much depends upon personal disposition.

446. Social Basis of Moral Education

The much and commonly lamented separation in the schools between intellectual and moral training, between acquiring information and growth of character, is simply one expression of the failure to conceive and construct the school as a social institution, having social life and value within itself. Expecting in so far as the school is an embryonic yet typical community life, moral training must be partly pathological and partly formal. It is pathological inasmuch as the stress comes to be laid upon correcting wrongdoing instead of upon forming habits of positive service. The teacher is necessarily forced into a position where his concern with the moral life of the pupils takes largely the form of being on the alert for failures to conform to the school rules and routine. These regulations, judged from the standpoint of the development of the child at the time, are more or less conventional and arbitrary. They are rules which have to be made in order that the existing modes of school work may go on; but the lack of inherent necessity in the school work reflects itself in a feeling, on the part of the child, that the moral discipline of the school is somewhat arbitrary. Any conditions which compel the teacher to take note of failures rather than of healthy growth put the emphasis in the wrong place and result in distortion and perversion. Attending to wrongdoing ought to be an incident rather than the important phase. The child ought to have a positive consciousness of what he is about, and to be able to judge and criticise his respective acts from the standpoint of their reference to the work which he has to do. Only in this way does he have a normal and healthy standard, enabling him properly to appreciate his failures and to estimate them at their right value.

By saying that the moral training of the school is partly formal I mean that the moral habits which are specially emphasized in the school are habits which are created, as it were, ad hoc. Even the habits of promptness, regularity, industry, non-interference with the work of others, faithfulness to tasks imposed, which are specially inculcated in the school, are habits which are morally necessary simply because the

446. John Dewey, *Ethical Principles Underlying Education* (Chicago: University of Chicago Press, 1903), pp. 14–15.

school system is what it is, and must be preserved intact. If we grant the inviolability of the school system as it is, these habits represent permanent and necessary moral ideas; but just in so far as the school system is itself isolated and mechanical, the insistence upon these moral habits is more or less unreal, because the ideal to which they relate is not itself necessary. The duties, in other words, are distinctly school duties, not life duties. If we compare this with the well-ordered home, we find that the duties and responsibilities which the child has to recognize and assume there are not such as belong to the family as a specialized and isolated institution, but flow from the very nature of the social life in which the family participates and to which it contributes. The child ought to have exactly the same motives for right doing, and be judged by exactly the same standard in the school, as the adult in the wider social life to which he belongs. Interest in the community welfare, an interest which is intellectual and practical, as well as emotional—an interest, that is to say, in perceiving whatever makes for social order and progress, and for carrying these principles into execution—is the ultimate ethical habit to which all the special school habits must be related if they are to be animated by the breath of moral life.

447. Moral Education Conditioned by Democracy

The interest of a socialized religious education in the public schools is not that they should teach religion in addition to reading, writing, and arithmetic, but that they should teach democracy, and that they should do it thoroughly. To "teach" democracy, it need hardly be argued at this stage of our discussion, means to develop intelligent democratic attitudes, activities, habits, and purposes—in short, to make the pupils democrats.

Here lies the acutest part of the problem of moral instruction and training in the public schools. Real educators are chary of proposals to "introduce moral education" into the schools. It is there already in every piece of work that the pupils are led to do thoroughly; it is there in everything that produces loyalty to the reasonable rules of the school; it is there in the co-operative life of schoolroom and play-ground; it is there in customs and measures that make for community consciousness and for political idealism—it cannot be introduced, it can

447. George A. Coe, *A Social Theory of Religious Education* (New York: Charles Scribner's Sons), 1918, pp. 263–264.

only be improved. The improvement for which we most need to strive, about which anxiety is most nearly justified, concerns, not a set of standard virtues that are the same under tyranny and under liberty, but measures for leading pupils to have as their own the great purposes of democracy, which are not only humane, but also constructive and aggressive. The problem of morals in the schools melts into the problem of creating ambition for a sort of society that is partly prefigured in our historic national ideals, but is still for the most part unachieved. Give us public schools that develop active interest in human welfare, passion for the basal rights of man as man, faith in the capacity of men for unselfishness, and the habit and purpose of co-operation—give us public schools like these, and social religion will look upon them as doing God's will even though they do not name His Name, but only that of His children.

448. Communist Moral Education

The overruling purpose of the school, according to Lenin, must be the cultivation of communist morality in the pupils. The entire business of the education of contemporary youth must be the development in them of communist morality.

Lenin showed that eternal and unchanging ethical standards do not exist. Ethical standards are determined by the development of society and by social relations. Also for every concrete social form there are corresponding ethical standards. The conduct of the individual is determined by social relations and by social position. The ruling ethics in society is the ethics of the ruling class. Wealthy classes, as Lenin says, regard their morality as the morality of all mankind and founded on "the commandments of god." "We reject any such morality which is derived from extra-human or extra-class conceptions. We say that it is a fraud, that it is a deception designed to dull the minds of workers and peasants in the interests of landlords and capitalists." *

In place of such ethics, created in the interests of exploiters, the working class creates a new ethics, which develops out of the interests of the struggle for a new society in which there will be no exploitation

448. Boris P. Esipov and N. K. Goncharov, *"I Want To Be Like Stalin,"* George S. Counts and Nucia P. Lodge, translators (New York: John Day Company, 1947), pp. 141–144.

---

* Nikolai Lenin, *Works,* Vol. XXX, p. 410.

of man by man. The new ethics, the ethics of the forward-looking class, serves the cause of the reconstruction of society. Communist ethics unites the workers for the struggle of the welfare of all mankind, for deliverance from oppression and violence. Communist ethics therefore is the most advanced, the most human, and the most noble; and it is devoted to the purpose of creating a communist society. "To this end," says Lenin, "we need a generation of youth transformed into responsible people by the conditions attending a disciplined and desperate struggle with the bourgeoisie. In this struggle genuine communists will be developed; to this struggle must be subjected and with this struggle must be linked every step in the education of youth." **

People who build a communist society must be devoted to the cause and be ready to defend it with all their strength and resources. They must be brave, courageous, honest, steadfast, and disciplined. They must hate their enemies, fear no difficulties, and overcome all obstacles. Such is the moral force of the new man, of the man of the new society. In the struggle and in the conquest of hardships the traits of firm Bolshevik character are cultivated.

Along with the revelation of the essence of communist morality Lenin outlines the basis and means of education in this morality.

Lenin taught youth to dedicate all of their strength and knowledge to the general good and to participate in life and in the building of a new society in such a way "that every day in every village and in every town youth will perform some task of socially useful labor, let it be ever so small or ever so simple." ***

In revealing the essence of communist morality, Lenin gave particular attention to the question of conscious discipline. Education in conscious discipline is an integral and essential part of education in communist morality. Through the study of morality in its historical development and in its dependence on social relations, Lenin shows that discipline varies in different periods of the development of society. Also there is a definite discipline which corresponds to every social order. The discipline of the whip harmonizes with the feudal order and the feudal discipline of labor. The capitalistic organization of production rests on the discipline of hunger. In either case submission is placid and absolute. In bourgeois society the discipline of hunger is often cloaked by "democratic" discourses on the freedom of labor. But if the workers are deprived of all means of production, such "democracy" merely marks the discipline of hunger. An entirely dif-

---

** *Ibid.*, p. 413.
*** *Ibid.*, p. 417.

ferent situation is created when the workers are the owners of the land and all means of production. "The farther communist organization of productive labor proceeds, toward which socialism is the first step," says Lenin, "the more will it rest on the free and conscious discipline of the workers themselves who overthrow the landlords as well as the capitalists." †

The new conscious discipline is not a consequence of good intentions. Nor does it appear ready-made. Such discipline is forged only through the long and stubborn struggle and labor of the workers. The younger generation must acquire discipline and habits of organized conduct from the earliest years.

The old school remained a school of drill, where measures of corporal punishment were applied and youth were crippled physically and morally. Education in conscious discipline must be put in the place of drill and the discipline of the whip. "It is necessary," says Lenin, "for the Young Communists to educate all youth from twelve years of age in conscious and disciplined labor." †† Conscious discipline is developed in the studies and the socially useful work of children. Conscious disciplined labor and conscious studies, that is, well and correctly thought-out instruction of children, is the means for the cultivation of conscious discipline. Lenin created a rigorous science of communist morality, as an integral part of communist education, and outlined the principal directives for the achievement of education in communist morality in the school.

449. Criteria of Moral Education

Here, then, is the moral standard, by which to test the work of the school upon the side of what it does directly for individuals. (a) Does the school as a system, at present, attach sufficient importance to the spontaneous instincts and impulses? Does it afford sufficient opportunity for these to assert themselves and work out their own results? Can we even say that the school in principle attaches itself, at present, to the active constructive powers rather than to processes of absorption and learning? Does not our talk about self-activity largely render

449. John Dewey, *Moral Principles in Education* (Boston: Houghton Mifflin Company, 1909), pp. 53–57. Used by permission of the publishers.

† *Ibid.*, p. 336.
†† *Ibid.*, p. 417.

itself meaningless because the self-activity we have in mind is purely "intellectual," out of relation to those impulses which work through hand and eye?

Just in so far as the present school methods fail to meet the test of such questions moral results must be unsatisfactory. We cannot secure the development of positive force of character unless we are willing to pay its price. We cannot smother and repress the child's powers, or gradually abort them (from failure of opportunity for exercise), and then expect a character with initiative and consecutive industry. I am aware of the importance attaching to inhibition, but mere inhibition is valueless. The only restraint, the only holding-in, that is of any worth is that which comes through holding powers concentrated upon a positive end. An end cannot be attained excepting as instincts and impulses are kept from discharging at random and from running off on side tracks. In keeping powers at work upon their relevant ends, there is sufficient opportunity for genuine inhibition. To say that inhibition is higher than power, is like saying that death is more than life, negation more than affirmation, sacrifice more than service.

(b) We must also test our school work by finding whether it affords the conditions necessary for the formation of good judgment. Judgment as the sense of relative values involves ability to select, to discriminate. Acquiring information can never develop the power of judgment. Development of judgment is in spite of, not because of, methods of instruction that emphasize simple learning. The test comes only when the information acquired has to be put to use. Will it do what we expect of it? . . .

The child cannot get power of judgment excepting as he is continually exercised in forming and testing judgments. He must have an opportunity to select for himself, and to attempt to put his selections into execution, that he may submit them to the final test, that of action. Only thus can he learn to discriminate that which promises success from that which promises failure; only thus can he form the habit of relating his purposes and notions to the conditions that determine their value. Does the school, as a system, afford at present sufficient opportunity for this sort of experimentation? Except so far as the emphasis of the school work is upon intelligent doing, upon active investigation, it does not furnish the conditions necessary for that exercise of judgment which is an integral factor in good character.

(c) I shall be brief with respect to the other point, the need of susceptibility and responsiveness. The informally social side of education, the aesthetic environment and influences, are all-important. In so far as the work is laid out in regular and formulated ways, so far as there are lacking opportunities for casual and free social intercourse between pupils and between the pupils and the teacher, this side of the child's nature is either starved, or else left to find haphazard expression along more or less secret channels. When the school system, under plea of the practical (meaning by the practical the narrowly utilitarian), confines the child to the three R's and the formal studies connected with them, shuts him out from the vital in literature and history, and deprives him of his right to contact with what is best in architecture, music, sculpture, and picture, it is hopeless to expect definite results in the training of sympathetic openness and responsiveness.

450. Indirect and Incidental Methods Inadequate for Moral Instruction

Many modern educators prefer the indirect or incidental method. This method implies that character education should be carried on *informally,* or incidentally, so that character may result as a concomitant rather than as a direct product from the formal study of it as a separate subject. The incidental technique or informal method permeate imperceptibly, as it were, the teaching of all subjects. In permeate imperceptibly, as it were, the teaching of all subjects. In regard to the indirect method, the reader should note carefully the lack therein of a positive moral sanction and an authoritative procedure which serve to discipline the child and cause him to discipline himself. "He that ruleth himself is greater than he that taketh a city." Unless sanction and authority are present, the usual consequence is that the child fails to develop in himself desirable character traits. Under the informal or incidental technique, moreover, many essential character traits are likely to be neglected, or insufficiently emphasized. This method, therefore, tends to eventuate in a one-sided, exclusive, and often haphazard form of character training, unless it is used in conjunction with the discussion method.

As indicated in earlier pages of this chapter, the direct training and disciplining of the will is necessary for all worthy character formation. It was stated, further, that the will is a blind faculty and needs the light of the intellect. In other words, the will needs to be "informed" by the intellect; it needs to have motives, worthy interests, desirable values proposed to it by the intellect to elicit its proper

450. John D. Redden and Francis A. Ryan, *A Catholic Philosophy of Education* (Milwaukee: The Bruce Publishing Company, 1955), pp. 230–231.

functioning. The direct method, therefore, is the most obvious and economical way by which ideas can be developed in the intellect. A skillful and artful use of the direct method is no mean task. This method is sometimes difficult for those who prefer to hide their lack of resourcefulness under the cloak of the "indirect method," which often has the saving convenience of covering a multitude of "pedagogical sins."

The advocates of the direct method hold that desirable traits of character must be presented directly to the child, and that he should be shown how to acquire them and make them function in his immediate life. This method involves a study of character traits; a selection of approved traits; a recognition of the training and discipline needed to acquire such traits; the fixing of definite standards to judge their desirability; and, finally, a definite plan wherein sufficient opportunity is given the child to acquire and express the approved traits. The aim of the direct method is to stimulate and influence the individual to acquire purposefully and deliberately the capacity to direct his own daily conduct in conformity to moral standards; and, *through his own volition*, to furnish himself with the necessary motivation to apply these standards consistently in life situations.

451. The Source of Obligation

The pedagogy of this section is as soft as any in Dewey . . .

Let us note first that there is no *ought* in this ethics, no universal binding moral principles, no obligatory duties, no rapturous apostrophe with Kant to the starry heavens above and the moral law within, no clear universal distinction between the right and the wrong. Instead there are preferences of the individual, there are contrasts between growing and limited selves and there is interest in one's occupation. The most used string on Dr. Dewey's harp is "occupation" and the most played tune is "continuity."

But, really, is there no ought? Any individual has received more than he has given; he has received life, capacities, and opportunities; he has given a measure of service, and in the giving he has received more. He owes a debt for what he has received; he owes it to his family and his fellows; perhaps he owes it to a spiritual universe which made him a spirit. What he owes is his *ought;* his debt is what is due; what is due is his duty. The obligation is binding whether he is

451. Herman H. Horne, *The Democratic Philosophy of Education* (New York: The Macmillan Company, 1935), p. 516.

interested in paying it or not; if he is interested in paying it, in a measure he discharges his obligation; if not, he remains the worse debtor.

452. Absolutism In Moral Education

Absolutism. Finally, moral concern is minimized whenever education is conducted in accordance with an absolute, unquestionable tradition received from an unchallengeable authority. When one derives his conceptions and values from uncritical obedience to another person or institution, he is not truly free and hence his acts are not genuinely moral. If submission to political, religious, or other authority is the basis for conduct, the only possible moral question is whether or not to remain subject to the system, and in many if not most instances even this choice is not open. Much of mankind's education is carried on within such a context. Human beings are frequently reluctant or unable to claim their freedom and to assume full responsibility for what they shall do, in education or in any other field. It is easier or safer to accept without question the prescription of another, who wields more power or enjoys more prestige.

Yet absolutist education is not really exempt from moral judgment. Though the absolutist educator himself may not act with moral responsibility, one standing outside the system can evaluate it in relation to alternative systems. The most rigid program of education handed down by a state, by a reigning intellectual elite, or by ecclesiastical authorities can be adjudged by an independent critic as better or worse than some other program. In this sense education is still a moral enterprise. But the full moral dimension of education is not realized until the educators themselves exercise their freedom to decide among alternative aims and methods for directing the development of personality.

453. Moral Education as Learning to Choose and Act Intelligently

The heart of behaving morally is to base action appropriately on thought. Situations do not come already labeled as right or wrong.

452. Philip Phenix, *Philosophy of Education* (New York: Henry Holt & Co., 1958), p. 284.
453. William H. Kilpatrick, *Remaking the Curriculum* (New York and Chicago: Newson and Company, 1936), pp. 82–83.

Man once fancied it ought to be so, and Moses and other lawgivers tried to make lists of the things that are right and wrong. But always some new and better dispensation has renounced the earlier effort and its error. No, we have to think about what to do. True enough, many situations so nearly repeat themselves that we need only recognize them and act upon the results of past thinking. And many parents, even today, try to bring up their children as if this with their commands would suffice. But no such will suffice. We live in a world that develops in novel fashion. When we face a new situation, we have to think in order to know what is right to do. We recognize some familiar elements in it but the new case demands novel consideration. In fact in every case of real doubt, both the alternatives are offering themselves as right. Only after we have deliberated on the alternative lines of consequences can we decide on one in preference to the other—and so label one as right and the other wrong. We may be mistaken; we often are. But we have to do the best we can. We must think as broadly as we can and as unselfishly and conscientiously as we can. If opportunity permits, we should talk it over with others. What we do thus conscientiously conclude, fixes "conscience" for us. It is in this sense that we can and should "follow conscience." But clearly the heart of it all is to base action on thinking and not on mere whim or impulse or past habits.

454. Morality and the Learning Curve

The beginner at target practice will miss the mark: that is a safe prediction. He is entirely free to hit it; and there is no assignable reason why he must miss it. "Good shooting," said a marksman to me, "is simply a matter of caring enough about each shot." Yet the beginner will miss. As time goes on, he will miss less frequently,— a curve of his progress in learning can be drawn. Some men progress more rapidly than others, and go farther toward a perfect score; but there is a similarity in all curves of learning. Is not sin a missing of the target, and hence a phenomenon of the curve of learning?

For any particular technique at which we try, the curve of learning holds; and so with the virtues, so far as they have a technique. Franklin's scheme of monthly practice was a prudent one. But right is not a matter of matching an objectively definable standard. In all such efforts the full will of the individual is on the side of striking the mark,

454. William E. Hocking, *Human Nature and Its Remaking* (New Haven, Conn.: Yale University Press, 1923), pp. 151–152.

and the adjustment is defeated by the physical obstacles of imperfect organization and control. In the moral effort there is no difficulty of this sort: the nature of right is to be always within reach, otherwise there is no obligation. The point is that my full will is *not* on the side of striking that mark. Hence the analogy breaks down; and there is no law of learning for morality. The sinful situation is not a failure to reach what was by some organic law beyond reach; it is a defection from what was within my power. I have, as a fact of history, preferred an easier course.

455. The Focus of Character Education

The first question is this: Are we to think of character as what a person is or as what he does? Unquestionably the weight of usage favors the first meaning. Character is commonly taken to indicate the person's essential nature. When we say that an individual has a good character, we mean that his conduct, desires, purposes, ambitions, and actions are such as we approve. We favor this interpretation also when we seek to learn what a person's motives are before we are ready to pass judgment on his actions.

Modern psychologists have raised serious objection to accepting this meaning as the basis of our theories of character. What a person is cannot be known directly by another person. The observer has to depend on the report which another person makes of his own motives. This report may or may not be honest or conscientious. If the report is relied on, the honesty of the reporter is assumed at the outset. Thus the judgment concerning his character is based on an assumption regarding one element of that character. Another difficulty is that no individual is capable of giving an adequate account of his own character because he does not know what it is himself. Much of it is inaccessible to his own self-observation and much of what he can observe is gravely distorted. What a person does represents him better on the whole than any picture he can give us of what he is. What a person does, moreover, is the significant thing about him. Our main concern is to explain his conduct and learn how to modify it. This is the behavioristic point of view, which looks at character from the outside.

The external approach to the study of character is a wholesome reaction from the uncontrolled subjective approach of the earlier

455. Department of Superintendence, Tenth Yearbook, *Character Education* (Washington, D.C.: National Education Association, 1932), pp. 60–61.

psychology. Nevertheless, some forms of modern psychology make use of the individual's own account of his experiences, desires, and aims. Psychoanalysis is based wholly on the person's own reports of his thoughts and feelings. It is a question whether the student of behavior and character by the external method can ever interpret his findings without imaginatively projecting himself into the other person's situation and explaining the other's reactions in the light of his own self-knowledge. If this is true, even the behavioristic method must make surreptitious use of introspection. This unrecognized use of subjective data incurs greater danger of error than their explicit use, because the technic of their use is not subjected to criticism. It seems necessary, then, in any complete study of character, to make full and explicit use of both the results of external observation and the individual's own report of his experiences.

456. Secular Moral Education

Even programs of so-called "moral education" fail, at times, to exhibit this regard for the nurture of intelligence which is an essential part of any educational program that has genuine respect for the individual human being. Whenever concern for a "revealed" code prompts those who serve as its trustees to try to transmit the code by a process of indoctrination that involves the withholding of pertinent knowledge, the young are not treated as ends in themselves. To treat a child as an end, means so to conduct his education that he will progressively grow in his ability to make up his own mind about that which he shall believe, and about that which is to be considered worthy of his allegiance. Measured by this standard, alleged interest in the ultimate welfare or future salvation of the child does not give adults the right to deprive him of the opportunity to develop a mind of his own. One of the deplorable features in the present confused situation is that certain groups, purporting to have the spiritual interests of man at heart, are trying to impose special programs of "moral education" on the public school that actually involve an abridgment of the processes of historical and critical study. There is nothing "spiritual" about suppression, and it is difficult to see how the moral life of a democratic community will be strengthened by a program of "moral education" that strives to keep the young in ignorance about any aspect of human experience. A faith that fears knowledge cannot be

456. John L. Childs, *Education and Morals* (New York: Appleton-Century-Crofts, Inc., copyright 1950), pp. 136–137.

counted on the side of the forces that are working to develop a democratic civilization based on respect for all men.

457. Moral Education Ineffective Without Religion

The Catholic Church, guided by superhuman wisdom and the experience of long centuries, declares that mere intellectual instruction will not prevent crime, make men honest and chaste, or insure the sanctity of the home or the security of the state. If there is a duty of self-restraint or an ethical duty of any kind to be done, there must be back of it a religious truth to be learned, so that morality in action and truth in religion are inseparable. Without religion there is no such thing as fixed principles of morality. Ignore religion and the power that sustains and the authority that sanctions all laws of human conduct are wanting. To exclude religion from education is to exclude morality. Morality not only means duty, but it also means obligation. It points out our duty and tells us the reason why we should do our duty. The reason why we are bound to be moral at all, or why some actions are to be designated as good and some as bad, cannot be determined or taught without religion. Moral duty is a law which binds the conscience, the source and the sanction of that law is God. There is then no morality or obligation to obey conscience without religion which teaches us the existence and the revelation of God and the obedience which we owe to our Supreme Law-giver and Judge.

457. Regis Canevin, "Religion First in Catholic Schools," *Catholic Educational Review,* 4:99–100, September 1912.

27

Religious Education

Problems in the Philosophy of Education Discussed in this Section

1. What is a religious situation? Does all education or just particular parts of it have religious significance?
2. Is a separate and distinct philosophy of education needed for religious education, or will the one for a lay curriculum serve equally well in religion too?
3. Might some children lack sensitivity to religion just as some are tone-deaf or color-blind?
4. Do secular and religious education make different assumptions as to the child's native predispositions? As to the nature of learning? What are the implications for learning of revelation and worship? Of conversion and regeneration? Of grace?
5. Is religion an area where indoctrination is more defensible as a method of instruction than elsewhere?
6. At how early an age should children be introduced to the metaphysical and theological bases of religion? Is religious education founded on metaphysical and theological absolutes an obstacle to or a guarantor of democracy?
7. If, as some say, democracy, nationalism, communism, and science have become religions to some people, what are the implications for religious education? Could education itself properly be a religion?

458. The Myth in Religious Education

The child knows terror and the dread of annihilation, it knows the anxiety of sin and the risk of being cut off and lost; it experiences the limitation of moral values in the breakdown of adult standards; it is the victim of political and other practical insanities. All of these

458. Gustav E. Mueller, *Education Limited* (Norman, Okla.: Copyright 1949, by the University of Oklahoma Press, pp. 113–114.) Reprinted by permission of the publisher.

together form the background through which the principle of a divine and unconditional and forgiving love can shine—regardless of socio-cultural tradition.

The growth of religious education, then, would seem to follow a dialectical law. The first step is the establishment of the myth, which is naively believed as story and accepted unquestioningly. Many will never need the second step, which, in adolescence, is the shattering of the myth through historical and logical criticism. For many people today the possibility of a religious education begins in this negation. The third step is the re-establishment of the myth as myth, at which point it is persuasive as an inadequate but human symbol of the religious truth. We then have the possibility of a sympathetic and catholic understanding of the same truth in other forms and symbols of incarnation. A religious man, having gone through this process of education, will respect the absolute in other forms of faith in spite of—even because of—their respective imaginative symbols. The symbol is necessary. It is the sign by which religions become social and historical.

459. Inclusiveness of Religious Education

The term "religious education" cannot be identified with education in any particular religion, such as the Mohammedan, Jewish, or Christian. It is an inclusive term which could be applied to any and all education in religion. But this does not mean that religious education is a vague sort of education in religion in general. As a matter of fact, all education takes place in a particular cultural situation and is influenced by it. This contemporary culture has a history and represents accumulated experience. Education "takes place in the growing generation where historical culture and contemporary living meet." This is true also of special aspects of education. Education in democracy is oriented to particular situations where democracy has been or is being tried; education in citizenship always assumes citizenship somewhere; education in morals has meaning only as it is related to attitudes and behavior in particular situations. Religious education also is carried on at a particular time and place, and is influenced both by contemporaneous cultural conditions and by current religious attitudes and practices.

＊   ＊   ＊

459. Harrison S. Elliott, *Can Religious Education Be Christian?* (New York: The Macmillan Company, 1940), pp. 307–309.

It is thus seen that religious education does not imply a general search for truth independent of any definite cultural or religious orientation, and that Christian education connotes an education which has its orientation within the Christian religion. That orientation requires full recognition of the historic origin and continuity of Christianity . . .

460. Religious Education as Broad as Education Itself

At the point of our knowledge of human nature and the ways by which it remakes itself there is not occasion, seemingly, for any theoretical distinction between education and religious education. In both cases is personality the central concept and respect for personality the foundation of method.

*   *   *

Religious education, we claim, is misconceived when it is regarded as a branch of education in respect to either function or subject-matter. It is rather education itself, but education so enlarged and enriched as to quite burst the confining walls of schoolrooms, school lessons, school objectives, and to overflow into the streets, the stores, the factories, the homes, playgrounds, the churches, where men work and play and worship together. If education is best accomplished through participation, then religious education is to be thought of as participation also, but that in which the child participates when he is being educated in religion is not a mere imitation or even sample of life but rather life itself—yet not life as it realistically *is*, but life as it is *becoming* through the efforts and sacrifices of those who see in the present the germ of a nobler future.

*   *   *

Religion, then, is not a method, like science, nor a body of knowledge, nor a collection of customs, nor the performance of rites and ceremonies, nor the seeking of this or that satisfaction. Religion is a discovery of kinship with the eternal, a discovery which is also, in this very act, an achievement of selfhood in a universe of coexistent selves.

*   *   *

Religious education to-day consists, therefore, of such experiences of reality as may issue in the discovery of the essential character of

460. Hugh Hartshorne, "The Relation of Religious to General Education," in P. Henry Lotz and L. W. Crawford, eds., *Studies in Religious Education* (Nashville, Tenn.: Copyright 1931, by Lamar and Whitmore), pp. 439–447. Used by permission of Abingdon-Cokesbury Press.

the universe, and of the part the self may play in forwarding the general movement of evolution toward the realization of more complete selfhood in a more humane society.

No more in religious education than in so-called general education are methods to be deduced entirely from principles. Every genuine educational process is at the moment it takes place a creative achievement. It is fresh growth from which one may learn how growth takes place. So in religious education there must be opportunity for growth. The child must be released, not bound. But the thing that is to grow is not an isolated skill, nor even a group of coordinated skills, attitudes, and knowledges, but a self; and as in the ordinary schoolroom the essential thing is the provision of appropriate materials and activities which are continuous with the life of society, so here the environment to which the child is to be exposed and the life in which he is to participate is the larger life of the beloved community, the ideal society, moving within the swift flow of events we call reality.

To interpose between a child and his adventurous contact with life a screen of dogma and ceremony is the antithesis of education in religion. A philosophy of life and certain reminders of its meaning are assuredly needed, and past or present formulas and rites are a part of the world of experience with which the child should come into touch; but meanings and forms are the genuine equipment of religion only for those who have thought them through for themselves or wrought them out by their own efforts. And furthermore, the contribution to our understanding and control of existence that might be made by the undimmed insight of childhood and youth is not to be despised. How much more hope of progress there would be if young and old, instead of continuing the drawn battle between them, would forget their jealousies and work shoulder to shoulder for the establishment of a spiritual commonwealth.

461. Religious Aspects of Education

Religion is not something that can be made an object of study, as is spelling, or algebra, or history. There could be a subject of instruction and a worthy one, too, worked up concerning religion, just as there has been such a subject worked up concerning the civil war; but the school subject about the war is not the war, has very little relation to it, and indeed may be of questionable value. Religion is not something mysteriously hidden away in language to be gotten into

461. Charles E. Rugh, *Essential Place of Religion in Education* (Ann Arbor, Mich.: National Education Association, 1916), pp. 12–21.

the child's memory or mind thru the eye or the ear by verbal instruction. Religious education is not instruction in the Bible . . .

            ❊   ❊   ❊

An attempt has been made to divide truth into two classes, sacred
and secular; if this foolish and erroneous attempt had not been made,
the religious implication and significance of much of the school work
would be perfectly evident. The laws of nature are permanent. The
multiplication table is as sacred as the ten commandments. No man
can break either of these laws. He may break himself against them, but
they remain permanent. Teaching that inculcates only the knowledge
of these eternal laws of God and does not develop the disposition to
employ and obey them, can hardly be called education. If a teacher
by examples and precept presents permanent values and induces
joyous obedience and loyalty, the teaching is religious both potentially and actually. Potentially because it is developing that psychic
machinery by which the learner may employ permanent standards for
evaluating things, persons and the self. The teaching is actually
religious because the learner is successfully adjusting himself to the
universe.

The religious development of human consciousness manifests itself
in its second phase in the disposition and ability to recover from
failure. In a world like this where both the child and its environment are developing, there are many failures of adjustment, many
failures in measuring things, persons, and self by eternal standards.
When behavior reveals the fact that one's standards were inadequate
or wrong, then the religious person repents, confesses, and consecrates
the will to what is believed to be higher and better standards of life.
In religious circles this is called conversion. Psychologically, the process is not confined to seeking spiritually perfect standards of life, but
may be employed in any fundamental interest, for example, in diet
or medicine, in politics, or family life.

As the ability to seek and employ a permanent system of values is
the supreme principle in instruction, so the development of the ability
and disposition to be converted from wrong ways of behaving is the
supreme principle, especially in cases of punishment.

But even if religious nurture has done all it can do and if we have
been converted from our wrong ways, and if we have experienced
forgiveness, still there will be sorrowful experiences of life, still there
will be mysteries. The religious life must develop the ability and
disposition to suffer the sorrows of accidents and storms and earth-
quake and death without bitterness, without the feeling of rebellion
and anarchy, without the feeling of utter defeat. The promise of all

ethnic religions is the triumph over the sorrows of life, even unto the last enemy, death. This aspect of life gives rise to the doctrine of religion as a warfare, a struggle against the forces of evil . . .

462. Whole Curriculum Related to God

She [the Church] feels that it is her duty to teach every branch in the curriculum since nothing can be understood by the pupil as it is, unless it is understood in the light which religion sheds upon it. Without God, the world consists of a multitude of fragments, and where God and religion are omitted from the curriculum, nothing else that the curriculum contains can be presented to the pupil as it is, since it cannot be presented to him in its relation to God and to the totality of created existence. It is not, therefore, for the sake of religion alone that the Church insists that religion and the so-called secular branches shall not be separated in her schools.

463. Religious and Secular Curriculum Differentiated

The principle of religious instruction is authority; that of secular instruction is demonstration and verification. It is obvious that these two principles should not be brought into the same school, but separated as widely as possible. Religious truth is revealed in allegoric and symbolic form, and is to be apprehended not merely by the intellect, but also by the imagination and the heart. The analytic understanding is necessarily hostile and skeptical in its attitude towards religious truth. The pupil is taught in mathematics to love demonstration and logical proof, and he is taught in history to verify its sources, and to submit all tradition to probabilities of common experience. The facts of common experience dealing with the ordinary operations of causality are not sufficient to serve for symbols of what is spiritual. They are opaque facts and do not serve for symbols— symbols are facts which serve as lenses with which to see divine things. On themes so elevated as religious faith deals with, the habit of thinking cultivated in secular instruction is out of place. Even the attitude of mind cultivated in secular instruction is unfitted for the

462. Thomas E. Shields, *Philosophy of Education* (Washington, D.C.: The Catholic Education Press, 1921), p. 404.

463. William T. Harris, "The Separation of the Church from the Tax-Supported School," *Educational Review*, 26:224–225, October 1903.

approach to religious truth. Religious instruction should be surrounded with solemnity. It should be approached with ceremonial preparation, so as to lift up the mind to the dignity of the lesson received. Christianity is indeed the religion of the revealed God, but there is no revelation possible to the mind immersed in trivialities and self-conceit. In religious lessons wherein the divine is taught as revealed to the human race, it is right that the raw, immature intellect of youth shall not be called upon to exercise a critical judgment, for the youth at his best cannot grasp the rationality of the dogmas which contain the deepest insights of the religious consciousness of the race.

464. Theories of Knowledge in Religious and Secular Curricula

Already the spirit of our schooling is permeated with the feeling that every subject, every topic, every fact, every professed truth must submit to a certain publicity and impartiality. All proffered samples of learning must go to the same assay-room and be subjected to common tests. It is the essence of all dogmatic faiths to hold that any such "showdown" is sacrilegious and perverse. The characteristic of religion, from their point of view, is that it is—intellectually—secret, not public; peculiarly revealed, not generally known; authoritatively declared, not communicated and tested in ordinary ways. What is to be done about this increasing antinomy between the standard for coming to know in other subjects of the school, and coming to know in religious matters? I am far from saying that the antinomy is an inherent one, or that the day may not come when religion will be so thoroughly naturalised in the hearts and minds of men that it can be considered publicly, openly, and by common tests, even among religious people. But it is pertinent to point out that, as long as religion is conceived as it now is conceived by the great majority of professed religionists, there is something self-contradictory in speaking of education in topics where the method of free inquiry has made its way. The "religious" would be the last to be willing that either the history or the content of religion should be taught in this spirit; while those to whom the scientific standpoint is not a merely technical device, but is the embodiment of integrity of mind, must protest against its being taught in any other spirit.

464. John Dewey, "Religion and Our Schools," *Hibbert Journal,* 6:804–805, July 1908.

465. Education and Evangelism

A mistaken antithesis has sometimes been drawn between evangelistic and educational ways of conceiving the function of the Church. Those who believe in religious education have been accused of ignoring the grace of God and of imagining that morality and religion may be educed from man himself or grown within him by processes of skillful cultivation, without need of the regenerating Spirit of God. Those, on the other hand, who have usurped to themselves the name of evangelists, have at times spoken as though the message of salvation were pre-eminently contained in Jesus' comparison of the Spirit to the wind, which "bloweth where it listeth, and thou hearest the sound thereof, but canst not tell whence it cometh and whither it goeth"; and they have relied upon spasmodic revivals of religion to the neglect of the more sober, constant, and constructive methods of *educational* evangelism. Less than a hundred years ago, debate was still waging in New England as to whether there really are or can be any *means* of grace.

It cannot be urged too strongly that the antithesis thus set up is mistaken and untrue. A scheme of Christian education that should fail to take account of man's dependence upon the Spirit of God would contradict the very gospel which it undertakes to teach. "By grace are ye saved through faith, and that not of yourselves; it is the gift of God." But the Spirit of God is not arbitrary; His grace does not baffle expectation. It is, in fact, a species of atheism—unintended yet practical atheism—to deny God's presence and power in the natural laws which He has ordained and to fail to recognize in these laws the accustomed means and channels of His will. Not evangelism *or* education, then, is the alternative before the Church; its work is that of evangelism *through* education . . .

466. Religious Means of Education

From the Catholic viewpoint, there are several excellent means of making changes in human beings, in addition to educational

465. Committee on the War and the Religious Outlook, *Teaching Work of the Church* (New York: Association Press, 1923), p. 40.

466. John D. Redden and Francis A. Ryan, *A Catholic Philosophy of Education* (Milwaukee: The Bruce Publishing Company, 1955), p. 299.

methods. Such means are prayer, the sacraments, and grace. They are intrinsically efficacious in that they cause human beings to make desirable changes in their own inner lives. When a teacher assists the child to set them in motion for himself, the desired changes and results are far more likely to be permanent. Furthermore, the proper shaping of the self-ideal of the individual, which is one of the most important outcomes of method, is much more likely to be effected by these spiritual means.

467. Educational View of Conversion

If by evangelism we mean the regenerating work of God's spirit in the soul of man, religious education has this as its highest aim. If, however, we identify evangelism with a sudden, momentary conversion experience, then religious education has a different method of work. Its very foundation is laid on Bushnell's proposition that the child is a child of God and should never know himself to be otherwise. Growth there must be, and decisions—not one, but many decisions for Christ as the countless situations of life unfold before the growing child. It is true that these decisions are of differing intensity, and one may even overtop all others as *the* decision. But no completed Christ-like character can be had in the twinkling of an eye. Religious educators do not deny the possibility of a momentary conversion experience. They maintain only that Christian nurture as a constant approach toward God, making unnecessary a turning-about experience, is a better and surer way. Even when birth into the Kingdom is by some sudden experience of conversion which completely reverses the former trends of life, it has usually been preceded by unnoted or forgotten educative influences, and must in any case be followed by a long process of education before Christ-like character is established.

468. Religious Character of the Public School

. . . We do not find it feasible or desirable to put upon the regular teachers the burden of teaching a subject which has the nature of religion. The alternative plan of parcelling out pupils among religious

467. Paul H. Vieth, "Objectives in Religious Education," *School and Society,* 34:360–361, September 1931.

468. John Dewey, "Religion and Our Schools," *Hibbert Journal,* 6:806–807. July 1908.

teachers drawn from their respective churches and denominations brings us up against exactly the matter which has done most to discredit the churches, and to discredit the cause, not perhaps of religion, but of organized and institutional religion: the multiplication of rival and competing religious bodies, each with its private inspiration and outlook. Our schools, in bringing together those of different nationalities, languages, traditions, and creeds, in assimilating them together upon the basis of what is common and public in endeavour and achievement, are performing an infinitely significant religious work. They are promoting the social unity out of which in the end genuine religious unity must grow. Shall we interfere with this work? Shall we run the risk of undoing it by introducing into education a subject which can be taught only by segregating pupils and turning them over at special hours to separate representatives of rival faiths? This would be deliberately to adopt a scheme which is predicated upon the maintenance of social divisions in just the matter, religion, which is empty and futile save as it expresses the basic unities of life . . .

469. Teachability of Religion

If religion comes by way of inner illumination, independent of instruction, as some have held, then obviously it cannot be taught. If it is a response of the individual to the social values of his group, then it is a question as to how far any formal training can make certain of eliciting such response. If there are tone-deaf persons who cannot learn music, may there not be emotionally stolid people who cannot sense the meaning and value of religion?

470. How the Child Learns Religion

In examining the results of such a lesson as this it will be found that the child will learn that God has made him and that his eye and ear and all the rest of him somehow came from God's thought. It is true that he fails utterly to comprehend how God's thought is realized in creation but he does reach the idea that God is the Creator

469. Edward S. Ames, "Can Religion Be Taught?" *Religious Education*, 25:42, January 1930.
470. Thomas E. Shields, *Philosophy of Education* (Washington, D.C.: The Catholic Education Press, 1921), p. 206.

and that secondary agents are employed to perfect and continue the original result of the creative act. It is true that he fails utterly to comprehend the doctrine of the Logos. He does not understand in the least how God's thought is realized in creation, but it is equally true that he has no desire and no need for such knowledge. In his state of mental development his dependence is overwhelmingly on authority instead of on internal evidence. Assertion is all he needs . . .

471. Incompatibility of Dogmatic Religion and Experimentalist Education

An experience-centered educational process does not imply lack of conviction. It only indicates how convictions are held. Convictions represent what seem to individuals or groups to be best. They act as if those convictions were final, but at the same time they take toward their action a critical attitude and seek ways of improving it. The two are not inconsistent . . .

An experience-centered educational process is inconsistent, however, with positions dogmatically and finally held. This is the source of much of the opposition to religious education and is also the cause of a conflict within education itself. There has often been a tendency for each religious faith to consider its own the only true religion. This results not only in the unwillingness to learn from other faiths, but also in the practice of branding them as false and untrue. Under these circumstances the followers of each faith feel the necessity of defending and propagating their own faith as the true religion. The search for truth is turned into dogmatic defense and counter-defense of a particular set of truths. Divisions arise and the fellowship of a true educational process is at an end. Religious education becomes a means for indoctrinating children and youth in a particular set of Christian interpretations or the propaganda by which others are influenced to accept that particular set of dogmas as the only true faith.

Religious leaders are not the only individuals with dogmatic certainty. Those who are at the extreme right in social and political outlook and wish to maintain the *status quo,* and those who have moved to the extreme left and wish to overthrow the existing order are often as dogmatic in their certainty as to the final right of their beliefs as are some of the followers of religion. Those at the right

471. Harrison S. Elliott, *Can Religious Education Be Christian?* (New York: The Macmillan Company, 1940), pp. 317–319.

wish to use education to maintain the *status quo* and they oppose free discussion of current problems as zealously as they do the direct teaching of radical notions. Those at the extreme left would like to use education for the propagation of their proposed theories and they also are opposed to free consideration of these problems. Thus, a true educational process is being challenged both from the extreme right and the extreme left. It is not surprising to find that those of a religious outlook who move to a dogmatically held extreme left in economic and political theory should at the same time move to a dogmatically held extreme right in religious faith, for the extreme right in religion and the extreme left in economics and politics are often alike in dogmatic certainty. The conflict then is not alone between authoritarian religion and experimental education. It is rather a more fundamental cleavage between those of dogmatic certainty in ethical and religious beliefs, and those who take the experimental attitude toward life and who are convinced that ethical standards and goals of endeavor as well as religious beliefs are worked out, by the same educational process as the means for their attainment. A true educational process is denied as soon as education is made the servant of any dogmatism, whether in religion or in any other area. The freedom of individuals and of groups to search for and find their own meaningful interpretations of life and destiny is important in religious education which is Christian. This liberty is in line with the spirit of the New Testament. It was a cardinal principle of the Reformation. It is true to the scientific spirit and method. It is that which gives Christian experience its vitality.

The issues in regard to religious education center in the source of authority. Those with an authoritarian approach seek to find authority for their interpretations outside of human responsibility in some direct revelation of God. Those with an educational approach recognize that while God has not left himself without witness, man has not been given any direct revelation of the meaning of these manifestations . . .

472. Transmissive Versus Critical Religious Education

Perhaps some one will raise the disturbing question: "What of the child to be educated? Has he no rights in the matter? Should he, just because he is born in a liberal or conservative environment, be sub-

472. Paul H. Vieth, *Objectives in Religious Education* (New York: Harper & Brothers, 1930), pp. 130–131. Reprinted by permission of the publishers.

mitted to the beliefs dominant in that particular environment?" We
may indeed pause to ponder this question. Every child has a right
to the truth, of course. But what if two equally competent and conscientious groups disagree as to what the truth is, when there is no
method of objective verification of the truth? Our modern educational approach holds a ray of light. Have we not assumed that in no
case is it to be a process of handing on a completed faith, but rather
one of giving the learner a share in developing a faith which is
reasonable and satisfactory to him? Are we not then under obligation
to bring the learner into contact with the best religious thought in its
various aspects and encourage him to weigh and choose? That this
lays a heavy strain on the teacher is evident. The strain is one of
representing fairly other viewpoints than his own, and of being
widely informed concerning the best thought on his subject. Yet the
discipline involved in responding to these strains is not too great for
the privilege of bearing the honored title of teacher. The compensa-
tions in the teacher's own enlargement of soul and development of
personality will more than repay him for the effort of being a teacher
according to the ideal here set forth.

473. Fallen Human Nature

The truth is that man, considered simply as natural man, is as whole
today, in intellect and will, as was man regarded in his purely natural
endowment when he came from the creative hand of God. In other
words original sin left man in no worse condition, on the purely
human level of his mind and will, than he was before Adam cast his
momentous decision against God.

What is true in all that we hear about the disastrous effects of
Adam's sin is this: the first man deliberately renounced God and
thereby lost the supernatural endowments which God had conferred
on him for the whole human race. Adam was created not only in a
state of natural perfection, but was elevated to the sonship of God by
sanctifying grace. Moreover, to complement this divine gift and to
enable Adam to preserve it for himself and the entire human family,
God added other remarkable gifts, notably the gift of integrity whereby
all his powers and faculties were perfectly subordinated to his reason
and will, and the gift of immortality whereby his body was subjected
to his soul so that it was liberated from the necessity of falling into

473. Cyril Vollert, "Original Sin and Education," *Review for Religious,* July
1946, 5:219–220, 223–226.

corruption and death. These inconceivably great bounties, all of them beyond the capacities of human nature, Adam received for himself and for all his descendants.

By sinning Adam lost them all. He lost original justice for himself and for his posterity . . .

＊　　　　＊　　　　＊

The same is the case with our intellect. Adam had a preternatural gift of infused knowledge. We have not. Therefore our understanding is dark as compared with his, for his was bathed with divine light. If Adam had not sinned, he would have handed on his special, infused gift of knowledge to his descendants. For this knowledge was a personal gift with which God equipped the first man, created as he was in adulthood in intimate communion with God and with a special office as teacher of the children he was to beget.

Adam had yet other endowments perfecting his intellect. Along with the sanctifying grace that elevated him to supernatural heights went the infused virtues, theological and moral. Among these are faith and prudence, which resided in his intellect. These he would have transmitted. But he sinned, and so could not transmit sanctifying grace and all the accompanying gifts. We, born without sanctifying grace, begin life deprived of the infused virtues, including those which would have equipped our minds with a habitual aptitude for higher truths. In this respect, too, our minds are defective as compared with his before the Fall.

But here we must consider another factor, which is seldom well brought out. In sinning, Adam lost, besides sanctifying grace with its cortege of infused virtues, the preternatural gifts of integrity and immortality. Along with the loss of immortality went the loss of impassibility, or immunity to suffering, disease, and death. His body was no longer perfectly subject to his soul.

From Adam we inherit bodies bereft of these gifts. Not only are we subject to concupiscence, but we have bodies unprotected from harm by the gifts of immortality and impassibility. Our souls are immortal, but they have not the power to impart immortality to our bodies. Thus left in their natural weakness, our bodies easily give in to fatigue, to a thousand different diseases, to the decrepitude of advancing age, and to dissolution. All this has weighty consequences for our knowledge and our capacity to learn.

Obviously, the pull of concupiscence is a tremendous obstacle to the acquisition of knowledge. We have a kinship for the concrete, the sensible. Higher truths, especially the truths of theology, religion, and metaphysics, have little charm for most people. They want to know and experience what is pleasant and easy. Whatever has a surface interest excites them. The clang of the fire-engine bell upsets the class; not only children in third grade but university students, and the professor himself, feel the urge to rush to the window. Philosophy is hard put to it to resist the seduction of the radio. Mathematics runs a poor second to movies. A game of ball in the nearby playground is more fun than geography or arithmetic. Shakespeare and Thackeray have less appeal than the funnies.

Another important consideration is the fatigue that goes with thinking. Continuity is essential to study. But the brain soon wearies and seeks distraction. Even under the most favorable circumstances, such as absolute quiet, freedom from interruption, and robust health, mental concentration is extremely hard work. We know how right Aristotle was when he remarked, "Learning is accompanied by pain." The experience of students is well formulated in a wise man's saying that has passed into a proverb: "Knowledge maketh a bloody entrance."

But ideal circumstances are rarely granted to us. Leisure for thinking is a luxury. The very necessity of caring for the body's needs takes up the most valuable portion of our time and energies. The majority of mankind must spend half or more of each working day in sheer toil for bread. What leisure is left is without the freshness of mind required for active thought.

Even when a person has leisure and opportunity for learning, his bodily condition is often a deterrent to efficient study. The eye too soon grows dim, and reading has to be rationed. Hayfever, sinus infection, a cold in the head, the hundred ills that plague mankind, all militate against the attention, correlation, and penetration required for sustained thinking and for the mastery of but a single province of human knowledge.

474. Revision of the Theories of Human Nature Demanded

Christian education has been very clearly dominated by theological theories of human nature; and they are still seriously complicating much of our church procedure. Certain of them are founded upon the narratives in the opening chapters of the Bible. Hebrew religious genius, seeking to account for the presence of evil, used material from ancient semitic mythology and pictured the temptation of Adam and

474. Theodore G. Soares, *Religious Education* (Chicago: University of Chicago Press, 1928), pp. 1–6.

Eve in the garden of innocence. The psychological truth, as well as the poetic beauty, of those stories ought to have saved them from the theologians. Paul employs them rabbinically and homiletically to make contrast between the heritage of evil that comes to us from our natural ancestry and the freedom effected by the regenerative power of grace. Here was the material for theological speculation, with the resulting orthodox Christian doctrine of the total depravity of man.

The effect of that doctrine upon the interpretation of childhood is inevitable and far reaching. Forced by the irrefutable logic of their system, men have held that the babe that lies in its mother's arms has a nature utterly corrupt. There is in it no possibility of good; all its tendencies are toward evil. It is alien from God and under His eternal wrath. Its spiritual father is the devil, and its fitting destiny is an unending hell. Of course this fearful doctrine was only the foundation of the glorious doctrine of salvation. God was graciously ready to change this depraved nature and to give to the child His own divine qualities. How was this to be brought about? There are two answers to this question, and the whole course of religious education has been, and is in many quarters today, affected by the theory that is espoused. For the sacramentalist, the regeneration of the child is effected by baptism, which is the channel of grace. When the sacred rite has been performed, an actual change has taken place in the essential nature of the infant. Not that the old evil is gone—it will wage a long struggle in the redeemed soul—but a new life has begun; and ability is now present to respond to spiritual guidance.

Childhood is easily interpreted on this theory. When the child does wrong, we see the outcropping of the old nature; when he is good, we behold the victory of the grace of God. Parents and teachers are encouraged to help the development of the better nature. Thus, in effect the dogma of baptismal regeneration offsets the dogma of human depravity. The sacramental churches have thus quite naturally been those in which religious education has been conceived as a fundamental responsibility of parents and pastors. To be sure, they have often spoiled it with intellectualistic catechisms; they have often routinized their technique and made of confirmation a kind of graduation from the childhood discipline. When they have done this, they have lost the opportunity which their sacramental theory afforded them. However, they have not been embarrassed by a theological theory of the ineducability of their children but have been so far free to develop their own training process.

A large section of the Christian church has rejected sacramentalism. To them it is little short of magic to think of a ceremony performed

upon an unconscious infant effecting any radical change in his fundamental nature. The evangelical theory is that the grace of God is
imparted to the repentant sinner. When one realizes his depraved
nature and exercises faith in the divine grace, then, and only then,
is the regenerating grace imparted; then, and only then, is the evil
nature changed. What place does this leave for the religious education of children? Manifestly you cannot religiously educate a child
of the devil. You should not teach him the Lord's prayer, for God is
not his Father. He should not learn the Twenty-third Psalm, for the
Lord is not his Shepherd. God is only his Judge.

✳   ✳   ✳

It is clear that all these theological theories are unscientific. They
are a priori, authoritative, based upon biblical interpretation. While
the biblical story upon which they rest was the outcome of human
experience, these theories have made no attempt to check that experience by direct observation of human nature itself.

What of the opposite theological theory of the divinity of man?
Rousseau laid down the doctrine of the essential goodness of nature
and formulated an educational theory based upon the goodness of
the natural impulses . . .

This theology equally with orthodoxy lacks both the sociological
and biological point of view. It fails to recognize that "goodness" and
"badness" are social terms deriving their meaning from social behavior
and that the original nature of man can be only his biological inheritance and therefore cannot have any qualities which belong to
social living.

475. Two Conceptions of Religious Education

The further question may now be asked whether Christian education
is not the chief support of vital piety. Three sets of contrasting notions
are here involved. First comes the dogmatic as contrasted with the
vital conception of discipleship. The dogmatic view makes the acceptance of a creed a preliminary to Christian living, the vital view
puts living first, and makes the creed a product and expression of
life. The one identifies education with instruction, while the other
identifies it with development of the personality. Underneath this

475. George A. Coe, *Education in Religion and Morals* (Chicago: Fleming H.
Revell, 1911), pp. 389–390.

opposition lies, in the scond place, the problem of authority. Here the opposing ideas are those of truth external to one's being and imposed upon one from without, and truth involved in one's being and realized in an inner experience. The one would make of education a bestowal upon the child, the other an unfolding of the child. But deeper still lies, in the third place, an opposition between two conceptions of God's relation to the world—God as existing in only external relations to creation, and God as immanent in the whole of it. The former conception, representing him as coming into our lives chiefly in special experiences, is well able to provide for religious crises, but not for continuous religious development. The doctrine of divine immanence, however, provides a basis for continuous development, or education proper.

The Christian thought of our time has already made choice between these alternative views. The immanent God, whose authority is internal and identical with the laws of self-realisation, and with whom we come into relations not primarily through belief but rather through the whole circle of impulses and aspirations that make us men—this is the standpoint that we have won. Here we find not only a basis for a theory of religious education, but also a practical condition of vital piety . . .

476. A Social Orientation of Religious Education

Coercion is not something—a technique to be used or to be avoided; it is an integral part of the organized state power! It will be used and is being used every day throughout the working-class front, not by the workers but by the bourgeoisie and their state power. And so to quibble academically about the possible use of coercion by the workers in the interests of the working class when the insurrectionary period arrives is sheer hypocrisy! And yet, such academic quibblings are typical of religious education in general. Modern religious education tries to orient the individual to a world that does not exist—it attempts to adjust the individual to a word of unreality. And I believe that just because of that fact, the laboring masses of our nation have divorced themselves from the Church and are periodically joined by the exodus of distracted and disgusted intellectuals.

And so, religious education must come to orient persons to those

476. Carleton Fisher, "The Place of Religious Education in the Social Revolution," *Religious Education*, 31:50–52, January 1936.

social techniques and instruments which give opportunities for the expression of their hopes and ambitions.

And in this connection, it seems necessary to me that we recognize the fact that religious education must more and more become "secularized," in that the organized expression of the social aspects of religion must take place in techniques foreign to the Church. The Church lacks a realistic program—it knows not how the City of God will be built . . .

I think we have to admit that a good deal of our real religious education is carried on outside the Church in these so-called secular agencies. Countless movements for social reconstruction are today expressing the religious passion of people to a degree that puts the Church to shame! In the by and large, the last vestige of truly social value left in the Church is that element that we know as worship, and to my way of thinking, such worship is coming more and more to the point where the old wine sack is about to fall in pieces.

*   *   *

In stressing these social objectives of religious education, I merely desire to emphasize the point that a healthy orientation to life must be based upon reality. The religion of Jesus has much more than that to offer, but it does include this much. To adjust a person to what is, is to make him conscious of what ought to be and what must not be! To see the inevitability of coercion versus coercion in the class struggle is necessary, but to see that coercion versus coercion will never produce love is also necessary. In the end, when one has been adjusted to society in a more or less stable fashion, the drive toward the ultimate good takes on vital meaning. It is this everlasting denouncing of the relative by a God-complexed Church that militates against the very expressions of Jesus' religion! To do something and be critically self-analytical about it, is one thing; to persistently do nothing and condemn, is quite another thing.

477. Agnosticism and Religious Education

Who is the philosophical agnostic? What does he ask of the state in the matter of public education?

The agnostic is one who recognizes the limitations, the finiteness, of

477. Lewis G. Janes, "Religious Instruction in State Schools," *Educational Review*, 4:121–125, September 1892.

the human intellect. He perceives, not that there is no infinite reality external to the human mind, but that this reality can only be known to man symbolically, as determined by the nature of his psychical limitations . . .

Religion, however, to the philosophical agnostic, is by no means to be identified with the theological garments in which it happens to be clothed. These it changes from age to age, to suit the intellectual requirements of various people in different stages of culture and development. The reality, however, persists in spite of these shifting phases of its manifestation, and will endure when the last vestige of anthropomorphic and man-made theology is stripped from its essential truth. Taking this view of religion, the agnostic would have no objection to the training of the religious nature of his children in precisely the same way as that in which the most enlightened educators aim to train their intellectual natures. He does object strongly, however, to the inculcation, even by inference or object-lesson, of theological dogmas, which, in his view, can never do otherwise than distort and unwisely bias and misdirect the normal activities of the religious sentiment.

Nor does the agnostic conceive it impossible to train and develop the religious sentiment, without the inculcation of dogma, or even apart from any technical Christian teaching. The essentials of the religious sentiment, which underlie all its specific manifestations, are reverence, faithfulness, and faith in the reality of the Unseen. All these sentiments and faculties may be stimulated along with the moral and intellectual training of children without any dogmatic teaching; and unless the teacher can arouse these sentiments in his pupils in connection with their daily tasks, he is lacking in complete preparation and qualification for his worthy and noble undertaking.

All teaching implies the fundamental distinction between truth and error—between that which conforms to reality and that which does not so conform, or merely appears so to conform. Reverence for truth, then, lies at the very foundation of all knowledge, and must be inculcated at every step of intellectual advancement. With the evolution and wise culture of the rational nature, and the cultivation of habits of reflection, the mind will naturally come to regard the order of nature, and those higher uniformities of conduct which constitute the perfect flower of human character, as phenomena of an underlying and indwelling reality, which is the source and nexus of all specific forms of truth, and merits the reverence which the mind has been taught to bestow upon the principle of truth everywhere.

❋   ❋   ❋

Faith in the Unseen Reality is inculcated by daily experience in all faithful work. It may seem strange to those who have studied agnosticism in the camp of its enemies to find this sentiment held up as a part of the agnostic's creed. He is ordinarily regarded as one who has no faith in anything—who repudiates faith as the mother of all superstitions, and accepts nothing which cannot be logically and inductively demonstrated. The existence of an Unseen Reality which, owing to the limitation of his faculties, is in its essential nature unknowable, is, however, the fundamental postulate of the agnostic's creed.

❊   ❊   ❊

The identification of morals with sectarian dogmas and ceremonial observances, has been well-nigh fatal to all the genuine springs of ethical effort. It has based morality upon the shifting sands of a verbal statement of truth, instead of upon the truth itself as revealed in the nature of things—in the constitution of the universe. By its emphasis on remote and extrinsic penalties for wrong-doing, it has robbed the soul of the finer ethical insight which declares that the effects of evil acts are instrinsic, and instantly enforced in the atrophy of character. In this era of crumbling creeds and shifting opinions, the greatest service to morality is to teach the momentous truth that the enforcement of the moral law is not dependent upon man's speculative opinions about God or the universe. It is the false teaching that it is so dependent, and not the contrary teaching which renders the moral law meaningless. This teaching of the instant penalty of wrong-doing will be as effective with the children of atheists and agnostics, of materialists and infidels, as with those of the most devout Christian; and there is no place, except the family, where it can be so effectively enforced as in the public school.

Though the public school may not teach dogma or ritual, or rightly force upon any pupil a stated reading of the Bible, or repetition of prayers, there is no reason, therefore, why it should not wisely cultivate the religious nature of the pupil and teach the soundest principles of morality. If the parent at home or in the Church chooses to have this teaching supplemented by instruction in the tenets of his particular faith, well and good. To this the agnostic can raise only a moral and rational objection, for over the action of sectarian parents in their individual and parental capacity he has no control. But when it is proposed to introduce sectarian teaching into public schools, or to appropriate the public educational funds to denominational institutions of learning, he is impelled to enter his most emphatic protest.

478. Humanism Versus Revelation in Religious Education

. . . Much religious education is conceived of as a sort of emotionalized social education. Emphasis upon personality and truth is minimized and in its place is put the emphasis upon social democracy or devotion to the highest social well-being. To be sure, God may be mentioned, but God is conceived as immanent in the social process, as a part of nature, capable of being experienced in man's high devotion to "ideal social ends." In short, the social "religious attitude" is substituted for definite personal relations to a personal God and definite ends. "The beyond" element is swallowed up in the present experience; it is conceived as the highest experience in a monistically conceived world. Thus religious education is a part of general education with no particular truth of its own. This is a thorough-going naturalism and humanism and immanentism. There is an unashamed continuity between God and man, and God is merely the unrealized possibilities of man.

❊ ❊ ❊

In the place of divine authority, man has placed himself. And the modern problem is: How can man find real meaning for life? On the one hand, we have *bourgeois* individualism with man the individual finding the meaning of life in his personal pursuit, and, on the other hand, we have man in mass fashion giving meaning to the lives of millions who have given up their chaotic liberal individualism by tired and fearful capitulation to coercion. The former denies community life, the latter denies individual freedom. Both are false types of life, for the center of life is usurped by a purpose that will never redeem man to his true self. They are God-less ways of life. There is no substitute for true divine content, to "fill" life with proper meaning. In fact, only by response to God through faith and in action can one possess true personality. Is there any salvation through humanism, whether individual or social?

Here, it seems to me, is the real problem of modern religious education. Religious education, if it would be truly religious, while it must deal primarily with man individually and socially, must not start with autonomous man, but with divine thought about man. Divine

478. Elmer G. Homrighausen, "The Real Problem of Religious Education," *Religious Education,* 34:13–17, January–March 1939.

thought about man is the criterion. True, a study of man's plight dimly, and negatively, reveals the need for divine revelation. For, even if we did start with man, and according to Froebel, say that man should be educated according to the "laws of his being," we might ask: How shall we determine what the real laws of man's being are? How shall we know what man is? Can we know man as he really is on the basis of man as he is? Man simply does not determine what he is on the basis of his own opinions. This method ends in confusion. All man's quest after life's meaning ends in hints about God's existence, but not in the nature of His being. Evaluation of man must come from beyond. The innate law of man may have some validity, but man has no power to determine what is ultimately valid about himself on the basis of what he thinks he is. Religious education must take the essential man more seriously. We cannot be content with a chart for the direction of man's growth that is as faulty as man himself, even though we will always have to deal with faulty man.

But is such a religion to be found, it may be asked. On the sheer basis of human need and the unfulfilled yearnings of man and society in this present hour, we might say we have the clearest demand for revelation from God.

But, on the other hand, if we would study history with the same zeal that we study the modern sciences we would discover that such a religion has dawned upon man's life, and has become a living force in human history. We should not be shied off because some have taken this religion by violence and have distorted it to their own ends, making it likewise a statistical, isolated, human possession of group or sect. The living Word became flesh and its personal claim has been proclaimed and effectuated these nineteen hundred years. It declares that God, the personal, condescending, righteous, loving God, is the center of history and the lord of life. He is the creator, sustainer, and the redeemer of life. In the light of this revelation we see light.

The solution is to be found in this religion given by divinely-initiated revelation, embracing a body of living, eternal truth through personality and history, capable of constant appropriation in and adaptation to the contemporary scene, through faith and the Divine Spirit, having social implications, and claiming to "fill" human life, both of man and men, with the true content for forgiven, purposeful, useful, reconciling, neighborly, realistic, victorious—yes, eternal—living.

This, to my mind, is found in the Hebrew-Christian tradition, and witnessed to it in the Scriptures, finding its culmination in divine incarnation, the Word became flesh, and issuing in constant realization, through the Holy Spirit. When this living Truth becomes active in life through obedient faith, life is meaningful and expresses itself in genuine love, in a true Christian secularism, if you please.

This proposal would not involve a complete break with modern methods of religious education, although such a religion would have distinctive methods of its own. But it would mean that modern methods would have to be christened to a new purpose and directed from a higher vantage ground. Every phase of religious education which was bent on keeping religion close to life will be maintained and utilized with a greater realism that is born of a clearer perception of the truth. True religion is not alien to the secular.

Religious education based upon this type of religion would result in freedom, for true freedom comes to man only when he is obedient to that for which he was created and to that for which he was meant to live—the will and the love of God. It would also result in democracy. We do not get freedom or democracy by direct method, they come only as results of true religion! This is the end of education as well as of religion, and pre-eminently the end of religious education. It is high time we began recovering the essential uniqueness of religious education. But before that can be done, we will need to define more adequately the precise meaning of "religion."

479. A Definite Body of Truth in Religious Education

. . . It has been claimed that the teaching of religion must be kept apart from the teaching of other subjects on the ground that its methods are incompatible with those that are employed in the "regular" work of the school; and it is worth while inquiring whether the Church in her long experience has not made use of methods that are free from any such objection.

It seems quite plain, to begin with, that the teaching of religion presupposes a definite body of truth. Statements that are vague and presentations of doctrine that leave a wide margin to views which may or may not be in accord with truth, cannot serve the purpose. The whole endeavor of scientific thought is to secure accuracy both in the work of investigation and in formulating the results. It is therefore all the more necessary that religious truth should be set forth in terms that admit no ambiguity or misinterpretation. If more generalities are to constitute the whole of religious instruction and if even these are

479. Edward A. Pace, "The Papacy and Education," *Catholic Education Review*, 1:3–7, January 1911.

fringed with uncertainty, they are not likely to take a firm hold on the mind; and they are less likely to do so when every other subject is taught in such a way as to make the child get clear-cut ideas about it.

There is consequently one obvious advantage in the Catholic system: it has a well-defined content. Its doctrines are expressed in statements no less careful and precise than the formulas of science. Should these require further interpretation, there is in the Church a living authority which decides on their meaning; and if as thus declared they are called in question or denied, the same authority draws the line plainly between Catholic truth and all opposing theories. The assent of faith which is the foundation of religion, is not given to hazy conceptions or shadowy abstractions; these are of no more avail in religious instruction than is the agnostic proposal to make the Unknowable an object of worship. For Christian faith especially they are not only useless but harmful in as much as Christianity has its basis in a positive revelation. Unless this is preserved in its integrity the spirit of faith will vanish, and the teaching of religion will disappear for the simple reason that there is nothing left to be taught.

From this point of view one can readily understand the vicissitudes through which religious thought and religious instruction have passed during the last four centuries. Once the duty and the task of determining what should be believed was committed to the individual judgment without respect to external authority, the way was opened to countless variations, and these more than anything else have complicated the problem of teaching religion in the school. But there is a further result which logically and practically makes that problem insoluble. Religion has become a purely subjective affair while the natural sciences deal with facts and laws that have an objective value. The teacher therefore may rightfully insist that the pupil's thought shall adjust itself to the reality which science describes and explains; but no such control is warranted in regard to the religious attitude which the pupil may assume, because there is no standard to which his ideas can be referred. He may be right or he may be wrong in his thought about God; that is his own concern. And it may also happen that he takes no thought of God at all, in which event, of course, both control and adjustment are out of the question. In other words, if education is correctly defined as a process of adjustment, and if this process implies an objective truth or reality to which the mind shall adjust itself, it follows that religion, as a merely subjective attitude, has no legitimate place in education.

While the Church has always upheld an objective criterion of belief and while the Papacy has authoritatively defined the doctrine of faith, it has never been a part of Catholic teaching that faith alone was sufficient either for complete living here or for winning eternal life. On the contrary, "faith without works is dead." Even the profession of Christian belief, however literally it may adhere to dogmatic pronouncement, cannot dispense from the obligation of doing the things that are in accordance with faith.

*   *   *

Here again the findings of psychology and sound educational theory are in accord with the traditional teaching and practice of the Church. It is generally recognized at present that any idea or item of knowledge, to get its full value, must be expressed in action . . .

A parallel to this sort of exaggeration is offered us in the notion of those who hold that religion should be divested of all external circumstance and of everything that appeals to sense. Liturgy and ritual, it is claimed, are mere outward forms that are foreign to Christianity. Worship is an internal act and prayer is a silent function of the soul. Logically, of course, it would follow that art should be dismissed from the service of religion, that symbolism and adornment should be swept from the temple and that the temple itself should become nothing more than a place of assembly, if indeed such a place be further required. Happily, this iconoclastic tendency, among Christian bodies at least, has been somewhat checked in recent times; and where it survives it is in open opposition to the principles of psychology not less than to the natural tendencies of the religious mind. Its effect on religious instruction would have been fatal, since it would have closed the senses to any impressions and consequently to any imagery in which the religious idea could find its setting and support. Thus while the eye and the ear would receive careful training in respect to the things that nature presents, and while the muscular sense would be duly exercised in actions of the ordinary type, none of these sensory activities would be allowed to suggest anything of a higher order.

480. Education as a Religion

I see no ground for criticizing those who regard education religiously. There have been many worse objects of faith and hope than the ideal possibilities of the development of human nature, and more harmful rites and cults than those which constitute a school system. Only if all faith that outruns sight is contemptible can education as

480. John Dewey, "Education As a Religion," *The New Republic,* 32:64–65, September 1922.

an object of religious faith be contemned. This particular form of faith testifies to a generous conception of human nature and to a deep belief in the possibilities of human achievement in spite of all its past failures and errors. Possibly all such faith involves credulity. But this particular credulity is not without its nobility. A faith becomes insincere and credulity injurious only when aspiration and credence are converted into dogmatic assertion; only when the importance of their objects is made the ground of asserting that we already have at hand the adequate means of attaining them, thereby attaining salvation. Worship of education as a symbol of unattained possibilities of realization of humanity is one thing; our obstinate devotion to existing forms—to our existing schools and their studies and methods of instruction and administration or to suggested specific programs of improvement—as if they embodied the object of worship—is quite another thing.

The first act evoked by a genuine faith in education is a conviction of sin and act of repentance as to the institutions and methods which we now call educational. This act must apply not to this and that, here and there, but to the idea which runs through all of it. It is no particular set of educators that is called to repentance. For everywhere there is the same absence of insight into the means by which our professed ends are to be realized, in consequence of which those ends remain nominal and sentimental. However much or little other religions may conflict with science, here we have a religion which can realize itself only through science: only, that is, through ways of understanding human nature in its concrete actuality and of discovering how its various factors are modified by interaction with the variety of conditions under which they operate. Without science this religion is bound to become formal, hypocritical and, in the end, a mass of dogmas called pedagogy and a mass of ritualistic exercises called school administration. Education may be a religion without being a superstition, and it may be a superstition when it is not even a religion but only an occupation of alleged hard-headed practical people.

481. Education and Death

Every man now living is going to die. What does this mean to him? Can a man suppose he is educated if he has not had to face this most

481. Ralph Harper, "Significance of Existence and Recognition for Education," in the 54th Yearbook of the National Society for the Study of Education, Part I, *Modern Philosophies and Education* (Published by the Society, Chicago, 1955), pp. 246–247.

depressing of questions? This is not merely a "religious" question. It is human and unavoidable. Every man becomes sick sooner or later, in mind as well as body. Every man fails himself and others many times. What do sickness and guilt mean to him? . . .

The reason this area cannot be left to the churches is not because the churches do not deal with it adequately—which is true—or because most men are not touched by the churches; the reason is that this area does not belong to the churches; it belongs to all men. Existentialism serves both mankind and organized religion by extracting the very experiential base on which religion is founded and by calling it existential rather than religious. The core of religion and the core of education are thus the same, those experiences which exhibit human finiteness and the need for redemption and resurrection.

482. The Role of Immortality in Education

Education apparently reveals in man a capacity for infinite growth. Will the education of man, which is never completed at any chosen moment in time, and for the eternal continuance of which man seems fit, go on unendingly? It would be a irrational universe, one in which the part did not manifest the whole, if a process with so much human significance in it as education has, and crying out so for an unending time, were to be cut short without conclusion, like a refreshing river in desert sands. If all the evidences are trustworthy and our world is rational; if the finite really manifests, though darkly, the infinite; if the fragmentary suggests, though imperfectly, the complete; if the part reveals, though in a riddle, the meaning of the whole; if, finally, all temporal values get their ultimate recognition; then there is for man an opportunity, guaranteed by his universe, and unabridged by the transitional incident in life named death, to finish his education, to achieve his destiny, and to grow unceasingly into the likeness of the Infinite Being. This is the hope of immortality.

482. Herman H. Horne, *The Philosophy of Education* (New York: The Macmillan Company, 1927), p. 283.

Index of Authors

(Numbers refer to selections.)

Adler, M. J., in American Catholic Philosophical Association, Proceedings of the Western Division, *The Philosophy of Christian Education*, 1941. **351**

—— in *The Educational Record.* **192**

—— in the *Journal of General Education.* **226**

—— in National Society for the Study of Education, 41st Yearbook, *Philosophies of Education.* **15, 134, 167**

—— in *The Social Frontier.* **49**

Adler, J. M., and M. Mayer, *The Revolution.* **14, 293**

American Historical Association, Report of the Commission on the Social Studies, *Conclusions and Recommendations.* New York: Charles Scribner's Sons, 1934. **33, 309**

Ames, E. S., in *Religious Education.* **469**

Aquinas, St. Thomas, in M. H. Mayer, *The Philosophy of Teaching of St. Thomas Aquinas.* Milwaukee: Bruce Publishing Co., 1929. **80, 331, 332**

Aristotle, in J. Burnet, *Aristotle on Education.* Cambridge: Harvard University Press, 1913. **253**

—— in *Metaphysics.* **105**

—— in *Nichomachean Ethics.* **158**

—— in *Politics.* **282**

Axtelle, G. E., in *Educational Method.* **93**

Bagley, W. C., *Education, Crime and Social Progress.* New York: Macmillan Co., 1930. **408**

—— *Education and Emergent Man.* New York: Thomas Nelson and Sons, 1934. **222, 297**

—— *The Education Process.* New York: Macmillan Co., 1926. **326**

—— in *Religious Education.* **116, 213**

Bayles, E. E., *Democratic Educational Philosophy.* New York: Harper & Bros., 1960. **107, 128, 430**

Beale, H. K., *Are American Teachers Free?* New York: Charles Scribner's Sons, 1936. **325**

Benne, K., in *The Teachers College Record.* **86**

—— in *Art Education Today.* **418**

Berkson, I. B., *Ideal and Community.* New York: Harper & Bros., 1958. **182**

Black, M., in *Ethics.* **416**

Blair, F. G., in *School and Society.* **232**

Boas, G., and S. Hook, *Academic Freedom, Logic, and Religion.* Philadelphia: University of Pennsylvania Press, 1951. **317**

Bode, B. H., *Conflicting Psychologies of Learning.* Boston: D. C. Heath & Co., 1929. **54, 60, 61**

—— *How We Learn.* Boston: D. C. Heath & Co., 1940. **92**

—— in *Progressive Education.* **361**

Bower, W. M., in P. H. Lotz and L. W. Crawford, editors, *Studies in Religious Education.* Nashville: Abingdon Cokesbury Press, 1931. **406**

Bowman, I., in *School and Society.* **247**

Brameld, T. B., in *The Social Frontier.* **290**

—— *Patterns of Educational Philosophy.* New York: World Book Co., 1950. **97**

—— *Toward a Reconstructed Philosophy of Education.* New York: Dryden Press, 1956. **306**

Breed, F. A., in *The Phi Delta Kappan.* **379**

—— in *School and Society.* **95**

Briggs, T. H., *The Great Investment.* Cambridge: Harvard University Press, 1930. **327**

Broudy, H. S., *Implications of Classical Realism for Philosophy of Education,* New York: Proceedings of the Association for Realistic Philosophy, 1949. **106, 208**

Brown, E. E., in *The Educational Review.* **38**

Bruce, W., in *Educational Administration and Supervision.* **178**

Bukarin, N., and E. Preobrazhensky, *The ABC of Communism.* New York: Workers Party of America, Lyceum Literature Department, 1921. **265**

Burnet, J., *Higher Education and the War.* London: Macmillan Co., 1917. **58**

Butler, N. M., *The Meaning of Education.* New York: Charles Scribner's Sons, 1915. **17**

Canevin, R., in *The Catholic Educational Review*. **457**

Chancellor, W. E., *Motives, Ideals, and Values in Education*. Boston: Houghton Mifflin Co., 1907. **235**

Chapman, J. C., and G. S. Counts, *Principles of Education*. Boston: Houghton Mifflin Co., 1924. **82, 85, 244, 263, 277**

Charters, W. W., *Curriculum Construction*. New York: Macmillan Co., 1929. **393**

Childs, J. L., *American Pragmatism and Education*. New York: Henry Holt & Co., 1956. **110, 337**

—— *Education and Morals*. New York: Appleton-Century-Crofts, Inc., 1950. **64, 123, 456**

—— *Education and the Philosophy of Experimentalism*. New York: Appleton-Century-Crofts, Inc., 1931. **18, 79, 99**

—— in *Progressive Education*. **39, 175**

Christian Century, editorial. **274**

Coe, G. A., *Educating for Citizenship*. New York: Charles Scribner's Sons, 1932. **368**

—— *Education in Religion and Morals*. New York: Fleming H. Revell Co., 1911. **475**

—— *Law and Freedom in the School*. Chicago: University of Chicago Press, 1924. **438**

—— in *Religious Education*. **444**

—— *A Social Theory of Religious Education*. New York: Charles Scribner's Sons, 1918. **447**

—— *What Is Christian Education?* New York: Charles Scribner's Sons, 1930. **114**

Cohen, R., in 54th Yearbook, National Society for the Study of Education, *Modern Philosophies and Education*. **55, 241**

Colvin, S. C., in *Education*. **389**

Committee on the War and the Religious Outlook, *Teaching Work of the Church*. New York: Association Press, 1923. **465**

Condorcet, in F. De La Fontainerie, *French Liberalism and Education in the Eighteenth Century*. New York: McGraw-Hill Book Co., 1932. **312**

Conference on the Scientific Spirit and Democratic Faith, *The Authoritarian Attempt to Capture Education*. New York: King's Crown Press, 1945. **271**

Conklin, E. G., in *School and Society*. **38**

Counts, G. S., *Dare the School Build a New Social Order?* New York: John Day Co., 1932. **237, 283**

—— in National Society for the Study of Education, 26th Yearbook. 145

—— *School and Society in Chicago.* New York: Harcourt, Brace and Co., 1928. 98

—— *The Social Composition of Boards of Education.* Chicago: University of Chicago Press, 1927. 243

Cummins, R. A., in *Educational Method.* 357

Cunningham, W. F., *The Pivotal Problems of Education.* New York: Macmillan Co., 1940. 25, 433

Davis, J., in *Journal of Educational Sociology.* 229

Day, J. F., in *Journal of Educational Sociology.* 214

DeHaas, J. A., in *Harvard Teachers Record.* 221

DeHovre, F., *Catholicism in Education.* New York: Benziger Bros., 1934. 177, 205

Dennis, L., *The Coming American Fascism.* New York: Harper and Bros., 1936. 201

—— in *The Social Frontier.* 262

Dewey, J., in *Art and Education.* Merion, Pennsylvania: The Barnes Foundation Press, 1929. 375

—— *The Child and Curriculum.* Chicago: University of Chicago Press, 1902. 350, 396

—— *Democracy and Education.* New York: Macmillan Co., 1916. 5, 56, 63, 101, 106, 111, 117, 118, 130, 138, 139, 142, 148, 150, 170, 185, 210, 352, 370, 397, 410, 414, 445

—— *Education Today.* New York: G. P. Putnam's Sons, 1940. 425

—— in *The Elementary School Journal.* 211

—— *Ethical Principles Underlying Education.* Chicago: University of Chicago Press, 1903. 362, 446

—— *Experience and Education.* New York: Macmillan Co., 1938. 330, 374, 423

—— in *Hibbert Journal.* 464, 468

—— *How We Think.* Boston: D. C. Heath & Co., 1933. 349

—— *Human Nature and Conduct.* New York: Henry Holt and Co., 1922. 346

—— *Ideals, Aims, and Methods in Education.* London: Sir Isaac Pitman & Sons, Ltd., 1922. 141, 172

—— in Paul Monroe, editor, *Cyclopedia of Education.* New York: Macmillan Co., 1911. 74, 173, 326

—— *Moral Principles in Education.* Boston: Houghton Mifflin Co., 1909. **47, 449**

—— in National Herbart Society Yearbook, 1895–1900. **369**

—— in National Society for the Study of Education, 33rd Yearbook, *The Activity Movement.* **358, 387**

—— in National Society for the Study of Education, 37th Yearbook, *The Scientific Movement in Education.* **8**

—— in *The New Republic.* **298, 480**

—— in *Progressive Education.* **381, 405**

—— *Reconstruction in Philosophy.* New York: Henry Holt and Co., 1920. **209**

—— in *School and Society.* **151, 219**

—— *The School and Society.* Chicago: University of Chicago Press, 1900. **223, 424**

—— in *The Social Frontier.* **245, 291**

—— *The Sources of a Science of Education.* New York: Liveright Co., 1931. **2, 13, 149, 380, 384**

—— and J. L. Childs, in W. H. Kilpatrick, editor, *Educational Frontier.* New York: Century Co., 1933. **281, 310, 344**

Donohue, J. W., *Work and Education.* Chicago: Loyola University Press, 1959. **227**

Ecclesiasticus. **419**

Eliot, T. S., *Notes toward the Definition of Culture.* New York: Harcourt, Brace & Co., 1949. **203**

Eliott, H. S., *Can Religious Education Be Christian?* New York: Macmillan Co., 1940. **459, 471**

—— in *Religious Education.* **78**

Emerson, R. W., *Education.* Boston: Houghton Mifflin Co., 1909. **176**

Esipov, B. P. and N. K. Goncharov, *I Want to Be Like Stalin* (G. S. Counts and N. P. Lodge, translators). New York: John Day Co., 1947. **448**

Esser, G., in *The Catholic Educational Review.* **120**

Ettinger, W. I., in *School and Society.* **244**

Fichte, J. G., in G. H. Turnbull, *Educational Theory of Johann Gottlieb Fichte.* Liverpool: University of Liverpool Press, 1926. **183**

Finney, R. L., *A Sociological Philosophy of Education.* New York: Macmillan Co., 1928. **62, 161, 206, 238, 288, 303, 367, 388, 428, 435**

Fischer, A., in *Educational Yearbook.* New York: Bureau of Publications, Teachers College, Columbia University, 1929. **168**

Fisher, C., in *Religious Education.* **476**

Fitzpatrick, E. A., editor, *St. Ignatius and the RATIO STUDIORUM.* New York: McGraw-Hill Book Co., 1933. **300**

Fleshman, A. C., *The Educational Process.* Philadelphia: J. B. Lippincott Co., 1908. **160, 193**

—— *The Metaphysics of Education.* Boston: Mayhew Publishing Co., 1914. **16**

Frankena, W. K., in *Harvard Educational Review.* **4**

Freeman, F. N., in *School and Society.* **376**

Froebel, F. W. A., in S. Fletcher and J. Welton, *Froebel's Chief Writings on Education.* New York: Longmans, Green & Co., 1912. **41**

Galbraith, J. K., in Association for Higher Education, *Current Issues in Higher Education,* 1959. **218**

Geiger, G. R., in 54th Yearbook, National Society for the Study of Education, *Modern Philosophies and Education.* **102, 390**

Gentile, G., *The Reform of Education.* New York: Harcourt, Brace and Co., 1922. **190, 431**

Greene, T. M., in 54th Yearbook, National Society for the Study of Education, *Modern Philosophies and Education.* **96, 127**

Haggerty, M. E., in *Annals of the American Academy of Political and Social Science.* **320**

Hans, N. A., *The Principles of Educational Policy.* London: King and Staples, Ltd., 1933. **248, 257**

Hardie, D. C., *Truth and Fallacy in Educational Theory.* London: Cambridge University Press, 1942. **125, 345**

Harper, R., in 54th Yearbook, National Society for the Study of Education, *Modern Philosophies and Education.* **71, 481**

Harris, W. T., in *Educational Review.* **353, 463**

—— in The Third Yearbook of the National Herbart Society. Chicago: University of Chicago Press, 1908. **421**

Hartshorne, H., *Character in Human Relations.* New York: Charles Scribner's Sons, 1932. **65, 225**

—— in C. M. Hill, editor, *Educational Progress and School Administration.* New Haven: Yale University Press, 1936. **217**

—— in *Religious Education.* **383**

—— in P. H. Lotz and L. W. Crawford, editors, *Studies in Religious Education.* Nashville: Abingdon-Cokesbury Press, 1931. **460**

Hegel, G. F. W., in F. L. Luqeer, *Hegel as Educator.* New York: Columbia University Press, 1896. **26**

—— in M. MacKenzie, *Hegel's Educational Theory and Practice.* London: Swann, Sonnenschein & Co., 1909. **186**

Henderson, E. N., *A Textbook in the Principles of Education.* New York: Macmillan Co., 1950. **319**

Hocking, W. E., *Human Nature and Its Remaking.* New Haven: Yale University Press, 1923. **70, 363, 437, 454**

Holaind, Rev. R. I., *The Parent First: An Answer to Dr. Bouquillon's Query.* New York: Benziger Bros., 1891. **252**

Homrighausen, E. G., in *Religious Education.* **478**

Hook, S., in *Journal of Educational Sociology.* **135**

Hopkins, L. T., *Integration: Its Meaning and Application.* New York: Appleton-Century-Crofts, Inc., 1937. **385**

Horn, E., in *Religious Education.* **371**

Horne, H. H., *The Democratic Philosophy of Education.* New York: Macmillan Co., 1935. **28, 31, 42, 45, 47, 104, 119, 171, 334, 338, 451**

—— *Idealism in Education.* New York: Macmillan Co., 1923. **422, 442**

—— *The Philosphy of Education.* New York: Macmillan Co., 1927. **19, 29, 30, 44, 59, 100, 355, 356, 365, 411, 482**

—— *This New Education.* Nashville: Abingdon-Cokesbury Press, 1931. **399**

Howerth, I. W., *The Theory of Education.* New York: Appleton-Century-Crofts, Inc., 1926. **143, 187**

Hutchins, R. M., *The Higher Learning in America.* New Haven: Yale University Press, 1936. **94**

—— in *William Rainey Memorial Conference.* Chicago: University of Chicago Press, 1938. **22**

Huxley, J., *UNESCO: Its Purpose and Philosophy.* Washington, D. C.: Public Affairs Press, 1947. **280**

Hyde, W. D., *The Teacher's Philosophy.* Boston: Houghton Mifflin, 1910. **426**

International Missionary Council, Jerusalem Meeting, 1928. **36**

Jackson, R. A., in *Board of Education v. Barnette.* **278**

Janes, L. G., in *Educational Review.* **477**

Jefferson, T., in *Writings of Thomas Jefferson.* New York: G. P. Putnam's Sons, 1899. **294**

Joad, C. E. M., *Introduction to Modern Political Theory.* New York: Oxford—Clarendon Press, 1933. **249**

Johnson, G., in *Catholic Educational Review.* **51**

Kallen, H. M., in *Progressive Education.* **124, 307**

Kandel, I. L., *Comparative Education.* Boston: Houghton Mifflin Co., 1933. **9, 191, 256, 275**

—— in *The Educational Forum.* **255**

—— *Kadelpian Review.* **295**

Kant, I., in E. F. Buchner, *The Educational Theory of Immanuel Kant.* Philadelphia: J. B. Lippincott Co., 1904. **37, 169, 377, 420**

Kelley, T. L., in *Science.* **11**

Kelly, W. A., *Educational Psychology,* Milwaukee: Bruce Publishing Co., 1933. **57, 69, 75**

Kilpatrick, W. H., in *Childhood Education.* **174**

—— *Education for a Changing Society.* New York: Macmillan Co., 1926. **404**

—— *Education and the Social Crisis.* New York: Liveright Publishing Corp., 1932. **311**

—— in *Progressive Education.* **27, 66, 89, 343, 354, 413**

—— *Remaking the Curriculum.* New York: Newson and Co., 1936. **453**

—— in *School and Society.* **12**

—— in National Society for the Study of Education, 26th Yearbook. **335**

Kirk, R., *Academic Freedom.* Chicago: Henry Regnery Co., 1955. **314**

Kluckholm, C., in Foundations for Integrated Education. *The Nature of Concepts, Their Relation and Role in Social Structure.* Stillwater, Oklahoma: Oklahoma A & M College, 1950. **132**

Laski, H. J., *A Grammar of Politics.* London: George Allen & Unwin, Ltd., 1925. **197**

Leary, D. B., *Educational Psychology.* New York: Thomas Nelson and Sons, 1934. **84**

Leighton, J. A., *Individuality and Education.* New York: Appleton-Century-Crofts, Inc., 1928. **194**

Lenin, *Collected Works,* vol. 23. New York: International Publishers Co., Inc., 1945. **285**

Leo XIII, in J. A. Ryan and F. J. Boland, *Catholic Principles of Politics.* New York: Macmillan Company, 1940. **315**

Lewis, C. L., *An Analysis of Knowledge and Valuation.* La Salle, Illinois: Open Court Publishing Co., 1946. **159**

Lieberman, M., in *Harvard Educational Review.* **181, 182**

Lippmann, W., *The Phantom Public.* New York: Harcourt, Brace and Co., 1925. **308**

Lodge, R. C., *Philosophy of Education*. New York: Harper and Bros., 1937.
348

Lowell, A. L., *At War with Academic Traditions in America*. Cambridge:
Harvard University Press, 1934.   **216, 321**

—— in *Harvard Teachers Record*.   **207**

Lusk, C., Report of Joint Legislative Committee of the State of New York,
Revolutionary Radicalism.   **292**

Machlup, F., in *Bulletin of the American Association of University Professors*.
318

McCall, W. A., in *Teachers College Record*.   **378**

McCallister, W. J., *The Growth of Freedom in Education*. New York: R. R.
Smith, Inc., 1931.   **372**

McGucken, W. J., *The Catholic Way in Education*. Milwaukee: Bruce Publishing Co., 1934.   **137, 301**

McMurry, F. M., in *Educational Review*.   **73**

McReynolds, J. C., in *Pierce v. Society of Sisters*, 268 U.S. 510, 535 (1924).
261

Mann, Horace, Tenth Annual Report as Secretary of State Board of Educa-
cation, Massachusetts.   **246**

—— Twelfth Annual Report as Secretary of State Board of Education, Massachusetts.   **236**

—— in Paul Monroe, *Founding of the American Public School System*. New
York: Macmillan Co., 1940.   **212**

Marique, P. J., *The Philosophy of Christian Education*. Englewood Cliffs,
N. J.: Prentice-Hall, Inc., 1939.   **436**

Maritain, J., *Education at the Crossroads*. New Haven: Yale University
Press, 1943.   **113**

—— in 54th Yearbook, National Society for the Study of Education, *Modern
Philosophies and Education*.   **109**

Mayer, M. H., *The Philosophy of Teaching of St. Thomas Aquinas*, Milwaukee: Bruce Publishing Co., 1929.   **333**

Meiklejohn, A., *Education between Two Worlds*. New York: Harper and
Bros., 1942.   **184, 269**

Mill, J. S., *On Liberty*. London: J. W. Parker & Sons, 1859.   **262**

Moberley, W., *Crisis in the University*. London: Student Christian Movement
Press, 1949.   **157**

Moore, E. C., *What Is Education?* Boston: Ginn & Co., 1915.   **3, 115, 122,
329, 395**

Morehouse, F. M., in *Historical Outlook*.   **342**

Morris, Van C., in *Educational Theory.* **364**

Morrison, H. C., *Basic Principles in Education.* Boston: Houghton Mifflin Co., 1934. **53**

Mueller, G. E., *Education Limited.* Norman, Oklahoma: University of Oklahoma Press, 1949. **458**

Munroe, J. P., in *Educational Review.* **260**

Murphy, A. E., in *The Humanist.* **323**

Mursell, J. L., in *Atlantic Monthly.* **87**

Nash, A. S., *The University and the Modern World.* New York: Macmillan Co., 1943. **133**

National Education Association, Department of Superintendence, Tenth Yearbook, *Character Education.* **391, 455**

—— Twelfth Yearbook, *Critical Problems of School Administration.* **284**

Navaratnam, R., *New Frontiers in East-West Philosophies of Education.* Bombay: Orient Longmans, 1958. **154**

National Education Association, Educational Policies Commission, *Education and Economic Well-Being in American Democracy.* **220**

—— *The Unique Function of Education in American Democracy.* **324**

National Society for the Study of Education, 26th Yearbook. **407**

Newman, J. H., *Idea of a University Sixth edition.* London: Longmans, Green & Co., 1886. **155, 156**

Niebuhr, R., *Moral Man and Immoral Society.* New York: Charles Scribner's Sons, 1932. **233, 239, 286**

Nietzsche, F., *On the Future of Our Educational Institutions,* J. Kennedy, translator. London: G. T. Foulis & Co., 1909. **200, 313**

Nock, A. J., *The Theory of Education in the United States.* New York: Harcourt, Brace and Co., 1932. **401**

Nunn, J. P., *Education, Its Data and First Principles.* New York: Longmans, Green & Co., 1920. **440**

O'Connor, D. J., *Introduction to Philosophy of Education.* New York: Philosophical Library, 1957. **6, 7**

Ogden, R. M., in *School and Society.* **91**

O'Shea, M. H., *Education as Adjustment.* New York: Longmans, Green & Co., 1906. **198**

Pace, E. A., in *Catholic Educational Review.* **479**

Palmer, G. H., *Ethical and Moral Instruction in the School.* Boston: Houghton Mifflin Co., 1909. **443**

Parker, F. W., *Talks on Pedagogies.* New York: John Day Co., 1939. **264**

Partridge, G. E., *Genetic Philosophy of Education*. New York: Sturgis and Walton Co., 1912. **46**

Patel, M. S., *The Educational Philosophy of Mahatma Gandhi*. Ahmedadbad, India: Narajivan Publishing House, 1953. **230**

Pécaut, F., in *Educational Yearbook*, 1929. **189**

Perry, C., in *International Journal of Ethics*. **400**

Peters, C. C., in *The Social Frontier*. **336**

Phenix, P., *Philosophy of Education*. New York: Henry Holt & Co., 1958. **35, 112, 452**

Pinkevitch, A. P., *The New Education in the Soviet Republic*. New York: John Day Co., 1929. **195, 228, 240, 254, 273, 287, 340, 432**

Pius XI, in *The Catholic Educational Review*. **23, 164, 267, 268, 302**

Plato, in B. Bosanquet, *The Education of the Young in the Republic of Plato*. **299**

—— *The Republic*, Cornford translation. Oxford University Press, 1953. **24**

Pring, B., *Education, Socialist and Capitalist*. London: Methuen and Co., Ltd., 1937. **231, 429, 439**

Raby, J. M., *A Critical Study of the New Education*. Washington, D.C.: Catholic Education Press, 1932. **67, 366**

Ragsdale, C., *Modern Psychologies and Education*. New York: Macmillan Co., 1936. **77, 434**

Randall, J. H., in *American Scholar*. **72**

Redden, J. D., and F. A. Ryan, *A Catholic Philosophy of Education*. Milwaukee: Bruce Publishing Co., 1942. **43, 166, 450, 466**

Reder, E. H., in *Teachers College Record*. **360**

Reisner, E. H., in *Teachers College Record*. **48, 304**

Renner, G. T., in *Social Frontier*. **215**

Ribicoff, A., in *New York Times*, July 9, 1961. **250**

Rosenkranz, K., *Pedagogies as a System*. St. Louis: R. P. Studley Co., 1872. **409, 427**

Rousseau, J. J., *Emile*, B. Foxley, translator. London: J. M. Dent & Sons, Ltd. (New York: E. P. Dutton Co.), 1911. **20, 129**

Royce, Josiah, in *Educational Review*. **40**

Rugg, H., *Culture and Education in America*. New York: Harcourt, Brace and Co., 1931. **415**

—— *The Great Technology*. New York: John Day Company, 1933. **1**

Rugh, C. E., *The Essential Place of Religion in Education*. National Education Association, Monograph, 1916. **461**

Russell, Bertrand, *Education and the Modern World*. New York: W. W. Norton & Co., Inc., 1932. **121, 204, 234, 266, 279**

Ryan, J. K., in *Journal of Higher Education*. **316**

Sanders, W. J., in *Harvard Educational Review*. **90, 165**

—— in John Dewey Society, Seventh Yearbook, *The Public School and Spiritual Values*. New York: Harper & Bros., 1944. **417**

Schoen, Max, in *Education*. **146**

Schoenchen, G. G., *The Activity School*. New York: Longmans, Green & Co., 1940. **21**

Second Conference on the Scientific Spirit and Democratic Faith, *The Authoritarian Attempt to Capture Education*. New York: Kings Crown Press, 1945. **271**

Sheehy, M. S., in P. H. Lotz and I. W. Crawford editors, *Studies in Religious Education*. Nashville: Abingdon-Cokesbury Press, 1931. **188**

Sheen, F. J., *Anti-Christ* (radio address). **441**

Shields, T. E., in *Catholic Educational Review*. **270**

—— *Philosophy of Education*, Washington, D. C.: The Catholic Education Press, 1921. **52, 259, 296, 462, 470**

Slesinger, Z., *Education and the Class Struggle*. New York: Covici Friede Co., 1937. **242, 289**

Smith, B. O., *Logical Aspects of Educational Measurement*. New York: Columbia University Press, 1938. **386**

—— in *Journal of Teacher Education*. **347**

——, W. O. Stanley, and J. H. Shores, *Fundamentals of Curriculum Development*. New York: World Book Co., 1951. **394, 398, 403**

Smith, I., in R. J. Deferrari, *Essays on Catholic Education in the United States*. Washington, D. C.: Catholic University of America Press, 1942. **276**

Smith, J. E., *Value Convictions and Higher Education*. New Haven, Connecticut: Edward W. Hazen Foundation, 1958. **136**

Smith, T. V., *The American Philosophy of Education*. Chicago: University of Chicago Press, 1927. **196**

Soares, T. G., *Religious Education*. Chicago: University of Chicago Press, 1928. **474**

Soper, E. D., in *School and Society*. **322**

Spencer, H., *Education: Intellectual, Moral, and Physical*. London: G. Manwaring, 1861. **144**

—— *Social Statics.* New York: D. Appleton Co., 1886.   **251**

Stevens, T., in Report of U. S. Commission of Education, 1898.   **258**

Stevenson, C. L., in *Harvard Educational Review.*   **10**

Taba, H., *The Dynamics of Education.* London: Kegan, Paul, Trench, Trubner and Co., Ltd., 1932.   **152**

Taeusch, C. F., *Professional and Business Ethics.* New York: Henry Holt and Co., 1926.   **179**

Thayer, V. T., in *Educational Theory.*   **272**

Thomas, L. G., in *Educational Administration and Supervision.*   **131**

—— in *Educational Forum.*   **50**

Thorndike, E. L., *Human Learning.* New York: The Century Company, 1931.   **83**

—— in *Journal of Adult Education.*   **402**

—— in *Journal of Educational Psychology.*   **76**

—— and A. I. Gates, *Elementary Principles of Education.* New York: Macmillan Co., 1930.   **81, 126, 153, 162**

Tucker, B. R., in *Educational Review.*   **373**

Vieth, P. H., *Objectives in Religious Education.* New York: Harper & Bros., 1930.   **472**

—— in *School and Society.*   **467**

Vollert, C., in *Review for Religious.*   **473**

Walker, H. M., in *Teachers College Record.*   **392**

Washburne, C., in *The Social Frontiers.*   **305**

Whipple, G. M., in *Progressive Education.*   **68**

Whitehead, Alfred North, *Aims of Education and Other Essays.* London: Williams and Norgate, Ltd., 1929.   **88, 412**

—— in *Atlantic Monthly.*   **34, 339**

—— *Essays in Science and Philosophy.* New York: Philosophical Library, 1947.   **341**

Wild, J., in 54th Yearbook, National Society for the Study of Education, *Modern Philosophies of Education.*   **108, 359**

Wilson, Logan, *Academic Man.* New York: Oxford University Press, 1952.   **180**

Index

Index

A

Absolute, the, 121, 150, 507
  truth as, 116
Absolutism, 11, 24, 189, 305, 306, 365
Acceptance, as interest, 405, 406
Administration, democracy in, 230, 231
Aesthetics, 460, 463–468
Agnosticism, 530–532
Aims, educational, 165ff. *See also* 27,
  30, 31, 45, 57, 80, 91, 111, 112,
  136, 146, 149–152, 155, 157–159,
  217, 219, 235, 404, 416, 421, 425,
  439, 458, 478, 530, 538
Analysis, method of, 432
  role in educational philosophy, 4
Anarchism, 280, 421
Anarchy, 492
Appearance, 110, 111, 145
Appreciation, 461, 462
Aristocracy, 224
Art, 460–472
  education as, 433
  of education, 48
  and play, 427
Asceticism, 415
Association, principles of, 98
Atheism, 519
Attention, 407
Authority, 33, 58, 59, 106, 107, 112,
  120, 121, 125, 152, 218, 224, 313,
  335, 352, 372, 388, 389, 427, 486,
  490, 517, 522, 529, 532
Autonomy, 204

B

Baptism, 527
Behaviorism, 63, 64, 92, 93, 100
Bible, 532
Biology, as basis of aims, 175
Body and soul, 49, 95
Buddhism, 180

C

Capitalism, 262, 284, 323–326
Caprice, 37, 83
Catholicism, 224
Causation, 476
Censorship, 369
Certainty, 43, 132
Chance, 45
Change, 109, 134, 193, 194, 450
  not all beneficial, 29
  and changeless, 34–42, 52, 53
  social, 323
Character, 257, 418, 436, 452, 474,
  505, 509, 510, 531, 532
Charity, 241
Church, 62, 196, 224, 298–304, 336,
  352, 353, 415, 530, 536, 539
  purpose of, 136
  and state, 305, 306
Citizen, 26
Civil liberty, 358, 367–371
Class, socio-economic, 292
  struggle, 274, 324, 325, 530
Code, of ethics, 201, 204
Collective bargaining, 200, 201
Collectivism, 323, 324
Common sense, 2
Communism, 218, 241, 258, 278, 279,
  363, 364
Competition, 246, 249, 250, 259, 260,
  411, 439
Compulsion, 416, 429, 480, 485
Compulsory attendance, 287, 288
Conditioned reflex, 98
Conscience, 511
  and consciousness, 497
Consciousness, 64
Consensus, 111–115, 342
Constitution, 318
Consumption, and education, 238, 240
Contemplation, 181–183
Convention, 28–33
Conversion, 131, 520
Craft, role in education, 259

Creation, 44, 45
Creativity, 462–465
Culture, 42, 104, 105, 170, 444, 453
Curriculum, the, 443ff. *See also* 31, 32, 36, 115, 119, 120, 126, 153, 171, 172, 174, 226, 239, 242, 255

D

Definition, 292, 293
Democracy, 179, 196, 212, 215–219, 221, 224, 225, 228–232, 279, 306, 337–339, 379, 480–482, 489, 500, 535
Destiny, of man, 47
Determinism, 85–87, 123
Development, 50, 169, 170
Discipline, student, 473ff. *See also* 49, 170, 199, 414–419, 428, 464, 465
formal, 69
Docility, 390, 482
Dogma, 522, 523, 528, 532, 538
Drill, 243, 503

E

Education, 25, 26, 129, 165, 201, 234, 235
as art, 433
Buddhist, 181
business of, 184
concern of, 132
and death, 338–339
defined, 107, 118, 168
as discipline, 55
both end and means, 240
its own end, 190–192
everywhere the same, 160
as experience, 133
and evangelism, 519, 520
general, 36. *See also* Liberal education.
nature of, 274–276, 323
as preparation, 343
purpose of, 48, 109. *See also* Aims.
as religion, 537, 538
right to, 226, 278
role distinguished from state's, 480
as social equalizer, 264
and socio-economic structure, 261ff.
universal, 262
Effort, 414, 418, 458
Elite, 222, 223
Emergence, 44

Emotion, 138
End, final, 49, 50
to treat as an, 510
Ends and means, 151, 152, 440
Equality, 26, 219, 221, 224, 226, 227
of opportunity, 218, 244, 267, 287
Essence, 48, 158
Ethics, 427, 494–496, 501
as principles of education, 195ff.
social, 238
Evaluation, 431–442
Evangelism, 131, 519, 520, 528
Evolution, 27, 29, 49, 52–55, 139, 316
Examinations, 439
Existentialism, 80, 412–414
Experience, 10, 12, 13, 19, 23, 24, 53, 95, 133, 198, 199, 384, 398, 408, 454, 466, 522, 523
Experimentalism, 59, 440, 523
Explanation, 392, 393

F

Faculty, of soul, 61, 66–69
Faith, 518, 532, 536–538
and morals, 102, 302, 305
Family, 298–303, 336
Fascism, 215, 216
Fatalism, 39, 83
Fear, 487
Field, theory, 99–101
Form and content, 40
Freedom, 33, 77, 81, 82, 215, 226, 227, 280–282, 284, 285, 306, 313, 314, 318, 327, 343, 445, 475, 476, 484, 485, 534
academic freedom, 347ff.

G

Gestalt, 91
Goal, *see* Aim.
God, 23, 25, 34, 48–50, 68, 72, 78, 103, 111, 121, 132, 136, 163, 182, 186, 196, 200, 298, 302, 303, 307, 336, 349–353, 377, 484, 486, 501, 511, 516–525, 530, 532–535
Good, absolute, 147
the good, 53, 109, 120, 130, 137, 156, 163, 198, 239
Government, student, 480, 489–492
Grace, 33, 75, 185, 299, 484, 519, 520, 524–528
Gradualism, 285, 323

"Great Books," 56
Group dynamics, 113, 115, 413
Growth, 118, 168, 169, 192

H

Habit, 98, 104, 156, 157
Habituation, 498
Happiness, 147, 155, 182, 404, 405
Hedonism, 154, 404–406
Heredity—environment, 223
Home, 162, 294–296
Humanism, 316, 533
Human nature, 60ff. See also 32, 36, 47,
    49, 50, 54, 55, 71, 87, 102, 103,
    105, 106, 157–161, 324, 325, 526–
    528, 538

I

Idea, as hypothesis, 116
Ideal, the, 47, 167
Idealism, 53, 116, 414
Ideals, 448
Imagination, 96, 129
Immortality, 525, 539
Impartiality, 344
Indeterminacy, 117, 122
Individual, dignity of, 286
Individualism, 217, 218, 245, 417, 487,
    533
Individuality, 28, 46, 217, 218, 373,
    408, 425, 426, 448
Indoctrination, 168, 219, 275, 308, 309,
    335, 336, 338–341
Induction—deduction, 400, 401
Industry, economic, 242–244
Infallibility, 102, 224, 302, 303
Information, 119, 444
Inhibition, 504
Inquiry, as teaching, 308–383
Instrumentalism, 97
Integration, 72–74
Integrity, 524
Intellect, 61, 77, 95, 96, 109, 110, 125,
    157, 181, 226, 227, 505, 506,
    525
Intelligence, 70, 104, 105, 107, 333,
    423, 510
    role of, 136–141, 158
Interest, 402ff. See also 32, 129, 247,
    445, 479, 481
Intuition, 68, 124, 125, 127–129, 137,
    157, 371

Investment, in people, 239–241
I.Q., 101–107

K

Knowledge, the nature of, 108ff. See
    also 13, 28, 29, 43, 82, 157, 171,
    172, 181, 188, 384, 385, 395, 399–
    401, 432, 438, 439, 449–451, 498,
    531
    as basis of interest, 406
    compared to information, 31, 119,
        126, 127
    infused, 525
    philosophy as, 20, 21
    preexisting, 377

L

Labor, see Work
Laissez-faire, 278, 285, 364, 365
Language, 142–144, 391
Law, 350, 427, 474, 485
    of effect, 405
    natural, 86, 87, 122, 282
    of thought, 394
Learning, 89ff. See also 68, 128, 399,
    400
    curve of, 508
    defined, 405
    by doing, 135
    incidental, 383
Leisure, 123, 238, 239, 251, 254, 263,
    264, 459
Liberal arts, 55, 109
Liberal education, 12, 80, 125, 181,
    242, 243, 253–255
Liberalism, 33, 284–286, 353
Liberty, see Freedom
    and license, 363
Life, 75
Linguistic analysis, 8, 9
Logic, 93
    psychological—logical, 392, 397–400,
        445
Loyalty, teacher, 327, 372, 373

M

Man, nature of, see Human nature
Marks, 259, 440
Marxism, 324–326
Materialism, 49
Matter and spirit, 36

Meaning, 125
Means—ends, 141, 171, 467
Measurement, 431–442
Mechanism, 91, 98, 429
Mental health, 424
Mental hygiene, 87, 88
Mental states, 69, 100
Metaphysics, 56–59, 371
Method of instruction, 374ff. *See also*
    356, 396
  as curriculum, 443–444
  of experimentalism, 23, 24
  incidental, 505
Mind, 24, 62–64, 67–70, 94, 100, 128,
    129, 135–138, 140, 395, 396, 486,
    524, 531, 532
Monopoly, 301
Moral code, 34
Moral education, 493ff., 254, 305, 487
  standards, 154
Morality, 532
Morals, and art, 468
Mortification, 415
Motivation, *see* Interest
Motive, 77, 83, 84
Mysticism, 130–132
Myth, 103

N

Nationalism and education, 308ff. *See
    also* 246, 301, 365, 366
Naturalism, 27–33, 306
Natural rights, 349
Natural—supernatural, 25–34, 304, 305,
    484
Nature, 25–33, 394
Need, 410
Neutrality, 344, 361
Normative function of philosophy, 3, 4
Novel—primordial, 43–47
Novelty, 37–40, 95

O

Obedience, 429, 474, 475, 487, 488
Objective, *see* Aim
Objectivity, 113, 361
Obligation, 414, 511
Opinion, 28, 29, 354

P

Parent, 282, 293, 294, 296, 340, 421,
    422

Paternalism, 365
Patriotism, 242, 308–311, 313, 471
Perennialism, 341
Personalism, 23
Personality, 196
Philistinism, 469
Philosophy, of education, 1ff. *See also*
    208
Planned economy, and education, 246–
    248
Play, 79, 239, 456–460. *See also*
    Work.
Politics, and education, 207ff. *See also*
    284, 320, 321, 328, 333
Positivism, 54, 371, 470, 471
  logical, 7, 8, 153
Potency—actuality, 156
Pragmatism, 40, 116, 155, 249, 432
Prayer, 520, 537
Predestination, 38, 100
Preparation, as aim, 169, 175, 416
Principles, first, 189
Private capital, and education, 246
Private profit system, 267
Privilege, education based on, 267, 272,
    278
Problem solving, 118, 343, 344, 383,
    462
Process, 39, 41, 42, 46
Profession, 200–204, 366, 367
Professional education, 254, 255
Profit motive, 245, 246, 249
Progress, 51–54, 102, 105–107, 112,
    109, 285, 365
  school and social, 317ff.
Progressive education, 32, 52–59, 148–
    152, 265, 266, 434, 456, 457, 478,
    490
Proletarian dictatorship, 218
Propaganda, 225, 308, 309, 327, 341
Property, private, and education, 260,
    267
Protestantism, 196
Public and private school, 277ff., *see
    also* 532
  parochial school, 292, 293
  religious character of, 520, 521
Punishment, 474, 475, 480, 483, 486–
    488
Puritanism, 469, 470
Purpose, *see* Aim

Q

Quality—quantity, 434

R

Rationalism, 52, 53
Rationality, 36
Realism, 394, 432
  classical, 121, 122, 226
Reality, traits of, 22ff., *see also* 40–42,
  110, 145, 198, 427, 449, 531, 532,
  536
  ultimate, 9–11, 122
Reason, 39, 40, 182, 350, 351, 448
Reasoning, 91, 92
Recapitulation, 51
Reconstructionism, 111, 115, 341
Reflex arc, 100
Regeneration, 527
Relations, 65
Relativity, 53, 112, 121–123, 153, 154
Reliability, 113
Religion, 200, 302, 511
Religious education, 500, 512ff.
Research, 381
Responsibility, 88, 475, 476, 480
Retribution, 489
Revelation, 49, 102, 352, 534, 536
Revolution, 326, 360
Reward, 483
Romanticism, 466

S

Sacraments, 520
Scepticism, 121, 354
Scholasticism, 151, 163
School, 123, 234
  and social progress, 317ff.
Science, and philosophy, 11–20
Secular education, 306
Self, 68
  activity, 135
  control, 424, 425, 484
  denial, 415, *see also* Inhibition
  expression, 49, 197, 217, 397, 405,
    448
  realization, 132, 169, 183, 217, 529
  selfhood, 195–198
Senses, 139
Sin, 494, 524–526
  original, 33, 49, 50, 102, 103
Social contract, 209
Socialism, 218, 241, 258, 284, 289, 290
Sociology, as basis of aim, 171

Soul, 74, 85, 96, 97, 100, 161, 196, 525,
  532, 537
  and body, *see* Body
Species, 29, 54, 55, 96
Spectator, theory of intelligence, 138,
  139
Speculation, 2, 3
Standards, 440
State, the, 120, 196, 209, 241, 270, 327,
  351, 364, 365, 489,
  see also Public and Private schools
Statistics, 437, 441, 442
Stimulus—response, 90, 97, 98, 100,
  101, 124
Stoicism, 80
Strike, teacher, 200, 201, 204–206
Supernatural, the, 415

T

Tabula rasa, 70, 96, 138
Tax, public school, 288
Teacher, as policeman, 479
  religious, 330
  as worker, 273
Teaching, 392
  art of, 376
  as inquiry, 380–383
Temporal—eternal, 41–43
Tenure, 359
Theology, 3, 526–528
Theory, 2, 123
Thinking, 36, 39, 40, 91, 124, 375, 380,
  392, 424
Thomism, 95, 97
Three R's, 55, 283
Time, 133
  and eternity, 48
Tolerance, 370
Totalitarianism, 285, 286
Trade, *see* Vocational education
Truth, 32, 43, 53, 57, 81, 96, 109–111,
  113, 114, 116, 119–123, 125, 126,
  131, 132, 137, 139, 141, 153, 182,
  183, 188, 227, 348, 349, 351–356,
  362, 391, 392, 427, 483, 516, 517,
  522, 524, 529, 531, 532, 535

U

UNESCO, 315, 316
Unfolding, education as, 50, 51, 529

Union, teacher, 272, 273
Units, of measurement, 435
Universals, 453

V

Validity, 438
Value, theory of, 317ff., *see also*, 14, 15,
    134, 146, 437, 452, 453
Virtue, 162, 186–188, 496–498
Vocational education, 12, 238, 242, 243,
    253, 270
  guidance, 243

W

"Warranted assertability," 97
Welfare state, 280
Whole child, 73, 75, 76
Will, 23, 61, 76–80, 85, 407, 415, 418,
    474, 475, 487, 524
  freedom of, 77–79, 83–85, 163, 350,
    486
  general, 209, 210, 214
Work, 238, 239, 269, 270, 250–259,
    456–460
  and play, 247, *see also* Play.
World state, 314, 315
Worship, 182, 537, 538